TITLES OF
UNITED STATES CODE
AND
UNITED STATES CODE ANNOTATED

**(See the note following Title 1, Section 204
for a list of the titles that have been
enacted into positive law.)**

UNITED STATES CODE ANNOTATED

TITLE 16

Conservation

§§ 411 to 460o-7

Comprising All Laws of a General
and Permanent Nature
Under Arrangement of the Official Code of
the Laws of the United States
with
Annotations from Federal Courts

WEST®

A Thomson Reuters business

Mat #40837103

TABLE OF CONTENTS

---

*

EXPLANATION

This volume, comprising sections 411 to 460o-7 of Title 16 of the United States Code, contains laws of a general and permanent nature relating to Conservation, including all amendments and enactments through Public Law 111-229, approved August 11, 2010.

Historical and Statutory Notes

This volume contains complete historical and statutory notes relating to amendments, effective dates, legislative reports, repeals, prior provisions, reorganization plans,executive orders, and other matters.

References

This volume contains cross references to constitutional and code provisions. Guidance to related materials in other publications is also provided, including references to the Code of Federal Regulations (CFR), the digest system collating judicial decisions from all jurisdictions, American Law Reports (ALR), encyclopedias, law review articles, forms and texts.

Notes of Decisions

The case annotations or constructions of the courts are arranged under numbered catchlines so that the user, by referring to the same catchline number in the supplementary pamphlets and pocket parts, can readily locate the latest decisions on any phase of the law. The catchlines are themselves collated and indexed to facilitate access to the judicial and administrative decisions classified to each section.

The annotations cover decisions of the Federal courts, the Comptroller General, the United States Merit Systems Protection Board, formal opinions of the Attorney General, and the informal opinions of the Office of Legal Counsel of the Department of Justice.

The annotations close with the following:

Reports	Abbreviations
Supreme Court Reporter	130 S.Ct. 2148
Federal Reporter, Third Series	605 F.3d 984
Federal Supplement, Second Series	691 F.Supp.2d 1381
Federal Rules Decisions	266 F.R.D. 501
United States Merit Systems Protection Board Reporter	113 M.S.P.R. 468
Federal Claims Reporter	92 Fed.Cl. 360
Military Justice Reporter	69 M.J.
	#2 C.M.A. 22
	#2 C.M.R. 512

EXPLANATION

Index to Text

A complete index to the text of the laws contained in Title 16 appears at the end of this title.

THE PUBLISHER

September 2010

VIII

RELATED PRODUCTS IN
FEDERAL LAW FROM WEST

FEDERAL PRACTICE

COURTROOM HANDBOOK ON FEDERAL EVIDENCE
Steven Goode and Olin Guy Wellborn III

FEDERAL CIVIL RULES HANDBOOK
Steven Baicker–McKee, William Janssen and John B. Corr

MODERN SCIENTIFIC EVIDENCE
David L. Faigman, David H. Kaye, Michael J. Saks,
Joseph Sanders, and Edward K. Cheng

FEDERAL JURY PRACTICE AND INSTRUCTIONS
Kevin F. O'Malley, Jay E. Grenig and William C. Lee
[Also available in CD–ROM]

FEDERAL PRACTICE AND PROCEDURE
Charles Alan Wright, Arthur R. Miller, Mary Kay Kane, Edward H. Cooper,
Richard L. Marcus, Kenneth W. Graham, Victor James Gold, Richard D.
Freer, Vikram David Amar, Joan E. Steinman, Andrew D. Leipold, Peter
J. Henning, Sarah H. Welling, Nancy J. King, Susan R. Klein, Charles H.
Koch, Jr., Catherine T. Struve, and Michael H. Graham
[Also available in CD–ROM]

WEST'S FEDERAL ADMINISTRATIVE PRACTICE
Authored by Federal Practice Experts

WEST'S FEDERAL FORMS
Authored by Federal Practice Experts
[Also available in CD–ROM]

FEDERAL COURT OF APPEALS MANUAL
David G. Knibb

**FEDERAL PRACTICE AND PROCEDURE—
FEDERAL PRACTICE DESKBOOK**
Charles Alan Wright and Mary Kay Kane

HANDBOOK OF FEDERAL EVIDENCE
Michael H. Graham

TREATISE ON CONSTITUTIONAL LAW
Ronald D. Rotunda and John E. Nowak

ADMINISTRATIVE LAW AND PRACTICE
Charles H. Koch, Jr.

FEDERAL TRIAL OBJECTIONS
Charles B. Gibbons

BUSINESS AND COMMERCIAL LITIGATION IN FEDERAL COURTS
Robert L. Haig, Editor–In–Chief

RELATED PRODUCTS

NEWBERG ON CLASS ACTIONS, 3rd
Herbert Newberg and Alba Conte
HANDBOOK OF FEDERAL CIVIL DISCOVERY AND DISCLOSURE
Jay E. Grenig and Jeffrey S. Kinsler
[Includes forms on Disk]
ANNOTATED MANUAL FOR COMPLEX LITIGATION
David F. Herr
MULTIDISTRICT LITIGATION MANUAL
David F. Herr
FEDERAL STANDARDS OF REVIEW
Hon. Harry T. Edwards and Linda A. Elliott

United States Code Annotated
West's Federal Practice Digest 4th
United States Code Congressional and Administrative News

CRIMINAL PRACTICE
SEARCH AND SEIZURE
Wayne R. LaFave
SUBSTANTIVE CRIMINAL LAW
Wayne R. LaFave
FEDERAL CRIMINAL RULES HANDBOOK
Laurie L. Levenson
CRIMINAL LAW DEFENSES
Paul H. Robinson
CRIMINAL PROCEDURE
Wayne R. LaFave, Jerold H. Israel, and Nancy J. King
FEDERAL SENTENCING LAW AND PRACTICE
Thomas W. Hutchison, Peter B. Hoffman, Deborah
Young, and Sigmund G. Popko
FEDERAL SENTENCING GUIDELINES HANDBOOK
Roger W. Haines, Jr., Frank O. Bowman III, and Jennifer C. Woll

---

Corpus Juris Secundum
West's Federal Case News
Federal Civil Judicial Procedure and Rules
Federal Criminal Code and Rules
Federal Environmental Laws
Federal Immigration Laws and Regulations

X

RELATED PRODUCTS

Federal Labor Laws
Federal Sentencing Guidelines
Federal Social Security Laws, Selected Statutes and Regulations
Federal Intellectual Property Laws and Regulations
Federal Litigator
Reference Manual on Scientific Evidence, Second
Manual for Complex Litigation, Fourth

TAX PUBLICATIONS

Federal Tax Regulations
Internal Revenue Code
Internal Revenue Acts

Westlaw®
WestCheck.com™
West CD–ROM Libraries™

To order any of these Federal practice tools, call your
West Representative or **1–800–328–9352**.

NEED RESEARCH HELP?

You can get quality research results with free help—call the West
Reference Attorneys when you have questions concerning Westlaw or West Publications at **1–800–REF–ATTY (1–800–733–
2889)**.

INTERNET ACCESS

Contact the West Editorial Department directly with your
questions and suggestions by e-mail at west.editor@thomson.com.
Visit West's home page at
west.thomson.com.

*

WestlawNext™

THE NEXT GENERATION OF ONLINE RESEARCH

WestlawNext is the world's most advanced legal research system. By leveraging more than a century of information and legal analysis from Westlaw, this easy-to-use system not only helps you find the information you need quickly, but offers time-saving tools to organize and annotate your research online. As with Westlaw.com, WestlawNext includes the editorial enhancements (e.g., case headnotes, topics, key numbers) that make it a perfect complement to West print resources.

- FIND ANYTHING by entering citations, descriptive terms, or Boolean terms and connectors into the WestSearch™ box at the top of every page.

- USE KEYCITE® to determine whether a case, statute, regulation, or administrative decision is good law.

- BROWSE DATABASES right from the home page.

- SAVE DOCUMENTS to folders and add notes and highlighting online.

SIGN ON: next.westlaw.com
LEARN MORE: West.Thomson.com/WestlawNext
FOR HELP: 1–800–WESTLAW (1–800–937–8529)

*

PREFACE
UNITED STATES CODE 2006 EDITION

———

This 2006 edition of the United States Code has been prepared and published under the supervision of Peter G. LeFevre, Law Revision Counsel of the House of Representatives, pursuant to section 285b of Title 2 of the Code. It contains the additions to and changes in the general and permanent laws of the United States enacted during the One Hundred Ninth Congress, Second Session. The last law of the 109th Congress was signed by the President on January 15, 2007. This 2006 edition establishes prima facie the general and permanent laws of the United States except for those titles of the Code that have been revised, codified, and enacted into positive law and are legal evidence of the law contained therein.

Nancy Pelosi

Speaker of the House of Representatives

Washington, D.C., *January 2007.*

*

ABBREVIATIONS

XVII

ABBREVIATIONS

Cite this Book

Thus: 16 U.S.C.A. § ——

*

UNITED STATES CODE ANNOTATED

TITLE 16

CONSERVATION

Sections 411 to 460o–7 appear in this Volume

1

CONSERVATION

CHAPTER 1—NATIONAL PARKS, MILITARY PARKS, MONUMENTS, AND SEASHORES

SUBCHAPTER I—NATIONAL PARK SERVICE

Sec.
1.   Service created; director; other employees.
1a.   Repealed.
1a–1.   National Park System: administration; declaration of findings and purpose.
1a–2.   Secretary of the Interior's authorization of activities.
1a–3.   Legislative jurisdiction; relinquishment by Secretary; submittal of proposed agreement to Congressional committees; concurrent legislative jurisdiction.
1a–4.   Uniform allowance.
1a–5.   Additional areas for National Park System.
1a–6.   Law enforcement personnel within National Park System.
1a–7.   National Park System development program.
1a–7a.   National Park System crime prevention assistance.
1a–7b.   Protecting Americans from violent crime.
1a–8.   Maintenance management system.
1a–9.   Periodic review of National Park System.
1a–10.   Consultation with affected agencies and organizations.
1a–11.   Contents of report.
1a–12.   Evaluation of proposed boundary changes.
1a–13.   Proposals for boundary changes.
1a–14.   National park system advisory committees.
1b.   Secretary of the Interior's authorization of additional activities; administration of National Park System.
1c.   General administration provisions; system defined; particular areas.
1d.   Appropriations.
1e.   National Capital region arts and cultural affairs; grant program.
1f.   Challenge cost–share agreement authority.
1g.   Cooperative agreements.
1h.   Sums provided by private entities for utility services.

4

9

18

Sec.

22

Sec.

39

41

50

51

58

Sec.

SUBCHAPTER LX—NATIONAL MILITARY PARKS

CROSS REFERENCES

Purchase of real estate for future military parks, see 16 USCA § 455c.

§ 411. Military maneuvers

In order to obtain practical benefits of great value to the country from the establishment of national military parks, said parks and their approaches are declared to be national fields for military maneuvers for the Regular Army of the United States and the National Guard or militia of the States. Said parks shall be opened for such purposes only in the discretion of the Secretary of the Army, and under such regulations as he may prescribe.

(May 15, 1896, c. 182, § 1, 29 Stat. 120.)

HISTORICAL AND STATUTORY NOTES

Change of Name

The Department of War was designated the Department of the Army and the title of the Secretary of War was changed to Secretary of the Army by section 205(a) of Act July 26, 1947, c. 343, Title II, 61 Stat. 501. Section 205(a) of Act July 26, 1947, was repealed by section 53 of Act Aug. 10, 1956, c. 1041, 70A Stat. 641. Section 1 of Act Aug. 10, 1956, enacted "Title 10, Armed Forces" which in sections 3011 to 3013 continued the military Department of the Army under the administrative supervision of a Secretary of the Army.

Transfer of Functions

Administrative functions of certain national military parks were transferred to the Department of the Interior by Ex. Ord. No. 6166, § 2, June 10, 1933, and

Ex. Ord. No. 6228, § 1, July 28, 1933, set out as a note under section 901 of Title 5, Government Organization and Employees.

National Park Service was substituted for Office of National Parks, Buildings, and Reservations referred to in Ex. Ord. No. 6166, § 2, June 10, 1933, by Act Mar. 2, 1934, c. 38, § 1, 48 Stat. 389.

Secretary of the Air Force

For transfer of certain real property functions, insofar as they pertain to the Air Force, to the Secretary of the Air Force and the Department of the Air Force, from the Secretary of the Army and the Department of the Army, see Secretary of Defense Transfer Order No. 14 [§ 2(31)], eff. July 1, 1948.

CODE OF FEDERAL REGULATIONS

Licensed guide service at national military parks, see 36 CFR § 25.1 et seq.
National cemeteries, use of, see 36 CFR § 12.1 et seq.

LIBRARY REFERENCES

American Digest System
Armed Services ☞54.
Woods and Forests ☞5.
Key Number System Topic Nos. 34, 411.

§ 412. Camps for military instruction; regulations for militia

The Secretary of the Army is authorized, within the limits of appropriations which may from time to time be available for such purpose, to assemble, at his discretion, in camp at such season of the year and for such period as he may designate, at such field of military maneuvers, such portions of the military forces of the United States as he may think best, to receive military instruction there.

The Secretary of the Army is further authorized to make and publish regulations governing the assembling of the National Guard or militia of the several States upon the maneuvering grounds, and he may detail instructors from the Regular Army for such forces during their exercises.

(May 15, 1896, c. 182, § 2, 29 Stat. 121.)

HISTORICAL AND STATUTORY NOTES

Change of Name

The Department of War was designated the Department of the Army and the title of the Secretary of War was changed to Secretary of the Army by section 205(a) of Act July 26, 1947, c. 343, Title II, 61 Stat. 501. Section 205(a) of Act July 26, 1947, was repealed by section 53 of Act Aug. 10, 1956, c. 1041, 70A Stat. 641. Section 1 of Act Aug. 10, 1956, enacted "Title 10, Armed Forces" which in sections 300 et seq. continued the military Department of the Army under the ad-

ministrative supervision of a Secretary of the Army.

Secretary of the Air Force

For transfer of certain functions, personnel and property, insofar as they pertain to the Air Force, from the Secretary of the Army and the Department of the Army to the Secretary of the Air Force and the Department of the Air Force, see Secretary of Defense Transfer Order Nos. 1, Sept. 26, 1947; 10, Apr. 27, 1948; and 40 [App. B(65)], July 22, 1949.

LIBRARY REFERENCES

American Digest System
    Armed Services ⊕54.
    Militia ⊕14.
    Woods and Forests ⊕5.
    Key Number System Topic Nos. 34, 259, 411.

§ 413. Offenses relating to structures and vegetation

Every person who willfully destroys, mutilates, defaces, injures, or removes any monument, statue, marker, guidepost, or other structure, or who willfully destroys, cuts, breaks, injures, or removes any tree, shrub, or plant within the limits of any national military parks shall be deemed guilty of a misdemeanor, punishable by a fine of not less than $10 nor more than $1,000 for each monument, statue, marker, guidepost, or other structure, tree, shrub, or plant destroyed, defaced, injured, cut, or removed, or by imprisonment for not less than fifteen days and not more than one year, or by both fine and imprisonment.

(Mar. 3, 1897, c. 372, §§ 1, 5, 29 Stat. 621, 622.)

LIBRARY REFERENCES

American Digest System
    Armed Services ⊕54.
    Woods and Forests ⊕10, 11.
    Key Number System Topic Nos. 34, 411.

§ 414. Trespassing for hunting, or shooting

Every person who shall trespass upon any national military parks for the purpose of hunting or shooting, or who shall hunt any kind of game thereon with gun or dog, or shall set trap or net or other device whatsoever thereon for the purpose of hunting or catching game of any kind, shall be guilty of a misdemeanor, punishable by a fine of not more than $1,000 or by imprisonment for not less than five days or more than thirty days, or by both fine and imprisonment.

(Mar. 3, 1897, c. 372, §§ 2, 5, 29 Stat. 621, 622.)

LIBRARY REFERENCES

American Digest System
  Game ⬤7, 8.
  Key Number System Topic No. 187.

§ 415.   Repealed.   Pub.L. 91–383, § 10(a)(1), as added Pub.L. 94–458, § 2, Oct. 7, 1976, 90 Stat. 1941

HISTORICAL AND STATUTORY NOTES

Section, Act Mar. 3, 1897, c. 372, §§ 3, 5, 29 Stat. 621, 622, authorized the superintendent or any guardian of a national military park to arrest and prosecute anyone engaged or who may have been engaged in committing any misdemeanor named in sections 413 and 414 of this title.

§ 416.   Refusal to surrender leased land; recovery

Any person to whom land lying within any national military parks may have been leased, who refuses to give up possession of the same to the United States after the termination of said lease, and after possession has been demanded for the United States by any park commissioner or the park superintendent, or any person retaining possession of land lying within the boundary of said park which he or she may have sold to the United States for park purposes and have received payment therefor, after possession of the same has been demanded for the United States by any park commissioner or the park superintendent, shall be deemed guilty of trespass, and the United States may maintain an action for the recovery of the possession of the premises so withheld in the courts of the United States, according to the statutes or code of practice of the State in which the park may be situated.

(Mar. 3, 1897, c. 372, §§ 4, 5, 29 Stat. 622.)

LIBRARY REFERENCES

American Digest System
  United States ⬤57.
  Woods and Forests ⬤10.
  Key Number System Topic Nos. 393, 411.

§ 417.   Omitted

HISTORICAL AND STATUTORY NOTES

Codifications
  Section, Act Aug. 18, 1894, c. 301, § 1, 28 Stat. 405, which authorized the acceptance, on behalf of the United States, of donations of land for road or other purposes, was considered obsolete by the Judge Advocate General. See JAG 601.1, June 27, 1935.

§ 418. Repealed. Feb. 20, 1931, c. 235, 46 Stat. 1191

HISTORICAL AND STATUTORY NOTES

Section, Act Mar. 3, 1925, c. 418, 43 Stat. 1104, authorizing the Secretary of War to convey to the States in which were located Government owned or controlled approach roads to national cemeteries and national military parks, was, in opinion of Judge Advocate General, repealed by Act Feb. 20, 1931, c. 235, 46 Stat. 1191, providing that no real estate of the Department of the Army should be disposed of without authority of Congress and providing "all existing acts or parts thereof in conflict with this proviso, other than special acts for the sale of stated tracts of land, are hereby repealed". See JAG 611, Dec. 3, 1931.

§ 419. Transferred

HISTORICAL AND STATUTORY NOTES

Codifications

Section, Act Feb. 15, 1901, c. 372, 31 Stat. 790, which related to rights-of-way for electrical plants, was transferred to section 79 of this title.

§ 420. Rights-of-way through military and other reservations for power and communications facilities

The head of the department having jurisdiction over the lands is authorized and empowered, under general regulations to be fixed by him, to grant an easement for rights-of-way, for a period not exceeding fifty years from the date of the issuance of such grant, over, across, and upon the public lands and reservations of the United States for electrical poles and lines for the transmission and distribution of electrical power, and for poles and lines for communication purposes, and for radio, television, and other forms of communication transmitting, relay, and receiving structures and facilities, to the extent of two hundred feet on each side of the center line of such lines and poles and not to exceed four hundred feet by four hundred feet for radio, television, and other forms of communication transmitting, relay, and receiving structures and facilities, to any citizen, association, or corporation of the United States, where it is intended by such to exercise the right-of-way herein granted for any one or more of the purposes herein named: *Provided*, That such right-of-way shall be allowed within or through any national park, military or any other reservation only upon the approval of the chief officer of the department under whose supervision or control such reservation falls, and upon a finding by him that the same is not incompatible with the public interest: *Provided further*, That all or any part of such right-of-way may be forfeited and annulled by declaration of the head of the department having jurisdiction over the lands for nonuse for a period of two years or for abandonment.

Any citizen, association, or corporation of the United States to whom there has been issued a permit prior to March 4, 1911, for any of the purposes specified herein under any law existing at that date, may obtain the benefit of this section upon the same terms and conditions as shall be required of citizens, associations, or corporations making application under the provisions of this section subsequent to such date.

(Mar. 4, 1911, c. 238, 36 Stat. 1253; May 27, 1952, c. 338, 66 Stat. 95.)

Repeals

Section repealed by Pub.L. 94–579, Title VII, § 706(a), Oct. 21, 1976, 90 Stat. 2793, effective on and after Oct. 21, 1976, insofar as applicable to the issuance of rights-of-way over, upon, under, and through the public lands and lands in the National Forest System.

HISTORICAL AND STATUTORY NOTES

Revision Notes and Legislative Reports
1952 Acts. House Report No. 1848, see 1952 U.S. Code Cong. and Adm. News, p. 1498.

Codifications
Section, in so far as it relates to rights-of-way in national parks and other reservations, is also set out as section 5 of this title; in so far as it relates to rights-of-way in national forests, is set out as section 523 of this title; and, in so far as it relates to rights-of-way on public lands generally, and Indian reservations, is set out as section 961 of Title 43, Public Lands.

Amendments
1952 Amendments. Act May 27, 1952, inserted reference to rights-of-way for radio, television, and other forms of communication, and increased from 40 feet to 400 feet the maximum width of rights-of-way for lines and poles.

Savings Provisions
Repeal by Pub.L. 94–579, Title VII, § 706(a), Oct. 21, 1976, 90 Stat. 2793, insofar as applicable to the issuance of rights-of-way, not to be construed as terminating any valid lease, permit, patent, etc., existing on Oct. 21, 1976, see note set out under section 1701 of Title 43, Public Lands.

CROSS REFERENCES

Issuance of licenses for construction, operation, and maintenance of transmission lines, for development, transmission, and utilization of power, across public lands and reservations, see 16 USCA § 797.

LIBRARY REFERENCES

American Digest System
Public Lands ⬤49.
Woods and Forests ⬤5.
Key Number System Topic Nos. 317, 411.

§ 421. Vacancies occurring in commissions in charge of parks not to be filled

Vacancies occurring by death or resignation in the membership of the several commissions in charge of national military parks shall not be filled, and the duties of the offices thus vacated shall devolve upon the remaining commissioners or commissioner for each of said parks. As vacancies occur the Secretary of the Army shall become ex officio a member of the commission effected with full authority to act with the remaining commissioners or commissioner, and in case of the vacation of all the offices of commissioner in any one park hereunder the duties of such commission shall thereafter be performed under the direction of the Secretary of the Army.

(Aug. 24, 1912, c. 355, § 1, 37 Stat. 442.)

HISTORICAL AND STATUTORY NOTES

Change of Name

The Department of War was designated the Department of the Army and the title of the Secretary of War was changed to Secretary of the Army by section 205(a) of Act July 26, 1947, c. 343, Title II, 61 Stat. 501. Section 205(a) of Act July 26, 1947, was repealed by section 53 of Act Aug. 10, 1956, c. 1041, 70A Stat. 641. Section 1 of Act Aug. 10, 1956, enacted "Title 10, Armed Forces" which in sections 3011 to 3013 continued the military Department of the Army under the administrative supervision of a Secretary of the Army.

Transfer of Functions

Administrative functions of certain national military parks were transferred to the Department of the Interior by Ex. Ord. No. 6166, § 2, June 10, 1933, and Ex. Ord. No. 6228, § 1, July 28, 1933, set out as a note under section 901 of Title 5, Government Organization and Employees.

National Park Service was substituted for Office of National Parks, Buildings, and Reservations referred to in Ex. Ord. No. 6166, § 2, June 10, 1933, by Act Mar. 2, 1934, c. 38, § 1, 48 Stat. 389.

Secretary of the Air Force

For transfer of certain membership functions to the Secretary of the Air Force, without prejudice to the continued membership of the Secretary of the Army, see Secretary of Defense Transfer Order No. 40, July 22, 1949.

LIBRARY REFERENCES

American Digest System

Woods and Forests ⚲7.
Key Number System Topic No. 411.

§ 422. Moores Creek National Battlefield; establishment

In order to preserve for historical and professional military study one of the most memorable battles of the Revolutionary War, the battlefield of Moores Creek, in the State of North Carolina, is declared to be a national battlefield whenever the title to the same shall have been acquired by the United States; that is to say, the area inclosed by the following lines:

Those tracts or parcels of land in the county of Pender, and State of North Carolina, more particularly described as follows:

First tract: Beginning at a stone at the run of Moores Creek, on the east bank of same, about twenty poles (in a straight line) above the new iron bridge, and running thence parallel to William Walker's line, south sixty-two and one-half degrees west eleven chains to a stake; thence south seven and one-half degrees east three and six-tenths chains to a stone at the south edge of the old stage road; thence along the south edge of said road south forty-six degrees east about five chains and eighty links to a stone; thence south thirty-seven and one-fourth degrees west fourteen chains and twelve links to a stone; thence north sixty-two and one-half degrees west ten chains and seventy-five links to a stone, a corner (4) of an eight-acre tract which the parties of the first part conveyed to Governor D. L. Russell, for the purposes aforesaid, by a deed dated January, 1898, and recorded in Pender County; thence with the lines of said tract north thirty-nine and one-half degrees east thirteen chains and twenty-seven links to a stake, the third corner of the said eight-acre tract; thence north fifty-one degrees west four chains to a stake about twenty feet from the old entrenchment (the second corner of the eight-acre tract); thence with the first line reversed north forty-four degrees west two chains to a sweet gum at the run of Moores Creek (the first corner of the eight-acre tract); thence up and with the run of said creek to the first station, containing twenty acres.

Second tract: Beginning at a sweet gum on the eastern edge of Moores Creek, running thence south forty-four degrees east two poles to a stake; thence south fifty-one degrees east four poles five links to a stake; thence south thirty-nine degrees west thirteen poles twenty-seven links to a stake; thence north fifty-one degrees west nine poles thirty-one links to a stake in the edge of Moores Creek; thence northerly with the creek to the beginning, containing eight acres more or less.

Third tract: Beginning at a cypress on the edge of the run of Moores Creek about twenty feet from the west end of the old entrenchments and running thence in a line parallel to and ten feet distance from the outside or east edge of the old line of entrenchments in all the various courses of the same to a stake ten feet distant on the east side of the north end of said entrenchments; thence a direct line to the run of said Moores Creek; thence down said creek to the beginning, containing two acres, be the same more or less (the intention is to include all lands now known and designated as Moores Creek battlefield and now so recognized as such and owned by the State of North Carolina), together with all the privileges and appurtenances thereunto belonging.

The aforesaid tracts of land containing in the aggregate thirty acres, more or less, and being the property of the State of North

Carolina, and the area thus inclosed shall be known as the Moores Creek National Battlefield.

(June 2, 1926, c. 448, § 1, 44 Stat. 684; Sept. 8, 1980, Pub.L. 96–344, § 12, 94 Stat. 1136.)

HISTORICAL AND STATUTORY NOTES

Change of Name

In the first undesignated paragraph, "battlefield" was substituted for "military park" and in the last undesignated paragraph "Battlefield" was substituted for "Military Park" on authority of Pub.L. 96–344, § 12, Sept. 8, 1980, 94 Stat. 1136, which redesignated the Moores Creek National Military Park as the Moores Creek National Battlefield.

LIBRARY REFERENCES

American Digest System

Armed Services ⬄54.
Woods and Forests ⬄1, 2.
Key Number System Topic Nos. 34, 411.

§ 422a.   Acceptance of lands

The establishment of the Moores Creek National Battlefield shall be carried forward under the control and direction of the Secretary of the Interior, who is authorized to receive from the State of North Carolina a deed of conveyance to the United States of all the lands belonging to the said State, embracing thirty acres, more or less, and described more particularly in section 422 of this title.

(June 2, 1926, c. 448, § 2, 44 Stat. 685; Ex. Ord. No. 6166, § 2, June 10, 1933; Ex. Ord. No. 6228, § 1, July 28, 1933; Sept. 8, 1980, Pub.L. 96–344, § 12, 94 Stat. 1136.)

HISTORICAL AND STATUTORY NOTES

Change of Name

"Battlefield" was substituted for "Military Park" on authority of Pub.L. 96–344, § 12, Sept. 8, 1980, 94 Stat. 1136, which redesignated the Moores Creek National Military Park as the Moores Creek National Battlefield.

Transfer of Functions

Administrative functions of Moores Creek National Military Park were transferred to the Department of the Interior by Ex. Ord. No. 6166 and Ex.Ord. No. 6228, set out as a note under section 901 of Title 5, Government Organization and Employees.

LIBRARY REFERENCES

American Digest System

Armed Services ⬄54.
United States ⬄55.
Woods and Forests ⬄2.
Key Number System Topic Nos. 34, 393, 411.

§ 422a–1. Acquisition of property

The Secretary of the Interior is authorized, in his discretion, to acquire by donation, purchase, or exchange lands, buildings, structures, and other property, or interests therein, which he may determine to be of historical interest in connection with the Moores Creek National Battlefield, the title to such property or interests to be satisfactory to the Secretary of the Interior: *Provided*, That the area acquired pursuant to this section shall not exceed one hundred acres. All such property and interests, upon acquisition by the Federal Government, shall be a part of the Moores Creek National Battlefield and shall be subject to all laws and regulations applicable thereto.

(Sept. 27, 1944, c. 417, § 1, 58 Stat. 746; Oct. 26, 1974, Pub.L. 93–477, Title IV, § 402, 88 Stat. 1447; Sept. 8, 1980, Pub.L. 96–344, § 12, 94 Stat. 1136.)

HISTORICAL AND STATUTORY NOTES

Amendments
  1974 Amendments. Pub.L. 93–477 substituted "acquire by donation, purchase, or exchange" for "accept in behalf of the United States donations of", and substituted "acquired" for "to be accepted".

Change of Name
  "Battlefield" was substituted for "Military Park" on authority of Pub.L. 96–344,

§ 12, Sept. 8, 1980, 94 Stat. 1136, which redesignated the Moores Creek National Military Park as the Moores Creek National Battlefield.

LIBRARY REFERENCES

American Digest System
  Armed Services ⊷54.
  United States ⊷55.
  Woods and Forests ⊷2.
  Key Number System Topic Nos. 34, 393, 411.

§ 422a–2. Authorization of appropriations

There are authorized to be appropriated such sums as may be necessary to carry out the purposes of section 422a–1 of this title, but not more than $243,000 shall be appropriated for the acquisition of lands and interests in lands and not more than $325,000 shall be appropriated for development.

(Sept. 27, 1944, c. 417, § 2, as added Oct. 26, 1974, Pub.L. 93–477, Title I, § 101(7), 88 Stat. 1445.)

§ 422b. Duties of Secretary of the Interior

The affairs of the Moores Creek National Battlefield shall be subject to the supervision and direction of the Secretary of the Interior, and it shall be the duty of the Interior Department, under the direction of the Secretary of the Interior, to open or repair such roads as may be necessary to the purposes of the battlefield, and to ascertain and mark with historical tablets or otherwise, as the Secretary of the Interior may determine, all lines of battle of the troops engaged in the Battle of Moores Creek, and other historical points of interest pertaining to the battle within the battlefield or its vicinity; and the Secretary of the Interior in establishing this battlefield is authorized to employ such labor and services and to obtain such supplies and material as may be considered best for the interest of the Government, and the Secretary of the Interior shall make and enforce all needed regulations for the care of the battlefield.

(June 2, 1926, c. 448, § 3, 44 Stat. 685; Ex.Ord. No. 6166, § 2, June 10, 1933; Ex.Ord. No. 6228, § 1, July 28, 1933; Sept. 8, 1980, Pub.L. 96–344, § 12, 94 Stat. 1136.)

HISTORICAL AND STATUTORY NOTES

Change of Name

"Battlefield" and "battlefield" were substituted for "Military Park" and "park", respectively, on authority of Pub.L. 96–344, § 12, Sept. 8, 1980, 94 Stat. 1136, which redesignated the Moores Creek National Military Park as the Moores Creek National Battlefield.

Transfer of Functions

Transfer of administrative functions of park [now battlefield], see note set out under section 422a of this title.

LIBRARY REFERENCES

American Digest System

United States ⬤57.
Woods and Forests ⬤5.
Key Number System Topic Nos. 393, 411.

§ 422c. Ascertaining and marking of lines of battle

It shall be lawful for any State that had troops engaged in the battle of the Moores Creek National Battlefield, to enter upon the same for the purpose of ascertaining and marking the lines of battle of its troops engaged therein: *Provided*, That before any such lines are permanently designated the position of the lines and the proposed methods of marking them by monuments, tablets, or otherwise, shall be submitted to and approved by the Secretary of the Interior; and all such lines, designs, and inscriptions for the same shall first receive the written approval of the Secretary of the Interior.

(June 2, 1926, c. 448, § 4, 44 Stat. 686; Ex.Ord. No. 6166, § 2, June 10, 1933; Ex.Ord. No. 6228, § 1, July 28, 1933; Sept. 8, 1980, Pub.L. 96–344, § 12, 94 Stat. 1136.)

HISTORICAL AND STATUTORY NOTES

Change of Name

"Battlefield" was substituted for "Military Park" on authority of Pub.L. 96–344, § 12, Sept. 8, 1980, 94 Stat. 1136, which redesignated the Moores Creek National

Military Park as the Moores Creek National Battlefield.

Transfer of Functions
   Transfer of administrative functions of park [now battlefield], see note set out under section 422a of this title.

LIBRARY REFERENCES

American Digest System
   Armed Services ☜54.
   Key Number System Topic No. 34.

§ 422d.   Monuments, etc., protected

If any person shall, except by permission of the Secretary of the Interior, destroy, deface, injure, or remove any monument, column, statues, memorial structures, or work of art, which shall be placed upon the grounds of the park by lawful authority, or shall destroy or remove any fence, railing, inclosure, or other mark for the protection or ornamentation of said park, or any portion thereof, or shall destroy, cut, hack, bark, break down, or otherwise injure any tree, brush, or shrubbery that may be growing upon said park, or shall cut down or remove or fell any timber, battle relic, tree, or tree growing upon said park, or hunt within the limits of the park, any person so offending and found guilty thereof before any justice of the peace of the county of Pender, State of North Carolina, shall, for each and every offense, forfeit and pay a fine, in the discretion of the justice, according to the aggravation of the offense, of not less than $5 nor more than $50, one-half for the use of the park and the other half to the informer, to be enforced and recovered before such justice in like manner as fines of like nature were, on June 2, 1926, by law recoverable in the said county of Pender, State of North Carolina.

(June 2, 1926, c. 448, § 5, 44 Stat. 686; Ex.Ord. No. 6166, § 2, June 10, 1933; Ex.Ord. No. 6228, § 1, July 28, 1933.)

HISTORICAL AND STATUTORY NOTES

Transfer of Functions
   Transfer of administrative functions of park, see note set out under section 422a of this title.

LIBRARY REFERENCES

American Digest System
   Armed Services ☜54.
   Woods and Forests ☜5, 10, 11.
   Key Number System Topic Nos. 34, 411.

§ 423.   Petersburg National Battlefield;   establishment

In order to commemorate the campaign and siege and defense of Petersburg, Virginia, in 1864 and 1865 and to preserve for historical purposes the breastworks, earthworks, walls, or other defenses or shelters used by the armies therein, the battle fields at Petersburg, in the State of Virginia, are declared a national battlefield whenever the title to the same shall have been acquired by the United States by donation and the usual jurisdiction over the lands and roads of the same shall have been granted to the United States by the State of Virginia—that is to say, one hundred and eighty-five acres or so much thereof as the Secretary of the Interior may deem necessary in and about the city of Petersburg, State of Virginia.

(July 3, 1926, c. 746, § 1, 44 Stat. 822; Ex. Ord. No. 6166, § 2, June 10, 1933; Ex. Ord. No. 6228, § 1, July 28, 1933; Aug. 24, 1962, Pub.L. 87–603, § 1, 76 Stat. 403.)

HISTORICAL AND STATUTORY NOTES

Change of Name

"National battlefield" was substituted for "national military park" in view of the redesignation of the Petersburg National Military Park as the Petersburg National Battlefield by Pub.L. 87–603. See section 423h–1 of this title.

Transfer of Functions

Administrative functions of Petersburg National Military Park [now Petersburg National Battlefield] were transferred to the Department of the Interior by Ex. Ord. No. 6166 and Ex. Ord. No. 6228, set out as a note under section 901 of Title 5, Government Organization and Employees.

National Park Service was substituted for Office of National Parks, Buildings, and Reservations referred to in Ex. Ord.

No. 6166, § 2, by Act Mar. 2, 1934, c. 38, § 1, 48 Stat. 389.

Transfer of Portion of Lands to Secretary of the Army

Act June 5, 1942, c. 345, 56 Stat. 322, provided: "That the Secretary of the Interior shall transfer to the Secretary of War [Army] jurisdiction over all lands owned by the United States lying south and east of the Hickory Hill Road within the Petersburg National Military Park [now Petersburg National Battlefield] in the Commonwealth of Virginia. Upon the date of the transfer, the lands shall cease to be a part of the Petersburg National Military Park [now Petersburg National Battlefield] and the Secretary of War [Army] shall thereafter administer the lands for military purposes."

CROSS REFERENCES

Acquisition of lands, see 16 USCA § 423h–2.
Duties of commission, see 16 USCA § 423c.
Petersburg National Battlefield Fund, acceptance and disposition of gifts, see 16 USCA § 423d.
Redesignation of park, see 16 USCA § 423h–1.

LIBRARY REFERENCES

American Digest System

Armed Services ☞54.
Woods and Forests ☞2.
Key Number System Topic Nos. 34, 411.

§ 423a.   Acceptance of donations of lands

The Secretary of the Interior is authorized to accept, on behalf of the United States, donations of lands, interests therein, or rights pertaining thereto required for the Petersburg National Battlefield.

(July 3, 1926, c. 746, § 2, 44 Stat. 822; Ex.Ord. No. 6166, § 2, June 10, 1933; Ex.Ord. No. 6228, § 1, July 28, 1933; Aug. 24, 1962, Pub.L. 87–603, § 1, 76 Stat. 403.)

HISTORICAL AND STATUTORY NOTES

Change of Name

"Petersburg National Battlefield" was substituted for "Petersburg National Military Park" pursuant to Pub.L. 87–603, § 1, Aug. 24, 1962, 76 Stat. 403, which redesignated the "Petersburg National Military Park" as the "Petersburg Nation-al Battlefield". See section 423h–1 of this title.

Transfer of Functions

Transfer of administrative functions of park [now battlefield], see note set out under section 423 of this title.

CROSS REFERENCES

Acceptance of gifts by commission, see 16 USCA § 423d.
Acquisition of lands, see 16 USCA § 423h–2.
Duties of commission, see 16 USCA § 423c.
Redesignation of park, see 16 USCA § 423h–1.

LIBRARY REFERENCES

American Digest System

Armed Services ☞54.
United States ☞55.
Key Number System Topic Nos. 34, 393.

§ 423a–1.   Addition of lands

The Department of the Army is authorized and directed to transfer to the Department of the Interior, without reimbursement, two tracts of land, comprising two hundred six acres, more or less, situated on either side of Siege Road adjacent to Petersburg National Battlefield, Virginia. Upon completion of such transfer, all lands, interest in lands, and other property in Federal ownership and under the administration of the National Park Service as a part of or in conjunction with Petersburg National Battlefield, in and about the city of Petersburg, Virginia, and comprising one thousand five hundred thirty-one acres, more or less, upon publication of the description thereof in the Federal Register by the Secretary of the Interior, shall constitute the Petersburg National Battlefield.

(Sept. 7, 1949, c. 543, § 1, 63 Stat. 691; Aug. 24, 1962, Pub.L. 87–603, § 1, 76 Stat. 403.)

HISTORICAL AND STATUTORY NOTES

Revision Notes and Legislative Reports
1949 Acts. Senate Report No. 932, see 1949 U.S. Code Cong. Service, p. 1947.

Change of Name
"Petersburg National Battlefield" was substituted for "Petersburg National Military Park" pursuant to Pub.L. 87–603, § 1, Aug. 24, 1962, 76 Stat. 403, which redesignated the "Petersburg National Military Park" as the "Petersburg National Battlefield". See section 423h–1 of this title.

Transfer of Functions
All functions of all other officers of the Department of the Interior and all func-

tions of all agencies and employees of such Department were, with two exceptions, transferred to the Secretary of the Interior, with power vested in him to authorize their performance or the performance of any of his functions by any of such officers, agencies, and employees, by 1950 Reorg. Plan No. 3, §§ 1, 2, eff. May 24, 1950, 15 F.R. 3174, 64 Stat. 1262, set out in Appendix 1 to Title 5, Government Organization and Employees.

CROSS REFERENCES

Redesignation of park, see 16 USCA § 423h–1.

LIBRARY REFERENCES

American Digest System
Armed Services ⏘54.
United States ⏘55.
Woods and Forests ⏘4.
Key Number System Topic Nos. 34, 393, 411.

§ 423a–2. Adjustment of boundary

The Secretary of the Interior is further authorized to adjust the boundary of the Petersburg National Battlefield through purchase, exchange, or transfer: *Provided,* That in doing so the total area of the battlefield will not be increased and that such changes will become effective upon publication of the description thereof in the Federal Register by the Secretary of the Interior.

(Sept. 7, 1949, c. 543, § 2, 63 Stat. 692; Aug. 24, 1962, Pub.L. 87–603, § 1, 76 Stat. 403.)

HISTORICAL AND STATUTORY NOTES

Revision Notes and Legislative Reports
1949 Acts. Senate Report No. 932, see 1949 U.S. Code Cong. Service, p. 1947.

Change of Name
"Petersburg National Battlefield" and "battlefield" were substituted for "Peters-

burg National Military Park" and "park", respectively, pursuant to Pub.L. 87–603, § 1, Aug. 24, 1962, 76 Stat. 403, which redesignated the "Petersburg National Military Park" as the "Petersburg National Battlefield". See section 423h–1 of this title.

CROSS REFERENCES

Redesignation of park, see 16 USCA § 423h–1.

LIBRARY REFERENCES

American Digest System
  Armed Services ⚷54.
  United States ⚷55.
  Woods and Forests ⚷1.
  Key Number System Topic Nos. 34, 393, 411.

§ 423b. Commission; organization

The affairs of the Petersburg National Battlefield shall, subject to the supervision and direction of the Secretary of the Interior, be in charge of three commissioners, consisting of Army officers, civilians, or both, to be appointed by the Secretary of the Interior, one of whom shall be designated as chairman and another as secretary of the commission.

(July 3, 1926, c. 746, § 3, 44 Stat. 822; Ex.Ord. No. 6166, § 2, June 10, 1933; Ex.Ord. No. 6228, § 1, July 28, 1933; Aug. 24, 1962, Pub.L. 87–603, § 1, 76 Stat. 403.)

HISTORICAL AND STATUTORY NOTES

Change of Name
  "Petersburg National Battlefield" was substituted for "Petersburg National Military Park" pursuant to Pub.L. 87–603, § 1, Aug. 24, 1962, 76 Stat. 403, which redesignated the "Petersburg National Military Park" as the "Petersburg National Battlefield". See section 423h–1 of this title.

Transfer of Functions
  Transfer of administrative functions of park [now battlefield], see note set out under section 423 of this title.

CROSS REFERENCES

  Acceptance of gifts, see 16 USCA § 423d.
  Acquisition of lands by Secretary of Interior, see 16 USCA § 423h–2.
  Duties, see 16 USCA § 423c.
  Redesignation of park, see 16 USCA § 423h–1.

LIBRARY REFERENCES

American Digest System
  Armed Services ⚷54.
  Woods and Forests ⚷7.
  Key Number System Topic Nos. 34, 411.

§ 423c. Duties of commission

It shall be the duties of the commissioners, under the direction of the Secretary of the Interior, to superintend the opening or repair of such roads as may be necessary to the purposes of the battlefield, and to ascertain and mark with historical tablets or otherwise, as the Secretary of the Interior may determine, all breastworks, earthworks, walls, or other defenses or shelters, lines of battle, location of troops, buildings, and other historical points of interest within the battlefield or in its vicinity, and the said commission in establishing the battlefield shall have authority, under the direction of the Secretary of the Interior, to employ such labor and service at rates to be fixed by the Secretary of the Interior, and to obtain such supplies and materials as may be necessary to carry out the provisions of sections 423, 423a, and 423b to 423h of this title.

(July 3, 1926, c. 746, § 4, 44 Stat. 822; Ex.Ord. No. 6166, § 2, June 10, 1933; Ex.Ord. No. 6228, § 1, July 28, 1933; Aug. 24, 1962, Pub.L. 87–603, § 1, 76 Stat. 403.)

HISTORICAL AND STATUTORY NOTES

Change of Name

"Battlefield" was substituted for "park" wherever appearing in view of the redesignation of the "Petersburg National Military Park" as the "Petersburg National Battlefield" by Pub.L. 87–603. See section 423h–1 of this title.

Transfer of Functions

Transfer of administrative functions of park [now battlefield], see note set out under section 423 of this title.

CROSS REFERENCES

Acceptance of gifts, see 16 USCA § 423d.
Acquisition of lands by Secretary of Interior, see 16 USCA § 423h–2.
Redesignation of park, see 16 USCA § 423h–1.

LIBRARY REFERENCES

American Digest System

Woods and Forests ☞7.
Key Number System Topic No. 411.

§ 423d. Acceptance and disposition of gifts

The commission, acting through the Secretary of the Interior, is authorized to receive gifts and contributions from States, Territories, societies, organizations, and individuals for the Petersburg National Battlefield: *Provided,* That all contributions of money received shall be deposited in the Treasury of the United States and credited to a fund to be designated "Petersburg National Battlefield Fund", which fund shall be applied to and expended under the direction of the Secretary of the Interior, for carrying out the provisions of sections 423, 423a, and 423b to 423h of this title.

(July 3, 1926, c. 746, § 5, 44 Stat. 822; Ex.Ord. No. 6166, § 2, June 10, 1933; Ex.Ord. No. 6228, § 1, July 28, 1933; Aug. 24, 1962, Pub.L. 87–603, § 1, 76 Stat. 403.)

HISTORICAL AND STATUTORY NOTES

Change of Name

"Petersburg National Battlefield" was substituted for "Petersburg National Military Park" pursuant to Pub.L. 87–603,

§ 1, Aug. 24, 1962, 76 Stat. 403, which redesignated the "Petersburg National Military Park" as the "Petersburg National Battlefield". See section 423h–1 of this title.

Transfer of Functions
Transfer of administrative functions of park [now battlefield], see note set out under section 423 of this title.

CROSS REFERENCES

Acquisition of lands by Secretary of Interior, see 16 USCA § 423h–2.
Duties of commission, see 16 USCA § 423c.
Redesignation of park, see 16 USCA § 423h–1.

LIBRARY REFERENCES

American Digest System
Armed Services ☞54.
United States ☞55.
Key Number System Topic Nos. 34, 393.

§ 423e.   Ascertaining and marking lines of battle

It shall be lawful for the authorities of any State having had troops engaged at Petersburg, to enter upon the lands and approaches of the Petersburg National Battlefield for the purpose of ascertaining and marking the lines of battle of troops engaged therein: *Provided,* That before any such lines are permanently designated, the position of the lines and the proposed methods of marking them by monuments, tablets, or otherwise, including the design and inscription for the same, shall be submitted to the Secretary of the Interior and shall first receive written approval of the Secretary, which approval shall be based upon formal written reports to be made to him in each case by the commissioners of the battlefield: *Provided,* That no discrimination shall be made against any State as to the manner of designating lines, but any grant made to any State by the Secretary of the Interior may be used by any other State.

(July 3, 1926, c. 746, § 6, 44 Stat. 823; Ex.Ord. No. 6166, § 2, June 10, 1933; Ex.Ord. No. 6228, § 1, July 28, 1933; Aug. 24, 1962, Pub.L. 87–603, § 1, 76 Stat. 403.)

HISTORICAL AND STATUTORY NOTES

Change of Name
"Petersburg National Battlefield" and "battlefield" were substituted for "Petersburg National Military Park" and "park", respectively, pursuant to Pub.L. 87–603, § 1, Aug. 24, 1962, 76 Stat. 403, which redesignated the "Petersburg National Military Park" as the "Petersburg National Battlefield". See section 423h–1 of this title.

Transfer of Functions
Transfer of administrative functions of park [now battlefield], see note set out under section 423 of this title.

CROSS REFERENCES

Acquisition of lands, see 16 USCA § 423h–2.
Duty of commission to ascertain and mark historical points of interest, see 16 USCA § 423c.
Petersburg National Battlefield Fund, acceptance and disposition of gifts, see 16 USCA § 423d.

85

Redesignation of park, see 16 USCA § 423h–1.

LIBRARY REFERENCES

American Digest System
Armed Services ⊂⇒54.
Woods and Forests ⊂⇒5.
Key Number System Topic Nos. 34, 411.

§ 423f. Protection of monuments, etc.

If any person shall, except by permission of the Secretary of the Interior, destroy, mutilate, deface, injure, or remove any monument, column, statues, memorial structures, or work of art that shall be erected or placed upon the grounds of the battlefield by lawful authority, or shall destroy or remove any fence, railing, inclosure, or other work for the protection or ornament of said battlefield, or any portion thereof, or shall destroy, cut, hack, bark, break down, or otherwise injure any tree, bush, or shrubbery that may be growing upon said battlefield, or shall cut down or fell or remove any timber, battle relic, tree or trees growing or being upon said battlefield, or hunt within the limits of the battlefield, or shall remove or destroy any breastworks, earthworks, walls, or other defenses or shelter or any part thereof constructed by the armies formerly engaged in the battles on the lands or approaches to the battlefield, any person so offending and found guilty thereof, before any United States magistrate judge or court, justice of the peace of the county in which the offense may be committed, or any other court of competent jurisdiction, shall for each and every such offense forfeit and pay a fine, in the discretion of the said United States magistrate judge or court, justice of the peace or other court, according to the aggravation of the offense, of not less than $5 nor more than $500, one-half for the use of the battlefield and the other half to the informant, to be enforced and recovered before such United States magistrate judge or court, justice of the peace or other court, in like manner as debts of like nature were, on July 3, 1926, by law recoverable in the several counties where the offense may be committed.

(July 3, 1926, c. 746, § 7, 44 Stat. 823; Ex.Ord. No. 6166, § 2, June 10, 1933; Ex.Ord. No. 6228, § 1, July 28, 1933; Aug. 24, 1962, Pub.L. 87–603, § 1, 76 Stat. 403; Oct. 17, 1968, Pub.L. 90–578, Title IV, § 402(b)(2), 82 Stat. 1118; Dec. 1, 1990, Pub.L. 101–650, Title III, § 321, 104 Stat. 5117.)

HISTORICAL AND STATUTORY NOTES

Revision Notes and Legislative Reports
1968 Acts. House Report No. 1629, see 1968 U.S. Code Cong. and Adm. News, p. 4252.

1990 Acts. Senate Report No. 101–416, see 1990 U.S. Code Cong. and Adm. News, p. 6802.

Change of Name
"United States magistrate judge" substituted for "United States magistrate" wherever appearing in text pursuant to section 321 of Pub.L. 101–650, set out as a note under section 631 of Title 28, Judiciary and Judicial Procedure. Previously, "United States magistrate" substituted for "United States commissioner" pursuant to Pub.L. 90–578. See chapter 43 (section 631 et seq.) of Title 28.

"Battlefield" was substituted for "park" wherever appearing in view of the redesignation of the Petersburg National Military Park as the Petersburg National Battlefield by Pub.L. 87–603. See section 423h–1 of this title.

Transfer of Functions
Transfer of administrative functions of park [now battlefield], see note set out under section 423 of this title.

CROSS REFERENCES

Acquisition of lands, see 16 USCA § 423h–2.
Duties of commission, see 16 USCA § 423c.
Petersburg National Battlefield Fund, acceptance and disposition of gifts, see 16 USCA § 423d.
Redesignation of park, see 16 USCA § 423h–1.

LIBRARY REFERENCES

American Digest System
Armed Services ☞54.
Woods and Forests ☞5.
Key Number System Topic Nos. 34, 411.

§ 423g. Rules and regulations

The Secretary of the Interior, subject to the approval of the President, shall have the power to make and shall make all needful rules and regulations for the care of the battlefield, and for the establishment and marking of lines of battle and other historical features of the battlefield.

(July 3, 1926, c. 746, § 8, 44 Stat. 823; Ex.Ord. No. 6166, § 2, June 10, 1933; Ex.Ord. No. 6228, § 1, July 28, 1933; Aug. 24, 1962, Pub.L. 87–603, § 1, 76 Stat. 403.)

HISTORICAL AND STATUTORY NOTES

Change of Name
"Battlefield" was substituted for "park" in two instances in view of the redesignation of Petersburg National Military Park as the Petersburg National Battlefield by Pub.L. 87–603. See section 423h–1 of this title.

Transfer of Functions
Transfer of administrative functions of park [now battlefield], see note set out under section 423 of this title.

CROSS REFERENCES

Acquisition of lands, see 16 USCA § 423h–2.
Duty of commission to ascertain and mark historical points of interest, see 16 USCA § 423c.
Petersburg National Battlefield Fund, acceptance and disposition of gifts, see 16 USCA § 423d.
Redesignation of park, see 16 USCA § 423h–1.

LIBRARY REFERENCES

American Digest System
Armed Services ⬤⇒54.
United States ⬤⇒57.
Woods and Forests ⬤⇒5.
Key Number System Topic Nos. 34, 393, 411.

§ 423h. Report of completion; superintendent of battlefield

Upon completion of the acquisition of the land and the work of the commission, the Secretary of the Interior shall render a report thereon to Congress, and thereafter the battlefield shall be placed in charge of a superintendent at a salary to be fixed by the Secretary of the Interior and paid out of the appropriation available for the maintenance of the battlefield.

(July 3, 1926, c. 746, § 9, 44 Stat. 823; Ex.Ord. No. 6166, § 2, June 10, 1933; Ex.Ord. No. 6228, § 1, July 28, 1933; Aug. 24, 1962, Pub.L. 87–603, § 1, 76 Stat. 403.)

HISTORICAL AND STATUTORY NOTES

Change of Name

"Battlefield" was substituted for "park" in two instances in view of the redesignation of Petersburg National Military Park as the Petersburg National Battlefield by Pub.L. 87–603. See section 423h–1 of this title.

Transfer of Functions

Transfer of administrative functions of park [now battlefield], see note set out under section 423 of this title.

CROSS REFERENCES

Acquisition of lands, see 16 USCA § 423h–2.
Duties of commission, see 16 USCA § 423c.
Petersburg National Battlefield Fund, acceptance and disposition of gifts, see 16 USCA § 423d.
Redesignation of park, see 16 USCA § 423h–1.

LIBRARY REFERENCES

American Digest System
Armed Services ⬤⇒54.
Woods and Forests ⬤⇒5.
Key Number System Topic Nos. 34, 411.

§ 423h–1. Redesignation of park

The Petersburg National Military Park, established under authority of sections 423, 423a and 423b to 423h of this title, and enlarged pursuant to sections 423a–1 and 423a–2 of this title, is redesignated the Petersburg National Battlefield.

(Pub.L. 87–603, § 1, Aug. 24, 1962, 76 Stat. 403.)

LIBRARY REFERENCES

American Digest System
    Armed Services ⊕54.
    Woods and Forests ⊕1.
    Key Number System Topic Nos. 34, 411.

§ 423h–2.   Acquisition of lands; publication in Federal Register; administration

The Secretary of the Interior, in furtherance of the purposes of sections 423, 423a and 423b to 423h of this title referred to in section 423h–1 of this title, may acquire by purchase with donated or appropriated funds, exchange, transfer, or by such other means as he deems to be in the public interest, not to exceed twelve hundred acres of land or interests in land at the site of the Battle of Five Forks for addition to the Petersburg National Battlefield. Lands and interests in lands acquired by the Secretary pursuant to this section shall, upon publication of a description thereof in the Federal Register, become a part of the Petersburg National Battlefield, and thereafter shall be administered by the Secretary of the Interior in accordance with the provisions of sections 1, 2, 3, and 4 of this title, as amended and supplemented.

(Pub.L. 87–603, § 2, Aug. 24, 1962, 76 Stat. 403.)

LIBRARY REFERENCES

American Digest System
    Armed Services ⊕54.
    United States ⊕55.
    Woods and Forests ⊕5.
    Key Number System Topic Nos. 34, 393, 411.

§ 423h–3.   Authorization of appropriation

There are authorized to be appropriated such sums, but not more than $90,000, as are necessary to acquire land pursuant to section 423h–2 of this title.

(Pub.L. 87–603, § 3, Aug. 24, 1962, 76 Stat. 403.)

§ 423i.   Omitted

HISTORICAL AND STATUTORY NOTES

Codifications
    Section, Act July 3, 1926, c. 746, § 10, 44 Stat. 823, appropriated $15,000 for carrying out provisions of sections 423, 423a and 423b to 423h of this title to be available until expended.

§§ 423j to 423*l*. Repealed. Pub.L. 106–511, Title V, § 507, Nov. 13, 2000, 114 Stat. 2376

HISTORICAL AND STATUTORY NOTES

Section 423j, Act Mar. 2, 1936, c. 113, § 1, 49 Stat. 1155, related to the establishment of Richmond National Battlefield Park.

Section 423k, Act Mar. 2, 1936, c. 113, § 2, 49 Stat. 1156, related to the acceptance of donations of lands, buildings, structures and other property, and funds for the purchase and/or maintenance of the Richmond National Battlefield Park.

Section 423*l*, Act Mar. 2, 1936, c. 113, § 3, 49 Stat. 1156, related to the administration, protection, and development of the Richmond National Battlefield Park.

§ 423*l*–1. Short title; definitions

(a) Short title

Sections 423*l*-1 to 423*l*-6 of this title may be cited as the "Richmond National Battlefield Park Act of 2000".

(b) Definitions

In sections 423*l*-1 to 423*l*-6 of this title:

(1) Battlefield park

The term "battlefield park" means the Richmond National Battlefield Park.

(2) Secretary

The term "Secretary" means the Secretary of the Interior.

(Pub.L. 106–511, Title V, § 501, Nov. 13, 2000, 114 Stat. 2373.)

HISTORICAL AND STATUTORY NOTES

Revision Notes and Legislative Reports
   2000 Acts. House Report No. 106–944, see 2000 U.S. Code Cong. and Adm. News, p. 2176.

References in Text
   Sections 423*l*–1 to 423*l*–6 of this title, referred to in text, was in the original "this title", meaning Pub.L. 106–511, Title V, Nov. 13, 2000, 114 Stat. 2373, which enacted 16 U.S.C.A. §§ 423*l*–1 to 423*l*–6, and repealed 16 U.S.C.A. §§ 423j to 423*l*. For complete classification of Title V to the Code, see Tables.

LIBRARY REFERENCES

American Digest System
   Armed Services ⏂54.
   Woods and Forests ⏂8.
   Key Number System Topic Nos. 34, 411.

§ 423*l*–2. Findings and purpose

(a) Findings

The Congress finds the following:

(1) In the Act of March 2, 1936 (Chapter 113; 49 Stat. 1155; 16 U.S.C. 423j), Congress authorized the establishment of the Richmond National Battlefield Park, and the boundaries of the battlefield park were established to permit the inclusion of all military battlefield areas related to the battles fought during the Civil War in the vicinity of the City of Richmond, Virginia. The battlefield park originally included the area then known as the Richmond Battlefield State Park.

(2) The total acreage identified in 1936 for consideration for inclusion in the battlefield park consisted of approximately 225,000 acres in and around the City of Richmond. A study undertaken by the congressionally authorized Civil War Sites Advisory Committee determined that of these 225,000 acres, the historically significant areas relating to the campaigns against and in defense of Richmond encompass approximately 38,000 acres.

(3) In a 1996 general management plan, the National Park Service identified approximately 7,121 acres in and around the City of Richmond that satisfy the National Park Service criteria of significance, integrity, feasibility, and suitability for inclusion in the battlefield park. The National Park Service later identified an additional 186 acres for inclusion in the battlefield park.

(4) There is a national interest in protecting and preserving sites of historical significance associated with the Civil War and the City of Richmond.

(5) The Commonwealth of Virginia and its local units of government have authority to prevent or minimize adverse uses of these historic resources and can play a significant role in the protection of the historic resources related to the campaigns against and in defense of Richmond.

(6) The preservation of the New Market Heights Battlefield in the vicinity of the City of Richmond is an important aspect of American history that can be interpreted to the public. The Battle of New Market Heights represents a premier landmark in black military history as 14 black Union soldiers were awarded the Medal of Honor in recognition of their valor during the battle. According to National Park Service historians, the sacrifices of the United States Colored Troops in this battle helped to ensure the passage of the Thirteenth Amendment to the United States Constitution to abolish slavery.

(b) Purpose

It is the purpose of sections 423*l*-1 to 423*l*-6 of this title—

(1) to revise the boundaries for the Richmond National Battlefield Park based on the findings of the Civil War Sites Advisory Committee and the National Park Service; and

(2) to direct the Secretary of the Interior to work in cooperation with the Commonwealth of Virginia, the City of Richmond, other political subdivisions of the Commonwealth, other public entities, and the private sector in the management, protection, and interpretation of the resources associated with the Civil War and the Civil War battles in and around the City of Richmond, Virginia.

(Pub.L. 106–511, Title V, § 502, Nov. 13, 2000, 114 Stat. 2373.)

HISTORICAL AND STATUTORY NOTES

Revision Notes and Legislative Reports
  2000 Acts. House Report No. 106–944, see 2000 U.S. Code Cong. and Adm. News, p. 2176.

References in Text
  The Act of March 2, 1936, referred to in subsec. (a)(1), is Act March 2, 1936, c. 113, 49 Stat. 1155, and was repealed by the Richmond National Battlefield Park Act of 2000, Pub.L. 106–511, Title V, § 507, Nov. 13, 2000, 114 Stat. 2376.

  Sections 423*l*–1 to 423*l*–6 of this title, referred to in subsec. (b), was in the original "this title", meaning Pub.L. 106–511, Title V, Nov. 13, 2000, 114 Stat. 2373, which enacted 16 U.S.C.A. §§ 423*l*–1 to 423*l*–6, and repealed 16 U.S.C.A. §§ 423j to 423*l*. For complete classification of Title V to the Code, see Tables.

LIBRARY REFERENCES

American Digest System
  Armed Services ⬦54.
  United States ⬦57.
  Woods and Forests ⬦8.
  Key Number System Topic Nos. 34, 393, 411.

§ 423*l*–3. Richmond National Battlefield Park; boundaries

(a) Establishment and purpose

For the purpose of protecting, managing, and interpreting the resources associated with the Civil War battles in and around the City of Richmond, Virginia, there is established the Richmond National Battlefield Park consisting of approximately 7,307 acres of land, as generally depicted on the map entitled "Richmond National Battlefield Park Boundary Revision", numbered 367N.E.F.A.80026A, and dated September 2000. The map shall be on file in the appropriate offices of the National Park Service.

(b) Boundary adjustments

The Secretary may make minor adjustments in the boundaries of the battlefield park consistent with section 460*l*–9(c) of this title.

(Pub.L. 106–511, Title V, § 503, Nov. 13, 2000, 114 Stat. 2374.)

HISTORICAL AND STATUTORY NOTES

Revision Notes and Legislative Reports
  2000 Acts. House Report No. 106–944,
see 2000 U.S. Code Cong. and Adm.
News, p. 2176.

LIBRARY REFERENCES

American Digest System
  Armed Services ☞54.
  United States ☞57.
  Woods and Forests ☞8.
  Key Number System Topic Nos. 34, 393, 411.

§ 423*l*–4.   Land acquisition

(a) Acquisition authority

(1) In general

The Secretary may acquire lands, waters, and interests in
lands within the boundaries of the battlefield park from willing
landowners by donation, purchase with donated or appropriated
funds, or exchange. In acquiring lands and interests in lands
under sections 423*l*–1 to 423*l*–6 of this title, the Secretary shall
acquire the minimum interest necessary to achieve the purposes
for which the battlefield is established.

(2) Special rule for private lands

Privately owned lands or interests in lands may be acquired
under sections 423*l*-1 to 423*l*-6 of this title only with the consent
of the owner.

(b) Easements

(1) Outside boundaries

The Secretary may acquire an easement on property outside
the boundaries of the battlefield park and around the City of
Richmond, with the consent of the owner, if the Secretary
determines that the easement is necessary to protect core Civil
War resources as identified by the Civil War Sites Advisory
Committee. Upon acquisition of the easement, the Secretary
shall revise the boundaries of the battlefield park to include the
property subject to the easement.

(2) Inside boundaries

To the extent practicable, and if preferred by a willing landowner, the Secretary shall use permanent conservation easements to acquire interests in land in lieu of acquiring land in fee
simple and thereby removing land from non-Federal ownership.

(c) Visitor center

The Secretary may acquire the Tredegar Iron Works buildings and associated land in the City of Richmond for use as a visitor center for the battlefield park.

(Pub.L. 106–511, Title V, § 504, Nov. 13, 2000, 114 Stat. 2374.)

HISTORICAL AND STATUTORY NOTES

Revision Notes and Legislative Reports
  2000 Acts. House Report No. 106–944, see 2000 U.S. Code Cong. and Adm. News, p. 2176.

References in Text
  Sections 423*l*–1 to 423*l*–6 of this title, referred to in subsec. (a), was in the origi-

nal "this title", meaning Pub.L. 106–511, Title V, Nov. 13, 2000, 114 Stat. 2373, which enacted 16 U.S.C.A. §§ 423*l*–1 to 423*l*–6, and repealed 16 U.S.C.A. §§ 423j to 423*l*. For complete classification of Title V to the Code, see Tables.

LIBRARY REFERENCES

American Digest System
  Armed Services ⚫=54.
  United States ⚫=55, 57.
  Woods and Forests ⚫=8.
  Key Number System Topic Nos. 34, 393, 411.

§ 423*l*–5. Park administration

(a) Applicable laws

The Secretary, acting through the Director of the National Park Service, shall administer the battlefield park in accordance with sections 423*l*-1 to 423*l*-6 of this title and laws generally applicable to units of the National Park System, including sections 1, 2, 3, and 4 of this title and sections 461 to 467 of this title.

(b) New Market Heights Battlefield

The Secretary shall provide for the establishment of a monument or memorial suitable to honor the 14 Medal of Honor recipients from the United States Colored Troops who fought in the Battle of New Market Heights. The Secretary shall include the Battle of New Market Heights and the role of black Union soldiers in the battle in historical interpretations provided to the public at the battlefield park.

(c) Cooperative agreements

The Secretary may enter into cooperative agreements with the Commonwealth of Virginia, its political subdivisions (including the City of Richmond), private property owners, and other members of the private sector to develop mechanisms to protect and interpret the historical resources within the battlefield park in a manner that would allow for continued private ownership and use where compatible with the purposes for which the battlefield is established.

(d) Technical assistance

The Secretary may provide technical assistance to the Commonwealth of Virginia, its political subdivisions, nonprofit entities, and private property owners for the development of comprehensive plans, land use guidelines, special studies, and other activities that are consistent with the identification, protection, interpretation, and commemoration of historically significant Civil War resources located inside and outside of the boundaries of the battlefield park. The technical assistance does not authorize the Secretary to own or manage any of the resources outside the battlefield park boundaries.

(Pub.L. 106–511, Title V, § 505, Nov. 13, 2000, 114 Stat. 2375.)

HISTORICAL AND STATUTORY NOTES

Revision Notes and Legislative Reports
2000 Acts. House Report No. 106–944, see 2000 U.S. Code Cong. and Adm. News, p. 2176.

References in Text
Sections 423*l*–1 to 423*l*–6 of this title, referred to in subsec. (a), was in the original "this title", meaning Pub.L. 106–511, Title V, Nov. 13, 2000, 114 Stat. 2373, which enacted 16 U.S.C.A. §§ 423*l*–1 to 423*l*–6, and repealed 16 U.S.C.A. §§ 423j to 423*l*. For complete classification of Title V to the Code, see Tables.

LIBRARY REFERENCES

American Digest System
Armed Services ⟨key⟩54.
United States ⟨key⟩57.
Woods and Forests ⟨key⟩8.
Key Number System Topic Nos. 34, 393, 411.

§ 423*l*–6. Authorization of appropriations

There are authorized to be appropriated such sums as are necessary to carry out sections 423*l*-1 to 423*l*-6 of this title.

(Pub.L. 106–511, Title V, § 506, Nov. 13, 2000, 114 Stat. 2375.)

HISTORICAL AND STATUTORY NOTES

Revision Notes and Legislative Reports
2000 Acts. House Report No. 106–944, see 2000 U.S. Code Cong. and Adm. News, p. 2176.

References in Text
Sections 423*l*–1 to 423*l*–6 of this title, referred to in text, was in the original "this title", meaning Pub.L. 106–511, Title V, Nov. 13, 2000, 114 Stat. 2373, which enacted 16 U.S.C.A. §§ 423*l*–1 to 423*l*–6, and repealed 16 U.S.C.A. §§ 423j to 423*l*. For complete classification of Title V to the Code, see Tables.

§ 423m. Eutaw Springs Battlefield Site; establishment; purpose

For the purpose of commemorating the battle which occurred at Eutaw Springs, in the State of South Carolina, during the Revolutionary War, when title to such lands on the site of the Battle of Eutaw Springs as may be designated by the Secretary of the Interior in the exercise of his discretion as necessary or desirable for battlefield-site purposes, shall be vested in the United States, said area shall be set apart as a battlefield site for the benefit and inspiration of the people and shall be called the Eutaw Springs Battlefield Site.

(June 26, 1936, c. 840, § 1, 49 Stat. 1975.)

LIBRARY REFERENCES

American Digest System
Armed Services ⊕54.
Woods and Forests ⊕2, 8.
Key Number System Topic Nos. 34, 411.

§ 423n. Acceptance of lands and funds; acquisition of lands

The Secretary of the Interior is authorized to accept donations of land, interests in land, and/or buildings, structures, and other property within the boundaries of the said battlefield site as determined and fixed hereunder, and donations of funds for the purchase and/or maintenance thereof, the title and evidence of title to lands acquired to be satisfactory to the Secretary of the Interior: *Provided*, That he may acquire on behalf of the United States out of any donated funds, either by purchase at prices deemed by him reasonable, or by condemnation under the provisions of section 3113 of Title 40, such tracts of land on the said battlefield site as may be necessary for the completion thereof.

(June 26, 1936, c. 840, § 2, 49 Stat. 1975.)

HISTORICAL AND STATUTORY NOTES

Codifications

In text, "section 3113 of Title 40" substituted for "sections 257 and 258 of Title 40", which originally read "the Act of August 1, 1888" on authority of Pub.L. 107–217, § 5(c), Aug. 21, 2002, 116 Stat. 1301, which is set out as a note preceding 40 U.S.C.A. § 101. Pub.L. 107–217, § 1, enacted Title 40 into positive law. The Act of August 1, 1888, is Act, Aug. 1,

1888, c. 728, 25 Stat. 357, which was classified to former 40 U.S.C.A. §§ 257 and 258, prior to being repealed by Pub.L. 107–217, § 6(b), Aug. 21, 2002, 116 Stat. 1305, and its substance reenacted as 40 U.S.C.A. § 3113. Section 258 of Title 40 was previously omitted from the Code as superseded by Rule 71A, Federal Rules of Civil Procedure, Title 28.

LIBRARY REFERENCES

American Digest System
Armed Services ⊕54.

United States ⊶55.
Key Number System Topic Nos. 34, 393.

§ 423*o*.   Administration, protection, and development

The administration, protection, and development of the aforesaid battlefield site shall be exercised under the direction of the Secretary of the Interior by the National Park Service, subject to the provisions of sections 1, 2, 3, and 4 of this title, as amended.

(June 26, 1936, c. 840, § 3, 49 Stat. 1975.)

HISTORICAL AND STATUTORY NOTES

Transfer of Functions
All functions of all other officers of the Department of the Interior and all functions of all agencies and employees of such Department were, with two exceptions, transferred to the Secretary of the Interior, with power vested in him to authorize their performance or the performance of any of his functions by any of such officers, agencies, and employees, by 1950 Reorg. Plan No. 3, §§ 1, 2, eff. May 24, 1950, 15 F.R. 3174, 64 Stat. 1262, set out in Appendix 1 to Title 5, Government Organization and Employees.

LIBRARY REFERENCES

American Digest System
Armed Services ⊶54.
Woods and Forests ⊶5.
Key Number System Topic Nos. 34, 411.

§ 424.   Chickamauga and Chattanooga National Military Park

For the purpose of preserving and suitably marking for historical and professional military study, the fields of some of the most remarkable maneuvers and most brilliant fighting in the War of the Rebellion, those portions of highways in the States of Georgia and Tennessee in the vicinity of the battlefields of Chickamauga and Chattanooga, respectively, jurisdiction over which has heretofore been ceded to the United States by those States respectively and as to which the United States has heretofore acquired a perfect title, shall be approaches to and parts of the Chickamauga and Chattanooga National Military Park, and each and all of such roads shall remain open as free and public highways, and all rights of way which existed on August 19, 1890, through the grounds of the said Park and its approaches shall be continued.   The lands and roads embraced in the area at and near the battlefield of Chickamauga and around Chattanooga, jurisdiction over which has heretofore been ceded to the United States by the State of Georgia and as to which a perfect title has heretofore been secured, together with the roads hereinbefore described, shall be a national military park, to be known as Chickamauga and Chattanooga National Park.   The said Chickamauga and Chattanooga National Park and the approaches thereto shall be under the control of the Secretary of the Interior. The Secretary of the Interior is authorized to enter into agreements upon such nominal terms as he may prescribe, with such persons, who were owners of the land on August 19, 1890, as may desire to remain upon it, to occupy and cultivate their then holdings, upon condition that they will preserve the then buildings and roads, and the then outlines of field and forest, and that they will only cut trees or underbrush under such regulations as the Secretary may prescribe, and that they will assist in caring for and protecting all tablets, monuments, or such other artificial works as may from time to time be erected by proper authority. It shall be the duty of the Secretary of the Interior to superintend the opening of such roads as may be necessary to the purposes of the park, and the repair of the roads of the same, and to ascertain and definitely mark the lines of battle of all troops engaged in the battles of Chickamauga and Chattanooga, so far as the same shall fall within the lines of the park. It shall be the duty of the Secretary of the Interior to cause to be ascertained and substantially marked the locations of the regular troops within the boundaries of the park, and to erect monuments upon those positions as Congress may provide the necessary appropriations; and the Secretary of the Interior in the same way may ascertain and mark all lines of battle within the boundaries of the park and erect plain and substantial historical tablets at such points in the vicinity of the park and its approaches as he may deem fitting and necessary to clearly designate positions and movements, which, although without the limits of the park, were directly connected with the battles of Chickamauga and Chattanooga. It shall be lawful for the authorities of any State having troops engaged either at Chattanooga or Chickamauga, and for the officers and directors of the Chickamauga Memorial Association, a corporation chartered under the laws of Georgia, to enter upon the lands and approaches of the Chickamauga and Chattanooga National Park for the purpose of ascertaining and marking the lines of battle of troops engaged therein: *Provided*, That before any such lines are permanently designated the position of the lines and the proposed methods of marking them by monuments, tablets, or otherwise shall be submitted to the Secretary of the Interior, and shall first receive the written approval of the Secretary. The Secretary of the Interior, subject to the approval of the President of the United States, shall have the power to make, and shall make, all needed regulations for the care of the park and for the establishment and marking of the lines of battle and other historical features of the park: *Provided further*, That State memorials shall be placed on brigade lines of battle under the direction of the National Park Service.

No monuments or memorials shall be erected upon any lands of the park, or remain upon any lands which may be purchased for the park, except upon ground actually occupied in the course of the battle by troops of the State which the proposed monuments are intended to commemorate, except upon those sections of the park set apart for memorials to troops which were engaged in the campaigns, but operated outside of the legal limits of the park.   Notwithstanding the restrictive provisions of this paragraph, the Secretary of the Interior is authorized in his discretion to permit without cost to the United States the erection of monuments or memorials to commemorate encampments of Spanish War organizations which were encamped in said park during the period of the Spanish-American War.

(Aug. 19, 1890, c. 806, 26 Stat. 333; Mar. 3, 1891, c. 542, 26 Stat. 978; Feb. 26, 1896, c. 33, 29 Stat. 21; June 4, 1897, c. 2, § 1, 30 Stat. 43; Apr. 15, 1926, c. 146, Title II, 44 Stat. 289; Feb. 23, 1927, c. 167, Title II, 44 Stat. 1140; Ex. Ord. No. 6166, § 2, June 10, 1933; Ex. Ord. No. 6228, § 1, July 28, 1933.)

HISTORICAL AND STATUTORY NOTES

Codifications

Act Mar. 3, 1891, and Act Apr. 5, 1926 provided for a reduced area of the park and provided that title to such reduced area should be procured by the Secretary of War [now Army] as provided and that the Secretary of War [now Army] should proceed with the establishment of the park as rapidly as jurisdiction of the roads and approaches and title to the land might be obtained.

The first sentence of the last paragraph relating to the erection of monuments or memorials was added by Act Feb. 26, 1896.

The proviso that State memorials shall be placed on brigade lines of battle under the direction of the Park Commission was added by Act June 4, 1897.

Act Feb. 23, 1927 made appropriations for items specified and added provisions relating to monuments or memorials to commemorate encampments of Spanish War organizations.

Transfer of Functions

Administrative functions of Chickamauga and Chattanooga National Military Park were transferred to the Department of the Interior by Ex. Ord. No. 6166, and by Ex. Ord. No. 6228, set out as a note under section 901 of Title 5, Government Organization and Employees.

National Park Service was substituted for Office of National Parks, Buildings, and Reservations referred to in Ex. Ord. No. 6166, § 2, by Act Mar. 2, 1934, c. 38, § 1, 48 Stat. 389.

LIBRARY REFERENCES

American Digest System

Armed Services ☞54.
Woods and Forests ☞5.
Key Number System Topic Nos. 34, 411.

§ 424–1. Acquisition of land

(a) In general

The Secretary of the Interior may acquire private land, easements, and buildings within the areas authorized for acquisition for the Chickamauga and Chattanooga National Military Park, by donation, purchase with donated or appropriated funds, or exchange.

(b) Limitation

Land, easements, and buildings described in subsection (a) may be acquired only from willing sellers.

(c) Administration

Land, easements, and buildings acquired by the Secretary under subsection (a) shall be administered by the Secretary as part of the park.

(Aug. 19, 1890, c. 806, § 12, as added Oct. 21, 1998, Pub.L. 105–277, Div. A, § 101(e) [Title I, § 138], 112 Stat. 2681–266.)

HISTORICAL AND STATUTORY NOTES

Revision Notes and Legislative Reports
   1998 Acts. Statement by President, see 1998 U.S. Code Cong. and Adm. News, p. 582.

LIBRARY REFERENCES

American Digest System
   Armed Services ☞54.
   United States ☞55.
   Key Number System Topic Nos. 34, 393.

§ 424a. Acceptance of donations of lands

The Secretary of the Interior is authorized, in his discretion, to accept in behalf of the United States lands, easements, and buildings as may be donated for an addition to the Chickamauga and Chattanooga National Military Park lying within what is known as the "Chattanooga-Lookout Mountain Park" (a corporation, Adolph S. Ochs, president) and/or any lands within one mile of said Chattanooga-Lookout Mountain Park in the States of Tennessee and Georgia.

(May 4, 1934, c. 218, § 1, 48 Stat. 666.)

CROSS REFERENCES

Laws applicable, see 16 USCA § 424b.

LIBRARY REFERENCES

American Digest System
   Armed Services ☞54.
   United States ☞55.
   Key Number System Topic Nos. 34, 393.

§ 424a–1. Acceptance of donations of lands and other property on Signal Mountain

The Secretary of the Interior, in his discretion, is authorized to accept, on behalf of the United States, donations of lands, buildings, structures, and other property, or interests therein, on Signal Mountain near Chattanooga, Tennessee, for addition to the Chickamauga-Chattanooga National Military Park, the title to such property or interests to be satisfactory to him.   Upon acquisition, such lands shall be a part of the Chickamauga-Chattanooga National Military Park and shall be subject to all laws and regulations applicable thereto. (Mar. 5, 1942, c. 148, § 1, 56 Stat. 133.)

LIBRARY REFERENCES

American Digest System
> Armed Services ⟐54.
> United States ⟐55.
> Key Number System Topic Nos. 34, 393.

§ 424a–2. Conveyance of portion of park to Georgia

The Secretary of the Interior, in his discretion, is authorized to convey, without consideration but under such terms and conditions as he may deem advisable, to the State of Georgia all of lot 78 and approximately one hundred and fifty acres of lot 114, Eleventh District, fourth section, of Dade County, Georgia, now a part of the Chickamauga-Chattanooga National Military Park.

(Mar. 5, 1942, c. 148, § 2, 56 Stat. 133.)

LIBRARY REFERENCES

American Digest System
> Armed Services ⟐54.
> Key Number System Topic No. 34.

§ 424a–3. Addition of surplus Government lands; publication of notice; effective date

Effective upon publication of notice, as hereinafter provided, there shall be added to the Chickamauga and Chattanooga National Military Park, a strip of land, comprising not more than one hundred acres, lying generally north of the present south line of Fort Ogle-thorpe and westward from the southeast corner thereof. The exact boundaries of the area added to the park shall be agreed upon by the Administrator, General Services Administration, and the Director of the National Park Service.

When the boundaries of the aforesaid area have been agreed upon, the General Services Administration shall furnish to the National Park Service a legal description of the lands to be added to the park, together with a map showing the boundaries and the acreage of the area.

Upon the receipt by the National Park Service of such legal description and map of the area, public notice that such lands are to become a part of the Chickamauga and Chattanooga National Military Park, effective on the date of publication of such notice, shall be given in the Federal Register.

(June 24, 1948, c. 630, 62 Stat. 646; June 30, 1949, c. 288, Title I, § 105, 63 Stat. 381.)

HISTORICAL AND STATUTORY NOTES

Revision Notes and Legislative Reports
1949 Acts. House Report No. 670 and Conference Report No. 935, see 1949 U.S. Code Cong. Service, p. 1475.

Transfer of Functions
All functions of all other officers of the Department of the Interior and all functions of all agencies and employees of such Department were, with two exceptions, transferred to the Secretary of the Interior, with power vested in him to authorize their performance or the performance of any of his functions by any of such officers, agencies, and employees, by 1950 Reorg. Plan No. 3, §§ 1, 2, eff. May 24, 1950, 15 F.R. 3174, 64 Stat. 1262, set out in Appendix 1 to Title 5, Government Organization and Employees.

Act June 30, 1949, transferred the functions, property and personnel of the War Assets Administration to the General Services Administration and the functions of the War Assets Administrator were transferred to the Administrator of General Services.

LIBRARY REFERENCES

American Digest System
Armed Services ⊕54.
United States ⊕55.
Woods and Forests ⊕2.
Key Number System Topic Nos. 34, 393, 411.

§ 424a–4. Repealed. Pub.L. 108–7, Div. F, Title I, § 160(e), Feb. 20, 2003, 117 Stat. 249

HISTORICAL AND STATUTORY NOTES

Section, Aug. 3, 1950, c. 532, §§ 1, 2, 64 Stat. 405, related to the acquisition of land in the Moccasin Bend of the Tennessee river as an addition to the Chickamauga and Chattanooga National Park.

§ 424b. Application of laws to donated lands

All laws affecting the Chickamauga and Chattanooga National Military Park shall be extended and apply to any addition or additions which may be added to said park under the authority of this section and section 424a of this title.

(May 4, 1934, c. 218, § 2, 48 Stat. 666.)

LIBRARY REFERENCES

American Digest System
Armed Services ⊕54.

Woods and Forests ⊶5.
Key Number System Topic Nos. 34, 411.

§ 424c. Moccasin Bend National Archeological District

(a) Short title

This section may be cited as the "Moccasin Bend National Archeological District Act".

(b) Definitions

As used in this section:

(1) Secretary

The term "Secretary" means the Secretary of the Interior.

(2) Archeological district

The term "archeological district" means the Moccasin Bend National Archeological District.

(3) State

The term "State" means the State of Tennessee.

(4) Map

The term "Map" means the map entitled, "Boundary Map Moccasin Bend National Archeological District", numbered 301/80098, and dated September 2002.

(c) Establishment

(1) In general

In order to preserve, protect, and interpret for the benefit of the public the nationally significant archeological and historic resources located on the peninsula known as Moccasin Bend, Tennessee, there is established as a unit of Chickamauga and Chattanooga National Military Park, the Moccasin Bend National Archeological District.

(2) Boundaries

The archeological district shall consist of approximately 780 acres generally depicted on the Map. The Map shall be on file and available for public inspection in the appropriate offices of the National Park Service, Department of the Interior.

(3) Acquisition of land and interests in land

(A) In general

The Secretary may acquire by donation, purchase from willing sellers using donated or appropriated funds, or ex-

103

change, lands and interests in lands within the exterior boundary of the archeological district. The Secretary may acquire the State, county and city-owned land and interests in land for inclusion in the archeological district only by donation.

(B) Easement outside boundary

To allow access between areas of the archeological district that on February 20, 2003, are noncontiguous, the Secretary may acquire by donation or purchase from willing owners using donated or appropriated funds, or exchange, easements connecting the areas generally depicted on the Map.

(d) Administration

(1) In general

The archeological district shall be administered by the Secretary in accordance with this section, with laws applicable to Chickamauga and Chattanooga National Military Park, and with the laws generally applicable to units of the National Park System.

(2) Cooperative agreement

The Secretary may consult and enter into cooperative agreements with culturally affiliated federally recognized Indian tribes, governmental entities, and interested persons to provide for the restoration, preservation, development, interpretation, and use of the archeological district.

(3) Visitor interpretive center

For purposes of interpreting the historical themes and cultural resources of the archeological district, the Secretary may establish and administer a visitor center in the archeological district.

(4) General management plan

Not later than 3 years after funds are made available under this section, the Secretary shall develop a general management plan for the archeological district. The general management plan shall describe the appropriate protection and preservation of natural, cultural, and scenic resources, visitor use, and facility development within the archeological district consistent with the purposes of this section, while ensuring continued access by private landowners to their property.

(Pub.L. 108–7, Div. F, Title I, § 160(a) to (d), Feb. 20, 2003, 117 Stat. 247.)

HISTORICAL AND STATUTORY NOTES

Revision Notes and Legislative Reports
2003 Acts. House Conference Report No. 108–10 and Statement by President, see 2003 U.S. Code Cong. and Adm. News, p. 4.

Codifications
Section is comprised of Pub.L. 108–7, Div. F, § 160. Subsec. (e) of this section,

shown as omitted, repealed former 16 U.S.C.A. § 424a–4.

LIBRARY REFERENCES

American Digest System
Environmental Law ⊙90.
Key Number System Topic No. 149E.

§ 425. Fredericksburg and Spotsylvania County Battle Fields Memorial; establishment

In order to commemorate the Civil War battles of Fredericksburg, Spotsylvania Court House, Wilderness, and Chancellorsville, including Salem Church, all located at or near Fredericksburg, Virginia, and to mark and preserve for historical purposes the breastworks, earthworks, gun emplacements, walls, or other defenses or shelters used by the armies in said battles, so far as the marking and preservation of the same are practicable, the land herein authorized to be acquired, or so much thereof as may be taken, and the highways and approaches herein authorized to be constructed, are declared to be a national military park to be known as the Fredericksburg and Spotsylvania County Battle Fields Memorial whenever the title to the same shall have been acquired by the United States, the said land so to be acquired being the land necessary for a park of the plan indicated on the index map sheet filed with the report of the Battle Field Commission appointed pursuant to an Act entitled "An Act to provide for the inspection of the battle fields in and around Fredericksburg and Spotsylvania Court House, Virginia," approved on the 7th day of June 1924, said index map sheet being referred to in said report, and particularly in the "Combined Plan—Antietam system," described in said report, the first of the plans mentioned in said report under the heading "Combined Plan—Antietam system" being the plan which is adopted, the said land herein authorized to be acquired being such land as the Secretary of the Interior may deem necessary to establish a park on the combined plan, Antietam system, above referred to, the particular boundaries of such land to be fixed by surveys made previous to the attempt to acquire the same, and authority is given to the Secretary of the Interior to acquire for the purposes of sections 425 to 425j of this title the land above mentioned, or so much thereof as he may deem necessary, together with all such existing breastworks, earthworks, gun emplacements, walls, defenses, shelters, or other historical points as the Secretary of the Interior may deem necessary, whether shown on said index map sheet or not, and together also with such additional land as the Secretary of the Interior may deem necessary for monuments, markers, tablets, roads, highways, paths, approaches, and to carry out the general purposes of said sections. As title is acquired to parts of the land herein authorized to be acquired, the Secretary of the Interior may proceed with the establishment of the park upon such portions so acquired, and the remaining portions of the lands desired shall be respectively brought within said park as titles to said portions are severally acquired.

(Feb. 14, 1927, c. 127, § 1, 44 Stat. 1091; Ex. Ord. No. 6166, § 2, June 10, 1933; Ex. Ord. No. 6228, § 1, July 28, 1933.)

HISTORICAL AND STATUTORY NOTES

References in Text

Act June 7, 1924, c. 339, 43 Stat. 646, referred to in text, was temporary and was not classified to the Code.

Transfer of Functions

Administrative functions of Fredericksburg and Spotsylvania County Battle Fields Memorial were transferred to the Department of the Interior by Ex. Ord. No. 6166, and by Ex. Ord. No. 6228, set out as a note under section 901 of Title 5, Government Organization and Employees.

National Park Service was substituted for Office of National Parks, Buildings, and Reservations referred to in Ex. Ord. No. 6166, § 2, by Act Mar. 2, 1934, c. 38, § 1, 48 Stat. 389.

CROSS REFERENCES

Acquisition of lands, see 16 USCA § 425a.
Authorization of appropriations, see 16 USCA § 425j.
Duties of commission, see 16 USCA § 425d.
Fredericksburg and Spotsylvania County Battle Fields Memorial fund, acceptance and distribution of gifts, see 16 USCA § 425e.
Revision of boundaries, see 16 USCA § 425k.

LIBRARY REFERENCES

American Digest System

Armed Services ☞54.
Woods and Forests ☞1, 8.
Key Number System Topic Nos. 34, 411.

§ 425a. Acquisition of lands

The Secretary of the Interior is authorized to cause condemnation proceedings to be instituted in the name of the United States under the provisions of section 3113 of Title 40, to acquire title to the lands, interests therein, or rights pertaining thereto within the said Fredericksburg and Spotsylvania County Battle Fields Memorial, authorized to be acquired in section 425 of this title, and the United States shall be entitled to immediate possession upon the filing of the petition in condemnation in the United States District Court for the Eastern

District of Virginia: *Provided*, That when the owner of such lands, interests therein, or rights pertaining thereto shall fix a price for the same, which in the opinion of the commission, referred to in section 425c of this title, and the Secretary of the Interior, shall be reasonable, the Secretary may purchase the same without further delay: *Provided further*, That the Secretary of the Interior is authorized to accept on behalf of the United States, donations of lands, interests therein or rights pertaining thereto required for the said Fredericksburg and Spotsylvania County Battle Fields Memorial: *And provided further*, That no public money shall be expended for title to any lands until a written opinion of the Attorney General shall be had in favor of the validity of title thereto.

(Feb. 14, 1927, c. 127, § 2, 44 Stat. 1092; Ex.Ord. No. 6166, § 2, June 10, 1933; Ex.Ord. No. 6228, § 1, July 28, 1933.)

HISTORICAL AND STATUTORY NOTES

Codifications

In text, "section 3113 of Title 40" substituted for "sections 257 and 258 of Title 40", which originally read "the Act of August 1, 1888, entitled 'An Act to authorize the condemnation of lands for sites for public buildings, and other purposes' (Twenty-fifth Statutes at Large, page 357)" on authority of Pub.L. 107–217, § 5(c), Aug. 21, 2002, 116 Stat. 1301, which is set out as a note preceding 40 U.S.C.A. § 101. Pub.L. 107–217, § 1, enacted Title 40 into positive law. The Act of August 1, 1888, is Act, Aug. 1, 1888, c. 728, 25 Stat. 357, which was classified to former 40 U.S.C.A. §§ 257 and 258, prior to being repealed by Pub.L. 107–217, § 6(b), Aug. 21, 2002, 116 Stat. 1305, and its substance reenacted as 40 U.S.C.A. § 3113. Section 258 of Title 40 was previously omitted from the Code as superseded by Rule 71A, Federal Rules of Civil Procedure, Title 28.

Transfer of Functions

Transfer of administrative functions of park, see note set out under section 425 of this title.

CROSS REFERENCES

Acceptance of gifts by commission, see 16 USCA § 425e.
Authorization of appropriations, see 16 USCA § 425j.
Duties of commission, see 16 USCA § 425d.
Fredericksburg and Spotsylvania County Battle Fields Memorial,
    Establishment, see 16 USCA § 425.
    Revision of boundaries, see 16 USCA § 425k.

LIBRARY REFERENCES

American Digest System

Armed Services ⬿54.
United States ⬿55.
Key Number System Topic Nos. 34, 393.

Research References

Treatises and Practice Aids

Federal Procedure, Lawyers Edition § 14:262, Who May Condemn; Procedures
    Governing Condemnation.

§ 425b.   Leasing lands for memorial

The Secretary of the Interior is authorized to enter into leases with the owners of such of the lands, works, defenses, and buildings thereon within the said Fredericksburg and Spotsylvania County Battle Fields Memorial, as in his discretion it is unnecessary to forthwith acquire title to, and such leases shall be on such terms and conditions as the Secretary of the Interior may prescribe, and may contain options to purchase, subject to later acceptance if in the judgment of the Secretary of the Interior it is as economical to purchase as condemn title to the property: *Provided*, That the Secretary of the Interior may enter into agreements upon such nominal terms as he may prescribe, permitting the present owners or their tenants to occupy or cultivate their present holdings, upon condition that they will preserve the present breastworks, earthworks, walls, defenses, shelters, buildings, and roads, and the present outlines of the battlefields, and that they will only cut trees or underbrush or disturb or remove the soil, under such regulations as the Secretary of the Interior may prescribe, and that they will assist in caring for and protecting all tablets, monuments, or such other artificial works as may from time to time be erected by proper authority: *Provided further*, That if such agreements to lease cover any lands the title to which shall have been acquired by the United States, the proceeds from such agreements shall be applied by the Secretary of the Interior toward the maintenance of the park.

(Feb. 14, 1927, c. 127, § 3, 44 Stat. 1092; Ex.Ord. No. 6166, § 2, June 10, 1933; Ex.Ord. No. 6228, § 1, July 28, 1933.)

HISTORICAL AND STATUTORY NOTES

Transfer of Functions

Transfer of administrative functions of park, see note set out under section 425 of this title.

CROSS REFERENCES

Authorization of appropriations, see 16 USCA § 425j.
Duties of commission, see 16 USCA § 425d.
Fredericksburg and Spotsylvania County Battle Fields Memorial,
    Establishment, see 16 USCA § 425.
    Fund, see 16 USCA § 425e.
    Revision of boundaries, see 16 USCA § 425k.

LIBRARY REFERENCES

American Digest System

Armed Services ☞54.
United States ☞55.
Key Number System Topic Nos. 34, 393.

§ 425c.   Commission; organization

The affairs of the said Fredericksburg and Spotsylvania County Battle Fields Memorial shall, subject to the supervision and direction of the Secretary of the Interior, be in charge of three commissioners, consisting of Army officers, civilians, or both, to be appointed by the Secretary of the Interior, one of whom shall be designated as chairman and another as secretary of the commission.

(Feb. 14, 1927, c. 127, § 4, 44 Stat. 1093; Ex.Ord. No. 6166, § 2, June 10, 1933; Ex.Ord. No. 6228, § 1, July 28, 1933.)

HISTORICAL AND STATUTORY NOTES

Transfer of Functions
Transfer of administrative functions of park, see note set out under section 425 of this title.

CROSS REFERENCES

Acceptance of gifts, see 16 USCA § 425e.
Acquisition of lands; determination of reasonableness of price fixed by owner, see
16 USCA § 425a.
Authorization of appropriations, see 16 USCA § 425j.
Duties, see 16 USCA § 425d.
Fredericksburg and Spotsylvania County Battle Fields Memorial,
Establishment, see 16 USCA § 425.
Revision of boundaries, see 16 USCA § 425k.

LIBRARY REFERENCES

American Digest System
Armed Services ☞54.
Woods and Forests ☞7.
Key Number System Topic Nos. 34, 411.

§ 425d.   Duties of commission

It shall be the duty of the commissioners, under the direction of the Secretary of the Interior, to survey, locate, and preserve the lines of the opposing armies in said battles, to open, construct, and repair such roads, highways, paths, and other approaches as may be necessary to make the historical points accessible to the public and to students of said battles and for the purposes of the park, to ascertain and mark with historical monuments, markers, tablets, or otherwise, as the Secretary of the Interior may determine, all breastworks, earthworks, gun emplacements, walls, or other defenses or shelters, lines of battle, location of troops, buildings, and other historical points of interest within the park or in its vicinity, and to establish and construct such observation towers as the Secretary of the Interior may deem necessary for said park, and the said commission in establishing the park shall have authority, under the direction of the

Secretary of the Interior to employ such labor and services at rates to be fixed by the Secretary of the Interior, and to obtain such supplies and materials as may be necessary to carry out the provisions of sections 425 to 425j of this title.

(Feb. 14, 1927, c. 127, § 5, 44 Stat. 1093; Ex.Ord. No. 6166, § 2, June 10, 1933; Ex.Ord. No. 6228, § 1, July 28, 1933.)

HISTORICAL AND STATUTORY NOTES

Transfer of Functions
Transfer of administrative functions of park, see note set out under section 425 of this title.

CROSS REFERENCES

Acceptance of gifts, see 16 USCA § 425e.
Authorization of appropriations, see 16 USCA § 425j.
Classification, appropriation and disbursement of Fredericksburg and Spotsylvania County Battle Fields memorial fund, see 31 USCA § 1321.
Fredericksburg and Spotsylvania County Battle Fields Memorial,
    Establishment, see 16 USCA § 425.
    Revision of boundaries, see 16 USCA § 425k.

LIBRARY REFERENCES

American Digest System
Armed Services ☞54.
Woods and Forests ☞7.
Key Number System Topic Nos. 34, 411.

§ 425e. Acceptance and distribution of gifts

The commission, acting through the Secretary of the Interior, is authorized to receive gifts and contributions from States, Territories, societies, organizations, and individuals for the said Fredericksburg and Spotsylvania County Battle Fields Memorial: *Provided*, That all contributions of money received shall be deposited in the Treasury of the United States and credited to a fund to be designated "Fredericksburg and Spotsylvania County Battle Fields Memorial fund", which fund shall be applied to and expended under the direction of the Secretary of the Interior for carrying out the provisions of sections 425 to 425j of this title.

(Feb. 14, 1927, c. 127, § 6, 44 Stat. 1093; Ex.Ord. No. 6166, § 2, June 10, 1933; Ex.Ord. No. 6228, § 1, July 28, 1933.)

HISTORICAL AND STATUTORY NOTES

Transfer of Functions
Transfer of administrative functions of park, see note set out under section 425 of this title.

§ 425f.   Ascertaining and marking lines of battle

It shall be lawful for the authorities of any State having had troops
engaged in said battles of Fredericksburg, Spotsylvania Court House,
Wilderness, and Chancellorsville, including Salem Church, or in any
of said battles, to enter upon the lands and approaches of the
Fredericksburg and Spotsylvania County Battle Fields Memorial for
the purposes of ascertaining and marking the lines of battle of troops
engaged therein: *Provided*, That before any such lines are permanently designated, the position of the lines and the proposed methods of
marking them by monuments, tablets, or otherwise, including the
design and inscription for the same, shall be submitted to the
Secretary of the Interior, and shall first receive written approval of
the Secretary, which approval shall be based upon formal written
reports to be made to him in each case by the commissioners of the
park: *Provided*, That no discrimination shall be made against any
State as to the manner of designing lines, but any grant made to any
State by the Secretary of the Interior may be used by any other State.

(Feb. 14, 1927, c. 127, § 7, 44 Stat. 1093; Ex.Ord. No. 6166, § 2, June 10,
1933; Ex.Ord. No. 6228, § 1, July 28, 1933.)

HISTORICAL AND STATUTORY NOTES

Transfer of Functions
  Transfer of administrative functions of
park, see note set out under section 425
of this title.

LIBRARY REFERENCES

American Digest System
  Armed Services ⇨54.
  Woods and Forests ⇨2, 5, 10.
  Key Number System Topic Nos. 34, 411.

§ 425g.   Protection of monuments, etc.

If any person shall, except by permission of the Secretary of the Interior, destroy, mutilate, deface, injure, or remove any monument, column, statue, memorial structure, or work of art that shall be erected or placed upon the grounds of the park by lawful authority, or shall destroy or remove any fence, railing, inclosure, or other work for the protection or ornament of said park, or any portion thereof, or shall destroy, cut, hack, bark, break down, or otherwise injure any tree, bush, or shrubbery that may be growing upon said park, or shall cut down or fell or remove any timber, battle relic, tree or trees growing or being upon said park, or hunt within the limits of the park, or shall remove or destroy any breastworks, earthworks, walls, or other defenses or shelter or any part thereof constructed by the armies formerly engaged in the battles on the lands or approaches to the park, any person so offending and found guilty thereof before any justice of the peace of the county in which the offense may be committed, or any court of competent jurisdiction, shall for each and every such offense forfeit and pay a fine, in the discretion of the justice, according to the aggravation of the offense, of not less than $5 nor more than $50, one-half for the use of the park and the other half to the informer, to be enforced and recovered before such justice in like manner as debts of like nature were, on February 14, 1927, by law recoverable in the several counties where the offense may be committed.

(Feb. 14, 1927, c. 127, § 8, 44 Stat. 1094; Ex.Ord. No. 6166, § 2, June 10, 1933; Ex.Ord. No. 6228, § 1, July 28, 1933.)

HISTORICAL AND STATUTORY NOTES

Transfer of Functions
  Transfer of administrative functions of park, see note set out under section 425 of this title.

CROSS REFERENCES

Authorization of appropriations, see 16 USCA § 425j.
Duties of commission, see 16 USCA § 425d.
Fredericksburg and Spotsylvania County Battle Fields Memorial,
    Establishment, see 16 USCA § 425.
    Fund, see 16 USCA § 425e.
    Revision of boundaries, see 16 USCA § 425k.

LIBRARY REFERENCES

American Digest System
Armed Services ☜54.
Woods and Forests ☜5, 10, 11.
Key Number System Topic Nos. 34, 411.

§ 425h. Rules and regulations

The Secretary of the Interior, subject to the approval of the President, shall have the power to make and shall make all needful rules and regulations for the care of the park, and for the establishment and marking of lines of battle and other historical features of the park.

(Feb. 14, 1927, c. 127, § 9, 44 Stat. 1094; Ex.Ord. No. 6166, § 2, June 10, 1933; Ex.Ord. No. 6228, § 1, July 28, 1933.)

HISTORICAL AND STATUTORY NOTES

Transfer of Functions
Transfer of administrative functions of park, see note set out under section 425 of this title.

CROSS REFERENCES

Authorization of appropriations, see 16 USCA § 425j.
Duty of commission to ascertain and mark historical points of interest, see 16 USCA § 425d.
Fredericksburg and Spotsylvania County Battle Fields Memorial,
Establishment, see 16 USCA § 425.
Fund, see 16 USCA § 425e.
Revision of boundaries, see 16 USCA § 425k.

LIBRARY REFERENCES

American Digest System
Armed Services ☜54.
Woods and Forests ☜5.
Key Number System Topic Nos. 34, 411.

§ 425i. Report of completion of acquisition of land and work of commission; superintendent of park

Upon completion of the acquisition of the land and the work of the commission, the Secretary of the Interior shall render a report thereon to Congress, and thereafter the park shall be placed in charge of a superintendent at a salary to be fixed by the Secretary of the Interior and paid out of the appropriation available for the maintenance of the park.

(Feb. 14, 1927, c. 127, § 10, 44 Stat. 1094; Ex.Ord. No. 6166, § 2, June 10, 1933; Ex.Ord. No. 6228, § 1, July 28, 1933.)

HISTORICAL AND STATUTORY NOTES

Transfer of Functions

Transfer of administrative functions of park, see note set out under section 425 of this title.

CROSS REFERENCES

Authorization of appropriations, see 16 USCA § 425j.
Duties of commission, see 16 USCA § 425d.
Fredericksburg and Spotsylvania County Battle Fields Memorial,
    Establishment, see 16 USCA § 425.
    Fund, see 16 USCA § 425e.
    Revision of boundaries, see 16 USCA § 425k.

LIBRARY REFERENCES

American Digest System

    Armed Services ☞54.
    United States ☞39(1).
    Woods and Forests ☞5.
    Key Number System Topic Nos. 34, 393, 411.

§ 425j. Authorization of appropriation

To enable the Secretary of the Interior to begin to carry out the provisions of sections 425 to 425j of this title, including the condemnation, purchase, or lease of the necessary lands, surveys, maps, marking the boundaries of the park, opening, constructing, or repairing necessary roads, pay and expenses of commissioners, salaries for labor and services, traveling expenses, supplies and materials, the sum of $50,000 is authorized to be appropriated out of any money in the Treasury not otherwise appropriated, to remain available until expended, and such additional sums are authorized to be appropriated from time to time as may be necessary for the completion of the project and for the proper maintenance of said park. All disbursements under said sections shall be annually reported by the Secretary of the Interior to Congress.

(Feb. 14, 1927, c. 127, § 11, 44 Stat. 1094; Ex.Ord. No. 6166, § 2, June 10, 1933; Ex.Ord. No. 6228, § 1, July 28, 1933.)

HISTORICAL AND STATUTORY NOTES

Transfer of Functions

Transfer of administrative functions of park, see note set out under section 425 of this title.

CROSS REFERENCES

Duties of commission, see 16 USCA § 425d.
Fredericksburg and Spotsylvania County Battle Fields Memorial,
    Establishment, see 16 USCA § 425.
    Fund, see 16 USCA § 425e.

Fredericksburg and Spotsylvania County Battle Fields Memorial,—Cont'd
Revision of boundaries, see 16 USCA § 425k.

§ 425k.   Revision of park boundaries

(a) Boundary revision

In furtherance of the purposes of sections 425 to 425j of this title, the Fredericksburg and Spotsylvania County Battlefields Memorial National Military Park (hereinafter in sections 425k to 425o of this title referred to as the "park") shall hereafter comprise the lands and interests in lands within the boundary generally depicted as "Proposed Park Boundary" on the maps entitled "Fredericksburg and Spotsylvania National Military Park", numbered 326–40075D/89, 326–40074E/89, 326–40069B/89, 326–40070D/89, 326–40071C/89, 326–40076A/89, and 326–40073D/89, and dated June 1989, and the map entitled "Fredericksburg and Spotsylvania National Military Park," numbered 326–40072E/89/A and dated September 1990. The maps shall be on file and available for public inspection in the Office of the National Park Service, Department of the Interior.

(b) Excluded lands

Lands and interests in lands within the boundary depicted on the maps referred to in subsection (a) of this section as "Existing Park Boundary" but outside of the boundary depicted as "Proposed Park Boundary" are hereby excluded from the park, in accordance with the provisions of section 425l(b) of this title. The Secretary of the Interior (hereinafter referred to as the "Secretary") may relinquish to the Commonwealth of Virginia exclusive or concurrent legislative jurisdiction over lands excluded from the park by this section by filing with the Governor a notice of relinquishment. Such relinquishment shall take effect upon acceptance thereof, or as the laws of the Commonwealth may otherwise provide.

(Pub.L. 101–214, § 2, Dec. 11, 1989, 103 Stat. 1849; Pub.L. 102–541, § 2(a), Oct. 27, 1992, 106 Stat. 3565; Pub.L. 106–150, § 1(c), Dec. 9, 1999, 113 Stat. 1730.)

HISTORICAL AND STATUTORY NOTES

Amendments
1999   Amendments. Subsec.   (a). Pub.L. 106–150, § 1(c), struck out "Spotslyvania" and inserted "Spotsylvania".

1992   Amendments. Subsec.   (a). Pub.L.   102–541,   § 2(a),   substituted "1989, and the map entitled 'Fredericksburg and Spotsylvania National Military Park,' numbered 326–40072E/89/A and dated September, 1990." for "1989." and struck out "326–40072E/89" following "326-400171C/89,".

Effective and Applicability Provisions
1992 Acts. Pub.L. 102–541, § 2(a)(2), Oct. 27, 1992, 106 Stat. 2565, provided in part: "That this subsection [amending subsec. (a)] shall not be effective until the lands included within the proposed new boundaries of the Fredricksburg and Spotsylvania County Battlefields Memori-

al National Military Park pursuant to this Act [Pub.L. 102–541, for classification of which, see Tables] have been donated to the Secretary of the Interior." This portion of section 2(a)(2) of Pub.L. 102–541 was repealed by Pub.L. 106–150, § 1(a), Dec. 9, 1999, 113 Stat. 1730.

Short Title
  1989 Acts. Pub.L. 101–214, § 1, Dec. 11, 1989, 103 Stat. 1849, provided that: "This Act [enacting sections 425k to 425o of this title] may be cited as the 'Fredericksburg and Spotsylvania County Battlefields Memorial National Military Park Expansion Act of 1989'."

Congressional Findings Relating to Park Expansion
  Pub.L. 102–541, § 1, Oct. 27, 1992, 106 Stat. 3565, provided that: "Congress finds that the land area near Fredericksburg and Spotsylvania County Battlefields Memorial National Military Park,

Virginia, located south and west of the intersection of the Orange Plank Road and Brock Road in Spotsylvania County was strategically significant ground associated with the battle of the Civil War known as the Battle of the Wilderness, and that the tract of land adjacent to such area known as 'Longstreet's Flank Attack' was also strategically significant to that battle."

Acquisition of Certain Lands by Donation Only
  Pub.L. 102–541, § 2(b), Oct. 27, 1992, 106 Stat. 3565, which provided that: "Lands included within the boundaries of the Fredericksburg and Spotsylvania County Battlefields Memorial National Military Park pursuant to this section [amending subsec. (a) of this section] may be acquired only by donation.", was repealed by Pub.L. 106–150, § 1(b)(2), Dec. 9, 1999, 113 Stat. 1730.

LIBRARY REFERENCES

American Digest System
  Armed Services ☞54.
  United States ☞55.
  Woods and Forests ☞1.
  Key Number System Topic Nos. 34, 393, 411.

§ 425*l*. Acquisitions and conveyances

(a) Acquisition

(1) Except as provided in paragraph (2), the Secretary is authorized to acquire lands and interests in lands within the park, by donation, purchase with donated or appropriated funds or by exchange.

(2) The lands designated "P04–04" on the map referred to in section 425k(a) of this title numbered 326–40072E/89/A and dated September 1990 may be acquired only by donation, and the lands designated "P04–01", "P04–02", and "P04–03" on such map may be acquired only by donation, purchase from willing sellers, or exchange.

(b) Conveyance of lands excluded from park

(1) The Secretary is authorized, in accordance with applicable existing law, to exchange Federal lands and interests excluded from the park pursuant to section 425k(b) of this title for the purpose of acquiring lands within the park boundary.

(2) If any such Federal lands or interests are not exchanged within five years after December 11, 1989, the Secretary may sell any or all such lands or interests to the highest bidder, in accordance with such regulations as the Secretary may prescribe, but any such conveyance shall be at not less than the fair market value of the land or interest, as determined by the Secretary.

(3) All Federal lands and interests sold or exchanged pursuant to this subsection shall be subject to such terms and conditions as will assure the use of the property in a manner which, in the judgment of the Secretary, will protect the battlefield setting.   Notwithstanding any other provision of law, the net proceeds from any such sale or exchange shall be used, subject to appropriations, to acquire lands and interests within the park.

(c) Alternative access

In order to facilitate the acquisition by the United States of existing easements or rights of access across Federal lands within the park and to provide the owners of such easements or rights of access with alternative rights of access across nonpark lands, the Secretary may acquire, by donation, purchase with donated or appropriated funds, or exchange, interests in land of similar estate across lands which are not within the park.   With or without the acceptance of payment of cash to equalize the values of the properties, the Secretary may convey such nonpark lands or interests in lands to the holders of such existing easements or rights of access across Federal lands within the park in exchange for their conveyance to the United States of such easements or rights.   Nothing in sections 425k to 425*o* of this title shall prohibit the Secretary from acquiring any outstanding easements or rights of access across Federal lands by donation, purchase with donated or appropriated funds or by exchange.

(d) Conservation easements

The Secretary is authorized to accept donations of conservation easements on lands adjacent to the park.   Such conservation easements shall have the effect of protecting the scenic and historic resources on park lands and the adjacent lands or preserving the undeveloped or historic appearance of the park when viewed from within or without the park.

(e) Other provisions

Within the area bounded by the Orange Turnpike, the Orange Plank Road, and McLaws Drive no improved property (as defined in section 425m of this title) may be acquired without the consent of the owner thereof unless the Secretary determines that, in his judgment, the property is subject to, or threatened with, uses which are having, or would have, an adverse impact on the park.

(Pub.L. 101–214, § 3, Dec. 11, 1989, 103 Stat. 1849; Pub.L. 106–150, § (b)(1), Dec. 9, 1999, 113 Stat. 1730.)

HISTORICAL AND STATUTORY NOTES

Amendments
  1999   Amendments. Subsec.   (a).
Pub.L.   106–150,   § 1(b)(1),   struck   out

"The Secretary" and inserted "(1) Except as provided in paragraph (2), the Secretary" and added par. (2).

LIBRARY REFERENCES

American Digest System
  Armed Services ☞54.
  United States ☞55.
  Key Number System Topic Nos. 34, 393.

§ 425m.   Retained rights

(a) Retention of use and occupancy

With the exception of property which the Secretary determines is necessary for development or public use, the owner or owners of improved property acquired pursuant to sections 425k to 425o of this title may retain a right of use and occupancy of such improved property for noncommercial residential purposes for a definite term of not more than twenty-five years, or for a term ending at the death of the owner or the owner's spouse. The owner shall elect the term to be reserved, except that if the owner is a corporation, trust, partnership, or any entity other than an individual, the term shall not exceed twenty-five years. Ownership shall be determined as of June 1, 1989. Unless the property is wholly or partially donated, the Secretary shall pay to the owner the fair market value of the property on the date of such acquisition, less the fair market value of the right retained by the owner.

(b) Terms and conditions

Any rights retained pursuant to this section shall be subject to such terms and conditions as the Secretary may prescribe and may be terminated by the Secretary upon his determination and after reasonable notice to the owner thereof that such property is being used for any purpose which is incompatible with the administration, protection, or public use of the park. Such right shall terminate by operation of law upon notification of the owner by the Secretary and tendering to the owner an amount equal to the fair market value of that portion of the right which remains unexpired.

(c) "Improved property" defined

As used in this section, the term "improved property" means a year-round noncommercial single-family dwelling together with such land, in the same ownership as the dwelling, as the Secretary determines is reasonably necessary for the enjoyment of the dwelling for single-family residential use.

(Pub.L. 101–214, § 4, Dec. 11, 1989, 103 Stat. 1850.)

LIBRARY REFERENCES

American Digest System
   Armed Services ⊕54.
   United States ⊕57.
   Woods and Forests ⊕2.
   Key Number System Topic Nos. 34, 393, 411.

§ 425n.   Interpretation

In administering the park, the Secretary shall take such action as is necessary and appropriate to interpret, for the benefit of visitors to the park and the general public, the battles of Fredericksburg, Chancellorsville, Spotsylvania Courthouse, and the Wilderness in the larger context of the Civil War and American history, including the causes and consequences of the Civil War and including the effects of the war on all the American people, especially on the American South.

(Pub.L. 101–214, § 5, Dec. 11, 1989, 103 Stat. 1851.)

LIBRARY REFERENCES

American Digest System
   Armed Services ⊕54.
   United States ⊕57.
   Woods and Forests ⊕5.
   Key Number System Topic Nos. 34, 393, 411.

§ 425o.   Authorization of appropriations

There are authorized to be appropriated such sums as may be necessary to carry out the purposes of sections 425k to 425o of this title.

(Pub.L. 101–214, § 6, Dec. 11, 1989, 103 Stat. 1851.)

§ 426.   Stones River National Battlefield; establishment; appointment of commission

A commission is created, to be composed of the following members, who shall be appointed by the Secretary of the Interior:

(1) A commissioned officer of the Corps of Engineers, United States Army;

(2) A veteran of the Civil War who served honorably in the military forces of the United States; and

(3) A veteran of the Civil War who served honorably in the military forces of the Confederate States of America.

(Mar. 3, 1927, c. 374, § 1, 44 Stat. 1399; Ex. Ord. No. 6166, § 2, June 10, 1933; Ex. Ord. No. 6228, § 1, July 28, 1933; Apr. 22, 1960, Pub.L. 86–443, §§ 2, 3, 74 Stat. 82.)

HISTORICAL AND STATUTORY NOTES

Change of Name

The Stones River National Military Park was redesignated as the Stones River National Battlefield by Pub.L. 86–443. See section 426*l* of this title.

Transfer of Functions

Administrative functions of Stones River National Military Park [now Stones River National Battlefield] were transferred to the Department of the Interior by Ex. Ord. No. 6166, and by Ex. Ord. No. 6228, set out as a note under section 901 of Title 5, Government Organization and Employees. Administrative functions of Stones River National Battlefield were assigned to the Department of the Interior by section 3 of Pub.L. 86–443, set out as section 426m of this title.

National Park Service was substituted for Office of National Parks, Buildings, and Reservations referred to in Ex. Ord. No. 6166, § 2, by Act Mar. 2, 1934, c. 38, § 1, 48 Stat. 389.

CROSS REFERENCES

Acquisition of additional lands, see 16 USCA § 426k.
Authorization of appropriations, see 16 USCA § 426j.
Boundary revision, see 16 USCA § 426n.
Establishment of national battlefield, see 16 USCA § 426e.
Payment of reasonable expenses of commission, see 16 USCA § 426c.
Qualifications of members of commission, see 16 USCA § 426a.

LIBRARY REFERENCES

American Digest System

Armed Services ☞54.
Woods and Forests ☞8.
Key Number System Topic Nos. 34, 411.

§ 426a. Qualifications of members of commission

In appointing the members of the commission created by section 426 of this title the Secretary of the Interior shall, as far as practicable, select persons familiar with the terrain of the battlefield of Stones River, Tennessee, and the historical events associated therewith.

(Mar. 3, 1927, c. 374, § 2, 44 Stat. 1399; Ex.Ord. No. 6166, § 2, June 10, 1933; Ex.Ord. No. 6228, § 1, July 28, 1933.)

HISTORICAL AND STATUTORY NOTES

Transfer of Functions

Transfer of administrative functions of park [now battlefield], see note set out under section 426 of this title.

CROSS REFERENCES

Acquisition of additional lands, see 16 USCA § 426k.
Authorization of appropriations, see 16 USCA § 426j.
Boundary revision of Stones River National Battlefield, see 16 USCA § 426n.
Establishment of national battlefield, see 16 USCA § 426e.
Payment of reasonable expenses, see 16 USCA § 426c.

LIBRARY REFERENCES

American Digest System
Armed Services ☞54.
Woods and Forests ☞7.
Key Number System Topic Nos. 34, 411.

§ 426b. Duties of commission

It shall be the duty of the commission, acting under the direction of the Secretary of the Interior, to inspect the battlefield of Stones River, Tennessee, and to carefully study the available records and historical data with respect to the location and movement of all troops which engaged in the battle of Stones River, and the important events connected therewith, with a view of preserving and marking such field for historical and professional military study.

(Mar. 3, 1927, c. 374, § 3, 44 Stat. 1399; Ex.Ord. No. 6166, § 2, June 10, 1933; Ex.Ord. No. 6228, § 1, July 28, 1933.)

HISTORICAL AND STATUTORY NOTES

Codifications
A provision of Act Mar. 3, 1927, authorizing the submission of a report by the commission to the Secretary of War not later than Dec. 1, 1927, and describing the contents of such report was omitted as executed.

Transfer of Functions
Transfer of administrative functions of park [now battlefield], see note set out under section 426 of this title.

CROSS REFERENCES

Acquisition of additional lands by Secretary of Interior, see 16 USCA § 426k.
Authorization of appropriations, see 16 USCA § 426j.
Boundary revision of Stones River National Battlefield, see 16 USCA § 426n.
Establishment of national battlefield, see 16 USCA § 426e.
Payment of reasonable expenses, see 16 USCA § 426c.

LIBRARY REFERENCES

American Digest System
Armed Services ☞54.
Woods and Forests ☞7.
Key Number System Topic Nos. 34, 411.

§ 426c. Assistants to commission; expenses of commission

The Secretary of the Interior is authorized to assign any officials of the Interior Department to the assistance of the commission if he deems it advisable. He is authorized to pay the reasonable expenses of the commission and their assistants incurred in the actual performance of the duties imposed upon them by sections 426 to 426j of this title.

(Mar. 3, 1927, c. 374, § 4, 44 Stat. 1400; Ex.Ord. No. 6166, § 2, June 10, 1933; Ex.Ord. No. 6228, § 1, July 28, 1933.)

HISTORICAL AND STATUTORY NOTES

Transfer of Functions
Transfer of administrative functions of park [now battlefield], see note set out under section 426 of this title.

CROSS REFERENCES

Acquisition of additional lands by Secretary of Interior, see 16 USCA § 426k.
Authorization of appropriations, see 16 USCA § 426j.
Boundary revision of Stones River National Battlefield, see 16 USCA § 426n.
Establishment of national battlefield, see 16 USCA § 426e.

LIBRARY REFERENCES

American Digest System
Armed Services ⬥54.
Woods and Forests ⬥7.
Key Number System Topic Nos. 34, 411.

§ 426d. Receipt of report of commission by Secretary of the Interior; acquisition of land for battlefield; other duties of Secretary

Upon receipt of the report of said commission, the Secretary of the Interior is authorized and directed to acquire, by purchase, when purchasable at prices deemed by him reasonable, otherwise by condemnation, such tract or tracts of lands as are recommended by the commission as necessary and desirable for a national battlefield; to establish and substantially mark the boundaries of the said battlefield; to definitely mark all lines of battle and locations of troops within the boundaries of the battlefield and erect substantial historical tablets at such points within the battlefield and in the vicinity of the battlefield and its approaches as are recommended by the commission, together with such other points as the Secretary of the Interior may deem appropriate; to construct the necessary roads and walks, plant trees and shrubs, restore and care for the grounds, including the Hazen Monument: *Provided*, That the entire cost of acquiring said land, including cost of condemnation proceedings, if any, ascertainment of title, surveys, and compensation for the land, the cost of marking the battlefield, the expenses of the commission, and the establishment of the national military battlefield, shall not exceed the sum of $100,000.

(Mar. 3, 1927, c. 374, § 5, 44 Stat. 1400; Apr. 15, 1930, c. 167, 46 Stat. 167; Ex.Ord. No. 6166, § 2, June 10, 1933; Ex.Ord. No. 6228, § 1, July 28, 1933; Apr. 22, 1960, Pub.L. 86–443, § 2, 74 Stat. 82.)

HISTORICAL AND STATUTORY NOTES

Amendments

1930 Amendments. Act Apr. 15, 1930 inserted "military" between "national" and "park" authorized construction of roads and walks, the planting of trees and shrubs, the restoration and care of the grounds, including the Hazen Monument, and added "and the establishment of the national military park" in the proviso.

Change of Name

"National battlefield" was substituted for "national military park", and "battle-field" for "park", respectively, wherever appearing, and "battlefield" was substituted for "battle field" following "the cost of marking the", in view of the redesignation of Stones River National Military Park as Stones River National Battlefield by Pub.L. 86–443. See section 4261*l* of this title.

Transfer of Functions

Transfer of administrative functions of park [now battlefield], see note set out under section 426 of this title.

CROSS REFERENCES

Acquisition of additional lands, see 16 USCA § 426k.
Authorization of appropriations, see 16 USCA § 426j.
Boundary revision of Stones River National Battlefield, see 16 USCA § 426n.
Establishment of national battlefield, see 16 USCA § 426e.
Payment of reasonable expenses of commission, see 16 USCA § 426c.

LIBRARY REFERENCES

American Digest System

Armed Services ⬯54.
United States ⬯55.
Woods and Forests ⬯2, 5.
Key Number System Topic Nos. 34, 393, 411.

Research References

Treatises and Practice Aids

Wright & Miller: Federal Prac. & Proc. § 3042, Relation to Other Rules and Statutes.

§ 426e. Lands acquired declared national battlefield; name

Upon the ceding of jurisdiction by the legislature of the State of Tennessee and the report of the Attorney General of the United States that a perfect title has been acquired, the lands acquired under the provisions of sections 426 to 426j of this title, together with the area already inclosed within the national cemetery at the battlefield of Stones River and the Government reservation in said battlefield upon which is erected a large monument to the memory of the officers and soldiers of General Hazen's brigade who fell on the spot, are declared to be a national battlefield, to be known as the Stones River National Battlefield.

(Mar. 3, 1927, c. 374, § 6, 44 Stat. 1400; Apr. 22, 1960, Pub.L. 86–443, § 2, 74 Stat. 82.)

HISTORICAL AND STATUTORY NOTES

Change of Name

"Stones River National Battlefield" and "national battlefield" were substituted for "Stones River National Park" and "national park", respectively, pursuant to Pub.L. 86–443, § 2, Apr. 22, 1960, 74 Stat. 82, which redesignated the Stones River National Military Park as the Stones River National Battlefield. See section 426*l* of this title.

CROSS REFERENCES

Acquisition of additional lands, see 16 USCA § 426k.
Authorization of appropriations, see 16 USCA § 426j.
Boundary revision of Stones River National Battlefield, see 16 USCA § 426n.
Payment of reasonable expenses of commission, see 16 USCA § 426c.

LIBRARY REFERENCES

American Digest System
Armed Services ⚬⚬54.
United States ⚬⚬55.
Key Number System Topic Nos. 34, 393.

§ 426f.   Control of battlefield; regulations

The said Stones River National Battlefield shall be under the control of the Secretary of the Interior, and he is authorized to make all needed regulations for the care of the battlefield. The superintendent of the Stones River National Cemetery shall likewise be the superintendent of and have the custody and care of the Stones River National Battlefield, under the direction of the Secretary of the Interior.

(Mar. 3, 1927, c. 374, § 7, 44 Stat. 1400; Ex.Ord. No. 6166, § 2, June 10, 1933; Ex.Ord. No. 6228, § 1, July 28, 1933; Apr. 22, 1960, Pub.L. 86–443, § 2, 74 Stat. 82.)

HISTORICAL AND STATUTORY NOTES

Change of Name

"Stones River National Battlefield" and "battlefield" were substituted for "Stones River National Park" and "park", respectively, pursuant to Pub.L. 86–443, § 2, Apr. 22, 1960, 74 Stat. 82, which redesignated the Stones River National Military Park as the Stones River National Battlefield. See section 426*l* of this title.

Transfer of Functions

Transfer of administrative functions of park [now battlefield], see note set out under section 426 of this title.

CROSS REFERENCES

Acquisition of additional lands, see 16 USCA § 426k.
Authorization of appropriations, see 16 USCA § 426j.
Boundary revision of Stones River National Battlefield, see 16 USCA § 426n.
Establishment of national battlefield, see 16 USCA § 426e.
Payment of reasonable expenses of commission, see 16 USCA § 426c.

LIBRARY REFERENCES

American Digest System
Armed Services ⚬⚬54.

Woods and Forests ☞5.
Key Number System Topic Nos. 34, 411.

§ 426g.   Occupation of lands by former owners

The Secretary of the Interior is authorized to enter into agreements, upon such nominal terms as he may prescribe, with such
present owners of the land as may desire to remain upon it, to
occupy and cultivate their present holdings, upon condition that they
will preserve the present buildings and roads, and the present outlines of field and forest, and that they will only cut trees or underbrush under such regulations as the Secretary may prescribe, and
that they will assist in caring for and protecting all tablets, monuments, or such other artificial works as may from time to time be
erected by proper authority.

(Mar. 3, 1927, c. 374, § 8, 44 Stat. 1400; Ex.Ord. No. 6166, § 2, June 10,
1933; Ex.Ord. No. 6228, § 1, July 28, 1933.)

HISTORICAL AND STATUTORY NOTES
Transfer of Functions
   Transfer of administrative functions of
park [now battlefield], see note set out
under section 426 of this title.

CROSS REFERENCES
   Acquisition of additional lands, see 16 USCA § 426k.
   Authorization of appropriations, see 16 USCA § 426j.
   Boundary revision of Stones River National Battlefield, see 16 USCA § 426n.
   Establishment of national battlefield, see 16 USCA § 426e.
   Payment of reasonable expenses of commission, see 16 USCA § 426c.

LIBRARY REFERENCES
American Digest System
   Armed Services ☞54.
   United States ☞57.
   Key Number System Topic Nos. 34, 393.

§ 426h.   Ascertaining and marking lines of battle

It shall be lawful for the authorities of any State having troops
engaged in the battle of Stones River to enter upon the lands and
approaches of the Stones River National Battlefield for the purpose
of ascertaining and marking the lines of battle of troops engaged
therein: *Provided*, That before any such lines are permanently designated, the position of the lines and the proposed methods of marking
them by monuments, tablets, or otherwise shall be submitted to the
Secretary of the Interior, and shall first receive the written approval
of the Secretary.

(Mar. 3, 1927, c. 374, § 9, 44 Stat. 1401; Ex.Ord. No. 6166, § 2, June 10,
1933; Ex.Ord. No. 6228, § 1, July 28, 1933; Apr. 22, 1960, Pub.L. 86–443,
§ 2, 74 Stat. 82.)

HISTORICAL AND STATUTORY NOTES

Change of Name

"Stones River National Battlefield" was substituted for "Stones River National Park" pursuant to Pub.L. 86–443, § 2, Apr. 22, 1960, 74 Stat. 82, which redesignated the Stones River National Military Park as the Stones River National Battlefield. See section 426*l* of this title.

Transfer of Functions

Transfer of administrative functions of park [now battlefield], see note set out under section 426 of this title.

CROSS REFERENCES

Acquisition of additional lands, see 16 USCA § 426k.
Authorization of appropriations, see 16 USCA § 426j.
Boundary revision of Stones River National Battlefield, see 16 USCA § 426n.
Establishment of national battlefield, see 16 USCA § 426e.
Payment of reasonable expenses of commission, see 16 USCA § 426c.

LIBRARY REFERENCES

American Digest System

Armed Services ☞54.
Key Number System Topic No. 34.

§ 426i. Protection of monuments, etc.

If any person shall willfully destroy, mutilate, deface, injure, or remove any monument, column, statue, memorial structure, or work of art that shall be erected or placed upon the grounds of the battlefield by lawful authority, or shall willfully destroy or remove any fence, railing, inclosure, or other work for the protection or ornament of said battlefield, or any portion thereof or shall willfully destroy, cut, hack, bark, break down, or otherwise injure any tree, bush, or shrubbery that may be growing upon said battlefield, or shall cut down or fell or remove any timber, battle relic, tree, or trees growing or being upon such battlefield, except by permission of the Secretary of the Interior, or shall willfully remove or destroy any breastworks, earthworks, walls, or other defenses or shelter, or any part thereof, constructed by the armies formerly engaged in the battle on the lands or approaches to the battlefield, any person so offending shall be guilty of a misdemeanor, and upon conviction thereof before any court of competent jurisdiction, shall for each and every such offense be fined not less than $5 nor more than $100.

(Mar. 3, 1927, c. 374, § 10, 44 Stat. 1401; Ex.Ord. No. 6166, § 2, June 10, 1933; Ex.Ord. No. 6228, § 1, July 28, 1933; Apr. 22, 1960, Pub.L. 86–443, § 2, 74 Stat. 82.)

HISTORICAL AND STATUTORY NOTES

Change of Name

"Battlefield" was substituted for "park" wherever appearing in view of the redesignation of Stones River National Military Park as Stones River National Battlefield by Pub.L. 86–443. See section 426*l* of this title.

Transfer of Functions
Transfer of administrative functions of park [now battlefield], see note set out under section 426 of this title.

CROSS REFERENCES

Acquisition of additional lands, see 16 USCA § 426k.
Authorization of appropriations, see 16 USCA § 426j.
Boundary revision of Stones River National Battlefield, see 16 USCA § 426n.
Establishment of national battlefield, see 16 USCA § 426e.
Payment of reasonable expenses of commission, see 16 USCA § 426c.

LIBRARY REFERENCES

American Digest System
Armed Services ⏥54.
Woods and Forests ⏥2, 5, 10, 11.
Key Number System Topic Nos. 34, 411.

§ 426j. Authorization of appropriation; fixing of boundaries as condition to purchase of lands

The sum of $100,000, or so much thereof as may be necessary, is authorized to be appropriated, out of any moneys in the Treasury not otherwise appropriated, to be expended for the purposes of sections 426 to 426j of this title: *Provided*, That no obligation for the purchase of lands shall be incurred until the commission has fixed the boundaries of said battlefield.

(Mar. 3, 1927, c. 374, § 11, 44 Stat. 1401; Apr. 22, 1960, Pub.L. 86–443, § 2, 74 Stat. 82.)

HISTORICAL AND STATUTORY NOTES

Change of Name
"Battlefield" was substituted for "park" in view of the redesignation of Stones River National Military Park as Stones River National Battlefield by Pub.L. 86–443. See section 426*l* of this title.

CROSS REFERENCES

Acquisition of additional lands, see 16 USCA § 426k.
Boundary revision of Stones River National Battlefield, see 16 USCA § 426n.
Establishment of national battlefield, see 16 USCA § 426e.
Payment of reasonable expenses of commission, see 16 USCA § 426c.

LIBRARY REFERENCES

American Digest System
Armed Services ⏥54.
United States ⏥57.
Woods and Forests ⏥2.
Key Number System Topic Nos. 34, 393, 411.

§ 426k.   Acquisition of additional lands

In furtherance of the purposes of sections 426 to 426j of this title, authorizing establishment of the Stones River National Battlefield, the Secretary of the Interior is authorized to acquire by such means as he may deem to be in the public interest, for inclusion in the Stones River National Battlefield, such additional lands and interests in lands, not to exceed seven acres, as in the discretion of the Secretary are necessary for the preservation and interpretation of the battlefield of Stones River, Tennessee.

(Pub.L. 86–443, §§ 1, 2, Apr. 22, 1960, 74 Stat. 82.)

HISTORICAL AND STATUTORY NOTES

Change of Name
"Stones River National Battlefield" was substituted for "Stones River National Park" in view of the redesignation of Stones River National Military Park as Stones River National Battlefield by Pub.L. 86–443. See section 426*l* of this title.

LIBRARY REFERENCES

American Digest System
  Armed Services ☞54.
  United States ☞55.
  Key Number System Topic Nos. 34, 393.

§ 426*l*.   Redesignation; availability of appropriations

Stones River National Military Park is redesignated as the Stones River National Battlefield, and any remaining balance of funds appropriated for the purpose of the Stones River National Military Park shall be available for the purpose of Stones River National Battlefield.

(Pub.L. 86–443, § 2, Apr. 22, 1960, 74 Stat. 82.)

§ 426m.   Administration, protection and development

The administration, protection and development of the Stones River National Battlefield shall be exercised by the Secretary of the Interior in accordance with the provisions of sections 1, 2, 3, and 4 of this title, as amended.

(Pub.L. 86–443, § 3, Apr. 22, 1960, 74 Stat. 82.)

LIBRARY REFERENCES

American Digest System
  Armed Services ☞54.
  Woods and Forests ☞5.
  Key Number System Topic Nos. 34, 411.

§ 426n.   Boundary revision of Stones River National Battlefield

(a) Expansion of Stones River National Battlefield

In furtherance of sections 426 to 426j of this title, the boundary of Stones River National Battlefield (hereinafter referred to as "battlefield") is hereby revised to include the lands generally depicted on the map entitled "Boundary Map, Stones River National Battlefield" numbered 327/80,004B, and dated November 1991. The map shall be on file and available for public inspection in the offices of the National Park Service, Department of the Interior and in the office of the Superintendent of the Stones River National Battlefield.

(b) Acquisition of lands

(1) The Secretary of the Interior (hereinafter referred to as "Secretary") is hereby authorized to acquire lands or interests therein within the boundary of the battlefield by donation, purchase with donated or appropriated funds, or exchange. Any lands or interests in lands owned by the State of Tennessee or any political subdivision thereof may be acquired only by donation. Lands and interests therein acquired pursuant to sections 426n to 426p of this title shall become part of the battlefield, subject to all the laws and regulations applicable thereto.

(2)(A) Before acquiring any lands under sections 426n to 426p of this title where the surface of such lands has been substantially disturbed or which are believed by the Secretary to contain hazardous substances, the Secretary shall prepare a report on the potential hazardous substances associated with such lands and the estimated cost of restoring such lands, together with a plan of the remedial measures necessary to allow acquisition of such lands to proceed in a timely manner, consistent with the requirements of subparagraph (B). The Secretary shall submit such report to the Committee on Energy and Natural Resources of the United States Senate and the Committee on Natural Resources of the United States House of Representatives.

(B) The Secretary shall not acquire any lands under sections 426n to 426p of this title if the Secretary determines that such lands, or any portion thereof, have become contaminated with hazardous substances (as defined in the Comprehensive Environmental Response, Compensation, and Liability Act (42 U.S.C. 9601) [42 U.S.C.A. § 9601 et seq.]).

(3)(A) Except for property which the Secretary determines to be necessary for the purposes of administration, development, access, or public use, an owner of improved property which is used solely for noncommercial residential purposes on the date of its acquisition by the Secretary may retain, as a condition of such acquisition, a right of use and occupancy of the property for such residential purposes. The right retained may be for a definite term which shall not exceed 25 years or, in lieu thereof, for a term ending at the death of the owner or the death of the spouse, whichever is later. The owner shall elect the term to be retained. The Secretary shall pay the owner the fair market value of the property on the date of such acquisition, less the fair market value of the term retained by the owner.

(B) Any right of use and occupancy retained pursuant to this section may, during its existence, be conveyed or transferred, but all rights of use and occupancy shall be subject to such terms and conditions as the Secretary deems appropriate to assure the use of the property in accordance with the purposes of sections 426n to 426p of this title. Upon his determination that the property, or any portion thereof, has ceased to be so used in accordance with such terms and conditions, the Secretary may terminate the right of use and occupancy by tendering to the holder of such right an amount equal to the fair market value, as of the date of the tender, of that portion of the right which remains unexpired on the date of termination.

(C) This paragraph applies only to owners who have reached the age of majority.

(D) As used in this paragraph, the term "improved property" means a detached, year-round noncommercial residential dwelling, the construction of which was begun before December 11, 1991, together with so much of the land on which the dwelling is situated, such land being in the same ownership as the dwelling, as the Secretary shall designate to be reasonably necessary for the enjoyment of the dwelling for the sole purpose of noncommercial residential use, together with any structures accessory to the dwelling which are situated on the land so designated.

(Pub.L. 100–205, § 1, Dec. 23, 1987, 101 Stat. 1433; Pub.L. 102–225, § 1(1), (2), Dec. 11, 1991, 105 Stat. 1682; Pub.L. 103–437, § 6(d)(15), Nov. 2, 1994, 108 Stat. 4584.)

HISTORICAL AND STATUTORY NOTES

Revision Notes and Legislative Reports
 1994 Acts. House Report No. 103–779, see 1994 U.S. Code Cong. and Adm. News, p. 3639.

References in Text
 The Comprehensive Environmental Response, Compensation, and Liability Act, referred to in subsec. (b)(2)(B), probably means the Comprehensive Environmental Response, Compensation, and Liability Act of 1980, Pub.L. 96–510, Dec. 11, 1980, 94 Stat. 2767, as amended, which is classified generally to chapter 103 (section 9601 et seq.) of Title 42, The Public

Health and Welfare. For the purpose of such Act, the definition of the term "hazardous substance" is classified to section 9601(14) of Title 42. For complete classification of this Act to the Code, see Short Title note set out under section 9601 of Title 42 and Tables.

Amendments

1994 Amendments. Subsec. (b)(2)(A). Pub.L. 103–437, § 6(d)(15), substituted reference to Committee on Natural Resources of the House of Representatives for reference to Committee on Interior and Insular Affairs of the House of Representatives.

1991 Amendments. Subsec. (a). Pub.L. 102–225, § 1(1), substituted "numbered 327/80,004B, and dated November 1991" for "numbered 327/80,001 and dated March 1987".

Subsec. (b)(1). Pub.L. 102–225, § 1(2), redesignated former subsec. (b) as par. (1).

Subsec. (b)(2), (3). Pub.L. 102–225, § 1(2), added pars. (2) and (3).

Change of Name

Committee on Natural Resources of House of Representatives treated as referring to Committee on Resources of House of Representatives by section 1(a) of Pub.L. 104–14, set out as a note preceding 2 U.S.C.A. § 21. Committee on Resources of House of Representatives changed to Committee on Natural Resources of House of Representatives by House Resolution No. 6, One Hundred Tenth Congress, Jan. 5, 2007.

LIBRARY REFERENCES

American Digest System
Armed Services ⚙54.
Woods and Forests ⚙2.
Key Number System Topic Nos. 34, 411.

§ 426o.   Agreement with Murfreesboro, Tennessee, respecting battlefield

The Secretary is authorized to enter into an agreement with the city of Murfreesboro, Tennessee, containing each of the following provisions—

    (1) If the city agrees to acquire sufficient interest in land to construct a trail linking the battlefield with Fortress Rosecrans, to construct such trail, and to operate and maintain the trail in accordance with standards approved by the Secretary, the Secretary shall (A) transfer to the city the funds available to the Secretary for the acquisition of such lands and for the construction of the trail, and (B) provide technical assistance to the city and to Rutherford County for the purpose of development and planning of the trail.

    (2) The Secretary shall agree to accept the transfer by donation from the city of the remnants of Fortress Rosecrans at Old Fort Park, and following such transfer, to preserve and interpret the fortress as part of the battlefield.

    (3) In administering the Fortress Rosecrans, the Secretary is authorized to enter a cooperative agreement with the city of Murfreesboro, Tennessee, for the rendering, on a nonreimbursable basis, of rescue, firefighting, and law enforcement services and cooperative assistance by nearby law enforcement and fire preventive agencies.

(Pub.L. 100–205, § 2, Dec. 23, 1987, 101 Stat. 1433; Pub.L. 102–225, § 1(3), Dec. 11, 1991, 105 Stat. 1683.)

HISTORICAL AND STATUTORY NOTES

Amendments
1991 Amendments. Pub.L. 102–225 amended section generally, substituting provisions authorizing the Secretary to enter into an agreement with the city of Murfreesboro which provides that the Secretary will transfer funds to the city for acquisition of land for a trail linking the battlefield with Fortress Rosecrans, and provide technical assistance in planning and developing the trail, if the city agrees to acquire land and construct, maintain and operate the trail, that the Secretary will accept transfer of the fortress for preservation and interpretation as part of the battlefield, and that the city will provide, on a cooperative basis with the Secretary and with nearby law enforcement and fire preventive agencies, rescue, firefighting, and law enforcement services for the fortress, for provisions authorizing the Secretary to enter into an agreement with the city under which the Secretary acquired land and built the trail, the city operated and maintained the trail, the Secretary preserved the fortress, and the city operated and maintained the fortress.

LIBRARY REFERENCES

American Digest System
Armed Services ⬤54.
United States ⬤60.
Key Number System Topic Nos. 34, 393.

§ 426o–1. Planning

(a) Preparation of plan for Redoubt Brannan

The Secretary shall, on or before February 1, 1992, prepare a plan for the preservation and interpretation of Redoubt Brannan.

(b) Update of General Management Plan

The Secretary shall, on or before March 31, 1993, update the General Management Plan for the Stones River National Battlefield.

(c) Technical assistance

The Secretary is authorized to provide technical assistance to the city and to Rutherford County in the development of zoning ordinances and other land use controls that would help preserve historically significant areas adjacent to the battlefield.

(d) Minor boundary revisions

If the planning activities conducted under subsections (a) and (b) of this section show a need for minor revisions of the boundaries indicated on the map referred to in section 426n of this title, the Secretary may, following timely notice in writing to the Committee on Natural Resources of the United States House of Representatives and to the Committee on Energy and Natural Resources of the United States Senate of his intention to do so and providing an opportunity for public comment, make such minor revisions by publication of a revised boundary map or other description in the Federal Register.

(Pub.L. 100–205, § 3, as added Pub.L. 102–225, § 1(4), Dec. 11, 1991, 105 Stat. 1683, and amended Pub.L. 103–437, § 6(d)(15), Nov. 2, 1994, 108 Stat. 4584.)

HISTORICAL AND STATUTORY NOTES

Revision Notes and Legislative Reports
1994 Acts. House Report No. 103–779, see 1994 U.S. Code Cong. and Adm. News, p. 3639.

Amendments
1994 Amendments. Subsec. (c). Pub.L. 103–437, § 6(d)(15), substituted reference to Committee on Natural Resources of the House of Representatives for reference to Committee on Interior and Insular Affairs of the House of Representatives.

Change of Name
Committee on Natural Resources of House of Representatives treated as referring to Committee on Resources of House of Representatives by section 1(a) of Pub.L. 104–14, set out as a note preceding 2 U.S.C.A. § 21. Committee on Resources of House of Representatives changed to Committee on Natural Resources of House of Representatives by House Resolution No. 6, One Hundred Tenth Congress, Jan. 5, 2007.

LIBRARY REFERENCES

American Digest System
Armed Services ⬿54.
Woods and Forests ⬿2.
Key Number System Topic Nos. 34, 411.

§ 426p. Authorization of appropriations

There is hereby authorized to be appropriated such sums as may be necessary to carry out the purposes of sections 426n to 426p of this title.

(Pub.L. 100–205, § 4, formerly § 3, Dec. 23, 1987, 101 Stat. 1433, renumbered § 4, Pub.L. 102–225, § 1(4), Dec. 11, 1991, 105 Stat. 1683.)

CROSS REFERENCES

Acquisition of lands within boundary of Stones River National Battlefield, see 16 USCA § 426n.

§ 427. Site of battle with Sioux Indians; purchase; erection of monument

The Secretary of the Interior is authorized and directed to acquire, by condemnation or otherwise, such land as may be deemed appropriate, not exceeding one hundred and sixty acres, on the site of the battle with the Sioux Indians in which the commands of Major Marcus A. Reno and Major Frederick W. Benteen were engaged, and to erect thereon a suitable monument and historical tablet.

(Apr. 14, 1926, c. 138, § 1, 44 Stat. 251.)

LIBRARY REFERENCES

American Digest System
　Armed Services ⊖54.
　United States ⊖55.
　Key Number System Topic Nos. 34, 393.

§ 427a.　Omitted

HISTORICAL AND STATUTORY NOTES

Codifications
　Section, Act Apr. 14, 1926, c. 138, § 2, 44 Stat. 251, made appropriation of $2,500 for carrying out of provisions of section 427 of this title.

§ 428.　Fort Donelson National Battlefield; establishment; appointment of commission

A commission is created, to be composed of the following members, who shall be appointed by the Secretary of the Interior:

(1) A commissioned officer of the Corps of Engineers, United States Army;

(2) A veteran of the Civil War who served honorably in the military forces of the United States; and

(3) A veteran of the Civil War who served honorably in the military forces of the Confederate States of America.

(Mar. 26, 1928, c. 248, § 1, 45 Stat. 367; Ex. Ord. No. 6166, § 2, June 10, 1933; Ex. Ord. No. 6228, § 1, July 28, 1933; Sept. 8, 1960, Pub.L. 86–738, § 5, 74 Stat. 876.)

HISTORICAL AND STATUTORY NOTES

Revision Notes and Legislative Reports
　1960 Acts. House Report No. 2009, see 1960 U.S. Code Cong. and Adm. News, p. 3488.

Change of Name
　The "Fort Donelson National Military Park" was redesignated the "Fort Donelson National Battlefield" by Pub.L. 86–738, § 4. See section 428n of this title.

Transfer of Functions
　Administrative functions of Fort Donelson National Military Park were transferred to the Department of the Interior by Ex. Ord. Nos. 6166 and 6228, set out as notes under section 901 of Title 5, Government Organization and Employees. Administrative functions of Fort Do-nelson National Battlefield were assigned to the Department of the Interior by section 5 of Pub.L. 86–738, set out as section 428o of this title.

　National Park Service was substituted for Office of National Parks, Buildings, and Reservations referred to in Ex. Ord. No. 6166, § 2, by Act Mar. 2, 1934, c. 38, § 1, 48 Stat. 389.

Short Title
　2004 Amendments. Pub.L. 108–367, § 1, Oct. 25, 2004, 118 Stat. 1743, provided that: "This Act [enacting 16 U.S.C.A. §§ 428p, 428p–1, and 428p–2, and amending 16 U.S.C.A. § 428k] may be cited as the 'Fort Donelson National Battlefield Expansion Act of 2004'."

CROSS REFERENCES

Addition of lands designated by Secretary of Interior, see 16 USCA § 428k.

Establishment of national battlefield, see 16 USCA § 428c.
Members of commission, see 16 USCA § 428a.

LIBRARY REFERENCES

American Digest System
Armed Services ☞54.
Woods and Forests ☞7.
Key Number System Topic Nos. 34, 411.

§ 428a.   Qualifications of members of commission

In appointing the members of the commission created by section 428 of this title the Secretary of the Interior shall, as far as practicable, select persons familiar with the terrain of the battlefield of Fort Donelson, Tennessee, and the historical events associated therewith.

(Mar. 26, 1928, c. 248, § 2, 45 Stat. 367; Ex.Ord. No. 6166, § 2, June 10, 1933; Ex.Ord. No. 6228, § 1, July 28, 1933; Sept. 8, 1960, Pub.L. 86–738, § 5, 74 Stat. 876.)

HISTORICAL AND STATUTORY NOTES

Transfer of Functions
Transfer of administrative functions of park [now battlefield], see note set out under section 428 of this title.

CROSS REFERENCES

Addition of lands designated by Secretary of Interior, see 16 USCA § 428k.
Establishment of national battlefield, see 16 USCA § 428e.

LIBRARY REFERENCES

American Digest System
Armed Services ☞54.
Woods and Forests ☞7.
Key Number System Topic Nos. 34, 411.

§ 428b.   Duties of commission

It shall be the duty of the commission, acting under the direction of the Secretary of the Interior, to inspect the battlefield of Fort Donelson, Tennessee, and to carefully study the available records and historical data with respect to the location and movement of all troops which engaged in the Battle of Fort Donelson, and the important events connected therewith, with a view of preserving and marking such field for historical and professional military study.

(Mar. 26, 1928, c. 248, § 3, 45 Stat. 367; Ex.Ord. No. 6166, § 2, June 10, 1933; Ex.Ord. No. 6228, § 1, July 28, 1933; Sept. 8, 1960, Pub.L. 86–738, § 5, 74 Stat. 876.)

HISTORICAL AND STATUTORY NOTES

Transfer of Functions
Transfer of administrative functions of park [now battlefield], see note set out under section 428 of this title.

CROSS REFERENCES

Addition of lands designated by Secretary of Interior, see 16 USCA § 428k.
Establishment of national battlefield, see 16 USCA § 428e.

LIBRARY REFERENCES

American Digest System
Armed Services ☞54.
Woods and Forests ☞7.
Key Number System Topic Nos. 34, 411.

§ 428c. Assistants to commission; expenses of commission

The Secretary of the Interior is authorized to assign any officials of the Interior Department to the assistance of the commission if he deems it advisable. He is authorized to pay the reasonable expenses of the commission and their assistants incurred in the actual performance of the duties herein imposed upon them.

(Mar. 26, 1928, c. 248, § 4, 45 Stat. 367; Ex.Ord. No. 6166, § 2, June 10, 1933; Ex.Ord. No. 6228, § 1, July 28, 1933; Sept. 8, 1960, Pub.L. 86–738, § 5, 74 Stat. 876.)

HISTORICAL AND STATUTORY NOTES

References in Text
Herein, referred to in text, means Act Mar. 26, 1928, c. 248, which is classified to sections 428 to 428d and 428e to 428i of this title. For complete classification of this Act to the Code, see Tables.

Transfer of Functions
Transfer of administrative functions of park [now battlefield], see note set out under section 428 of this title.

CROSS REFERENCES

Addition of lands designated by Secretary of Interior, see 16 USCA § 428k.
Establishment of national battlefield, see 16 USCA § 428e.

LIBRARY REFERENCES

American Digest System
Armed Services ☞54.
Woods and Forests ☞7.
Key Number System Topic Nos. 34, 411.

§ 428d. Receipt of report of commission by Secretary of the Interior; acquisition of land for battlefield; other duties of Secretary

Upon receipt of the report of said commission the Secretary of the Interior is authorized and directed to acquire, by purchase, when purchasable at prices deemed by him reasonable, otherwise by condemnation, such tract or tracts of lands as are recommended by the commission as necessary and desirable for a national battlefield; to establish and substantially mark the boundaries of the said battlefield; to definitely mark all lines of battle and locations of troops within the boundaries of the battlefield and erect substantial historical tablets at such points within the battlefield and in the vicinity of the battlefield and its approaches as are recommended by the commission, together with such other points as the Secretary of the Interior may deem appropriate; to construct the necessary roads and walks, plant trees and shrubs, restore and care for the grounds, including the restoration and maintenance of those portions of old Fort Donelson, and of the Confederate water batteries that are located on the present engineer reservation: *Provided*, That the entire cost of acquiring said land, including cost of condemnation proceedings, if any, ascertainment of title, surveys, and compensation for the land, the cost of marking the battlefield, the expenses of the commission, and the establishment of the national battlefield shall not exceed the sum of $50,000.

(Mar. 26, 1928, c. 248, § 5, 45 Stat. 368; Feb. 18, 1930, c. 49, 46 Stat. 69; Ex.Ord. No. 6166, § 2, June 10, 1933; Ex.Ord. No. 6228, § 1, July 28, 1933; Sept. 8, 1960, Pub.L. 86–738, § 4, 74 Stat. 876; Sept. 8, 1960, Pub.L. 86–738, § 5, 74 Stat. 876.)

HISTORICAL AND STATUTORY NOTES

Revision Notes and Legislative Reports
 1960 Acts. House Report No. 2009, see 1960 U.S. Code Cong. and Adm. News, p. 3488.

Amendments
 1930 Amendments. Act Feb. 18, 1930 inserted "military" between "national" and "park", authorized construction of roads and walks, the planting of trees and shrubs, the restoration and care of the grounds, including portions of Fort Donelson and the Confederate water batteries, and added "and the establishment of the national military park" in the proviso.

Change of Name
 "National battlefield" and "battlefield" were substituted for "national military park" and "park", respectively, in view of the redesignation of Fort Donelson National Military Park as Fort Donelson National Battlefield by Pub.L. 86–738. See section 428n of this title.

Transfer of Functions
 Transfer of administrative functions of park [now battlefield], see note set out under section 428 of this title.

CROSS REFERENCES

Addition of lands designated by Secretary of Interior, see 16 USCA § 428k.
Establishment of national battlefield, see 16 USCA § 428e.

LIBRARY REFERENCES

American Digest System
 Armed Services ☞54.
 United States ☞55.
 Woods and Forests ☞8.
 Key Number System Topic Nos. 34, 393, 411.

§ 428d–1. Acquisition of additional lands

The following-described tracts or parcels of land, lying and being within the seventh civil district of Stewart County, Tennessee, are transferred from the jurisdiction of the Secretary of War to the jurisdiction of the Secretary of the Interior as additions to the Fort Donelson National Battlefield, and shall after August 30, 1937, be subject to all laws and rules and regulations applicable to said battlefield:

Tract numbered 1, a right-of-way, fifty feet wide, lying twenty-five feet on each side of a center line, beginning at a point in the southerly boundary line of lock D reservation, seven hundred and thirty-four and eight-tenths feet from the southwest corner of this reservation; thence south thirty-one degrees five minutes west seventy-seven and one-tenth feet, thence south eighty-six degrees twenty-one minutes west four hundred and seventy-nine and nine-tenths feet, thence south sixty-three degrees fifty-three minutes west two hundred and sixty-two and three-tenths feet, thence south thirty-nine degrees thirty-six minutes west one hundred and eighty-six and seven-tenths feet, thence south exactly forty minutes east exactly one hundred and ninety-four feet, thence south thirty degrees fifty-eight minutes east three hundred and fourteen and five-tenths feet, thence south twenty-eight degrees fifteen minutes east exactly eighty-five feet, thence south twenty-eight degrees thirty-seven minutes east two hundred and fifty and five-tenths feet, thence south four degrees six minutes east two hundred and sixty-one and seven-tenths feet, thence south thirty-six degrees twenty-seven minutes east two hundred and eighty-two and three-tenths feet, thence south twenty-three degrees forty-five minutes east one hundred and seventy-eight and three-tenths feet to center line of county road, reserving, however, to the Department of the Army the right to the continued use of the road over this tract as a means of access to lock D.

Tract numbered 2, beginning at a point in the southern boundary line of lock D reservation, seven hundred and fifty-three and five-tenths feet from the southwest corner of this reservation, thence north seventy-four degrees twenty-eight minutes east one hundred and ninety-one and ninety-eight one-hundredths feet, thence south eighty-five degrees twelve minutes east fifty-two and nine-tenths feet, thence south fifty-one degrees thirty-six minutes east thirty-two and nine-tenths feet, thence south nine degrees thirty-three minutes east one hundred and seventeen and two one-hundredths feet, thence south thirty-one degrees three minutes west sixty-nine and eighty-two one-hundredths feet, thence north fifty-eight degrees fifty-seven minutes west two hundred and eighty-eight and eight one-hundredths feet to beginning.

Tract numbered 3, beginning at a point in the southern boundary line of lock D reservation, five hundred and ninety feet from the southwest corner of this reservation, this point being marked by an iron fence post, thence north fifty-eight degrees fifty-seven minutes west five hundred and ninety feet along the southern boundary line of lock D reservation, thence north thirty-one degrees three minutes east four hundred and eighty-eight feet along the western boundary line of the lock D reservation to low-water mark on bank of Cumberland River, thence along low-water line of Cumberland River in a southeasterly direction three hundred and thirty-five feet, thence south thirty-four degrees five minutes west one hundred and twenty-three feet to an iron pin, thence south fifty-five degrees fifty-five minutes east three hundred and seven and five-tenths feet to an iron pin, thence south forty degrees five minutes west three hundred and ten and five-tenths feet to beginning.

(Aug. 30, 1937, c. 888, § 1, 50 Stat. 881; Sept. 8, 1960, Pub.L. 86–738, § 4, 74 Stat. 876.)

HISTORICAL AND STATUTORY NOTES

Revision Notes and Legislative Reports
  1960 Acts. House Report No. 2009, see 1960 U.S. Code Cong. and Adm. News, p. 3488.

Change of Name
  The Department of War was designated the Department of the Army and the title of the Secretary of War was changed to Secretary of the Army by section 205(a) of Act July 26, 1947, c. 343, Title II, 61 Stat. 501. Section 205(a) of Act July 26, 1947, was repealed by section 53 of Act Aug. 10, 1956, c. 1041, 70A Stat. 641. Section 1 of Act Aug. 10, 1956, enacted

"Title 10, Armed Forces" which in sections 3011 to 3013 continued the military Department of the Army under the administrative supervision of a Secretary of the Army.

  "Fort Donelson National Battlefield" and "battlefield" were substituted for "Fort Donelson National Military Park" and "park", respectively, in view of the redesignation of Fort Donelson National Military Park as Fort Donelson National Battlefield by Pub.L. 86–738. See section 428n of this title.

LIBRARY REFERENCES

American Digest System
  Armed Services ☞54.
  United States ☞55.
  Woods and Forests ☞2.
  Key Number System Topic Nos. 34, 393, 411.

§ 428d–2. Acceptance of donations by Secretary of the Interior

The Secretary of the Interior is authorized to accept donations of land, interests in land, buildings, structures, and other property within a distance of one mile from the boundaries of said Fort Donelson National Battlefield, as extended by section 428d–1 of this title, and donations of funds for the purchase or maintenance thereof, the title and evidence of title to lands acquired to be satisfactory to the Secretary of the Interior: *Provided*, That he may acquire on behalf of the United States out of any donated funds, by purchase at prices deemed by him reasonable or by condemnation, such tracts of land within a distance of one mile from the boundaries of the said national battlefield as may be necessary for the completion thereof. Upon the acquisition of such land, the same shall become a part of the Fort Donelson National Battlefield and shall be subject to the laws and rules and regulations applicable to said battlefield.

(Aug. 30, 1937, c. 888, § 2, 50 Stat. 882; Sept. 8, 1960, Pub.L. 86–738, § 4, 74 Stat. 876.)

HISTORICAL AND STATUTORY NOTES

Revision Notes and Legislative Reports
 1960 Acts. House Report No. 2009, see 1960 U.S. Code Cong. and Adm. News, p. 3488.

Change of Name
 "Fort Donelson National Battlefield" "national battlefield" and "battlefield" were substituted for "Fort Donelson National Military Park", "national military park" and "park", respectively, pursuant to Pub.L. 86–738, § 4, Sept. 8, 1960, 74 Stat. 876, which redesignated the "Fort Donelson National Military Park" as the "Fort Donelson National Battlefield". See section 428n of this title.

LIBRARY REFERENCES

American Digest System
 Armed Services ☞54.
 United States ☞55.
 Key Number System Topic Nos. 34, 393.

§ 428d–3.   Administration, protection, and development

The administration, protection, and development of the lands authorized to be added to the Fort Donelson National Battlefield by sections 428d–1 and 428d–2 shall be exercised under the direction of the Secretary of the Interior by the National Park Service, subject to the provisions of sections 1, 2, 3, and of this title, as amended.

(Aug. 30, 1937, c. 888, § 3, 50 Stat. 883; Sept. 8, 1960, Pub.L. 86–738, § 4, 74 Stat. 876.)

HISTORICAL AND STATUTORY NOTES

Revision Notes and Legislative Reports
 1960 Acts. House Report No. 2009, see 1960 U.S. Code Cong. and Adm. News, p. 3488.

Change of Name
 "Fort Donelson National Battlefield" was substituted for "Fort Donelson National Military Park" pursuant to Pub.L. 86–738, § 4, Sept. 8, 1960, 74 Stat. 876, which redesignated the "Fort Donelson National Military Park" as the "Fort Donelson National Battlefield". See section 428n of this title.

LIBRARY REFERENCES

American Digest System
Armed Services ⬤54.
Woods and Forests ⬤5.
Key Number System Topic Nos. 34, 411.

§ 428e.   Lands acquired declared national battlefield;   name

Upon the ceding of jurisdiction by the Legislature of the State of Tennessee and the report of the Attorney General of the United States that a perfect title has been acquired, the lands acquired under the provisions of sections 428 to 428d and 428e to 428i of this title, together with the area already inclosed within the national cemetery at the battle field of Fort Donelson, are declared to be a national battlefield, to be known as the Fort Donelson National Battlefield.

(Mar. 26, 1928, c. 248, § 6, 45 Stat. 368; Sept. 8, 1960, Pub.L. 86–738, § 4, 74 Stat. 876.)

HISTORICAL AND STATUTORY NOTES

Revision Notes and Legislative Reports
1960 Acts. House Report No. 2009, see 1960 U.S. Code Cong. and Adm. News, p. 3488.

Change of Name
"Fort Donelson National Battlefield" and "battlefield" were substituted for "Fort Donelson National Military Park" and "park", respectively, pursuant to Pub.L. 86–738, § 4, Sept. 8, 1960, 74 Stat. 876, which redesignated the "Fort Donelson National Military Park" as the "Fort Donelson National Battlefield". See section 428n of this title.

CROSS REFERENCES

Addition of lands designated by Secretary of Interior, see 16 USCA § 428k.

LIBRARY REFERENCES

American Digest System
Armed Services ⬤54.
United States ⬤55.
Key Number System Topic Nos. 34, 393.

§ 428f.   Control of battlefield;   regulations

The said Fort Donelson National Battlefield shall be under the control of the Secretary of the Interior, and he is authorized to make all needed regulations for the care of the battlefield. The superintendent of the Fort Donelson National Cemetery shall likewise be the superintendent of and have the custody and care of the Fort Donelson National Battlefield, under the direction of the Secretary of the Interior.

(Mar. 26, 1928, c. 248, § 7, 45 Stat. 368; Ex.Ord. No. 6166, § 2, June 10, 1933; Ex.Ord. No. 6228, § 1, July 28, 1933; Sept. 8, 1960, Pub.L. 86–738, § 4, 74 Stat. 876; Sept. 8, 1960, Pub.L. 86–738, § 5, 74 Stat. 876.)

HISTORICAL AND STATUTORY NOTES

Revision Notes and Legislative Reports
 1960 Acts. House Report No. 2009, see 1960 U.S. Code Cong. and Adm. News, p. 3488.

Change of Name
 "Fort Donelson National Battlefield" and "battlefield" were substituted for "Fort Donelson National Military Park" and "park", respectively, pursuant to

Pub.L. 86–738, § 4, Sept. 8, 1960, 74 Stat. 876, which redesignated the "Fort Donelson National Military Park" as the "Fort Donelson National Battlefield". See section 428n of this title.

Transfer of Functions
 Transfer of administrative functions of park [now battlefield], see note set out under section 428 of this title.

CROSS REFERENCES

Addition of lands designated by Secretary of Interior, see 16 USCA § 428k.
Establishment of national battlefield, see 16 USCA § 428e.

LIBRARY REFERENCES

American Digest System
 Armed Services ☜54.
 Woods and Forests ☜5.
 Key Number System Topic Nos. 34, 411.

§ 428g. Occupation of lands by former owners

The Secretary of the Interior is authorized to enter into agreements, upon such nominal terms as he may prescribe, with such present owners of the land as may desire to remain upon it, to occupy and cultivate their present holdings, upon condition that they will preserve the present buildings and roads, and the present outlines of field and forest, and that they will only cut trees or underbrush under such regulations as the Secretary may prescribe, and that they will assist in caring for and protecting all tablets, monuments, or such other artificial works as may from time to time be erected by proper authority.

(Mar. 26, 1928, c. 248, § 8, 45 Stat. 368; Ex.Ord. No. 6166, § 2, June 10, 1933; Ex.Ord. No. 6228, § 1, July 28, 1933; Sept. 8, 1960, Pub.L. 86–738, § 5, 74 Stat. 876.)

HISTORICAL AND STATUTORY NOTES

Transfer of Functions
 Transfer of administrative functions of park [now battlefield], see note set out under section 428 of this title.

CROSS REFERENCES

Addition of lands designated by Secretary of Interior, see 16 USCA § 428k.
Establishment of national battlefield, see 16 USCA § 428e.

LIBRARY REFERENCES

American Digest System
 Armed Services ☜54.

United States ⊕57.
Woods and Forests ⊕2.
Key Number System Topic Nos. 34, 393, 411.

§ 428h. Ascertaining and marking line of battle

It shall be lawful for the authorities of any State having troops engaged in the Battle of Fort Donelson to enter upon the lands and approaches of the Fort Donelson National Battlefield for the purpose of ascertaining and marking the lines of battle of troops engaged therein: *Provided*, That before any such lines are permanently designated, the position of the lines and the proposed methods of marking them by monuments, tablets, or otherwise shall be submitted to the Secretary of the Interior and shall first receive the written approval of the Secretary.

(Mar. 26, 1928, c. 248, § 9, 45 Stat. 368; Ex.Ord. No. 6166, § 2, June 10, 1933; Ex.Ord. No. 6228, § 1, July 28, 1933; Sept. 8, 1960, Pub.L. 86–738, § 4, 74 Stat. 876; Sept. 8, 1960, Pub.L. 86–738, §§ 4, 5, 74 Stat. 876.)

HISTORICAL AND STATUTORY NOTES

Revision Notes and Legislative Reports
  1960 Acts. House Report No. 2009, see 1960 U.S. Code Cong. and Adm. News, p. 3488.

Change of Name
  "Fort Donelson National Battlefield" was substituted for "Fort Donelson National Military Park" pursuant to Pub.L. 86–738, § 4, Sept. 8, 1960, 74 Stat. 876, which redesignated the "Fort Donelson National Military Park" as the "Fort Donelson National Battlefield". See section 428n of this title.

Transfer of Functions
  Transfer of administrative functions of park [now battlefield], see note set out under section 428 of this title.

CROSS REFERENCES

Addition of lands designated by Secretary of Interior, see 16 USCA § 428k.
Establishment of national battlefield, see 16 USCA § 428e.

LIBRARY REFERENCES

American Digest System
  Armed Services ⊕54.
  Woods and Forests ⊕2.
  Key Number System Topic Nos. 34, 411.

§ 428i. Protection of monuments, etc.

If any person shall willfully destroy, mutilate, deface, injure, or remove any monument, column, statue, memorial structure, or work of art that shall be erected or placed upon the grounds of the battlefield by lawful authority, or shall willfully destroy or remove any fence, railing, inclosure, or other work for the protection or ornament of said battlefield, or any portion thereof, or shall willfully destroy, cut, hack, bark, break down, or otherwise injure any tree, bush, or shrubbery that may be growing upon said battlefield, or shall cut down or fell or remove any timber, battle relic, tree, or trees growing or being upon such battlefield, except by permission of the Secretary of the Interior, or shall willfully remove or destroy any breastworks, earthworks, walls, or other defenses or shelter, or any part thereof, constructed by the armies formerly engaged in the battle on the lands or approaches to the battlefield, any person so offending shall be guilty of a misdemeanor, and upon conviction thereof before any court of competent jurisdiction shall for each and every such offense be fined not less than $5 nor more than $100.

(Mar. 26, 1928, c. 248, § 10, 45 Stat. 368; Ex.Ord. No. 6166, § 2, June 10, 1933; Ex.Ord. No. 6228, § 1, July 28, 1933; Sept. 8, 1960, Pub.L. 86–738, §§ 4, 5, 74 Stat. 876.)

HISTORICAL AND STATUTORY NOTES

Revision Notes and Legislative Reports
   1960 Acts. House Report No. 2009, see 1960 U.S. Code Cong. and Adm. News, p. 3488.

Change of Name
   "Battlefield" was substituted for "park" wherever appearing in view of the redesignation of Fort Donelson National

Military Park as Fort Donelson National Battlefield by Pub.L. 86–738. See section 428n of this title.

Transfer of Functions
   Transfer of administrative functions of park [now battlefield], see note set out under section 428 of this title.

CROSS REFERENCES

Addition of lands designated by Secretary of Interior, see 16 USCA § 428k.
Establishment of national battlefield, see 16 USCA § 428e.

LIBRARY REFERENCES

American Digest System
   Armed Services ⊜54.
   Woods and Forests ⊜5.
   Key Number System Topic Nos. 34, 411.

§ 428j.   Omitted

HISTORICAL AND STATUTORY NOTES

Codifications
   Section, Act Mar. 26, 1928, c. 248, § 11, 45 Stat. 369, authorized the appro-

priation of $50,000 to be expended for purposes of sections 428 to 428d and 428e to 428i of this title.

§ 428k.   Addition of lands

In furtherance of the purposes of sections 428 to 428d and 428e to 428i of this title, and to facilitate an appropriate observance of the one hundredth anniversary of the Battle of Fort Donelson, the Secretary of the Interior is authorized to designate for addition to the present Fort Donelson National Battlefield such lands and interests in lands adjacent to said battlefield as in his discretion are necessary to preserve and interpret this historic battleground, including the nearby historic Surrender House and the land upon which it is situated on Spring Street in the town of Dover, Tennessee.

(Pub.L. 86–738, §§ 1, 4, Sept. 8, 1960, 74 Stat. 875, 876, and amended Pub.L. 108–367, § 6, Oct. 25, 2004, 118 Stat. 1745.)

HISTORICAL AND STATUTORY NOTES

Revision Notes and Legislative Reports
  1960 Acts. House Report No. 2009, see 1960 U.S. Code Cong. and Adm. News, p. 3488.

  2004 Acts. Senate Report No. 108–230, see 2004 U.S. Code Cong. and Adm. News, p. 1920.

Amendments
  2004 Amendments. Pub.L. 108–367, § 6, struck out "Tennessee, but the total area commemorating the battle of Fort

Donelson shall not exceed 600 acres." and substituted "Tennessee.".

Charge of Name
  "Fort Donelson National Battlefield" and "battlefield" were substituted for "Fort Donelson National Military Park" and "park", respectively, in view of the redesignation of Fort Donelson National Military Park as Fort Donelson National Battlefield by Pub.L. 86–738, § 4, Sept. 8, 1960, 74 Stat. 876. See section 428n of this title.

LIBRARY REFERENCES

American Digest System
  Armed Services ☞54.
  United States ☞55.
  Key Number System Topic Nos. 34, 393.

§ 428*l*. Acquisition of lands; agreement for transfer of jurisdiction

Within the area designated for addition to such battlefield under section 428k of this title, the Secretary is authorized to acquire non-Federal lands and interests in lands by purchase, by donation, by purchase with donated funds, or in such other manner and by such means as he may deem to be in the public interest, except that the Surrender House and land upon which it is situated shall be acquired only by donation or by purchase with donated funds. Administrative jurisdiction and control over lands administered by the Corps of Engineers, Department of the Army, above contour elevation 369 and which, under authority of section 428k of this title, are designated for inclusion in the battlefield, shall, upon agreement of the administering agency, be transferred to the Secretary of the Interior without a transfer of funds.

(Pub.L. 86–738, §§ 2, 4, Sept. 8, 1960, 74 Stat. 876.)

HISTORICAL AND STATUTORY NOTES

Revision Notes and Legislative Reports
  1960 Acts. House Report No. 2009, see 1960 U.S. Code Cong. and Adm. News, p. 3488.

Change of Name
  "Battlefield" was substituted for "park" in view of the redesignation of Fort Donelson National Military Park as Fort Donelson National Battlefield by Pub.L. 86–738, § 4, Sept. 8, 1960, 74 Stat. 876. See section 428n of this title.

LIBRARY REFERENCES

American Digest System
  Armed Services ⬡54.
  United States ⬡55.
  Key Number System Topic Nos. 34, 393.

§ 428m. Authorization of appropriation

There is authorized to be appropriated the sum of not to exceed $454,000 for the purpose of acquiring lands, interests in lands, and improvements thereon as may be necessary for carrying out sections 428k to 428*o* of this title.

(Pub.L. 86–738, § 3, Sept. 8, 1960, 74 Stat. 876; Pub.L. 92–272, Title I, § 101(5), Apr. 11, 1972, 86 Stat. 120.)

HISTORICAL AND STATUTORY NOTES

Revision Notes and Legislative Reports
  1960 Acts. House Report No. 2009, see 1960 U.S. Code Cong. and Adm. News, p. 3488.

Amendments
  1972 Amendments. Pub.L. 92–272 increased the authorization of appropria-tions from a sum not to exceed $226,000 to a sum not to exceed $454,000.

Research References

ALR Library
  33 ALR, Fed. 9, Uniform Relocation Assistance and Real Property Acquisition Policies Act of 1970 (42 U.S.C.A. §§ 4601-4655).

§ 428n. Change in name to Fort Donelson National Battlefield

Upon acquisition of the additional lands pursuant to authority contained in sections 428k to 428*o* of this title, the Fort Donelson National Military Park shall be redesignated by the Secretary of the Interior as the Fort Donelson National Battlefield, notice thereof shall be published in the Federal Register, and any remaining balance of funds appropriated for purposes of the Fort Donelson National Military Park shall be available for the purposes of the Fort Donelson National Battlefield.

(Pub.L. 86–738, § 4, Sept. 8, 1960, 74 Stat. 876.)

HISTORICAL AND STATUTORY NOTES

Revision Notes and Legislative Reports
1960 Acts. House Report No. 2009, see
1960 U.S. Code Cong. and Adm. News, p.
3488.

LIBRARY REFERENCES

American Digest System
Armed Services ⊕54.
Woods and Forests ⊕1.
Key Number System Topic Nos. 34, 411.

§ 428*o*.   Administration, protection, and development

The administration, protection, and development of the Fort Donelson National Battlefield shall be exercised by the Secretary of the Interior in accordance with the provisions of sections 1, 2, 3, and 4 of this title, as amended.

(Pub.L. 86–738, § 5, Sept. 8, 1960, 74 Stat. 876.)

HISTORICAL AND STATUTORY NOTES

Revision Notes and Legislative Reports
1960 Acts. House Report No. 2009, see
1960 U.S. Code Cong. and Adm. News, p.
3488.

LIBRARY REFERENCES

American Digest System
Armed Services ⊕54.
Woods and Forests ⊕5.
Key Number System Topic Nos. 34, 411.

§ 428p.   Fort Donelson National Battlefield

(a) Designation; purpose

There exists as a unit of the National Park System the Fort Donelson National Battlefield to commemorate—

(1) the Battle of Fort Donelson in February 1862; and

(2) the campaign conducted by General Ulysses S. Grant and Admiral Andrew H. Foote that resulted in the capture of Fort Donelson by Union forces.

(b) Boundaries

The boundary of the Fort Donelson National Battlefield is revised to include the site of Fort Donelson and associated land that has been acquired by the Secretary of the Interior for administration by the National Park Service, including Fort Donelson National Cemetery, in Stewart County, Tennessee and the site of Fort Heiman and associated land in Calloway County, Kentucky, as generally depicted on the map entitled "Fort Donelson National Battlefield Boundary Adjustment" numbered 328/80024, and dated September 2003. The map shall be on file and available for public inspection in the appropriate offices of the National Park Service.

(c) Expansion of boundaries

The Fort Donelson National Battlefield shall also include any land acquired pursuant to section 428p–1 of this title.

(Pub.L. 108–367, § 2, Oct. 25, 2004, 118 Stat. 1743.)

HISTORICAL AND STATUTORY NOTES

Revision Notes and Legislative Reports
 2004 Acts. Senate Report No. 108–230, see 2004 U.S. Code Cong. and Adm. News, p. 1920.

LIBRARY REFERENCES

American Digest System
 Armed Services ⚭54.
 Key Number System Topic No. 34.

§ 428p–1. Land acquisition related to Fort Donelson National Battlefield

(a) Acquisition authority

Subject to subsections (b) and (c) of this section, the Secretary of the Interior may acquire land, interests in land, and improvements thereon for inclusion in the Fort Donelson National Battlefield. Such land, interests in land, and improvements may be acquired by the Secretary only by purchase from willing sellers with appropriated or donated funds, by donation, or by exchange with willing owners.

(b) Land eligible for acquisition

The Secretary of the Interior may acquire land, interests in land, and improvements thereon under subsection (a) of this section—

  (1) within the boundaries of the Fort Donelson National Battlefield described in section 428p(b) of this title; and

  (2) outside such boundaries if the land has been identified by the American Battlefield Protection Program as part of the battlefield associated with Fort Donelson or if the Secretary otherwise determines that acquisition under subsection (a) of this section will protect critical resources associated with the Battle of Fort Donelson in 1862 and the Union campaign that resulted in the capture of Fort Donelson.

(c) Boundary revision

Upon acquisition of land or interests in land described in subsection (b)(2) of this section, the Secretary of the Interior shall revise the boundaries of the Fort Donelson National Battlefield to include the acquired property.

(d) Limitation on total acreage of park

The total area encompassed by the Fort Donelson National Battlefield may not exceed 2,000 acres.

(Pub.L. 108–367, § 3, Oct. 25, 2004, 118 Stat. 1743.)

HISTORICAL AND STATUTORY NOTES

Revision Notes and Legislative Reports
 2004 Acts. Senate Report No. 108–230, see 2004 U.S. Code Cong. and Adm. News, p. 1920.

LIBRARY REFERENCES

American Digest System
  Armed Services ☞54.
  United States ☞55.
  Key Number System Topic Nos. 34, 393.

§ 428p–2. Administration of Fort Donelson National Battlefield

The Secretary of the Interior shall administer the Fort Donelson National Battlefield in accordance with sections 428p to 428p–2 of this title and the laws generally applicable to units of the National Park System, including sections 1, 2, 3, and 4 of this title and section 461 to 467 of this title.

(Pub.L. 108–367, § 4, Oct. 25, 2004, 118 Stat. 1744.)

HISTORICAL AND STATUTORY NOTES

Revision Notes and Legislative Reports
 2004 Acts. Senate Report No. 108–230, see 2004 U.S. Code Cong. and Adm. News, p. 1920.

References in Text
 Sections 428p to 428p–2 of this title, referred to in text, was in the original "this Act", meaning Pub.L. 108–367, Oct. 25, 2004, 118 Stat. 1743, the Fort Donelson National Battlefield Expansion Act of 2004, which enacted this section and 16 U.S.C.A. §§ 428p and 428p–1, amended 16 U.S.C.A. § 428k, and enacted provisions set out as a note under 16 U.S.C.A. § 428 of this title. For complete classifi-

cation, see Short Title note set out under 16 U.S.C.A. § 428 and Tables.

 Sections 1, 2, 3, and 4 of this title, referred to in text, was in the original "the Act of August 25, 1916 (commonly known as the National Park Service Organic Act; 16 U.S.C. 1 et seq.)", meaning the Act of August 25, 1916, the National Park Service Organic Act, Act Aug. 25, 1916, c. 408, 39 Stat. 535, which is principally classified to chapter 1 of this title, 16 U.S.C.A. § 1 et seq.; see Tables for complete classification.

 Sections 461 to 467 of this title, referred to in text, was in the original "The Act of August 21, 1935 (commonly known

as the Historic Sites, Buildings, and An-   Historic Sites Act and is classified princi-
tiquities Act;   16 U.S.C. 461 et seq.)'',   pally to chapter 1A of this title, 16
meaning the Historic Sites, Buildings,   U.S.C.A. § 461 et seq.; see Tables for
and Antiquities Act, Aug. 21, 1935, c. 593,   complete classification.
49 Stat. 666, which is also known as the

LIBRARY REFERENCES

American Digest System
> Armed Services ☞54.
> Key Number System Topic No. 34.

§ 429. Brices Cross Roads and Tupelo battlefields in Mississippi; establishment

For the purpose of commemorating the battles of Brices Cross Roads, Mississippi, and Tupelo, Mississippi, the Secretary of the Interior is authorized and directed to (1) acquire not to exceed one acre of land, free of cost to the United States, at each of the above-named battle fields, (2) fence each parcel of land so acquired, (3) build an approach to each such parcel of land, and (4) erect a suitable marker on each such parcel of land.

(Feb. 21, 1929, c. 289, § 1, 45 Stat. 1254.)

HISTORICAL AND STATUTORY NOTES

Transfer of Functions
"Secretary of the Interior" substituted in text for "Secretary of War" pursuant to Reorg. Plan No. 3 of 1950, § 1, 2; Ex. Ord. No. 6166, 2; and Ex. Ord. No. 6228, 1. See below.

Reorg. Plan No. 3 of 1950, Secs. 1, 2, eff. May 24, 1950, 15 F.R. 3174, 64 Stat. 1262, set out in the Appendix to Title 5, transferred the functions of other officers,

employees, and agencies of the Department of the Interior, with certain exceptions, to the Secretary of the Interior, with power to delegate.

Ex. Ord. No. 6166, § 2, and Ex. Ord. No. 6228, § 1, set out as a note under 5 U.S.C.A. § 901, transferred the administrative functions of Brices Cross Roads and Tupelo battlefield sites to the Department of the Interior.

LIBRARY REFERENCES

American Digest System
> Armed Services ☞54.
> Woods and Forests ☞8.
> Key Number System Topic Nos. 34, 411.

WESTLAW ELECTRONIC RESEARCH

See WESTLAW guide following the Explanation pages of this volume.

§ 429a. Jurisdiction and control; authorization of annual appropriation

Each parcel of land acquired under section 429 of this title shall be under the jurisdiction and control of the Secretary of the Interior, and there is authorized to be appropriated for the maintenance of

each such parcel of land, fence, approach, and marker a sum not to
exceed $250 per annum.

(Feb. 21, 1929, c. 289, § 3, 45 Stat. 1254; Ex. Ord. No. 6166, § 2, June 10,
1933; Ex. Ord. No. 6228, § 1, July 28, 1933.)

HISTORICAL AND STATUTORY NOTES

Transfer of Functions
Administrative functions of Brices
Cross Roads and Tupelo battlefield sites
were transferred to the Department of the
Interior by Ex. Ord. No. 6166, § 2 and
Ex. Ord. No. 6228, § 1, set out as a note
under section 901 of Title 5, Government
Organization and Employees.

National Park Service was substituted
for Office of National Parks, Buildings,
and Reservations referred to in Ex. Ord.
No. 6166, § 2, by Act Mar. 2, 1934, c. 38,
§ 1, 48 Stat. 389.

LIBRARY REFERENCES

American Digest System
 Armed Services ☞54.
 United States ☞57.
 Key Number System Topic Nos. 34, 393.

§ 429a–1. Tupelo National Battlefield; acquisition of additional lands

To further the purposes of sections 429 and 429a of this title, the
Secretary of the Interior may acquire by donation or with donated
funds not to exceed one-half acre of land and interests in land for
addition to the adjoining Tupelo National Battlefield site.

(Pub.L. 87–133, § 1, Aug. 10, 1961, 75 Stat. 336.)

LIBRARY REFERENCES

American Digest System
 Armed Services ☞54.
 United States ☞55.
 Key Number System Topic Nos. 34, 393.

§ 429a–2. Change in name to Tupelo National Battlefield; administration

The Tupelo National Battlefield site is redesignated the Tupelo
National Battlefield which shall continue to be administered pursuant to sections 1, 2, 3, and 4 of this title, as amended and supplemented.

(Pub.L. 87–133, § 2, Aug. 10, 1961, 75 Stat. 336.)

LIBRARY REFERENCES

American Digest System
 Armed Services ☞54.
 Woods and Forests ☞1, 5.
 Key Number System Topic Nos. 34, 411.

§ 429b.   Manassas National Battlefield Park

(a) Establishment; boundaries

There is established as a unit of the national park system in the Commonwealth of Virginia the Manassas National Battlefield Park, which shall contain within its boundaries the important historical lands relating to the two battles of Manassas. The total area of the park shall not be greater than four thousand five hundred and twenty-five acres. The boundaries of the park shall be the boundaries depicted on the map entitled "Boundary Map, Manassas National Battlefield Park", dated October 1980, and numbered 379/80,009, which shall be on file and available for public inspection in the offices of the National Park Service, Department of the Interior. The Secretary shall publish in the Federal Register, as soon as practicable after the date of the enactment of this Act, but no later than one year from the effective date of this section, a detailed description and map of the boundaries. Notwithstanding section 460*l*–9(c) of this title, the Secretary may not make any changes in the boundaries of the park. The Secretary shall administer the park in accordance with laws, rules, and regulations applicable to the national park system.

(b) Addition to park

(1) In addition to subsection (a) of this section, the boundaries of the park shall include the area, comprising approximately 600 acres, which is south of U.S. Route 29, north of Interstate Route 66, east of Route 705, and west of Route 622. Such area shall hereafter in sections 429b to 429b–5 of this title be referred to as the "Addition".

(2)(A) Notwithstanding any other provision of law, effective on November 10, 1988, there is hereby vested in the United States all right, title, and interest in and to, and the right to immediate possession of, all the real property within the Addition.

(B) The United States shall pay just compensation to the owners of any property taken pursuant to this paragraph and the full faith and credit of the United States is hereby pledged to the payment of any judgment entered against the United States with respect to the taking of such property. Payment shall be in the amount of the agreed negotiated value of such property or the valuation of such property awarded by judgment and shall be made from the permanent judgment appropriation established pursuant to 31 U.S.C. 1304. Such payment shall include interest on the value of such property which shall be compounded quarterly and computed at the rate applicable for the period involved, as determined by the Secretary of the Treasury on the basis of the current average market yield on outstanding marketable obligations of the United States of comparable maturities from November 10, 1988, to the last day of the month preceding the date on which payment is made.

(C) In the absence of a negotiated settlement, or an action by the owner, within 1 year after November 10, 1988, the Secretary may initiate a proceeding at anytime seeking in a court of competent jurisdiction a determination of just compensation with respect to the taking of such property.

(3) Not later than 6 months after November 10, 1988, the Secretary shall publish in the Federal Register a detailed description and map depicting the boundaries of the Addition. The map shall be on file and available for public inspection in the offices of the National Park Service, Department of the Interior.

(c) Use of addition

The Secretary shall not allow any unauthorized use of the Addition after November 10, 1988, except that the Secretary may permit the orderly termination of all operations on the Addition and the removal of equipment, facilities, and personal property from the Addition.

(Apr. 17, 1954, c. 153, § 1, 68 Stat. 56; renumbered § 1 and amended Oct. 13, 1980, Pub.L. 96–442, § 2, 94 Stat. 1885; Nov. 10, 1988, Pub.L. 100–647, Title X, § 10002, 102 Stat. 3810.)

HISTORICAL AND STATUTORY NOTES

Revision Notes and Legislative Reports
    1988 Acts. Senate Report No. 100–445 and House Conference Report No. 100–1104, see 1988 U.S. Code Cong. and Adm. News, p. 4515.

References in Text
    The date of the enactment of this Act, and effective date of this section, referred to in subsec. (a), probably means the date of the enactment of the Manassas National Battlefield Park Amendments of 1980, Pub.L. 96–442, which was approved Oct. 13, 1980.

Amendments
    1988   Amendments. Subsec.   (a). Pub.L. 100–647, § 10002(1), designated existing provisions as subsec. (a).
    Subsecs. (b), (c).   Pub.L. 100–647, § 10002(2), added subsecs. (b) and (c).
    1980 Amendments. Pub.L. 96–442 substituted a referenced map for specific boundaries, limited the expanded battlefield park to 4525 acres, included the

park in the National Park System, required the Secretary to publish a more detailed map, prohibited the Secretary from making boundary adjustments and required him to administer the Park in accordance with the laws and regulations applicable to the National Park System.

Short Title
    1988   Amendments. Pub.L.   100–647, Title X, § 10001, Nov. 10, 1988, 102 Stat. 3810, provided that: "This title [amending this section and section 429b–1 of this title and enacting provisions set out as a note under this section] may be cited as the 'Manassas National Battlefield Park Amendments of 1988'."
    1980 Acts. Pub.L. 96–442, § 1, Oct. 13, 1980, 94 Stat. 1885, provided: "That this Act [enacting sections 429b–1 to 429b–5 of this title, amending this section and enacting provisions set out as a note under section 460cc of this title] may be cited as the 'Manassas National Battlefield Park Amendments of 1980'."

Highway Relocation

Pub.L. 100–647, Title X, § 10004, Nov. 10, 1988, 102 Stat. 3811, provided that:

"**(a) Study.**—The Secretary of the Interior (hereafter in this section referred to as the 'Secretary'), in consultation and consensus with the Commonwealth of Virginia, the Federal Highway Administration, and Prince William County, shall conduct a study regarding the relocation of highways (known as routes 29 and 234) in, and in the vicinity of, the Manassas National Battlefield Park (hereinafter in this section referred to as the 'park'). The study shall include an assessment of the available alternatives, together with cost estimates and recommendations regarding preferred options. The study shall specifically consider and develop plans for the closing of those public highways (known as routes 29 and 234) that transect the park and shall include analysis of the timing and method of such closures and of means to provide alternative routes for traffic now transecting the park. The Secretary shall provide for extensive public involvement in the preparation of the study.

"**(b) Determination.**—Within 1 year after the enactment of this Act [Nov. 10, 1988], the Secretary shall complete the study under subsection (a). The study shall determine when and how the highways (known as routes 29 and 234) should be closed.

"**(c) Assistance.**—The Secretary shall provide funds to the appropriate construction agency for the construction and improvement of the highways to be used for the rerouting of traffic now utilizing highways (known as routes 29 and 234) to be closed pursuant to subsection (b) if the construction and improvement of such alternatives are deemed by the Secretary to be in the interest of protecting the integrity of the park. Not more than 75 percent of the costs of such construction and improvement shall be provided by the Secretary and at least 25 percent shall be provided by State or local governments from any source other than Federal funds. Such construction and improvement shall be approved by the Secretary of Transportation.

"**(d) Authorization.**—There is authorized to be appropriated to the Secretary not to exceed $30,000,000 to prepare the study required by subsection (a) and to provide the funding described in subsection (c)."

LIBRARY REFERENCES

American Digest System
Armed Services ⬡54.
Woods and Forests ⬡1, 2, 8.
Key Number System Topic Nos. 34, 411.

§ 429b–1. Acquisition and use of lands

(a) Acquisition of property or interests in property; scenic preservation of views

(1) In order to effectuate the purposes of sections 429b to 429b–5 of this title, the Secretary is authorized to acquire by donation, purchase with donated or appropriated funds or exchange, any property or interests therein which are located within the boundaries of the park, except that property owned by the Commonwealth of Virginia or by any political subdivision thereof may be acquired only by donation.

(2) The Secretary shall cooperate with the Commonwealth of Virginia, the political subdivisions thereof, and other parties as designated by the Commonwealth or its political subdivisions in order to promote and achieve scenic preservation of views from

154

within the park through zoning and such other means as the parties determine feasible.

(b) Acquisition of fee simple title with the consent of owner; hearing and review

With respect to areas within the 1954 boundaries of the park, as identified on the map referred to in section 429b of this title, the Secretary may not acquire fee simple title to such areas without the consent of the owner so long as the lands continue to be devoted to a use which is the same as that in effect on September 1, 1980. Further, if the Secretary proposes to acquire fee simple title to such property because of a change in use, the owner of such property may seek a review of the proposed acquisition of his or her property and is entitled to a hearing on the record in accordance with section 554 of Title 5.

(c) Secretary authorized to make land available for Route 234 bypass

If the Virginia Department of Highways and Transportation determines that the proposed Route 234 bypass should be properly located between the Virginia Electric Power Company powerline easement and Route 705, the Secretary shall make available the land necessary for such bypass, subject to such revisions, terms, and conditions as the Secretary deems are necessary and appropriate to assure that such bypass is located, constructed, operated, and maintained in a manner consistent with the administration of the park.

(d) Secretary not to close State roads

The Secretary may not close any State roads within the park unless action permitting the closing of such roads has been taken by appropriate officials of the Commonwealth of Virginia.

(Apr. 17, 1954, c. 153, § 2, as added Oct. 13, 1980, Pub.L. 96–442, § 2, 94 Stat. 1885, and amended Nov. 10, 1988, Pub.L. 100–647, Title X, § 10003, 102 Stat. 3811.)

HISTORICAL AND STATUTORY NOTES

Revision Notes and Legislative Reports
  1988 Acts. Senate Report No. 100–445 and House Conference Report No. 100–1104, see 1988 U.S. Code Cong. and Adm. News, p. 4515.

Amendments
  1988 Amendments. Subsec. (a)(1). Pub.L. 100–647, § 10003(1), designated existing provisions, as par. (1).

Subsec. (a)(2). Pub.L. 100–647, § 10003(2), added par. (2).

LIBRARY REFERENCES

American Digest System
    Armed Services ☞54.
    United States ☞55.
    Woods and Forests ☞5.
    Key Number System Topic Nos. 34, 393, 411.

§ 429b–2. Retention of right of use and occupation of improved property by owner

(a) Time limits; compensation

Subsequent to October 13, 1980, the owner of improved property on the date of its acquisition by the Secretary may, as a condition of such acquisition, retain for himself and his heirs and assigns a right of use and occupancy of the improved property for noncommercial residential purposes for a definite term of not more than twenty-five years or for a term ending at the death of the owner or the death of the spouse of the owner, whichever is later. The owner shall elect the term to be reserved. Unless this property is wholly or partially donated to the United States, the Secretary shall pay the owner an amount equal to the fair market value of the property on the date of its acquisition less the value on such date of the right retained by the owner. If such property is donated (in whole or in part) to the United States, the Secretary may pay to the owner such lesser amount as the owner may agree to. A right retained pursuant to this section shall be subject to termination by the Secretary upon his determination that it is being exercised in a manner inconsistent with the purposes of sections 429b to 429b–5 of this title, and it shall terminate by operation of law upon the Secretary's notifying the holder of the right of such determination and tendering to him an amount equal to the fair market value of that portion of the right which remains unexpired.

(b) Displaced person; waiver of benefits

No property owner who elects to retain a right of use and occupancy under this section shall be considered a displaced person as defined in section 4601(6) of Title 42. Such owners shall be considered to have waived any benefits which would otherwise accrue to them under sections 4623 to 4626 of Title 42.

(Apr. 17, 1954, c. 153, § 3, as added Oct. 13, 1980, Pub.L. 96–442, § 2, 94 Stat. 1886.)

LIBRARY REFERENCES

American Digest System
    Armed Services ☞54.
    United States ☞57.

Woods and Forests ⊕2.
Key Number System Topic Nos. 34, 393, 411.

§ 429b–3. Definitions

For purposes of sections 429b to 429b–5 of this title—

(1) The term "improved property" means a detached, one-family dwelling, construction of which was begun before January 1, 1979, which is used for noncommercial residential purposes, together with not to exceed three acres of land on which the dwelling is situated and together with such additional lands or interests therein as the Secretary deems to be reasonably necessary for access thereto, such lands being in the same ownership as the dwelling, together with any structures accessory to the dwelling which are situated on such land.

(2) The term "park" means the Manassas National Battlefield Park established under sections 429b to 429b–5 of this title.

(3) The term "Secretary" means the Secretary of the Interior.

(4) The term "owner" means the owner of record as of September 1, 1980.

(Apr. 17, 1954, c. 153, § 4, as added Oct. 13, 1980, Pub.L. 96–442, § 2, 94 Stat. 1886.)

LIBRARY REFERENCES

American Digest System
Armed Services ⊕54.
Key Number System Topic No. 34.

§ 429b–4. Funds from Land and Water Conservation Fund

(a) Maximum amount usable for acquisition of property

In addition to sums heretofore expended for the acquisition of property and interests therein for the park, from funds available for expenditure from the Land and Water Conservation Fund, as established under the Land and Water Conservation Fund Act of 1965 [16 U.S.C.A. § 460*l*–4 et seq.], not more than a total of $8,700,000 may be expended for the acquisition of property and interests therein under sections 429b to 429b–5 of this title.

(b) Completion of acquisition in two years

It is the express intent of Congress that, except for property referred to in section 429b–1(b) of this title, the Secretary shall acquire property and interests therein under sections 429b to 429b–5 of this title within two complete fiscal years after October 13, 1980.

(Apr. 17, 1954, c. 153, § 5, as added Oct. 13, 1980, Pub.L. 96–442, § 2, 94 Stat. 1886.)

HISTORICAL AND STATUTORY NOTES

References in Text

The Land and Water Conservation Fund Act of 1965, referred to in subsec. (a), is Pub.L. 88–578, Sept. 3, 1964, 78 Stat. 897, as amended, which is classified generally to Part B (§ 460*l*–4 et seq.) of subchapter LXIX of this chapter. For complete classification of this Act to the Code, see Short Title note set out under section 460*l*–4 of this title and Tables.

LIBRARY REFERENCES

American Digest System

Armed Services ⚎54.
United States ⚎55.
Key Number System Topic Nos. 34, 393.

§ 429b–5. Funding limitations; contracting authority, etc.

(a) Effective date of authorizations

Authorizations of moneys to be appropriated under sections 429b to 429b–5 of this title from the Land and Water Conservation Fund for acquisition of properties and interests shall be effective on October 1, 1981.

(b) Authority limited by appropriations

Notwithstanding any other provision of sections 429b to 429b–5 of this title, authority to enter into contracts, to incur obligations, or to make payments under sections 429b to 429b–5 of this title shall be effective only to the extent, and in such amounts as are provided in advance in appropriation Acts.

(Apr. 17, 1954, c. 153, § 6, as added Oct. 13, 1980, Pub.L. 96–442, § 2, 94 Stat. 1887.)

§ 430. Kings Mountain National Military Park; establishment

In order to commemorate the Battle of Kings Mountain, which was fought on the 7th day of October 1780, the Kings Mountain battle ground, in the State of South Carolina, including such adjacent and contiguous lands as may be useful and proper in effectually carrying out the purpose of sections 430, 430a, and 430b to 430e of this title, is declared to be a national military park, to be known as the Kings Mountain National Military Park, when such land including said battle ground, shall become the property of the United States.

(Mar. 3, 1931, c. 437, § 1, 46 Stat. 1508.)

LIBRARY REFERENCES

American Digest System

Armed Services ⚎54.
Woods and Forests ⚎8.
Key Number System Topic Nos. 34, 411.

§ 430a. Acquisition of land

The Secretary of the Interior shall ascertain on what land the Battle of Kings Mountain was fought and, subject to the provisions of sections 3111 and 3112 of Title 40, shall proceed to acquire title to such land together with such adjacent and contiguous lands as he may deem useful and proper in effectually carrying out the purposes of sections 430, 430a, and 430b of this title, either by purchase or gift or by condemnation under the provisions of section 3113 of Title 40.

(Mar. 3, 1931, c. 437, § 2, 46 Stat. 1508; Ex.Ord. No. 6166, § 2, June 10, 1933; Ex.Ord. No. 6228, § 1, July 28, 1933.)

HISTORICAL AND STATUTORY NOTES

Codifications

In text, "sections 3111 and 3112 of Title 40" substituted for "section 255 of Title 40", which originally read "section 355 of the Revised Statutes", on authority of Pub.L. 107–217, § 5(c), Aug. 21, 2002, 116 Stat. 1301, which is set out as a note preceding 40 U.S.C.A. § 101. Pub.L. 107–217, § 1, enacted Title 40 into positive law. Section 355 of the Revised Statutes was classified to former 40 U.S.C.A. § 255 and its provisions were carried forward into revised Title 40 at 40 U.S.C.A. §§ 3111, 3112.

In text, "section 3113 of Title 40" substituted for "sections 257 and 258 of Title 40", which originally read "the Act of August 1, 1888, entitled 'An Act to authorize the condemnation of lands for sites for public buildings, and other purposes'" on authority of Pub.L. 107–217, § 5(c), Aug. 21, 2002, 116 Stat. 1301, which is set out as a note preceding 40 U.S.C.A. § 101. Pub.L. 107–217, § 1, enacted Title 40 into positive law. The Act of August 1, 1888, is Act, Aug. 1, 1888, c. 728, 25 Stat. 357, which was classified to former 40 U.S.C.A. §§ 257 and 258, prior to being repealed by Pub.L. 107–217, § 6(b), Aug. 21, 2002, 116 Stat. 1305, and its substance reenacted as 40 U.S.C.A. § 3113. Section 258 of Title 40 was previously omitted from the Code as superseded by Rule 71A, Federal Rules of Civil Procedure, Title 28.

Transfer of Functions

Administrative functions of Kings Mountain National Military Park were transferred to the Department of the Interior by Ex.Ord. No. 6166, and by Ex.Ord. No. 6228, set out as a note under section 901 of Title 5, Government Organization and Employees.

National Park Service was substituted for Office of National Parks, Buildings, and Reservations referred to in Ex.Ord. No. 6166, § 2, by Act Mar. 2, 1934, c. 38, § 1, 48 Stat. 389.

LIBRARY REFERENCES

American Digest System
Armed Services ☞54.
United States ☞55.
Key Number System Topic Nos. 34, 393.

§ 430a–1. Revision of boundaries

In order to consolidate the Federal ownership of lands in, and to facilitate protection and preservation of, Kings Mountain National Military Park, South Carolina, the boundaries are revised as follows:

  (1) Federally owned lands lying west of the easterly right-of-way line of State Route P–11–123, containing approximately two hundred acres, are excluded from the park;

(2) Privately owned lands lying east of the easterly right-of-way line of State Route P–11–123, containing approximately eighty acres, are included in the park; and

(3) Lands of the Mary Morris estate lying south of the southerly right-of-way line of the historic Yorkville-Shelbyville Road, and forming the triangle bounded by the new State Route P–11–86, the historic Yorkville-Shelbyville Road and the present park boundary (Old Houser tract), aggregating approximately sixty acres, are included in the park.

(Pub.L. 86–62, § 1, June 23, 1959, 73 Stat. 108.)

HISTORICAL AND STATUTORY NOTES

Revision Notes and Legislative Reports
1959 Acts. Senate Report No. 374, see 1959 U.S. Code Cong. and Adm. News, p. 1569.

LIBRARY REFERENCES

American Digest System
Armed Services ⟜54.
Woods and Forests ⟜1.
Key Number System Topic Nos. 34, 411.

§ 430a–2. Acquisition of lands within revised boundary

The Secretary of the Interior is authorized to acquire lands and interests in lands within the revised boundary by purchase, donation, with donated funds, or by exchange, utilizing for such exchanges federally owned lands of approximately equal value excluded from the park pursuant to sections 430a–1 to 430a–3 of this title. Federally owned lands so excluded which the Secretary of the Interior determines are not needed for such exchanges shall be disposed of in accordance with the provisions of the Federal Property and Administrative Services Act of 1949, as amended.

(Pub.L. 86–62, § 2, June 23, 1959, 73 Stat. 108.)

HISTORICAL AND STATUTORY NOTES

Revision Notes and Legislative Reports
1959 Acts. Senate Report No. 374, see 1959 U.S. Code Cong. and Adm. News, p. 1569.

References in Text
The Federal Property and Administrative Services Act of 1949, referred to in text, is Act June 30, 1949, c. 288, 63 Stat. 377, as amended, Title III of which is currently classified to subchapter IV of chapter 4 of Title 41, 41 U.S.C.A. § 251 et seq., and the remainder of which was formerly classified to chapter 10 of former Title 40, 40 U.S.C.A. § 471 et seq., prior to being repealed by Pub.L. 107–217, § 6(b), Aug. 21, 2002, 116 Stat. 1313; see now generally chapter 1 of Title 40, 40 U.S.C.A. § 101 et seq.

LIBRARY REFERENCES

American Digest System
Armed Services ☞54.
United States ☞55.
Key Number System Topic Nos. 34, 393.

§ 430a–3. Applicability of laws and regulations to acquired lands and interests therein

Lands and interests therein acquired pursuant to sections 430a–1 to 430a–3 of this title shall thereupon become a part of the Kings Mountain National Military Park and be subject to all the laws and regulations applicable thereto.

(Pub.L. 86–62, § 3, June 23, 1959, 73 Stat. 108.)

HISTORICAL AND STATUTORY NOTES

Revision Notes and Legislative Reports
1959 Acts. Senate Report No. 374, see 1959 U.S. Code Cong. and Adm. News, p. 1569.

LIBRARY REFERENCES

American Digest System
Armed Services ☞54.
United States ☞57.
Woods and Forests ☞5.
Key Number System Topic Nos. 34, 393, 411.

§ 430b. Control; regulations for care and management

Such park shall be under the control and direction of the Secretary of the Interior. The Secretary is authorized to prescribe from time to time such regulations for the care and management of such park as he may deem necessary.

(Mar. 3, 1931, c. 437, § 3, 46 Stat. 1508; Ex.Ord. No. 6166, § 2, June 10, 1933; Ex.Ord. No. 6228, § 1, July 28, 1933.)

HISTORICAL AND STATUTORY NOTES

Transfer of Functions
Transfer of administrative functions of park, see note set out under section 430a of this title.

CROSS REFERENCES

Establishment of Kings Mountain National Military Park, see 16 USCA § 430.

LIBRARY REFERENCES

American Digest System
Armed Services ☞54.

Woods and Forests ☞5.
Key Number System Topic Nos. 34, 411.

§ 430c. Permits to occupy land

Upon such terms and conditions as he may prescribe, the Secretary of the Interior is authorized to permit any person occupying any land within the boundaries of such park to continue to occupy such land, but the Secretary may revoke such permit at any time.

(Mar. 3, 1931, c. 437, § 4, 46 Stat. 1508; Ex.Ord. No. 6166, § 2, June 10, 1933; Ex.Ord. No. 6228, § 1, July 28, 1933.)

HISTORICAL AND STATUTORY NOTES

Transfer of Functions
    Transfer of administrative functions of park, see note set out under section 430a of this title.

CROSS REFERENCES

Establishment of Kings Mountain National Military Park, see 16 USCA § 430.

LIBRARY REFERENCES

American Digest System
    Armed Services ☞54.
    United States ☞57.
    Woods and Forests ☞5.
    Key Number System Topic Nos. 34, 393, 411.

§ 430d. Repair of roads; historical markers

The Secretary of the Interior shall open or repair such roads in such park as may be necessary, and ascertain and mark with tablets or otherwise, as he may determine, all lines of battle of the American troops and British troops engaged in the Battle of Kings Mountain and other historical points of interest pertaining to the battle which are within the boundaries of the park. The Secretary is authorized to employ such labor and services and to obtain such supplies and materials as may be necessary to carry out the provisions of this section.

(Mar. 3, 1931, c. 437, § 5, 46 Stat. 1508; Ex.Ord. No. 6166, § 2, June 10, 1933; Ex.Ord. No. 6228, § 1, July 28, 1933.)

HISTORICAL AND STATUTORY NOTES

Transfer of Functions
    Transfer of administrative functions of park, see note set out under section 430a of this title.

§ 430e.   Monuments and tablets within park; approval

The authorities of any State which had troops engaged in the Battle of Kings Mountain may enter the Kings Mountain National Military Park for the purpose of ascertaining and marking the lines of battle of such troops, but before any such lines are permanently designated the position of the lines and the proposed methods of marking them by monuments, tablets, or otherwise shall be approved by the Secretary of the Interior. Any State organization or individual may, with the approval of the Secretary of the Interior, erect monuments or place tablets within such park.

(Mar. 3, 1931, c. 437, § 6, 46 Stat. 1508; Ex.Ord. No. 6166, § 2, June 10, 1933; Ex.Ord. No. 6228, § 1, July 28, 1933.)

HISTORICAL AND STATUTORY NOTES

Transfer of Functions
    Transfer of administrative functions of
park, see note set out under section 430a
of this title.

§ 430f.   Shiloh National Military Park

In order that the armies of the southwest which served in the civil war, like their comrades of the eastern armies at Gettysburg and those of the central west at Chickamauga, may have the history of one of their memorable battles preserved on the ground where they fought, that part of the battlefield of Shiloh, in the State of Tennessee, title to which has heretofore been acquired by the United States, and as to which the usual jurisdiction over the lands and the roads of same has been granted to the United States by the State of Tennessee, containing 3,000 acres, more or less, shall be a national military park, and shall be known as the Shiloh National Military Park. The Secretary of the Interior is authorized to enter into agreements whereby he may lease, upon such terms as he may prescribe, with such persons, who were owners or tenants of the land on December 27, 1894, as may desire to remain upon it to occupy and cultivate their then holdings upon condition that they will preserve the then buildings and roads and the then outlines of field and forest, and that they only will cut trees or underbrush under such regulations as the Secretary may prescribe, and that they will assist in caring for and protecting all tablets, monuments, or such other artificial works as may from time to time be erected by proper authority. It shall be the duty of the Secretary of the Interior to cause to be opened or repaired such roads as may be necessary for the purposes of the park and to cause to be ascertained and marked with historical tablets or otherwise, as he may determine, all lines of battle of the troops engaged in the battle of Shiloh and other historical points of interest pertaining to the battle within the park or its vicinity, and the Secretary of the Interior shall make and enforce all needed regulations for the care of the park. It shall be lawful for any State that had troops engaged in the battle of Shiloh to enter upon the lands of the Shiloh National Military Park for the purpose of ascertaining and marking the lines of battle of its troops therein: *Provided*, That before any such lines are permanently designated the position of the lines and the proposed methods of marking them by monuments, tablets, or otherwise shall be submitted to and approved by the Secretary of the Interior, and all such lines, designs and inscriptions for the same shall first receive the written approval of the Secretary: *Provided*, That no discrimination shall be made against any State as to the manner of designating lines, but any grant made to any State by the Secretary of the Interior may be used by any other State.

(Dec. 27, 1894, c. 12, 28 Stat. 597; Ex.Ord. No. 6166, § 2, June 10, 1933; Ex.Ord. No. 6228, § 1, July 28, 1933; Sept. 6, 1966, Pub.L. 89–554, § 8(a), 80 Stat. 637.)

HISTORICAL AND STATUTORY NOTES

Codifications

Section is based on sections 1 to 6 of Act Dec. 27, 1894. Section 7 of the Act, which established fines for offenses against park property, and section 8, which authorized initial appropriations for the park, were not classified to the Code.

Amendments

1966 Amendments. Pub.L. 89–554 eliminated provisions which required that the affairs of the Shiloh National Military Park be subject to the supervision and direction of the Secretary of the Interior.

Transfer of Functions

Administrative functions of Shiloh National Military Park were transferred to the Department of the Interior by Ex.Ord. No. 6166, and by Ex.Ord. No. 6228, set out as a note under section 901 of Title 5, Government Organization and Employees.

National Park Service was substituted for Office of National Parks, Buildings, and Reservations, referred to in Ex.Ord. No. 6166, by Act Mar. 2, 1934, c. 38, § 1, 48 Stat. 389.

Exchange of Lands
Act June 25, 1947, c. 126, 61 Stat. 173, provided:

"[Section 1.] That the Secretary of the Interior is authorized, in his discretion, and under such terms and conditions as he may deem necessary, to convey, without consideration, to W. A. Shaw and E. L. Shaw, or nominees, the following described lands within Shiloh National Military Park in Hardin County in the State of Tennessee: Beginning at a point from which the intersection of Shiloh National Military Park boundary between boundary corners numbered 228 and 229 with center line of Confederate Road bears south eight degrees fifty-seven minutes east, eighty and thirty-seven one-hundredths feet (said intersection bears north eighty-eight degrees ten minutes fourteen seconds west, one thousand one hundred and thirty-one and eighty-nine one-hundredths feet from boundary corner numbered 228); thence north twenty-nine degrees thirty-one minutes west, three hundred and twenty-six feet; thence south seventy-six degrees nineteen minutes east, three hundred and thirty-seven and fifty-four one-hundredths feet; and thence running sixty feet from and parallel to center line of Confederate Road south thirty-nine degrees twenty minutes west, two hundred and sixty-three and forty-six one-hundredths feet to the point of beginning. The tract as described contains approximately ninety-two one-hundredths acre.

"Sec. 2.   For the purpose of consolidating Federal holdings within the park, the Secretary of the Interior is authorized, in his discretion and under such terms and conditions as he may deem necessary, to accept any non-Federal real or personal property within the authorized boundaries of the park.   In exchange for such properties, he may, in his discretion, convey to the grantors of such properties any Federally owned lands or interests in lands within the authorized boundaries of the park which are of approximately equal value, as determined by the Secretary, to the properties being acquired in each case."

LIBRARY REFERENCES

American Digest System
    Armed Services ⬥54.
    Woods and Forests ⬥8.
    Key Number System Topic Nos. 34, 411.

§ 430f–1.   Conveyance of lands

In order that existing roads within Shiloh National Military Park may be devoted primarily to use by park visitors and that traffic hazards and nonconforming uses may be eliminated from the park by providing a more suitable road location and related area for the highways designated State Routes Numbered 22 and 142 which now traverse the central portion of the park, the Secretary of the Interior is authorized to convey certain lands within Shiloh National Military Park on the terms and conditions hereinafter provided.

(Pub.L. 85–406, § 1, May 16, 1958, 72 Stat. 114.)

HISTORICAL AND STATUTORY NOTES

Revision Notes and Legislative Reports
  1958 Acts. Senate Report No. 1497, see 1958 U.S. Code Cong. and Adm. News, p. 2438.

§ 430f–2. Conveyance of right-of-way; construction and maintenance of roadways

The Secretary may convey to the State of Tennessee for road purposes a right-of-way located in Hardin County, Tennessee, as shown on National Park Service map NMP–SH–7006, revised June 1956, being a minimum of one hundred and twenty feet and a maximum of one hundred and forty feet in width, and a length of approximately eighteen thousand and nine hundred feet, said right-of-way containing approximately fifty-one acres: *Provided*, That, in exchange, the State constructs and thereafter maintains a roadway on said lands and thereupon releases those portions of the present highways within the park designated State Routes Numbered 22 and 142 from such designation and subsequent use for State highway purposes.

(Pub.L. 85–406, § 2, May 16, 1958, 72 Stat. 114.)

HISTORICAL AND STATUTORY NOTES

Revision Notes and Legislative Reports
1958 Acts. Senate Report No. 1497, see 1958 U.S. Code Cong. and Adm. News, p. 2438.

§ 430f–3. Conveyance of lands for recreational area; development and use

The Secretary may convey to the State of Tennessee for use as a recreational area contiguous and incident to the relocated State Route Numbered 22 certain lands situated in Hardin County, Tennessee, as shown on National Park Service map NMP–SH–7006, revised June 1956, and designated thereon as parcel A, said lands containing one hundred and fifty-one acres, more or less: *Provided*, That in exchange the lands so conveyed shall be developed and used exclusively by the State or its political subdivisions for recreational purposes only, thereby removing certain incompatible uses from the military park.

(Pub.L. 85–406, § 3, May 16, 1958, 72 Stat. 114.)

HISTORICAL AND STATUTORY NOTES

Revision Notes and Legislative Reports
1958 Acts. Senate Report No. 1497, see 1958 U.S. Code Cong. and Adm. News, p. 2438.

LIBRARY REFERENCES

American Digest System
Armed Services ⬩54.
United States ⬩57.
Woods and Forests ⬩4, 5.
Key Number System Topic Nos. 34, 393, 411.

§ 430f–4. Jurisdiction of lands

Upon the delivery and acceptance of the conveyance herein authorized, any jurisdiction heretofore ceded to the United States by the State of Tennessee over the lands conveyed shall thereby cease and determine and shall thereafter vest and be in the State of Tennessee.

(Pub.L. 85–406, § 4, May 16, 1958, 72 Stat. 115.)

HISTORICAL AND STATUTORY NOTES

Revision Notes and Legislative Reports
1958 Acts. Senate Report No. 1497, see 1958 U.S. Code Cong. and Adm. News, p. 2438.

References in Text
Herein, referred to in text, means Pub.L. 85–406, May 16, 1958, 72 Stat.

114, which is classified to sections 430f–1 to 430f–4 of this title. For complete classification of this Act to the Code, see Tables.

LIBRARY REFERENCES

American Digest System
Armed Services ⬩54.
United States ⬩3.
Key Number System Topic Nos. 34, 393.

§ 430f–5. Siege and Battle of Corinth

(a) Purpose

The purpose of this section is to provide for a center for the interpretation of the Siege and Battle of Corinth and other Civil War actions in the Region and to enhance public understanding of the significance of the Corinth Campaign in the Civil War relative to the Western theater of operations, in cooperation with State or local governmental entities and private organizations and individuals.

(b) Acquisition of property at Corinth, Mississippi

The Secretary of the Interior (referred to in this title as the "Secretary") shall acquire by donation, purchase with donated or appropriated funds, or exchange, such land and interests in land in the vicinity of the Corinth Battlefield, in the State of Mississippi, as the Secretary determines to be necessary for the construction of an interpretive center to commemorate and interpret the 1862 Civil War Siege and Battle of Corinth.

(c) Publicly owned land

Land and interests in land owned by the State of Mississippi or a political subdivision of the State of Mississippi may be acquired only by donation.

(d) Interpretive center and marking

(1) Interpretive center

The Secretary shall construct, operate, and maintain on the property acquired under subsection (b) of this section a center for the interpretation of the Siege and Battle of Corinth and associated historical events for the benefit of the public.

(2) Marking

The Secretary may mark sites associated with the Siege and Battle of Corinth National Historic Landmark, as designated on May 6, 1991, if the sites are determined by the Secretary to be protected by State or local governmental agencies.

(3) Administration

The land and interests in land acquired, and the facilities constructed and maintained pursuant to this section, shall be administered by the Secretary as a part of Shiloh National Military Park, subject to the appropriate laws (including regulations) applicable to the Park, sections 1, 2, 3, and 4 of this title, and sections 461 to 467 of this title.

(e) Authorization of appropriations

There are authorized to be appropriated $6,000,000 for development to carry out this section.

(Pub.L. 104–333, Div. I, Title VI, § 602, Nov. 12, 1996, 110 Stat. 4171.)

HISTORICAL AND STATUTORY NOTES

References in Text

This title, referred to in subsec. (b), is Title VI (§§ 601 to 607) of Pub.L. 104–333, Nov. 12, 1996, 110 Stat. 4171. For complete classification of this Title to the Code, see Tables.

§ 430f–6.   Corinth unit of Shiloh National Military Park; findings and purposes

(a) Findings

Congress finds that—

(1) in 1996, Congress authorized the establishment and construction of a center—

(A) to facilitate the interpretation of the Siege and Battle of Corinth and other Civil War actions in the area in and around the city of Corinth, Mississippi; and

(B) to enhance public understanding of the significance of the Corinth campaign and the Civil War relative to the western theater of operations, in cooperation with—

(i) State or local governmental entities;

(ii) private organizations; and

(iii) individuals;

(2) the Corinth Battlefield was ranked as a priority 1 battlefield having critical need for coordinated nationwide action by the year 2000 by the Civil War Sites Advisory Commission in its report on Civil War Battlefields of the United States;

(3) there is a national interest in protecting and preserving sites of historic significance associated with the Civil War; and

(4) the States of Mississippi and Tennessee and their respective local units of government—

(A) have the authority to prevent or minimize adverse uses of these historic resources; and

(B) can play a significant role in the protection of the historic resources related to the Civil War battles fought in the area in and around the city of Corinth.

(b) Purposes

The purposes of sections 430f-6 to 430f-12 of this title are—

(1) to establish the Corinth Unit of the Shiloh National Military Park—

(A) in the city of Corinth, Mississippi; and

(B) in the State of Tennessee;

169

(2) to direct the Secretary of the Interior to manage, protect, and interpret the resources associated with the Civil War Siege and the Battle of Corinth that occurred in and around the city of Corinth, in cooperation with—

    (A) the State of Mississippi;

    (B) the State of Tennessee;

    (C) the city of Corinth, Mississippi;

    (D) other public entities; and

    (E) the private sector; and

(3) to authorize a special resource study to identify other Civil War sites in and around the city of Corinth that—

    (A) are consistent with the themes of the Siege and Battle of Corinth;

    (B) meet the criteria for designation as a unit of the National Park System; and

    (C) are considered appropriate for inclusion in the Unit.

(Pub.L. 106–271, § 2, Sept. 22, 2000, 114 Stat. 792.)

HISTORICAL AND STATUTORY NOTES

Revision Notes and Legislative Reports
  2000 Acts. Senate Report No. 106–186, see 2000 U.S. Code Cong. and Adm. News, p. 648.

Short Title
  2000 Acts. Pub.L. 106–271, § 1, Sept. 22, 2000, 114 Stat. 792, provided that:

"This Act [enacting this section and sections 430f–7 to 430f–12 of this title] may be cited as the 'Corinth Battlefield Preservation Act of 2000'."

§ 430f–7. Definitions

In sections 430f-6 to 430f-12 of this title:

(1) Map

The term "Map" means the map entitled "Park Boundary–Corinth Unit", numbered 304A/80009, and dated April 2007.

(2) Park

The term "Park" means the Shiloh National Military Park.

(3) Secretary

The term "Secretary" means the Secretary of the Interior.

(4) Unit

The term "Unit" means the Corinth Unit of Shiloh National Military Park established under section 430f–8 of this title.

(Pub.L. 106–271, § 3, Sept. 22, 2000, 114 Stat. 793; Pub.L. 110–161, Div. F, Title I, § 127(1), Dec. 26, 2007, 121 Stat. 2122.)

HISTORICAL AND STATUTORY NOTES

Revision Notes and Legislative Reports
   2000 Acts. Senate Report No. 106–186, see 2000 U.S. Code Cong. and Adm. News, p. 648.
   2007 Acts. House Report No. 110–197, see 2007 U.S. Code Cong. and Adm. News, p. 661.
   Statement by President, see 2007 U.S. Code Cong. and Adm. News, p. S34.

Amendments
   2007 Amendments. Par. (1). Pub.L. 110–161, Div. F, § 127(1), struck out "304/80,007, and dated October 1998" and inserted "304A/80009, and dated April 2007".

§ 430f–8. Establishment of Unit

(a) In general

There is established in the States of Mississippi and Tennessee the Corinth Unit of the Shiloh National Military Park.

(b) Composition of Unit

The Unit shall be comprised of—

   (1) approximately 950 acres, as generally depicted on the Map; and

   (2) any additional land that the Secretary determines to be suitable for inclusion in the Unit that—

      (A) is under the ownership of a public entity or nonprofit organization; and

      (B) has been identified by the Siege and Battle of Corinth National Historic Landmark Study, dated January 8, 1991.

(c) Availability of Map

The Map shall be on file and available for public inspection in the office of the Director of the National Park Service .

(Pub.L. 106–271, § 4, Sept. 22, 2000, 114 Stat. 793; Pub.L. 110–161, Div. F, Title I, § 127(2), Dec. 26, 2007, 121 Stat. 2122.)

HISTORICAL AND STATUTORY NOTES

Revision Notes and Legislative Reports
   2000 Acts. Senate Report No. 106–186, see 2000 U.S. Code Cong. and Adm. News, p. 648.
   2007 Acts. House Report No. 110–197, see 2007 U.S. Code Cong. and Adm. News, p. 661.
   Statement by President, see 2007 U.S. Code Cong. and Adm. News, p. S34.

Amendments
   2007 Amendments. Subsec. (b)(1). Pub.L. 110–161, Div. F, § 127(2), rewrote par. (1), which formerly read: "the tract consisting of approximately 20 acres generally depicted as 'Battery Robinett Boundary' on the Map; and".

LIBRARY REFERENCES

American Digest System
   Armed Services ☞54.
   United States ☞57.
   Key Number System Topic Nos. 34, 393.

171

§ 430f–9. Land acquisition

(a) In general

The Secretary may acquire land and interests in land within the boundary of the Park described in section 430f–8(b) of this title, by—

(1) donation;

(2) purchase with donated or appropriated funds; or

(3) exchange.

(b) Exception

Land may be acquired only by donation from—

(1) the State of Mississippi (including a political subdivision of the State);

(2) the State of Tennessee (including a political subdivision of the State); or

(3) the organization known as "Friends of the Siege and Battle of Corinth".

(Pub.L. 106–271, § 5, Sept. 22, 2000, 114 Stat. 793; Pub.L. 110–161, Div. F, Title I, § 127(3), Dec. 26, 2007, 121 Stat. 2122.)

HISTORICAL AND STATUTORY NOTES

Revision Notes and Legislative Reports
2000 Acts. Senate Report No. 106–186, see 2000 U.S. Code Cong. and Adm. News, p. 648.
2007 Acts. House Report No. 110–197, see 2007 U.S. Code Cong. and Adm. News, p. 661.
Statement by President, see 2007 U.S. Code Cong. and Adm. News, p. S34.

Amendments
2007   Amendments. Subsec.   (a). Pub.L. 110–161, Div. F, § 127(3), in the introductory matter preceding par. (1), struck out "as depicted on the Map" and inserted "described in section 430f–8(b) of this title".

LIBRARY REFERENCES

American Digest System
Armed Services ⟪54.
United States ⟪55.
Key Number System Topic Nos. 34, 393.

§ 430f–10. Park management and administration

(a) In general

The Secretary shall administer the Unit in accordance with sections 430f–6 to 430f–12 of this title and the laws generally applicable to units of the National Park System, including—

(1) sections 1, 2, 3, and 4 of this title; and

(2) sections 461 to 467 of this title.

(b) Duties

In accordance with section 430f-5 of this title, the Secretary shall—

(1) commemorate and interpret, for the benefit of visitors and the general public, the Siege and Battle of Corinth and other Civil War actions in the area in and around the city of Corinth within the larger context of the Civil War and American history, including the significance of the Civil War Siege and Battle of Corinth in 1862 in relation to other operations in the western theater of the Civil War; and

(2) identify and preserve surviving features from the Civil War era in the area in and around the city of Corinth, including both military and civilian themes that include—

(A) the role of railroads in the Civil War;

(B) the story of the Corinth contraband camp; and

(C) the development of field fortifications as a tactic of war.

(c) Cooperative agreements

(1) In general

To carry out sections 430f-6 to 430f-12 of this title, the Secretary may enter into cooperative agreements with entities in the public and private sectors, including—

(A) colleges and universities;

(B) historical societies;

(C) State and local agencies; and

(D) nonprofit organizations.

(2) Technical assistance

To develop cooperative land use strategies and conduct activities that facilitate the conservation of the historic, cultural, natural, and scenic resources of the Unit, the Secretary may provide technical assistance, to the extent that a recipient of technical assistance is engaged in the protection, interpretation, or commemoration of historically significant Civil War resources in the area in and around the city of Corinth, to—

(A) the State of Mississippi (including a political subdivision of the State);

(B) the State of Tennessee (including a political subdivision of the State);

(C) a governmental entity;

(D) a nonprofit organization; and

(E) a private property owner.

(d) Resources outside the Unit

Nothing in subsection (c)(2) of this section authorizes the Secretary to own or manage any resource outside the Unit.

(Pub.L. 106–271, § 6, Sept. 22, 2000, 114 Stat. 794.)

HISTORICAL AND STATUTORY NOTES

Revision Notes and Legislative Reports
 2000 Acts. Senate Report No. 106–186, see 2000 U.S. Code Cong. and Adm. News, p. 648.

LIBRARY REFERENCES

American Digest System
 Armed Services ⊶54.
 United States ⊶57.
 Key Number System Topic Nos. 34, 393.

§ 430f–11. Repealed. Pub.L. 110–161, Div. F, Title I, § 127(4), Dec. 26, 2007, 121 Stat. 2122

HISTORICAL AND STATUTORY NOTES

Section, Pub.L. 106–271, § 7, Sept. 22, 2000, 114 Stat. 795, authorized a special resource study to determine whether certain additional properties were appropriate for inclusion in the Corinth Unit of the Shiloh National Military Park.

§ 430f–12. Authorization of appropriations

There are authorized to be appropriated such sums as are necessary to carry out sections 430f–6 to 430f–12 of this title, including $3,000,000 for the construction of an interpretive center under section 430f–5d of this title.

(Pub.L. 106–271, § 7, formerly § 8, Sept. 22, 2000, 114 Stat. 796; renumbered § 7, Pub.L. 110–161, Div. F, Title I, § 127(5), Dec. 26, 2007, 121 Stat. 2122.)

HISTORICAL AND STATUTORY NOTES

Revision Notes and Legislative Reports
 2000 Acts. Senate Report No. 106–186, see 2000 U.S. Code Cong. and Adm. News, p. 648.
 2007 Acts. House Report No. 110–197, see 2007 U.S. Code Cong. and Adm. News, p. 661.

Statement by President, see 2007 U.S. Code Cong. and Adm. News, p. S34.

§ 430g. Gettysburg National Military Park

The lands heretofore conveyed by the Gettysburg Battlefield Memorial Association to the United States, embracing about 800 acres, more or less, and being a considerable part of the battlefield of Gettysburg, and such other lands on the battlefield as the United States has heretofore acquired or shall hereafter acquire by purchase or condemnation proceedings, shall be designated and known as the "Gettysburg National Park." Nothing contained in this section shall be deemed and held to prejudice the rights acquired by any State or by any military organization to the ground on which its monuments or markers are placed, nor the right-of-way to the same. It shall be the duty of the Secretary of the Interior to establish and enforce proper regulations for the custody, preservation, and care of the monuments erected or which may be hereafter erected within the limits of the said national military park; and such rules shall provide for convenient access by visitors to all such monuments within the park, and the ground included therein, on such days and within such hours as may be designated and authorized by the Secretary of the Interior. The Secretary of the Interior may lease the lands of the park at his discretion either to former owners or other persons for agricultural purposes, the proceeds to be applied by the Secretary of the Interior, through the proper disbursing officer, to the maintenance of the park.

(Feb. 11, 1895, c. 80, 28 Stat. 651; June 4, 1897, c. 2, § 1, 30 Stat. 44; Ex.Ord. No. 6166, § 2, June 10, 1933; Ex.Ord. No. 6228, § 1, July 28, 1933; Sept. 6, 1966, Pub.L. 89–554, § 8(a), 80 Stat. 637.)

HISTORICAL AND STATUTORY NOTES

Amendments

1966 Amendments. Pub.L. 89–544 eliminated provisions which required that the affairs of the park be subject to the supervision and direction of the Secretary of the Interior.

Transfer of Functions

Administrative functions of Gettysburg National Military Park were transferred to the Department of the Interior by Ex. Ord. No. 6166, as amended by Ex.Ord. No. 6228, set out as a note under section 901 of Title 5, Government Organization and Employees.

National Park Service was substituted for Office of National Parks, Buildings, and Reservations referred to in Ex.Ord. No. 6166, by Act Mar. 2, 1934, c. 38, § 1, 48 Stat. 389.

Acquisition of Additional Lands for Gettysburg National Military Park; Study and Report

Pub.L. 100–132, § 2, Oct. 16, 1987, 101 Stat. 807, provided that:

"(a) **Acquisition of additional lands.**—Except as provided in section 1 of this Act [enacting section 430g–3 of this title], until Congress receives the study under subsection (b), the Secretary of the Interior may not acquire by purchase, donation, exchange, or any other means any additional land for the Gettysburg National Military Park which is not within the boundaries of the 3,874 acre area depicted on the map dated July 25, 1974, numbered 305–92,004 and entitled 'Gettysburg National Military Park'.

"(b) **Study by National Park Service.**—The Secretary of the Interior through the National Park Service shall conduct a boundary study and shall submit a report to Congress within one year of the date of enactment of this Act [Oct. 16, 1987], with recommendations with respect to the final development of the Gettysburg National Military Park. In conducting the study, the Secretary shall consult with the people of the community and their elected representatives at all levels as well as with other interested individuals and groups."

175

CROSS REFERENCES

Revision of boundary, see 16 USCA § 430g–4.

LIBRARY REFERENCES

American Digest System
     Armed Services ☜28, 54.
     Woods and Forests ☜8.
     Key Number System Topic Nos. 34, 411.

Notes of Decisions

Guide licensing   1
_____

1. Guide licensing
    The Secretary could make regulations as to licensing of guides in the Gettysburg National Military Park, and unlicensed guides could be enjoined in suit by the government. U.S. v. Gilbert, M.D.Pa. 1932, 58 F.2d 1031.

§ 430g–1.   Exchange of lands

For the purpose of consolidating Federal holdings of land within Gettysburg National Military Park, Pennsylvania, the Secretary of the Interior is authorized, in his discretion, to accept, on behalf of the United States, approximately four acres of non-Federal land within the park boundaries, such land to be conveyed to the United States without cost by the Evergreen Cemetery Association, of Gettysburg. Upon acceptance of title thereto by the United States, such property shall be subject to all laws and regulations applicable to the park. In exchange for the conveyance to the United States of the aforesaid property, the Secretary of the Interior is authorized to convey to the Evergreen Cemetery Association approximately one and one-quarter acres of federally owned land within the park, such property constituting a right-of-way through the Evergreen Cemetery property: *Provided*, That the aforesaid exchange shall be consummated only upon condition that the Secretary is satisfied that such exchange is in the public interest and that the properties to be exchanged are of approximately equal value.

(Jan. 31, 1948, c. 41, 62 Stat. 16.)

LIBRARY REFERENCES

American Digest System
     Armed Services ☜54.
     Woods and Forests ☜4.
     Key Number System Topic Nos. 34, 411.

§ 430g–2.   Exchange of lands

The Secretary of the Interior is authorized to have competent and disinterested appraisals made as to the value of not more than twenty-three acres of land in Gettysburg National Military Park, in the State of Pennsylvania, such land lying generally between East Confederate Avenue and Wainwright Avenue, and being situated adjacent to the present high-school property in that area. Upon the basis of such appraisals, the Secretary is authorized to convey such property for public-school purposes to the State of Pennsylvania, or the appropriate local agency thereof, the conveyance to be made in exchange for non-Federal land of approximately equal value, which land, upon acceptance by the United States, shall become a part of Gettysburg National Military Park.

(July 31, 1953, c. 290, 67 Stat. 243.)

LIBRARY REFERENCES

American Digest System

Armed Services ⚷54.
United States ⚷55.
Woods and Forests ⚷4.
Key Number System Topic Nos. 34, 393, 411.

§ 430g-3. Donation of non-Federal lands

The Secretary of the Interior shall accept on behalf of the United States, the donation of approximately 31 acres of land known as the "Taney Farm" for administration as part of the Gettysburg National Military Park in Pennsylvania if such land is offered to be conveyed to the United States without cost to the United States by the Gettysburg Battlefield Preservation Association. Upon acceptance of title thereto by the United States, such property shall be subject to all laws and regulations applicable to the park.

(Pub.L. 100-132, § 1, Oct. 16, 1987, 101 Stat. 807.)

LIBRARY REFERENCES

American Digest System

Armed Services ⚷54.
Woods and Forests ⚷2, 5.
Key Number System Topic Nos. 34, 411.

§ 430g-4. Gettysburg National Military Park boundary revision

(a) Lands included in park

In furtherance of the purposes of section 430g of this title, the Gettysburg National Military Park (hereafter in sections 430g-4 to 430g-10 of this title referred to as the "park") shall on and after August 17, 1990, comprise the lands and interests in lands within the boundary generally depicted as "Park Boundary" on the map entitled

"Gettysburg National Military Park Boundary Map", numbered NPS 305/80034–B, and dated March 1990, which shall be on file and available for public inspection in the Office of the Director of the National Park Service, Department of the Interior.

(b) Additional land

In addition to the land identified in subsection (a) of this section, the park shall also include the property commonly known as the Wills House located in the Borough of Gettysburg and identified as Tract P02–1 on the map entitled "Gettysburg National Military Park" numbered MARO 305/80,011 Segment 2, and dated April 1981, revised May 14, 1999.

(c) Lands excluded from park

Lands and interests in lands outside of the boundary so depicted as "Park Boundary" on the maps referred to in subsections (a) and (b) of this section are hereby excluded from the park and shall be disposed of in accordance with the provisions of section 430g–5(c) of this title.

(Pub.L. 101–377, § 1, Aug. 17, 1990, 104 Stat. 464; Pub.L. 106–290, § 1, Oct. 10, 2000, 114 Stat. 921.)

HISTORICAL AND STATUTORY NOTES

Revision Notes and Legislative Reports
  2000 Acts. Senate Report No. 106–787, see 2000 U.S. Code Cong. and Adm. News, p. 752.

Amendments
  2000 Amendments. Subsec. (b). Pub.L. 106–290, § 1(1), (2), added sub-sec. (b) and redesignated former subsec. (b) as (c).
  Subsec. (c). Pub.L. 106–290, § 1(1), (3), redesignated former subsec. (b) as (c), and as so redesignated, substituted "maps referred to in subsections (a) and (b) of this section" for "map referred to in subsection (a) of this section".

CROSS REFERENCES

Acquisition of lands,
    In general, see 16 USCA § 430g–5.
    Within Gettysburg Battlefield Historic District on which historic monuments and tablets have been erected, see 16 USCA § 430g–6.
Advisory Commission, see 16 USCA § 430g–8.
Authorization of appropriations, see 16 USCA § 430g–10.

LIBRARY REFERENCES

American Digest System
    Armed Services ⟊54.
    Woods and Forests ⟊1, 8.
    Key Number System Topic Nos. 34, 411.

Notes of Decisions

Jurisdiction   2
Taking for public use   1

1. Taking for public use

Taking of land to be added to Gettysburg National Military Park was for public use specifically authorized by Congress when it approved boundary map for the Park and authorized the Secretary of the Interior to acquire lands and interest in lands within the Park. U.S. v. 18.67 Acres of Land, M.D.Pa.1992, 793 F.Supp. 582. Eminent Domain ⚬ 2.2

2. Jurisdiction

Given that taking of land within boundary of Gettysburg National Military Park was for public use and with specific congressional approval, district court had no jurisdiction to review decision of the Secretary of the Interior that particular tract taken was necessary for the administration, preservation and development of the Park, and the timing of the taking was entirely within the hands of the Secretary. U.S. v. 18.67 Acres of Land, M.D.Pa.1992, 793 F.Supp. 582. Eminent Domain ⚬ 67

§ 430g–5. Acquisition and disposal of lands

(a) General authority

The Secretary is authorized to acquire lands and interests in lands within the park by donation, purchase with donated or appropriated funds, exchange, or otherwise. In acquiring lands and interests in lands under sections 430g–4 to 430g–10 of this title, the Secretary shall acquire the minimum Federal interests necessary to achieve the objectives identified for specific areas and the park.

(b) Authority to convey freehold and leasehold interests within park

The Secretary may convey lands and interests in lands within the park authorized in accordance with subsection (a) of section 460l–22 of this title except that, notwithstanding subsection (d) of that section, the net proceeds from any such conveyance may be used, subject to appropriations, to acquire lands and interests within the park.

(c) Conveyance of lands excluded from park

(1) The Secretary is authorized, in accordance with applicable existing law, to exchange Federal lands and interests excluded from the park pursuant to section 430g–4(c) of this title for the purpose of acquiring lands within the park boundary.

(2) If any such Federal lands or interests are not exchanged within five years after August 17, 1990, the Secretary may sell any or all such lands or interests to the highest bidder, in accordance with such regulations as the Secretary may prescribe, but any such conveyance shall be at not less than the fair market value of the land or interest, as determined by the Secretary.

(3) All Federal lands and interests sold or exchanged pursuant to this subsection shall be subject to such terms and conditions as will

assure the use of the property in a manner which, in the judgment of the Secretary, will protect the park and the Gettysburg Battlefield Historic District (hereafter in sections 430g–5 to 430g–10 of this title referred to as the "historic district"). Notwithstanding any other provision of law, the net proceeds from any such sale or exchange shall be used, subject to appropriations, to acquire lands and interests within the park.

(d) Relinquishment of legislative jurisdiction to Pennsylvania

With respect to any lands over which the United States exercises exclusive or concurrent legislative jurisdiction and which are excluded from the park pursuant to section 430g–4(c) of this title, the Secretary may relinquish to the State of Pennsylvania such exclusive or concurrent legislative jurisdiction by filing with the Governor a notice of relinquishment to take effect upon acceptance thereof, unless otherwise provided by the laws of the State.

(Pub.L. 101–377, § 2, Aug. 17, 1990, 104 Stat. 464; Pub.L. 106–290, § 2, Oct. 10, 2000, 114 Stat. 921.)

HISTORICAL AND STATUTORY NOTES

Revision Notes and Legislative Reports

  2000 Acts. Senate Report No. 106–787, see 2000 U.S. Code Cong. and Adm. News, p. 752.

References in Text

  Section 460*l*–22 of this title, referred to in subsec. (b), was in the original "subsection (a) of the Act of July 15, 1968 (16 U.S.C. 460*l*–22)" and was translated as reading subsection (a) of section 5 of the Act of July 15, 1968 (16 U.S.C. 460*l*–22) to reflect the probable intent of Congress.

Amendments

  2000 Amendments. Subsec. (c)(1). Pub.L. 106–290, § 2, substituted "section 430g–4(c) of this title" for "section 430g–4(b) of this title".

  Subsec. (d). Pub.L. 106–290, § 2, substituted "section 430g–4(c) of this title" for "section 430g–4(b) of this title".

CROSS REFERENCES

Advisory Commission, see 16 USCA § 430g–8.
Authorization of appropriations, see 16 USCA § 430g–10.
Lands excluded from park, see 16 USCA § 430g–4.

LIBRARY REFERENCES

American Digest System

  Armed Services ⬅⮕54.
  United States ⬅⮕55.
  Woods and Forests ⬅⮕8.
  Key Number System Topic Nos. 34, 393, 411.

Notes of Decisions

Minimum Federal interests 1   Review 2

1. Minimum Federal interests

  Defense in condemnation suit of abuse of discretion by the Secretary of the Interior in determining that fee simple represented the minimum federal interest necessary was not insufficient, so as to be subject to being stricken, in light of restriction on authority of Secretary to acquire lands and interests within boundary of the Gettysburg National Military Park, that the Secretary "shall acquire the minimum Federal interests necessary to achieve the objectives identified for specific areas and the park." U.S. v. 18.67 Acres of Land, M.D.Pa.1992, 793 F.Supp. 582. Eminent Domain ☞ 58

2. Review

In reviewing decision of Secretary of Interior to acquire fee simple interest in tract within Gettysburg National Military Park, in light of statutory provision requiring acquisition of minimum interest necessary, district court would do no more than review administrative record to determine whether Secretary's action was arbitrary or capricious or otherwise an abuse of discretion, and scope of review should give proper measure of deference to both legislative and executive branches in carrying out legislative mandates regarding boundary revision of the Park. U.S. v. 18.67 Acres of Land, M.D.Pa.1992, 793 F.Supp. 582. Eminent Domain ☞ 67

§ 430g–6.   Agreements with respect to monuments and tablets located outside park boundary

The Secretary is authorized to enter into agreements with the owners of property in proximity to but outside the boundary of the park on which historic monuments and tablets commemorating the Battle of Gettysburg have been erected on or before January 1, 1990. The Secretary may make funds available, subject to appropriations, for the maintenance, protection, and interpretation of such monuments and tablets pursuant to such agreements. In addition, within the area depicted as the "Gettysburg Battlefield Historic District" on the map referred to in section 430g–4(a) of this title, or in proximity thereto, the Secretary may, with the consent of the owner, acquire, by donation, purchase, or exchange, lands and interests comprising such monuments and tablets together with lands and interests necessary to provide adequate public access thereto.

(Pub.L. 101–377, § 3, Aug. 17, 1990, 104 Stat. 465.)

CROSS REFERENCES

Acquisition of lands, see 16 USCA § 430g–5.
Advisory Commission, see 16 USCA § 430g–8.
Authorization of appropriations, see 16 USCA § 430g–10.
Revision of park boundary, see 16 USCA § 430g–4.

LIBRARY REFERENCES

American Digest System
Armed Services ☞54.
United States ☞60.
Key Number System Topic Nos. 34, 393.

§ 430g–7. Conservation within Gettysburg Battlefield historic district

(a) Encouragement of conservation

The Secretary shall take appropriate action to encourage conservation of the historic district by landowners, local governments, organizations, and businesses.

(b) Prioritization of grants

Within the historic district, the Secretary shall give priority in making grants under section 101(d), and in providing technical assistance, information, and advice under section 101(h), of the National Historic Preservation Act (16 U.S.C. 470a(d), (h)) to those programs and activities in the historic district that will assure development and use of natural and cultural resources in a manner that is consistent with the conservation and maintenance of the district's historic character.

(c) Provision of technical assistance

The Secretary may provide technical assistance to assist local governments in cooperative efforts which complement the values of the park and the historic district and to help landowners prepare individual property plans which meet landowner and conservation objectives in the historic district.

(d) Reimbursement of planning costs

The Secretary, under such terms and conditions as the Secretary may prescribe and at the request of any local or county government within the historic district, shall provide matching reimbursements for up to 50 percent of the planning costs incurred by such government in the development of comprehensive plans and land use guidelines which are consistent with conserving the historic character of the historic district. Reimbursements may only be provided under this subsection to the extent or in such amounts as are provided in appropriation Acts.

(e) Acceptance of easement donations

The Secretary, upon recommendation from the Director of the National Park Service, in consultation with the Advisory Commission established under section 430g–8 of this title, is authorized to accept donations of conservation easements on land located within the historic district.

(f) Federal consistency

(1) Any Federal or federally assisted activity or undertaking in the historic district, shall be consistent to the maximum extent possible with the purposes of the preservation of the historic district, including its rural, agricultural, and town elements, and shall also comply with the National Historic Preservation Act [16 U.S.C.A. § 470 et seq.] and other applicable laws.

(2) The head of any Federal agency (hereafter in this subsection referred to as the "agency") having direct or indirect jurisdiction over a proposed Federal or federally assisted undertaking in the historic district, and the head of any Federal agency having authority to license or permit any undertaking in such area, shall at the earliest feasible date prepare a detailed analysis of any proposed action and submit it to the Secretary.

(3) The Secretary shall review the analysis and consult with the agency. If after such review and consultation, the Secretary finds that the proposed action is not consistent with the purposes identified in this subsection, the agency shall not proceed with the action until after a justification for the action has been submitted to the appropriate committees of Congress with adequate time allowed for Congressional comment. Such justification shall include the following elements: the anticipated effects on the historic and commemorative character of the historic district, the social and economic necessity for the proposed action, all possible alternatives to the proposed action, the comparative benefits of proposed alternative actions, and the mitigation measures outlined in the proposed action.

(Pub.L. 101–377, § 4, Aug. 17, 1990, 104 Stat. 465.)

HISTORICAL AND STATUTORY NOTES

References in Text

Subsections (d) and (h) of section 101 of the National Historic Preservation Act, referred to in subsec. (b), were redesignated as subsecs. (e) and (i), respectively, of that section by Pub.L. 102–575, Title XL, 4006(a)(1), Oct. 30, 1992, 106 Stat. 4755, and are classified to subsecs. (e) and (i), respectively, of 16 U.S.C.A. § 470a.

CROSS REFERENCES

Advisory Commission, see 16 USCA § 430g–8.
Authorization of appropriations, see 16 USCA § 430g–10.
Revision of park boundary, see 16 USCA § 430g–4.
Sale or exchange of lands and interests; terms and conditions for protection of historic district, see 16 USCA § 430g–5.

LIBRARY REFERENCES

American Digest System

Armed Services ⚷54.
United States ⚷57.
Woods and Forests ⚷8.
Key Number System Topic Nos. 34, 393, 411.

§ 430g–8. Advisory Commission

(a) Establishment

There is hereby established the Gettysburg National Military Park Advisory Commission (hereafter in sections 430g–8 to 430g–10 of this title referred to as the "Advisory Commission"). The Advisory Commission shall be composed of eleven members, as follows:

(1) One member representing each of the local governments from the four townships surrounding the park and the Borough of Gettysburg, appointed by the Secretary.

(2) One member representing the Adams County, Pennsylvania government, appointed by the Secretary.

(3) One member representing the State Historic Preservation Office of the State of Pennsylvania, appointed by the Secretary.

(4) Two members who are residents of Adams County and who are knowledgeable about the park and its resources, appointed by the Secretary, one of whom shall own land or interests in land within the park boundary.

(5) One member with expertise in local historic preservation, appointed by the Secretary.

(6) The Director of the National Park Service or his designee, ex officio.

Members shall be appointed for staggered terms of three years, as designated by the Secretary at the time of the initial appointments. Any member of the Advisory Commission appointed for a definite term may serve after the expiration of his term until his successor is appointed. The Advisory Commission shall designate one of its members as Chairperson. Six members of the Advisory Commission shall constitute a quorum.

(b) Management and development issues

The Secretary, or his designee, shall from time to time, but at least semiannually, meet and consult with the Advisory Commission to coordinate the management of the park and the historic district with local jurisdictions.

(c) Meetings

The Advisory Commission shall meet on a regular basis. Notice of meetings and agenda shall be published in local newspapers which have a distribution which generally covers the area affected by the park. Advisory Commission meetings shall be held at locations and in such a manner as to ensure adequate public involvement.

(d) Expenses

Members of the Advisory Commission shall serve without compensation as such, but the Secretary may pay expenses reasonably incurred in carrying out their responsibilities under sections 430g–4 to 430g–10 of this title on vouchers signed by the Chairperson.

(e) Charter

The provisions of section 14 of the Federal Advisory Committee Act (5 U.S.C.App.) are hereby waived with respect to this Advisory Commission.

(Pub.L. 101–377, § 5, Aug. 17, 1990, 104 Stat. 466.)

HISTORICAL AND STATUTORY NOTES

References in Text

The Federal Advisory Committee Act, including section 14 of the Act, referred to in subsec. (e), is Pub.L. 92–463, Oct. 6, 1972, 86 Stat. 770, as amended, which is set out in Appendix 2 to Title 5, Government Organization and Employees.

CROSS REFERENCES

Acquisition of lands, see 16 USCA § 430g–5.
Authorization of appropriations, see 16 USCA § 430g–10.
Consultation with Secretary of Interior regarding acceptance of donations of conservation easements within historic district, see 16 USCA § 430g–7.
Revision of park boundary, see 16 USCA § 430g–4.

LIBRARY REFERENCES

American Digest System

Armed Services ⬩54.
Woods and Forests ⬩7.
Key Number System Topic Nos. 34, 411.

§ 430g–9. Interpretation

In administering the park, the Secretary shall take such action as is necessary and appropriate to interpret, for the benefit of visitors to the park and the general public, the Battle of Gettysburg in the larger context of the Civil War and American history, including the causes and consequences of the Civil War and including the effects of the war on all the American people.

(Pub.L. 101–377, § 6, Aug. 17, 1990, 104 Stat. 467.)

CROSS REFERENCES

Acquisition of lands, see 16 USCA § 430g–5.
Advisory Commission, see 16 USCA § 430g–8.
Authorization of appropriations, see 16 USCA § 430g–10.
Revision of park boundary, see 16 USCA § 430g–4.

§ 430g–10. Authorization of appropriations

There are authorized to be appropriated such sums as may be necessary to carry out the purposes of sections 430g–4 to 430g–10 of this title.

(Pub.L. 101–377, § 7, Aug. 17, 1990, 104 Stat. 467.)

CROSS REFERENCES

Acquisition of lands, see 16 USCA § 430g–5.
Advisory Commission, see 16 USCA § 430g–8.
Revision of park boundary, see 16 USCA § 430g–4.

§ 430h. Vicksburg National Military Park

In order to commemorate the campaign, siege, and defense of Vicksburg, and to preserve the history of the battles and operations of the siege and defense on the ground where they were fought and carried on, the battlefield of Vicksburg, in the State of Mississippi, insofar as title to the same has been acquired by the United States and as the usual jurisdiction over the lands and roads of the same has heretofore been granted to the United States by the State of Mississippi, shall be a National Military Park. The Secretary of the Interior is authorized to enter into agreements of leasing upon such terms as he may prescribe with such persons, who were on February 21, 1899, occupants or tenants of the lands, as may desire to remain upon them to occupy and cultivate their holdings, upon condition that they will preserve the then buildings and roads and the then outlines of field and forest, and that they will only cut trees and underbrush under such regulations as the Secretary of the Interior may prescribe, and that they will assist in caring for and protecting all tablets, monuments, or such other historical works as may from time to time be erected by proper authority: *Provided*, That the United States shall at all times have and retain their right, power, and authority to take possession of any and all parts and portions of said premises, and to remove and expel therefrom any such occupant, tenant, or other person or persons found thereon whenever the Secretary of the Interior shall deem it proper or necessary; and such right, power, and authority shall be reserved in express terms in all leases and agreements giving or granting such occupant or tenant the right to remain in possession as herein contemplated; and thereupon said occupant or tenant or other persons who may be required to vacate said premises shall each and all of them at once surrender and deliver up the possession thereof. It shall be the duty of the Secretary of the Interior to cause to be restored the forts and lines of fortification, the parallels and the approaches of the two armies, or so much thereof as may be necessary to the purposes of this Park; to open and construct and repair such roads as may be necessary to said purposes, and to ascertain and to mark with historical tablets, or otherwise, the lines of battle of the troops engaged in the assaults, and the lines held by the troops during the siege and defense of Vicksburg, the headquarters of General Grant and of General Pemberton, and other historical points of interest pertaining to the siege and defense of Vicksburg within the Park or its vicinity; and the Secretary of the Interior shall have authority to do all things necessary to the purposes of the park, and he shall make and enforce all needful regulations for the care of the Park. It shall be lawful for any State that had troops engaged in the siege and defense of Vicksburg to enter upon the lands of the Vicksburg National Military Park for the purpose of ascertaining and marking the lines of battle of its troops engaged therein: *Provided*, That before any such lines are permanently designated the position of the lines and the proposed methods of marking them by monuments, tablets, or otherwise shall be submitted to and approved by the Secretary of the Interior, and all such lines, designs, and inscriptions for the same shall first receive the written approval of the Secretary of the Interior; and no monument, tablet, or other designating indication shall be erected or placed within said park or vicinity without such written authority of the Secretary of the Interior: *Provided*, That no discrimination shall be made against any State as to the manner of designating lines, but any grant made to any State by the Secretary of the Interior may be used by any other State. The provisions of this section shall also apply to organizations and persons; and as the Vicksburg National Cemetery is on ground partly occupied by Federal lines during the siege of Vicksburg, the provisions of this section, as far as may be practicable, shall apply to monuments or tablets designating such lines within the limits of that cemetery. If any person shall, except by permission of the Secretary of the Interior, destroy, mutilate, deface, injure, or remove any monument, column, statue, memorial structure, tablet, or work of art that shall be erected or placed upon the grounds of the park by lawful authority, or shall destroy or remove any fence, railing, inclosure, or other work intended for the protection or ornamentation of said park, or any portion thereof, or shall destroy, cut, hack, bark, break down, or otherwise injure any tree, bush, or shrub that may be growing upon said park, or shall cut down or fell or remove any timber, battle relic, tree, or trees growing or being upon said park, or hunt within the limits of the park, or shall remove or destroy any breastworks, earthworks, walls, or other defenses or shelter or any part thereof constructed by the armies formerly engaged in the battles, on the lands or approaches to the park, any person so offending and found guilty thereof before any United States magistrate judge or court, justice of the peace of the county in which the offense may be committed, or any court of competent jurisdiction, shall for each and every such offense forfeit and pay a fine in the discretion of the said magistrate judge or court of the United States or justice of the peace, according to the aggravation of the offense, of not less than five nor more than five hundred dollars, one half for the use of the park and the other half to the informant, to be enforced and recovered before such United States magistrate judge or court or justice of the peace or other court in like manner as debts of like nature were, on February 21, 1899, by law recoverable in the several counties where the offense may be committed.

(Feb. 21, 1899, c. 176, 30 Stat. 841; Ex.Ord. No. 6166, § 2, June 10, 1933; Ex.Ord. No. 6228, § 1, July 28, 1933; Sept. 6, 1966, Pub.L. 89–554, § 8(a), 80 Stat. 638; Oct. 17, 1968, Pub.L. 90–578, Title IV, § 402(b)(2), 82 Stat. 1118; Dec. 1, 1990, Pub.L. 101–650, Title III, § 321, 104 Stat. 5117.)

HISTORICAL AND STATUTORY NOTES

Revision Notes and Legislative Reports
1968 Acts. House Report No. 1629, see 1968 U.S. Code Cong. and Adm. News, p. 4252.

Amendments
1966 Amendments. Pub.L. 89–554 struck out provisions relating to appointment and pay of three commissioners to supervise Vicksburg National Military Park, and of a secretary.

Change of Name
"United States magistrate judge" and "magistrate judge" substituted for "United States magistrate" and "magistrate", respectively, wherever appearing in text pursuant to section 321 of Pub.L. 101–650, set out as a note under section 631 of Title 28, Judiciary and Judicial Procedure. Previously, "magistrate" substituted for "commissioner" pursuant to Pub.L. 90–578. See chapter 43 (§ 631 et seq.) of Title 28.

"Magistrate" was substituted for "commissioner" in view of Pub.L. 90–578, Title IV, § 402(b)(2), Oct. 17, 1968, 82 Stat. 1118, which provided that within each district, references in previously enacted statutes and previously promulgated rules and regulations to United States commissioners are to be deemed, within such district, references to United States magistrates duly appointed under section 631 of Title 28, Judiciary and Judicial Procedure. See Applicable Law note under section 631 of Title 28.

Transfer of Functions
Administrative functions of Vicksburg National Military Park were transferred to the Department of the Interior, by Ex. Ord. No. 6166, as amended by Ex.Ord. No. 6228, set out as a note under section 901 of Title 5, Government Organization and Employees.

National Park Service was substituted for Office of National Parks, Buildings, and Reservations referred to in Ex.Ord. No. 6166, by Act March 2, 1934, c. 38, § 1, 48 Stat. 389.

Short Title
2002 Acts. Pub.L. 107–238, § 1, Oct. 11, 2002, 116 Stat. 1486, provided that: "This Act [enacting 16 U.S.C.A. §§ 430h–10 to 430h–13] may be cited as the 'Vicksburg National Military Park Boundary Modification Act of 2002'."

§ 430h–1.   Donations of land and property

The Secretary of the Interior is authorized, in his discretion, to accept, in behalf of the United States, donations of lands, buildings, structures, and other property, or interests therein, within a distance of one mile of the present boundaries of the Vicksburg National Military Park, which he may determine to be of historical interest in connection with said park, the title to such property or interests therein to be satisfactory to the Secretary of the Interior.

All such property or interests therein, upon acceptance thereof, shall become a part of the Vicksburg National Military Park and shall be subject to all laws and regulations applicable thereto.

(Oct. 9, 1940, c. 790, 54 Stat. 1061.)

§ 430h–2.   Exchange of certain lands authorized

In order to further the consolidation of land comprising Vicksburg National Military Park, the Secretary of the Interior is authorized, upon such terms and conditions as he may deem necessary, to transfer to the city of Vicksburg, Mississippi, for school purposes, a tract of park land containing three and one-tenth acres, more or less, now under revocable permit to said city, acting through its board of education, and to transfer to the Mississippi State Highway Commission a tract of park land containing one and thirty-two hundredths acres, more or less, now under revocable permit to said commission for use as a site for a weighing station: *Provided*, That, from among the land designated as tracts 199, 201, 202, 203, 204, 205, 206, and 216 on map Numbered NMP–VIC–7007, said city and highway commission shall transfer in exchange to the United States, for addition to Vicksburg National Military Park, such land or interests therein as may be mutually agreed upon and which are approximately equal in value to the properties being acquired in each case.

(Pub.L. 85–667, Aug. 14, 1958, 72 Stat. 617.)

Revision Notes and Legislative Reports
1958 Acts. Senate Report No. 2086,
see 1958 U.S. Code Cong. and Adm.
News, p. 3570.

LIBRARY REFERENCES

American Digest System
   Armed Services ☞54.
   Woods and Forests ☞2, 8.
   Key Number System Topic Nos. 34, 411.

§ 430h–3. Consolidation of lands and installation of park tour road

In order to preserve and protect the essential historical features of Vicksburg National Military Park in the State of Mississippi and to enhance visitor enjoyment and safety by means of a park tour road and through the consolidation of park lands, the Secretary of the Interior is authorized, in his discretion, and under such terms and conditions as he determines are in the public interest—

(a) Disposition of lands and roads; incorporation into municipal road system; reversion on failure of conditions; reservation of title to monuments and easements

to quitclaim to the city of Vicksburg, Mississippi, approximately one hundred and fifty-four acres of land, including the roads thereon and the park land abutting said roads, in exchange for the city's agreeing to place the roads in its road system and thereby assume jurisdiction and maintenance thereof, and upon the further agreement of the city to maintain the parklike character of so much of the park land conveyed to it and abutting the road as the Secretary may prescribe, said land being generally that part of Vicksburg National Military Park lying south of Fort Garrott with the exception of Navy Circle, South Fort, and Louisiana Circle: *Provided*, That title to so much of said abutting park land prescribed by the Secretary and covered by said agreement of the city to maintain the parklike character thereof shall revert to the United States if its parklike character is not maintained; to quitclaim to Warren County, Mississippi, upon like terms and conditions approximately twenty-four acres of land, including the road and abutting park land, being known as Sherman Avenue and the Sherman Avenue spur; to release or quitclaim to Warren County or any other appropriate political subdivision of the State all interest which the United States of America has, if any, in those portions of any public road located on park land which are no longer required for park purposes:

Provided, That the United States shall reserve from the conveyance or conveyances made pursuant to this subsection title to all
historical monuments, means of access thereto, and such other
easements as the Secretary determines are required for the
continued administration of said monuments as a part of Vicksburg National Military Park; and

(b) Acquisition of lands: purchases, condemnations and dona-tions

to acquire not in excess of five hundred and forty-four acres of
land, or interests in land, for addition to Vicksburg National
Military Park, such authority to include purchase and condemnation with appropriated funds but not to constitute a limitation
upon existing authority to accept donations; and

(c) Municipal agreements of park tour road's effect upon local road systems; Federal obligations for local roads directly attributable to installation of park tour road

to enter into agreements with duly authorized officials of the
city of Vicksburg and Warren County relative to the effect which
the installation of a one-way park tour road with controlled
access will have upon the existing local road systems; subject to
the availability of funds, to obligate the United States to make
provision for such alterations, relocations and construction of
local roads, including procurement of rights-of-way therefor and
the subsequent transfer thereof to the State or its appropriate
political subdivisions which shall thereupon assume jurisdiction
and maintenance, as the Secretary and said officials agree are
directly attributable to the installation of the park tour road; and
to transfer to the city or county jurisdiction and maintenance of
service roads which the Secretary constructs on park lands to
properties that otherwise would be denied access because of the
installation of the park tour road.

The Secretary of the Interior shall not, without first obtaining the
consent of the city and county officials referred to in subsection (c),
convert the portion of the existing road known as Confederate
Avenue lying between Graveyard Road and Fort Garrott into a one-
way park tour road with controlled access, or otherwise limit the use
of such portion by local traffic, until the United States has provided
for such alterations, relocations, and construction of local roads
(including procurement of rights-of-way) as the Secretary and said
officials agree are directly attributable to the installation of such park
tour road.

(Pub.L. 88–37, § 1, June 4, 1963, 77 Stat. 55.)

LIBRARY REFERENCES

American Digest System
> Armed Services ☞54.
> United States ☞55.
> Woods and Forests ☞4.
> Key Number System Topic Nos. 34, 393, 411.

§ 430h–4. Jurisdiction over lands and roads

Upon the delivery and acceptance of the conveyances herein authorized, any jurisdiction heretofore ceded to the United States by the State of Mississippi over the lands and roads transferred shall thereby cease and thereafter rest in the State of Mississippi.

(Pub.L. 88–37, § 2, June 4, 1963, 77 Stat. 56.)

LIBRARY REFERENCES

American Digest System
> Armed Services ☞54.
> United States ☞3.
> Key Number System Topic Nos. 34, 393.

§ 430h–5. Authorization of appropriations

There are hereby authorized to be appropriated such sums, but not more than $3,850,000, as are required for acquisition of lands and interests in lands and for construction and relocation of roads pursuant to sections 430h–3 to 430h–5 of this title.

(Pub.L. 88–37, § 3, June 4, 1963, 77 Stat. 56; Pub.L. 94–578, Title II, § 201(8), Oct. 21, 1976, 90 Stat. 2733.)

HISTORICAL AND STATUTORY NOTES

Amendments
1976 Amendments. Pub.L. 94–578 substituted "$3,850,000" for "$2,050,000".

§ 430h–6. Addition of lands to Vicksburg National Military Park

(a) Grant's Canal, Louisiana

The Secretary of the Interior (hereinafter in sections 430h–6 to 430h–9 of this title referred to as the "Secretary") is authorized to acquire by donation, exchange, or purchase with donated or appropriated funds, approximately two and five-tenths acres of land in Madison Parish, Louisiana, known generally as the Grant's Canal property.

(b) Warren County, Mississippi

(1) The Secretary is authorized to acquire by donation approximately two and eighty-two one-hundredths acres of land adjacent to

the entrance of Vicksburg National Military Park owned by Warren County, Mississippi.

(2) The Secretary may contribute, in cash or services, to the relocation and construction of a maintenance facility to replace the facility located on the land to be donated, all in accordance with an agreement between the Secretary and the Board of Supervisors.

(3) The Secretary is authorized to restore and landscape the property acquired pursuant to this subsection.

(c) Boundary revision

Upon acquisition of the properties referred to in subsections (a) and (b) of this section, the Secretary shall, after the publication of notice in the Federal Register, revise the boundary of Vicksburg National Military Park (hereinafter in sections 430h–6 to 430h–9 of this title referred to as the "park") to reflect the inclusion of such properties within the park.

(Pub.L.101–442, Title I, § 101, Oct. 18, 1990, 104 Stat. 1019.)

LIBRARY REFERENCES

American Digest System
> Armed Services ☜54.
> United States ☜55.
> Key Number System Topic Nos. 34, 393.

§ 430h–7. Exclusion of lands from park

(a) Exclusion of certain lands

The park boundary is hereby revised to exclude those lands depicted as "Proposed Deletions" on the map entitled "Vicksburg National Military Park" numbered 306–80,007 and dated May 1990, which map shall be on file and available for public inspection in the Office of the National Park Service, Department of the Interior. Exclusive jurisdiction over the lands excluded from the park is hereby retroceded to the State of Mississippi.

(b) Transfer to adjacent owners

(1) For a period ending four years after October 18, 1990, and subject to the provisions of paragraph (2), the Secretary is authorized to convey title to all or part of the lands referred to in subsection (a) of this section to an owner of property adjacent to such lands, upon the application of such owner.

(2) No property shall be conveyed unless the application referred to in paragraph (1) is accompanied by a payment in an amount equal to—

(A) the fair market value of the land to be conveyed; and

(B) the administrative costs of such transfer incurred by the Secretary, including the costs of surveys, appraisals, and filing and recording fees.

(c) Excess property

Any lands not conveyed pursuant to subsection (b) of this section shall be reported to the Administrator of General Services as excess to the needs of the Department of the Interior and shall be subject to transfer or disposition in accordance with the Federal Property and Administrative Services Act of 1949, as amended.

(Pub.L.101–442, Title I, § 102, Oct. 18, 1990, 104 Stat. 1019.)

HISTORICAL AND STATUTORY NOTES

References in Text

The Federal Property and Administrative Services Act of 1949, referred to in subsec. (c), is Act June 30, 1949, c. 288, 63 Stat. 377, as amended, Title III of which is currently classified to subchapter IV of chapter 4 of Title 41, 41 U.S.C.A. § 251 et seq., and the remainder of which was formerly classified to chapter 10 of former Title 40, 40 U.S.C.A. § 471 et seq., prior to being repealed by Pub.L. 107–217, § 6(b), Aug. 21, 2002, 116 Stat. 1313; see now generally chapter 1 of Title 40, 40 U.S.C.A. § 101 et seq.

LIBRARY REFERENCES

American Digest System
Armed Services ⟋54.
Woods and Forests ⟋1, 8.
Key Number System Topic Nos. 34, 411.

§ 430h–8. Park interpretation

In administering Vicksburg National Military Park, the Secretary shall interpret the campaign and siege of Vicksburg from April 1862 to July 4, 1863, and the history of Vicksburg under Union occupation during the Civil War and Reconstruction.

(Pub.L.101–442, Title I, § 103, Oct. 18, 1990, 104 Stat. 1020.)

LIBRARY REFERENCES

American Digest System
Armed Services ⟋54.
Key Number System Topic No. 34.

§ 430h–9. Authorization of appropriations

There are hereby authorized to be appropriated such sums as may be necessary to carry out the purposes of sections 430h–6 to 430h–9 of this title.

(Pub.L.101–442, Title I, § 104, Oct. 18, 1990, 104 Stat. 1020.)

§ 430h–10.   Boundary modification

The boundary of Vicksburg National Military Park is modified to include the property known as Pemberton's Headquarters, as generally depicted on the map entitled "Boundary Map, Pemberton's Headquarters at Vicksburg National Military Park", numbered 306/80015A, and dated August, 2001. The map shall be on file and available for inspection in the appropriate offices of the National Park Service.

(Pub.L. 107–238, § 2, Oct. 11, 2002, 116 Stat. 1486.)

HISTORICAL AND STATUTORY NOTES

Revision Notes and Legislative Reports
2002 Acts. Senate Report No. 107–183 and Statement by President, see 2002 U.S. Code Cong. and Adm. News, p. 978.

§ 430h–11.   Acquisition of property

(a) Pemberton's Headquarters

The Secretary of the Interior is authorized to acquire the properties described in section 430h–10 of this title and subsection (b) of this section by purchase, donation, or exchange, except that each property may only be acquired with the consent of the owner thereof.

(b) Parking

The Secretary is also authorized to acquire not more than one acre of land, or interest therein, adjacent to or near Pemberton's Headquarters for the purpose of providing parking and other facilities related to the operation of Pemberton's Headquarters. Upon the acquisition of the property referenced in this subsection, the Secretary shall add the property to Vicksburg National Military Park and shall modify the boundaries of the park to reflect its inclusion.

(Pub.L. 107–238, § 3, Oct. 11, 2002, 116 Stat. 1486; Pub.L. 108–352, § 15, Oct. 21, 2004, 118 Stat. 1397.)

HISTORICAL AND STATUTORY NOTES

Revision Notes and Legislative Reports
2002 Acts. Senate Report No. 107–183 and Statement by President, see 2002 U.S. Code Cong. and Adm. News, p. 978.
2004 Acts. Senate Report No. 108–239, see 2004 U.S. Code Cong. and Adm. News, p. 1332.

Amendments
2004 Amendments. Subsec. (b). Pub.L. 108–352, § 15, struck out "the Secretary add it" and inserted "the Secretary shall add the property".

LIBRARY REFERENCES

American Digest System
Armed Services ⊕54.

United States ☞55.
Key Number System Topic Nos. 34, 393.

§ 430h–12. Administration

The Secretary shall administer any properties acquired under this Act as part of the Vicksburg National Military Park in accordance with applicable laws and regulations.

(Pub.L. 107–238, § 4, Oct. 11, 2002, 116 Stat. 1486.)

HISTORICAL AND STATUTORY NOTES

Revision Notes and Legislative Reports
  2002 Acts. Senate Report No. 107–183 and Statement by President, see 2002 U.S. Code Cong. and Adm. News, p. 978.

References in Text
  This Act, referred to in text, is the Vicksburg National Military Park Bound-ary Modification Act of 2002, Pub.L. 107–238, Oct. 11, 2002, 116 Stat. 1486, which enacted 16 U.S.C.A. §§ 430h–10 to 430h–13.

LIBRARY REFERENCES

American Digest System
  Armed Services ☞54.
  United States ☞57.
  Key Number System Topic Nos. 34, 393.

§ 430h–13. Authorization of appropriations

There is authorized to be appropriated such sums as may be necessary to carry out sections 430h-10 to 430h-13 of this title.

(Pub.L. 107–238, § 5, Oct. 11, 2002, 116 Stat. 1487.)

HISTORICAL AND STATUTORY NOTES

Revision Notes and Legislative Reports
  2002 Acts. Senate Report No. 107–183 and Statement by President, see 2002 U.S. Code Cong. and Adm. News, p. 978.

§ 430i. Guilford Courthouse National Military Park

In order to preserve for historical and professional military study one of the most memorable battles of the Revolutionary War, the Battlefield of Guilford Courthouse, in the State of North Carolina, containing in the aggregate 125 acres, more or less, together with all privileges and appurtenances thereunto belonging, title to which has heretofore been acquired by the United States, shall be a national military park and shall be known as the Guilford Courthouse National Military Park. The Secretary of the Interior is authorized and directed to acquire at such times and in such manner such additional lands adjacent to the Guilford Courthouse National Military Park as may be necessary for the purposes of the park and for its improvement. It shall be the duty of the Secretary of the Interior, to open or repair such roads as may be necessary to the purposes of the park, and to ascertain and mark with historical tablets or otherwise, as the Secretary of the Interior may determine, all lines of battle of the troops engaged in the Battle of Guilford Courthouse and other historical points of interest pertaining to the battle within the park or its vicinity; and the Secretary of the Interior shall make and enforce all needed regulations for the care of the park. It shall be lawful for any State that had troops engaged in the battle of Guilford Courthouse to enter upon the lands of the Guilford Courthouse National Military Park for the purpose of ascertaining and marking the lines of battle of its troops engaged therein: *Provided*, That before any such lines are permanently designated the position of the lines and the proposed methods of marking them, by monuments, tablets, or otherwise, shall be submitted to and approved by the Secretary of the Interior; and all such lines, designs, and inscriptions for the same shall first receive the written approval of the Secretary of the Interior. If any person shall, except by permission of the Secretary of the Interior, destroy, mutilate, deface, injure, or remove any monument, column, statues, memorial structures, or work of art that shall be erected or placed upon the grounds of the park by lawful authority, or shall destroy or remove any fence, railing, inclosure, or other work for the protection or ornamentation of said park, or any portion thereof, or shall destroy, cut, hack, bark, break down, or otherwise injure any tree, brush, or shrubbery that may be growing upon said park, or shall cut down or fell or remove any timber, battle relic, tree, or trees growing or being upon said park, or hunt within the limits of the park, any person so offending and found guilty thereof before any justice of the peace of the county of Guilford, State of North Carolina, shall, for each and every such offense, forfeit and pay a fine, in the discretion of the justice, according to the aggravation of the offense, of not less than $5 nor more than $50, one-half for the use of the park and the other half to the informer, to be enforced and recovered before such justice in like manner as debts of like nature were on March 2, 1917, by law recoverable in the said county of Guilford, State of North Carolina.

(Mar. 2, 1917, c. 152, 39 Stat. 996; Ex.Ord. No. 6166, § 2, June 10, 1933; Ex.Ord. No. 6228, § 1, July 28, 1933; Sept. 6, 1966, Pub.L. 89–554, § 8(a), 80 Stat. 643.)

HISTORICAL AND STATUTORY NOTES

Amendments

1966　Amendments. Pub.L.　89–554 eliminated provisions which required that the affairs of the park, subject to the supervision and direction of the Secretary of the Interior, be in charge of three commissioners.

Transfer of Functions

Administrative functions of Guilford Courthouse National Military Park were transferred to the Department of the Interior by Ex.Ord. No. 6166, as amended by Ex.Ord. No. 6228, set out as a note under section 901 of Title 5, Government Organization and Employees.

National Park Service was substituted for Office of National Parks, Buildings, and Reservations referred to in Ex.Ord. No. 6166, by Act Mar. 2, 1934, c. 38, § 1, 48 Stat. 389.

Abolishment of Commission

Act Oct. 9, 1942, c. 583, 56 Stat. 778, provided: "That the Guilford Courthouse National Military Park Commission, established pursuant to the Act of March 2, 1917 (39 Stat. 996; 16 U.S.C. 430i), is abolished effective at the expiration, on October 13, 1941, of the current appointment of the resident commissioner."

LIBRARY REFERENCES

American Digest System
Armed Services ⊕54.
Woods and Forests ⊕1, 5, 8, 10, 11.
Key Number System Topic Nos. 34, 411.

§ 430j. Monocacy National Battlefield; establishment

That in order to commemorate the Battle of Monocacy, Maryland, and to preserve for historical purposes the breastworks, earthworks, walls, or other defenses or shelters used by the armies therein, the battlefield at Monocacy in the State of Maryland is hereby established as the Monocacy National Battlefield. The battlefield shall comprise the area within the boundary generally depicted on the map entitled "Monocacy National Battlefield," numbered 894/40,001A, and dated April 1980, which shall be on file and available for public inspection in the Office of the National Park Service, Department of the Interior.

(June 21, 1934, c. 694, § 1, 48 Stat. 1198; Oct. 21, 1976, Pub.L. 94–578, Title III, § 319(1), 90 Stat. 2738; Dec. 28, 1980, Pub.L. 96–607, Title XIV, § 140(a), 94 Stat. 3546.)

HISTORICAL AND STATUTORY NOTES

Amendments

1980 Amendments. Pub.L. 96–607 substituted provision directing that the battlefield be comprised of the area within the boundary generally depicted on the map entitled Monocacy National Battlefield, numbered 894/40,001A, dated April 1980, which map is to be on file and available for public inspection for provision directing that the battlefield be comprised of the area generally depicted on the drawing entitled Boundary, Monocacy National Battlefield, numbered 894–40,000, dated May 1976.

1976 Amendments. Pub.L. 94–578 substituted "is declared a national battlefield to be known as the 'Monocacy National Battlefield' (hereinafter referred to as 'the battlefield'). The battlefield shall comprise the area generally depicted on the drawing entitled 'Boundary Monocacy National Battlefield', numbered 894–40,000 and dated May 1976" for "is declared a national military park to be known as the 'Monocacy National Military Park', whenever the title to the lands deemed necessary by the Secretary of the Interior shall have been acquired by the United States and the usual jurisdiction over the lands and roads of the same shall have been granted to the United States by the State of Maryland."

CROSS REFERENCES

Authority of Secretary of Interior to,
   Accept gifts and contributions, see 16 USCA § 430*o*.
   Lease to immediately preceding owners any lands acquired, see 16 USCA
      § 430*l*.
Authorization of appropriations, see 16 USCA § 430s.

LIBRARY REFERENCES

American Digest System
   Armed Services ☞54.
   Woods and Forests ☞1, 8.
   Key Number System Topic Nos. 34, 411.

§ 430k.   Condemnation proceedings; purchase without condemnation; acceptance of donations of land

The Secretary of the Interior is authorized to cause condemnation proceedings to be instituted in the name of the United States under the provisions of section 3113 of Title 40, to acquire title to the lands, interests therein, or rights pertaining thereto within the said battlefield, and the United States shall be entitled to immediate possession upon the filing of the petition in condemnation in the United States District Court for the District of Maryland: *Provided*, That when the owner of such lands, interests therein, or rights pertaining thereto shall fix a price for the same, which, in the opinion of the Secretary of the Interior, shall be reasonable, the Secretary may purchase the same without further delay: *Provided further*, That the Secretary of the Interior is authorized to accept, on behalf of the United States, donations of lands, interests therein, or rights pertaining thereto required for the battlefield: *And provided further*, That title and evidence of title to lands and interests therein acquired for said battlefield shall be satisfactory to the Secretary of the Interior.

(June 21, 1934, c. 694, § 2, 48 Stat. 1199; Oct. 21, 1976, Pub.L. 94–578, Title III, § 319(2), 90 Stat. 2738.)

HISTORICAL AND STATUTORY NOTES

Codifications

In text, "section 3113 of Title 40" substituted for "sections 257 and 258 of Title 40", which originally read "the Act of August 1, 1888, entitled 'An Act to authorize the condemnation of lands for sites for public buildings and other purposes' (25 Stat.L. 357)" on authority of Pub.L. 107–217, § 5(c), Aug. 21, 2002, 116 Stat. 1301, which is set out as a note preceding 40 U.S.C.A. § 101.   Pub.L. 107–217, § 1, enacted Title 40 into positive law.   The Act of August 1, 1888, is Act, Aug. 1, 1888, c. 728, 25 Stat. 357,

which was classified to former 40 U.S.C.A. §§ 257 and 258, prior to being repealed by Pub.L. 107–217, § 6(b), Aug. 21, 2002, 116 Stat. 1305, and its substance reenacted as 40 U.S.C.A. § 3113. Section 258 of Title 40 was previously omitted from the Code as superseded by Rule 71A, Federal Rules of Civil Procedure, Title 28.

Amendments

1976 Amendments. Pub.L. 94–578 substituted "battlefield" for "Monocacy National Military Park" wherever appearing.

nocacy National Battlefield by Pub. L.
94–578, § 319(1), set out as section 430j
of this title.

CROSS REFERENCES

Authority of Secretary of Interior to,
    Accept gifts and contributions, see 16 USCA § 430o.
    Lease to immediately preceding owners any lands acquired, see 16 USCA
       § 430l.
Authorization of appropriations, see 16 USCA § 430s.

LIBRARY REFERENCES

American Digest System
    Armed Services ⚏54.
    Eminent Domain ⚏5.
    Key Number System Topic Nos. 34, 148.

Research References

Encyclopedias
    Am. Jur. 2d Eminent Domain § 74, Parks, Squares, Playgrounds, and Forest
    Preserves--Condemnation by Federal Government.

§ 430l. Leases with preceding owners of acquired lands; conditions

The Secretary of the Interior is authorized to lease to the immediately preceding owner or owners any lands acquired pursuant to an agreement that such lessee or lessees will occupy such lands in a manner consistent with the purposes of sections 430j to 430m and 430o to 430s of this title and that they will preserve the present breastworks, earthworks, walls, defenses, shelters, buildings, and roads, and the present outlines of the battlefields, and that they will only cut trees or underbrush or disturb or remove the soil, under such regulations as the Secretary of the Interior may prescribe, and that they will assist in protecting all tablets, monuments, or such other artificial works as may from time to time be erected by proper authority.

(June 21, 1934, c. 694, § 3, 48 Stat. 1199; Oct. 21, 1976, Pub.L. 94–578, Title III, § 319(3), 90 Stat. 2738.)

HISTORICAL AND STATUTORY NOTES

Amendments
  1976 Amendments. Pub.L. 94–578 substituted "lease to the immediately preceding owner or owners any lands acquired pursuant to an agreement that such lessee or lessees will occupy such lands in a manner consistent with the purposes of sections 430j to 430m and 430o to 430s, of this title and" for "enter into leases

with the owners of such of the lands, works, defenses, and buildings thereon within the Monocacy National Military Park, as in his discretion it is unnecessary to forthwith acquire title to, and such leases shall be on such terms and conditions as the Secretary of the Interior may prescribe, and may contain options to purchase, subject to later acceptance, if, in the judgment of the Secretary of the Interior, it is as economical to purchase as condemn title to the property: *Provided*, That the Secretary of the Interior may enter into agreements upon such nominal terms as he may prescribe, permitting the present owners or their tenants to occupy or cultivate their present holdings, upon condition".

CROSS REFERENCES

Acceptance of gifts and contributions by Secretary of Interior, see 16 USCA § 430o.
Authorization of appropriations, see 16 USCA § 430s.

LIBRARY REFERENCES

American Digest System
Armed Services ⊕54.
United States ⊕57.
Key Number System Topic Nos. 34, 393.

§ 430m. Administration

The administration, development, preservation, and maintenance of the battlefield shall be exercised by the Secretary of the Interior in accordance with sections 1, 2, 3, and 4 of this title, as amended and supplemented, and sections 461 to 467 of this title.

(June 21, 1934, c. 694, § 4, 48 Stat. 1199;   Oct. 21, 1976, Pub.L. 94–578, Title III, § 319(4), 90 Stat. 2738.)

HISTORICAL AND STATUTORY NOTES

Amendments
1976 Amendments. Pub.L. 94–578 substituted "The administration, development, preservation, and maintenance of the battlefield shall be exercised by the Secretary of the Interior in accordance with sections 1 and 2 to 4 of this title, as amended and supplemented, and sections 461 to 467 of this title" for "The affairs of the Monocacy National Military Park shall, subject to the supervision and direction of the National Park Service of the Interior Department, be in charge of a superintendent, to be appointed by the Secretary of the Interior".

CROSS REFERENCES

Authority of Secretary of Interior to,
    Accept gifts and contributions, see 16 USCA § 430o.
    Lease to immediately preceding owners any lands acquired, see 16 USCA § 430l.
Authorization of appropriations, see 16 USCA § 430s.

LIBRARY REFERENCES

American Digest System
Armed Services ⊕54.
Woods and Forests ⊕5.
Key Number System Topic Nos. 34, 411.

§ 430n.   Repealed. Pub.L. 94–578, Title III, § 319(5), Oct. 21, 1976, 90 Stat. 2738

HISTORICAL AND STATUTORY NOTES

Section, Act June 21, 1934, c. 694, § 5, 48 Stat. 1199, provided for the opening and repair of necessary roads in the bat-tlefield and the erection of historical tablets.

§ 430o.   Gifts and donations; acceptance by Secretary

The Secretary of the Interior,[1] is authorized to receive gifts and contributions from States, Territories, societies, organizations, and individuals for the battlefield for carrying out the provisions of sections 430j to 430m and 430o to 430s of this title.

(June 21, 1934, c. 694, § 6, 48 Stat. 1199; Oct. 21, 1976, Pub.L. 94–578, Title III, § 319(6), 90 Stat. 2738.)

[1] So in original. The comma probably should not appear.

HISTORICAL AND STATUTORY NOTES

Amendments

1976 Amendments. Pub.L. 94–578 substituted "The Secretary of the Interior, is authorized to receive gifts and contributions from States, Territories, societies, organizations, and individuals for the battlefield" for "The National Park Service, acting through the Secretary of the Interior, is authorized to receive gifts and contributions from States, Territories, societies, organizations, and individuals for the Monocacy National Military Park: *Provided,* That all contributions of money received shall be deposited in the Treasury of the United States and credited to a fund to be designated 'Monocacy National Military Park fund', which fund shall be applied to and expended under the direction of the Secretary of the Interior,".

CROSS REFERENCES

Authorization of appropriations, see 16 USCA § 430s.
Leases with immediately preceding owners of acquired lands, see 16 USCA § 430*l*.

LIBRARY REFERENCES

American Digest System
Armed Services ☞54.
United States ☞55.
Key Number System Topic Nos. 34, 393.

§ 430p.   Right of States to enter and mark battle lines

It shall be lawful for the authorities of any State having had troops at the Battle of Monocacy to enter upon the lands and approaches of the battlefield for the purpose of ascertaining and marking the line of battle of troops engaged therein: *Provided,* That before any such lines are permanently designated the position of the lines and the proposed methods of marking them by monuments, tablets, or otherwise, including the design and inscription for the same, shall be submitted to the Secretary of the Interior and shall first receive written approval of the Secretary: *Provided further*, That no discrimination shall be made against any State as to the manner of designating lines, but any grant made to any State by the Secretary of the Interior may be used by any other State.

(June 21, 1934, c. 694, § 7, 48 Stat. 1200; Oct. 21, 1976, Pub.L. 94–578, Title III, § 319(7), 90 Stat. 2738.)

HISTORICAL AND STATUTORY NOTES

Amendments
  1976 Amendments. Pub.L. 94–578 substituted "battlefield" for "Monocacy National Military Park" and ": *Provided further*," for ", which approval shall be based upon formal written reports to be made to him in each case by the National Park Service: *Provided*,".

CROSS REFERENCES

Acceptance of gifts and contributions by Secretary of Interior, see 16 USCA § 430*o*.
Authorization of appropriations, see 16 USCA § 430s.
Leases with immediately preceding owners of acquired lands, see 16 USCA § 430*l*.

LIBRARY REFERENCES

American Digest System
  Armed Services ⊕54.
  Key Number System Topic No. 34.

§ 430q. Offenses

If any person shall, except by permission of the Secretary of the Interior, destroy, mutilate, deface, injure, or remove any monument, column, statue, memorial structure, or work of art that shall be erected or placed upon the grounds of the park by lawful authority, or shall destroy or remove any fence, railing, enclosure, or other work for the protection or ornament of said park, or any portion thereof, or shall destroy, cut, hack, bark, break down, or otherwise injure any tree, bush, or shrubbery that may be growing upon said park, or shall cut down or fell or remove any timber, battle relic, tree or trees growing or being upon said park, or hunt within the limits of the park, or shall remove or destroy any breastworks, earthworks, walls, or other defenses or shelter or any part thereof constructed by the armies formerly engaged in the battles on the lands or approaches to the park, any person so offending and found guilty thereof, before any United States magistrate judge or court, of the jurisdiction in which the offense may be committed, shall for each and every such offense forfeit and pay a fine, in the discretion of the

United States magistrate judge or court, according to the aggravation of the offense.

(June 21, 1934, c. 694, § 8, 48 Stat. 1200; Oct. 17, 1968, Pub.L. 90–578, Title IV, § 402(b)(2), 82 Stat. 1118; Oct. 21, 1976, Pub.L. 94–578, Title III, § 319(8), 90 Stat. 2739; Dec. 1, 1990, Pub.L. 101–650, Title III, § 321, 104 Stat. 5117.)

HISTORICAL AND STATUTORY NOTES

Revision Notes and Legislative Reports

  1968 Acts. House Report No. 1629, see 1968 U.S. Code Cong. and Adm. News, p. 4252.

Amendments

  1976 Amendments. Pub.L. 94–578 struck out provisions which had limited fines to not less than $5 nor more than $500.

Change of Name

  "United States magistrate judge" substituted for "United States magistrate" wherever appearing in text pursuant to section 321 of Pub.L. 101–650, set out as a note under section 631 of Title 28, Judiciary and Judicial Procedure. Previously, "United States magistrate" substituted for "United States commissioner" pursuant to Pub.L. 90–578. See chapter 43 (section 631 et seq.) of Title 28.

  "Magistrate" was substituted for "commissioner" in view of Pub.L. 90–578, Title IV, § 402(b)(2), Oct. 17, 1968, 82 Stat. 1118, which provided that within each district, references in previously enacted statutes and previously promulgated rules and regulations to United States commissioners are to be deemed, within such district, references to United States magistrates duly appointed under section 631 of Title 28, Judiciary and Judicial Procedure. See Applicable Law note under section 631 of Title 28.

LIBRARY REFERENCES

American Digest System
  Armed Services ⚯54.
  Woods and Forests ⚯10, 11.
  Key Number System Topic Nos. 34, 411.

§ 430r. Rules and regulations

The Secretary of the Interior shall have the power to make all needful rules and regulations for the care of the park, and for the establishment and marking of lines of battle and other historical features of the park.

(June 21, 1934, c. 694, § 9, 48 Stat. 1200.)

CROSS REFERENCES

  Acceptance of gifts and contributions, see 16 USCA § 430o.
  Authorization of appropriations, see 16 USCA § 430s.
  Leases with immediately preceding owners of acquired lands, see 16 USCA § 430l.

LIBRARY REFERENCES

American Digest System
  Armed Services ⚯54.
  Woods and Forests ⚯5.
  Key Number System Topic Nos. 34, 411.

§ 430s.   Authorization of appropriations

There are hereby authorized to be appropriated such sums as may be necessary, but not more than $3,525,000 for the acquisition of lands and interests in lands, and not to exceed $500,000 for the development of essential public facilities. Within three years from October 21, 1976, the Secretary shall develop and transmit to the Committees on Interior and Insular Affairs of the United States Congress a final master plan for the full development of the battle-field consistent with the preservation objectives of sections 430j to 430m and 430o to 430s of this title, indicating:

(1) the facilities needed to accommodate the health, safety, and interpretive needs of the visiting public;

(2) the location and estimated cost of all facilities; and

(3) the projected need for any additional facilities within the battlefield.

No funds authorized to be appropriated pursuant to this section shall be available prior to October 1, 1977.

(June 21, 1934, c. 694, § 10, 48 Stat. 1200; Oct. 21, 1976, Pub.L. 94–578, Title III, § 319(9), 90 Stat. 2739.)

HISTORICAL AND STATUTORY NOTES

Amendments
1976 Amendments. Pub.L. 94–578 substituting provisions authorizing appropriations of not more than $3,525,000 for the acquisition of lands and interests in lands, and not to exceed $500,000 for the development of essential public facilities for provisions which had authorized the appropriation of $50,000 to carry out the provisions of sections 430j to 430m and 430o to 430s of this title and added provisions for the development and transmittal within three years from Oct. 21, 1976, of a final master plan for the full development of the battlefield.

Change of Name
Committee on Interior and Insular Affairs of the House of Representatives changed to Committee on Natural Resources of the House of Representatives on Jan. 5, 1993, by House Resolution No. 5, One Hundred Third Congress. Committee on Natural Resources of House of Representatives treated as referring to Committee on Resources of House of

Representatives by section 1(a) of Pub.L. 104–14, set out as a note preceding 2 U.S.C.A. § 21. Committee on Resources of House of Representatives changed to Committee on Natural Resources of House of Representatives by House Resolution No. 6, One Hundred Tenth Congress, Jan. 5, 2007.

Prior Provisions
Section, Act June 21, 1934, c. 694, § 10, 48 Stat. 1200, authorized the appropriation of $50,000 for carrying out provisions of sections 430j to 430s of this title.

Authorization of Appropriations for Additional Land Acquisition
Pub.L. 102–202, Dec. 10, 1991, 105 Stat. 1634, provided that: "There are authorized to be appropriated up to $20,000,000 for acquisition of lands and interests in lands for purposes of the Monocacy National Battlefield, Maryland; such sums shall be in addition to other funds available for such purposes."

§ 430t. Kennesaw Mountain National Battlefield Park; establishment

When title to all the lands, structures, and other property within the military battlefield area and other areas of Civil War interest at and in the vicinity of Kennesaw Mountain in the State of Georgia, as shall be designated by the Secretary of the Interior, in the exercise of his discretion, as necessary or desirable for national battlefield park purposes, shall have been vested in the United States, such areas shall be, and they are, established, dedicated, and set apart as a public park for the benefit and inspiration of the people and shall be known as the "Kennesaw Mountain National Battlefield Park."

(June 26, 1935, c. 315, § 1, 49 Stat. 423.)

LIBRARY REFERENCES

American Digest System
    Armed Services ⚮54.
    Woods and Forests ⚮8.
    Key Number System Topic Nos. 34, 411.

§ 430u. Donations of land; purchase and condemnation

The Secretary of the Interior is authorized to accept donations of land, interests in land, buildings, structures, and other property within the boundaries of said national battlefield park as determined and fixed hereunder, the title and evidence of title to lands purchased to be satisfactory to the Secretary of the Interior: *Provided*, That under such funds available therefor he may acquire on behalf of the United States by purchase when purchasable at prices deemed by him reasonable, otherwise by condemnation under the provisions of section 3113 of Title 40, such tracts of land within the said national battlefield park as may be necessary for the completion thereof.

(June 26, 1935, c. 315, § 2, 49 Stat. 423.)

HISTORICAL AND STATUTORY NOTES

Codifications

In text, "section 3113 of Title 40" substituted for "sections 257 and 258 of Title 40", which originally read "the Act of August 1, 1888" on authority of Pub.L. 107–217, § 5(c), Aug. 21, 2002, 116 Stat. 1301, which is set out as a note preceding 40 U.S.C.A. § 101. Pub.L. 107–217, § 1, enacted Title 40 into positive law. The Act of August 1, 1888, is Act, Aug. 1,

1888, c. 728, 25 Stat. 357, which was classified to former 40 U.S.C.A. §§ 257 and 258, prior to being repealed by Pub.L. 107–217, § 6(b), Aug. 21, 2002, 116 Stat. 1305, and its substance reenacted as 40 U.S.C.A. § 3113. Section 258 of Title 40 was previously omitted from the Code as superseded by Rule 71A, Federal Rules of Civil Procedure, Title 28.

LIBRARY REFERENCES

American Digest System
    Armed Services ⚮54.

United States ⚏55.
Key Number System Topic Nos. 34, 393.

Research References

Encyclopedias
Am. Jur. 2d Eminent Domain § 74, Parks, Squares, Playgrounds, and Forest Preserves--Condemnation by Federal Government.

§ 430v. Monuments and memorials; regulations; historical markers

Upon creation of the national battlefield park the Secretary of the Interior shall—

(a) Allow monuments and memorials to be erected in the park by and to the various organizations and individuals of either the Union or Confederate Armies, subject to the written approval of said Secretary as to the location and character of such monuments and memorials.

(b) Make such regulations as are necessary from time to time for the care and protection of the park. Any person violating such regulations shall be guilty of an offense punishable by a fine of not more than $500, or imprisonment not exceeding six months, or both.

(c) Provide for the ascertainment and marking of the route of march of the Union and Confederate armies from Chattanooga, Tennessee, through Georgia, and of principal battle lines, breastworks, fortifications, and other historical features along such route, and for the maintenance of such markers to such extent as deemed advisable and practicable.

(June 26, 1935, c. 315, § 3, 49 Stat. 423.)

LIBRARY REFERENCES

American Digest System
Armed Services ⚏54.
Woods and Forests ⚏5, 8.
Key Number System Topic Nos. 34, 411.

§ 430w. Administration, protection, and development

The administration, protection, and development of the aforesaid national battlefield park shall be exercised under the direction of the Secretary of the Interior by the National Park Service subject to the provisions of sections 1, 2, 3, and 4 of this title, as amended.

(June 26, 1935, c. 315, § 4, 49 Stat. 424.)

HISTORICAL AND STATUTORY NOTES

Transfer of Functions

All functions of all other officers of the Department of the Interior and all functions of all agencies and employees of such Department were, with two exceptions, transferred to the Secretary of the Interior, with power vested in him to authorize their performance or the performance of any of his functions by any of those such agencies, and employees, by 1950 Reorg. Plan No. 3, §§ 1, 2, eff. May 24, 1950, 15 F.R. 3174, 64 Stat. 1262, set out in Appendix 1 to Title 5, Government Organization and Employees.

LIBRARY REFERENCES

American Digest System
    Armed Services ☞54.
    United States ☞57.
    Woods and Forests ☞5.
    Key Number System Topic Nos. 34, 393, 411.

§ 430x. Authorization of appropriations; authorization to expand boundaries

The sum of $100,000 is authorized to be appropriated out of any sums in the Treasury not otherwise appropriated for the purposes herein designated: *Provided*, That if, after the expenditure of the funds herein authorized, the Secretary of the Interior shall determine that the acquisition of additional lands is necessary in order to perfect the symmetry of the park area or to acquire locations of historic interest adjacent to the park area already acquired upon which fortifications or entrenchments are located which are likely to deteriorate or be destroyed under private ownership, he is authorized to acquire additional lands for such purposes.

(June 26, 1935, c. 315, § 5, 49 Stat. 424; Aug. 9, 1939, c. 614, § 1, 53 Stat. 1274.)

HISTORICAL AND STATUTORY NOTES

References in Text

Herein, referred to in text, means Act June 26, 1935, c. 315, 49 Stat. 423, which is classified to sections 430t to 430x of this title. For complete classification of this Act to the Code, see Tables.

Amendments
1939 Amendments. Act Aug. 9, 1939 added proviso.

Appropriation

Additional $55,000 was authorized to be appropriated by section 2 of Act Aug. 9, 1939.

§ 430y. Spanish War Memorial Park; establishment

When title to such lands located on Davis Island in the city of Tampa, Florida, as shall be designated by the Secretary of the Interior, in the exercise of his judgment and discretion as necessary and suitable for the purpose, shall have been vested in the United States, said area shall be set apart as the Spanish War Memorial

Park, for the benefit and inspiration of the people: *Provided*, That said lands shall be donated without cost to the United States by the city of Tampa, Florida, and the Secretary of the Interior is authorized to accept such conveyance of lands.

(Aug. 20, 1935, c. 575, § 1, 49 Stat. 661.)

LIBRARY REFERENCES

American Digest System
    Armed Services ⬤⇒54.
    Woods and Forests ⬤⇒1, 8.
    Key Number System Topic Nos. 34, 411.

§ 430z. Monument within park; construction authorized

There is authorized to be located and constructed within said memorial park a suitable monument or memorial to commemorate the patriotic services of the American forces in the War with Spain. The cost of establishing such monument or memorial, of constructing suitable sidewalks and approaches, and of landscaping such site, may be paid from any fund or moneys available for such purpose, except from the general fund of the Treasury; and the Secretary is for that purpose further authorized and empowered to determine upon a suitable location, plan, and design for said monument or memorial, by and with the advice of the National Commission of Fine Arts.

(Aug. 20, 1935, c. 575, § 2, 49 Stat. 661.)

LIBRARY REFERENCES

American Digest System
    Armed Services ⬤⇒54.
    United States ⬤⇒56.
    Key Number System Topic Nos. 34, 393.

§ 430z–1. Landscaping park; employment of architects and engineers

In the discharge of his duties hereunder, the Secretary of the Interior, through the National Park Service, is authorized to employ, in his discretion, by contract or otherwise, landscape architects, architects, artists, engineers, and/or other expert consultants in accordance with the usual customs of the several professions and that expenditures for such employment shall be construed to be included in any appropriations hereafter authorized for any work under the objectives of sections 430y to 430z–3 of this title.

(Aug. 20, 1935, c. 575, § 3, 49 Stat. 662.)

HISTORICAL AND STATUTORY NOTES

Codifications

Provisions which authorized employment of landscape architects, architects, artists, engineers, and/or other expert consultants in accordance with the usual customs of the several professions "without reference to civil-service requirements or to the Classification Act of 1923, as amended" were omitted as obsolete. Such employment is subject to the civil service laws unless specifically excepted by those laws or by laws enacted subsequent to Ex.Ord. No. 8743, Apr. 23, 1941, issued by the President pursuant to the Act of Nov. 26, 1940, c. 919, Title I, § 1, 54 Stat. 1211, which covered most excepted positions into the classified (competitive) civil service. The Order is set out as a note under section 3301 of Title 5, Government Organization and Employees.

As to the compensation of such personnel, sections 1202 and 1204 of the Classification Act of 1949, 63 Stat. 972, 973, repealed the Classification Act of 1923 and all other laws or parts of laws inconsistent with the 1949 Act. The Classification Act of 1949 was repealed by Pub.L. 89–554, Sept. 6, 1966, § 8(a), 80 Stat. 632, and reenacted as chapter 51 and subchapter III of chapter 53 of Title 5. Section 5102 of Title 5 contains the applicability provisions of the 1949 Act, and section 5103 of Title 5 authorizes the Office of Personnel Management to determine the applicability to specific positions and employees.

Transfer of Functions

All functions of all other officers of the Department of the Interior and all functions of all agencies and employees of such Department were, with two exceptions, transferred to the Secretary of the Interior, with power vested in him to authorize their performance or the performance of any of his functions by any of such officers, agencies, and employees, by 1950 Reorg. Plan No. 3, §§ 1, 2, eff. May 24, 1950, 15 F.R. 3174, 64 Stat. 1262, set out in Appendix 1 to Title 5, Government Organization and Employees.

LIBRARY REFERENCES

American Digest System
   Armed Services ⚵54.
   United States ⚵57.
   Woods and Forests ⚵5.
   Key Number System Topic Nos. 34, 393, 411.

§ 430z–2. Memorials within park; erection authorized

The Secretary of the Interior is further authorized, by and with the advice of the National Commission of Fine Arts, to authorize and permit the erection in said memorial park of suitable memorials in harmony with the monument and/or memorial herein authorized that may be desired to be constructed by Spanish War organizations, States, and/or foreign governments: *Provided*, That the design and location of such memorials must be approved by the Secretary of the Interior, by and with the advice of the National Commission of Fine Arts, before construction is undertaken.

(Aug. 20, 1935, c. 575, § 4, 49 Stat. 662.)

LIBRARY REFERENCES

American Digest System
   Armed Services ⚵54.
   United States ⚵56.
   Woods and Forests ⚵8.
   Key Number System Topic Nos. 34, 393, 411.

§ 430z–3.   Administration, protection, and development

The administration, protection, and development of the aforesaid Spanish War Memorial Park, including any and all memorials that may be erected thereon, shall be exercised under the direction of the Secretary of the Interior by the National Park Service.

(Aug. 20, 1935, c. 575, § 5, 49 Stat. 662.)

HISTORICAL AND STATUTORY NOTES

Transfer of Functions

All functions of all other officers of the Department of the Interior and all functions of all agencies and employees of such Department were, with two exceptions, transferred to the Secretary of the Interior, with power vested in him to authorize their performance or the performance of any of his functions by any of such officers, agencies, and employees, by 1950 Reorg. Plan No. 3, §§ 1, 2, eff. May 24, 1950, 15 F.R. 3174, 64 Stat. 1262, set out in Appendix 1 to Title 5, Government Organization and Employees.

LIBRARY REFERENCES

American Digest System

  Armed Services ⬥54.
  Woods and Forests ⬥5.
  Key Number System Topic Nos. 34, 411.

§ 430aa.   Pea Ridge National Military Park;   establishment

When not less than one thousand two hundred acres of the non-Federal lands hereinafter described (together with improvements thereon) and known as the Pea Ridge Battlefield, near Bentonville, Arkansas, shall have been acquired and transferred free and clear of all encumbrances to the United States without expense to the Federal Government, such areas shall be, and are hereby, dedicated and set apart as a unit of the National Park System for the benefit and enjoyment of the people of the United States, under the name of the Pea Ridge National Military Park.

(July 20, 1956, c. 653, § 1, 70 Stat. 592.)

HISTORICAL AND STATUTORY NOTES

Revision Notes and Legislative Reports

  1956 Acts. Senate Report No. 2514, see 1956 U.S. Code Cong. and Adm. News, p. 3394.

LIBRARY REFERENCES

American Digest System

  Armed Services ⬥54.
  Woods and Forests ⬥1, 8.
  Key Number System Topic Nos. 34, 411.

§ 430bb. Determination of desirable areas

The Secretary of the Interior is authorized and directed to make an examination of the Pea Ridge Battlefield with a view to determining the area or areas thereof deemed desirable for inclusion in the Pea Ridge National Military Park and which—except for not more than twenty acres of any other lands adjacent to such battlefield found by the Secretary to be necessary to carry out the provisions of sections 430aa to 430ee of this title—lie within the lands particularly described as follows: sections 17, 18, 19, 20, 29, 30, 31, 32, and 33, all township 21 north, range 28 west, Fifth principal meridian; sections 4, 5, 6, 7, and 8, all township 20 north, range 28 west, Fifth principal meridian; sections 13, 14, 20, 21, 22, 23, 24, 25, 26, 27, 28, 29, 31, 32, 33, 34, 35, and 36, all township 21 north, range 29 west, Fifth principal meridian; and sections 1, 2, 3, 4, 5, 6, 7, 8, 9, 10, 11, and 12, all township 20 north, range 29 west, Fifth principal meridian.

(July 20, 1956, c. 653, § 2, 70 Stat. 592.)

HISTORICAL AND STATUTORY NOTES

Revision Notes and Legislative Reports
 1956 Acts. Senate Report No. 2514, see 1956 U.S. Code Cong. and Adm. News, p. 3394.

LIBRARY REFERENCES

American Digest System
 Armed Services ☜54.
 Woods and Forests ☜1.
 Key Number System Topic Nos. 34, 411.

§ 430cc. Administration, protection, and development; improvements

(a) The National Park Service under the direction of the Secretary of the Interior, shall administer, protect, and develop the park, subject to the provisions of sections 1, 2, 3, and 4 of this title, as amended.

(b) In order to provide for the proper development and maintenance of the park, the Secretary of the Interior shall construct and maintain therein such roads, trails, markers, buildings, and other improvements, and such facilities for the care and accommodation of visitors, as he may deem necessary.

(July 20, 1956, c. 653, § 3, 70 Stat. 593.)

HISTORICAL AND STATUTORY NOTES

Revision Notes and Legislative Reports
  1956 Acts. Senate Report No. 2514,
see 1956 U.S. Code Cong. and Adm.
News, p. 3394.

LIBRARY REFERENCES

American Digest System
  Armed Services ⊂54.
  Woods and Forests ⊂5.
  Key Number System Topic Nos. 34, 411.

§ 430dd. Dedication

Sections 430aa to 430ee of this title shall become effective if and when the requirements of sections 430aa and 430bb of this title shall have been fully complied with to the satisfaction of the President of the United States, who shall then issue a notice declaring that the requirements herein have been met, and said notice shall formally dedicate and set aside the areas transferred to the United States in accordance with the provisions of section 430aa of this title.

(July 20, 1956, c. 653, § 4, 70 Stat. 593.)

HISTORICAL AND STATUTORY NOTES

Revision Notes and Legislative Reports
  1956 Acts. Senate Report No. 2514,
see 1956 U.S. Code Cong. and Adm.
News, p. 3394.

LIBRARY REFERENCES

American Digest System
  Armed Services ⊂54.
  Key Number System Topic No. 34.

§ 430ee. Authorization of appropriations

There are authorized to be appropriated such sums as may be necessary to carry out the provisions of sections 430aa to 430ee of this title.

(July 20, 1956, c. 653, § 5, 70 Stat. 593.)

HISTORICAL AND STATUTORY NOTES

Revision Notes and Legislative Reports
  1956 Acts. Senate Report No. 2514,
see 1956 U.S. Code Cong. and Adm.
News, p. 3394.

§ 430ff.   Horseshoe Bend National Military Park;   establishment

When not less than five hundred acres of the non-Federal lands hereinafter described (together with improvements thereon) and known as the Horseshoe Bend Battle Ground on the Tallapoosa River, in the State of Alabama, shall have been acquired and transferred free and clear of all encumbrances to the United States without expense to the Federal Government, such areas shall be, and are hereby, dedicated and set apart as a unit of the National Park System for the benefit and enjoyment of the people of the United States, under the name of the Horseshoe Bend National Military Park.

(July 25, 1956, c. 729, § 1, 70 Stat. 651.)

HISTORICAL AND STATUTORY NOTES

Revision Notes and Legislative Reports
 1956 Acts. Senate Report No. 2515, see 1956 U.S. Code Cong. and Adm. News, p. 3528.

LIBRARY REFERENCES

American Digest System
  Armed Services ⟞54.
  Woods and Forests ⟞1, 8.
  Key Number System Topic Nos. 34, 411.

§ 430gg.   Determination of desirable areas

The Secretary of the Interior is authorized and directed to make an examination of the Horseshoe Bend Battle Ground with a view to determining the area or areas thereof deemed desirable for inclusion in the Horseshoe Bend National Military Park and which, except for not more than twenty acres of any other lands adjacent to such battleground found by the Secretary to be necessary to carry out the provisions of sections 430ff to 430jj of this title, lie within the lands particularly described as follows: Sections 13, 14, 15, 22, and 23, all township 23 north, range 23 east, Saint Stephens meridian.

(July 25, 1956, c. 729, § 2, 70 Stat. 651.)

HISTORICAL AND STATUTORY NOTES

Revision Notes and Legislative Reports
 1956 Acts. Senate Report No. 2515, see 1956 U.S. Code Cong. and Adm. News, p. 3528.

LIBRARY REFERENCES

American Digest System
  Armed Services ⟞54.

Woods and Forests ⚭1.
Key Number System Topic Nos. 34, 411.

§ 430hh. Administration, protection, and development; improvements

(a) The National Park Service, under the direction of the Secretary of the Interior, shall administer, protect, and develop the park, subject to the provisions of sections 1, 2, 3, and 4 of this title, as amended.

(b) In order to provide for the proper development and maintenance of the park, the Secretary of the Interior shall construct and maintain therein such roads, trails, markers, buildings, and other improvements, and such facilities for the care and accommodation of visitors, as he may deem necessary.

(July 25, 1956, c. 729, § 3, 70 Stat. 651.)

HISTORICAL AND STATUTORY NOTES

Revision Notes and Legislative Reports
  1956 Acts. Senate Report No. 2515,
see 1956 U.S. Code Cong. and Adm.
News, p. 3528.

LIBRARY REFERENCES

American Digest System
  Armed Services ⚭54.
  Woods and Forests ⚭5.
  Key Number System Topic Nos. 34, 411.

§ 430ii. Dedication

Sections 430ff to 430jj of this title shall become effective if and when the requirements of sections 430ff and 430gg of this title shall have been fully complied with to the satisfaction of the President of the United States, who shall then issue a notice declaring that the requirements herein have been met, and said notice shall formally dedicate and set aside the areas transferred to the United States in accordance with the provisions of section 430ff of this title.

(July 25, 1956, c. 729, § 4, 70 Stat. 651.)

HISTORICAL AND STATUTORY NOTES

Revision Notes and Legislative Reports
  1956 Acts. Senate Report No. 2515,
see 1956 U.S. Code Cong. and Adm.
News, p. 3528.

PROCLAMATIONS
PROCLAMATION NO. 3308
Aug. 11, 1959, 24 F.R. 6607
ESTABLISHMENT OF PARK

WHEREAS the battle of Horseshoe Bend, fought on March 27, 1814, on the Tallapoosa River in Alabama, resulted in a decisive victory for the forces of General Andrew Jackson over a strong body of Creek Indians and broke the power of the Creek Confederacy; and

WHEREAS this significant historic event on the Indian border opened the way for settlement in Alabama and other parts of the old Southwest; and

WHEREAS section 1 of an act approved July 25, 1956 (70 Stat. 651) [section 430ff of this title], provides that when not less than five hundred acres of non-Federal lands (together with improvements thereon), known as the Horseshoe Bend Battle Ground, shall have been acquired and transferred free and clear of all encumbrances to the United States without expense to the Federal Government, such area shall be dedicated and set apart as the Horseshoe Bend National Military Park; and

WHEREAS section 2 of that act [section 430gg of this title] authorizes and directs the Secretary of the Interior to make an examination of the Horseshoe Bend Battle Ground with a view to determining the area or areas thereof deemed desirable for inclusion in the Horseshoe Bend National Military Park; and

WHEREAS the Secretary of the Interior on June 11, 1957, approved a map showing an area of 2,040 acres on the Horseshoe Bend Battle Ground as being desirable for inclusion in the Horseshoe Bend National Military Park, and such land was donated to, and accepted on behalf of, the United States of America on April 24, 1959; and

WHEREAS the requirements of sections 1 and 2 of the act of July 25, 1956 (70 Stat. 651) [sections 430ff and 430gg of this title], have been fully complied with:

NOW, THEREFORE, I, DWIGHT D. EISENHOWER, President of the United States of America, by virtue of the authority vested in me by section 4 of the abovementioned act of July 25, 1956 [this section], do hereby dedicate and set aside the following-described lands in Tallapoosa County, Alabama, as the Horseshoe Bend National Military Park:

Northeast quarter (NE¼), northeast quarter of northwest quarter (NE¼ of NW ¼), northeast quarter of southeast quarter (NE¼ of SE¼), fractions A, B, C and E of section 15; fractions B, D, and E of section 22; all in township 23 north, range 23 east; also one-half acre known as the Ferry Landing on the south side of the Tallapoosa River in said section 15, more particularly described as follows: Commence at the southwest corner of section 15, township 23 north, range 23 east, Tallapoosa County, Alabama; thence south 89 degrees 00 minutes east 1968 feet to a point; thence north 1 degree 00 minutes west 1267 feet to a point on the southerly bank of the Tallapoosa River and the point of beginning of the parcel herein intended to be described; thence south 52 degrees 00 minutes west 147.6 feet to a point; thence north 38 degrees 00 minutes west 147.6 feet to a point; thence north 52 degrees 00 minutes east 147.6 feet to a point on the southerly bank of the said river; thence upstream along the southerly bank of the river south 38 degrees 00 minutes east 147.6 feet to the point of beginning, and being situated in the east half of the southwest quarter of section 15, township 23 north, range 23 east, Tallapoosa County, Alabama; also a parcel of land known as Miller's Island in the Tallapoosa River just south of the river bridge more particularly described as follows: Commencing at the southwest corner of said section 15, township 23 north, range 23 east, Tallapoosa County, Alabama; thence south 89 degrees 00 minutes east 2605 feet to a point on the west bank of said island, which is the point of beginning; thence north 5 degrees 00 minutes east 220 feet to a point; thence north 8 degrees 00 minutes west 510 feet to a point; thence north 82 degrees 00 minutes east 350 feet to a point; thence north 55 degrees 30 minutes east 75 feet to a point; thence north 82 degrees 00 minutes east

115 feet to a point; thence south 17 degrees 00 minutes east 330 feet to a point; thence south 8 degrees 00 minutes east 270 feet to a point; thence south 77 degrees 45 minutes west 270 feet to a point; thence south 59 degrees 35 minutes west 160 feet to a point; thence south 36 degrees 06 minutes west 650 feet to a point; thence north 5 degrees 00 minutes east 530 feet to the point of beginning, containing 14.11 acres, more or less, and being situated in sections 15 and 22, township 23 north, range 23 east, Tallapoosa County, Alabama. Less and except 5.1 acres in said section 15, township 23 north, range 23 east, previously conveyed by Nora E. Miller to Horseshoe Bend Battle Park Commission, described as follows: Beginning at a point which is 13 chains and 51 links south 75 degrees 30 minutes west of a point on the west line of section 14, township 23 north, range 23 east, which is 69 chains south of the northwest corner of said section 14; thence west 8 chains and 50 links, thence south 6 chains, thence east 8 chains and 50 links thence north 6 chains to the point of beginning.

The above described lands contain 560.66 acres, more or less.

Section 14, township 23 north, range 23 east; west half of northwest quarter and northeast quarter of northwest quarter of section 23, township 23 north, range 23 east; section 15 and section 22, township 23 north, range 23 east, less and except the following described parts of said sections 15 and 22, township 23 north, range 23 east, known as Alabama Power Company lands, described as follows: Northeast quarter (NE¼), northeast quarter of northwest quarter (NE¼ of NW ¼), northeast quarter of southeast quarter (NE¼ of SE¼), fractions A, B, C and E of section 15; fractions B, D, and E of section 22; all in township 23 north, range 23 east; also one-half acre known as the Ferry Landing on the south side of the Tallapoosa River in section 15, more particularly described as follows: Commence at the southwest corner of section 15, township 23 north, range 23 east, Tallapoosa County, Alabama; thence south 89 degrees 00 minutes east 1968 feet to a point; thence north 1 degree 00 minutes west 1267 feet to a point on the southerly bank of the Tallapoosa River and the point of beginning of the parcel herein intended to be described; thence south 52 degrees 00 minutes west 147.6

feet to a point; thence north 38 degrees 00 minutes west 147.6 feet to a point; thence north 52 degrees 00 minutes east 147.6 feet to a point on the southerly bank of said river; thence upstream along the southerly bank of the river south 38 degrees 00 minutes east 147.6 feet to the point of beginning, and being situated in the east half of the southwest quarter of section 15, township 23 north, range 23 east, Tallapoosa County, Alabama; also a parcel of land known as Miller's Island in the Tallapoosa River just south of the river bridge more particularly described as follows: Commencing at the southwest corner of said section 15, township 23 north, range 23 east, Tallapoosa County, Alabama; thence south 89 degrees 00 minutes east 2605 feet to a point on the west bank of said island, which is the point of beginning; thence north 5 degrees 00 minutes east 220 feet to a point; thence north 8 degrees 00 minutes west 510 feet to a point; thence north 82 degrees 00 minutes east 350 feet to a point; thence north 55 degrees 30 minutes east 75 feet to a point; thence north 82 degrees 00 minutes east 115 feet to a point; thence south 17 degrees 00 minutes east 330 feet to a point; thence south 8 degrees 00 minutes east 270 feet to a point; thence south 77 degrees 45 minutes west 270 feet to a point; thence south 59 degrees 35 minutes west 160 feet to a point; thence south 36 degrees 06 minutes west 650 feet to a point; thence north 5 degrees 00 minutes east 530 feet to the point of beginning, containing 14.11 acres, more or less, and being situated in sections 15 and 22, township 23 north, range 23 east, Tallapoosa County, Alabama. Less and except 5.1 acres in said section 15, township 23 north, range 23 east, previously conveyed by Nora E. Miller to Horseshoe Bend Battle Park Commission, described as follows: Beginning at a point which is 13 chains and 51 links south 75 degrees 30 minutes west of a point on the west line of section 14, township 23 north, range 23 east, which is 69 chains south of the northwest corner of said section 14; thence west 8 chains and 50 links, thence south 6 chains, thence east 8 chains and 50 links, thence north 6 chains to the point of beginning. Said 5.1-acre exception in said section 15 has heretofore been conveyed to the United States of America by patent from the State of Alabama.

The above-described lands contain 1,474.24 acres, more or less.

Beginning at a point which is 13 chains and 51 links south 75 degrees 30 minutes west of a point on the west line of section 14 which is 69 chains south of the northwest corner of section 14, thence west 8 chains and 50 links, thence south 6 chains, thence east 8 chains and 50 links, thence north 6 chains to the point of beginning, the said land lying and being in section 15, township 23 north, range 23 east.

The above-described lands contain 5.1 acres, more or less.

IN WITNESS WHEREOF, I have hereunto set my hand and caused the Seal of the United States of America to be affixed.

DONE at the City of Washington this eleventh day of August in the year of our Lord nineteen hundred and fifty-nine, and of the Independence of the United States of America the one hundred and eighty-fourth.

[SEAL] DWIGHT D. EISENHOWER

LIBRARY REFERENCES

American Digest System
 Armed Services ☞54.
 Woods and Forests ☞1.
 Key Number System Topic Nos. 34, 411.

§ 430jj. Authorization of appropriations

There are authorized to be appropriated such sums as may be necessary to carry out the provisions of sections 430ff to 430jj of this title.

(July 25, 1956, c. 729, § 5, 70 Stat. 651.)

HISTORICAL AND STATUTORY NOTES

Revision Notes and Legislative Reports
 1956 Acts. Senate Report No. 2515, see 1956 U.S. Code Cong. and Adm. News, p. 3528.

§ 430kk. Wilson's Creek National Battlefield: establishment and acquisition of lands

(a) Establishment, initial boundaries

The Secretary of the Interior shall acquire, by gift, purchase, condemnation, or otherwise, the lands (together with any improvements thereon) comprising the Wilson's Creek Battlefield site near Springfield, Missouri, and any other lands adjacent to such site which in his opinion are necessary or desirable to carry out the purposes of sections 430kk to 430mm of this title.

(b) Expansion of boundaries

(1) The boundaries of the Wilson's Creek National Battlefield are revised to include lands and interests therein consisting of six parcels totaling 615 acres and identified as parcels "1, 2, 3, 4, 5, and 6" on the map entitled "Wilson's Creek National Battlefield Proposed

Boundary'', numbered 410/80,037 and dated January 27, 2004.   The map shall be on file and available for public inspection in the appropriate offices of the National Park Service.

(2) The Secretary is authorized to acquire the lands referred to in paragraph (1) by donation, by purchase from willing sellers with donated or appropriated funds, or by exchange.   The Secretary may acquire by the same methods personal property associated with, and appropriate for, interpretation of the park.

(c) Access to private property

Nothing in sections 430kk to 430mm of this title shall be construed to—

> **(1)** require any private property owner to allow public access (including Federal, State, or local government access) to such private property; or

> **(2)** modify any provision of Federal, State, or local law with regard to public access to or use of private property.

(d) Liability

The revision of the boundaries of the Wilson's Creek National Battlefield by subsection (b) of this section shall not be considered to create any liability for, or to have any effect on any liability under any other law of, any owner of private property with respect to any person injured on that private property.

(e) Recognition of authority to control land use

Nothing in sections 430kk to 430mm of this title shall be construed to modify the authority of Federal, State, or local governments to regulate land use.

(f) Participation of private property owners

Nothing in sections 430kk to 430mm of this title shall be construed to require the owner of any private property located within the boundaries of the Wilson's Creek National Battlefield to participate in, or be associated with, the National Battlefield.

(g) Effect of expansion

The boundaries of the Wilson's Creek National Battlefield, as revised by subsection (b) of this section, represent the area within which Federal funds appropriated for the purpose of sections 430kk to 430mm of this title may be expended.   The boundary revision shall not be construed to provide any nonexisting regulatory authority on

219

land use within the National Battlefield or its viewshed by the Secretary or the National Park Service.

(Pub.L. 86–434, § 1, Apr. 22, 1960, 74 Stat. 76; Pub.L. 108–394, § 2(a), Oct. 30, 2004, 118 Stat. 2247.)

HISTORICAL AND STATUTORY NOTES

Revision Notes and Legislative Reports
  1960 Acts. Senate Report No. 1213, see 1960 U.S. Code Cong. and Adm. News, p. 1892.
  2004 Acts. House Report No. 108–651, see 2004 U.S. Code Cong. and Adm. News, p. 2273.

References in Text
  Sections 430kk to 430mm of this title, referred to in text, originally read "this Act", meaning Pub.L. 86–434, Apr. 22, 1960, 74 Stat. 76, which enacted 16 U.S.C.A. §§ 430kk to 430mm.

Amendments
  2004 Amendments. Subsec. (a). Pub.L. 108–394, § 2(a)(1), struck out

"That the Secretary" and inserted "Wilson's Creek National Battlefield: establishment and acquisition of lands" and "(a) Establishment, initial boundaries— The Secretary".

  Subsecs. (b) to (g). Pub.L. 108–394, § 2(a)(2), added subsecs. (b) to (g).

Short Title
  2004 Acts. Pub.L. 108–394, § 1, Oct. 30, 2004, 118 Stat. 2247, provided that: "This Act [amending this section and 16 U.S.C.A. § 430mm] may be cited as the 'Wilson's Creek National Battlefield Boundary Adjustment Act of 2004'."

LIBRARY REFERENCES

American Digest System
  Armed Services ⚲54.
  United States ⚲55.
  Woods and Forests ⚲1, 8.
  Key Number System Topic Nos. 34, 393, 411.

§ 430*ll*.   Designation

(a) Administration, protection, and development

The lands acquired under section 430kk of this title shall be set aside as a public park for the benefit and enjoyment of the people of the United States, and shall be designated as the Wilson's Creek National Battlefield. The National Park Service, under the direction of the Secretary of the Interior, shall administer, protect, and develop the park, subject to the provisions of sections 1, 2, 3, and 4 of this title.

(b) Improvements

In order to provide for the proper development and maintenance of the park, the Secretary of the Interior shall construct and maintain therein such roads, trails, markers, buildings, and other improvements, and such facilities for the care and accommodation of visitors, as he may deem necessary.

(Pub.L. 86–434, § 2, Apr. 22, 1960, 74 Stat. 76; Pub.L. 91–554, § 1(a), Dec. 16, 1970, 84 Stat. 1441.)

HISTORICAL AND STATUTORY NOTES

Revision Notes and Legislative Reports
   1960 Acts. Senate Report No. 1213, see 1960 U.S. Code Cong. and Adm. News, p. 1892.

Amendments
   1970 Amendments. Pub.L. 91–554 substituted "Wilson's Creek National Battle-field" for "Wilson's Creek Battlefield National Park".

LIBRARY REFERENCES

American Digest System
   Armed Services ☞54.
   Woods and Forests ☞5.
   Key Number System Topic Nos. 34, 411.

§ 430mm. Authorization of appropriations

For development of the Wilson's Creek National Battlefield, there are authorized to be appropriated not more than $5,640,000. There are authorized to be appropriated such sums as may be necessary to carry out section 430kk(b) of this title.

(Pub.L. 86–434, § 3, Apr. 22, 1960, 74 Stat. 76; Pub.L. 91–554, § 1(b), Dec. 16, 1970, 84 Stat. 1441; Pub.L. 95–625, Title I, § 101(29), Nov. 10, 1978, 92 Stat. 3472; Pub.L. 108–394, § 2(b), Oct. 30, 2004, 118 Stat. 2248.)

HISTORICAL AND STATUTORY NOTES

Revision Notes and Legislative Reports
   1960 Acts. Senate Report No. 1213, see 1960 U.S. Code Cong. and Adm. News, p. 1892.

   2004 Acts. House Report No. 108–651, see 2004 U.S. Code Cong. and Adm. News, p. 2273.

Amendments
   2004 Amendments. Pub.L. 108–394, § 2(b), added at the end the following new sentence: "There are authorized to be appropriated such sums as may be necessary to carry out section 430kk(b) of this title.".

   1978 Amendments. Pub.L. 95–625 substituted "$5,640,000." for "$2,285,000 (March 1969 prices), plus or minus such amounts, if any, as may be justified by reason of ordinary fluctuations in construction cost indices applicable to the types of construction involved herein."

   1970 Amendments. Pub.L. 91–554 increased the authorization of appropriations from not more than $120,000 to not more than $2,285,000 (March 1969 prices), plus or minus such amounts, if any, as may be justified by reason of ordinary fluctuations in construction costs as indicated by engineering cost indices.

§ 430nn. Antietam Battlefield site; acquisition of lands, buildings, structures, and other property

The Secretary of the Interior is authorized, in his discretion, to acquire in behalf of the United States, through donations or by purchase at prices deemed by him reasonable or by condemnation in accordance with section 3113 of Title 40, lands, buildings, structures, and other property, or interests therein, which he may determine to be of historical interest in connection with the Antietam Battlefield site, the title to such property or interests to be satisfactory to the Secretary of the Interior: *Provided*, That payment for such property or interests shall be made solely from donated funds. All such property and interests shall be a part of the Antietam Battlefield site and shall be subject to all laws and regulations applicable thereto.

(May 14, 1940, c. 191, 54 Stat. 212.)

HISTORICAL AND STATUTORY NOTES

Codifications

In text, "section 3113 of Title 40" substituted for "sections 257 and 258 of Title 40", which originally read "the Act of August 1, 1888 (25 Stat. 357)" on authority of Pub.L. 107–217, § 5(c), Aug. 21, 2002, 116 Stat. 1301, which is set out as a note preceding 40 U.S.C.A. § 101. Pub.L. 107–217, § 1, enacted Title 40 into positive law. The Act of August 1, 1888, is Act, Aug. 1, 1888, c. 728, 25 Stat. 357, which was classified to former 40 U.S.C.A. §§ 257 and 258, prior to being repealed by Pub.L. 107–217, § 6(b), Aug. 21, 2002, 116 Stat. 1305, and its substance reenacted as 40 U.S.C.A. § 3113. Section 258 of Title 40 was previously omitted from the Code as superseded by Rule 71A, Federal Rules of Civil Procedure, Title 28.

Antietam National Battlefield Site Redesignated as Antietam National Battlefield; Boundary Revision

Pub.L. 95–625, Title III, § 319(b), Nov. 10, 1978, 92 Stat. 3488, as amended Pub.L. 100–528, § 1(c), Oct. 25, 1988, 102 Stat. 2649, provided that: "The Antietam National Battlefield Site established pursuant to such Act of April 22, 1960 [section 430oo of this title] is hereby redesignated the 'Antietam National Battlefield'. The boundaries of such battlefield are hereby revised to include the area generally depicted on the map referenced in subsection (a) of this section [set out as a note under section 430oo of this title], which shall be on file and available for public inspection in the offices of the National Park Service, Department of the Interior."

LIBRARY REFERENCES

American Digest System

Armed Services ⚬54.
United States ⚬55.
Woods and Forests ⚬8.
Key Number System Topic Nos. 34, 393, 411.

§ 430oo. Acquisition of lands for preservation, protection and improvement; limitation

The Secretary of the Interior is authorized to acquire such lands and interests in land and to enter into such agreements with the owners of land on behalf of themselves, their heirs and assigns with respect to the use thereof as the Secretary finds necessary to preserve, protect and improve the Antietam Battlefield comprising approximately 1,800 acres in the State of Maryland and the property of the United States thereon, to assure the public a full and unimpeded view thereof, and to provide for the maintenance of the site (other than those portions thereof which are occupied by public buildings and monuments and the Antietam National Cemetery) in, or its restoration to, substantially the condition in which it was at the time of the battle of Antietam.   Any acquisition authorized by this section may be made without regard to the limitation set forth in the proviso contained in section 430nn of this title.

(Pub.L. 86–438, Apr. 22, 1960, 74 Stat. 79; Pub.L. 93–608, § 1(11), Jan. 2, 1975, 88 Stat. 1969; Pub.L. 100–528, § 1(a), Oct. 25, 1988, 102 Stat. 2649.)

HISTORICAL AND STATUTORY NOTES

Revision Notes and Legislative Reports
   1975 Acts. Senate Report No. 93–1332, see 1974 U.S. Code Cong. and Adm. News, p. 7159.

Amendments
   1988 Amendments. Pub.L. 100–528 struck out provision limiting acquisition by purchase or condemnation to 600 acres, with exception for acquisition and immediate reconveyance with covenants as will accomplish purposes of this section, with proviso relating to cost.
   1975 Amendments. Pub.L. 93–608 struck out requirement that Secretary report to Congress at least once each year on any acquisition made or agreement entered into under provisions of this section.

Scenic Easements; Acquisition
   Pub.L. 95–625, Title III, § 319(a), Nov. 10, 1978, 92 Stat. 3488, as amended Pub.L. 100–528, § 1(b), Oct. 25, 1988, 102 Stat. 2649, provided that: "In furtherance of the purposes of the Act entitled 'An Act to provide for the protection and preservation of the Antietam Battlefield in the State of Maryland', approved April 22, 1960 (74 Stat. 79) [this section], and other Acts relative thereto [see section 430nn of this title], the Secretary is hereby authorized to acquire the additional lands generally depicted on the map entitled 'Boundary Map, Antietam National Battlefield, Washington County, Maryland,' numbered 302–80.005–A and dated June 1977."

LIBRARY REFERENCES

American Digest System
   Armed Services ⚭54.
   United States ⚭55.
   Key Number System Topic Nos. 34, 393.

§ 430pp. Fort Necessity National Battlefield; acquisition of land

In furtherance of the purposes of the Act of March 4, 1931 (46 Stat. 1522), the Secretary of the Interior is authorized to acquire by purchase, exchange, donation, with donated funds or otherwise by such means as he may deem to be in the public interest, lands and interests in lands adjoining or near the Fort Necessity National Battlefield site which in his discretion are necessary to preserve the historic battleground, together with not to exceed 25 acres at the detached Braddock Monument: *Provided*, That the total area acquired pursuant to sections 430pp to 430tt of this title shall not exceed 500 acres, except that in order to avoid the undesirable severance of parcels in private ownership such parcels may be purchased in the entirety.

(Pub.L. 87–134, § 1, Aug. 10, 1961, 75 Stat. 336.)

HISTORICAL AND STATUTORY NOTES

References in Text
Act of March 4, 1931 (46 Stat. 1522),
referred to in text, was not classified to
the Code.

LIBRARY REFERENCES

American Digest System
Armed Services ⚏54.
United States ⚏55.
Key Number System Topic Nos. 34, 393.

§ 430qq.   Exchange of lands

The Secretary of the Interior, in order to implement the purposes of section 430pp of this title, is authorized to exchange lands which may be acquired pursuant to sections 430pp to 430tt of this title for other lands or interests therein of approximately equal value lying within the original George Washington land patent at Fort Necessity.

(Pub.L. 87–134, § 2, Aug. 10, 1961, 75 Stat. 336.)

LIBRARY REFERENCES

American Digest System
Armed Services ⚏54.
Woods and Forests ⚏4.
Key Number System Topic Nos. 34, 411.

§ 430rr.   Change in name to Fort Necessity National Battlefield

The Fort Necessity National Battlefield site is redesignated as the Fort Necessity National Battlefield and any remaining balance of funds appropriated for the purposes of the site shall be available for the purposes of the Fort Necessity National Battlefield.

(Pub.L. 87–134, § 3, Aug. 10, 1961, 75 Stat. 336.)

LIBRARY REFERENCES

American Digest System
Armed Services ⚏54.
Woods and Forests ⚏1.
Key Number System Topic Nos. 34, 411.

§ 430ss.   Administration, protection, and development

The administration, protection, and development of the Fort Necessity National Battlefield shall be exercised by the Secretary of the Interior in accordance with provisions of sections 1, 2, 3, and 4 of this title, as amended and supplemented.

(Pub.L. 87–134, § 4, Aug. 10, 1961, 75 Stat. 336.)

LIBRARY REFERENCES

American Digest System
  Armed Services ⇔54.
  Woods and Forests ⇔5.
  Key Number System Topic Nos. 34, 411.

§ 430tt. Authorization of appropriation

There are authorized to be appropriated such sums, but not more than $722,000, as are necessary to carry out the provisions of sections 430pp to 430tt of this title.

(Pub.L. 87–134, § 5, Aug. 10, 1961, 75 Stat. 336; Pub.L. 93–477, Title I, § 101(4), Oct. 26, 1974, 88 Stat. 1445.)

HISTORICAL AND STATUTORY NOTES

Amendments
  1974 Amendments. Pub.L. 93–477 substituted "$722,000" for "$115,000".

§ 430uu. Big Hole National Battlefield; redesignation of monument

The Big Hole Battlefield National Monument, established by Executive Order Numbered 1216 of June 23, 1910, and enlarged by Proclamation Numbered 2339 of June 29, 1939, is hereby redesignated as the Big Hole National Battlefield.

(Pub.L. 88–24, § 1, May 17, 1963, 77 Stat. 18.)

HISTORICAL AND STATUTORY NOTES

References in Text
  Executive Order Numbered 1216 of June 23, 1910, referred to in text, was not classified to the Code.

Proclamation Numbered 2339 of June 29, 1939 (53 Stat. 2544), referred to in text, was not classified to the Code.

LIBRARY REFERENCES

American Digest System
  Armed Services ⇔54.
  Woods and Forests ⇔1, 8.
  Key Number System Topic Nos. 34, 411.

§ 430uu–1. Revision of boundaries

In order to preserve historic features and sites associated with the Battle of the Big Hole and to facilitate their administration and interpretation, the boundaries of the Big Hole National Battlefield are hereby revised to include the following described lands:

Montana Principal Meridian

Township 2 south, range 17, west: Section 13, southwest quarter southeast quarter, southeast quarter southwest quarter, east half

southwest quarter southwest quarter; section 23, east half northeast
quarter southeast quarter; section 24, west half east half, north half
southwest quarter, southeast quarter southwest quarter, east half
southwest quarter southwest quarter; section 25, those portions of
the northeast quarter northwest quarter and the northwest quarter
northeast quarter lying north of the north right-of-way line of relocated Montana State Route 43; consisting of approximately 466 acres.

(Pub.L. 88–24, § 2, May 17, 1963, 77 Stat. 18.)

LIBRARY REFERENCES

American Digest System
    Armed Services ⟾54.
    Woods and Forests ⟾1.
    Key Number System Topic Nos. 34, 411.

§ 430uu–2. Acquisition of land; exclusion from Beaverhead National Forest; administration

(a) The Secretary of the Interior may acquire by donation, purchase, exchange, or otherwise, lands and interests in lands within the
area described in section 430uu–1 of this title.

(b) Any lands described in section 430uu–1 of this title that are a
part of the Beaverhead National Forest on May 17, 1963, are hereby
excluded from the forest and added to the Big Hole National Battlefield.

(c) Lands included in the Big Hole National Battlefield pursuant to
sections 430uu to 430uu–4 of this title shall be administered in
accordance with the provisions of sections 1, 2, 3, and 4 of this title.

(Pub.L. 88–24, § 3, May 17, 1963, 77 Stat. 19.)

LIBRARY REFERENCES

American Digest System
    Armed Services ⟾54.
    United States ⟾55.
    Woods and Forests ⟾2, 5.
    Key Number System Topic Nos. 34, 393, 411.

§ 430uu–3. Jurisdiction

There is hereby retroceded to the State of Montana, effective when
accepted by said State in accordance with its laws, such jurisdiction
as has been ceded by such State to the United States over any lands
within the boundaries of the Big Hole National Battlefield reserving
in the United States, however, concurrent legislative jurisdiction over
such lands.

(Pub.L. 88–24, § 4, May 17, 1963, 77 Stat. 19.)

§ 430uu–4. Authorization of appropriation

There are authorized to be appropriated such sums not exceeding $42,500 as are necessary for the acquisition of lands and interests in land pursuant to sections 430uu to 430uu–4 of this title.

(Pub.L. 88–24, § 5, May 17, 1963, 77 Stat. 19; Pub.L. 92–272, Title I, § 101(2), Apr. 11, 1972, 86 Stat. 120.)

HISTORICAL AND STATUTORY NOTES

Amendments
  1972 Amendments. Pub.L. 92–272 substituted "$42,500" for "$20,000".

§ 430vv. River Raisin National Battlefield Park

(a) Establishment

(1) In general

If Monroe County or Wayne County, Michigan, or other willing landowners in either County offer to donate to the United States land relating to the Battles of the River Raisin on January 18 and 22, 1813, or the aftermath of the battles, the Secretary of the Interior (referred to in this section as the "Secretary") shall accept the donated land.

(2) Designation of Park

On the acquisition of land under paragraph (1) that is of sufficient acreage to permit efficient administration, the Secretary shall designate the acquired land as a unit of the National Park System, to be known as the "River Raisin National Battlefield Park" (referred to in this section as the "Park").

(3) Legal description

(A) In general

The Secretary shall prepare a legal description of the land and interests in land designated as the Park by paragraph (2).

(B) Availability of map and legal description

A map with the legal description shall be on file and available for public inspection in the appropriate offices of the National Park Service.

(b) Administration

(1) In general

The Secretary shall manage the Park for the purpose of preserving and interpreting the Battles of the River Raisin in accordance with sections 1, 2, 3, and 4 of this title and sections 461 to 467 of this title.

(2) General management plan

(A) In general

Not later than 3 years after the date on which funds are made available, the Secretary shall complete a general management plan for the Park that, among other things, defines the role and responsibility of the Secretary with regard to the interpretation and the preservation of the site.

(B) Consultation

The Secretary shall consult with and solicit advice and recommendations from State, county, local, and civic organizations and leaders, and other interested parties in the preparation of the management plan.

(C) Inclusions

The plan shall include—

(i) consideration of opportunities for involvement by and support for the Park by State, county, and local governmental entities and nonprofit organizations and other interested parties; and

(ii) steps for the preservation of the resources of the site and the costs associated with these efforts.

(D) Submission to Congress

On the completion of the general management plan, the Secretary shall submit a copy of the plan to the Committee on Natural Resources of the House of Representatives and the Committee on Energy and Natural Resources of the Senate.

(3) Cooperative agreements

The Secretary may enter into cooperative agreements with State, county, local, and civic organizations to carry out this section.

(c) Report

Not later than 3 years after March 30, 2009, the Secretary shall submit to the Committee on Energy and Natural Resources of the

Senate and the Committee on Natural Resources of the House a report describing the progress made with respect to acquiring real property under this section and designating the River Raisin National Battlefield Park.

(d) Authorization of appropriations

There are authorized to be appropriated such sums as are necessary to carry out this section.

(Pub.L. 111–11, Title VII, § 7003, Mar. 30, 2009, 123 Stat. 1188.)

HISTORICAL AND STATUTORY NOTES

Revision Notes and Legislative Reports
  2009 Acts. Statement by President, see 2009 U.S. Code Cong. and Adm. News, p. S13.

References in Text
  Sections 1, 2, 3, and 4 of this title, referred to in subsec. (b)(1), originally read "the National Park Service Organic Act (16 U.S.C. 1 et seq.)", meaning Act Aug. 25, 1916, c. 408, 39 Stat. 535, which is principally classified to sections 1 to 4 of this title. For complete classification,

see Short Title note set out under 16 U.S.C.A. § 1 and Tables.
  Sections 461 to 467 of this title, referred to in subsec. (b)(1), originally read "the Act of August 21, 1935 (16 U.S.C. 461 et seq.)', meaning the Historic Sites, Buildings and Antiquities Act, Aug. 21, 1935, c. 593, 49 Stat. 666, which is principally classified to chapter 1–A of this title, 16 U.S.C.A. 461 et seq. For complete classification, see Short Title note set out under 16 U.S.C.A. § 461 and Tables.

SUBCHAPTER LXI—NATIONAL AND INTERNATIONAL MONUMENTS AND MEMORIALS

CROSS REFERENCES

Protection of timber upon national monuments from fire, disease, or insect ravages, see 16 USCA § 594.

§ 431. National monuments; reservation of lands; relinquishment of private claims

The President of the United States is authorized, in his discretion, to declare by public proclamation historic landmarks, historic and prehistoric structures, and other objects of historic or scientific interest that are situated upon the lands owned or controlled by the Government of the United States to be national monuments, and may reserve as a part thereof parcels of land, the limits of which in all cases shall be confined to the smallest area compatible with the proper care and management of the objects to be protected. When such objects are situated upon a tract covered by a bona fide unperfected claim or held in private ownership, the tract, or so much thereof as may be necessary for the proper care and management of the object, may be relinquished to the Government, and the Secretary of the Interior is authorized to accept the relinquishment of such tracts in behalf of the Government of the United States.

(June 8, 1906, c. 3060, § 2, 34 Stat. 225.)

HISTORICAL AND STATUTORY NOTES

Short Title

1906 Acts. Act June 8, 1906, c. 3060, 34 Stat. 225, which is classified generally to sections 431, 432 and 433 of this title, is popularly known as the National Monument Act (Preservation of Antiquities), the Antiquities Act of 1906, and the American Antiquities Preservation Act.

Albert Einstein Memorial

Conveyance of property to National Academy of Sciences for erection and maintenance of a Memorial to Albert Einstein on south side of Square Numbered 88 between 21st Street, 22d Street and Constitution Avenue, District of Columbia, with reverter of title when no longer used for memorial purposes or public access is restricted, was authorized by Pub.L. 95–625, Title VI, § 612, Nov. 10, 1978, 92 Stat. 3521, as amended Pub.L. 96–87, Title IV, § 401(*o*), Oct. 12, 1979, 93 Stat. 666.

National Law Enforcement Officers Memorial Maintenance Fund

Pub.L. 104–329, Title II, § 201, Oct. 20, 1996, 110 Stat. 4011, which provided for National Law Enforcement Officers Memorial Maintenance Fund, was editorially transferred to the National Memorials table by Pub.L. 109–314, §§ 1, 2, Oct. 6, 2006, 120 Stat. 1739.

National Monument Commission

Act Aug. 31, 1954, c. 1160, §§ 1 to 6, 68 Stat. 1029, provided for a Commission to obtain plans and designs for a useful monument to the Nation symbolizing to the United States and the world the ideals of a democracy as embodied in the five freedoms (speech, religion, press, assembly, and petition) and to submit such plans to Congress for legislative authorization after approval by the Secretary of the Interior, the National Capital Planning Commission, and the Commission of Fine Arts. The Commission terminated 30 days after submission of required report which was submitted in 1957 but audit of business was not completed until September 1964.

Study to Add Alaska and Hawaii to Lincoln National Memorial

Pub.L. 94–556, Oct. 19, 1976, 90 Stat. 2632, provided:

"[Section 1.] That, for the purpose of providing appropriate commemoration at the Lincoln National Memorial of the addition of the States of Alaska and Hawaii to the Union, the Secretary of the Interior is authorized and directed to study the feasibility of and make recommendations for the recognition at an appropriate place at such memorial of the addition to the Union of the States of Alaska and Hawaii. Such recommendations shall after review and approval by the Commission of Fine Arts, the National Capital Planning Commission, and the Advisory Council on Historic Preservation be submitted to the Committees on Interior and Insular Affairs of the Senate and the House of Representatives of the United States [now the Committee on Energy and Natural Resources of the Senate and the Committee on Natural Resources of the House of Representatives]. If, at the end of sixty days (not counting days on which the Senate or the House of Representatives has adjourned for more than three consecutive days) following receipt of such recommendations, neither committee has adopted a resolution of disapproval, the Secretary is authorized and directed to carry out said recommendations.

"**Sec. 2.** There are authorized to be appropriated such sums as may be necessary to carry out the purposes of this Act, but not to exceed $20,000. No funds authorized to be appropriated pursuant to this Act shall be available prior to October 1, 1977."

National Monuments Established Under Presidential Proclamation

Ackia Battleground National Monument, Mississippi [see 16 U.S.C.A. § 450r].—Proc. No. 2307, Oct. 25, 1938, 53 Stat. 2494.

Admiralty Island National Monument, Alaska [Monument established within Tongass National Forest by Pub.L. 96–487, Title V, § 503(b), Dec. 2, 1980, 94 Stat. 2399; Pub.L. 104–123, §§ 1 to 6, Apr. 1, 1996, 110 Stat. 879; Pub.L. 105–60, §§ 1 to 6, Oct. 10, 1997, 111 Stat. 1269].—Proc. No. 4611, Dec. 1, 1978, 93 Stat. 1446.

African Burial Ground National Monument, New York.—Proc. No. 7984, Feb. 27, 2006, 71 F.R. 10793.

Agua Fria National Monument, Arizona.—Proc. No. 7263, Jan. 11, 2000, 114 Stat. 3230.

Andrew Johnson National Monument, Tennessee [Monument redesignated Andrew Johnson National Historical Site, see 16 U.S.C.A. § 450o].—Proc. No. 2554, Apr. 27, 1942, 56 Stat. 1955.

Aniakchak National Monument, Alaska [Monument established as unit of National Park System, see 16 U.S.C.A. § 410hh(1)].—Proc. No. 4612, Dec. 1, 1978, 93 Stat. 1448.

Arches National Monument, Utah [Monument abolished and funds made available to Arches National Park, see section 272 of this title].—Proc. No. 1875, Apr. 12, 1929, 46 Stat. 2988; Proc. No. 2312, Nov. 25, 1938, 53 Stat. 2504; Proc. No. 3360, July 22, 1960, 74 Stat. c79; Proc. No. 3887, Jan. 20, 1969, 83 Stat. 920.

Aztec Ruins National Monument, New Mexico.—Proc. No. 1650, Jan. 24, 1923, 42 Stat. 2295; Proc. No. 1840, July 2, 1928, 45 Stat. 2954; Proc. No. 1928, Dec. 19, 1930, 46 Stat. 3040; Proc. No. 2787, May 27, 1948, 62 Stat. 1513; Pub.L. 100–559, Title VI, §§ 601 to 604, Oct. 28, 1988, 102 Stat. 2800.

Badlands National Monument, South Dakota [Monument redesignated Badlands National Park, see 16 U.S.C.A. § 441e–1].—Proc. No. 2320, Jan. 25, 1939, 53 Stat. 2521.

Bandelier National Monument, New Mexico.—Proc. No. 1322, Feb. 11, 1916, 39 Stat. 1764; Proc. No. 1991, Feb. 25, 1932, 47 Stat. 2503; Proc. No. 3388, Jan. 9, 1961, 75 Stat. 1014; Proc. No. 3539, May 27, 1963, 77 Stat. 1006; Pub.L. 94–578, § 309, Oct. 21, 1976, 90 Stat. 2736; Pub.L. 105–85, Div. C, Title XXXI, § 3164, Nov. 18, 1997, 111 Stat. 2050; Pub.L. 105–376, Nov. 12, 1998, 112 Stat. 3388.

Becharof National Monument, Alaska.—Proc. No. 4613, Dec. 1, 1978, 93 Stat. 1450.

Bering Land Bridge National Monument, Alaska.—Proc. No. 4614, Dec. 1, 1978, 93 Stat. 1451.

Big Hole Battlefield National Monument, Montana [Monument redesignated Big Hole National Battlefield, see section 430uu of this title].—Ex.Ord. No. 1216, June 23, 1910; Proc. No. 2339, June 29, 1939, 53 Stat. 2544.

Black Canyon of the Gunnison National Monument, Colorado.—Proc. No. 2033, Mar. 2, 1933, 47 Stat. 2558; Proc. No. 2286, May 16, 1938, 52 Stat. 1548; Proc. No. 2372, Oct. 28, 1939, 54 Stat. 2669; Proc. No. 3344, Apr. 8, 1960, 74 Stat. c56; Pub.L. 98–357, July 13, 1984, 98 Stat. 397.

Bryce Canyon National Monument, Utah.—Proc. No. 1664, June 8, 1923, 43 Stat. 1914; Proc. No. 1930, Jan. 5, 1931, 46 Stat. 3042; Proc. No. 1952, May 4, 1931, 47 Stat. 2455.

Buck Island Reef National Monument, Virgin Islands.—Proc. No. 3443, Dec. 28, 1961, 76 Stat. 1441; Proc. No. 4346, Feb. 1, 1975, 89 Stat. 1237; Proc. No. 4359, Mar. 28, 1975, 89 Stat. 1254; Proc. No. 7392, Jan. 17, 2001, 115 Stat. 2562.

Cabrillo National Monument, California.—Proc. No. 1255, Oct. 14, 1913, 38 Stat. 1965; Proc. No. 3273, Feb. 2, 1959, 73 Stat. c19; Proc. No. 4319, Sept. 28, 1974, 88 Stat. 2514.

California Coastal National Monument.—Proc. No. 7264, Jan. 11, 2000, 114 Stat. 3233.

Canyon De Chelly National Monument, Arizona [see section 445 of this title].—Proc. No. 1945, Apr. 1, 1931, 47 Stat. 2448; Proc. No. 2036, Mar. 3, 1933, 47 Stat. 2562.

Canyons of the Ancients National Monument, Colorado.—Proc. No. 7317, June 9, 2000, 115 Stat. 3319.

Cape Krusenstern National Monument, Alaska [Monument established as unit of National Park System, see 16 U.S.C.A. § 410hh(3)].—Proc. No. 4615, Dec. 1, 1978, 93 Stat. 1453.

Capitol Reef National Monument, Utah [Monument abolished and funds made available to Capitol Reef National Park, see section 273 of this title].—Proc. No. 2246, Aug. 2, 1937, 50 Stat. 1856; Proc. No. 3249, July 2, 1958, 72 Stat. c48; Proc. No. 3888, Jan. 20, 1969, 83 Stat. 922.

Capulin Volcano National Monument, New Mexico [see 16 U.S.C.A. § 460uu–46(g)].—Proc. No. 1340, Aug. 9, 1916, 39 Stat. 1792.

Carlsbad Cave National Monument, New Mexico [Monument redesignated Carlsbad Caverns National Park, see section 16 U.S.C.A. § 407].—Proc.

No. 1679, Oct. 25, 1923, 43 Stat. 1929.

Carrizo Plain National Monument—Proc. No. 7393, Jan. 17, 2001, 115 Stat. 2566.

Casa Grande National Monument, Arizona.—Proc. No. 1470, Aug. 3, 1918, 40 Stat. 1818.

Cascade-Siskiyou National Monument, Oregon.—Proc. No. 7318, June 9, 2000, 114 Stat. 3323; Pub.L. 111–11, Title I, §§ 1401 to 1406, Mar. 30, 2009, 123 Stat. 1026.

Castillo de San Marcos National Monument, Florida [Monument changed from Fort Marion National Monument by Act June 5, 1942, c. 337, 56 Stat. 312].—Proc. No. 1713, Oct. 15, 1924, 43 Stat. 1968; Pub.L. 108–480, Dec. 23, 2004, 118 Stat. 3907.

Castle Pinckney National Monument, South Carolina.—Proc. No. 1713, Oct. 15, 1924, 43 Stat. 1968.

Cedar Breaks National Monument, Utah.—Proc. No. 2054, Aug. 22, 1933, 48 Stat. 1705.

Chaco Canyon National Monument, New Mexico [Monument abolished and funds made available to Chaco Culture National Historical Park, see 16 U.S.C.A. § 410ii–1(a)].—Proc. No. 740, Mar. 11, 1907, 35 Stat. 2119; Proc. No. 1826, Jan. 10, 1928, 45 Stat. 2937.

Channel Islands National Monument, California [Monument abolished and incorporated in Channel Islands National Park, see 16 U.S.C.A. § 410ff].—Proc. No. 2281, Apr. 26, 1938, 52 Stat. 1541; Proc. No. 2825, Feb. 9, 1949, 63 Stat. 1258.

Chesapeake and Ohio Canal National Monument, Maryland.—Proc. No. 3391, Jan. 18, 1961, 75 Stat. 1023.

Chiricahua National Monument, Arizona.—Proc. No. 1692, Apr. 18, 1924, 43 Stat. 1946; Proc. No. 2288, June 10, 1938, 52 Stat. 1551.

Cinder Cone National Monument, California.—Proc. No. 753, May 6, 1907, 35 Stat. 2131.

Colonial National Monument, Virginia [Monument redesignated Colonial National Historical Park, see 16 U.S.C.A. § 81].—Proc. No. 1929, Dec. 30, 1930, 46 Stat. 3041; Proc. No. 2055, Aug. 22, 1933, 48 Stat. 1706.

Colorado National Monument, Colorado.—Proc. No. 1126, May 24, 1911, 37 Stat. 1681; Proc. No. 2037, Mar. 3, 1933, 47 Stat. 2563; Proc. No. 3307, Aug. 7, 1959, 73 Stat. c69.

Craters of the Moon National Monument, Idaho.—Proc. No. 1694, May 2, 1924, 43 Stat. 1947; Proc. No. 1843, July 23, 1928, 45 Stat. 2959; Proc. No. 1916, July 9, 1930, 46 Stat. 3029; Proc. No. 2499, July 18, 1941, 55 Stat. 1660; Proc. No. 3506, Nov. 19, 1962, 77 Stat. 960; Pub.L. 104–333, Div. I, Title II, § 205, Nov. 12, 1996, 110 Stat. 4106; Proc. No. 7373, Nov. 9, 2000, 65 FR 69221; Pub.L. 107–213, § 1, Aug. 21, 2002, 116 Stat. 1052.

Death Valley National Monument, California and Nevada [Monument abolished and land incorporated in Death Valley National Park, see 16 U.S.C.A. § 410aaa–1].—Proc. No. 2028, Feb. 11, 1933, 47 Stat. 2554; Proc. No. 2228, Mar. 26, 1937, 50 Stat. 1823; Proc. No. 2961, Jan. 17, 1952, 66 Stat. c18; Pub.L. 103–433, Title III, § 302, Oct. 31, 1994, 108 Stat. 4485.

Denali National Monument, Alaska.— Proc. No. 4616, Dec. 1, 1978, 93 Stat. 1455.

Devil Postpile National Monument, California.—Proc. No. 1166, July 6, 1911, 37 Stat. 1715.

Devils Tower National Monument, Wyoming.—Proc. No. 658, Sept. 24, 1906, 34 Stat. 3236; Act Aug. 9, 1955, c. 647, 69 Stat. 575.

Dinosaur National Monument, Utah–Colorado.—Proc. No. 1313, Oct. 4, 1915, 39 Stat. 1752; Proc. No. 2290, July 14, 1938, 53 Stat. 2454; Pub.L. 100–701, §§ 2 to 4, Nov. 19, 1988, 102 Stat. 4641.

Edison Laboratory National Monument, New Jersey [Monument and Edison Home National Historic Site together with certain adjacent lands redesignated Edison National Historic Site by Pub.L. 87–628, § 1, Sept. 5, 1962, 76 Stat. 428; Edison National Historic Site redesignated Thomas Edison National Historical Park by Pub.L. 111–11, Title VI, § 7110(c)(4), (5), Mar. 30, 2009, 123 Stat. 1198; see 16 U.S.C.A. § 410mmm].—Proc. No. 3148, July 14, 1956, 70 Stat. c49.

Effigy Mounds National Monument, Iowa.—Proc. No. 2860, Oct. 25,

1949, 64 Stat. A371; Pub.L. 106–323, Oct. 19, 2000, 114 Stat. 1289.

El Morro National Monument, New Mexico.—Proc. No. 695, Dec. 8, 1906, 34 Stat. 3264; Proc. No. 1377, June 18, 1917, 40 Stat. 1673.

Fort Jefferson National Monument, Florida [included in Dry Tortugas National Park, Pub.L. 102–525, Title II, Oct. 26, 1992, 106 Stat. 3439 (16 U.S.C.A. § 410xx et seq.)].—Proc. No. 2112, Jan. 4, 1935, 49 Stat. 3430; abolished by Pub.L. 102–525, Title II, § 201(c), Oct. 26, 1992, 102 Stat. 3440.

Fort Laramie National Monument, Wyoming [Monument redesignated Fort Laramie Historic Site by Pub.L. 86–444, § 3, Apr. 29, 1960, 74 Stat. 84].—Proc. No. 2292, July 16, 1938, 53 Stat. 2461.

Fort Marion National Monument, Florida [Monument redesignated Castillo de San Marcos National Monument by Act June 5, 1942, c. 337, 56 Stat. 312].—Proc. No. 1713, Oct. 15, 1924, 43 Stat. 1968.

Fort Matanzas National Monument, Florida.—Proc. No. 1713, Oct. 15, 1924, 43 Stat. 1968; Proc. No. 2114, Jan. 9, 1935, 49 Stat. 3433; Proc. No. 2773, Mar. 24, 1948, 62 Stat. 1491; Pub.L. 106–524, Nov. 22, 2000, 114 Stat. 2493.

Fort Niagara National Monument, New York.—Proc. No. 1745, Sept. 5, 1925, 44 Stat. 2582.

Fort Pulaski National Monument, Georgia.—Proc. No. 1713, Oct. 15, 1924, 43 Stat. 1968; June 26, 1936, c. 844, 49 Stat. 1979; Nov. 12, 1996, Pub.L. 104–333, Div. I, Title VIII, § 807, Nov. 12, 1996, 110 Stat. 4188.

Fort Wood National Monument, New York.—Proc. No. 1713, Oct. 15, 1924, 43 Stat. 1968.

Fossil Cycad National Monument, South Dakota.—Proc. No. 1641, Oct. 21, 1922, 42 Stat. 2286.

Gates of the Arctic National Monument, Alaska.—Proc. No. 4617, Dec. 1, 1978, 93 Stat. 1457.

Giant Sequoia National Monument, California–Proclamation No. 7295, Apr. 15, 2000, 114 Stat. 3286.

Gila Cliff-Dwellings National Monument, New Mexico.—Proc. No. 781, Nov. 16, 1907, 35 Stat. 2162; Proc. No. 3467, Apr. 17, 1962, 76 Stat. 1465.

Glacier Bay National Monument, Alaska [Monument redesignated Glacier Bay National Park, see 16 U.S.C.A. § 410hh–1(1)].—Proc. No. 1733, Feb. 26, 1925, 43 Stat. 1988; Proc. No. 2330, Apr. 18, 1939, 53 Stat. 2534; Proc. No. 3089, Mar. 31, 1955, 69 Stat. c27; Proc. No. 4618, Dec. 1, 1978, 93 Stat. 1458.

Governors Island National Monument, New York—Proc. No. 7402, Jan. 19, 2001, 115 Stat. 2595; Proc. No. 7647, Feb. 7, 2003, 117 Stat. 2998.

Gran Quivira National Monument, New Mexico [Monument abolished and funds made available to Salinas National Monument by Pub.L. 96–550, Title VI, § 601(b), Dec. 19, 1980, 94 Stat. 3231. Salinas National Monument redesignated Salinas Pueblo Missions National Monument by Pub.L. 100–559, Title I, § 101, Oct. 28, 1988, 102 Stat. 2797].—Proc. No. 882, Nov. 1, 1909, 36 Stat. 2503; Proc. No. 1545, Nov. 25, 1919, 41 Stat. 1778.

Grand Canyon National Monument, Arizona.—Proc. No. 794, Jan. 11, 1908, 35 Stat. 2175; Proc. No. 2022, Dec. 22, 1932, 47 Stat. 2547; Proc. No. 2393, Apr. 4, 1940, 54 Stat. 2692.

Grand Canyon-Parashant National Monument, Arizona.—Proc. No. 7265, Jan. 11, 2000, 114 Stat. 3236.

Grand Staircase-Escalante National Monument, Utah.—Proc. No. 6920, Sept. 18, 1996, 110 Stat. 4561; Pub.L. 105–335, Oct. 31, 1998, 112 Stat. 3139; Pub.L. 105–355, Title II, § 201, Nov. 6, 1998, 112 Stat. 3252; Pub.L. 106–176, Title III, § 307, Mar. 10, 2000, 114 Stat. 33.

Great Sand Dunes National Monument, Colorado.—Proc. No. 1994, Mar. 17, 1932, 47 Stat. 2506; Proc. No. 2681, Mar. 12, 1946, 60 Stat. 1339; Proc. No. 3138, June 7, 1956, 70 Stat. c31. For provisions relating to abolishment of Monument, see 16 U.S.C.A. § 410hhh–2.

Hanford Reach National Monument, Washington.—Proc. No. 7319, June 9, 2000, 114 Stat. 3327.

Holy Cross National Monument, Colorado [Monument abolished by Act Aug. 3, 1950, c. 530, 64 Stat. 404].—Proc.

No. 1877, May 11, 1929, 46 Stat. 2993.

Hovenweep National Monument, Colorado–Utah.—Proc. No. 1654, Mar. 2, 1923, 42 Stat. 2299; Proc. No. 2924, Apr. 26, 1951, 65 Stat. c8; Proc. No. 2998, Nov. 20, 1952, 67 Stat. c21; Proc. No. 3132, Apr. 6, 1956, 70 Stat. c26.

Ironwood Forest National Monument, Arizona.—Proc. No. 7320, June 9, 2000, 114 Stat. 3332.

Jackson Hole National Monument, Wyoming [Monument abolished and incorporated in Grand Teton National Park, see section 406d–1 of this title].—Proc. No. 2578, Mar. 15, 1943, 57 Stat. 731.

Jewel Cave National Monument, South Dakota.—Proc. No. 799, Feb. 7, 1908, 35 Stat. 2180.

Joshua Tree National Monument, California [Monument abolished and land incorporated in Joshua Tree National Park, see section 410aaa–22 of this title].—Proc. No. 2193, Aug. 10, 1936, 50 Stat. 1760; Pub.L. 103–433, Title IV, § 402, Oct. 31, 1994, 108 Stat. 4488.

Kasha–Katuwe Tent Rocks National Monument—Proc. No. 7394, Jan. 17, 2001, 66 F.R. 7343.

Katmai National Monument, Alaska [Monument redesignated Katmai National Park, see 16 U.S.C.A. § 410hh–1(2)].—Proc. No. 1487, Sept. 24, 1918, 40 Stat. 1855; Proc. No. 1950, Apr. 24, 1931, 47 Stat. 2453; Proc. No. 2177, June 15, 1936, 49 Stat. 3523; Proc. No. 2564, Aug. 4, 1942, 56 Stat. 1972; Proc. No. 3890, Jan. 20, 1969, 83 Stat. 926; Proc. No. 4619, Dec. 1, 1978, 93 Stat. 1460.

Kenai Fjords National Monument, Alaska.—Proc. No. 4620, Dec. 1, 1978, 93 Stat. 1462.

Kobuk Valley National Monument, Alaska.—Proc. No. 4621, Dec. 1, 1978, 93 Stat. 1463.

Lake Clark National Monument, Alaska.—Proc. No. 4622, Dec. 1, 1978, 93 Stat. 1465.

Lassen Peak National Monument, California.—Proc. No. 754, May 6, 1907, 35 Stat. 2132.

Lava Beds National Monument, California.—Proc. No. 1755, Nov. 21, 1925,

44 Stat. 2591; Proc. No. 2925, Apr. 27, 1951, 65 Stat. c9.

Lehman Caves National Monument, Nevada [Monument abolished and lands incorporated in, and funds made available for, Great Basin National Park, see 16 U.S.C.A. § 410mm(d)].—Proc. No. 1618, Jan. 24, 1922, 42 Stat. 2260.

Lewis and Clark Cavern National Monument, Montana.—Proc. No. 807, May 11, 1908, 35 Stat. 2187; Proc. No. 1123, May 16, 1911, 37 Stat. 1679.

Marble Canyon National Monument, Arizona.—Proc. No. 3889, Jan. 20, 1969, 83 Stat. 924.

Marianas Trench Marine National Monument.—Proc. No. 8335, Jan. 6, 2009, 74 F.R. 1557.

Meriwether Lewis National Monument, Tennessee [Monument included in Natchez Trace Parkway, see 16 U.S.C.A. § 460–1].—Proc. No. 1730, Feb. 6, 1925, 43 Stat. 1986; Proc. No. 1825, Dec. 6, 1927, 45 Stat. 2935.

Minidoka Internment National Monument [Monument abolished and incorporated in Minidoka National Historic Site by Pub.L. 110–229, Title III, § 313, May 8, 2008, 122 Stat. 770, see 16 U.S.C.A. § 461 note [Table]].—Proc. No. 7395, Jan. 17, 2001, 115 Stat. 2572.

Misty Fjords National Monument, Alaska [Monument established within Tongass National Forest by Pub.L. 96–487, Title V, § 503(a), Dec. 2, 1980, 94 Stat. 2399].—Proc. No. 4623, Dec. 1, 1978, 93 Stat. 1466.

Montezuma Castle National Monument, Arizona.—Proc. No. 696, Sept. 8, 1906, 93 Stat. 3265; Proc. No. 2226, Feb. 23, 1937, 50 Stat. 1817; Pub.L. 108–190, Dec. 19, 2003, 117 Stat. 2867.

Mound City Group National Monument, Ohio [Monument redesignated Hopewell Culture National Historic Park, see 16 U.S.C.A. § 401uu].—Proc. No. 1653, Mar. 2, 1923, 42 Stat. 2298; Pub.L. 96–607, Title VII, § 701, Dec. 28, 1980, 94 Stat. 3540.

Mount Olympus National Monument, Washington [Monument abolished and lands incorporated in Olympic National Park, see section 251 of this title].—Proc. No. 869, Mar. 2, 1909,

35 Stat. 2247; Proc. No. 1191, Apr. 17, 1912, 37 Stat. 1737; Proc. No. 1293, May 11, 1915, 39 Stat. 1726; Proc. No. 1862, Jan. 7, 1929, 45 Stat. 2984.

Muir Woods National Monument, California.—Proc. No. 793, Jan. 9, 1908, 35 Stat. 2174; Proc. No. 1608, Sept. 22, 1921, 42 Stat. 2249; Proc. No. 2122, Apr. 5, 1935, 49 Stat. 3443; Proc. No. 2932, June 26, 1951, 65 Stat. c20; Proc. No. 3311, Sept. 8, 1959, 73 Stat. c76.

Mukuntuweap National Monument, Utah [Monument redesignated Zion National Monument by Proc. No. 1435, Mar. 18, 1918, 40 Stat. 1760, and later redesignated Zion National Park, see 16 U.S.C.A. § 344].—Proc. No. 877, July 31, 1909, 36 Stat. 2498.

Natural Bridges National Monument, Utah.—Proc. No. 804, Apr. 16, 1908, 35 Stat. 2183; Proc. No. 881, Sept. 25, 1909, 36 Stat. 2502; Proc. No. 1323, Feb. 11, 1916, 39 Stat. 1764; Proc. No. 3486, Aug. 14, 1962, 76 Stat. 1495.

Navajo National Monument, Arizona.—Proc. No. 873, May 20, 1909, 36 Stat. 2491; Proc. No. 1186, Mar. 14, 1912, 37 Stat. 1733.

Noatak National Monument, Alaska.—Proc. No. 4624, Dec. 1, 1978, 93 Stat. 1468.

Northwestern Hawaiian Islands Marine National Monument, Hawaii [Monument redesignated Papahanaumokuakea Marine National Monument by Proc. No. 8112, Feb. 28, 2007, 72 F.R. 10031].—Proc. No. 8031, June 15, 2006, 71 F.R. 36443.

Ocmulgee National Monument, Georgia [see section 447a of this title].—Proc. No. 2212, Dec. 23, 1936, 50 Stat. 1798; Proc. No. 2493, June 13, 1941, 55 Stat. 1654; Pub.L. 102–67, July 9, 1991, 105 Stat. 325.

Old Kasaan National Monument, Alaska [Monument abolished and incorporated in Tongass National Forest by Act July 26, 1955, c. 387, 69 Stat. 380].—Proc. No. 1351, Oct. 25, 1916, 39 Stat. 1812.

Oregon Caves National Monument, Oregon.—Proc. No. 876, July 12, 1909, 36 Stat. 2497.

Organ Pipe Cactus National Monument, Arizona.—Proc. No. 2232, Apr. 13, 1937, 50 Stat. 1827; Pub.L. 108–64, §§ 1, 2, July 29, 2003, 117 Stat. 874.

Pacific Remote Islands Marine National Monument.—Proc. No. 8336, Jan. 6, 2009, 74 F.R. 1565.

Papago Saguaro National Monument, Arizona.—Proc. No. 1262, Jan. 31, 1914, 38 Stat. 1991; Pub.L. 109–163, Div. B, Title XXVIII, § 2873, Jan. 6, 2006, 119 Stat. 3535; abolished by Act Apr. 7, 1930, c. 107, 46 Stat. 142.

Papahanaumokuakea Marine National Monument, Hawaii [formerly Northwestern Hawaiian Islands Marine National Monument, Proc. No. 8031, June 15, 2006, 71 F.R. 3644, was redesignated Papahanaumokuakea Marine National Monument].—Proc. No. 8112, Feb. 28, 2007, 72 F.R. 10031.

Perry's Victory and International Peace Memorial National Monument, Ohio.—Proc. No. 2182, July 6, 1936, 50 Stat. 1734.

Petrified Forest National Monument [Monument disestablished on establishment of Petrified Forest National Park, see sections 119 and 444 of this title].—Proc. No. 697, Dec. 8, 1906, 34 Stat. 3266; Proc. No. 1167, July 31, 1911, 37 Stat. 1716; Proc. No. 1927, Nov. 14, 1930, 46 Stat. 3040; Proc. No. 1975, Nov. 30, 1931, 47 Stat. 2486; Proc. No. 2011, Sept. 23, 1932, 47 Stat. 2532.

Pinnacles National Monument, California.—Proc. No. 796, Jan. 16, 1908, 35 Stat. 2177; Proc. No. 1660, May 7, 1923, 43 Stat. 1911; Proc. No. 1704, July 2, 1924, 43 Stat. 1961; Proc. No. 1948, Apr. 13, 1931, 47 Stat. 2451; Proc. No. 2050, July 11, 1933, 48 Stat. 1701; Proc. No. 2528, Dec. 5, 1941, 55 Stat. 1709; Proc. No. 7266, Jan. 11, 2000, 114 Stat. 3241.

Pipe Spring National Monument, Arizona.—Proc. No. 1663, May 31, 1923, 43 Stat. 1913.

Pompeys Pillar National Monument—Proc. No. 7396, Jan. 17, 2001, 115 Stat. 2576.

Port Chicago National Memorial, California.—Pub.L. 102–562, Title II, Oct. 28, 1992, 106 Stat. 4235; Pub.L. 111–84, Div. B, Title XXVIII, § 2853(a), Oct. 28, 2009, 123 Stat. 2685.

President Lincoln and Soldiers' Home National Monument, Washington D.C.—Proc. No. 7329, July 7, 2000, 114 Stat. 3349.

Rainbow Bridge National Monument, Utah.—Proc. No. 1043, May 30, 1910, 36 Stat. 2703.

Rose Atoll Marine National Monument.—Proc. No. 8337, Jan. 6, 2009, 74 F.R. 1577.

Russell Cave National Monument, Alabama.—Proc. No. 3413, May 11, 1961, 75 Stat. 1058.

Saguaro National Monument, Arizona [Monument incorporated into Saguaro National Park by Pub.L. 103–364, Oct. 14, 1994, 108 Stat. 3467].—Proc. No. 2032, Mar. 1, 1933, 47 Stat. 2557; Proc. No. 3439, Nov. 15, 1961, 76 Stat. 1437; Pub.L. 102–61, June 19, 1991, 105 Stat. 303.

Santa Rosa Island National Monument, Florida.—Proc. No. 2337, May 17, 1939, 53 Stat. 2542; Proc. No. 2659, Aug. 13, 1945, 59 Stat. 877.

Scotts Bluff National Monument, Nebraska.—Proc. No. 1547, Dec. 12, 1919, 41 Stat. 1779; Proc. No. 1999, June 1, 1932, 47 Stat. 2512; Proc. No. 2391, Mar. 29, 1940, 54 Stat. 2690.

Shoshone Cavern National Monument, Wyoming [Monument abolished by Act May 17, 1954, c. 203, 68 Stat. 98].—Proc. No. 880, Sept. 21, 1909, 36 Stat. 2501.

Sieur de Monts National Monument, Maine.—Proc. No. 1339, July 8, 1916, 39 Stat. 1785.

Sitka National Monument, Alaska [Monument redesignated Sitka National Historical Park by Pub.L. 92–501, Oct. 18, 1972, 86 Stat. 904].—Proc. No. 959, Mar. 23, 1910, 36 Stat. 2601; Proc. No. 2965, Feb. 25, 1952, 66 Stat. c22; Pub.L. 106–291, Title I, § 130, Oct. 11, 2000, 114 Stat. 946.

Sonoran Desert National Monument—Proc. No. 7397, Jan. 17, 2001, 115 Stat. 2578.

Statue of Liberty National Monument.—Proc. No. 1713, Oct. 15, 1924, 43 Stat. 1968; Proc. No. 2250, Sept. 7, 1937, 51 Stat. 393; Proc. No. 3656, May 11, 1965, 79 Stat. 1490.

Sunset Crater Volcano National Monument, Arizona [Monument changed from Sunset Crater National Monument by Pub.L. 101–612, § 15, Nov.

16, 1990, 104 Stat. 3222].—Proc. No. 1911, May 26, 1930, 46 Stat. 3023.

Timpanogos Cave National Monument, Utah.—Proc. No. 1640, Oct. 14, 1922, 42 Stat. 2285; Proc. No. 3457, Mar. 27, 1962, 76 Stat. 1457; Pub.L. 107–329, Title I, §§ 101 to 107, Dec. 6, 2002, 116 Stat. 2815.

Tonto National Monument, Arizona.—Proc. No. 787, Dec. 19, 1907, 35 Stat. 2168; Proc. No. 2230, Apr. 1, 1937, 50 Stat. 1825.

Tumacacori National Monument, Arizona [Monument abolished and lands incorporated in, and funds made available for, Tumacacori National Historical Park, see 16 U.S.C.A. § 410ss].—Proc. No. 821, Sept. 15, 1908, 35 Stat. 2205; Proc. No. 3228, Mar. 28, 1958, 72 Stat. c30.

Tuzigoot National Monument, Arizona.—Proc. No. 2344, July 25, 1939, 53 Stat. 2548.

Upper Missouri River Breaks National Monument—Proc. No. 7398, Jan. 17, 2001, 115 Stat. 2583.

Verendrye National Monument, North Dakota.—Proc. No. 1380, June 29, 1917, 40 Stat. 1677.

Vermilion Cliffs National Monument.—Proc. No. 7374, Nov. 9, 2000, 114 Stat. 3422.

Virgin Islands Coral Reef National Monument—Proc. No. 7399, Jan. 17, 2001, 115 Stat. 2588.

Walnut Canyon National Monument, Arizona.—Proc. No. 1318, Nov. 30, 1915, 39 Stat. 1761; Proc. No. 2300, Sept. 24, 1938, 53 Stat. 2469; Pub.L. 104–333, Div. I, Title II, § 208, Nov. 12, 1996, 110 Stat. 4107.

Wheeler National Monument, Colorado [Monument abolished by Act Aug. 3, 1950, c. 534, 64 Stat. 405].—Proc. No. 831, Dec. 7, 1908, 35 Stat. 2214.

White Sands National Monument, New Mexico.—Proc. No. 2025, Jan. 18, 1933, 47 Stat. 2551; Proc. No. 2108, Nov. 28, 1934, 49 Stat. 3426; Proc. No. 2295, Aug. 29, 1938, 53 Stat. 2465; Proc. No. 3024, June 24, 1953, 67 Stat. c53; Pub.L. 104–201, Div. B, Title XXVIII, § 2854, Sept. 23, 1996, 110 Stat. 2803.

World War II Valor In the Pacific National Monument.—Proc. No. 8327, Dec. 5, 2008, 73 F.R. 75293.

Wrangell-St. Elias National Monument, Alaska.—Proc. No. 4625, Dec. 1, 1978, 93 Stat. 1470.

Wupatki National Monument, Arizona.— Proc. No. 1721, Dec. 9, 1924, 43 Stat. 1977; Proc. No. 2243, July 9, 1937, 52 Stat. 1841; Proc. No. 2454, Jan. 20, 1941, 55 Stat. 1608; Pub.L. 104–333, Div. I, Title II, §207, Nov. 12, 1996, 110 Stat. 4107.

Yucca House National Monument, Colorado.—Proc. No. 1549, Dec. 19, 1919, 41 Stat. 1781; Pub.L. 104–333, Div. I, Title II, § 201, Nov. 12, 1996, 110 Stat. 4105.

Yukon-Charley National Monument, Alaska.—Proc. No. 4626, Dec. 1, 1978, 93 Stat. 1472.

Yukon Flats National Monument, Alaska.—Proc. No. 4627, Dec. 1, 1978, 93 Stat. 1473.

Zion National Monument, Utah [Monument combined with Zion National Park into a single National Park unit, see 16 U.S.C.A. § 346b. A prior Zion National Monument, formerly Mukuntuweap National Monument, Proc. No. 877, July 31, 1909, 36 Stat. 2498, and Proc. No. 1435, Mar. 18, 1918, 40 Stat. 1760, was redesignated Zion National Park, see 16 U.S.C.A. § 344].—Proc. No. 2221, Jan. 22, 1937, 50 Stat. 1809.

Miscellaneous National Monuments
Agate Fossil Beds National Monument, Nebraska.—Pub.L. 89–33, June 5, 1965, 79 Stat. 123.

Alibates Flint Quarries National Monument, Texas.—Pub.L. 89–154, Aug. 31, 1965, 79 Stat. 587. Name changed from Alibates Flint Quarries and Texas Panhandle Pueblo Culture National Monument by Pub.L. 95–625, Title III, § 321(c), Nov. 10, 1978, 92 Stat. 3488.

Congaree Swamp National Monument, South Carolina.—Pub.L. 94–545, Oct. 18, 1976, 90 Stat. 2517, as amended Pub.L. 100–524, §§ 5, 6, Oct. 24, 1988, 102 Stat. 2607; Pub.L. 108–108, Title I, § 148, Nov. 10, 2003, 117 Stat. 1281. [Monument redesignated Congaree National Park, see 16 U.S.C.A. § 410jjj et seq.]

El Malpais National Monument, New Mexico.—Pub.L. 100–225, Title I, §§ 101 to 104, Dec. 31, 1987, 101 Stat. 1539 (16 U.S.C.A. § 460uu et seq.).

Florissant Fossil Beds National Monument, Colorado.—Pub.L. 91–60, Aug. 20, 1969, 83 Stat. 101.

Fossil Butte National Monument, Wyoming.—Pub.L. 92–537, Oct. 23, 1972, 86 Stat. 1069.

Hagerman Fossil Beds National Monument, Idaho.—Pub.L. 100–696, Title III, §§ 301 to 308, Nov. 18, 1988, 102 Stat. 4575; Pub.L. 101–512, Title I, Nov. 5, 1990, 104 Stat. 1923; Pub.L. 104–333, Div. I, Title II, § 206, Nov. 12, 1996, 110 Stat. 4106; Pub.L. 106–421, §§ 1 to 4, Nov. 1, 2000, 114 Stat. 1870.

Hohokam Pima National Monument, Arizona.—Pub.L. 92–525, Oct. 21, 1972, 86 Stat. 1047.

John Day Fossil Beds National Monument, Oregon.—Pub.L. 93–486, Title I, § 101(a)(2), Oct. 26, 1974, 88 Stat. 1461.

Kill Devil National Monument, North Carolina.—Act Mar. 2, 1927, c. 251, 44 Stat. 1264. Name change to Wright Brothers National Memorial, Dec. 1, 1953.

Little Bighorn Battlefield National Monument, Montana.—Pub.L. 102–201, Titles I, II, Dec. 10, 1991, 105 Stat. 1631 to 1633.

Mount St. Helens National Volcanic Monument, Washington.—Pub.L. 97–243, Aug. 26, 1982, 96 Stat. 301; Pub.L. 105–279, Oct. 23, 1998, 112 Stat. 2690.

National Military Working Dog Teams National Monument, Virginia.— Pub.L. 110–181, Div. B, Title XXVIII, § 2877, Jan. 28, 2008, 122 Stat. 563; Pub.L. 111–84, Div. B, Title XXVIII, § 2871(a), Oct. 28, 2009, 123 Stat. 2696.

Newberry National Volcanic Monument, Oregon—Pub.L. 101–522, Nov. 5, 1990, 104 Stat. 2288.

Pecos National Monument, New Mexico [included in Pecos National Historical Park by Pub.L. 101–313, Title II, § 202(b), June 27, 1990, 104 Stat. 278 (16 U.S.C.A. § 410rr–1(b))].— Pub.L. 89–54, June 28, 1965, 79 Stat. 195; repealed by Pub.L. 101–313, Title II, § 202(c), June 27, 1990, 104 Stat. 278 (16 U.S.C.A. § 410rr–1(c)).

Petroglyph National Monument, New Mexico.—Pub.L. 101–313, Title I, June 27, 1990, 104 Stat. 272, as amended Pub.L. 103–50, § 401, July 2, 1993, 107 Stat. 252; Pub.L. 104–333, Div. I, Title VIII, § 814(d)(2)(D), Nov. 12, 1996, 110 Stat. 4196; Pub.L. 105–174, § 3005, May 1, 1998, 112 Stat. 82.

Poverty Point National Monument, Louisiana.—Pub.L. 100–560, Oct. 31, 1988, 102 Stat. 2803.

Prehistoric Trackways National Monument, New Mexico.—Pub.L. 111–11, Title II, §§ 2101 to 2105, May 30, 2003, 123 Stat. 1096.

Salinas Pueblo Missions National Monument, New Mexico.—Pub.L. 96–550, Title VI, § 601, Dec. 19, 1980, 94 Stat. 3231, as amended Pub.L. 100–559, Title I, § 101, Oct. 28, 1988, 102 Stat. 2797.

Santa Rosa and San Jacinto Mountains National Monument, California.— Pub.L. 106–351, Oct. 24, 2000, 114 Stat. 1362, as amended Pub.L. 106–434, § 2, Nov. 6, 2000, 114 Stat. 1913; Pub.L. 111–11, Title I, § 1853, Mar. 30, 2009, 123 Stat. 1068.

National Memorials

AIDS Memorial Grove, California.— Pub.L. 104–333, Div. I, Title V, § 516, Nov. 12, 1996, 110 Stat. 4170.

Arkansas Post National Memorial, Arkansas.—Pub.L. 86–595, July 6, 1960, 74 Stat. 333, as amended Pub. L. 105–83, Title I, § 126, Nov. 14, 1997, 111 Stat. 1567.

Astronauts Memorial, John F. Kennedy Space Center, Florida.—Recognized as national memorial to astronauts who die in line of duty by Pub.L. 102–41, May 8, 1991, 105 Stat. 242.

Battle of Midway National Memorial, Midway Atoll—Pub.L. 106–113, Div. B, § 1000(a)(3) [Title I, § 126], Nov. 29, 1999, 113 Stat. 1535, 1501A–164.

Benjamin Franklin National Memorial, Pennsylvania.—Designation of Benjamin Franklin Memorial Hall as National Memorial by Pub.L. 92–551, Oct. 25, 1972, 86 Stat. 1164.

Bosque Redondo Memorial, New Mexico.—Pub.L. 106–511, Title II, §§ 201 to 206, Nov. 13, 2000, 114 Stat. 2369, as amended Pub.L. 108–204, Title I, § 101, Mar. 2, 2004, 118 Stat. 543.

Buffalo Soldiers Memorial, New Orleans.—Pub.L. 109–152, Dec. 30, 2005, 119 Stat. 2887.

Chamizal National Memorial, Texas.— Pub.L. 89–479, June 30, 1966, 80 Stat. 232.

Coronado National Memorial, Arizona.— Acts Aug. 18, 1941, c. 365, § 1, 55 Stat. 630, and July 9, 1952, c. 610, 66 Stat. 510 (16 U.S.C.A. § 450y); Proc. No. 2995, Nov. 5, 1952, 67 Stat. c18.

Custis-Lee Mansion National Memorial, Virginia.—Act Mar. 4, 1925, c. 562, 43 Stat. 1356. Made permanent memorial by Act June 29, 1955, c. 223, 69 Stat. 190.

David Berger Memorial, Ohio.—Pub.L. 96–199, Title I, § 116, Mar. 5, 1980, 94 Stat. 71.

Disabled American Veterans Vietnam Veterans National Memorial, New Mexico.—Recognized as a memorial of national significance by Pub.L. 100–164, Nov. 13, 1987, 101 Stat. 905.

Dwight D. Eisenhower Memorial.— Pub.L. 106–79, Title VIII, § 8162, Oct. 25, 1999, 113 Stat. 1724. Memorial authorized as a Commemorative Work by Pub.L. 107–117, Div. A, Title VIII, § 8120(a), (b), Jan. 10, 2002, 115 Stat. 2273, 2274. See, Pub.L. 107–117, Div. A, Title VIII, § 8120(a), (b) set out as a note under 40 U.S.C.A. § 8903.

Father Marquette National Memorial, Michigan.—Pub.L. 94–160, Dec. 20, 1975, 89 Stat. 848.

Federal Hall National Memorial, New York.—Designated May 26, 1939. Designation changed from Federal Hall Memorial Historic Site by Act Aug. 11, 1955, c. 779, 69 Stat. 632.

Flight 93 National Memorial, Pennsylvania.—Pub.L. 107–226, §§ 1 to 6, Sept. 25, 2002, 116 Stat. 1345; Pub.L. 110–161, Div. F, Title I, § 128, Dec. 26, 2007, 121 Stat. 2122.

Fort Caroline National Memorial, Florida.—Act Sept. 21, 1950, c. 973, 64 Stat. 897. Established Jan. 16, 1953.

Franklin Delano Roosevelt National Memorial, District of Columbia.—Act Aug. 11, 1955, c. 833, 69 Stat. 694; Sept. 1, 1959, Pub.L. 86–214, 73 Stat. 445; Oct. 18, 1962, Pub.L. 87–842, 76 Stat. 1079; Oct. 30, 1965, Pub.L. 89–305, 79 Stat. 1126; Sept.

8, 1970, Pub.L. 91–398, 84 Stat. 837; June 30, 1972, Pub.L. 92–332, 86 Stat. 401; July 28, 1982, Pub.L. 97–224, 96 Stat. 243; Oct. 1, 1996, Pub.L. 104–221, §§ 3, 4, 110 Stat. 3024; July 24, 1997, Pub.L. 105–29, §§ 1 to 4, 111 Stat. 246; Nov. 14, 1997, Pub.L. 105–83, Title III, § 335, 111 Stat. 1601.

Hamilton Grange National Memorial, New York.—Pub.L. 87–438, Apr. 27, 1962, 76 Stat. 57, as amended Pub.L. 100–701, § 1, Nov. 19, 1988, 102 Stat. 4640; Pub.L. 106–482, Nov. 9, 2000, 114 Stat. 2192.

House Where Lincoln Died National Memorial, District of Columbia.—Act June 11, 1896, c. 420, 29 Stat. 439.

Johnstown Flood National Memorial, Pennsylvania.—Pub.L. 88–546, Aug. 31, 1964, 78 Stat. 752; Pub.L. 108–313, Oct. 5, 2004, 118 Stat. 1196.

Lincoln Boyhood National Memorial, Indiana.—Pub.L. 87–407, Feb. 19, 1962, 76 Stat. 9.

Lincoln Museum National Memorial, District of Columbia.—Act Apr. 7, 1866, c. 28, § 1, 14 Stat. 23.

Lincoln National Memorial, District of Columbia.—Act Feb. 9, 1911, c. 42, 36 Stat. 898.

Mount Rushmore National Memorial, South Dakota.—Act Feb. 25, 1929, c. 315, 45 Stat. 1300.

Mt. Soledad Veterans Memorial, San Diego, California.—Pub.L. 108–447, Div. J, Title I, § 116, Dec. 8, 2004, 118 Stat. 3346; Pub.L. 109–272, §§ 1, 2, Aug. 14, 2006, 120 Stat. 770; Pub.L. 109–364, Div. A, Title X, § 1071(d), Oct. 17, 2006, 120 Stat. 2401.

National D-Day Memorial, Virginia.—Pub.L. 104–201, Div. A, Title X, § 1080, Sept. 23, 1996, 110 Stat. 2670.

National Fallen Firefighter's Memorial, Maryland.—Pub.L. 101–347, Aug. 9, 1990, 104 Stat. 398.

National Law Enforcement Officers Memorial, District of Columbia.—Establishment of Maintenance Fund by Pub.L. 104–329, Title II, § 201, Oct. 20, 1996, 110 Stat. 4011, as amended Pub.L. 109–314, §§ 1, 2, Oct. 6, 2006, 120 Stat. 1739.

National Medal of Honor Sites.—Pub.L. 106–83, Oct. 28, 1999, 113 Stat. 1293.

Patrick Henry National Memorial, Virginia.—Pub.L. 99–296, May 12, 1986, 100 Stat. 429.

Prisoner of War/Missing in Action National Memorial, California.—Pub.L. 108–454, Title VI, § 601, Dec. 10, 2004, 118 Stat. 3623.

Richard L. Kohnstamm Memorial Area, Oregon.—Pub.L. 111–11, Title I, § 1202(b), Mar. 30, 2009, 123 Stat. 1009.

Seabees of the United States Navy Memorial.—Pub.L. 92–422, Sept. 18, 1972, 86 Stat. 678.

Signers of the Declaration of Independence Memorial, District of Columbia.—Pub.L. 95–260, Apr. 17, 1978, 92 Stat. 197.

Thomas Jefferson National Memorial, District of Columbia.—Act June 26, 1934, c. 763, 48 Stat. 1243.

United States Marine Corps Memorial, Virginia.—Act July 1, 1947, c. 196, 61 Stat. 242, as amended July 7, 1952, c. 585, 66 Stat. 441; June 16, 1953, c. 120, 67 Stat. 64.

United States National Civil Defense Monument, Maryland.—Pub.L. 106–103, Nov. 13, 1999, 113 Stat. 1482.

United States Navy Memorial, District of Columbia.—Pub.L. 96–199, Title I, § 113, Mar. 5, 1980, 94 Stat. 70.

U.S.S. Indianapolis Memorial, Indianapolis, Indiana.—Pub.L. 103–160, Div. A, Title XI, § 1165, Nov. 30, 1993, 107 Stat. 1765.

U.S.S. Oklahoma Memorial, Hawaii.—Pub.L. 109–163, Div. A, Title X, § 1017, Jan. 6, 2006, 119 Stat. 3425.

Vietnam Veterans Memorial, District of Columbia.—Pub.L. 96–297, July 1, 1980, 94 Stat. 827; Pub.L. 106–214, June 15, 2000, 114 Stat. 335; Pub.L. 108–126, § 101, Nov. 17, 2003, 117 Stat. 1348.

Washington Monument National Memorial, District of Columbia.—Act Aug. 2, 1876, c. 250, § 1, 19 Stat. 123.

White Cross World War I Memorial, California.—Pub.L. 107–117, Div. A, Title VIII, § 8137, Jan. 10, 2002, 115 Stat.

2278; Pub.L. 108–87, Title VIII, § 8121, Sept. 30, 2003, 117 Stat. 1100.

World War II Memorials on Guam.— Pub.L. 106–398, § 1 [Div. B, Title XXVIII, § 2886], Oct. 30, 2000, 114 Stat. 1654, 1654A–441; Pub.L.

107–107, Div. B, Title XXVIII, § 2868, 115 Stat. 1334.

Wright Brothers National Memorial, North Carolina.—Kill Devil Hill National Monument authorized by Act Mar. 2, 1927, c. 251, 44 Stat. 1264. Name changed to Wright Brothers National Memorial, Dec. 1, 1953.

CROSS REFERENCES

Applicability of other Federal laws withdrawing lands, see 43 USCA § 1714.
Disposition of archaeological resources, see 16 USCA § 470dd.
Establishment of,
    Carlsbad Caverns National Park, see 16 USCA § 407.
    Great Basin National Park, see 16 USCA § 410mm.
Excavation and removal, see 16 USCA § 470cc.
National monument in Riverside County, California, see 16 USCA § 434.
Permits to examine ruins, excavations and gathering of objects; regulations, see
    16 USCA § 432.
Use of wilderness areas, see 16 USCA § 1133.

CODE OF FEDERAL REGULATIONS

National cemeteries, use of, see 36 CFR § 12.1 et seq.
Special regulations for particular areas, see 36 CFR § 7.1 et seq.

LAW REVIEW AND JOURNAL COMMENTARIES

A synopsis of the laws protecting our cultural heritage. Marilyn Phelan, 28 New
    Eng.L.Rev. 63 (1993).
Identity and cultural property: The protection of cultural property in the United
    States. Patty Gerstenblith, 75 B.U.L.Rev. 559 (1995).
Preserving monumental landscapes under the Antiquities Act. Christine A. Klein,
    87 Cornell L. Rev. 1333 (2002).
Protection of the ethnobiological knowledge of indigenous peoples. Lester I.
    Yano, 41 UCLA L.Rev. 443 (1993).
Requiem for Indiana Jones: Federal law, Native Americans, and the treasure
    hunters. Comment, 30 Tulsa L.J. 213 (1994).
Secularizing the sacrosanct: Defining 'sacred' for Native American sacred sites
    protection legislation. Note, 33 Hofstra L. Rev. 751 (2004).

LIBRARY REFERENCES

American Digest System
    Armed Services ⚲54.
    United States ⚲3.
    Woods and Forests ⚲2.
    Key Number System Topic Nos. 34, 393, 411.

Research References

ALR Library
    11 ALR, Fed. 2nd Series 623, Validity, Construction, and Application of Antiquities
        Act of 1906, 16 U.S.C.A. §§ 431 et seq.
    184 ALR, Fed. 139, Validity, Construction, and Operation of Archaeological
        Resources Protection Act of 1979, 16 U.S.C.A. §§ 470aa to 470mm.
    33 ALR, Fed. 9, Uniform Relocation Assistance and Real Property Acquisition
        Policies Act of 1970 (42 U.S.C.A. §§ 4601-4655).
    14 ALR, Fed. 508, Construction and Application of Wilderness Act (16 U.S.C.A.
        §§ 1131 et seq.) Providing for National Wilderness Preservation System.

14 ALR 2nd 992, What Actions Arise Under the Laws and Treaties of the United
   States So as to Vest Jurisdiction of Federal Courts.
109 ALR 300, Amount in Controversy for Purposes of Jurisdiction in Case
   Involving Tax or License Fee.

Encyclopedias
25 Am. Jur. Proof of Facts 2d 685, Abandonment of Tangible Personal Property.
63 Am. Jur. Proof of Facts 3d 195, Interference with the Right to Free Exercise of
   Religion.
73 Am. Jur. Proof of Facts 3d 89, Proof of Religion in the Courtroom that Violates
   the Right to a Fair Trial.

Treatises and Practice Aids
West's Federal Administrative Practice § 5274, Additional Environmental Statutes.

Notes of Decisions

Abolishment of monuments   9
Action against United States   11
Construction with other laws   1
Declaratory judgment   13
Designation of area in proclamation   2
Grounds for proclamation   4
Jurisdiction   12
Mining claims   5
Objects of historic or scientific interest
   3
Preexisting property rights   8
Review   15
Stays   14
Submerged lands   7
Transfer of monuments   10
Water rights   6

_____

1. Construction with other laws

Agency directives in presidential proclamation designating federal lands as national monument that required Bureau of
Land Management (BLM) to prepare
management plan and conduct grazing
compatibility determination, in reliance
upon "all applicable legal authorities,"
necessarily referred to BLM's independent statutory obligations under Federal
Land Policy and Management Act
(FLPMA), and therefore proclamation's
directives relied on specific statutory authority sufficient to subject agency action
or inaction taken in accordance with
those directives to judicial review under
Administrative Procedure Act (APA).
Western Watersheds Project v. Bureau of
Land Management, D.Ariz.2009, 629
F.Supp.2d 951.   Public Lands ☞ 17

President's designation of 1.7 million
acres of federal land in Utah as Grand
Staircase National Monument, under Antiquities Act, was not subject to requirements of National Environmental Policy
Act (NEPA), even if idea for designation

originated with Department of the Interi-
or (DOI), rather than with President;
there was no requirement of presidential
inspiration in Antiquities Act's grant of
authority to President.   Utah Ass'n of
Counties v. Bush, D.Utah 2004, 316
F.Supp.2d 1172, appeal dismissed 455
F.3d 1094.   Environmental Law ☞ 577

President's proclamation designating
national forest as national monument
pursuant to Antiquities Act did not withdraw land from national forest system,
and explicitly stated that Secretary of
Agriculture, through Forest Service,
would continue to manage monument
and underlying forest, and thus proclamation did not violate National Forest
Management Act (NFMA).   Tulare County v. Bush, D.D.C.2001, 185 F.Supp.2d
18, affirmed 306 F.3d 1138, 353 U.S.App.
D.C. 312, rehearing en banc denied 317
F.3d 227, 354 U.S.App.D.C. 325, certiorari denied 124 S.Ct. 63, 540 U.S. 813, 157
L.Ed.2d 28.

Any recommendations by Secretary of
Interior on the exercise of President's
powers under section 431 et seq. of this
title, which recommendations have been
requested by President, do not come under impact statement process of the National Environmental Policy Act, section
4332 of Title 42.   State of Alaska v. Car-
ter, D.C.Alaska 1978, 462 F.Supp. 1155.
Environmental Law ☞ 595(2)

2. Designation of area in proclamation

That the area designated in Proclamation No. 2578, Mar. 15, 1943, 57 Stat.
731, establishing the Jackson Hole National Monument was not consistent with
the preface to such proclamation was not
material, where the area over which control was threatened was in any event lim-

241

ited to that defined in such proclamation. State of Wyoming v. Franke, D.C.Wyo. 1945, 58 F.Supp. 890. Public Lands ☞ 49

3. Objects of historic or scientific interest

The pool of water in Devil's Hole, and rare fish inhabiting the pool, were "objects of historic or scientific interest" and president had authority under sections 431, 432 and 433 of this title for the protection of American Antiquities to reserve Devil's Hole as a national monument. Cappaert v. U.S., U.S.Nev.1976, 96 S.Ct. 2062, 426 U.S. 128, 48 L.Ed.2d 523. Environmental Law ☞ 527; Environmental Law ☞ 90

Under this section, the President was authorized to establish a monument reserve embracing the Grand Canyon, of the Colorado River; it being an "object of scientific interest." Cameron v. U.S., U.S.Ariz.1920, 40 S.Ct. 410, 252 U.S. 450, 64 L.Ed. 659.

Proclamation No. 2578, Mar. 15, 1943, 57 Stat. 731, declaring the Jackson Hole Country in Wyoming a national monument because of its historic landmarks, prehistoric structures, and other objects of historic or scientific interest, was not shown to be arbitrary so as to justify interference by the courts. State of Wyoming v. Franke, D.C.Wyo.1945, 58 F.Supp. 890. Public Lands ☞ 49

4. Grounds for proclamation

Presidential proclamation withdrawing Devil's Hole from the public domain and making it a part of the Death Valley National Monument was not solely for purpose of preserving only the Devil's Hole pool with its unique limestone formation but also to protect the pupfish, a unique and endangered species living in pool. U.S. v. Cappaert, C.A.9 (Nev.) 1974, 508 F.2d 313, certiorari granted 95 S.Ct. 2654, 422 U.S. 1041, 45 L.Ed.2d 692, affirmed 96 S.Ct. 2062, 426 U.S. 128, 48 L.Ed.2d 523. Environmental Law ☞ 528

President clearly acted pursuant to Antiquities Act in designating 1.7 million acres of federal land in Utah as Grand Staircase National Monument, and thus judicial review of President's exercise of discretion was not available; President's Proclamation spoke in detail of monument's natural and archeological resources and indicated that designated area was smallest consistent with protection of those resources. Utah Ass'n of Counties v. Bush, D.Utah 2004, 316 F.Supp.2d 1172, appeal dismissed 455 F.3d 1094. United States ☞ 57

5. Mining claims

To bring a lode mining claim within the saving clause in the withdrawal of public lands for a monument reserve, under this section, in respect of any "valid" mining claim theretofore acquired, the discovery must have preceded the creation of that reserve. Cameron v. U.S., U.S.Ariz.1920, 40 S.Ct. 410, 252 U.S. 450, 64 L.Ed. 659.

Any injury resulting from voiding of association member's mining claims could not be basis for associational standing to challenge creation of national monument under Antiquities Act or Wilderness Act, inasmuch as voiding of claims was not caused by government's actions in designating monument, but by member's failure to comply with filing requirements. Utah Ass'n of Counties v. Bush, C.A.10 (Utah) 2006, 455 F.3d 1094. United States ☞ 57

6. Water rights

The implied reservation of water rights, as applied to Devil's Hole which was reserved as a national monument by presidential proclamation, was applicable to both surface water and ground water. Cappaert v. U.S., U.S.Nev.1976, 96 S.Ct. 2062, 426 U.S. 128, 48 L.Ed.2d 523. Water Law ☞ 1720

Federal government was not entitled to reserved water for minimum stream flows in the Yampa River through Dinosaur National Monument for recreational purposes; however, determination of federal government's reserved water rights for stream flows for purpose of preserving fish habitats of historic and scientific interest could not be made without further proceedings bearing on the issue of whether Presidential Proclamation of 1938, which enlarged Dinosaur National Monument to protect "objects of historic and scientific interest," intended to reserve water for fish habitats. U.S. v. City and County of Denver, By and Through Bd. of Water Com'rs, Colo.1982, 656 P.2d 1. Water Law ☞ 1703

7. Submerged lands

In creating Glacier Bay National Monument, which later became a national park, the United States reserved the sub-

merged lands underlying Glacier Bay and
the remaining waters within the monument's boundaries, supporting federal
government's claim of submerged lands
in dispute with Alaska; the president issued a proclamation, pursuant to the Antiquities Act, to create the Monument,
and later expanded the Monument to include all of Glacier Bay's waters, exclusion of submerged lands from the monument would have undermined purposes
behind creation of the Monument, and by
the time Alaska achieved statehood, the
Monument had already existed as a federal reservation for 34 years. Alaska v.
U.S., U.S.2005, 125 S.Ct. 2137, 545 U.S.
75, 162 L.Ed.2d 57, entered 126 S.Ct.
1014, 546 U.S. 413, 163 L.Ed.2d 995.
Water Law ☞ 2647

California, and not the United States,
has dominion over submerged lands and
waters within one-mile belts surrounding
Santa Barbara and Anacapa Islands within Channel Islands National Monument.
U.S. v. California, U.S.Cal.1978, 98 S.Ct.
1662, 436 U.S. 32, 56 L.Ed.2d 94. Water
Law ☞ 2647

8. Preexisting property rights

Presidential proclamation, under Antiquities Act, designating national forest as
national monument did not violate any
preexisting property rights; prior settlement which had provided that commercial logging would continue to be available in area did not create right in any
party to actual timber harvest, and no
claimant actually possessed contract for
timber harvest. Tulare County v. Bush,
C.A.D.C.2002, 306 F.3d 1138, 353
U.S.App.D.C. 312, rehearing en banc denied 317 F.3d 227, 354 U.S.App.D.C. 325,
certiorari denied 124 S.Ct. 63, 540 U.S.
813, 157 L.Ed.2d 28. Environmental
Law ☞ 78

9. Abolishment of monuments

Section 431 et seq. of this title, authorizing the President to establish national
monuments, does not authorize him to
abolish them after they have been established. 39 Op.Atty.Gen. 185 (Sept. 26,
1938), 1938 WL 1497.

10. Transfer of monuments

It was not within executive authority to
transfer national monuments under administration of War Department and Department of Agriculture to National Park
Service in Department of the Interior.

36 Op.Atty.Gen. 75 (July 8, 1929), 1929
WL 1723.

11. Action against United States

Where mineral claimants did not con-
tend that federal government officers had
acted beyond authority or under unconstitutional law or orders in withdrawing
an area as a national monument or in
causing default judgment to be entered
voiding claimants' mining claim location
thereon and transferring the property to
the Atomic Energy Commission, claimants' action against the Commission and
Secretary of Interior for declaratory and
other relief was in effect an action against
United States and, in absence of government's consent to be sued, could not be
maintained. Oyler v. McKay, C.A.10
(Utah) 1955, 227 F.2d 604. United States
☞ 125(28.1)

A suit by the State of Wyoming against
a federal officer in the Department of
Interior, alleging that defendant was exceeding his authority in exercising control over the area known as the Jackson
Hole National Monument, was not a suit
against the United States which was not
maintainable, nor was it a suit in which it
was necessary to join defendant's superi-
or officers. State of Wyoming v. Franke,
D.C.Wyo.1945, 58 F.Supp. 890. Declaratory Judgment ☞ 203; Federal Civil Procedure ☞ 219; United States ☞ 125(32);
United States ☞ 135

12. Jurisdiction

An action by the State of Wyoming
challenging the validity of Proclamation
No. 2578, Mar. 15, 1943, 57 Stat. 731,
with respect to the creation of the Jackson Hole National Monument, was an
"action arising under the laws of the
United States" of which the federal district court had jurisdiction. State of Wyoming v. Franke, D.C.Wyo.1945, 58
F.Supp. 890. Federal Courts ☞ 193

13. Declaratory judgment

Where injunction would not lie to enjoin federal interference with the state's
control over the Jackson Hole Country in
Wyoming, designated by Proclamation
No. 2578, Mar. 15, 1943, 57 Stat. 731, as
a national monument, a declaratory judgment could not be substituted for injunction. State of Wyoming v. Franke,
D.C.Wyo.1945, 58 F.Supp. 890. Declaratory Judgment ☞ 41; Declaratory Judgment ☞ 203

14. Stays

City was entitled to stay pending appeal of district court order requiring city to remove Latin cross from veterans' memorial on city property; any harm in brief delay pending the Court of Appeals' expedited consideration of the case was slight compared to the irreparable harm of altering the memorial and removing the cross, Congress had recently deemed the monument a national memorial and authorized the Secretary of the Interior to take title to the memorial if city offered to donate it, and parallel state court litigation presented an opportunity for state courts to address state-law issues pertinent to district court's order. (Per Justice Kennedy, as Circuit Justice.) San Diegans For Mt. Soledad Nat. War Memorial v. Paulson, U.S.2006, 126 S.Ct. 2856, 548

U.S. 1301, 165 L.Ed.2d 941. Federal Courts ☞ 446

15. Review

Agency directives in presidential proclamation designating federal lands as national monument which required, inter alia, that Bureau of Land Management (BLM) prepare management plan and conduct grazing compatibility determination, as well as standards set forth in Federal Land Policy and Management Act (FLPMA) and other applicable statutes concerning BLM's management of federal lands, were sufficiently specific and objective to subject agency action or inaction taken in violation of proclamation to judicial review under Administrative Procedure Act (APA). Western Watersheds Project v. Bureau of Land Management, D.Ariz.2009, 629 F.Supp.2d 951. Public Lands ☞ 17

§ 431a. Limitation on further extension or establishment of national monuments in Wyoming

No further extension or establishment of national monuments in Wyoming may be undertaken except by express authorization of Congress.

(Sept. 14, 1950, c. 950, § 1, 64 Stat. 849.)

HISTORICAL AND STATUTORY NOTES

Revision Notes and Legislative Reports

1950 Acts. House Report No. 2910, see 1950 U.S. Code Cong. Service, p. 3746.

Codifications

Section comprises only part of the last sentence of section 1 of Act Sept. 14, 1950. The remainder of such section, except that part of the last sentence

which repealed sections 406 to 406d of this title, is set out as sections 406d–1 and 451a of this title.

Repeal of Inconsistent Laws

Repeal of laws inconsistent with Act Sept. 14, 1950, see note under section 406d–1 of this title.

CROSS REFERENCES

Grand Teton National Park, see 16 USCA §§ 406d–1 to 406d–3 and 406d–5.

National parks in Wyoming, limitation on further extension or establishment, see 16 USCA § 451a.

LIBRARY REFERENCES

American Digest System

Armed Services ☞54.

United States ☞57.

Woods and Forests ☞1, 2.

Key Number System Topic Nos. 34, 393, 411.

§ 432. Permits to examine ruins, excavations, and gathering of objects; regulations

Permits for the examination of ruins, the excavation of archaeological sites, and the gathering of objects of antiquity upon the lands under their respective jurisdictions may be granted by the Secretaries of the Interior, Agriculture, and Army to institutions which they may deem properly qualified to conduct such examination, excavation, or gathering, subject to such rules and regulations as they may prescribe: *Provided,* That the examinations, excavations, and gatherings are undertaken for the benefit of reputable museums, universities, colleges, or other recognized scientific or educational institutions, with a view to increasing the knowledge of such objects, and that the gatherings shall be made for permanent preservation in public museums. The Secretaries of the departments aforesaid shall make and publish from time to time uniform rules and regulations for the purpose of carrying out the provisions of this section and sections 431 and 433 of this title.

(June 8, 1906, c. 3060, §§ 3, 4, 34 Stat. 225.)

HISTORICAL AND STATUTORY NOTES

Codifications

The last sentence only of this section was derived from section 4 of Act June 8, 1906, the remainder being from section 3.

Change of Name

The Department of War was designated the Department of the Army and the title of the Secretary of War was changed to Secretary of the Army by section 205(a) of Act July 26, 1947, c. 343, Title II, 61 Stat. 501. Section 205(a) of Act July 26, 1947, was repealed by section 53 of Act Aug. 10, 1956, c. 1041, 70A Stat. 641. Section 1 of Act Aug. 10, 1956, enacted "Title 10, Armed Forces" which in sections 3011 to 3013 continued the military Department of the Army under the administrative supervision of a Secretary of the Army.

Transfer of Functions

Enforcement functions of Secretary or other official in Department of Interior related to compliance with permits issued under sections 431, 432 and 433 of this title and such functions of Secretary or other official in Department of Agricul-

ture, insofar as they involve lands and programs under jurisdiction of that Department, related to compliance with removal of objects of antiquity under sections 431, 432, and 433 with respect to pre-construction, construction, and initial operation of transportation system for Canadian and Alaskan natural gas were transferred to the Federal Inspector, Office of Federal Inspector for the Alaska Natural Gas Transportation System, until the first anniversary of date of initial operation of the Alaska Natural Gas Transportation System, see Reorg. Plan No. 1 of 1979, §§ 102(e), (f), 203(a), 44 F.R. 33663, 33666, 93 Stat. 1373, 1376, effective July 1, 1979, set out in Appendix 1 to Title 5, Government Organization and Employees.

Secretary of the Air Force

For transfer of certain functions relating to real property under the jurisdiction of the Department of the Air Force, to the Secretary of the Air Force from the Secretary of the Army, see Secretary of Defense Transfer Order No. 14 [§ 2(25)], eff. July 1, 1948.

CROSS REFERENCES

Disposition and custody of archaeological resources, see 16 USCA § 470dd.
Establishment; Great Basin National Park, see 16 USCA § 410mm.

Excavation and removal, see 16 USCA § 470cc.
National monument in Riverside County, California, see 16 USCA § 434.
Smithsonian Institution, see 20 USCA § 78a.
Use of wilderness areas, see 16 USCA § 1133.
Withdrawals of lands, see 43 USCA § 1714.

CODE OF FEDERAL REGULATIONS

Preservation of antiquities, see 43 CFR § 3.1 et seq.

LIBRARY REFERENCES

American Digest System
> Armed Services ☞54.
> United States ☞57.
> Woods and Forests ☞5.
> Key Number System Topic Nos. 34, 393, 411.

Research References

ALR Library
> 11 ALR, Fed. 2nd Series 623, Validity, Construction, and Application of Antiquities Act of 1906, 16 U.S.C.A. §§ 431 et seq.

Notes of Decisions

Hearing 4
Power of Secretary 1
Procedure for permits 3
Removal of objects 2

1. Power of Secretary

This section gives the Secretary of the Interior broad discretionary power to dispose of objects of antiquity found on federal land under his jurisdiction. People of State of Cal. ex rel. Younger v. Mead, C.A.9 (Cal.) 1980, 618 F.2d 618. Environmental Law ☞ 90

2. Removal of objects

Complaint wherein the state of California and a county museum alleged that the Secretary of the Interior violated this section and regulations promulgated thereunder when he permitted the Smithsonian Institute to remove and study a 6,070 pound meteorite that was found on federal land in Southern California did not state a cause of action. People of State of Cal. ex rel. Younger v. Mead, C.A.9 (Cal.) 1980, 618 F.2d 618. Environmental Law ☞ 90

3. Procedure for permits

Though regulations issued under this section establish a uniform method of applying for antiquities permits, the regulations do not limit the ability of the Secretary of the Interior to act in absence of application nor do they require that the Secretary solicit and choose between competing applications for antiquities permits. People of State of Cal. ex rel. Younger v. Mead, C.A.9 (Cal.) 1980, 618 F.2d 618. Environmental Law ☞ 92; Environmental Law ☞ 90

4. Hearing

Neither the State of California nor the San Bernardino County Museum demonstrated the kind of interest in a 6,070 pound meteorite that had been found on federal land in Southern California which would entitle them to a hearing, as a matter of constitutional right, before the Secretary of the Interior could act under this section to authorize an out-of-state museum to remove the meteorite for study. People of State of Cal. ex rel. Younger v. Mead, C.A.9 (Cal.) 1980, 618 F.2d 618. Environmental Law ☞ 95

§ 433. American antiquities

Any person who shall appropriate, excavate, injure, or destroy any historic or prehistoric ruin or monument, or any object of antiquity, situated on lands owned or controlled by the Government of the United States, without the permission of the Secretary of the Department of the Government having jurisdiction over the lands on which said antiquities are situated, shall, upon conviction, be fined in a sum of not more than $500 or be imprisoned for a period of not more than ninety days, or shall suffer both fine and imprisonment, in the discretion of the court.

(June 8, 1906, c. 3060, § 1, 34 Stat. 225.)

HISTORICAL AND STATUTORY NOTES

Transfer of Functions

Enforcement functions of Secretary or other official in Department of Interior related to compliance with permits issued under sections 431, 432, and 433 of this title and such functions of Secretary or other official in Department of Agriculture, insofar as they involve lands and programs under jurisdiction of that Department, related to compliance with removal of objects of antiquity under sections 431, 432, and 433 with respect to pre-construction, construction, and initial operation of transportation system for Canadian and Alaskan natural gas were transferred to the Federal Inspector, Office of Federal Inspector for the Alaska Natural Gas Transportation System, until the first anniversary of date of initial operation of the Alaska Natural Gas Transportation System, see Reorg. Plan No. 1 of 1979, §§ 102(e), (f), 203(a), 44 F.R. 33663, 33666, 93 Stat. 1373, 1376, effective July 1, 1979, set out in Appendix 1 to Title 5, Government Organization and Employees.

CROSS REFERENCES

Disposition and custody of archaeological resources, see 16 USCA § 470dd.
Establishment; Great Basin National Park, see 16 USCA § 410mm.
Excavation and removal, see 16 USCA § 470cc.
National monument in Riverside County, California, see 16 USCA § 434.
Permits to examine ruins, excavations, and gathering of objects, see 16 USCA § 432.
Smithsonian Institution, see 20 USCA § 78a.
Use of wilderness areas, see 16 USCA § 1133.
Withdrawals of lands, see 43 USCA § 1714.

CODE OF FEDERAL REGULATIONS

Criminal law enforcement, see 43 CFR § 9260.0–1.

LAW REVIEW AND JOURNAL COMMENTARIES

A synopsis of the laws protecting our cultural heritage. Marilyn Phelan, 28 New Eng.L.Rev. 63 (1993).
Bones of contention: Regulation of paleontological resources on the federal public lands. Note, 69 Ind.L.J. 601 (1994).
Preserving Utah's cultural resources: A proposal for new legislation. Comment, 10 J.Energy L. & Pol'y 93 (1989).

LIBRARY REFERENCES

American Digest System
Armed Services ☞54.
United States ☞57.
Woods and Forests ☞5, 10, 11.
Key Number System Topic Nos. 34, 393, 411.

Corpus Juris Secundum
CJS Public Lands § 5, Trespasses on Public Lands.

Research References

ALR Library

11 ALR, Fed. 2nd Series 623, Validity, Construction, and Application of Antiquities Act of 1906, 16 U.S.C.A. §§ 431 et seq.

184 ALR, Fed. 139, Validity, Construction, and Operation of Archaeological Resources Protection Act of 1979, 16 U.S.C.A. §§ 470aa to 470mm.

110 ALR, Fed. 313, Reports of Tests, Experiments, or Analyses as Subject to Discovery by Defendant under Rule 16 of Federal Rules of Criminal Procedure.

42 ALR, Fed. 901, Validity, Construction, and Application of 18 U.S.C.A. § 1361, Making It Unlawful to Willfully Injure or Commit Any Depredation Against Any Property of the United States.

Encyclopedias

25 Am. Jur. Proof of Facts 2d 685, Abandonment of Tangible Personal Property.

Treatises and Practice Aids

Wright & Miller: Federal Prac. & Proc. § 142, Misjoinder, Duplicity, and Multiplicity.

Notes of Decisions

Constitutionality 1
Construction with other laws 2
Hearing 5
Jury trial 6
Lands owned or controlled by United States 4
Purpose 3
Weight and sufficiency of evidence 7

1. Constitutionality

As applied in prosecution of defendants for taking artifacts from ancient sites for commercial motives, this section was not unconstitutionally vague or uncertain. U.S. v. Smyer, C.A.10 (N.M.) 1979, 596 F.2d 939, certiorari denied 100 S.Ct. 84, 444 U.S. 843, 62 L.Ed.2d 55. Public Lands ☞ 8

This section which prohibited the appropriation, excavation, or injuring of any historic or prehistoric ruin or monument or any object of antiquity situated on lands owned or controlled by the United States Government, which did not define such terms as "ruin," "monument," or "object of antiquity," and which was asserted by Government to protect objects not only on the basis of their age but also on basis of use for which they were made and to which they were put, was fatally vague in violation of due process clause of the Fifth Amendment. U.S. v. Diaz, C.A.9 (Ariz.) 1974, 499 F.2d 113. Constitutional Law ☞ 4509(1); Public Lands ☞ 8

2. Construction with other laws

In enacting this section, Congress did not mean to limit applicability of general theft and malicious mischief statutes, sections 641 and 1361 of Title 18, nor did Congress, in enacting general theft and malicious mischief statutes, intend that they would not apply to conduct covered by this section; thus, government was not precluded from prosecuting defendants under the more general statutes for alleged conduct which was prohibited by express language of the general statutes. U.S. v. Jones, C.A.9 (Ariz.) 1979, 607 F.2d 269, certiorari denied 100 S.Ct. 1043, 444 U.S. 1085, 62 L.Ed.2d 771. Criminal Law ☞ 29(10)

3. Purpose

This section was intended to facilitate preservation of objects of historical importance, and it did not subrogate United States to prerogative rights of English Crown. Treasure Salvors, Inc. v. Unidentified Wrecked and Abandoned Sailing Vessel, C.A.5 (Fla.) 1978, 569 F.2d 330. Environmental Law ☞ 90

This section, prohibiting inter alia, the appropriation of "any object of antiquity" situated on government lands, was intended to protect American Indians from those who would appropriate, excavate or injure any historic monument or object of "antiquity" situated on Indian lands. U.S. v. Diaz, D.C.Ariz.1973, 368 F.Supp. 856, reversed on other grounds 499 F.2d 113. Public Lands ☞ 8

4. Lands owned or controlled by United States

Where wreck of vessel thought to be Spanish vessel which sank in 1622 rested on continental shelf outside territorial waters of United States, remains of vessel were not situated on lands owned or controlled by United States under this section. Treasure Salvors, Inc. v. Unidentified Wrecked and Abandoned Sailing Vessel, C.A.5 (Fla.) 1978, 569 F.2d 330. United States ☞ 2

5. Hearing

Hearing was required to determine temporary custodian for rare dinosaur fossil found on land owned by federal government pending final disposition of main action to determine ownership, despite government's contention that fossil was evidence from investigation of Antiquities Act violations, since seizure deprived public and scientific community from viewing and studying rare find, parties which sought return had interest in preserving fossil, fossil continued to deteriorate while being stored at machine shop, and government did not need to retain "priceless" fossil in order to preserve evidence in petty misdemeanor criminal prosecution. Black Hills Institute of Geological Research v. U.S. Dept. of Justice, C.A.8 (S.D.) 1992, 967 F.2d 1237, rehearing denied. Searches And Seizures ☞ 84

6. Jury trial

Record in prosecution for violation of this section established that defendants knowingly and voluntarily waived their right to jury trial; in any case, defendants had no right to jury trial where concurrent sentences of less than six months were imposed. U.S. v. Smyer, C.A.10 (N.M.) 1979, 596 F.2d 939, certiorari denied 100 S.Ct. 84, 444 U.S. 843, 62 L.Ed.2d 55. Jury ☞ 22(2); Jury ☞ 29(6)

7. Weight and sufficiency of evidence

In prosecution for violation of this section, evidence failed to support defendants' contention that they believed that they were on private property when they excavated for artifacts. U.S. v. Smyer, C.A.10 (N.M.) 1979, 596 F.2d 939, certiorari denied 100 S.Ct. 84, 444 U.S. 843, 62 L.Ed.2d 55. Public Lands ☞ 8

§ 433a. Perry's Victory and International Peace Memorial; establishment

The President of the United States is authorized to establish by proclamation the following-described Government lands, together with the Perry's Victory Memorial proper, its approaches, retaining walls, and all buildings, structures, and other property thereon, situated in Put-in-Bay Township, South Bass Island, Ottawa County, Lake Erie, State of Ohio, as the "Perry's Victory and International Peace Memorial", for the preservation of the historical associations connected therewith, to inculcate the lessons of international peace by arbitration and disarmament, and for the benefit and enjoyment of the people: Commencing at the intersection of the middle line of Delaware Avenue and Chapman Avenue, in the village of Put-in-Bay, and running thence south eighty-eight degrees fifty-nine minutes east in the middle line of said Delaware Avenue, and the same extended four hundred and ninety-five feet to Lake Erie; thence north forty-nine degrees fifty-nine minutes east along said lake shore three hundred and forty-six feet; thence north forty-three degrees fourteen minutes east along said lake shore two hundred and twelve feet; thence north fifty-three degrees thirteen minutes east four hundred feet along said lake shore; thence north forty-six degrees six minutes west about seven hundred and thirty feet to Lake Erie; thence southwesterly and westerly along said lake shore to the middle line, extended, of said Chapman Avenue; thence south one degree thirty minutes west along said middle line, and the same extended, about five hundred and twenty feet to the place of beginning, and containing fourteen and twenty-five one-hundredths acres of land and known as a part of lots numbered 1 and 2, range south of county road, and a part of lot numbered 12, East Point, in South Bass Island, in the township of Put-in-Bay, county of Ottawa, State of Ohio.

(June 2, 1936, c. 477, § 1, 49 Stat. 1393; Oct. 26, 1972, Pub.L. 92–568, § 1, 86 Stat. 1181.)

HISTORICAL AND STATUTORY NOTES

Change of Name
"Perry's Victory and International Peace Memorial" was substituted for "Perry's Victory and International Peace Memorial National Monument" to conform to the redesignation provided in section 1 of Pub.L. 92–568, classified to section 433f–1 of this title.

Establishment of Memorial; Boundaries
Memorial and boundaries established by Presidential Proc. No. 2182, July 6, 1936, 50 Stat. 1734.

LIBRARY REFERENCES

American Digest System
Armed Services ⊗⇒54.
United States ⊗⇒57.
Woods and Forests ⊗⇒1, 8.
Key Number System Topic Nos. 34, 393, 411.

§ 433b. Administration, protection, and development

The administration, protection and development of the aforesaid peace memorial shall be exercised under the direction of the Secretary of the Interior by the National Park Service, subject to the provisions of sections 1, 2, 3, and 4 of this title, as amended.

(June 2, 1936, c. 477, § 2, 49 Stat. 1394; Oct. 26, 1972, Pub.L. 92–568, § 1, 86 Stat. 1181.)

HISTORICAL AND STATUTORY NOTES

Change of Name
"Peace memorial" was substituted for "national monument" to conform to the redesignation of Perry's Victory and International Peace Memorial National Monument as Perry's Victory and International Peace Memorial provided in section 1 of Pub.L. 92–568, classified to section 433f–1 of this title.

Transfer of Functions
All functions of all other officers of the Department of the Interior and all functions of all agencies and employees of such Department were, with two exceptions, transferred to the Secretary of the Interior, with power vested in him to authorize their performance or the performance of any of his functions by any of such officers, agencies, and employees by 1950 Reorg. Plan. No. 3, §§ 1, 2, eff. May 24, 1950, 15 F.R. 3174, 64 Stat. 1262, set out in Appendix 1 to Title 5, Government Organization and Employees.

§ 433c.   Acceptance of donations of lands and funds;   acquisition of land

After the said peace memorial has been established as provided in section 433a of this title the Secretary of the Interior is authorized to accept donations of land, interests in land, buildings, structures, and other property as may be donated for the extension and improvement of the said peace memorial, and donations of funds for the purchase and maintenance thereof, the title and evidence of title to lands acquired to be satisfactory to the Secretary of the Interior: *Provided*, That he may acquire on behalf of the United States out of any donated funds by purchase when purchasable at prices deemed by him reasonable, otherwise by condemnation under the provisions of section 3113 of Title 40, such tracts of land within the said peace memorial as may be necessary for the completion thereof.   The Secretary of the Interior is authorized to purchase with appropriated funds not to exceed four acres of land, or interests in land, for addition to the Perry's Victory and International Peace Memorial.

(June 2, 1936, c. 477, § 3, 49 Stat. 1394;   Oct. 26, 1972, Pub.L. 92–568, §§ 1, 2, 86 Stat. 1181, 1182.)

HISTORICAL AND STATUTORY NOTES

Codifications

In text, "section 3113 of Title 40" substituted for "sections 257 and 258 of Title 40", which originally read "the Act of August 1, 1888" on authority of Pub.L. 107–217, § 5(c), Aug. 21, 2002, 116 Stat. 1301, which is set out as a note preceding 40 U.S.C.A. § 101. Pub.L. 107–217, § 1, enacted Title 40 into positive law. The Act of August 1, 1888, is Act, Aug. 1, 1888, c. 728, 25 Stat. 357, which was classified to former 40 U.S.C.A. §§ 257 and 258, prior to being repealed by Pub.L. 107–217, § 6(b), Aug. 21, 2002, 116 Stat. 1305, and its substance reenacted as 40 U.S.C.A. § 3113.   Section 258 of Title 40 was previously omitted from the Code as superseded by Rule 71A, Federal Rules of Civil Procedure, Title 28.

Amendments

1972 Amendments. Pub.L. 92–568, § 2, authorized acquisition of an additional four acres of land.

Change of Name

"Peace memorial" was substituted for "national monument" to conform to the redesignation of Perry's Victory and International Peace Memorial National Monument as Perry's Victory and International Peace Memorial provided in section 1 of Pub.L. 92–568, classified to section 433f–1 of this title.

Transfer of Functions

All functions of all other officers of the Department of the Interior and all functions of all agencies and employees of such Department were, with two exceptions, transferred to the Secretary of the Interior, with power vested in him to authorize their performance or the performance of any of his functions by any of such officers, agencies, and employees, by 1950 Reorg. Plan No. 3, §§ 1, 2, eff. May 24, 1950, 15 F.R. 3174, 64 Stat. 1262, set out in Appendix 1 to Title 5,

Government Organization and Employees.

Authorization of Appropriations
Pub.L. 92–568, § 4, Oct. 26, 1972, 86 Stat. 1182, as amended Pub.L. 95–625, Title I, § 101(21), Nov. 10, 1978, 92 Stat. 3472; Pub.L. 98–141, § 7(a), Oct. 31, 1983, 97 Stat. 910; Pub.L. 98–181, Title I, § 1401, Nov. 30, 1983, 97 Stat. 1294, provided that: "There are authorized to be appropriated such sums as may be necessary to carry out the purposes of this Act [enacting section 433f–1, amending sections 433a to 433c and 433e, and repealing section 433d of this title, and enacting provisions set out as a note hereunder], but not more than $370,000 shall be appropriated for the acquisition of lands and interests in lands and not more than $10,500,000 shall be appropriated for development. The sums authorized in this section shall be available for acquisition and development undertaken subsequent to the approval of this Act [such sections]."

LIBRARY REFERENCES

American Digest System
Armed Services ⊗54.
United States ⊗55.
Key Number System Topic Nos. 34, 393.

§ 433d. Repealed. Pub.L. 92–568, § 3(2), Oct. 26, 1972, 86 Stat. 1182

HISTORICAL AND STATUTORY NOTES

Section, Act June 2, 1936, c. 477, § 4, 49 Stat. 1394, provided that members of Perry's Victory Memorial Commission created by Act Mar. 3, 1919, c. 116, 40 Stat. 1322, act as a board of advisors, and also provided for number of members, method of filling vacancies, and travel expenses but no compensation for the members.

§ 433e. Repealed. Pub.L. 98–141, § 7(b), Oct. 31, 1983, 97 Stat. 910

HISTORICAL AND STATUTORY NOTES

Section, Act June 2, 1936, c. 477, § 5, 49 Stat. 1395; Oct. 26, 1972, Pub.L. 92–568, § 1, 86 Stat. 1181, provided that employees of the Perry's Victory Memorial Commission on June 2, 1936, could, in the discretion of the Secretary of the Interior, be employed by the National Park Service in the administration, protection, and development of the memorial.

§ 433f. Inconsistent laws repealed

The provisions of the Act of March 3, 1919 (c. 116, 40 Stat. 1322–1324), and Acts supplemental thereof and amendatory thereto and all other Acts inconsistent with the provisions of sections 433a to 433f of this title are repealed to the extent of such inconsistency.

(June 2, 1936, c. 477, § 6, 49 Stat. 1395.)

HISTORICAL AND STATUTORY NOTES

References in Text

The Act of March 3, 1919 (c. 116, 40 Stat. 1322–1324), referred to in text, made provision for the creation of the Perry's Victory Memorial Commission. Neither that Act nor any Acts supplementary thereof and amendatory thereto, also referred to in text, were classified to the Code.

Section 433d of this title, included within the reference to sections 433a to 433f of this title, was repealed by Pub.L. 92–568, § 3(2), Oct. 26, 1972, 86 Stat. 1182.

Section 433e of this title, included within the reference to sections 433a to 433f of this title, was repealed by Pub.L. 98–141, § 7(b), Oct. 31, 1983, 97 Stat. 910.

§ 433f–1. Change in name of Perry's Victory and International Peace Memorial National Monument

The Perry's Victory and International Peace Memorial National Monument, established in accordance with section 433a of this title, is redesignated the Perry's Victory and International Peace Memorial.

(Pub.L. 92–568, § 1, Oct. 26, 1972, 86 Stat. 1181.)

LIBRARY REFERENCES

American Digest System

Armed Services ⇝54.
Woods and Forests ⇝1.
Key Number System Topic Nos. 34, 411.

§ 433g. Fort Frederica National Monument; establishment

When title to the site of Fort Frederica, on Saint Simon Island, Georgia, and such other related sites located thereon, as may be designated by the Secretary of the Interior, in the exercise of his discretion, as necessary or desirable for national-monument purposes, shall have been vested in the United States, said area not to exceed two hundred and fifty acres shall be, and is, set apart as a national monument for the benefit and inspiration of the people, and shall be called the "Fort Frederica National Monument."

(May 26, 1936, c. 451, § 1, 49 Stat. 1373; Sept. 20, 1950, c. 957, § 1, 64 Stat. 869; May 16, 1958, Pub.L. 85–401, § 1, 72 Stat. 110.)

HISTORICAL AND STATUTORY NOTES

Revision Notes and Legislative Reports

1950 Acts. Senate Report No. 2553, see 1950 U.S. Code Cong. Service, p. 3762.

1958 Acts. Senate Report No. 1499, see 1958 U.S. Code Cong. and Adm. News, p. 2433.

Amendments

1958 Amendments. Pub.L. 85–401 increased the maximum acreage from one hundred acres to two hundred and fifty acres.

1950 Amendments. Act Sept. 20, 1950, increased the maximum acreage from eighty to one hundred acres.

Land Exchange and Boundary Adjustment

Pub.L. 108–417, §§ 1, 2, Nov. 30, 2004, 118 Stat. 2339, provided that:

"**Section 1.   Exchange of lands.**

"**(a) In general.**—Notwithstanding section 5(b) of Public Law 90–401 (16 U.S.C. 460l–22(b)), the Secretary of the Interior is authorized to convey to Christ Church of St. Simons Island, Georgia, the approximately 6.0 acres of land within the boundary of Fort Frederica National Monument adjacent to Christ Church and depicted as 'NPS Lands for Exchange' on the map entitled 'Fort Frederica National Monument 2003 Boundary Revision' numbered 369/ 80016, and dated April 2003, in exchange for approximately 8.7 acres of land to be acquired by Christ Church, which is depicted as 'Private Lands for Addition' on the same map.

"**(b) Map availability.**—The map referred to in subsection (a) shall be on file and available for public inspection in the appropriate offices of the National Park Service.

"**Sec. 2.   Boundary adjustment.**

"Upon completion of the land exchange under subsection (a) of section 1 [of this note], the Secretary of the Interior shall revise the boundary of Fort Frederica National Monument to reflect the exchange and shall administer the land acquired through the exchange as part of that monument."

Authorization of Appropriations

Act Sept. 20, 1950, c. 957, § 2, 64 Stat. 869, provided that: "There is hereby authorized to be appropriated not to exceed $5,000 for the acquisition of land and interests in land for the said national monument. The Secretary of the Interior is authorized to use any funds so appropriated, together with any donated funds made available pursuant to the aforesaid Act of May 26, 1936 [sections 433g, 433h, 433i, and 433j of this title], for the procurement of land and interests in land for the national monument."

LIBRARY REFERENCES

American Digest System
Armed Services ⬆54.
Woods and Forests ⬆1, 8.
Key Number System Topic Nos. 34, 411.

§ 433h. Donation of property; acquisition of lands

The Secretary of the Interior is authorized to accept donations of land, interests in land, buildings, structures, and other property within the boundaries of the said national monument as determined and fixed hereunder, and donations of funds for the purchase and maintenance thereof, the title and evidence of title to lands acquired to be satisfactory to the Secretary of the Interior: *Provided*, That he may acquire on behalf of the United States out of any donated funds, either by purchase at prices deemed by him reasonable, or by condemnation under the provisions of section 3113 of Title 40, such tracts of land within the said national monument as may be necessary for the completion thereof.

(May 26, 1936, c. 451, § 2, 49 Stat. 1373.)

HISTORICAL AND STATUTORY NOTES

Codifications

In text, "section 3113 of Title 40" substituted for "sections 257 and 258 of Title 40", which originally read "the Act of August 1, 1888" on authority of Pub.L. 107–217, § 5(c), Aug. 21, 2002, 116 Stat. 1301, which is set out as a note preceding 40 U.S.C.A. § 101. Pub.L. 107–217, § 1,

enacted Title 40 into positive law. The
Act of August 1, 1888, is Act, Aug. 1,
1888, c. 728, 25 Stat. 357, which was
classified to former 40 U.S.C.A. §§ 257
and 258, prior to being repealed by
Pub.L. 107–217, § 6(b), Aug. 21, 2002,

116 Stat. 1305, and its substance reenacted as 40 U.S.C.A. § 3113. Section
258 of Title 40 was previously omitted
from the Code as superseded by Rule
71.1, Federal Rules of Civil Procedure,
Title 28.

LIBRARY REFERENCES

American Digest System
> Armed Services ⊙54.
> United States ⊙55.
> Key Number System Topic Nos. 34, 393.

§ 433h–1. Acquisition of additional lands

The Secretary of the Interior is authorized and directed to acquire
by purchase, condemnation, or otherwise, subject to the acreage
limitation contained in section 433g of this title, the site known as the
Bloody Marsh Battle memorial monument located on Saint Simon
Island, Georgia, together with such additional land, including the
marshland across the river to the west of Fort Frederica National
Monument, or interest in land, as in the judgment of the Secretary of
the Interior might be desirable for the protection of such national
monument. Such lands or interest in lands acquired by the Secretary pursuant to this section shall be made a part of the Fort
Frederica National Monument.

(Pub.L. 85–401, § 2, May 16, 1958, 72 Stat. 110.)

HISTORICAL AND STATUTORY NOTES

Revision Notes and Legislative Reports
   1958 Acts. Senate Report No. 1499,
see 1958 U.S. Code Cong. and Adm.
News, p. 2433.

Authorization of Appropriations
   Pub.L. 85–401, § 3, May 16, 1958, 72
Stat. 110, provided that: "There are here-

by authorized to be appropriated, out of
any money in the Treasury not otherwise
appropriated, such amounts, not to exceed $20,000, as may be necessary to
carry out the provisions of this Act [this
section]."

LIBRARY REFERENCES

American Digest System
> Armed Services ⊙54.
> United States ⊙55.
> Key Number System Topic Nos. 34, 393.

§ 433i. Museum; historical markers

(a) Maintenance; donations

The Secretary of the Interior is authorized, in his discretion, to
maintain in some suitable structure within the national monument a
museum for relics and records pertaining to Fort Frederica, and for

other articles of national and patriotic interest, and in his discretion to accept, on behalf of the United States, for installation in such museum, articles which may be offered as additions to the museum.

(b) State and local participation

Any State or political subdivision thereof, organization, or individual may, with the approval of the Secretary of the Interior, erect monuments or place tablets commemorating historic events or persons connected with the history of the area, within the boundaries of the Fort Frederica National Monument.

(May 26, 1936, c. 451, § 3, 49 Stat. 1373.)

LIBRARY REFERENCES

American Digest System
Armed Services ⚖54.
United States ⚖57.
Woods and Forests ⚖5.
Key Number System Topic Nos. 34, 393, 411.

§ 433j. Administration, protection, and development

The administration, protection, and development of the aforesaid national monument shall be exercised under the direction of the Secretary of the Interior by the National Park Service, subject to the provisions of sections 1, 2, 3, and 4 of this title, as amended.

(May 26, 1936, c. 451, § 4, 49 Stat. 1373.)

HISTORICAL AND STATUTORY NOTES

Transfer of Functions

All functions of all other officers of the Department of the Interior and all functions of all agencies and employees of such Department were, with two exceptions, transferred to the Secretary of the Interior, with power vested in him to authorize their performance or the performance of any of his functions by any of such officers, agencies, and employees, by 1950 Reorg. Plan No. 3, §§ 1, 2, eff. May 24, 1950, 15 F.R. 3174, 64 Stat. 1262, set out in Appendix 1 to Title 5, Government Organization and Employees.

LIBRARY REFERENCES

American Digest System
Armed Services ⚖54.
Woods and Forests ⚖5.
Key Number System Topic Nos. 34, 411.

§ 433k. Whitman Mission National Historic Site; acquisition of land; establishment, supervision and maintenance

The Secretary of the Interior is authorized and directed to acquire, on behalf of the United States, by gift, the site of the Indian mission established in 1836 by Marcus Whitman on the Walla Walla River in what is now Walla Walla County, Washington, together with such additional land, including a right-of-way to the nearest highway, as the Secretary may deem necessary to carry out the purposes of this section.

The property acquired under the provisions of the first paragraph of this section shall constitute the Whitman Mission National Historic Site and shall be a public national memorial to Marcus Whitman and his wife, Narcissa Prentiss Whitman, who here established their Indian mission and school, and ministered to the physical and spiritual needs of the Indians until massacred with twelve others [1] persons in 1847. The Director of the National Park Service, under the direction of the Secretary of the Interior, shall have the supervision, management, and control of such national historic site, and shall maintain and preserve it for the benefit and enjoyment of the people of the United States.

(June 29, 1936, c. 863, §§ 1, 2, 49 Stat. 2028; May 31, 1962, Pub.L. 87–471, 76 Stat. 90.)

[1] So in original. Probably should be "other".

HISTORICAL AND STATUTORY NOTES

Change of Name

"Whitman Mission National Historic Site" and "national historic site" were substituted for "Whitman National Monument" and "national monument", respectively, pursuant to Pub.L. 87–471, May 31, 1962, 76 Stat. 90, which redesignated the Whitman National Monument as the Whitman Mission National Historic Site. See section 433n of this title.

Transfer of Functions

All functions of all other officers of the Department of the Interior and all functions of all agencies and employees of such Department were, with two exceptions, transferred to the Secretary of the Interior, with power vested in him to authorize their performance or the performance of any of his functions by any of such officers, agencies, and employees, by 1950 Reorg. Plan No. 3, §§ 1, 2, eff. May 24, 1950, 15 F.R. 3174, 64 Stat. 1262, set out in Appendix 1 to Title 5, Government Organization and Employees.

LIBRARY REFERENCES

American Digest System
  Armed Services ⚷54.
  United States ⚷55.
  Woods and Forests ⚷5, 8.
  Key Number System Topic Nos. 34, 393, 411.

§ 433k–1. Acquisition of additional land

For the purpose of including within Whitman Mission National Historic Site, Washington, certain properties that are of historic significance in connection with the site area and which are needed to provide suitable monument facilities, the Secretary of the Interior is authorized to procure not to exceed fifty acres of land adjacent to the existing site and a right-of-way thereto from United States Highway

410, using therefor any land acquisition funds available for the purposes of the national park system, such property to be acquired in such manner as the Secretary shall consider to be in the public interest. Following the acquisition by the United States of land for addition to the site pursuant to this section, such addition shall be effective in each instance upon the publication of notice thereof in the Federal Register.

(Pub.L. 85–388, May 1, 1958, 72 Stat. 101; Pub.L. 87–471, May 31, 1962, 76 Stat. 90.)

HISTORICAL AND STATUTORY NOTES

Revision Notes and Legislative Reports
  1958 Acts. House Report No. 1577, see 1958 U.S. Code Cong. and Adm. News, p. 2417.

Change of Name
"Whitman Mission National Historic Site" and "site" were substituted for "Whitman National Monument" and "monument", respectively, pursuant to Pub.L. 87–471, May 31, 1962, 76 Stat. 90, which redesignated the Whitman National Monument as the Whitman Mission National Historic Site. See section 433n of this title.

LIBRARY REFERENCES

American Digest System
  Armed Services ☞54.
  United States ☞55.
  Key Number System Topic Nos. 34, 393.

§ 433*l*. Erection of monuments and tablets

Any State, or political subdivision thereof, organization, or individual may, with the approval of the Secretary of the Interior, erect monuments or place tablets within the boundaries of the Whitman Mission National Historic Site.

(June 29, 1936, c. 863, § 3, 49 Stat. 2029; May 31, 1962, Pub.L. 87–471, 76 Stat. 90.)

HISTORICAL AND STATUTORY NOTES

Change of Name
"Whitman Mission National Historic Site" was substituted for "Whitman National Monument" pursuant to Pub.L. 87–471, May 31, 1962, 76 Stat. 90, which redesignated the Whitman National Monument as the Whitman Mission National Historic Site. See section 433n of this title.

LIBRARY REFERENCES

American Digest System
  Armed Services ☞54.
  United States ☞57.
  Key Number System Topic Nos. 34, 393.

§ 433m.   Authorization of appropriation

There are authorized to be appropriated such sums as may be necessary to carry out the provisions of sections 433k and 433*l* of this title.

(June 29, 1936, c. 863, § 4, 49 Stat. 2029.)

§ 433n.   Change in name of Whitman National Monument

Effective January 1, 1963, the Whitman National Monument, established pursuant to sections 433k, 433*l* and 433m of this title, shall be known as the Whitman Mission National Historic Site.

(Pub.L. 87–471, May 31, 1962, 76 Stat. 90.)

LIBRARY REFERENCES

American Digest System
> Armed Services ☞54.
> Woods and Forests ☞1.
> Key Number System Topic Nos. 34, 411.

§ 434.   National monument in Riverside County, California

The Secretary of the Interior is authorized to set apart the following-described lands located in the county of Riverside, in the State of California, as a national monument, which shall be under the exclusive control of the Secretary of the Interior, who shall administer and protect the same under the provisions of sections 431, 432 and 433 of this title, and under such regulations as he may prescribe: The west half of the southwest quarter of section 2, the southeast quarter of section 3, all of section 10, the west half of the northwest quarter of section 11, all of section 14, all in township 5 south, range 4 east, San Bernardino base and meridian, containing one thousand six hundred acres: *Provided*, That before such reservation and dedication as herein authorized shall become effective the consent and relinquishment of the Agua Caliente Band of Indians shall first be obtained, covering its right, title, and interest in and to the lands herein described, and payment therefor to the members of said band on a per capita basis, at a price to be agreed upon, when there shall be donated for such purposes to the Secretary of the Interior a fund in an amount to be fixed and determined by him as sufficient to compensate the Indians therefor.

(Aug. 26, 1922, c. 295, § 1, 42 Stat. 832.)

LIBRARY REFERENCES

American Digest System
> Armed Services ☞54.

Woods and Forests ⊙1, 8.
Key Number System Topic Nos. 34, 411.

§ 435. Acquiring reservation land

In order to determine the amount to be paid under section 434 of this title the Secretary of the Interior is authorized and directed to negotiate with said Indians to obtain their consent and relinquishment, and when such consent and relinquishment has been obtained and an agreement reached the Secretary of the Interior is further authorized to make payment from said donated fund for the lands relinquished to the enrolled members of the said Agua Caliente Band as authorized by section 434 of this title. The consent and relinquishment of the Indians may be obtained and payment made for the lands in such manner as the Secretary of the Interior may deem advisable. The water rights, dam, pipe lines, canals, and irrigation structures located in sections 2 and 3 of township 5 south, range 4 east, San Bernardino meridian, and also all water and water rights in Palm Canyon, are excepted from this reserve and shall remain under the exclusive control and supervision of the Bureau of Indian Affairs. The provisions of the Federal Power Act [16 U.S.C.A. § 791a et seq.] shall not apply to this monument.

(Aug. 26, 1922, c. 295, §§ 2, 3, 42 Stat. 832.)

HISTORICAL AND STATUTORY NOTES

References in Text

The Federal Power Act, referred to in text, was in the original the "Act of Congress approved June 10, 1920, known as the Federal Water Power Act", and was redesignated as the Federal Power Act by section 791a of this title. The Federal Power Act is Act June 10, 1920, c. 285, 41 Stat. 1063, as amended, and is classified generally to chapter 12 (section 791a et seq.) of this title. For complete classification of this Act to the Code, see section 791a of this title and Tables.

Codifications

This section is a combination provision, the last sentence of which is from section 3 of Act Aug. 26, 1922, the remainder being derived from section 2 of that Act.

Transfer of Functions

All functions of all other officers of the Department of the Interior and all functions of all agencies and employees of such Department were, with two exceptions, transferred to the Secretary of the Interior, with power vested in him to authorize their performance or the performance of any of his functions by any of such officers, agencies, and employees, by 1950 Reorg. Plan No. 3, §§ 1, 2, eff. May 24, 1950, 15 F.R. 3174, 64 Stat. 1262, set out in Appendix 1 to Title 5, Government Organization and Employees.

LIBRARY REFERENCES

American Digest System

Armed Services ⊙54.
Indians ⊙150.
United States ⊙55.
Key Number System Topic Nos. 34, 209, 393.

§ 436. Omitted

HISTORICAL AND STATUTORY NOTES

Codifications

Section, Act Apr. 9, 1924, c. 86, § 3, 43 Stat. 90, related to the transfer by the Secretary of the Agriculture to the Secre-tary of the Interior for road purposes of part of the material, equipment and supplies received from the Secretary of War.

§ 437. Fort McHenry; restoration and preservation

The Secretary of the Interior is authorized and directed to begin the restoration of Fort McHenry, in the State of Maryland, including the restoration of the old Fort McHenry proper to such a condition as would make it suitable for preservation permanently as a national monument and perpetual national memorial shrine as the birthplace of the immortal "Star-Spangled Banner" written by Francis Scott Key, and he is further authorized and directed, as are his successors, to hold the said Fort McHenry in perpetuity as a military reservation, national monument and historic shrine, and to maintain it as such, except that part mentioned in section 439 of this title, and that part in use on March 3, 1925, by the Department of Commerce for a light and fog-signal station under revocable license from the Interior Department with the maintenance of the electric lines thereto and such portion of the reservation, including improvement, as may be reserved by the Secretary of the Army for the use of the Chief of Engineers, the said reservation to be maintained as a national public monument, subject to such regulations as may from time to time be issued by the Secretary of the Interior.

(May 26, 1914, c. 100, 38 Stat. 382; Mar. 3, 1925, c. 425, 43 Stat. 1109; Ex.Ord. No. 6166, § 2, June 10, 1933; Ex.Ord. No. 6228, § 1, July 28, 1933; Aug. 11, 1939, c. 686, 53 Stat. 1405.)

HISTORICAL AND STATUTORY NOTES

Codifications

This section and sections 438 to 440 of this title were derived from Act Mar. 3, 1925, which was entitled "An act to repeal and reenact chapter 100, 1914, Public, Numbered 108, to provide for the restoration of Fort McHenry, in the State of Maryland, and its permanent preservation as a national park and perpetual national memorial shrine as the birthplace of the immortal 'Star-Spangled Banner,' written by Francis Scott Key, for the appropriation of the necessary funds, and for other purposes." The enacting clause reads as follows: "Be it enacted by the Senate and House of Representatives of the United States of America in Congress assembled, That an Act authorizing the Secretary of War to grant the use of the Fort McHenry Military Reservation in the State of Maryland to the mayor and city council of Baltimore, a municipal corporation of the State of Maryland, making certain provisions in connection therewith, providing access to and from the site of the new immigration station heretofore set aside be, and hereby is, repealed and reenacted to read as follows."

As reenacted in 1925 this section recites that Fort McHenry is "now" occupied and used as a military reservation and authorized the restoration "so soon as it may no longer be needed for uses and needs growing out of the late war."

The foregoing provisions have been omitted as temporary.

The words of this section "on March 3, 1925" refer to the date of passage of the Act.

Change of Name

"National monument", "national monument and historic shrine" and "national public monument" were substituted for "national park", "national park, and memorial" and "national public park" respectively, in view of the change in name effected by Act Aug. 11, 1939. See section 440a of this title.

The Department of War was designated the Department of the Army and the title of the Secretary of War was changed to Secretary of the Army by section 205(a) of Act July 26, 1947, c. 343, Title II, 61 Stat. 501. Section 205(a) of Act July 26, 1947, was repealed by section 53 of Act Aug. 10, 1956, c. 1041, 70A Stat. 641. Section 1 of Act Aug. 10, 1956, enacted "Title 10, Armed Forces" which in sections 3010 to 3013 continued the military Department of the Army under the administrative supervision of a Secretary of the Army.

Transfer of Functions

Administrative functions of Fort McHenry National Park were transferred to the Department of the Interior by Ex. Ord. No. 6166, as amended by Ex.Ord. No. 6228, set out as a note under section 901 of Title 5, Government Organization and Employees.

National Park Service was substituted for Office of National Parks, Buildings, and Reservations referred to in Ex.Ord. No. 6166, by Act Mar. 2, 1934, c. 38, § 1, 48 Stat. 389.

Termination of War and Emergencies

Joint Res. July 25, 1947, c. 327, § 3, 61 Stat. 451, provided that in the interpretation of these sections, the date July 25, 1947, shall be deemed to be the date of termination of any state of war theretofore declared by Congress and of the national emergencies proclaimed by the President on Sept. 8, 1939, and May 27, 1941.

LIBRARY REFERENCES

American Digest System

Armed Services ⚲54.
Woods and Forests ⚲5, 8.
Key Number System Topic Nos. 34, 411.

§ 438. Repairs and improvements; how made

Any and all repairs, improvements, changes, and alterations in the grounds, buildings, and other appurtenances to the reservation shall be made only according to detailed plans which shall be approved by the Secretary of the Interior, and all such repairs, improvements, or alterations shall be made at the expense of the United States, and all such improvements, together with the reservation itself, shall become and remain permanently the property of the United States.

(May 26, 1914, c. 100, 38 Stat. 382; Mar. 3, 1925, c. 425, 43 Stat. 1109; Ex.Ord. No. 6166, § 2, June 10, 1933; Ex.Ord. No. 6228, § 1, July 28, 1933.)

HISTORICAL AND STATUTORY NOTES

Codifications

This section and sections 437, 439, and 440 of this title were derived from Act Mar. 3, 1925. See Codifications note set out under section 437 of this title.

Transfer of Functions

Transfer of administrative functions of park, see note set out under section 437 of this title.

Termination of War and Emergencies
  Joint Res. July 25, 1947, c. 327, § 3, 61
Stat. 451, provided that in the interpretation of these sections, the date July 25,
1947, shall be deemed to be the date of

termination of any state of war theretofore declared by Congress and of the national emergencies proclaimed by the
President on Sept. 8, 1939, and May 27,
1941.

LIBRARY REFERENCES

American Digest System
  Armed Services ⟊54.
  United States ⟊57.
  Woods and Forests ⟊5.
  Key Number System Topic Nos. 34, 393, 411.

§ 439.   Land for use of Secretary of the Treasury

Permission is granted the Secretary of the Treasury to use permanently a strip of land sixty feet wide belonging to said fort grounds,
beginning at the north corner of the grounds of the fort and extending south sixty-three degrees thirty minutes east, six hundred and
eighty feet to the south corner of the site set aside for the immigration station at Baltimore, said strip of land being located along the
northwest boundary of the land ceded to the Baltimore Dry Dock
Company and the land of the said immigration station, the same to
be used, if so desired, in lieu of acquiring, by purchase or condemnation, any of the lands of the dry dock company so that the Secretary
of the Treasury may, in connection with land acquired from the
Baltimore and Ohio Railroad Company, have access to and from said
immigration station and grounds over the right-of-way so acquired to
the city streets and railroads beyond, the Secretary of the Treasury to
have the same power to construct, contract for, and arrange for
railroad and other facilities upon said outlet as fully as provided in
the Act approved March 4, 1913, chapter 147, Thirty-seventh Statutes
889, setting aside a site for an immigration station and providing for
an outlet therefrom, but the Interior Department shall have equal use
of the railroad track and other roads so constructed, over which to
reach the city streets and railroads beyond from the other part of the
fort grounds.

(May 26, 1914, c. 100, 38 Stat. 382; Mar. 3, 1925, c. 425, 43 Stat. 1109;
Ex.Ord. No. 6166, § 2, June 10, 1933; Ex.Ord. No. 6228, § 1, July 28, 1933;
June 5, 1936, c. 528, 49 Stat. 1484.)

HISTORICAL AND STATUTORY NOTES

References in Text
  The Act approved March 4, 1913, chapter 147, Thirty-seventh Statutes 889, referred to in text, was a building authorization statute. The portion of the Act
covering the Fort McHenry work was

section 29, which section was not classified to the Code.

Codifications
  This section and sections 437, 438 and
440 of this title were derived from Act

Mar. 3, 1925. See Codifications note set out under section 437 of this title.

Amendments

1936 Amendments. Act June 5, 1936 substituted "six hundred and eighty feet" for "six hundred and fifty feet".

Transfer of Functions

Transfer of administrative functions of park, see note set out under section 437 of this title.

Termination of War and Emergencies

Joint Res. July 25, 1947, c. 327, § 3, 61 Stat. 451, provided that in the interpretation of these sections, the date July 25, 1947, shall be deemed to be the date of termination of any state of war theretofore declared by Congress and of the national emergencies proclaimed by the President on Sept. 8, 1939, and May 27, 1941.

LIBRARY REFERENCES

American Digest System

Armed Services ☞54.
United States ☞57.
Woods and Forests ☞1, 2, 8.
Key Number System Topic Nos. 34, 393, 411.

§ 440. Closure in times of national emergency

The Secretary of the Interior may, in case of a national emergency, close the said Fort McHenry and it may be used for any and all military purposes during the period of the emergency and for such period of time thereafter, as the public needs may require.

(May 26, 1914, c. 100, 38 Stat. 382; Mar. 3, 1925, c. 425, 43 Stat. 1109; Ex.Ord. No. 6166, § 2, June 10, 1933; Ex.Ord. No. 6228, § 1, July 28, 1933.)

HISTORICAL AND STATUTORY NOTES

Codifications

A proviso at the close of Act Mar. 3, 1925, authorizing the disposal of the useless temporary buildings constructed during the World War and appropriating a sum from the proceeds thereof for the purposes of the Act has been omitted as temporary and executed.

This section and sections 437 to 439 of this title were derived from Act Mar. 3, 1925. See Codifications note set out under section 437 of this title.

Transfer of Functions

Transfer of administrative functions of park, see note set out under section 437 of this title.

Termination of War and Emergencies

Joint Res. July 25, 1947, c. 327, § 3, 61 Stat. 451, provided that in the interpretation of these sections, the date July 25, 1947, shall be deemed to be the date of termination of any state of war theretofore declared by Congress and of the national emergencies proclaimed by the President on Sept. 8, 1939, and May 27, 1941.

LIBRARY REFERENCES

American Digest System

Armed Services ☞54.
War and National Emergency ☞1103.
Woods and Forests ☞5.
Key Number System Topic Nos. 34, 402, 411.

§ 440a. Change in name of Fort McHenry Park

The Fort McHenry National Park, in the State of Maryland, authorized by sections 437 to 440 of this title, shall hereafter be called and known as the "Fort McHenry National Monument and Historic Shrine", and all moneys heretofore or hereafter appropriated for this area under previous designations may be used in this area as redesignated.

(Aug. 11, 1939, c. 686, 53 Stat. 1405.)

HISTORICAL AND STATUTORY NOTES

Codifications
Section consists of a part of Act Aug. 11, 1939. The remainder, relating to changing the name of "Abraham Lincoln National Park" to "Abraham Lincoln National Historical Park" is set out as section 217 of this title.

LIBRARY REFERENCES

American Digest System
Armed Services ⚖54.
Woods and Forests ⚖1.
Key Number System Topic Nos. 34, 411.

§ 441. Badlands National Park; establishment

When a quantum, satisfactory to the Secretary of the Interior, of the privately owned lands lying within the area hereinafter described shall have been acquired and transferred to the United States for park purposes, without expense to the Federal Treasury, such areas are dedicated and set apart as a national park for the benefit and enjoyment of the people, under the name of the Badlands National Park: *Provided*, That the State of South Dakota shall have first constructed the highways hereinafter described.

(Mar. 4, 1929, c. 693, § 1, 45 Stat. 1553; Nov. 10, 1978, Pub.L. 95–625, Title VI, § 611, 92 Stat. 3521.)

HISTORICAL AND STATUTORY NOTES

References in Text
Hereinafter, referred to in text, means Act Mar. 4, 1929, which is classified to sections 441 to 441e of this title. For complete classification of this Act to the Code, see Tables.

Change of Name
In text, "park" and "Park" were substituted for "monument" and "Monument", respectively, on authority of Pub.L. 95–625, Title VI, § 611, Nov. 10, 1978, 92 Stat. 3521, classified to section 441e–1 of this title, which redesignated the Badlands National Monument as the Badlands National Park.

Ben Reifel Visitor Center
Pub.L. 101–512, Title I, Nov. 5, 1990, 104 Stat. 1923, provided in part that: "hereafter the Cedar Pass Visitor Center at Badlands National Park, South Dakota, shall be known as the Ben Reifel Visitor Center".

§ 441a. Boundaries

The areas to be included in said Badlands National Park are situated in the State of South Dakota and lie within the boundaries particularly described as follows: Beginning at the northeast corner section 13, township 3 south, range 18 east, Black Hills meridian; thence west one-fourth mile; thence south one mile; thence west one-fourth mile; thence south one-fourth mile; thence west one mile; thence south one-fourth mile; thence west one-fourth mile; thence north one mile; thence west one and one-fourth miles; thence north one-half mile; thence west three miles, to the northwest corner section 18, township 3 south, range 18 east, Black Hills meridian.

Thence north one-fourth mile; thence west one-half mile; thence north one-fourth mile; thence west three-fourths mile; thence south one-fourth mile; thence west one-fourth mile; thence north one-fourth mile; thence west one-fourth mile; thence north one-fourth mile; thence west three-fourths mile; thence south one-fourth mile; thence west one-half mile; thence south one-half mile; thence west one mile; thence north one-fourth mile; thence west one-fourth mile; thence north one-fourth mile; thence west one and one-fourth miles; thence north one-fourth mile; thence west one-fourth mile; thence north three-fourths mile; thence west one and one-fourth miles; thence north one-half mile, to the northeast corner section 2, township 3 south, range 16 east, Black Hills meridian.

Thence west one-half mile; thence north one mile; thence west one-fourth mile; thence north one-half mile; thence west three-fourths mile; thence north one-half mile; thence west one-half mile; thence north two miles; thence west eight miles; thence south one-half mile; thence west one mile; thence north one-half mile, to the northeast corner section 13, township 2 south, range 14 east, Black Hills meridian.

Thence west one mile; thence south one mile; thence east one-half mile; thence south one-half mile; thence west one-half mile; thence south two and one-half miles; thence east one and one-fourth miles; thence south one mile; thence east three-fourths mile, to the northeast corner section 7, township 3 south, range 15 east, Black Hills meridian.

Thence south one-fourth mile; thence east one-fourth mile; thence south one-half mile; thence west one-fourth mile; thence south one-fourth mile; thence west one mile; thence south one and three-fourths miles; thence east one mile; thence north three-fourths mile; thence east two miles; thence north one-half mile; thence east three-fourths mile; thence north one-fourth mile; thence east one-half mile; thence north three-fourths mile; thence west one-fourth mile; thence north three-fourths mile; thence west one-fourth mile; thence north one-fourth mile; thence west one-fourth mile; thence north one-fourth mile; thence east one-fourth mile; thence north one-half mile; thence east one mile; thence south one-fourth mile; thence east one and three-fourths miles; thence north one-half mile; thence west one-half mile; thence north one-half mile, to the northwest corner section 31, township 2 south, range 16 east, Black Hills meridian.

Thence east one-half mile; thence south one-fourth mile; thence east one mile; thence south one-fourth mile; thence east one and three-fourths miles; thence south three-fourths mile; thence east three-fourths mile; thence south three-fourths mile; thence east one-half mile; thence south one-fourth mile; thence east one-fourth mile; thence south one-fourth mile; thence east one-fourth mile; thence south one-fourth mile; thence east one-fourth mile; thence south one-fourth mile; thence east one-fourth mile; thence south one-fourth mile; thence east one-half mile; thence south one and one-fourth miles; thence east three-fourths mile; thence north one-half mile; thence east one-fourth mile, to the northeast corner section 19, township 3 south, range 17 east, Black Hills meridian.

Thence north one-half mile; thence east three-fourths mile; thence south two miles; thence east one and one-half miles; thence north one and one-half miles; thence east two miles; thence south one-fourth mile; thence east one-fourth mile; thence south one-fourth mile; thence east one-half mile; thence south one-fourth mile; thence east one-half mile; thence south one-fourth mile; thence east one-half mile, to the northeast corner section 30, township 3 south, range 18 east, Black Hills meridian.

Thence south three-fourths mile; thence east one-fourth mile; thence south one-fourth mile; thence east one-half mile; thence north one-fourth mile; thence east one and one-fourth miles; thence south one-fourth mile; thence east three miles, to the northeast corner of section 36, township 3 south, range 18 east, Black Hills meridian.

Thence north one mile; thence east one mile; thence north one-half mile; thence west one-fourth mile; thence north one-fourth mile; thence west one-fourth mile; thence north one and one-fourth miles; thence west one-half mile to the point of beginning.

(Mar. 4, 1929, c. 693, § 2, 45 Stat. 1554; Nov. 10, 1978, Pub.L. 95–625, Title VI, § 611, 92 Stat. 3521.)

HISTORICAL AND STATUTORY NOTES

Change of Name

In first undesignated paragraph, "Park" was substituted for "Monument" on authority of Pub.L. 95–625, Title VI, § 611, Nov. 10, 1978, 92 Stat. 3521, classified to section 441e–1 of this title, which redesignated the Badlands National Monument as the Badlands National Park.

Extension of Boundaries

Act June 26, 1936, c. 842, Title II, § 1, 49 Stat. 1979, provided that the boundaries of the Badlands National Monument as established by this section shall be "extended to include such lands adjacent or contiguous thereto, in the State of South Dakota, including, but not being restricted to, lands designated as submarginal by the Resettlement Administration, as may be determined by the President, by proclamation, within five years following the approval of this Act, to be necessary for the proper rounding out of the boundaries of said Monument or the administration thereof, providing the entire area of such Monument shall not exceed 250,000 acres."

Laws Applicable

The provisions of sections 1 and 2 to 4 of this title were made applicable to the above added lands by Act June 26, 1936, c. 842, Title II, § 2, 49 Stat. 1979.

LIBRARY REFERENCES

American Digest System

Armed Services ☞54.
Woods and Forests ☞1.
Key Number System Topic Nos. 34, 411.

§ 441b. Construction of highway by State of South Dakota

The establishment of said park is conditioned upon the State of South Dakota first constructing the following highway in a manner satisfactory to the Secretary of the Interior: A highway commencing at the corporation limits of the town of Interior, thence going in a northwesterly direction to and over Big Foot Pass, and through the region known as The Pinnacles; thence in a westerly direction to Sage Creek, being a total distance of about thirty miles.

(Mar. 4, 1929, c. 693, § 3, 45 Stat. 1555; Nov. 10, 1978, Pub.L. 95–625, Title VI, § 611, 92 Stat. 3521.)

HISTORICAL AND STATUTORY NOTES

Change of Name

In text, "park" was substituted for "monument" on authority of Pub.L. 95–625, Title VI, § 611, Nov. 10, 1978, 92 Stat. 3521, classified to section 441e–1 of this title, which redesignated the Badlands National Monument as the Badlands National Park.

LIBRARY REFERENCES

American Digest System

Armed Services ☞54.
Woods and Forests ☞1, 8.
Key Number System Topic Nos. 34, 411.

§ 441c.   Administration, protection, and promotion;   franchises for hotel and lodge accommodations

The administration, protection, and promotion of said Badlands National Park shall be exercised under the direction of the Secretary of the Interior by the National Park Service, subject to the provisions of sections 1, 2, 3, and 4 of this title: *Provided*, That in advance of the fulfillment of the conditions herein the Secretary of the Interior may grant franchises for hotel and for lodge accommodations under the provisions of this section.

(Mar. 4, 1929, c. 693, § 4, 45 Stat. 1555; Nov. 10, 1978, Pub.L. 95–625, Title VI, § 611, 92 Stat. 3521.)

HISTORICAL AND STATUTORY NOTES

Change of Name

In text, "Park" was substituted for "Monument" on authority of Pub.L. 95–625, Title VI, § 611, Nov. 10, 1978, 92 Stat. 3521, classified to section 441e–1 of this title, which redesignated the Badlands National Monument as the Badlands National Park.

Transfer of Functions

All functions of all other officers of the Department of the Interior and all func-

tions of all agencies and employees of such Department were, with two exceptions, transferred to the Secretary of the Interior, with power vested in him to authorize their performance or the performance of any of his functions by any of such officers, agencies, and employees, by 1950 Reorg. Plan No. 3, §§ 1, 2, eff. May 24, 1950, 15 F.R. 3174, 64 Stat. 1262, set out in Appendix 1 to Title 5, Government Organization and Employees.

LIBRARY REFERENCES

American Digest System
Armed Services ⬤54.
Woods and Forests ⬤5.
Key Number System Topic Nos. 34, 411.

§ 441d.   Examinations, excavations, and gathering of objects of interest within park

The Secretary of the Interior is authorized to permit examinations, excavations, and gathering of objects of interest within said park by any person or persons whom he may deem properly qualified to conduct such examinations, excavations, or gatherings, subject to such rules and regulations as he may prescribe: *Provided*, That the examinations, excavations, and gatherings are undertaken only for the benefit of some reputable museum, university, college, or other recognized scientific or educational institution, with a view to increasing the knowledge of such objects and aiding the general advancement of geological and zoological science.

(Mar. 4, 1929, c. 693, § 5, 45 Stat. 1555; Nov. 10, 1978, Pub.L. 95–625, Title VI, § 611, 92 Stat. 3521.)

HISTORICAL AND STATUTORY NOTES

Change of Name

In text, "park" was substituted for "monument" on authority of Pub.L. 95–625, Title VI, § 611, Nov. 10, 1978, 92 Stat. 3521, classified to section 441e–1 of this title, which redesignated the Badlands National Monument as the Badlands National Park.

LIBRARY REFERENCES

American Digest System

Armed Services ☞54.
Woods and Forests ☞5.
Key Number System Topic Nos. 34, 411.

§ 441e. Effective date of sections 441 to 441d

Sections 441 to 441d of this title shall become effective if and when all of the above conditions shall have been fully complied with to the satisfaction of the President of the United States, who shall then issue a proclamation declaring that the conditions precedent herein required have been complied with, and said proclamation shall formally dedicate and set aside the areas herein described in accordance with the provisions of section 441 of this title.

(Mar. 4, 1929, c. 693, § 6, 45 Stat. 1555.)

PROCLAMATIONS
PROCLAMATION NO. 2320

Proclamation declaring that conditions precedent required by sections 441 to 441d of this title had been complied with, and formally dedicating and setting aside as the Badlands National Monument the areas therein described was issued by the President on Jan. 25, 1939. See Proc. No. 2320, Jan. 25, 1939, 4 F.R. 457, 53 Stat. 2521.

LIBRARY REFERENCES

American Digest System

Armed Services ☞54.
Key Number System Topic No. 34.

§ 441e–1. Change in name of Badlands National Monument

The area formerly known as the "Badlands National Monument", established by Presidential Proclamation of January 25, 1939 (53 Stat. 2521), shall henceforth be known as the "Badlands National Park".

(Pub.L. 95–625, Title VI, § 611, Nov. 10, 1978, 92 Stat. 3521.)

LIBRARY REFERENCES

American Digest System

Armed Services ☞54.
Woods and Forests ☞1.
Key Number System Topic Nos. 34, 411.

Research References

Treatises and Practice Aids

Federal Procedure, Lawyers Edition § 46:93, Notice to Former Owners--Of Right to Repurchase Land Outside Monument or Gunnery Range Boundaries.

Federal Procedure, Lawyers Edition § 46:95, Notice to Former Owners--Of Right to Acquire Life Estates in, or Land in Lieu of, Parkland.

Federal Procedure, Lawyers Edition § 46:98, What Application Forms to Use; Time Within Which to File.

§ 441f. Adjustment and redefinition of boundaries

In order to establish a more appropriate boundary for the Badlands National Park and to consolidate Federal land ownership therein, the Secretary of the Interior, in his discretion, is authorized to adjust and redefine the exterior boundaries of the national park by appropriate reductions or additions of land: *Provided*, That the total acreage of the national park, as revised pursuant to sections 441f to 441i of this title, shall not exceed its area of approximately one hundred fifty-four thousand one hundred and nineteen acres as of May 7, 1952.

(May 7, 1952, c. 244, § 1, 66 Stat. 65; Nov. 10, 1978, Pub.L. 95–625, Title VI, § 611, 92 Stat. 3521.)

HISTORICAL AND STATUTORY NOTES

Revision Notes and Legislative Reports
   1952 Acts. Senate Report No. 1064, see 1952 U.S. Code Cong. and Adm. News, p. 1415.

Codifications
   Reference to the monument's approximately 154,119 acre area "as of May 7, 1952" was substituted for a reference in the original to the monument's "present" area.

Change of Name
   In text, "Park" and "park" were substituted for "Monument" and "monument", respectively, on authority of Pub.L. 95–625, Title VI, § 611, Nov. 10, 1978, 92 Stat. 3521, classified to section 441e–1 of this title, which redesignated the Badlands National Monument as the Badlands National Park.

LIBRARY REFERENCES

American Digest System
   Armed Services ⊕54.
   Woods and Forests ⊕1, 2.
   Key Number System Topic Nos. 34, 411.

§ 441g. Orders to effectuate revision of boundaries; publication

The revision of boundaries of the national park, as authorized in section 441f of this title, shall be accomplished by the issuance, by the Secretary of the Interior, of an appropriate order, or orders, such order or orders to be effective upon publication in the Federal Register: *Provided*, That federally owned land under the administrative jurisdiction of any other department or agency of the Federal

Government shall be included within the park only with the approval of the head of such department or agency.

(May 7, 1952, c. 244, § 2, 66 Stat. 65; Nov. 10, 1978, Pub.L. 95–625, Title VI, § 611, 92 Stat. 3521.)

HISTORICAL AND STATUTORY NOTES

Revision Notes and Legislative Reports
1952 Acts. Senate Report No. 1064, see 1952 U.S. Code Cong. and Adm. News, p. 1415.

References in Text
Section 441f of this title, referred to in text, was in the original "sections 1 and 5 of this Act". Section 1 of the Act is classified to section 441f of this title. Section 5 is probably a reference to section 5 of the original bill, which would have authorized the inclusion of up to 4,000 acres of the Pine Ridge Indian Res-

ervation within the Badlands National Monument. Such section 5 was stricken from the bill by Senate amendment, and as enacted the Act contained only four sections.

Change of Name
In text, "park" was substituted for "monument" on authority of Pub.L. 95–625, Title VI, § 611, Nov. 10, 1978, 92 Stat. 3521, classified to section 441e–1 of this title, which redesignated the Badlands National Monument as the Badlands National Park.

LIBRARY REFERENCES

American Digest System
 Armed Services ⚿54.
 Woods and Forests ⚿1 to 2.
 Key Number System Topic Nos. 34, 411.

§ 441h. Jurisdiction of mining and mineral rights; patents

Administrative jurisdiction over all Federal lands eliminated from the park, by the issuance of an order or orders of the Secretary of the Interior, is transferred to the Secretary of Agriculture for use, administration, and disposition in accordance with the provisions of title III of the Bankhead-Jones Farm Tenant Act [7 U.S.C.A. § 1010 et seq.] and the related provisions of title IV thereof: *Provided*, That all of such lands formerly set apart and reserved from the public domain shall be subject to the mining and minerals-leasing laws: *And provided further*, That any disposition of any such lands formerly set apart and reserved from the public domain shall be evidenced by patents issued by the Secretary of the Interior.

(May 7, 1952, c. 244, § 3, 66 Stat. 65; Nov. 10, 1978, Pub.L. 95–625, Title VI, § 611, 92 Stat. 3521.)

HISTORICAL AND STATUTORY NOTES

Revision Notes and Legislative Reports
1952 Acts. Senate Report No. 1064, see 1952 U.S. Code Cong. and Adm. News, p. 1415.

References in Text
The Bankhead-Jones Farm Tenant Act, referred to in text, is Act July 22, 1937, c.

517, 50 Stat. 522, as amended. Title III of the Act is classified generally to subchapter III (section 1010 et seq.) of chapter 33 of Title 7, Agriculture. Title IV thereof, referred to in text, which was classified to sections 1014 to 1029 of title 7, was repealed by Act June 25, 1948, c.

645, § 21, 62 Stat. 862, and by Pub.L. 87–128, Title III, § 341(a), Aug. 8, 1961, 75 Stat. 318. For complete classification of this Act to the Code, see section 1000 of Title 7 and Tables.

The mining and minerals-leasing laws, referred to in text, are classified generally to Title 30, Mineral Lands and Mining.

Change of Name

In text, "park" was substituted for "monument" on authority of Pub.L. 95–625, Title VI, § 611, Nov. 10, 1978, 92 Stat. 3521, classified to section 441e–1 of this title, which redesignated the Badlands National Monument as the Badlands National Park.

LIBRARY REFERENCES

American Digest System

Armed Services ⊜54.
United States ⊜3.
Key Number System Topic Nos. 34, 393.

§ 441i.   Exchanges of land

In order that exchanges of land may be effectuated for the purposes of sections 441f to 441i of this title, the Secretary of the Interior is authorized, in his discretion and in accordance with the provisions of sections 3111 and 3112 of Title 40, to accept, on behalf of the United States, title to any land or interests in land within the exterior boundaries of the Badlands National Park as revised pursuant to sections 441f to 441i of this title, and, in exchange therefor, with the approval and concurrence of the Secretary of Agriculture, the Secretary of the Interior may patent lands of approximately equal value which were formerly set apart and reserved from the public domain within the Badlands Fall River soil conservation project, SD–LU–1. In effectuating such exchanges, in lieu of conveyances by the Secretary of the Interior, the Secretary of Agriculture may convey lands of approximately equal value within said project which have been acquired heretofore by the United States. All such exchanges shall, in all other respects, be considered as exchanges under the provisions of section 32c, title III, of the Bankhead-Jones Farm Tenant Act [7 U.S.C.A. § 1011(c)] and shall otherwise be in accordance with provisions of said Act [7 U.S.C.A. § 1000 et seq.], except that, upon acceptance of title to any lands so acquired by the United States under this section, such lands and any other lands acquired otherwise by the United States within the park boundaries shall be a part of that area. In consummating land exchanges hereunder upon an equitable basis, patents and instruments of conveyance may be issued, and property may be accepted, by the United States, subject to such reservations as may be necessary or in the public interest.

(May 7, 1952, c. 244, § 4, 66 Stat. 66; Nov. 10, 1978, Pub.L. 95–625, Title VI, § 611, 92 Stat. 3521.)

HISTORICAL AND STATUTORY NOTES

Revision Notes and Legislative Reports
1952 Acts. Senate Report No. 1064, see 1952 U.S. Code Cong. and Adm. News, p. 1415.

References in Text
The Bankhead-Jones Farm Tenant Act, referred to in text, is Act July 22, 1937, c. 517, 50 Stat. 522, as amended, which is classified generally to chapter 33 (section 1000 et seq.) of Title 7, Agriculture. The reference to section "32c" of such Act was probably meant as a reference to section 32(c) of such Act, which is classified to section 1011(c) of Title 7. For complete classification of this Act to the Code, see section 1000 of Title 7 and Tables.

Codifications
In text, "sections 3111 and 3112 of Title 40" substituted for "section 255 of

Title 40", which originally read "section 355, Revised Statutes", on authority of Pub.L. 107–217, § 5(c), Aug. 21, 2002, 116 Stat. 1301, which is set out as a note preceding 40 U.S.C.A. § 101. Pub.L. 107–217, § 1, enacted Title 40 into positive law. Section 355 of the Revised Statutes was classified to former 40 U.S.C.A. § 255 and its provisions were carried forward into revised Title 40 at 40 U.S.C.A. §§ 3111, 3112.

Change of Name
In text, "Park" and "park" were substituted for "Monument" and "monument", respectively, on authority of Pub.L. 95–625, Title VI, § 611, Nov. 10, 1978, 92 Stat. 3521, classified to section 441e–1 of this title, which redesignated the Badlands National Monument as the Badlands National Park.

LIBRARY REFERENCES

American Digest System
Armed Services ☞54.
Woods and Forests ☞4.
Key Number System Topic Nos. 34, 411.

§ 441j. Revision of boundaries

In order to include lands of outstanding scenic and scientific character in the Badlands National Park, the boundaries of the park are revised as generally depicted on the map entitled "Badlands National Monument", numbered NM–BL–7021B, dated August 1967, which is on file and available for public inspection in the offices of the National Park Service, Department of the Interior. The Secretary of the Interior may make minor adjustments in the boundaries, but the total acreage in the park may not exceed the acreage within the boundaries depicted on the map referred to herein. Lands within the boundaries of the park that are acquired by the United States shall be subject to the laws and regulations applicable to the park.

(Pub.L. 90–468, § 1, Aug. 8, 1968, 82 Stat. 663; Pub.L. 95–625, Title VI, § 611, Nov. 10, 1978, 92 Stat. 3521.)

HISTORICAL AND STATUTORY NOTES

Revision Notes and Legislative Reports
1968 Acts. Senate Report No. 1349, see 1968 U.S. Code Cong. and Adm. News, p. 3163.

Change of Name
In text, "Park" and "park" were substituted for "Monument" and "monument", respectively, on authority of Pub.L. 95–625, Title VI, § 611, Nov. 10, 1978, 92

Stat. 3521, classified to section 441e–1 of this title, which redesignated the Badlands National Monument as the Badlands National Park.

CROSS REFERENCES

Pine Ridge Indian Reservation; conditions on conveyed lands, see 25 USCA § 459.

LIBRARY REFERENCES

American Digest System
Armed Services ☞54.
Woods and Forests ☞1, 2.
Key Number System Topic Nos. 34, 411.

Research References

Treatises and Practice Aids
Federal Procedure, Lawyers Edition § 46:96, Who May Purchase Gunnery Range Land.

§ 441k. Acquisition of property for park

(a) Consent of State or Oglala Sioux Tribe of South Dakota; transfer from Federal agency

Subject to the provisions of subsection (b) of this section, the Secretary of the Interior may, within the boundaries of the park, acquire lands and interests in lands by donation, purchase with donated or appropriated funds, or exchange, except that any lands or interests in lands owned by the State of South Dakota, a political subdivision thereof, or the Oglala Sioux Tribe of South Dakota may be acquired only with the consent of owner. Notwithstanding any other provision of law, lands and interests in lands located within the park under the administrative jurisdiction of any other Federal agency may be transferred to the administrative jurisdiction of the Secretary without a transfer of funds.

(b) Easements

As to lands located within the boundaries of the park but outside the boundaries of the gunnery range referred to in section 441l of this title, the Secretary of the Interior may acquire only rights-of-way and scenic easements.

(Pub.L. 90–468, § 2, Aug. 8, 1968, 82 Stat. 663; Pub.L. 95–625, Title VI, § 611, Nov. 10, 1978, 92 Stat. 3521.)

HISTORICAL AND STATUTORY NOTES

Revision Notes and Legislative Reports
  1968 Acts. Senate Report No. 1349, see 1968 U.S. Code Cong. and Adm. News, p. 3163.

Change of Name
  In text, "park" was substituted for "monument" on authority of Pub.L. 95–625, Title VI, § 611, Nov. 10, 1978, 92 Stat. 3521, classified to section 441e–1 of

this title, which redesignated the Badlands National Monument as the Badlands National Park.

CROSS REFERENCES

Pine Ridge Indian Reservation; conditions on conveyed lands, see 25 USCA § 459.

LIBRARY REFERENCES

American Digest System
    Armed Services ☞54.
    United States ☞55.
    Key Number System Topic Nos. 34, 393.

§ 441*l*. Exchange of lands; transfer from Federal agency to administrative jurisdiction of Secretary; terms and conditions of purchase

Inasmuch as (A) most of the lands added to the Badlands National Park by section 441j of this title are inside the boundaries of the Pine Ridge Sioux Indian Reservation, (B) such lands are also within a tract of land forty-three miles long and twelve and one-half miles wide which is in the northwestern part of such Indian reservation and has been used by the United States Air Force as a gunnery range since the early part of World War II, (C) the tribal lands within such gunnery range were leased by the Federal Government and the other lands within such gunnery range were purchased by the Federal Government from the individual owners (mostly Indians), (D) the Department of the Air Force has declared most of such gunnery range lands excess to its needs and such excess lands have been requested by the National Park Service under the Federal Property and Administrative Services Act of 1949, (E) the leased tribal lands and the excess lands within the enlarged Badlands National Park are needed for the park, (F) the other excess lands in such gunnery range should be restored to the former Indian owners of such lands, and (G) the tribe is unwilling to sell its tribal lands for inclusion in the national park, but is willing to exchange them or interests therein for the excess gunnery range lands, which, insofar as the lands within the gunnery range formerly held by the tribe are concerned, should be returned to Indian ownership in any event, the Congress hereby finds that such exchange would be in the national interest and authorizes the following actions:

(a) All Federal lands and interests in lands within the Badlands Air Force gunnery range that are outside the boundaries of the park and that heretofore or hereafter are declared excess to the needs of the Department of the Air Force shall be transferred to the administrative jurisdiction of the Secretary of the Interior without a transfer of funds.

(b) Any former Indian or non-Indian owner of a tract of such land, whether title was held in trust or fee, may purchase such tract from the Secretary of the Interior under the following terms and conditions:

(1) The purchase price to a former Indian owner shall be the total amount paid by the United States to acquire such tract and all interests therein, plus interest thereon from the date of acquisition at a rate determined by the Secretary of the Treasury taking into consideration the average market yield of all outstanding marketable obligations of the United States at the time the tract was acquired by the United States, adjusted to the nearest one-eighth of 1 per centum. The purchase price to a former non-Indian owner shall be present fair market value of the tract as determined by the Secretary of the Interior.

(2) Not less than $100 or 20 per centum of the purchase price, whichever is less, shall be paid at the time of purchase, and the balance shall be payable in not to exceed 20 years with interest at a rate determined by the Secretary of the Treasury taking into account the current average market yield on outstanding marketable obligations of the United States with twenty years remaining to date of maturity, adjusted to the nearest one-eighth of 1 per centum.

(3) Title to the tract purchased shall be held in trust for the purchaser if it was held in trust status at the time the tract was acquired by the United States; otherwise, the title to the tract purchased shall be conveyed to the purchaser subject to a mortgage and such other security instruments as the Secretary deems appropriate. If a tract purchased under this subsection is offered for resale during the following ten-year period, the tribe must be given the first right to purchase it.

(4) The unpaid balance of the purchase price shall be a lien against the land if the title is held in trust and against all rents, bonuses, and royalties received therefrom. In the event of default in the payment of any installment of the purchase price the Secretary may take such action to enforce the lien as he deems appropriate, including foreclosure and conveyance of the land to the Oglala Sioux Tribe.

(5) An application to purchase the tract must be filed with the Secretary of the Interior within one year from the date a notice is published in the Federal Register that the tract has been transferred to the jurisdiction of the Secretary.

(6) No application may be filed by more than five of the former owners of an interest in the tract. If more than one such application is filed for a tract the applicants must agree on not more than five of the former owners who shall make the purchase, and failing such agreement all such applications for the tract shall be rejected by the Secretary.

(7) "Former owner" means, for the purposes of subsection (b) of this section, each person from whom the United States acquired an interest in the tract, or if such person is deceased, his spouse, or if such spouse is deceased, his children.

(Pub.L. 90–468, § 3, Aug. 8, 1968, 82 Stat. 663; Pub.L. 95–625, Title VI, § 611, Nov. 10, 1978, 92 Stat. 3521.)

HISTORICAL AND STATUTORY NOTES

Revision Notes and Legislative Reports
1968 Acts. Senate Report No. 1349, see 1968 U.S. Code Cong. and Adm. News, p. 3163.

References in Text
The Federal Property and Administrative Services Act of 1949, referred to in the provision preceding subsec. (a), is Act June 30, 1949, c. 288, 63 Stat. 377, as amended, Title III of which is currently classified to subchapter IV of chapter 4 of Title 41, 41 U.S.C.A. § 251 et seq., and the remainder of which was formerly classified to chapter 10 of former Title 40, 40 U.S.C.A. § 471 et seq., prior to being repealed by Pub.L. 107–217, § 6(b), Aug. 21, 2002, 116 Stat. 1313; see now generally chapter 1 of Title 40, 40 U.S.C.A. § 101 et seq.

Change of Name
In provision preceding subsec. (a) and in subsec. (a), "Park" and "park" were substituted for "Monument" and "monument", respectively, on authority of Pub.L. 95–625, Title VI, § 611, Nov. 10, 1978, 92 Stat. 3521, classified to section 441e–1 of this title, which redesignated the Badlands National Monument as the Badlands National Park.

CROSS REFERENCES

Pine Ridge Indian Reservation; conditions on conveyed lands, see 25 USCA § 459.

LIBRARY REFERENCES

American Digest System
Armed Services ☞54.
United States ☞55.
Woods and Forests ☞4, 5, 8.
Key Number System Topic Nos. 34, 393, 411.

Research References

Treatises and Practice Aids
Federal Procedure, Lawyers Edition § 46:96, Who May Purchase Gunnery Range Land.
Federal Procedure, Lawyers Edition § 46:98, What Application Forms to Use; Time Within Which to File.

Notes of Decisions

Offer for resale   1
_____

1. Offer for resale
   Application for an issuance of fee patent on individual Indians' "in lieu" tract did not constitute "offer for resale" triggering Indian tribe's right of first preference to purchase contained in this section which provided for Indian reacquisition

of lands on reservation which had been purchased by United States for Air Force gunnery range during World War II, but which were in excess of needs of United States, or acquisition of other tracts "in lieu" of such excess lands. Oglala Sioux Tribe of Pine Ridge Indian Reservation v. Hallett, C.A.8 (S.D.) 1983, 708 F.2d 326. Indians ⊗ 160

§ 441m.   Disposition of excess gunnery range lands and reservation lands; purchase; terms and conditions; life estates and use restrictions

(a) Gunnery range lands; reservation lands

All Federal lands and interests in lands within the Badlands Air Force gunnery range that are outside the boundaries of the park, and that have been declared excess to the needs of the Department of the Air Force, and that are not purchased by former owners under section 441*l*(b) of this title, and all lands that have been acquired by the United States under authority of title II of the National Industrial Recovery Act of June 16, 1933 (48 Stat. 200), and subsequent relief Acts, situated within the Pine Ridge Indian Reservation, administrative jurisdiction over which has heretofore been transferred by the President from the Secretary of Agriculture to the Secretary of the Interior by Executive Order Numbered 7868, dated April 15, 1938, shall be subject to the following provisions of this section.

(b) Purchases

Any former Indian owner of land that is within the Badlands Air Force gunnery range and outside the boundaries of the park and that has not been declared excess to the needs of the Department of the Air Force on August 8, 1968, may, within the period specified in section 441*l*(b)(5) of this title, elect (i) to purchase an available tract of land described in subsection (a) of this section of substantially the same value, or (ii) to purchase the tract formerly owned by him at such time as such tract is declared excess and transferred to the Secretary of the Interior as provided in section 441*l*(a) of this title.

(c) Life estates and use restrictions

Any former Indian owner of a tract of land within the boundaries of the park that was acquired by the United States for the Badlands Air Force gunnery range, and that is transferred to the Secretary of the Interior pursuant to section 441k of this title, may, within the period specified in section 441*l*(b)(5) of this title, elect (i) to acquire from the Secretary of the Interior a life estate in such tract at no cost, subject to restrictions on use that may be prescribed in regulations applicable to the park, or (ii) to purchase an available tract of land described in subsection (a) of this section of substantially the same value.

(d) Purchase restrictions

Purchases under subsection (b) and clause (ii) of subsection (c) of this section shall be made on the terms provided in section 441*l*(b) of this title.

(Pub.L. 90–468, § 4, Aug. 8, 1968, 82 Stat. 664; Pub.L. 95–625, Title VI, § 611, Nov. 10, 1978, 92 Stat. 3521.)

HISTORICAL AND STATUTORY NOTES

Revision Notes and Legislative Reports
  1968 Acts. Senate Report No. 1349, see 1968 U.S. Code Cong. and Adm. News, p. 3163.

References in Text
  Title II of the National Industrial Recovery Act of June 16, 1933, referred to in subsec. (a), is Act June 16, 1933, c. 90, Title II, 48 Stat. 200, as amended, which was classified generally to chapter 8 of former Title 40, former 40 U.S.C.A. § 401 et seq. The provisions were terminated

June 30, 1943 by Act June 27, 1942, c. 450, § 1, 56 Stat. 410.
  Executive Order Numbered 7868, dated April 15, 1938, referred to in subsec. (a), was not classified to the Code.

Change of Name
  In subsecs. (a), (b), and (c), "park" was substituted for "monument" on authority of Pub.L. 95–625, Title VI, § 611, Nov. 10, 1978, 92 Stat. 3521, classified to section 441e–1 of this title, which redesignated the Badlands National Monument as the Badlands National Park.

CROSS REFERENCES

Pine Ridge Indian Reservation; conditions on conveyed lands, see 25 USCA § 459.

LIBRARY REFERENCES

American Digest System
  Armed Services ⚮54.
  United States ⚮3.
  Woods and Forests ⚮4.
  Key Number System Topic Nos. 34, 393, 411.

§ 441n.   Lands outside gunnery range; exchange of lands; reservation of mineral rights; grazing and mineral development rights of Indians; execution of instruments; trust title

(a) Exchange of lands; mineral and grazing rights

Title to all Federal lands and interests in lands within the boundaries of the Badlands Air Force gunnery range that are outside the boundaries of the park, and that are transferred to the administrative jurisdiction of the Secretary of the Interior as provided in section 441*l*(a) of this title, including lands hereafter declared to be excess, and that are not selected under sections 441*l*(b) or 441m of this title, and title to all lands within the boundaries of the park that were acquired by the United States for the Badlands Air Force gunnery range, subject to any life estate conveyed pursuant to section 441m(c) of this title and subject to restrictions on use that may be prescribed in regulations applicable to the park, which regulations may include provisions for the protection of the black-footed ferret, may be conveyed to the Oglala Sioux Tribe in exchange (i) for the right of the United States to use all tribal land within the park for park purposes, including the right to manage fish and wildlife and other resources and to construct visitor use and administrative facilities thereon, and (ii) for title to three thousand one hundred fifteen and sixty-three one-hundredths acres of land owned by the Oglala Sioux Tribe and located in the area of the Badlands Air Force gunnery range which is not excess to the needs of the Department of the Air Force and which is encompassed in civil action numbered 859 W.D. in the United States District Court for the District of South Dakota, if such exchange is approved by the Oglala Sioux Tribal Council. The lands acquired under paragraph (ii) shall become a part of the Badlands Air Force gunnery range retained by the Department of the Air Force. The United States and the Oglala Sioux Tribe shall reserve all mineral rights in the lands so conveyed. The right of the United States to use for park purposes lands that were tribally owned prior to August 8, 1968, shall not impair the right of the Oglala Sioux Tribe to use such lands for grazing purposes and mineral development, including development for oil and gas.

(b) Execution of instruments

The Oglala Sioux Tribal Council may authorize the execution of the necessary instruments to effect the exchange on behalf of the tribe, and the Secretary may execute the necessary instruments on behalf of the United States.

(c) Trust title

After the exchange is effected the title of the Oglala Sioux Tribe to the property acquired by the exchange shall be held in trust subject to the same restrictions and authorities that apply to other lands of the tribe that are held in trust.

(Pub.L. 90–468, § 5, Aug. 8, 1968, 82 Stat. 665; Pub.L. 95–625, Title VI, § 611, Nov. 10, 1978, 92 Stat. 3521.)

HISTORICAL AND STATUTORY NOTES

Revision Notes and Legislative Reports
  1968 Acts. Senate Report No. 1349, see 1968 U.S. Code Cong. and Adm. News, p. 3163.

Change of Name
  In subsec. (a), "park" was substituted for "monument" on authority of Pub.L. 95–625, Title VI, § 611, Nov. 10, 1978, 92

Stat. 3521, classified to section 441e–1 of this title, which redesignated the Bad-

lands National Monument as the Badlands National Park.

CROSS REFERENCES

Pine Ridge Indian Reservation; conditions on conveyed lands, see 25 USCA § 459.

LIBRARY REFERENCES

American Digest System
  Armed Services ⊕54.
  United States ⊕55.
  Woods and Forests ⊕4.
  Key Number System Topic Nos. 34, 393, 411.

§ 441o. Facilities for interpretation of park and history of Sioux Nation; conveyance of reservation lands; submission of terms to Congressional committees

The Oglala Sioux Tribe may convey and the Secretary of the Interior may acquire not to exceed forty acres of tribally owned lands on the Pine Ridge Indian Reservation for the purpose of erecting thereon permanent facilities to be used to interpret the natural phenomena of the park and the history of the Sioux Nation: *Provided*, That no such conveyance shall be made until sixty days after the terms thereof have been submitted to the Interior and Insular Affairs Committees of the House of Representatives and the Senate.

(Pub.L. 90–468, § 6, Aug. 8, 1968, 82 Stat. 666; Pub.L. 95–625, Title VI, § 611, Nov. 10, 1978, 92 Stat. 3521.)

HISTORICAL AND STATUTORY NOTES

Revision Notes and Legislative Reports
  1968 Acts. Senate Report No. 1349, see 1968 U.S. Code Cong. and Adm. News, p. 3163.

Change of Name
  Committee on Interior and Insular Affairs of the House of Representatives changed to Committee on Natural Resources of the House of Representatives on Jan. 5, 1993, by House Resolution No. 5, One Hundred Third Congress. Committee on Natural Resources of House of Representatives treated as referring to Committee on Resources of House of Representatives by section 1(a) of Pub.L. 104–14, set out as a note preceding 2 U.S.C.A. § 21. Committee on Resources of House of Representatives changed to Committee on Natural Resources of

House of Representatives by House Resolution No. 6, One Hundred Tenth Congress, Jan. 5, 2007.

The Committee on Interior and Insular Affairs of the Senate was abolished and replaced by the Committee on Energy and Natural Resources of the Senate, effective Feb. 11, 1977. See Rule XXV of the Standing Rules of the Senate, as amended by Senate Resolution 4 (popularly cited as the "Committee System Reorganization Amendments of 1977"), approved Feb. 4, 1977.

Committee on Interior and Insular Affairs of the House of Representatives changed to Committee on Natural Resources of the House of Representatives on Jan. 5, 1993, by House Resolution No. 5, One Hundred Third Congress.

§ 442.   George Washington Birthplace National Monument

The land owned by the United States at Wakefield, Westmoreland County, Virginia, and all structures thereon shall constitute the George Washington Birthplace National Monument at Wakefield, Virginia, which is established and set apart for the preservation of the historical associations connected therewith, for the benefit and enjoyment of the people, and the said national monument shall be after January 23, 1930, administered by the National Park Service under the direction of the Secretary of the Interior subject to the provisions of sections 1, 2, 3, and 4 of this title, as amended.

(Jan. 23, 1930, c. 24, §§ 1, 2, 46 Stat. 58.)

HISTORICAL AND STATUTORY NOTES

Transfer of Functions

All functions of all other officers of the Department of the Interior and all functions of all agencies and employees of such Department were, with two exceptions, transferred to the Secretary of the Interior, with power vested in him to authorize their performance or the performance of any of his functions by any of such officers, agencies, and employees, by 1950 Reorg. Plan No. 3, §§ 1, 2, eff. May 24, 1950, 15 F.R. 3174, 64 Stat. 1262, set out in Appendix 1 to Title 5, Government Organization and Employees.

Revision of Boundaries; Acquisition of Lands; Administration; Authorization of Appropriations

Pub.L. 107–354, §§ 1 to 3, Dec. 17, 2002, 116 Stat. 2984, provided that:

"Sec. 1.   Addition to National Monument.

"The boundaries of the George Washington Birthplace National Monument (hereinafter referred to as the 'National Monument') are hereby modified to include the area comprising approximately 115 acres, as generally depicted on the map entitled 'George Washington Birthplace National Monument Boundary Map', numbered 332/80,023 and dated October 2001, which shall be on file and available for public inspection in the appropriate offices of the National Park Service, Department of the Interior.

"Sec. 2.   Acquisition of Lands.

"Within the boundaries of the National Monument, the Secretary of the Interior (hereinafter referred to as the 'Secretary') is authorized to acquire lands, or interests therein, from willing owners by donation, purchase with donated money or appropriated funds, or exchange.

"Sec. 3.   Administration of National Monument.

"In administering the National Monument, the Secretary shall take actions necessary to preserve and interpret the history and resources associated with George Washington, the generations of the Washington family who lived in the vicinity and their contemporaries, and 18th century plantation life and society."

George Washington's Boyhood Home, Ferry Farm

Pub.L. 105–355, Title V, § 509, Nov. 6, 1998, 112 Stat. 3264, provided that:

"(a) Acquisition of easement.—The Secretary of the Interior may acquire no more than a less than fee interest in the property generally known as George Washington's Boyhood Home, Ferry Farm, located in Stafford County, Virginia, across the Rappahannock River from Fredericksburg, Virginia, comprising approximately 85 acres as generally depicted on the map entitled 'George Washington Birthplace National Monument Boundary Map', numbered 322/80,020, and dated April 1998, to ensure the preservation of the important cultural and natural resources associated with Ferry Farm. The Secretary of the Interior shall keep the map on file and available for public inspection in appropriate offices of the National Park Service.

"**(b) Management of easement.**—The Secretary shall enter into a cooperative agreement with Kenmore Association, Inc., for the management of Ferry Farm pending completion of the study referred to in subsection (c).

"**(c) Resource study.**—Not later than 18 months after the date on which funds are made available to carry out this section, the Secretary of the Interior shall submit to the Committee on Energy and Natural Resources of the Senate and the Committee on Resources [now Natural Resources] of the House of Representatives a resource study of the property described in subsection (a). The study shall—

"**(1)** identify the full range of resources and historic themes associated with Ferry Farm, including those associated with George Washington's tenure at the property and those associated with the Civil War period;

"**(2)** identify alternatives for further National Park Service involvement at the property beyond those that may be provided for in the acquisition authorized under subsection (a); and

"**(3)** include cost estimates for any necessary acquisition, development, interpretation, operation, and maintenance associated with the alternatives identified.

"**(d) Agreements.**—Upon completion of the resource study under subsection (c), the Secretary of the Interior may enter into an agreement with the owner of the property described in subsection (a) or other entities for the purpose of providing programs, services, facilities, or technical assistance that further the preservation and public use of the property."

Boundary Revision and Administration of National Monument

Pub.L. 103–25, May 3, 1993, 107 Stat. 68, provided that:

"**Section 1. Addition to National Monument.**

"The boundaries of the George Washington Birthplace National Monument (hereinafter referred to as the 'National Monument') are hereby modified to include the area comprising approximately 12 acres, as generally depicted on the map entitled 'George Washington Birthplace National Monument Boundary Map', numbered 382/80,011A and dated September 1992, which shall be on file and available for public inspection in the appropriate offices of the National Park Service, Department of the Interior.

"**Sec. 2. Acquisition of lands.**

"Within the boundaries of the National Monument, the Secretary of the Interior (hereinafter referred to as the 'Secretary') is authorized to acquire lands, or interests therein, by donation, purchase with donated or appropriated funds, or exchange.

"**Sec. 3. Administration of National Monument.**

"In administering the National Monument, the Secretary shall take such action as is necessary to preserve and interpret the history and resources associated with George Washington, the generations of the Washington family who lived in the vicinity, and their contemporaries, as well as 18th century plantation life and society.

"**Sec. 4. Authorization of appropriations.**

"There are authorized to be appropriated such sums as may be necessary to carry out this Act [this note]."

Additional Lands

Additional lands were added to and made part of the monument by Presidential Proc. No. 1944, Mar. 30, 1931, 47 Stat. 2446.

LIBRARY REFERENCES

American Digest System
    Armed Services ⊙–54.
    Woods and Forests ⊙–1, 5, 8.
    Key Number System Topic Nos. 34, 411.

§§ 443 to 443f.   Transferred

HISTORICAL AND STATUTORY NOTES

Codifications
Sections, Acts July 3, 1930, c. 837, §§ 1 to 7, 46 Stat. 856; Mar. 3, 1931, c. 405, 46 Stat. 1490; June 5, 1936, c. 525, §§ 1, 2, 49 Stat. 1483, relating to the Colonial National Historical Park, were transferred to sections 81, 81a, 81c and 81e to 81i of this title.

§ 444.   Petrified Forest National Monument; elimination of private holdings of land within boundaries; exchange of lands

The Secretary of the Interior, for the purpose of eliminating private holdings of land within the Petrified Forest National Monument, Arizona, is empowered, in his discretion, to obtain for the United States the complete title to any or all of the lands held in private ownership within the boundaries of the Petrified Forest National Monument, Arizona, as now or as may be hereafter defined, by accepting from the owners of such privately owned lands complete relinquishment thereof and by granting and patenting to such owners in exchange therefor, in each instance, like public lands of equal value situated in Navajo and/or Apache Counties, in the State of Arizona, after due notice of the proposed exchange has been given by publication for not less than thirty days in the counties where the lands proposed to be exchanged or taken in exchange are located: *Provided*, That the Secretary of the Interior shall, on application or otherwise, designate public lands located outside the extreme boundaries of the said monument subject to exchange under this section which are, in his opinion, chiefly valuable for grazing and raising forage crops, do not contain merchantable timber, are not susceptible of irrigation from any known source of water supply, and are of character similar to the privately owned lands offered in exchange.

(May 14, 1930, c. 271, § 1, 46 Stat. 278.)

HISTORICAL AND STATUTORY NOTES

Disestablishment of Petrified Forest National Monument
Disestablishment of Petrified Forest National Monument upon establishment of Petrified Forest National Park, see section 119 of this title.

CROSS REFERENCES

Petrified Forest National Park, exchange of lands, see 16 USCA § 119.

LIBRARY REFERENCES

American Digest System
Armed Services ☞54.
Woods and Forests ☞4.
Key Number System Topic Nos. 34, 411.

§ 444a. Ascertainment of value of lands offered for exchange; evidence of title

The value of all patented lands within said monument offered for exchange, and the value of the lands of the United States to be given in exchange therefor, shall be ascertained in such manner as the Secretary of the Interior may direct; and the owners of such privately owned lands within said monument shall, before any exchange is effective, furnish the Secretary of the Interior evidence satisfactory to him of title to the patented lands offered in exchange; and lands conveyed to the United States under section 444 of this title shall be and remain a part of the Petrified Forest National Monument.

(May 14, 1930, c. 271, § 2, 46 Stat. 278.)

HISTORICAL AND STATUTORY NOTES

Disestablishment of Petrified Forest National Monument

Disestablishment of Petrified Forest National Monument upon establishment of Petrified Forest National Park, see section 119 of this title.

CROSS REFERENCES

Petrified Forest National Park, exchange of lands, see 16 USCA § 119.

LIBRARY REFERENCES

American Digest System
    Armed Services ⊕54.
    Woods and Forests ⊕1, 2.
    Key Number System Topic Nos. 34, 411.

§ 445. Canyon De Chelly National Monument; establishment; boundaries

With the consent of the tribal council of the Navajo Tribe of Indians, the President of the United States is authorized to establish by presidential proclamation the Canyon De Chelly National Monument, within the Navajo Indian Reservation, Arizona, including the lands hereinafter described.

All lands in Del Muerto, De Chelly, and Monument Canyons, in the canyons tributary thereto, and the lands within one-half mile of the rims of the said canyons, situated in unsurveyed townships 4 and 5 north, range 7 west; townships 4, 5, and 6 north, range 8 west; townships 4 and 5 north, range 9 west; and in surveyed townships 4 and 5 north, range 6 west; townships 3, 6, and 7 north, range 7 west; township 6 north, range 9 west; and township 5 north, range 10 west; embracing about eighty-three thousand eight hundred and forty acres, all of the Navajo meridian, in Arizona.

(Feb. 14, 1931, c. 188, § 1, 46 Stat. 1161; Mar. 1, 1933, c. 161, 47 Stat. 1419.)

HISTORICAL AND STATUTORY NOTES

Amendments
1933 Amendments. Act Mar. 1, 1933, changed the description of lands to read as set out in the second paragraph of this section.

Establishment of Monument; Boundaries
Monument and boundaries established by Presidential Proc. No. 1945, Apr. 1,

1931, 47 Stat. 2448; Proc. No. 2036, Mar. 3, 1933, 47 Stat. 2562.

LIBRARY REFERENCES

American Digest System
Armed Services ⊛54.
Woods and Forests ⊛1, 8.
Key Number System Topic Nos. 34, 411.

§ 445a. Rights and privileges of Navajo Indians in canyons

Nothing herein shall be construed as in any way impairing the right, title, and interest of the Navajo Tribe of Indians which they now have and hold to all lands and minerals, including oil and gas, and the surface use of such lands for agricultural, grazing, and other purposes, except as defined in section 445b of this title; and the said tribe of Indians is granted the preferential right, under regulations to be prescribed by the Secretary of the Interior, of furnishing riding animals for the use of visitors to the monument.

(Feb. 14, 1931, c. 188, § 2, 46 Stat. 1161.)

HISTORICAL AND STATUTORY NOTES

References in Text
Herein, referred to in text, means Act Feb. 14, 1931, which is classified to sec-

tions 445 to 445b of this title. For complete classification of this Act to the Code, see Tables.

LIBRARY REFERENCES

American Digest System
Armed Services ⊛54.
Indians ⊛150.
Key Number System Topic Nos. 34, 209.

§ 445b. Administration by National Park Service; powers and duties

The National Park Service, under the direction of the Secretary of the Interior, is charged with the administration of the area of said national monument, so far as it applies to the care, maintenance, preservation and restoration of the prehistoric ruins, or other features of scientific or historical interest within the area, and shall have the right to construct upon the lands such roads, trails, or other structures or improvements as may be necessary in connection with the administration and protection of the monument, and also the right to provide facilities of any nature whatsoever required for the care and accommodation of visitors to the monument.

(Feb. 14, 1931, c. 188, § 3, 46 Stat. 1161.)

HISTORICAL AND STATUTORY NOTES

Transfer of Functions

All functions of all other officers of the Department of the Interior and all functions of all agencies and employees of such Department were, with two exceptions, transferred to the Secretary of the Interior, with power vested in him to authorize their performance or the performance of any of his functions by any of such officers, agencies, and employees, by 1950 Reorg. Plan No. 3, §§ 1, 2, eff. May 24, 1950, 15 F.R. 3174, 64 Stat. 1262, set out in Appendix 1 to Title 5, Government Organization and Employees.

CODE OF FEDERAL REGULATIONS

Special regulations for particular areas of system, see 36 CFR § 7.1 et seq.

LIBRARY REFERENCES

American Digest System

Armed Services ☞54.
Woods and Forests ☞5.
Key Number System Topic Nos. 34, 411.

§ 445c. Pipestone National Monument

(a) Establishment; boundaries

The lands lying in Pipestone County, Minnesota, within the area hereinafter described are dedicated and set apart as a national monument for the benefit and enjoyment of the people of the United States, under the name of the "Pipestone National Monument": Beginning at a point twenty-two and four-tenths feet north and forty-five and eight one-hundredths feet west of the southwest corner of section 1, township 106 north, range 46 west, fifth principal meridian; thence north one thousand six hundred and fifty-five feet; thence north eighty-nine degrees fifteen minutes east, seven hundred and eight feet; thence north no degrees forty-five minutes west, six hundred and seven and three-tenths feet; thence north sixty-two degrees five minutes east, nine hundred and eighty-seven and one-tenth feet; thence south twenty-seven degrees fifty-five minutes east, two hundred and sixty-four and five-tenths feet; thence south eighty-eight degrees nineteen minutes east, nine hundred and sixty-seven and five-tenths feet; thence south no degrees twenty-four minutes east, one hundred and forty-four and three-tenths feet; thence south eighty-three degrees forty-three minutes west, four hundred and seventy-two and four-tenths feet; thence south two degrees seventeen minutes east, two thousand two hundred and forty-nine feet; thence south eighty-nine degrees twenty minutes west, four hundred and fifty-eight and two-tenths feet; thence south no degrees no minutes east, one hundred and one and one-tenth feet; thence south ninety degrees no minutes west, one hundred and thirty-seven and two-tenths feet; thence north no degrees no minutes west, one hundred feet; thence south eighty-nine degrees twenty minutes west, one thousand six hundred and eighty-three and eight-tenths feet to the point of beginning; containing approximately one hundred and fifteen and eighty-six one-hundredths acres, including concourse, excluding from the area described herein forty-seven one-hundredths acres, constituting a right-of-way of the Chicago, Rock Island and Pacific Railway.

(b) Administration, protection, and development

The administration, protection, and development of such monument shall be exercised under the direction of the Secretary of the Interior by the National Park Service, subject to the provisions of sections 1, 2, 3, and 4 of this title, as amended.

(c) Quarry rights of Indians

The quarrying of the red pipestone in the lands described in subsection (a) of this section is expressly reserved to Indians of all tribes, under regulations to be prescribed by the Secretary of the Interior.

(Aug. 25, 1937, c. 768, §§ 1–3, 50 Stat. 804, 805.)

HISTORICAL AND STATUTORY NOTES

Transfer of Functions

All functions of all other officers of the Department of the Interior and all functions of all agencies and employees of such Department were, with two exceptions, transferred to the Secretary of the Interior, with power vested in him to authorize their performance or the performance of any of his functions by any of such officers, agencies, and employees, by 1950 Reorg. Plan No. 3, §§ 1, 2, eff. May 24, 1950, 15 F.R. 3174, 64 Stat. 1262, set out in Appendix 1 to Title 5, Government Organization and Employees.

CODE OF FEDERAL REGULATIONS

Special regulations for particular areas of system, see 36 CFR § 7.1 et seq.

LIBRARY REFERENCES

American Digest System

Armed Services ⬤54.
Woods and Forests ⬤1, 8.
Key Number System Topic Nos. 34, 411.

§ 445d. Acquisition of additional lands, Pipestone School Reserve and non–Federal land; redefining of boundaries; quarry rights of Indians

The Secretary of the Interior is authorized to add to the Pipestone National Monument such part of the Pipestone school reserve, not exceeding two hundred and fifty acres, as he deems necessary to protect archeological remains, to acquire by purchase or condemnation not exceeding ten acres of non–Federal land, as he deems necessary to improve the boundary and administration of the Pipestone National Monument Federal land, and to redefine the exterior boundaries of the Pipestone National Monument to include the lands so transferred and acquired pursuant to this section. All lands added to the Pipestone National Monument pursuant to this section shall be subject to the provisions of subsections (b) and (c) of section 445c of this title.

(June 18, 1956, c. 401, 70 Stat. 290.)

HISTORICAL AND STATUTORY NOTES

Revision Notes and Legislative Reports
1956 Acts. Senate Report No. 2037, see 1956 U.S. Code Cong. and Adm. News, p. 2748.

LIBRARY REFERENCES

American Digest System
    Armed Services ⬥54.
    United States ⬥55.
    Woods and Forests ⬥2.
    Key Number System Topic Nos. 34, 393, 411.

§ 446. Sites for tablets at Antietam; care and supervision

All lands acquired by the United States, whether by purchase, gift, or otherwise, for the purposes of sites for tablets for the marking of the lines of battle of the Army of the Potomac and of the Army of Northern Virginia at Antietam, and of the position of each of the forty-three different commands of the Regular Army engaged in the battle of Antietam, shall be under the care and supervision of the Secretary of the Interior.

(Aug. 30, 1890, c. 837, § 1, 26 Stat. 401; Ex.Ord. No. 6166, § 2, June 10, 1933; Ex.Ord. No. 6228, § 1, July 28, 1933.)

HISTORICAL AND STATUTORY NOTES

Transfer of Functions
    Administrative functions of certain national military parks were transferred to the Department of the Interior by Ex.Ord. No. 6166, as amended by Ex.Ord. No. 6228, set out as a note under section 901 of Title 5, Government Organization and Employees.

National Park Service was substituted for Office of National Parks, Buildings, and Reservations referred to in Ex.Ord.

No. 6166, by Act Mar. 2, 1934, c. 38, § 1, 48 Stat. 389.

LIBRARY REFERENCES

American Digest System
 Armed Services ☞54.
 Woods and Forests ☞5.
 Key Number System Topic Nos. 34, 411.

§ 447. Repealed. Pub.L. 94–429, § 3(d), Sept. 28, 1976, 90 Stat. 1342

HISTORICAL AND STATUTORY NOTES

Section, Act June 13, 1933, c. 70, 48 Stat. 139, extended the mining laws of the United States to the lands within Death Valley National Monument subject to regulation by the Secretary of the Interior.

Mining Rights Existing Prior to Sept. 28, 1976
 Pub.L. 94–429, § 3, Sept. 28, 1976, 90 Stat. 1342, provided in part that this sec-

tion was repealed in order to close area to entry and location under the Mining Law of 1872, subject to valid existing rights.

§ 447a. Ocmulgee National Monument; establishment; acquisition of property

When title to lands commonly known as the "Old Ocmulgee Fields", upon which certain Indian mounds of great historical importance are located, comprising approximately two thousand acres, in and around the city of Macon, County of Bibb, State of Georgia, as shall be designated by the Secretary of the Interior, in the exercise of his judgment and discretion as necessary for national-monument purposes, shall have been vested in the United States, said area shall be set aside as a national monument, by proclamation of the President, and shall be known as the "Ocmulgee National Monument": *Provided,* That the United States shall not purchase by appropriation of public moneys any lands within the aforesaid area, but such lands shall be secured by the United States only by public or private donation.

(June 14, 1934, c. 519, § 1, 48 Stat. 958.)

HISTORICAL AND STATUTORY NOTES

Establishment of Monument; Boundaries
 Monument and boundaries established by Presidential Proc. No. 2212, Dec. 23,

1936, 50 Stat. 1798; Proc. No. 2493, June 13, 1941, 55 Stat. 1655.

LIBRARY REFERENCES

American Digest System
   Armed Services ☞54.
   United States ☞55.
   Woods and Forests ☞1, 8.
   Key Number System Topic Nos. 34, 393, 411.

§ 447b. Donation of property; condemnation proceedings

The Secretary of the Interior is authorized to accept donations of land, interests in land, buildings, structures, and other property, within the boundaries of said national monument as determined and fixed hereunder and donations of funds for the purchase and/or maintenance thereof, the title and evidence of title to lands acquired to be satisfactory to the Secretary of the Interior: *Provided*, That he may acquire on behalf of the United States under any donated funds by purchase when purchasable at prices deemed by him reasonable, otherwise by condemnation under the provisions of section 3113 of Title 40, such tracts of land within the said national monument as may be necessary for the completion thereof.

(June 14, 1934, c. 519, § 2, 48 Stat. 959.)

HISTORICAL AND STATUTORY NOTES

Codifications

In text, "section 3113 of Title 40" substituted for "sections 257 and 258 of Title 40", which originally read "the Act of August 1, 1888" on authority of Pub.L. 107–217, § 5(c), Aug. 21, 2002, 116 Stat. 1301, which is set out as a note preceding 40 U.S.C.A. § 101. Pub.L. 107–217, § 1, enacted Title 40 into positive law. The Act of August 1, 1888, is Act, Aug. 1, 1888, c. 728, 25 Stat. 357, which was classified to former 40 U.S.C.A. §§ 257 and 258, prior to being repealed by Pub.L. 107–217, § 6(b), Aug. 21, 2002, 116 Stat. 1305, and its substance reenacted as 40 U.S.C.A. § 3113. Section 258 of Title 40 was previously omitted from the Code as superseded by Rule 71A, Federal Rules of Civil Procedure, Title 28.

LIBRARY REFERENCES

American Digest System
   Armed Services ☞54.
   United States ☞55.
   Woods and Forests ☞2.
   Key Number System Topic Nos. 34, 393, 411.

Research References

Encyclopedias
   Am. Jur. 2d Eminent Domain § 77, Preservation of Historical Sites; Monuments--
   Under Federal Statutes.

§ 447c. Administration, protection, and development

The administration, protection, and development of the Ocmulgee National Monument shall be under the supervision of the Secretary of the Interior subject to the provisions of sections 1, 2, 3, and 4 of this title, as amended.

(June 14, 1934, c. 519, § 3, 48 Stat. 959.)

LIBRARY REFERENCES

American Digest System
  Woods and Forests ☞5.
  Key Number System Topic No. 411.

§ 448. Pioneer National Monument; establishment

When title to the sites of Fort Boonesborough, Boones Station, Bryans Station, and Blue Licks Battlefield, in the State of Kentucky, comprising noncontiguous tracts to be united by a Memorial Highway, together with such historical structures and remains thereon, as may be designated by the Secretary of the Interior as necessary or desirable for national-monument purposes and for the proper commemoration of the valor and sacrifices of the pioneers of "the West", shall have been vested in the United States, said areas and improvements shall be designated and set apart by proclamation of the President for preservation as a national monument for the benefit and inspiration of the people, and shall be called the "Pioneer National Monument."

(June 18, 1934, c. 573, § 1, 48 Stat. 982.)

LIBRARY REFERENCES

American Digest System
  Armed Services ☞54.
  Woods and Forests ☞1, 8.
  Key Number System Topic Nos. 34, 411.

§ 449. Acceptance of donations of land and funds; acquisition of land

The Secretary of the Interior be, and he is, authorized to accept donations of land, interests in land and/or buildings, structures, and other property within the boundaries of said national monument as determined and fixed hereunder, and donations of funds for the purchase and/or maintenance thereof, the title and evidence of title to lands acquired to be satisfactory to the Secretary of the Interior: *Provided*, That he may acquire on behalf of the United States out of any donated funds, by purchase at prices deemed by him reasonable, or by condemnation under the provisions of section 3113 of Title 40, such tracts of land within the said national monument as may be necessary for the completion thereof.

(June 18, 1934, c. 573, § 2, 48 Stat. 983.)

HISTORICAL AND STATUTORY NOTES

Codifications

In text, "section 3113 of Title 40" substituted for "sections 257 and 258 of Title 40", which originally read "the Act of August 1, 1888" on authority of Pub.L. 107–217, § 5(c), Aug. 21, 2002, 116 Stat. 1301, which is set out as a note preceding 40 U.S.C.A. § 101. Pub.L. 107–217, § 1, enacted Title 40 into positive law. The Act of August 1, 1888, is Act, Aug. 1, 1888, c. 728, 25 Stat. 357, which was classified to former 40 U.S.C.A. §§ 257 and 258, prior to being repealed by Pub.L. 107–217, § 6(b), Aug. 21, 2002, 116 Stat. 1305, and its substance reenacted as 40 U.S.C.A. § 3113. Section 258 of Title 40 was previously omitted from the Code as superseded by Rule 71A, Federal Rules of Civil Procedure, Title 28.

LIBRARY REFERENCES

American Digest System
Armed Services ☞54.
United States ☞55.
Woods and Forests ☞2.
Key Number System Topic Nos. 34, 393, 411.

Research References

Encyclopedias
Am. Jur. 2d Eminent Domain § 77, Preservation of Historical Sites; Monuments-- Under Federal Statutes.

§ 450. Administration, protection, and development

The administration, protection, and development of the aforesaid national monument shall be exercised under the direction of the Secretary of the Interior by the National Park Service, subject to the provisions of sections 1, 2, 3, and 4 of this title, as amended.

(June 18, 1934, c. 573, § 3, 48 Stat. 983.)

HISTORICAL AND STATUTORY NOTES

Transfer of Functions

All functions of all other officers of the Department of the Interior and all functions of all agencies and employees of such Department were, with two exceptions, transferred to the Secretary of the Interior, with power vested in him to authorize their performance or the performance of any of his functions by any of such officers, agencies, and employees, by 1950 Reorg. Plan No. 3, §§ 1, 2, eff. May 24, 1950, 15 F.R. 3174, 64 Stat. 1262, set out in Appendix 1 to Title 5, Government Organization and Employees.

LIBRARY REFERENCES

American Digest System
Armed Services ☞28, 54.
Woods and Forests ☞7.
Key Number System Topic Nos. 34, 411.

§ 450a. Chalmette, Louisiana, Monument

The sum of twenty-five thousand dollars is appropriated, or so much thereof as may be necessary, out of any money in the Treasury of the United States not otherwise appropriated, for the completion of a monument to the memory of the soldiers who fell in the battle of New Orleans in the war of eighteen hundred and twelve, said monument to be completed under the direction and approval of the Secretary of the Army: *Provided*, That the State of Louisiana shall cede and transfer its jurisdiction to the property on which said monument is to be completed in accordance with the provisions of act numbered forty-one of the legislature of that State, approved July nineteenth, nineteen hundred and two: *Provided further*, That when said monument is completed the responsibility of maintaining the same and keeping the grounds surrounding it shall hereafter rest with the Government of the United States; and there is authorized to be appropriated from time to time, out of any money in the Treasury not otherwise appropriated, such sums as may be necessary for such expenses.

(Mar. 4, 1907, c. 2928, 34 Stat. 1411; June 2, 1930, c. 369, 46 Stat. 489.)

HISTORICAL AND STATUTORY NOTES

Amendments

1930 Amendments. Act June 2, 1930, placed the responsibility for maintaining monument and grounds with United States Government and authorized appropriations for expenses.

Change of Name

The Department of War was designated the Department of the Army and the title of the Secretary of War was changed to Secretary of the Army by section 205(a) of Act July 26, 1947, c. 343, Title II, 61 Stat. 501.   Section 205(a) of Act July 26, 1947, was repealed by section 53 of Act Aug. 10, 1956, c. 1041, 70A Stat. 641. Section 1 of Act Aug. 10, 1956, enacted "Title 10, Armed Forces" which in sections 3010 to 3013 continued the military Department of the Army under the administrative supervision of a Secretary of the Army.

Transfer of Functions

Administrative functions of Chalmette Monument and Grounds, Louisiana were transferred to the Department of the Interior by Ex.Ord. No. 6166, § 2, as amended by Ex.Ord. No. 6228, set out as a note under section 901 of Title 5, Government Organization and Employees.   National Park Service was substituted for Office of National Parks, Buildings and Reservations referred to in Ex.Ord. No. 6166, § 2, set out as a note under section 901 of Title 5, by Act Mar. 2, 1934, c. 38, § 1, 48 Stat. 389.

Chalmette Unit of Jean Lafitte National Historical Park

Designation of lands on which monument erected as Chalmette Unit of Jean Lafitte National Historical Park, see sections 230h and 231 of this title.

LIBRARY REFERENCES

American Digest System

Armed Services ⚬➡54.
Key Number System Topic No. 34.

§§ 450b to 450e. Repealed. Pub.L. 94–578, Title III, § 308(e), Oct. 21, 1976, 90 Stat. 2736

HISTORICAL AND STATUTORY NOTES

Section 450b, Acts June 18, 1930, c. 520, § 1, 46 Stat. 777; Aug. 13, 1935, c. 520, § 1, 49 Stat. 613; Apr. 15, 1954, c. 142, 68 Stat. 54, provided for the creation of the Appomattox Court House National Historical Park.

Section 450c, Acts June 18, 1930, c. 520, § 2, 46 Stat. 777; Aug. 13, 1935, c. 520, § 1, 49 Stat. 613, authorized the appropriation of $100,000 for the Appomattox Court House National Historical Park.

Section 450d, Acts June 18, 1930, c. 520, § 3, 46 Stat. 777; Aug. 13, 1935, c. 520, § 1, 49 Stat. 613, authorized the

Secretary of the Interior to accept donations of land or buildings within the boundaries of the park.

Section 450d–1, Acts July 17, 1953, c. 227, 67 Stat. 181; Apr. 15, 1954, c. 142, 68 Stat. 54, authorized the exchange of land in the park for adjacent non-Federal land.

Section 450e, Act June 18, 1930, c. 520, § 4, as added Aug. 13, 1935, c. 520, § 2, 49 Stat. 614, and amended Apr. 15, 1954, c. 142, 68 Stat. 54, provided for the administration of the park by the National Park Service under the direction of the Secretary of the Interior.

§ 450e–1. Appomattox Court House National Historical Park

(a) Boundaries

The Appomattox Court House National Historical Park shall hereafter comprise the area depicted on the map entitled "Boundary Map, Appomattox Court House National Historical Park", numbered 340/80,015 and dated June 1992, which is on file and available for public inspection in the offices of the National Park Service, Department of the Interior.

(b) Land acquisition by donation, purchase, or exchange; limitation on acquisition of State land

Within the boundaries of the park, the Secretary may acquire lands and interests in lands, by donation, purchase with donated or appropriated funds, or exchange. Any lands or interests in lands owned by the State of Virginia or its political subdivisions may be acquired only by donation.

(c) Owner's reservation of right of use and occupancy of improved property for residential purposes for life or fixed term of years; compensation at fair market value; termination of right retained by owner; "improved property" defined; waiver of rights and benefits by owner

(1) The owner of an improved property on the date of its acquisition by the Secretary may, as a condition of such acquisition, retain for himself and his heirs and assigns a right of use and occupancy of the improved property for noncommercial residential purposes for a definite term of not more than twenty-five years or, in lieu thereof, for a term ending at the death of the owner or the death of his

spouse, whichever is later. The owner shall elect the term to be reserved. Unless this property is wholly or partially donated to the United States, the Secretary shall pay the owner the fair market value of the property on the date of acquisition, less the fair market value, on that date, of the right retained by the owner. A right retained pursuant to this section shall be subject to termination by the Secretary upon his determination that it is being exercised in a manner inconsistent with the purposes of this section, and it shall terminate by operation of law upon the Secretary's notifying the holder of the right of such determination and tendering to him an amount equal to the fair market value of that portion of the right which remains unexpired.

(2) As used in this section, the term "improved property" means a detached, single-family dwelling, construction of which was begun before June 8, 1976, which is used for noncommercial residential purposes, together with such additional lands or interests therein as the Secretary deems to be reasonably necessary for access thereto, such lands being in the same ownership as the dwelling, together with any structures accessory to the dwelling which are situated on such land.

(3) Whenever an owner of property elects to retain a right of use and occupancy as provided in this section, such owner shall be deemed to have waived any benefits or rights accruing under sections 4623, 4624, 4625, and 4626 of Title 42, and for the purposes of such sections such owner shall not be considered a displaced person as defined in section 4601(6) of Title 42.

(d) Administration

The Secretary shall administer the park in accordance with sections 1, 2, 3, and 4 of this title, as amended and supplemented, and sections 461 to 467 of this title.

(e) Omitted

(f) Authorization of appropriation

There are authorized to be appropriated not to exceed $1,335,000 to carry out the purposes of this section.

(Pub.L. 94–578, Title III, § 308, Oct. 21, 1976, 90 Stat. 2735; Pub.L. 102–541, § 3(a), Oct. 27, 1992, 106 Stat. 3565.)

HISTORICAL AND STATUTORY NOTES

References in Text

This "Act", in the original, has been changed to this "section" as the probable intent of Congress.

Codifications

Section is comprised of 308 of Pub.L. 94–578. Subsec. (e) of section 308 of Pub.L. 94–578 repealed sections 450b to 450e of this title.

Amendments

1992 Amendments. Subsec. (a). Pub.L. 102–541, § 3(a), substituted "numbered 340/80,015 and dated June 1992," for "numbered 340–20,000A, and dated September 1976,".

Effective and Applicability Provisions

1992 Acts. Pub.L. 102–541, § 3(a), Oct. 27, 1992, 106 Stat. 3565, provided in part: "That this subsection [amending subsec. (a) of this section] shall not be effective until the lands included within the proposed new boundaries of the Appomattox Court House National Historical Park pursuant to this Act [Pub.L. 102–541, for distribution of which, see Tables] have been donated to the Secretary of the Interior." [Lands included within proposed new boundaries were donated on Sept. 14, 1993, and Sept. 15, 1993.]

Acquisition of Certain Lands by Donation Only

Pub.L. 102–541, § 3(b), Oct. 27, 1992, 106 Stat. 3566, provided that: "Lands included within the boundaries of the Appomattox Court House National Historical Park pursuant to this section [amending subsec. (a) of this section] may be acquired only by donation."

LIBRARY REFERENCES

American Digest System

Armed Services ⊕54.
Woods and Forests ⊕1, 2, 8.
Key Number System Topic Nos. 34, 411.

§§ 450f to 450k. Repealed. Dec. 21, 1944, c. 634, § 1, 58 Stat. 852

HISTORICAL AND STATUTORY NOTES

Section 450f, Act Aug. 15, 1935, c. 547, § 1, 49 Stat. 652, related to the establishment of the Patrick Henry National Monument.

Sections 450f–1 and 450f–2, Act Jan. 29, 1940, c. 16, 54 Stat. 18, related to the acquisition of Patrick Henry's estate and the erection of a permanent public memorial.

Sections 450g to 450k, Act Aug. 15, 1935, c. 547, §§ 2 to 6, 49 Stat. 652, 653, related to the administration, etc., of the monument.

Unexpended Funds

Section 2 of Act Dec. 21, 1944, c. 634, 58 Stat. 853 provided that all unexpended balances of amounts appropriated were to be covered into the surplus fund of the Treasury.

§ 450*l*. Fort Stanwix National Monument; establishment

When title to the site or portion thereof at Fort Stanwix, in the State of New York, together with such buildings and other property located thereon as may be designated by the Secretary of the Interior as necessary or desirable for national monument purposes, shall have been vested in the United States, said area and improvements, if any, shall be designated and set apart by proclamation of the President for preservation as a national monument for the benefit and inspiration of the people and shall be called the "Fort Stanwix National Monument": *Provided*, That such area shall include at least that part of Fort Stanwix now belonging to the State of New York.

(Aug. 21, 1935, c. 592, § 1, 49 Stat. 665.)

LIBRARY REFERENCES

American Digest System
    Armed Services ⟐54.
    Woods and Forests ⟐1, 8.
    Key Number System Topic Nos. 34, 411.

§ 450m. Acceptance of donations of lands and funds; acquisition of land

The Secretary of the Interior is authorized to accept donations of land, interests in land and/or buildings, structures, and other property within the boundaries of said national monument as determined and fixed hereunder, and donations of funds for the purchase and/or maintenance thereof, the title and evidence of title to lands acquired to be satisfactory to the Secretary of the Interior: *Provided*, That he may acquire on behalf of the United States out of any donated funds, by purchase at prices deemed by him reasonable, or by condemnation under the provisions of section 3113 of Title 40, such tracts of land within the said national monument as may be necessary for the completion thereof.

(Aug. 21, 1935, c. 592, § 2, 49 Stat. 666.)

HISTORICAL AND STATUTORY NOTES

References in Text
    Hereunder, referred to in text, means Act Aug. 21, 1935, which is classified to sections 450*l* to 450n of this title. For complete classification of this Act to the Code, see Tables.

Codifications
    In text, "section 3113 of Title 40" substituted for "sections 257 and 258 of Title 40", which originally read "the Act of August 1, 1888" on authority of Pub.L. 107–217, § 5(c), Aug. 21, 2002, 116 Stat. 1301, which is set out as a note preceding

40 U.S.C.A. § 101. Pub.L. 107–217, § 1, enacted Title 40 into positive law. The Act of August 1, 1888, is Act, Aug. 1, 1888, c. 728, 25 Stat. 357, which was classified to former 40 U.S.C.A. §§ 257 and 258, prior to being repealed by Pub.L. 107–217, § 6(b), Aug. 21, 2002, 116 Stat. 1305, and its substance reenacted as 40 U.S.C.A. § 3113. Section 258 of Title 40 was previously omitted from the Code as superseded by Rule 71A, Federal Rules of Civil Procedure, Title 28.

LIBRARY REFERENCES

American Digest System
    Armed Services ⟐54.
    United States ⟐55.
    Woods and Forests ⟐2.
    Key Number System Topic Nos. 34, 393, 411.

§ 450n. Administration, protection, and development

The administration, protection, and development of the aforesaid national monument shall be exercised under the direction of the Secretary of the Interior by the National Park Service, subject to the provisions of sections 1, 2, 3, and 4 of this title, as amended.

(Aug. 21, 1935, c. 592, § 3, 49 Stat. 666.)

HISTORICAL AND STATUTORY NOTES

Transfer of Functions

All functions of all other officers of the Department of the Interior and all functions of all agencies and employees of such Department were, with two exceptions, transferred to the Secretary of the Interior, with power vested in him to authorize their performance or the performance of any of his functions by any of such officers, agencies, and employees, by 1950 Reorg. Plan No. 3, §§ 1, 2, eff. May 24, 1950, 15 F.R. 3174, 64 Stat. 1262, set out in Appendix 1 to Title 5, Government Organization and Employees.

LIBRARY REFERENCES

American Digest System

  Armed Services ☞54.
  Woods and Forests ☞5.
  Key Number System Topic Nos. 34, 411.

§ 450o. Andrew Johnson National Historic Site; authorization

When title to the site of the Andrew Johnson Homestead and the site of the tailor shop in which Andrew Johnson worked (now owned and administered by the State of Tennessee), located in Greeneville, Tennessee, together with such buildings and property located thereon as may be designated by the Secretary of the Interior as necessary or desirable for national-historic site purposes shall have been vested in the United States, said area and improvements, if any, together with the burial place of Andrew Johnson, now administered as a national cemetery, shall be designated and set apart by proclamation of the President for preservation as a national historic site for the benefit and inspiration of the people and shall be called the "Andrew Johnson National Historic Site."

(Aug. 29, 1935, c. 801, § 1, 49 Stat. 958; Dec. 11, 1963, Pub.L. 88–197, § 1, 77 Stat. 349.)

HISTORICAL AND STATUTORY NOTES

Change of Name

References to national historic sites were substituted for references to national monuments on authority of Pub.L. 88–197, which redesignated the "Andrew Johnson National Monument" as the "Andrew Johnson National Historic Site".

Establishment of Monument; Boundaries

Monument and boundaries established by Presidential Proc. No. 2554, Apr. 27, 1942, 56 Stat. 1955.

LIBRARY REFERENCES

American Digest System

  Armed Services ☞54.
  Woods and Forests ☞1, 2.
  Key Number System Topic Nos. 34, 411.

§ 450p. Acquisition of property; donations

The Secretary of the Interior is authorized to acquire on behalf of the United States out of any funds allotted and made available for this project by proper authority or out of any donated funds, by purchase at prices deemed by him reasonable, or by condemnation under the provisions of section 3113 of Title 40, or to accept by donation, such land, interest in land, and/or buildings, structures, and other property within the boundaries of said national historic site as determined and fixed hereunder, and he is further authorized to accept donations of funds for the purchase and/or maintenance thereof.

(Aug. 29, 1935, c. 801, § 2, 49 Stat. 958; Dec. 11, 1963, Pub.L. 88–197, § 1, 77 Stat. 349.)

HISTORICAL AND STATUTORY NOTES

References in Text

Hereunder, referred to in text, means Act Aug. 29, 1935, which is classified to sections 450o to 450q of this title. For complete classification of this Act to the Code, see Tables.

Codifications

In text, "section 3113 of Title 40" substituted for "sections 257 and 258 of Title 40", which originally read "the Act of August 1, 1888 (25 Stat. 357)" on authority of Pub.L. 107–217, § 5(c), Aug. 21, 2002, 116 Stat. 1301, which is set out as a note preceding 40 U.S.C.A. § 101. Pub.L. 107–217, § 1, enacted Title 40 into positive law. The Act of August 1, 1888, is Act, Aug. 1, 1888, c. 728, 25 Stat. 357,

which was classified to former 40 U.S.C.A. §§ 257 and 258, prior to being repealed by Pub.L. 107–217, § 6(b), Aug. 21, 2002, 116 Stat. 1305, and its substance reenacted as 40 U.S.C.A. § 3113. Section 258 of Title 40 was previously omitted from the Code as superseded by Rule 71A, Federal Rules of Civil Procedure, Title 28.

Change of Name

"Historic site" was substituted for "monument" on authority of Pub.L. 88–197, which redesignated the "Andrew Johnson National Monument" as the "Andrew Johnson National Historic Site".

LIBRARY REFERENCES

American Digest System

Armed Services ⟐54.
United States ⟐55.
Woods and Forests ⟐2.
Key Number System Topic Nos. 34, 393, 411.

§ 450q. Administration, protection, and development

The administration, protection, and development of the aforesaid national historic site shall be exercised under the direction of the Secretary of the Interior by the National Park Service, subject to the provisions of sections 1, 2, 3, and 4 of this title, as amended.

(Aug. 29, 1935, c. 801, § 3, 49 Stat. 958; Dec. 11, 1963, Pub.L. 88–197, § 1, 77 Stat. 349.)

HISTORICAL AND STATUTORY NOTES

Change of Name

"Historic site" was substituted for "monument" on authority of Pub.L. 88–197, which redesignated the "Andrew Johnson National Monument" as the "Andrew Johnson National Historic Site".

Transfer of Functions

All functions of all other officers of the Department of the Interior and all functions of all agencies and employees of such Department were, with two exceptions, transferred to the Secretary of the Interior, with power vested in him to authorize their performance or the performance of any of his functions by any of such officers, agencies, and employees, by 1950 Reorg. Plan No. 3, §§ 1, 2, eff. May 24, 1950, 15 F.R. 3174, 64 Stat. 1262, set out in Appendix 1 to Title 5, Government Organization and Employees.

LIBRARY REFERENCES

American Digest System

Armed Services ☞54.
Woods and Forests ☞5.
Key Number System Topic Nos. 34, 411.

§ 450r. Ackia Battleground National Monument; establishment

The Secretary of the Interior is authorized in his discretion to acquire, by purchase or by condemnation and/or accept by donation in behalf of the United States, such lands, easements, and buildings not to exceed fifty acres, and when title satisfactory to the Secretary of the Interior shall have been vested in the United States such area or areas shall be, upon proclamation of the President, established, dedicated, and set apart as a public monument for the benefit and enjoyment of the people and shall be known as the "Ackia Battleground National Monument": *Provided*, That such area shall include the site of the Battle of Ackia.

(Aug. 27, 1935, c. 755, § 2, 49 Stat. 897.)

HISTORICAL AND STATUTORY NOTES

Boundaries of Monument

By Proc. No. 2307, Oct. 25, 1938, 3 F.R. 2579, 53 Stat. 2494, the following described lands in Lee County, Mississippi, were dedicated subject to the easement of the Tennessee Valley Authority, as the Ackia Battleground National Monument: "Beginning at a point which lies north 41 degrees 03 minutes east 138.53 feet from the quarter section corner between sections 23 and 26, T. 9 S., R. 5 E., of the Chickasaw Meridian; thence north 80 degrees 03 minutes east 1166.0 feet to a point; thence south 55 degrees 10 minutes east 300.94 feet to a point; thence south 55 degrees 12 minutes east 479.8 feet to a point; thence south 29 degrees 45 minutes west 695.31 feet to a point; thence south 60 degrees 21 minutes west 933.6 feet to a point; thence north 64 degrees 26 minutes west 1236.0 feet to a point; thence north 31 degrees 49 minutes east 912.75 feet to the place of beginning, containing 49.15 acres of land and being parts of sections 23 and 26 T. 9 S., R. 5 E., of the Chickasaw Meridian, County of Lee, State of Mississippi."

Inclusion in Natchez Trace Parkway

Ackia Battleground National Monument included in the Natchez Trace Parkway, see section 460–1 of this title.

LIBRARY REFERENCES

American Digest System
 Armed Services ⟐54.
 Woods and Forests ⟐1, 8.
 Key Number System Topic Nos. 34, 411.

§ 450s. Omitted.

HISTORICAL AND STATUTORY NOTES

Codifications
 Section, Act Aug. 27, 1935, c. 755, § 3, 49 Stat. 897, authorized the appropria- tion of $15,000 for purposes of section 450r of this title.

§ 450t. Administration, protection, and development

The administration, protection, and development of the aforesaid national monument shall be exercised under the direction of the Secretary of the Interior by the National Park Service, subject to the provisions of sections 1, 2, 3, and 4 of this title, as amended.
(Aug. 27, 1935, c. 755, § 4, 49 Stat. 897.)

HISTORICAL AND STATUTORY NOTES

Transfer of Functions
 All functions of all other officers of the Department of the Interior and all functions of all agencies and employees of such Department were, with two exceptions, transferred to the Secretary of the Interior, with power vested in him to authorize their performance or the performance of any of his functions by any of such officers, agencies, and employees, by 1950 Reorg. Plan No. 3, §§ 1, 2, eff. May 24, 1950, 15 F.R. 3174, 64 Stat. 1262, set out in Appendix 1 to Title 5, Government Organization and Employees.

LIBRARY REFERENCES

American Digest System
 Armed Services ⟐54.
 Woods and Forests ⟐5.
 Key Number System Topic Nos. 34, 411.

§ 450u. Homestead National Monument of America; establishment

The Secretary of the Interior is authorized and directed to acquire, on behalf of the United States, by gift, purchase, or condemnation, the south half of the northwest quarter, the northeast quarter of the northwest quarter, and the southwest quarter of the northeast quarter section 26, township 4 north, range 5 east, of the sixth principal meridian, Gage County, Nebraska, the same being the first homestead entered upon under the General Homestead Act of May 20, 1862, by Daniel Freeman, and that when so acquired, the said area be designated "The Homestead National Monument of America."
(Mar. 19, 1936, c. 157, § 1, 49 Stat. 1184.)

HISTORICAL AND STATUTORY NOTES

References in Text

The General Homestead Act, referred to in text, is Act May 20, 1862, c. 75, 12 Stat. 392, which was classified to former section 161 et seq. of Title 43, Public Lands, and repealed by Pub.L. 94–579, Title VII, § 702, Oct. 21, 1976, 90 Stat. 2787.

Additional Lands

Additional lands were added to and made part of the Homestead National Monument of America in Nebraska by the Homestead National Monument of America Additions Act, Pub.L. 107–332, §§ 1 to 4, Dec. 16, 2002, 116 Stat. 2871.

Freeman School Addition

Pub.L. 91–411, Sept. 25, 1970, 84 Stat. 863, provided for addition of the Freeman School to the Homestead National Monument of America in Nebraska and authorized appropriation of not more than $50,000 for rehabilitation and development of the Freeman School.

LIBRARY REFERENCES

American Digest System

Armed Services ⇐54.
Woods and Forests ⇐1, 8.
Key Number System Topic Nos. 34, 411.

§ 450v. Omitted.

HISTORICAL AND STATUTORY NOTES

Codifications

Section, Act Mar. 19, 1936, c. 157, § 2, 49 Stat. 1184, authorized the appropriation of $24,000 for purpose of acquiring tract described in section 450u of this title.

§ 450w. Administration; establishment of museum

It shall be the duty of the Secretary of the Interior to lay out said land in a suitable and enduring manner so that the same may be maintained as an appropriate monument to retain for posterity a proper memorial emblematical of the hardships and the pioneer life through which the early settlers passed in the settlement, cultivation, and civilization of the great West. It shall be his duty to erect suitable buildings to be used as a museum in which shall be preserved literature applying to such settlement and agricultural implements used in bringing the western plains to its present high state of civilization, and to use the said tract of land for such other objects and purposes as in his judgment may perpetuate the history of the country mainly developed by the homestead law.

(Mar. 19, 1936, c. 157, § 3, 49 Stat. 1184.)

HISTORICAL AND STATUTORY NOTES

References in Text

The homestead law, referred to in text, is set out in former section 161 et seq. of Title 43, Public Lands.

§ 450x. Authorization of annual appropriations

For the purpose of carrying out the suggestions and recommendations of the Secretary of the Interior, the necessary annual appropriations therefor are authorized.

(Mar. 19, 1936, c. 157, § 4, 49 Stat. 1184.)

§ 450y. Coronado National Memorial; establishment

For the purpose of permanently commemorating the explorations of Francisco Vásquez de Coronado, the President of the United States is authorized to declare, by proclamation, any lands within the following-described area, subject to all valid existing rights, to be established as the "Coronado National Memorial":

Gila and Salt River meridian: Township 24 south, range 20 east, section 10, south half southwest quarter, south half southeast quarter; section 11, south half southwest quarter; section 13, southwest quarter northwest quarter, south half; section 14, northwest quarter, south half, northwest quarter northeast quarter, south half northeast quarter; section 15, all; section 22, all; section 23, all; section 24, all; township 24 south, range 21 east, section 17, south half southwest quarter; section 18, southwest quarter, south half southeast quarter; section 19, all; section 20, lots 3 and 4; aggregating approximately two thousand eight hundred and eighty acres.

(Aug. 18, 1941, c. 365, § 1, 55 Stat. 630; July 9, 1952, c. 610, §§ 1, 2, 66 Stat. 510.)

HISTORICAL AND STATUTORY NOTES

Amendments
    1952 Amendments. Act July 9, 1952 changed the name of "Coronado International Memorial" to "Coronado National Memorial", and struck out proviso which required action of Mexican government prior to establishment of the Memorial.

PROCLAMATIONS
PROCLAMATION NO. 2995
Nov. 5, 1952, 17 F.R. 10157, 67 Stat. c18
ESTABLISHMENT OF MEMORIAL

NOW, THEREFORE, I, HARRY S. TRUMAN, President of the United States of America, under and by virtue of the authority vested in me by section 1 of the said act of August 18, 1941, as amended [this section] do proclaim and declare that, subject to all valid existing rights, the following-described public lands in the State of Arizona are hereby established as the Coronado National Memorial:

GILA AND SALT RIVER MERIDIAN T. 24 S., R. 20 E.,

Sec. 10, S½SW¼, S½SE¼;
Sec. 11, S½SW¼;
Sec. 13, SW¼NW¼, S½;
Sec. 14, NW¼, S½, NW¼NE¼, S½NE¼;
Sec. 15, all;
Sec. 22, all;
Sec. 23, all;
Sec. 24, all;

T. 24 S., R. 21 E.,

Sec. 17, lots 5 and 6;
Sec. 18, lots 3, 4, 8, 9, 10 and SE¼SW ¼;

Sec. 19, all;
Sec. 20, lots 3 and 4.

The areas described aggregate approximately 2,745.33 acres.

Warning is hereby expressly given to all unauthorized persons not to appropriate, injure, destroy, deface, or remove any feature of this Memorial or to settle upon any of the lands thereof as hereby established.

Subject to the provisions of the said act of August 18, 1941 [this section], the Director of the National Park Service, under the direction of the Secretary of the Interior, shall have the supervision, management, and control of the lands constituting the Coronado National Memorial in accordance with the act entitled "An Act to establish a National Park Service, and for other purposes", approved Aug. 25, 1916 (39 Stat. 535; 16 U.S.C. 1–3) [16 U.S.C.A. §§ 1 to 4], and acts supplementary thereto or amendatory thereof so far as the provisions of such acts may be applicable.

LIBRARY REFERENCES

American Digest System
　Armed Services ☞54.
　Woods and Forests ☞1, 8.
　Key Number System Topic Nos. 34, 411.

§ 450y–1. Administration

The National Park Service, under the direction of the Secretary of the Interior, shall promote and regulate the use of the Coronado National Memorial for the benefit and enjoyment of the people of the United States. Insofar as applicable and not in conflict with sections 450y to 450y–4 of this title, sections 1, 2, 3, and 4 of this title, as amended and supplemented, providing for the establishment of a National Park Service, shall govern the promotion and regulation of the designated memorial area: *Provided*, That nothing in sections 450y to 450y–4 of this title shall be construed to authorize any recreational or other development by the National Park Service within the sixty-foot strip north of the international boundary between the United States and Mexico withdrawn by proclamation of the President dated May 27, 1907 (35 Stat., part II, p. 2136), unless such development has received the prior approval of the Secretary of State.

(Aug. 18, 1941, c. 365, § 2, 55 Stat. 630; July 9, 1952, c. 610, § 1, 66 Stat. 510.)

HISTORICAL AND STATUTORY NOTES

Amendments
1952 Amendments. Act July 9, 1952, changed the name of "Coronado International Memorial" to "Coronado National Memorial".

Transfer of Functions
All functions of all other officers of the Department of the Interior and all functions of all agencies and employees of such Department were, with two exceptions, transferred to the Secretary of the Interior, with power vested in him to authorize their performance or the performance of any of his functions by any of such officers, agencies, and employees, by 1950 Reorg. Plan No. 3, §§ 1, 2, eff. May 24, 1950, 15 F.R. 3174, 64 Stat. 1262, set out in Appendix 1 to Title 5, Government Organization and Employees.

LIBRARY REFERENCES

American Digest System
  Armed Services ☞54.
  Woods and Forests ☞5.
  Key Number System Topic Nos. 34, 411.

§ 450y–2.   Grazing within memorial area

The Secretary of the Interior, under such regulations as shall be prescribed by him, which regulations shall be substantially similar to those now in effect, shall permit—

Grazing of livestock within the memorial area to the extent now permitted within the said area when such grazing will not interfere with recreational development authorized by sections 450y to 450y–4 of this title.

(Aug. 18, 1941, c. 365, § 3, 55 Stat. 631; Sept. 28, 1976, Pub.L. 94–429, § 3(f), 90 Stat. 1342.)

HISTORICAL AND STATUTORY NOTES

Revision Notes and Legislative Reports
1976 Acts. House Report No. 94–1428, see 1976 U.S. Code Cong. and Adm. News, p. 2487.

Amendments
1976 Amendments. Pub.L. 94–429 struck out "(a)" preceding "grazing of livestock" and deleted former subsec. (b) which related to the surface use of the land within the memorial area for prospecting and mining.

Mining Rights Existing Prior to 1976 Amendments
Pub.L. 94–429, § 3, Sept. 28, 1976, 90 Stat. 1342, provided in part that this section was amended as indicated in order to close area to entry and location under the Mining Law of 1872, subject to valid existing rights.

§ 450y–3. Construction of fences

In the administration of the memorial area the Secretary shall not permit the construction of fences except (a) along the international boundary, (b) beside memorial roads or approach roads, and (c) around memorial areas within which improvements have been located by the National Park Service: *Provided*, That any roads constructed within the memorial area by the National Park Service shall include necessary cattle underpasses properly located for the passage of cattle across such roads: *And provided further*, That the right to the exclusive beneficial consumptive use for stock-watering purposes of any water heretofore developed or used for such purposes within the memorial area shall remain in the present holders thereof, their heirs, assigns, successors, and administrators, so long as such water continues to be used exclusively for such purposes: *And provided further*, That nothing in sections 450y to 450y–4 of this title shall be construed to alter or affect any water right in the State of Arizona or the jurisdiction of said State over its waters: *And provided further*, That neither roads nor public campgrounds shall be constructed by the National Park Service within the south half southwest quarter of said section 10.

(Aug. 18, 1941, c. 365, § 4, 55 Stat. 631.)

HISTORICAL AND STATUTORY NOTES

Transfer of Functions

All functions of all other officers of the Department of the Interior and all functions of all agencies and employees of such Department were, with two exceptions, transferred to the Secretary of the Interior, with power vested in him to authorize their performance or the performance of any of his functions by any of such officers, agencies, and employees, by 1950 Reorg. Plan No. 3, §§ 1, 2, eff. May 24, 1950, 15 F.R. 3174, 64 Stat. 1262, set out in Appendix 1 to Title 5, Government Organization and Employees.

§ 450y–4. Acquisition of property; donations

Upon submission of title satisfactory to him, the Secretary of the Interior, on behalf of the United States, may accept lands and interests in lands which are within the memorial area but are not in Federal ownership and which are offered to the United States without cost.

(Aug. 18, 1941, c. 365, § 5, 55 Stat. 631.)

LIBRARY REFERENCES

American Digest System
  Armed Services ⊗54.
  United States ⊗55.
  Key Number System Topic Nos. 34, 393.

§ 450y–5. Revision of boundaries

In furtherance of the purposes of sections 450y to 450y–4 of this title and to facilitate the administration and development of the Coronado National Memorial, Arizona, the boundaries thereof are revised by the following additions and deletions of land:

(1) Inclusion in the memorial and exclusion from the Coronado National Forest of lots 2 and 7 and a portion of Homestead Entry Survey 310 situated in section 18, township 24 south, range 21 east, Gila and Salt River base and meridian, said portion of Homestead Entry Survey 310 being more particularly described as follows: Beginning at the southwest corner (identified as corner number 1), of Homestead Entry Survey 310, said point being located on the present boundary of Coronado National Memorial and marked by an iron pipe with a brass cap and a rock cairn placed by the United States Bureau of Land Management in 1955; thence north zero degrees thirty-three minutes west, one thousand two hundred ninety-four and twenty-six hundredths feet, more or less, along the west boundary of said tract, which line is also the present boundary of said memorial, to the northeast corner of lot 8, section 18, said point being marked by an iron pipe with a brass cap and a rock cairn placed by the United States Bureau of Land Management in 1955; thence north zero degrees twenty-three minutes east, two hundred thirty and eight-tenths feet, more or less, along the west boundary of Homestead Entry Survey 310 to a point on a circular curve marked by an iron pipe with a National Park Service brass cap, said point being located south eighty-one degrees forty-four minutes east, exactly one hundred forty feet from the point of curvature of said curve; thence southeasterly five hundred forty-eight and two-tenths feet along said circular curve to the right of radius one thousand seven hundred thirty-two and four-tenths feet and having a beginning tangent bearing of south eighty-four degrees three minutes east (from point of curvature to point of intersection), to the point of tangency of

said curve; thence south sixty-one degrees sixteen minutes east, two hundred twenty-four and eight-tenths feet to the point of curvature of a circular curve to the right; thence southeasterly two hundred ninety-two and six-tenths feet along said circular curve to the right of radius six thousand twenty-nine and six-tenths feet to the point of tangency of said curve; thence south fifty-eight degrees twenty-nine minutes east, five hundred eighty-eight and seven-tenths feet to the point of curvature of a circular curve to the right; thence southeasterly two hundred twenty-five and nine-tenths feet along said circular curve to the right of radius two thousand two hundred nine and nine-tenths feet to the point of tangency of said curve; thence south fifty-two degrees thirty-eight minutes east, twenty-eight and eight-tenths feet to the point of curvature of a circular curve to the left; thence southeasterly two hundred sixteen and nine-tenths feet along said circular curve to the left of radius one thousand six hundred nine and nine-tenths feet to the point of tangency of said curve; thence south sixty degrees twenty-one minutes east, thirty and seven-tenths feet to the point of curvature of a circular curve to the right; thence southeasterly seven hundred thirteen and six-tenths feet, more or less, along said circular curve to the right of radius one thousand two hundred fifty-four and nine-tenths feet to a point on the southern boundary line of Homestead Entry Survey 310 marked by an iron pipe with a National Park Service brass cap, said point also being located on the present northern boundary line of Coronado National Memorial; thence north eighty-nine degrees forty-nine minutes west two thousand three hundred and sixty-one feet, more or less, along the southern boundary line of Homestead Entry Survey 310, which line is also the present northern boundary of the said memorial, to the point of beginning (all bearings referred to the true meridian).

(2) Inclusion in the Memorial and exclusion from the Coronado National Forest of lots 5 and 6 in section 20, township 24 south, range 21 east, Gila and Salt River base and meridian.

(3) Exclusion from the Memorial and inclusion in the Coronado National Forest of the north half southwest quarter northwest quarter section 13, and the north half southeast quarter northeast quarter section 14, all in township 24 south, range 20 east, Gila and Salt River base and meridian.

(Pub.L. 86–689, § 1, Sept. 2, 1960, 74 Stat. 736.)

HISTORICAL AND STATUTORY NOTES

Revision Notes and Legislative Reports
  1960 Acts. House Report No. 2022, see 1960 U.S. Code Cong. and Adm. News, p. 3284.

LIBRARY REFERENCES

American Digest System
  Armed Services ☞54.
  Woods and Forests ☞1, 8.
  Key Number System Topic Nos. 34, 411.

§ 450y–6.   Acquisition of lands; administration

The Secretary of the Interior is authorized to acquire lands and interests in lands within the revised boundaries of the Coronado National Memorial by purchase, donation, with donated funds, or by such other means as he may consider to be in the public interest. Lands and interests in lands acquired pursuant to this Act shall become a part of the Memorial and be administered by the Secretary of the Interior in accordance with the provisions of sections 1, 2, 3, and 4 of this title, as amended, and pursuant to sections 450y–1 to 450y–3 of this title.

(Pub.L. 86–689, § 2, Sept. 2, 1960, 74 Stat. 737.)

HISTORICAL AND STATUTORY NOTES

Revision Notes and Legislative Reports
  1960 Acts. House Report No. 2022, see 1960 U.S. Code Cong. and Adm. News, p. 3284.

References in Text
  This Act, referred to in text, means Pub.L. 86–689, which added sections 450y–5 to 450y–7 of this title and amended section 17j–2 of this title. For complete classification of this Act to the Code, see Tables.

LIBRARY REFERENCES

American Digest System
  Armed Services ☞54.
  United States ☞55.
  Woods and Forests ☞5.
  Key Number System Topic Nos. 34, 393, 411.

§ 450y–7.   Authorization of appropriations

There is authorized to be appropriated the sum of not to exceed $3,000 for the purpose of acquiring lands, interests in lands, and improvements thereon as may be necessary for carrying out this Act.

(Pub.L. 86–689, § 4, Sept. 2, 1960, 74 Stat. 737.)

HISTORICAL AND STATUTORY NOTES

Revision Notes and Legislative Reports
 1960 Acts. House Report No. 2022, see 1960 U.S. Code Cong. and Adm. News, p. 3284.

References in Text
 This Act, referred to in text, means Pub.L. 86–689, which added sections 450y–5 to 450y–7 of this title and amended section 17j–2 of this title. For complete classification of this Act to the Code, see Tables.

§ 450z.   Repealed.   Pub.L. 94–429, § 3(g), Sept. 28, 1976, 90 Stat. 1343

HISTORICAL AND STATUTORY NOTES

Section, Act Oct. 27, 1941, c. 459, 55 Stat. 745, provided for the prospecting and mining of surface lands within the Organ Pipe Cactus National Monument, in Arizona, under regulations prescribed by the Secretary of the Interior.

Mining Rights Existing Prior to September 28, 1976
 Pub.L. 94–429, § 3, Sept. 28, 1976, 90 Stat. 1342, provided in part that this section was amended as indicated in order to close area to entry and location under the Mining Law of 1872, subject to valid existing rights.

§ 450aa.   George Washington Carver National Monument; acquisition of land

The Secretary of the Interior is authorized and directed to acquire, on behalf of the United States, by gift or purchase, the site of the birthplace of George Washington Carver, distinguished Negro scientist, located near Diamond, Missouri, together with such additional land or interests in land and any improvements thereon as the Secretary may deem necessary to carry out the purposes of sections 450aa to 450aa–2 of this title. In the event the Secretary is unable to acquire such property, or any part thereof, at a reasonable price, he is authorized and directed to condemn such property, or any part thereof, in the manner provided by law.

(July 14, 1943, c. 238, § 1, 57 Stat. 563.)

HISTORICAL AND STATUTORY NOTES

Authorization of Appropriations
 Section 4 of Act July 14, 1943, as amended Sept. 9, 1950, c. 940, 64 Stat. 828, provided that: "There are authorized to be appropriated such sums not to exceed $150,000 as may be necessary to carry out the provisions of this Act [sections 450aa to 450aa–2 of this title]."

LIBRARY REFERENCES

American Digest System
 Armed Services ☞54.
 United States ☞55.
 Woods and Forests ☞5.
 Key Number System Topic Nos. 34, 393, 411.

Research References

Treatises and Practice Aids

Wright & Miller: Federal Prac. & Proc. § 3042, Relation to Other Rules and Statutes.

§ 450aa–1. Establishment and supervision

The property acquired under the provisions of section 450aa of this title shall constitute the George Washington Carver National Monument and shall be a public national memorial to George Washington Carver. The Director of the National Park Service, under the direction of the Secretary of the Interior, shall have the supervision, management, and control of such national monument, and shall maintain and preserve it in a suitable and enduring manner which, in his judgment, will provide for the benefit and enjoyment of the people of the United States.

(July 14, 1943, c. 238, § 2, 57 Stat. 563.)

HISTORICAL AND STATUTORY NOTES

Transfer of Functions

All functions of all other officers of the Department of the Interior and all functions of all agencies and employees of such Department were with two exceptions, transferred to the Secretary of the Interior, with power vested in him to authorize their performance or the performance of any of his functions by any of such officers, agencies, and employees, by 1950 Reorg. Plan No. 3, §§ 1, 2, eff. May 24, 1950, 15 F.R. 3174, 64 Stat. 1262, set out in Appendix 1 to Title 5, Government Organization and Employees.

LIBRARY REFERENCES

American Digest System

Armed Services ⬅54.
Woods and Forests ⬅1, 5, 8.
Key Number System Topic Nos. 34, 411.

§ 450aa–2. Maintenance of museum; construction of roads and use of markers

The Secretary of [1] Interior is authorized to—

(1) Maintain, either in an existing structure acquired under the provisions of section 450aa of this title or in a building constructed by him for the purpose, a museum for relics and records pertaining to George Washington Carver, and for other articles of national and patriotic interest, and to accept, on behalf of the United States, for installation in such museum, articles which may be offered as additions to the museum; and

(2) Construct roads and mark with monuments, tablets, or otherwise, points of interest within the boundaries of the George Washington Carver National Monument.

(July 14, 1943, c. 238, § 3, 57 Stat. 564.)

¹ So in original. Probably should be "of the".

LIBRARY REFERENCES

American Digest System
    Armed Services ⬤⇒54.
    United States ⬤⇒57.
    Woods and Forests ⬤⇒5.
    Key Number System Topic Nos. 34, 393, 411.

§ 450bb.   Harpers Ferry National Historical Park

(a) In general

To carry out the purposes of sections 450bb to 450bb–2 of this title, the Secretary of the Interior (referred to in sections 450bb to 450bb–2 of this title as the "Secretary") is authorized to acquire, by purchase from a willing seller with donated or appropriated funds, by donation, or by exchange, land or an interest in land within the boundaries as generally depicted on the map entitled "Boundary Map, Harpers Ferry National Historical Park", numbered 385–80,021A, and dated April 1979.

(b) Bradley and Ruth Nash Addition

The Secretary is authorized to acquire, by donation only, approximately 27 acres of land or interests in land that are outside the boundary of the Harpers Ferry National Historical Park and generally depicted on the map entitled "Proposed Bradley and Ruth Nash Addition—Harpers Ferry National Historical Park", numbered 385–80056, and dated April 1, 1989.

(c) Boundary expansion

(1) In general

The Secretary is authorized to acquire, by purchase from a willing seller with donated or appropriated funds, by donation, or by exchange, land or an interest in land within the area depicted as "Private Lands" on the map entitled "Harpers Ferry National Historical Park Proposed Boundary Expansion", numbered 385/80,126, and dated July 14, 2003.

(2) Administration

The Secretary shall—

    (A) transfer to the National Park Service for inclusion in the Harpers Ferry National Historical Park (referred to in sections 450bb to 450bb–2 of this title as the "Park") the land depicted on the map referred to in paragraph (1) as "U.S. Fish and Wildlife Service Lands" and revise the boundary of the Park accordingly; and

(B) revise the boundary of the Park to include the land depicted on the map referred to in paragraph (1) as "Appalachian NST" and exclude that land from the boundary of the Appalachian National Scenic Trail.

(d) Maximum number of acres

The number of acres of the Park shall not exceed 3,745.

(e) Maps

The maps referred to in this section shall be on file and available for public inspection in the appropriate offices of the National Park Service.

(f) Acquired land

Land or an interest in land acquired under this section shall become a part of the Park, subject to the laws (including regulations) applicable to the Park.

(g) Authorization of appropriations

There are authorized to be appropriated such sums as are necessary to carry out this section.

(June 30, 1944, c. 328, § 1, 58 Stat. 645; May 29, 1963, Pub.L. 88–33, 77 Stat. 52; Oct. 24, 1974, Pub.L. 93–466, § 1(1), 88 Stat. 1420; Mar. 5, 1980, Pub.L. 96–199, Title I, § 108(1), 94 Stat. 69; Oct. 6, 1989, Pub.L. 101–109, § 1(a), 103 Stat. 681; Nov. 2, 1994, Pub.L. 103–437, § 6(h)(2), 108 Stat. 4585; Sept. 24, 2004, Pub.L. 108–307, § 2, 118 Stat. 1133.)

HISTORICAL AND STATUTORY NOTES

Revision Notes and Legislative Reports
1980 Acts. Senate Report No. 96–484, see 1980 U.S. Code Cong. and Adm. News, p. 133.

1994 Acts. House Report No. 103–779, see 1994 U.S. Code Cong. and Adm. News, p. 3639.

2004 Acts. House Report No. 108–655, see 2004 U.S. Code Cong. and Adm. News, p. 1026.

References in Text
Sections 450bb to 450bb–2 of this title, referred to in subsecs. (a) and (c)(2), originally read "this Act", meaning Act June 30, 1944, c. 328, 58 Stat. 645, which enacted 16 U.S.C.A. § 450bb to 450bb–2.

Amendments
2004 Amendments. Pub.L. 108–307, § 2, rewrote the section, which formerly read: "In order to carry out the purposes of sections 450bb to 450bb–2 of this title, the Secretary of the Interior is authorized to acquire lands or interests in lands, by donation, purchase with donated or appropriated funds, or exchange, within the boundaries as generally depicted on the drawing entitled 'Boundary Map, Harpers Ferry National Historical Park', numbered 385–80,021A and dated April 1979, which shall be on file and available for public inspection in the offices of the National Park Service, Department of the Interior: *Provided,* That after advising the Committee on Energy and Natural Resources of the Senate and the Committee

on Natural Resources of the House of Representatives, in writing, the Secretary may make minor revisions in the boundary, when necessary, by publication of a revised drawing or other boundary description in the Federal Register, but the total acreage shall not exceed two thousand five hundred and five acres: *Provided further*, That nothing herein shall be deemed to authorize the acquisition, without consent of the owner, of a fee simple interest in lands within the boundaries in which a less than fee interest has previously been acquired by the Secretary of the Interior. The Secretary is authorized to acquire, by donation only, approximately twenty-seven acres of land or interests therein which are outside the boundary of the Harpers Ferry National Historical Park and generally depicted on a map entitled 'Proposed Bradley and Ruth Nash Addition—Harpers Ferry National Historical Park,' dated April 1, 1989 and numbered 385–80056. Such map shall be on file and available for public inspection in the offices of the National Park Service, Department of the Interior, Washington, District of Columbia. When acquired, such lands or interests therein shall become a part of the park, subject to the laws and regulations applicable thereto. Any Federal land within the area designated by the Secretary of the Interior as necessary for park purposes shall be transferred to the administration of the Department of the Interior and when so transferred shall become a part of the park: *Provided*, That the Federal department or agency having administration over such land shall agree in advance to such transfer.

1994 Amendments. Pub.L. 103–437, § 6(h)(2), substituted "Committee on Energy and Natural Resources of the Senate and the Committee on Natural Resources of the House of Representatives" for "Committees on Interior and Insular Affairs of the Congress of the United States."

1989 Amendments. Pub.L. 101–109, § 1(a)(1), substituted "two thousand five hundred and five acres" for "two thousand four hundred and seventy-five acres" in the provision setting the maximum total acreage of the park.

Pub.L. 101–109, § 1(a)(2), added provisions authorizing the Secretary to acquire, by donation only, approximately twenty-seven acres of land or interests

therein which were outside the boundary of the Harpers Ferry National Historical Park and generally depicted on a map entitled "Proposed Bradley and Ruth Nash Addition—Harpers Ferry National Historical Park", dated April 1, 1989 and numbered 385–80056, directing that the map be on file and available for public inspection in the offices of the National Park Service, Department of the Interior, Washington, District of Columbia, and indicating that, when acquired, such lands or interests therein would become a part of the park, subject to the laws and regulations applicable thereto.

1980 Amendments. Pub.L. 96–199 substituted " 'Boundary Map, Harpers Ferry National Historical Park', numbered 385–80,021A and dated April 1979" for " 'Boundary Map, Harpers Ferry National Historical Park', numbered 385–40,000D and dated April 1974" and "two thousand four hundred and seventy-five acres" for "two thousand acres".

1974 Amendments. Pub.L. 93–466 inserted reference to updated map, prohibited the Secretary from exercising any power of condemnation on lands in which a less than fee interest has been previously acquired, authorized the acquisition of land with appropriated funds and by exchange, authorized an increase in total area from 1500 to 2000 acres, and authorized the Secretary to make minor boundary changes by publication of a revised description in the Federal Register, after advising the Committees on Interior and Insular Affairs.

Change of Name

The Committee on Interior and Insular Affairs of the Senate was abolished and replaced by the Committee on Energy and Natural Resources of the Senate, effective Feb. 11, 1977. See Rule XXV of the Standing Rules of the Senate, as amended by Senate Resolution 4 (popularly cited as the "Committee System Reorganization Amendments of 1977"), approved Feb. 4, 1977.

"Park" was substituted for "monument" in two instances in view of the redesignation of the Harpers Ferry National Monument as the Harpers Ferry National Historical Park by Pub.L. 88–33, set out as section 450bb–6 of this title.

Short Title

2004 Amendments. Pub.L. 108–307, § 1, Sept. 24, 2004, 118 Stat. 1133, provided that: "This Act [amending this section and 16 U.S.C.A. §§ 460bb–1 and 460bb–2] may be cited as the 'Harpers Ferry National Historical Park Boundary Revision Act of 2004'."

Acquisition of Clear and Marketable Title to Additional Park Lands

Pub.L. 101–109, § 1(b), Oct. 6, 1989, 103 Stat. 681, provided that: "Nothing in this Act [amending this section] shall be deemed to prohibit the Secretary from using such measures as may be necessary to acquire a clear and marketable title, free of any and all encumbrances, to the lands identified for acquisition in paragraph (a)(2) of this Act."

Authorization of Appropriations

Act June 30, 1944, c. 328, § 4, 58 Stat. 646, as amended Pub.L. 93–466, § 1(3), Oct. 24, 1974, 88 Stat. 1420; Pub.L. 95–625, Title I, § 101(14), Nov. 10, 1978, 92 Stat. 3471; Pub.L. 96–199, Title I, § 108(2), Mar. 5, 1980, 94 Stat. 69, provided that: "In addition to such sums as have heretofore been appropriated, there are authorized to be appropriated such sums as may be necessary to carry out the provisions of this Act [sections 450bb to 450bb–2 of this title], but not more than $1,600,000 for the acquisition of lands and interests in lands, and not more than $12,385,000 for development."

LIBRARY REFERENCES

American Digest System
    Armed Services ☞54.
    United States ☞55.
    Woods and Forests ☞1, 8.
    Key Number System Topic Nos. 34, 393, 411.

§ 450bb–1. Administration

The property acquired under the provisions of section 450bb of this title shall constitute the Harpers Ferry National Historical Park and shall be a public national memorial commemorating historical events at or near Harpers Ferry. The Director of the National Park Service under the direction of the Secretary, shall have the supervision, management, and control of such national historical park, and shall maintain and preserve it for the benefit and enjoyment of the people of the United States, subject to the provisions of sections 1, 2, 3 and 4 of this title, as amended.

(June 30, 1944, c. 328, § 2, 58 Stat. 646; May 29, 1963, Pub.L. 88–33, 77 Stat. 52; Sept. 24, 2004, Pub.L. 108–307, § 3, 118 Stat. 1134.)

HISTORICAL AND STATUTORY NOTES

Revision Notes and Legislative Reports
    2004 Acts. House Report No. 108–655, see 2004 U.S. Code Cong. and Adm. News, p. 1026.

    2004 Amendments. Pub.L. 108–307, § 3, struck out "Secretary of the Interior" and inserted "Secretary".

Change of Name
    "Harpers Ferry National Historical Park" and "national historical park" were substituted for "Harpers Ferry National Monument" and "national monument", respectively, in view of the redesignation of the "Harpers Ferry National

Monument" as the "Harpers Ferry National Historical Park" by Pub.L. 88–33, classified to section 450bb–6 of this title.

Transfer of Functions
    All functions of all other officers of the Department of the Interior and all functions of all agencies and employees of such Department were, with two exceptions, transferred to the Secretary of the Interior, with power vested in him to authorize their performance or the performance of any of his functions by any of such officers, agencies, and employees, by 1950 Reorg. Plan No. 3, §§ 1, 2, eff.

May 24, 1950, 15 F.R. 3174, 64 Stat.
1262, set out in Appendix 1 to Title 5,

Government Organization and Employees.

CODE OF FEDERAL REGULATIONS

Special regulations for particular areas of system, see 36 CFR § 7.1 et seq.

LIBRARY REFERENCES

American Digest System
  Armed Services ☜54.
  Woods and Forests ☜5.
  Key Number System Topic Nos. 34, 411.

§ 450bb-2.   Maintenance of museum; acceptance of museum articles; construction of roads, etc.

The Secretary is authorized to—

(1) Maintain, either in an existing structure acquired under the provisions of section 450bb of this title or in a building constructed by him for the purpose, a museum for relics and records pertaining to historic events that took place at Harpers Ferry, and for other relics of national and patriotic interest, and to accept on behalf of the United States, for installation in such museum, articles which may be offered as additions to the museum;

(2) Construct roads and facilities and mark with monuments, tablets, or otherwise, points of interest within the boundaries of the Harpers Ferry National Historical Park; and

(3) Provide, directly or by contract, subject to the provisions of the Act of June 7, 1974, an interpretive shuttle transportation service within, between, and among lands acquired for the purpose of sections 450bb to 450bb-2 of this title for such times and upon such terms as in his judgment will best accomplish the purposes of sections 450bb to 450bb-2 of this title.

(June 30, 1944, c. 328, § 3, 58 Stat. 646; May 29, 1963, Pub.L. 88–33, 77 Stat. 52; Oct. 24, 1974, Pub.L. 93–466, § 1(2), 88 Stat. 1420; Sept. 24, 2004, Pub.L. 108–307, § 3, 118 Stat. 1134.)

HISTORICAL AND STATUTORY NOTES

Revision Notes and Legislative Reports
  2004 Acts. House Report No. 108–655, see 2004 U.S. Code Cong. and Adm. News, p. 1026.

References in Text
  Sections 450bb to 450bb-2 of this title, referred to in par. (3), originally read "this Act", meaning Act June 30, 1944, c. 328, 58 Stat. 645, which enacted 16 U.S.C.A. §§ 450bb to 450bb-2.

The Act of June 7, 1974, referred to in par. (3), is Pub.L. 93–303, June 7, 1974, 88 Stat. 192, which amended sections 460*l*–6a, 460*l*–8, and 460*l*–10a of this title. For complete classification of this Act to the Code, see Tables.

Amendments
  2004 Amendments. Intro par. Pub.L. 108–307, § 3, struck out "Secretary of the Interior" and inserted "Secretary".

1974   Amendments. Par.   (3). Pub.L. 93–466 added par. (3).

Change of Name
"Harpers Ferry National Historical Park" was substituted for "Harpers Ferry National Monument" in view of the re-designation of the "Harpers Ferry National Monument" as the "Harpers Ferry National Historical park" by Pub.L. 88–33, classified to section 450bb–6 of this title.

LIBRARY REFERENCES

American Digest System
  Armed Services ☞54.
  Woods and Forests ☞5.
  Key Number System Topic Nos. 34, 411.

§ 450bb–3.   Acquisition of additional lands

To further the commemorative purposes of sections 450bb to 450bb–2 of this title, by providing historic properties and administrative facilities, the Secretary of the Interior is authorized to acquire, in the manner hereafter stated, the Storer College site, the original site of John Brown's "Fort" and the old Federal armory, comprising altogether approximately thirty acres, for addition to Harpers Ferry National Historical Park.

(Pub.L. 86–655, § 1, July 14, 1960, 74 Stat. 520; Pub.L. 88–33, May 29, 1963, 77 Stat. 52.)

HISTORICAL AND STATUTORY NOTES

Revision Notes and Legislative Reports
  1960   Acts. Senate Report No. 1219, see 1960 U.S. Code Cong. and Adm. News, p. 3155.

References in Text
  Sections 450bb to 450bb–2 of this title, referred to in text, originally read "Act of June 30, 1944 (58 Stat. 645)", which enacted 16 U.S.C.A. §§ 450bb to 450bb–2.

Change of Name
  "Harpers Ferry National Historical Park" was substituted for "Harpers Ferry National Monument" in view of the re-designation of the "Harpers Ferry National Monument" as the "Harpers Ferry National Historical Park" by Pub.L. 88–33, classified to section 450bb–6 of this title.

LIBRARY REFERENCES

American Digest System
  Armed Services ☞54.
  United States ☞55.
  Woods and Forests ☞2.
  Key Number System Topic Nos. 34, 393, 411.

§ 450bb–4.   Acceptance and purchase of lands and improvements; payment; exchange of lands

(a) The Secretary of the Interior may accept the conveyance of all right, title, and interest of the trustees of Storer College in and to the lands and improvements in Harpers Ferry, West Virginia, granted to their predecessors for educational purposes pursuant to section 2 of the Act of December 15, 1868 (15 Stat. 266), upon payment to said trustees of not more than the current fair market value of the improvements located upon such lands. The Secretary may also purchase lands, interests therein, and improvements thereon, which lands were granted to the trustees of Storer College pursuant to such Act of 1868 and subsequently were alienated by the trustees: *Provided,* That he may pay not in excess of the amount paid therefor by the then owners plus the cost of existing improvements placed thereon by them, and, in no event may he pay more than the current fair market value. The Secretary may also purchase from the trustees of Storer College, at not more than their fair market value, other lands and interests in lands acquired by them or their predecessors as a part of the college site, together with any improvements thereon. In addition, up to seven acres of privately owned lands, interests therein, and improvements thereon, which are interspersed with the aforesaid college lands may be purchased by the Secretary. Lands and interests purchased under this subsection may be exchanged for other lands, and interests therein, of approximately equal value, which comprise the college and interspersed lands otherwise authorized herein for purchase.

(b) To facilitate the acquisition of the original site of the engine house known as John Brown's "Fort" and the old Federal arsenal, the Secretary of the Interior is authorized to exchange therefor federally owned park lands or interests in lands of approximately equal value in the vicinity of Cumberland, Maryland, which he finds are no longer required for park purposes.

(Pub.L. 86–655, § 2, July 14, 1960, 74 Stat. 520.)

HISTORICAL AND STATUTORY NOTES

Revision Notes and Legislative Reports
  1960 Acts. Senate Report No. 1219, see 1960 U.S. Code Cong. and Adm. News, p. 3155.

References in Text
  Section 2 of the Act of December 15, 1868, referred to in subsec. (a), means

Act Dec. 15, 1868, c. 2, § 2, 15 Stat. 266, which was not classified to the Code.

LIBRARY REFERENCES

American Digest System
  Armed Services ⊂⇒54.
  United States ⊂⇒55.
  Woods and Forests ⊂⇒4.
  Key Number System Topic Nos. 34, 393, 411.

§ 450bb–5. Authorization of appropriations

There are authorized to be appropriated such sums, not to exceed $300,000, as may be necessary for the purchase of lands, interests therein, and improvements thereon pursuant to sections 450bb–3 to 450bb–5 of this title.

(Pub.L. 86–655, § 3, July 14, 1960, 74 Stat. 521.)

HISTORICAL AND STATUTORY NOTES

Revision Notes and Legislative Reports
  1960 Acts. Senate Report No. 1219, see 1960 U.S. Code Cong. and Adm. News, p. 3155.

§ 450bb–6. Change in name of Harpers Ferry National Monument

The Harpers Ferry National Monument established pursuant to sections 450bb to 450bb–2 of this title, shall on and after May 29, 1963, be known as Harpers Ferry National Historical Park, and any law, regulation, document, or record of the United States in which such monument is designated or referred to under the name of Harpers Ferry National Monument shall be held to refer to such monument under and by the name of Harpers Ferry National Historical Park.

(Pub.L. 88–33, May 29, 1963, 77 Stat. 52.)

HISTORICAL AND STATUTORY NOTES

References in Text
  Sections 450bb to 450bb–2 of this title, referred to in text, originally read "the Act entitled 'An Act to provide for the establishment of the Harpers Ferry National Monument', approved June 30, 1944 (58 Stat. 645)", which enacted 16 U.S.C.A. §§ 450bb to 450bb–2.

LIBRARY REFERENCES

American Digest System
  Armed Services ⊙54.
  United States ⊙3.
  Woods and Forests ⊙1.
  Key Number System Topic Nos. 34, 393, 411.

§ 450cc. Castle Clinton National Monument; establishment

The Secretary of the Interior is authorized to accept, on behalf of the United States, title to the site, comprising approximately one acre and situated in Battery Park, New York City, of the historic structure known as Castle Clinton, together with such structure and any other improvement on or appurtenant to such site. When title to such property is vested in the United States, it shall constitute the Castle Clinton National Monument.

(Aug. 12, 1946, c. 954, § 1, 60 Stat. 997.)

HISTORICAL AND STATUTORY NOTES

Preservation and Administration of Castle Clinton National Monument

Study by New York City National Shrines Advisory Board concerning preservation and administration of Castle Clinton National Monument, pursuant to Act Aug. 11, 1955, c. 779, 69 Stat. 632, formerly set out as a note under section 463 of this title.

LIBRARY REFERENCES

American Digest System
Armed Services ⊙54.
Woods and Forests ⊙1, 8.
Key Number System Topic Nos. 34, 411.

§ 450cc–1. Administration, protection, and development

The administration, protection, and development of the Castle Clinton National Monument shall be under the supervision of the Secretary of the Interior, subject to the provisions of sections 1, 2 3, and 4 of this title, as amended.

(Aug. 12, 1946, c. 954, § 2, 60 Stat. 997.)

HISTORICAL AND STATUTORY NOTES

Transfer of Functions

All functions of all other officers of the Department of the Interior and all functions of all agencies and employees of such Department were, with two exceptions, transferred to the Secretary of the Interior, with power vested in him to authorize their performance or the performance of any of his functions by any of such officers, agencies, and employees, by 1950 Reorg. Plan No. 3, §§ 1, 2, eff. May 24, 1950, 15 F.R. 3174, 64 Stat. 1262, set out in Appendix 1 to Title 5, Government Organization and Employees.

LIBRARY REFERENCES

American Digest System
Armed Services ⊙54.
Woods and Forests ⊙5.
Key Number System Topic Nos. 34, 411.

§ 450dd. De Soto National Memorial; establishment

For the purpose of establishing an appropriate memorial to Hernando De Soto, the Secretary of the Interior is authorized, in his discretion, to acquire on behalf of the United States, by donation, by purchase with donated funds when purchaseable [1] at prices deemed by him reasonable, or by condemnation with donated funds, such lands and interests in land within an area of not to exceed thirty acres as he may select in the vicinity of Tampa Bay and Bradenton, Florida, and to construct thereon a suitable memorial structure, together with such connecting roads and public facilities as may be desirable.

(Mar. 11, 1948, c. 109, § 1, 62 Stat. 78; Sept. 8, 1960, Pub.L. 86–728, § 1A, 74 Stat. 856.)

[1] So in original.   Probably should be "purchasable".

HISTORICAL AND STATUTORY NOTES

Revision Notes and Legislative Reports
1948 Acts. Senate Report No. 906, see 1948 U.S. Code Cong. Service, p. 1145.
1960 Acts. House Report No. 1609, see 1960 U.S. Code Cong. and Adm. News, p. 3457.

Amendments
1960 Amendments. Pub.L. 86–728 increased the limitation on acquisition of land from twenty-five to thirty acres.

Authorization of Appropriations
Act Mar. 11, 1948, c. 109, § 3, 62 Stat. 79, as amended Aug. 21, 1950, c. 768, 64

Stat. 469; Sept. 8, 1960, Pub.L. 86–728, § 1B, 74 Stat. 856; Nov. 10, 1978, Pub.L. 95–625, Title I, § 101(8), 92 Stat. 3471; Oct. 12, 1979, Pub.L. 96–87, Title IV, § 401(a), 93 Stat. 665, provided that: "There is hereby authorized to be appropriated such sums, not to exceed $292,000, as may be necessary to carry out the provisions of this Act [sections 450dd and 450dd–1 of this title]."

LIBRARY REFERENCES

American Digest System
Armed Services ☞54.
Woods and Forests ☞1, 8.
Key Number System Topic Nos. 34, 411.

§ 450dd–1. Administration

Upon a determination by the Secretary of the Interior that sufficient land has been acquired by the United States for the memorial, such property shall be established as the "De Soto National Memorial", and shall be administered by the Secretary of the Interior, through the National Park Service, for the benefit of the people of the United States.   An order of the Secretary of the Interior, constituting notice of such establishment, shall be published in the Federal Register.   Insofar as applicable and not in conflict with this section and section 450dd of this title, sections 1, 2, 3, and 4 of this title, providing for the establishment of a National Park Service, as amended and supplemented, shall govern the promotion and development of the national memorial.

(Mar. 11, 1948, c. 109, § 2, 62 Stat. 78.)

HISTORICAL AND STATUTORY NOTES

Revision Notes and Legislative Reports
1948 Acts. Senate Report No. 906, see 1948 U.S. Code Cong. Service, p. 1145.

Transfer of Functions
All functions of all other officers of the Department of the Interior and all functions of all agencies and employees of such Department were, with two exceptions, transferred to the Secretary of the

Interior, with power vested in him to authorize their performance or the performance of any of his functions by any of such officers, agencies, and employees, by 1950 Reorg. Plan No. 3, §§ 1, 2, eff. May 24, 1950, 15 F.R. 3174, 64 Stat. 1262, set out in Appendix 1 to Title 5, Government Organization and Employees.

LIBRARY REFERENCES

American Digest System
  Armed Services ⊕54.
  Woods and Forests ⊕5.
  Key Number System Topic Nos. 34, 411.

§ 450ee. Fort Sumter National Monument; establishment

The Secretary of the Army is authorized and directed to transfer, without consideration, to the Secretary of the Interior title to the site of the historic structure known as Fort Sumter, situated in Charleston Harbor, Charleston, South Carolina, together with such buildings and other improvements as are appurtenant to such site.

(Apr. 28, 1948, c. 239, § 1, 62 Stat. 204.)

HISTORICAL AND STATUTORY NOTES

Revision Notes and Legislative Reports
  1948 Acts. House Report No. 1670, see
1948 U.S. Code Cong. Service, p. 1491.

LIBRARY REFERENCES

American Digest System
  Armed Services ⊕54.
  Woods and Forests ⊕1, 8.
  Key Number System Topic Nos. 34, 411.

Notes of Decisions

Appurtenance　1
Concession　2

1. Appurtenance

Fort Sumter pier was within area deeded to United States by South Carolina and was an "appurtenance" transferred to Secretary when Fort Sumter was made a national monument and was "on or within" the monument within this section and § 450ee–1 of this title, and Secretary's regulation relating to permits for activities on or within monument, and Secretary had authority to restrict to one concessioner the privilege of maintaining fare-charging craft to discharge and embark passengers at pier. U.S. v. Gray Line Water Tours of Charleston, C.A.4 (S.C.) 1962, 311 F.2d 779. United States ⊕ 3

2. Concession

Record failed to show any unfair dealing in awarding concession to maintain fare-charging craft to discharge and embark passengers at pier at Fort Sumter National Monument. U.S. v. Gray Line Water Tours of Charleston, C.A.4 (S.C.) 1962, 311 F.2d 779. United States ⊕ 57

§ 450ee–1. Administration

The property acquired by the Secretary of the Interior under this joint resolution shall constitute the Fort Sumter National Monument and shall be a public national memorial commemorating historical events at or near Fort Sumter. The Director of the National Park Service under the direction of the Secretary of the Interior shall have the supervision, management, and control of such national monument, and shall maintain and preserve it for the benefit and enjoyment of the people of the United States, subject to the provisions of sections 1, 2, 3, and 4 of this title, as amended.

(Apr. 28, 1948, c. 239, § 2, 62 Stat. 204.)

HISTORICAL AND STATUTORY NOTES

Revision Notes and Legislative Reports
 1948 Acts. House Report No. 1670, see 1948 U.S. Code Cong. Service, p. 1491.

References in Text
 This joint resolution, referred to in text, means Act Apr. 28, 1948, which is classified to sections 450ee and 450ee–1 of this title.

Transfer of Functions
 All functions of all other officers of the Department of the Interior and all func-

tions of all agencies and employees of such Department were, with two exceptions, transferred to the Secretary of the Interior, with power vested in him to authorize their performance or the performance of any of his functions by any of such officers, agencies, and employees, by 1950 Reorg. Plan No. 3, §§ 1, 2, eff. May 24, 1950, 15 F.R. 3174, 64 Stat. 1262, set out in Appendix 1 to Title 5, Government Organization and Employees.

LIBRARY REFERENCES

American Digest System
 Armed Services ☞54.
 Woods and Forests ☞5.
 Key Number System Topic Nos. 34, 411.

§ 450ff.   Fort Vancouver National Historic Site; establishment

For the purpose of establishing a Federal area of national historical importance for the benefit of the people of the United States, to be known as the "Fort Vancouver National Historic Site," the Administrator of General Services and the Secretary of the Army are authorized to transfer to the Secretary of the Interior, without exchange of funds, administrative jurisdiction over such federally owned lands and other property, real or personal, under their jurisdiction, including the site of the old Hudson's Bay Company stockade in the State of Washington, as they shall find to be surplus to the needs of their respective agencies, such properties to be selected, with their approval, by the Secretary of the Interior for inclusion within the national historic site.

(June 19, 1948, c. 546, § 1, 62 Stat. 532; June 30, 1949, c. 288, Title I, § 105, 63 Stat. 381; June 30, 1961, Pub.L. 87–78, § 4, 75 Stat. 197.)

HISTORICAL AND STATUTORY NOTES

Revision Notes and Legislative Reports
 1948 Acts. Senate Report No. 1605, see 1948 U.S. Code Cong. Service, p. 1925.
 1949 Acts. House Report No. 670 and Conference Report No. 935, see 1949 U.S. Code Cong. Service, p. 1475.

Change of Name
 "Fort Vancouver National Historic Site" and "national historic site" were substituted for "Fort Vancouver National Monument" and "national monument", respectively, in view of the change in

name effected by Pub.L. 87–78. See section 450ff–6 of this title.

Transfer of Functions

"Administrator of General Services" was substituted for "Administrator of the War Assets Administration" pursuant to Act June 30, 1949, c. 288, Title I, § 105, 63 Stat. 381, which transferred all functions of the Administrator of the War Assets Administration and the War Assets Administration to the Administrator of General Services and the General Services Administration.

McLoughlin House Addition to Fort Vancouver National Historic Site

Pub.L. 108–63, July 29, 2003, 117 Stat. 872, provided that:

"Sec. 1. Short Title; definitions.

"(a) Short title.—This Act [this note] may be cited as the 'McLoughlin House Addition to Fort Vancouver National Historic Site Act'.

"(b) Definitions.—For the purposes of this Act [this note], the following definitions apply:

"(1) City.—The term 'City' means Oregon City, Oregon.

"(2) McLoughlin House.—The term 'McLoughlin House' means the McLoughlin House National Historic Site which is described in the Acting Assistant Secretary of the Interior's Order of June 27, 1941, and generally depicted on the map entitled 'McLoughlin House, Fort Vancouver National Historic Site', numbered 89/92,002, and dated 5/01/03, and includes the McLoughlin House, the Barclay House, and other associated real property, improvements, and personal property.

"(3) Secretary.—The term 'Secretary' means the Secretary of the Interior.

"Sec. 2. McLoughlin House addition to Fort Vancouver.

"(a) Acquisition.—The Secretary is authorized to acquire the McLoughlin House, from willing sellers only, by donation, purchase with donated or appropriated funds, or exchange, except that lands or interests in lands owned by the City may be acquired by donation only.

"(b) Map availability.—The map identifying the McLoughlin House referred to in section 1(b)(2) [of this note] shall be on file and available for inspection in the appropriate offices of the National Park Service, Department of the Interior.

"(c) Boundaries; administration.—Upon acquisition of the McLoughlin House, the acquired property shall be included within the boundaries of, and be administered as part of, the Fort Vancouver National Historic Site in accordance with all applicable laws and regulations.

"(d) Name change.—Upon acquisition of the McLoughlin House, the Secretary shall change the name of the site from the 'McLoughlin House National Historic Site' to the 'McLoughlin House'.

"(e) Federal laws.—After the McLoughlin House is acquired and added to Fort Vancouver National Historic Site, any reference in a law, map, regulation, document, paper, or other record of the United States to the 'McLoughlin House National Historic Site' (other than this Act) shall be deemed a reference to the 'McLoughlin House', a unit of Fort Vancouver National Historic Site."

LIBRARY REFERENCES

American Digest System
  Armed Services ☞54.
  Woods and Forests ☞1, 8.
  Key Number System Topic Nos. 34, 411.

§ 450ff–1. Size of site; effective date; additional lands

The total area of the national historic site as established or as enlarged by transfers pursuant to sections 450ff to 450ff–2 of this title shall not exceed ninety acres. Establishment of the historic site shall be effective, upon publication in the Federal Register of notice of such establishment, following the transfer to the Secretary of the

Interior of administrative jurisdiction over such lands as the Secretary of the Interior shall deem to be sufficient for purposes of establishing the national historic site. Additional lands may be added to the historic site in accordance with the procedure prescribed in section 450ff of this title, governing surplus properties, or by donation, subject to the maximum acreage limitation prescribed by sections 450ff to 450ff–2 of this title, upon publication of notice thereof in the Federal Register.

(June 19, 1948, c. 546, § 2, 62 Stat. 532; June 30, 1961, Pub.L. 87–78, § 4, 75 Stat. 197.)

HISTORICAL AND STATUTORY NOTES

Revision Notes and Legislative Reports
1948 Acts. Senate Report No. 1605, see 1948 U.S. Code Cong. Service, p. 1925.

Change of Name
"Historic site" was substituted for "monument" wherever appearing in view of the change in name effected by Pub.L. 87–78. See section 450ff–6 of this title.

LIBRARY REFERENCES

American Digest System
Armed Services ☜54.
United States ☜55.
Woods and Forests ☜1, 2, 8.
Key Number System Topic Nos. 34, 393, 411.

§ 450ff–2. Administration, protection, and development

The administration, protection, and development of the aforesaid national historic site shall be exercised under the direction of the Secretary of the Interior by the National Park Service, subject to the provisions of sections 1, 2, 3, and 4 of this title, as amended.

(June 19, 1948, c. 546, § 3, 62 Stat. 533; June 30, 1961, Pub.L. 87–78, § 4, 75 Stat. 197.)

HISTORICAL AND STATUTORY NOTES

Revision Notes and Legislative Reports
1948 Acts. Senate Report No. 1605, see 1948 U.S. Code Cong. Service, p. 1925.

Change of Name
"Historic site" was substituted for "monument" in view of the change in name effected by Pub.L. 87–78. See section 450ff–6 of this title.

Transfer of Functions
All functions of all other officers of the Department of the Interior and all functions of all agencies and employees of such Department were, with two exceptions, transferred to the Secretary of the Interior, with power vested in him to authorize their performance or the performance of any of his functions by any of such officers, agencies, and employees, by 1950 Reorg. Plan No. 3, §§ 1, 2, eff. May 24, 1950, 15 F.R. 3174, 64 Stat. 1262, set out in Appendix 1 to Title 5, Government Organization and Employees.

LIBRARY REFERENCES

American Digest System
　Armed Services ⚖54.
　Woods and Forests ⚖5.
　Key Number System Topic Nos. 34, 411.

§ 450ff–3.　Revision of boundaries

For the purpose of preserving certain historic properties associated with the Fort Vancouver National Historic Site, established pursuant to sections 450ff to 450ff–2 of this title, the Secretary of the Interior may revise the boundaries of the historic site to include therein not more than one hundred and thirty additional acres of land adjacent to, contiguous to, or in the vicinity of, the existing historic site.

(Pub.L. 87–78, § 1, June 30, 1961, 75 Stat. 196.)

HISTORICAL AND STATUTORY NOTES

Change of Name
　"Historic Site" and "historic site" were, in the original, "Monument" and "monument", respectively. Substitution of "Historic Site" and "historic site" for "Monument" and "monument", respectively, was made pursuant to section 4 of Pub.L. 87–78, set out as section 450ff–6 of this title, which redesignated the "Fort Vancouver National Monument" as the "Fort Vancouver National Historic Site".

LIBRARY REFERENCES

American Digest System
　Armed Services ⚖54.
　Woods and Forests ⚖1.
　Key Number System Topic Nos. 34, 411.

§ 450ff–4.　Acquisition of lands

The Secretary of the Interior may acquire in such manner as he may consider to be in the public interest the non-Federal lands and interests in lands within the revised boundaries.

(Pub.L. 87–78, § 2, June 30, 1961, 75 Stat. 197.)

LIBRARY REFERENCES

American Digest System
　Armed Services ⚖54.
　United States ⚖55.
　Woods and Forests ⚖2.
　Key Number System Topic Nos. 34, 393, 411.

§ 450ff–5.　Administrative jurisdiction of Federal lands

The heads of executive departments may transfer to the Secretary of the Interior, without exchange of funds, administrative jurisdiction over such federally owned lands and other property under their administrative jurisdictions within the revised boundary as may become excess to the needs of their respective agencies, for inclusion in the Fort Vancouver National Historic Site.

(Pub.L. 87–78, § 3, June 30, 1961, 75 Stat. 197.)

HISTORICAL AND STATUTORY NOTES

Change of Name

"Historic Site" was, in the original, "Monument". Substitution of "Historic Site" for "Monument" was made pursuant to section 4 of Pub.L. 87–78, set out as section 450ff–6 of this title, which redesignated the "Fort Vancouver National Monument" as the "Fort Vancouver National Historic Site".

LIBRARY REFERENCES

American Digest System

Armed Services ⬥54.
United States ⬥3.
Woods and Forests ⬥5.
Key Number System Topic Nos. 34, 393, 411.

§ 450ff–6.   Change in name of Fort Vancouver National Monument

Fort Vancouver National Monument is redesignated Fort Vancouver National Historic Site.

(Pub.L. 87–78, § 4, June 30, 1961, 75 Stat. 197.)

LIBRARY REFERENCES

American Digest System

Armed Services ⬥54.
Woods and Forests ⬥1.
Key Number System Topic Nos. 34, 411.

§§ 450gg to 450gg–3.   Repealed. Pub.L. 91–660, § 5, Jan. 8, 1971, 84 Stat. 1969

HISTORICAL AND STATUTORY NOTES

Sections, Act July 2, 1948, c. 806, §§ 1 to 4, 62 Stat. 1220, provided for the establishment of the Pensacola National Monument, the maintenance of a museum for relics and records of Pensacola and its harbor defenses, and the transfer of title to the land and jurisdiction of the area to the State of Florida, upon determination by the Secretary of the Interior that the area would be more suitably administered as a State historical park.

§ 450hh.   Saint Croix Island International Historic Site; establishment; acceptance of land; size

For the purpose of establishing a Federal area of national historical importance for the benefit of the people of the United States, the Secretary of the Interior is authorized to accept, for national monument purposes, on behalf of the United States, the donation of all non-Federal lands and interests in land situated on Saint Croix (Dochet) Island, located in the Saint Croix River, in the State of Maine. The Secretary is authorized to acquire, in such manner as he may consider to be in the public interest, not to exceed fifty acres of land or interests therein situated on the mainland, such property to be used for general administrative purposes and for a landing dock in order to provide a suitable approach and ready access to the island.

(June 8, 1949, c. 180, § 1, 63 Stat. 158.)

HISTORICAL AND STATUTORY NOTES

Revision Notes and Legislative Reports

1949 Acts. House Report No. 262, see 1949 U.S. Code Cong. Service, p. 1335.

Saint Croix Island Heritage Act

Pub.L. 106–529, §§ 1 to 5, Nov. 22, 2000, 114 Stat. 2524, provided that:

"**Sec. 1. Short title.**

"This Act [this note] may be cited as the 'Saint Croix Island Heritage Act'.

"**Sec. 2. Findings and purposes.**

"(a) **Findings.**—Congress finds that—

"(1) Saint Croix Island is located in the Saint Croix River, a river that is the boundary between the State of Maine and Canada;

"(2) the Island is the only international historic site in the National Park System;

"(3) in 1604, French nobleman Pierre Dugua Sieur de Mons, accompanied by a courageous group of adventurers that included Samuel Champlain, landed on the Island and began the construction of a settlement;

"(4) the French settlement on the Island in 1604 and 1605 was the initial site of the first permanent settlement in the New World, predating the English settlement of 1607 at Jamestown, Virginia;

"(5) many people view the expedition that settled on the Island in 1604 as the beginning of the Acadian culture in North America;

"(6) in October, 1998, the National Park Service completed a general management plan to manage and interpret the Saint Croix Island International Historic Site;

"(7) the plan addresses a variety of management alternatives, and concludes that the best management strate-

gy entails developing an interpretive trail and ranger station at Red Beach, Maine, and a regional heritage center in downtown Calais, Maine, in cooperation with Federal, State, and local agencies;

"(8) a 1982 memorandum of understanding, signed by the Department of the Interior and the Canadian Department for the Environment, outlines a cooperative program to commemorate the international heritage of the Saint Croix Island site and specifically to prepare for the 400th anniversary of the settlement in 2004; and

"(9) only 4 years remain before the 400th anniversary of the settlement at Saint Croix Island, an occasion that should be appropriately commemorated.

"(b) **Purpose.**—The purpose of this Act [this note] is to direct the Secretary of the Interior to take all necessary and appropriate steps to work with Federal, State, and local agencies, historical societies, and nonprofit organizations to facilitate the development of a regional heritage center in downtown Calais, Maine before the 400th anniversary of the settlement of Saint Croix Island.

"**Sec. 3. Definitions.**

"In this Act [this note]:

"(1) **Island.**—The term 'Island' means Saint Croix Island, located in the Saint Croix River, between Canada and the State of Maine.

"(2) **Secretary.**—The term 'Secretary' means the Secretary of the Interior, acting through the Director of the National Park Service.

"**Sec. 4. Saint Croix Island Regional Heritage Center.**

"(a) In general.—The Secretary shall provide assistance in planning, constructing, and operating a regional heritage center in downtown Calais, Maine, to facilitate the management and interpretation of the Saint Croix Island International Historic Site.

"(b) Cooperative agreements.—To carry out subsection (a), in administering the Saint Croix Island International Historic Site, the Secretary may enter into cooperative agreements under appropriate terms and conditions with other Federal agencies, State and local agencies and nonprofit organizations—

"(1) to provide exhibits, interpretive services (including employing individuals to provide such services), and technical assistance;

"(2) to conduct activities that facilitate the dissemination of information relating to the Saint Croix Island International Historic Site;

"(3) to provide financial assistance for the construction of the regional heritage center in exchange for space in the center that is sufficient to interpret the Saint Croix Island International Historic Site; and

"(4) to assist with the operation and maintenance of the regional heritage center.

"Sec. 5.   Authorization of appropriations.

"(a) Design and construction.—

"(1) In general.—There is authorized to be appropriated to carry out this Act [this note] (including the design and construction of the regional heritage center) $2,000,000.

"(2) Expenditure.—Paragraph (1) authorizes funds to be appropriated on the condition that any expenditure of those funds shall be matched on a dollar-for-dollar basis by funds from non-Federal sources.

"(b) Operation and maintenance.—There are authorized to be appropriated such sums as are necessary to maintain and operate interpretive exhibits in the regional heritage center."

Authorization of Appropriations

Act June 8, 1949, c. 180, § 4, 63 Stat. 158, provided that: "There are hereby authorized to be appropriated such sums as may be necessary to carry out the provisions of this Act [sections 450hh to 450hh–2 of this title]."

LIBRARY REFERENCES

American Digest System
    Armed Services ⏚54.
    United States ⏚55.
    Woods and Forests ⏚1, 2, 8.
    Key Number System Topic Nos. 34, 393, 411.

§ 450hh–1. Designation; acquisition of additional lands; lands excluded

Upon a determination by the Secretary of the Interior that sufficient land and interests in land situated on the island have been acquired by the United States for the establishment of a suitable national monument, such acquired property, and any Federal properties on the island that are not required for other public purposes, shall be established as the "Saint Croix Island International Historic Site". An order of the Secretary of the Interior, constituting notice of such determination, shall be published in the Federal Register. Following establishment of the national monument, other properties situated upon the island may become a part of the monument upon acquisition of title to such properties by the United States, and Federal properties situated upon the island, upon a determination by the agency administering such Federal properties that they are no longer required by that agency, may be transferred to the Secretary of the Interior by such agency to become a part of the national monument. Notice of the addition of any such properties to the monument shall be published in the Federal Register by the Secretary of the Interior. There shall be excluded from the national monument, for such time as the United States Coast Guard shall consider it to be necessary, any portion of the island which is being used and which is required for the purposes of a Coast Guard light station.

(June 8, 1949, c. 180, § 2, 63 Stat. 158; Sept. 25, 1984, Pub.L. 98–422, 98 Stat. 1615.)

HISTORICAL AND STATUTORY NOTES

Revision Notes and Legislative Reports
  1949 Acts. House Report No. 262, see 1949 U.S. Code Cong. Service, p. 1335.

Change of Name
  Pub.L. 98–422, Sept. 25, 1984, 98 Stat. 1615, provided that:
  "**(a)** in recognition of its historic significance to the United States and Canada, the Saint Croix Island National Monument in the State of Maine is hereby redesignated as the 'Saint Croix Island International Historic Site'.
  "**(b)** Any reference in a law, map, regulation, document, record, or other paper of the United States to such monument shall be deemed to be a reference to the 'Saint Croix Island International Historic Site'.

  "**(c)** Nothing in this joint resolution shall affect the status of the 'Saint Croix Island International Historic Site' as a national monument and a unit of the National Park System."

Transfer of Functions
  For transfer of authorities, functions, personnel, and assets of the Coast Guard, including the authorities and functions of the Secretary of Transportation relating thereto, to the Department of Homeland Security, and for treatment of related references, see 6 U.S.C.A. §§ 468(b), 551(d), 552(d) and 557, and the Department of Homeland Security Reorganization Plan of November 25, 2002, as modified, set out as a note under 6 U.S.C.A. § 542.

LIBRARY REFERENCES

American Digest System
  Armed Services ☞54.
  United States ☞55.
  Woods and Forests ☞1, 2, 8.
  Key Number System Topic Nos. 34, 393, 411.

§ 450hh–2. Administration

The national monument shall be administered by the Secretary of the Interior, through the National Park Service, subject to the provisions of sections 1, 2, 3, and 4 of this title, as amended and supplemented, and sections 461 to 467 of this title.

(June 8, 1949, c. 180, § 3, 63 Stat. 158.)

HISTORICAL AND STATUTORY NOTES

Revision Notes and Legislative Reports
  1949 Acts. House Report No. 262, see 1949 U.S. Code Cong. Service, p. 1335.

Transfer of Functions
  All functions of all other officers of the Department of the Interior and all functions of all agencies and employees of such Department were, with two exceptions, transferred to the Secretary of the Interior, with power vested in him to authorize their performance or the performance of any of his functions by any of such officers, agencies, and employees, by 1950 Reorg. Plan No. 3, §§ 1, 2, eff. May 24, 1950, 15 F.R. 3174, 64 Stat. 1262, set out in Appendix 1 to Title 5, Government Organization and Employees.

LIBRARY REFERENCES

American Digest System
  Armed Services ⬤54.
  Woods and Forests ⬤5.
  Key Number System Topic Nos. 34, 411.

§ 450ii. Joshua Tree National Monument; revision of boundaries

Joshua Tree National Monument, in the State of California, established by Proclamation Numbered 2193, of August 10, 1936 (50 Stat. 1760), after September 25, 1950, shall comprise the following-described area:

SAN BERNARDINO MERIDIAN

Township 1 south, range 5 east, sections 22 to 27, inclusive, and sections 34 to 36, inclusive; township 2 south, range 5 east, portion of east half lying north of the north right-of-way line of the Colorado River aqueduct but excluding therefrom that portion of the Long Canyon Camp and dump area in section 27; township 1 south, range 6 east, sections 19 to 36, inclusive; township 2 south, range 6 east, sections 1 to 30, inclusive, that portion of section 31 lying north of the north right-of-way line of the Colorado River aqueduct, and sections 32 to 36, inclusive; township 3 south, range 6 east, portion lying north of the north right-of-way line of the Colorado River aqueduct but excluding therefrom that portion of the Deception Camp and dump area in section 14, that portion of the West Deception Camp and dump area in section 10, and the portions of the East Wide Canyon Camps and dump areas in sections 5 and 6; township 1 south, range 7 east, sections 1 to 4, inclusive, and 9 to 15, inclusive, unsurveyed, section 16, sections 19 to 23, inclusive, section 24, unsurveyed, and sections 25 to 36, inclusive; township 2 south, range 7 east; township 3 south, range 7 east, portion lying north of the north right-of-way line of the Colorado River aqueduct but excluding therefrom that portion of the Fan Hill Camp and dump area in section 20; township 1 south, range 8 east, partly unsurveyed; townships 2 and 3 south, range 8 east; township 1 south, range 9 east, sections 5 to 9, inclusive, sections 16 to 23, inclusive, and sections 26 to 35, inclusive; township 2 south, range 9 east, sections 2 to 11, inclusive, and sections 14 to 36, inclusive, partly unsurveyed; township 3 south, range 9 east; township 4 south, range 9 east, sections 1 to 5, inclusive, and sections 11 to 14, inclusive; township 2 south, range 10 east, sections 25 to 36, inclusive, unsurveyed; township 3 south, range 10 east, partly unsurveyed; township 4 south, range 10 east, sections 1 to 18, inclusive, sections 22 to 26, inclusive, and sections 35 and 36; township 5 south, range 10 east, section 1; township 2 south, range 11 east, sections 25 to 36, inclusive, unsurveyed; townships 3 and 4 south, range 11 east, partly unsurveyed; township 5 south, range 11 east, sections 1 to 18, inclusive, sections 22 to 27, inclusive, and sections 34, 35, and 36; township 6 south, range 11 east, portion of sections 1, 2, and 3 lying north of north transmission line right-of-way which is adjacent to the north right-of-way line of the Colorado River aqueduct but excluding therefrom the Aggregate Deposit in section 3; township 2 south, range 12 east, section 13 and sections 23 to 36, inclusive, partly unsurveyed; townships 3 and 4 south, range 12 east, partly unsurveyed; township 5 south, range 12 east, sections 1 to 24, inclusive, and sections 26 to 34, inclusive, partly unsurveyed, and portions of sections 25 and 35 lying north of north transmission line right-of-way which is adjacent to the north right-of-way line of the Colorado River aqueduct; township 6 south, range 12 east, portions of sections 2, 3, 4, 5, 6, and 10, lying north of north transmission line right-of-way which is adjacent to the north right-of-way line of the Colorado River aqueduct, but excluding therefrom the Bumpani's Aggregate Deposit in section 4; township 2 south, range 13 east, sections 1 and 2 and sections 7 to 36, inclusive, partly unsurveyed; township 3 south, range 13 east, sections 1 to 18, inclusive, partly unsurveyed; township 5 south, range 13 east, sections 6, 7, 18, and 19, unsurveyed; township 1 south, range 14 east, sections 33 to 36, inclusive, partly unsurveyed; township 2 south, range 14 east, partly unsurveyed; township 3 south, range 14 east, sections 1 to 18, inclusive, partly unsurveyed; township 1 south, range 15 east, sections 31 to 35, inclusive, partly unsurveyed; township 2 south, range 15 east, sections 2 to 36, inclusive, partly unsurveyed; township 3 south, range 15 east, sections 1 to 12, inclusive, partly unsurveyed, and section 18, unsurveyed; township 2 south, range 16 east, sections 18, 19, 30, and 31, unsurveyed; and township 3 south, range 16 east, sections 6 and 7 unsurveyed. Also, all that portion of the south half of the northeast quarter and of the north half of the southeast quarter of section 33, township 1 north, range 9 east, San Bernardino base and meridian, in the county of San Bernardino, State of California, shown on map titled "Record of Survey" by H.F. Cameron, Junior, licensed engineer 6826, dated December 29, 1948, and James B. Hommon, licensed engineer 6916, dated October 5, 1949, and made for the National Park Service, Department of the Interior, and recorded October 17, 1949, in volume 7, page 72, of the official records of the county of San Bernardino, said land being described as follows:

Beginning at the United States Government Land Office monument marked as the east quarter corner of said section 33, thence proceeding on a true bearing south 89 degrees 02 minutes 10 seconds west a distance of 50.01 feet to the true point of beginning of the hereinafter described parcel of land;

Thence north 0 degrees 02 minutes 55 seconds west a distance of 250.08 feet to a point of curve; thence along the arc of a curve to the left having a radius of 20.00 feet a distance of 31.73 feet to a point of tangency; thence south 89 degrees 02 minutes 40 seconds west a distance of 2,559.24 feet; thence south 0 degrees 19 minutes 50 seconds east a distance of 270.76 feet;

Thence south 0 degrees 21 minutes 02 seconds east a distance of 409.32 feet to the beginning of a curve; thence along the arc of a curve to the left having a radius of 280.98 feet a distance of 275.93 feet to a point of compound curvature; thence along the arc of a curve to the left having a radius of 800.00 feet a distance of 753.98 feet to a point of tangency; thence north 69 degrees 22 minutes 58 seconds east a distance of 125.31 feet to the beginning of a curve;

Thence along the arc of a curve to the right having a radius of 1,400.00 feet a distance of 1,042.74 feet to a point of tangency; thence south 67 degrees 56 minutes 33 seconds east a distance of 94.55 feet to the beginning of a curve; thence along the arc of a curve to the left having a radius of 700.00 feet a distance of 366.52 feet to a point of compound curvature;

Thence along the arc of a curve to the left having a radius of 167.60 feet a distance of 240.17 feet to a point of tangency; thence north 0 degrees 02 minutes 55 seconds west a distance of 648.91 feet to the point of beginning containing 57.839 acres, more or less.

(Sept. 25, 1950, c. 1030, § 1, 64 Stat. 1033; June 30, 1961, Pub.L. 87–80, 75 Stat. 197.)

HISTORICAL AND STATUTORY NOTES

Amendments
1961 Amendments. Pub.L. 87–80 included within the boundaries of Joshua Tree National Monument certain federally owned lands situated in county of San Bernardino, California.

LIBRARY REFERENCES

American Digest System
    Armed Services ⚖54.
    Woods and Forests ⚖1, 8.
    Key Number System Topic Nos. 34, 411.

§ 450ii–1.   Excluded lands opened to entry under mining laws

All public-domain lands included before September 25, 1950, within the Joshua Tree National Monument which are eliminated from the National Monument by sections 450ii to 450ii–3 of this title are opened to location, entry, and patenting under the United States mining laws: *Provided*, That such public-domain lands or portions thereof shall be restored to application and entry under other applicable public land laws, including the mineral leasing laws.

(Sept. 25, 1950, c. 1030, § 2, 64 Stat. 1035.)

HISTORICAL AND STATUTORY NOTES

References in Text
    The United States mining laws, referred to in text, are classified generally to Title 30, Mineral Lands and Mining.
    The public land laws, referred to in text, are classified generally to Title 43, Public Lands.

The mineral leasing laws, referred to in text, are classified generally to section 181 et seq. of Title 30, Mineral Lands and Mining.

LIBRARY REFERENCES

American Digest System
    Armed Services ⚖54.
    Mines and Minerals ⚖1.
    Public Lands ⚖49.
    Key Number System Topic Nos. 34, 260, 317.

§ 450ii–2.   Continuation of leases, permits, and licenses

All leases, permits, and licenses issued or authorized by any department, establishment, or agency of the United States, with respect to the Federal lands excluded from the Joshua Tree National Monument by sections 450ii to 450ii–3 of this title, which are in effect on September 25, 1950, shall continue in effect, subject to compliance with the terms and conditions therein set forth, until terminated in accordance with the provisions thereof.

(Sept. 25, 1950, c. 1030, § 3, 64 Stat. 1035.)

LIBRARY REFERENCES

American Digest System
    Armed Services ⚖54.
    Mines and Minerals ⚖5.
    Public Lands ⚖49.
    Key Number System Topic Nos. 34, 260, 317.

§ 450ii–3.   Survey and report of mineral value

The Secretary of the Interior is authorized and directed, through the United States Bureau of Mines, the United States Geological Survey, and the National Park Service, to cause a survey to be made of the area within the revised boundaries of the Joshua Tree National Monument with a view to determining to what extent the said area is more valuable for minerals than for the National Monument purposes for which it was created. Report of said survey shall be filed with the President of the United States Senate and the Speaker of the House of Representatives on or before February 1, 1951.

(Sept. 25, 1950, c. 1030, § 4, 64 Stat. 1035; Nov. 13, 1991, Pub.L. 102–154, Title I, 105 Stat. 1000; May 18, 1992, Pub.L. 102–285, § 10, 106 Stat. 171.)

HISTORICAL AND STATUTORY NOTES

Revision Notes and Legislative Reports
  1992 Acts. House Report No. 102–333, see 1992 U.S. Code Cong. and Adm. News, p. 119.

Change of Name
  Pub.L. 102–285, § 10(a), May 18, 1992, 106 Stat. 171, redesignated the Geological Survey and provided that on and after May 18, 1992, it shall be known as the United States Geological Survey. An earlier statute [Pub.L. 102–154, Title I, Nov. 13, 1991, 105 Stat. 1000] had provided

for the identical change of name effective on and after Nov. 13, 1991. See note under section 31 of Title 43, Public Lands.

  Pub.L. 102–285, § 10(b), May 18, 1992, 106 Stat. 172, provided that, on and after May 18, 1992, the Bureau of Mines is redesignated and shall thereafter be known as the United States Bureau of Mines. See note under section 1 of Title 30, Mineral Lands and Mining.

LIBRARY REFERENCES

American Digest System
  Armed Services ⊸54.
  Mines and Minerals ⊸2.
  Public Lands ⊸49.
  Key Number System Topic Nos. 34, 260, 317.

§ 450jj.   Jefferson National Expansion Memorial; authorization

There is authorized to be constructed by the Secretary of the Interior upon the Jefferson National Expansion Memorial National Historic Site, Saint Louis, Missouri, an appropriate national memorial to those persons who made possible the territorial expansion of the United States, including President Thomas Jefferson and his aides, Livingston and Monroe, who negotiated the Louisiana Purchase, the great explorers, Lewis and Clark, and the hardy hunters, trappers, frontiersmen, pioneers, and others who contributed to such expansion.

(May 17, 1954, c. 204, § 1, 68 Stat. 98.)

HISTORICAL AND STATUTORY NOTES

Short Title

1984 Amendments. Pub.L. 98–398, Title II, § 203, Aug. 24, 1984, 98 Stat. 1472, provided that: "This title [enacting sections 450jj–3 to 450jj–9 of this title, enacting provisions set out as a note under section 450jj–3 of this title, and amending provisions set out as a note under this section] may be cited as the 'Jefferson National Expansion Memorial Amendments of 1984'."

Disposition of Funds Received by National Park Service as Reimbursement for Costs Incurred

Pub.L. 99–500, Title I, § 101(h) [Title I, § 100], Oct. 18, 1986, 100 Stat. 1783–251, provided: "That notwithstanding any other provision of law, hereafter funds received by the National Park Service as reimbursement for the cost of providing security, law enforcement, interpretive, and other services with respect to the operation of facilities at the Jefferson National Expansion Memorial National Historic Site shall be credited to the appropriation bearing the cost of providing such services."

[An identical provision is contained in Pub.L. 99–591, Title I, § 101(h) [Title I, § 100], Oct. 30, 1986, 100 Stat. 3341–251.]

Authorization of Appropriations; Federal and Non-Federal Ratio of Expenditures

Act May 17, 1954, c. 204, § 11, formerly § 4, 68 Stat. 99, as amended Pub.L. 85–936, Sept. 6, 1958, 72 Stat. 1794; Pub.L. 89–269, Oct. 19, 1965, 79 Stat. 991; Pub.L. 94–578, Title II, § 201(6), Oct. 21, 1976, 90 Stat. 2733; renumbered § 11 and amended Pub.L. 98–398, Title II, § 201(b), Aug. 24, 1984, 98 Stat. 1471; Pub.L. 102–355, § 1(3), Aug. 26, 1992, 106 Stat. 947, provided that:

"(a) There is hereby authorized to be appropriated not to exceed $32,750,000 to carry out the purposes of this Act [sections 450jj to 450jj–9 of this title]: *Provided*, That funds authorized to be appropriated by this Act shall be expended by the United States for construction of the memorial in the ratio of $3 of Federal funds for each $1 of money contributed hereafter by the city of Saint Louis or other non-Federal source for purposes of the memorial, and for such purposes the Secretary is authorized to accept from the said city or other non-Federal sources, and to utilize for purposes of this Act, and money so contributed: *Provided further*, That the value of any land hereafter contributed by the city of Saint Louis shall be excluded from the computation of the city's share."

"(b)(1) For the purposes of the East St. Louis portion of the memorial, there are authorized to be appropriated $2,000,000 for land acquisition and, subject to the provisions of paragraphs (2) and (3), such sums as may be necessary for development: *Provided*, That such authorization shall not include any sums for the acquisition, removal, or relocation of the grain elevator and business located within the East St. Louis unit of the Memorial. Such development shall be consistent with the level of development described in phase one of the draft Development and Management Plan and Environmental Assessment, East St. Louis Addition to Jefferson National Expansion Memorial—Illinois/Missouri, dated August 1987.

"(2) Federal funds expended under paragraph (1) for development may not exceed 75 percent of the actual cost of such development. The remaining share of such actual costs shall be provided from non-Federal funds, services, or materials, or a combination thereof, fairly valued as determined by the Secretary. Any non-Federal expenditures for the acquisition, removal, or relocation of the grain elevator and business shall be included as part of the non-Federal cost share: *Provided*, That credit shall not be given for any such expenditures which exceed the cost of acquisition, removal, or relocation of the grain elevator and business located within the East St. Louis unit of the Memorial if such action had been accomplished by the Federal Government as determined by the Secretary under existing law: *Provided further*, That only those non-Federal funds expended at least sixty days after the transmission of the report referred to in paragraph (3) for the removal of such grain elevator shall be credited towards the non-Federal cost share. For the purposes of this paragraph, the Secretary may accept and utilize for such purposes any non-Federal funds, services, and materials so contributed.

"(3) Within one year after the date of enactment of this paragraph [Aug. 26, 1992], the Secretary, in direct consultation with the city of East St. Louis, Gateway Arch Park Expansion, and the Southwestern Illinois Development Authority, shall develop and transmit to the Committee on Energy and Natural Resources of the United States Senate and the Committee on Interior and Insular Affairs [now the Committee on Natural Resources] of the United States House of Representatives a study of alternatives to, and costs associated with, the removal of the grain elevator located within the East St. Louis unit of the Memorial. The study shall contain, but need not be limited to, at least one alternative which would incorporate and retain the existing grain elevator into the draft development and management plan and environmental assessment referred to in paragraph (1).

"(c) Funds appropriated under subsection (b) of this section shall remain available until expended.

"(d) [Repealed.   Pub.L.   102–355, § 1(3), Aug. 26, 1992, 106 Stat. 947]."

LIBRARY REFERENCES

American Digest System
   Armed Services ⚷54.
   Woods and Forests ⚷1, 8.
   Key Number System Topic Nos. 34, 411.

§ 450jj–1. Construction of memorial

(a) Plan; contracts; employment and compensation of personnel

The memorial authorized herein shall be constructed in general, in accordance with the plan approved by the United States Territorial Expansion Memorial Commission on May 25, 1948. The Secretary of the Interior is authorized to enter into such contracts as may be necessary to carry out the purposes of sections 450jj to 450jj–9 of this title. The Secretary is also authorized to employ, in his discretion, by contract or otherwise, landscape architects, architects, engineers, sculptors, artists, other expert consultants, or firms, partnerships, or associations thereof, and to include in any such contract provision for the utilization of the services and facilities, and the payment of the travel and other expenses, of their respective organizations, in accordance with the usual customs of the several professions and at the prevailing rates for such services and facilities, without regard to the civil-service laws or regulations, chapter 51 and subchapter III of chapter 53 of Title 5, section 5 of Title 41, or any other law or regulation relating to either employment or compensation.

(b) Easements; above-ground parking

The Secretary of the Interior, in connection with the construction and operation of the memorial, is authorized to grant such easements as are in the public interest, and, in his discretion, to convey to the city of Saint Louis for above-ground parking structures, under such terms and conditions as he may consider to be compatible with maintaining the integrity, appearance, and purposes of said memorial, such portion of the historic site as may in his judgment be excluded therefrom without detriment thereto, subject, however, to reversion of such portion of the historic site to the United States if such excluded area ceases to be used for parking purposes by said city.

(c) Easements; public protection

The Secretary of the Interior is authorized to grant easements for the purpose of erecting underground structures suitable for public protection under such terms and conditions as he may consider to be compatible with maintaining the integrity, appearance, and purposes of said memorial.

(May 17, 1954, c. 204, § 2, 68 Stat. 99.)

HISTORICAL AND STATUTORY NOTES

References in Text

Herein, referred to in subsec. (a), means Act May 17, 1954, which is generally classified to sections 450jj to 450jj–9 of this title. For complete classification of this Act to the Code, see Tables.

The civil-service laws, referred to in subsec. (a), are classified generally to Title 5, Government Organization and Employees. See, particularly, section 3301 et seq. of Title 5.

Codifications

In subsec. (a), "chapter 51 and subchapter III of chapter 53 of Title 5" was substituted for "the Classification Act of 1949, as amended" on authority of Pub.L. 89–554, § 7(b), Sept. 6, 1966, 80 Stat. 631, the first section of which enacted Title 5, Government Organization and Employees.

LIBRARY REFERENCES

American Digest System

Armed Services ⚎54.
United States ⚎56.
Key Number System Topic Nos. 34, 393.

§ 450jj–2. Railroad agreement as condition precedent to undertaking memorial project

The memorial project authorized herein shall not be undertaken until there shall have been reached an agreement satisfactory to the Secretary of the Interior providing for the relocation of the railroad tracks and structures now situated on lands adjacent to the Jefferson National Expansion Memorial National Historic Site, between the boundary of the site and the river. Such agreement shall contain such terms as may be deemed desirable by the Secretary but shall contain a provision limiting the Federal expenditure of funds in connection with such relocation of the tracks and structures to work undertaken within the historic site area.

(May 17, 1954, c. 204, § 3, 68 Stat. 99.)

HISTORICAL AND STATUTORY NOTES

References in Text
Herein, referred to in text, means Act May 17, 1954, which is generally classi-

fied to sections 450jj to 450jj–9 of this title. For complete classification of this Act to the Code, see Tables.

LIBRARY REFERENCES

American Digest System
Armed Services ⬤➡54.
Railroads ⬤➡5.5(3).
United States ⬤➡60.
Key Number System Topic Nos. 34, 320, 393.

§ 450jj–3. Designation of additional land by Secretary; manner of acquiring additional land

(a) There is hereby designated for addition to the Jefferson National Expansion Memorial (hereinafter in sections 450jj–3 to 450jj–9 of this title referred to as the "Memorial") approximately one hundred acres in the city of East Saint Louis, Illinois, contiguous with the Mississippi River and between the Eads Bridge and the Poplar Street Bridge, as generally depicted on the map entitled "Boundary Map, Jefferson National Expansion Memorial", numbered 366–80013, dated January 1992, which shall be on file and available for public inspection in the offices of the National Park Service, Department of the Interior. The additional acreage authorized by this section is in recognition of the historical significance of the Memorial site to the westward expansion of the United States and the historical linkage of this site on the Mississippi in both Missouri and Illinois to such expansion, the international recognition of the Gateway Arch, designed by Eero Saarinen, as one of the world's great sculptural and architectural achievements, and the increasing use of the Memorial site by millions of people from all over the United States and the world.

(b) Within the area designated in accordance with this section, the Secretary of the Interior may acquire lands and interests in lands by donation, purchase with donated or appropriated funds, or exchange, except that lands owned by the State of Illinois or any political subdivision thereof may be acquired only by donation.

(May 17, 1954, c. 204, § 4, as added Aug. 24, 1984, Pub.L. 98–398, Title II, § 201(a), 98 Stat. 1467, and amended Aug. 26, 1992, Pub.L. 102–355, § 1(1), 106 Stat. 947.)

HISTORICAL AND STATUTORY NOTES

Amendments
1992   Amendments. Subsec.   (a).
Pub.L.   102–355,   § 1(1),   substituted "There is hereby designated" for "The

Secretary of the Interior is further authorized to designate", "approximately" for "not more than", and "366–80013, dated   January   1992"   for

341

"MWR–366/80,004, and dated February 9, 1984".

Prior Provisions

A prior section 4 of Act May 17, 1954, c. 204, was renumbered section 11 of such Act by Pub.L. 98–398, Title II, § 201(b)(1), Aug. 24, 1984, 98 Stat. 1472, and is set out as a note under section 450jj of this title.

Compliance With Congressional Budget Act

Pub.L. 98–398, Title II, § 202, Aug. 24, 1984, 98 Stat. 1472, provided that: "Any provision of this title (or any amendment made by this title) [enacting this section and sections 450jj–4 to 450jj–9 of this title and enacting and amending provisions set out as notes under section 450jj of this title] which, directly or indirectly, authorizes the enactment of new budget authority described in section 402(a) of the Congressional Budget Act of 1974 [section 652(a) of Title 2] shall be effective only for fiscal years beginning after September 30, 1983."

LIBRARY REFERENCES

American Digest System

Armed Services ⊂⇒54.
United States ⊂⇒55.
Woods and Forests ⊂⇒2.
Key Number System Topic Nos. 34, 393, 411.

§ 450jj–4. Transfer of land

Where appropriate in the discretion of the Secretary of the Interior, he may transfer by lease or otherwise, to any appropriate person or governmental entity, land owned by the United States (or any interest therein) which has been acquired by the Secretary under section 450jj–3 of this title. Any such transfer shall be consistent with the management plan for the area and with the requirements of section 460*l*–22 of this title and shall be subject to such conditions and restrictions as the Secretary deems necessary to carry out the purposes of sections 450jj to 450jj–9 of this title, including terms and conditions which provide for—

(1) the continuation of existing uses of the land which are compatible with the Memorial,

(2) the protection of the important historical resources of the leased area, and

(3) the retention by the Secretary of such access and development rights as the Secretary deems necessary to provide for appropriate visitor use and resource management.

In transferring any lands or interest in lands under this section, the Secretary shall take into account the views of the Commission established under section 450jj–6 of this title.

(May 17, 1954, c. 204, § 5, as added Aug. 24, 1984, Pub.L. 98–398, Title II, § 201(a), 98 Stat. 1468.)

HISTORICAL AND STATUTORY NOTES

References in Text

Section 450jj–6 of this title, referred to in text, originally read "section 8", meaning section 8 of Act May 17, 1954, c. 204, and was translated as reading "section 7" of such act, to reflect the probable intent of Congress, because section 7 related to the establishment of the Jefferson National Expansion Memorial Commission.

Prior Provisions

A prior section 5 of Act May 17, 1954, c. 204, which was classified as a note under section 450jj of this title and had prohibited the use of appropriated funds for the planning or construction of the so-called "Saarinen Plan" stainless-steel arch, approved May 25, 1948, was repealed by Pub.L. 85–936, Sept. 6, 1958, 72 Stat. 1794.

Compliance With Congressional Budget Act

For required compliance with Congressional Budget Act, see section 202 of Title II of Pub.L. 98–398 set out as a note under section 450jj–3 of this title.

LIBRARY REFERENCES

American Digest System

Armed Services ☞54.
United States ☞57.
Woods and Forests ☞4.
Key Number System Topic Nos. 34, 393, 411.

§ 450jj–5. Administration of Memorial; cooperation with State and local governments and private sector

Lands and interests in lands acquired pursuant to section 450jj–3 of this title shall, upon acquisition, be a part of the Memorial. The Secretary of the Interior shall administer the Memorial in accordance with sections 450jj to 450jj–9 of this title and the provisions of law generally applicable to units of the national park system, including sections 1, 2, 3, and 4 of this title and sections 461 to 467 of this title. In the development, management, and operation of that portion of the Memorial which is added to the Memorial under section 450jj–3 of this title, the Secretary shall, to the maximum extent feasible, utilize the assistance of State and local government agencies and the private sector. For such purposes, the Secretary may, consistent with the management plan for the area, enter into cooperative agreements with the State, with any political subdivision of the State, or with any person. Any such cooperative agreement shall, at a minimum, establish procedures for providing notice to the Secretary of any action proposed by the State, such political subdivision, or such person, which may affect the area.

(May 17, 1954, c. 204, § 6, as added Aug. 24, 1984, Pub.L. 98–398, Title II, § 201(a), 98 Stat. 1468.)

HISTORICAL AND STATUTORY NOTES

Compliance With Congressional Budget Act

For required compliance with Congressional Budget Act, see section 202 of Title II of Pub.L. 98–398 set out as a note under section 450jj–3 of this title.

§ 450jj–6. Jefferson National Expansion Memorial Commission

(a) Establishment

There is hereby established the Jefferson National Expansion Memorial Commission (hereinafter in sections 450jj–6 to 450jj–9 of this title referred to as the "Commission").

(b) Composition

The Commission shall be composed of twenty members as follows:

(1) The county executive of Saint Louis County, Missouri, ex officio, or a delegate.

(2) The chairman of the Saint Clair County Board of Supervisors, Illinois, ex officio, or a delegate.

(3)(A) The executive director of the Bi-State Development Agency, Saint Louis, Missouri, ex officio, or a delegate.

(B) A member of the Bi-State Development Agency, Saint Louis, Missouri, who is not a resident of the same State as the executive director of such agency, appointed by a majority of the members of such agency, or a delegate.

(4) The mayor of the city of East Saint Louis, Illinois, ex officio, or a delegate.

(5) The mayor of Saint Louis, Missouri, ex officio, or a delegate.

(6) The Governor of the State of Illinois, ex officio, or a delegate.

(7) The Governor of the State of Missouri, ex officio, or a delegate.

(8) The Secretary of the Interior, ex officio, or a delegate.

(9) The Secretary of Housing and Urban Development, ex officio, or a delegate.

(10) The Secretary of Transportation, ex officio, or a delegate.

(11) The Secretary of the Treasury, ex officio, or a delegate.

(12) The Secretary of Commerce, ex officio, or a delegate.

(13) The Secretary of the Smithsonian Institution, ex officio, or a delegate.

(14) Three individuals appointed by the Secretary of the Interior from a list of individuals nominated by the mayor of East Saint Louis, Illinois, and the Governor of the State of Illinois.

(15) Three individuals appointed by the Secretary of the Interior from a list of individuals nominated by the mayor of Saint Louis, Missouri, and the Governor of the State of Missouri.

Individuals nominated for appointment under paragraphs (14) and (15) shall be individuals who have knowledge and experience in one or more of the fields of parks and recreation, environmental protection, historic preservation, cultural affairs, tourism, economic development, city planning and management, finance, or public administration.   A vacancy in the Commission shall be filled in the manner in which the original appointment was made.

(c) Term of office of members

(1) Except as provided in paragraphs (2) and (3), members of the Commission shall be appointed for terms of three years.

(2) Of the members of the Commission first appointed under paragraphs (14) and (15) of subsection (c) [1] of this section—

(A) two shall be appointed for terms of one year;

(B) two shall be appointed for terms of two years; and

(C) two shall be appointed for terms of three years;

as designated by the Secretary of the Interior at the time of appointment.

(3) Any member of the Commission appointed to fill a vacancy occurring before the expiration of the term for which his predecessor was appointed shall be appointed only for the remainder of such term.   A member of the Commission may serve after the expiration of his term until his successor has taken office.

(d) Compensation of members; travel expenses and per diem

Members of the Commission shall receive no pay on account of their service on the Commission, but while away from their homes or regular places of business in the performance of services for the Commission, members of the Commission shall be allowed travel expenses, including per diem in lieu of subsistence, in the same manner as persons employed intermittently in the Government service are allowed expenses under section 5703 of Title 5.

(e) Chairperson

The chairperson of the Commission shall be elected by the members of the Commission.

(f) Assistance from Federal agencies

Upon request of the Commission, the head of any Federal agency represented by members on the Commission may detail any of the personnel or [2] such agency, or provide administrative services to the Commission to assist the Commission in carrying out the Commission's duties under section 450jj–7 of this title.

(g) Gifts, bequests, or donations

The Commission may, for the purposes of carrying out the Commission's duties under section 450jj–7 of this title, seek, accept, and dispose of gifts, bequests, or donations of money, personal property, or services, received from any source.

(h) Termination; extension

(1) Except as provided in paragraph (2), the Commission shall terminate on the day occurring ten years after August 24, 1984.

(2) The Secretary of the Interior may extend the life of the Commission for a period of not more than five years beginning on the day referred to in paragraph (1) if the Commission determines that such extension is necessary in order for the Commission to carry out sections 450jj to 450jj–9 of this title.

(May 17, 1954, c. 204, § 7, as added Aug. 24, 1984, Pub.L. 98–398, Title II, § 201(a), 98 Stat. 1469.)

[1] So in original. Subsection "(b)" was probably intended.
[2] So in original. Probably should be "of".

HISTORICAL AND STATUTORY NOTES

Compliance With Congressional Budget Act
For required compliance with Congressional Budget Act, see section 202 of Title II of Pub.L. 98–398 set out as a note under section 450jj–3 of this title.

LIBRARY REFERENCES

American Digest System
Armed Services ☞54.
Woods and Forests ☞7.
Key Number System Topic Nos. 34, 411.

§ 450jj–7. Development and management plan for East Saint Louis, Illinois, portion of Memorial

(a) Within two years from August 24, 1984, the Commission shall develop and transmit to the Secretary a development and management plan for the East Saint Louis, Illinois, portion of the Memorial. The plan shall include—

    (1) measures for the preservation of the area's resources;

(2) indications of types and general intensities of development (including visitor circulation and transportation patterns, systems, and modes) associated with public enjoyment and use of the area, including general locations, timing of implementation, and cost estimates;

(3) identification of any implementation commitments for visitor carrying capacities for all areas of the area;

(4) indications of potential modifications to the external boundaries of the area, the reasons therefore,[1] and cost estimates;

(5) measures and commitments for insuring that the development, management, and operation of the area in the State of Illinois are compatible with the portion of the Memorial in the State of Missouri;

(6) opportunities and commitments for cooperative activities in the development, management, and operation of the East Saint Louis portion of the Memorial with other Federal, State, and local agencies, and the private sector; and

(7) effective and appropriate ways to increase local participation in the management of the East Saint Louis portion of the Memorial to help reduce the day-to-day operational and management responsibilities of the National Park Service and to increase opportunities for local employment.

(b) The plan shall also identify and include—

(1) needs, opportunities, and commitments for the aesthetic and economic rehabilitation of the entire East Saint Louis, Illinois, waterfront and adjacent areas, in a manner compatible with and complementary to, the Memorial, including the appropriate commitments and roles of the Federal, State, and local governments and the private sector; and

(2) cost estimates and recommendations for Federal, State, and local administrative and legislative actions.

In carrying out its duties under this section, the Commission shall take into account Federal, State, and local plans and studies respecting the area, including the study by the National Park Service on the feasibility of a museum of American ethnic culture to be a part of any development plans for the Memorial.

(May 17, 1954, c. 204, § 8, as added Aug. 24, 1984, Pub.L. 98–398, Title II, § 201(a), 98 Stat. 1470.)

[1] So in original. Probably should be "therefor,".

HISTORICAL AND STATUTORY NOTES

Compliance With Congressional Budget Act

For required compliance with Congressional Budget Act, see section 202 of Title II of Pub.L. 98–398 set out as a note under section 450jj–3 of this title.

LIBRARY REFERENCES

American Digest System

Armed Services ☜54.
United States ☜57.
Key Number System Topic Nos. 34, 393.

§ 450jj–8. Repealed. Pub.L. 102–355, § 1(2), Aug. 26, 1992, 106 Stat. 947

HISTORICAL AND STATUTORY NOTES

Section, Act May 17, 1954, c. 204, § 9, as added Aug. 24, 1984, Pub.L. 98–398, Title II, § 201(a), 98 Stat. 1471, related to the approval of the development and management plan for the East Saint Louis, Illinois portion of the Jefferson National Expansion Memorial, and transmission of such approved plan to the Committee on Interior and Insular Affairs [now Committee on Resources] of the House of Representatives and to the Committee on Energy and Natural Resources of the United States Senate.

§ 450jj–9. Activities in Memorial area pending submission of plan

Pending submission of the Commission's plan, any Federal entity conducting or supporting significant activities directly affecting East Saint Louis, Illinois, generally and the site specifically referred to in section 450jj–3 of this title shall—

(1) consult with the Secretary of the Interior and the Commission with respect to such activities;

(2) cooperate with the Secretary of the Interior and the Commission in carrying out their duties under sections 450jj to 450jj–9 of this title, and to the maximum extent practicable, coordinate such activities with the carrying out of such duties; and

(3) to the maximum extent practicable, conduct or support such activities in a manner which the Secretary determines will not have an adverse effect on the Memorial.

(May 17, 1954, c. 204, § 10, as added Aug. 24, 1984, Pub.L. 98–398, Title II, § 201(a), 98 Stat. 1471.)

HISTORICAL AND STATUTORY NOTES

Compliance With Congressional Budget Act
For required compliance with Congressional Budget Act, see section 202 of Title

II of Pub.L. 98–398 set out as a note under section 450jj-3 of this title.

LIBRARY REFERENCES

American Digest System
Armed Services ⬤54.
United States ⬤57.
Key Number System Topic Nos. 34, 393.

§ 450kk. Fort Union National Monument; acquisition of site and other lands; reversions and reservations

In order to preserve and protect, in the public interest, the historic Old Fort Union, situated in the county of Mora, State of New Mexico, and to provide adequate public access thereto, the Secretary of the Interior is authorized to acquire on behalf of the United States by donation, or he may procure with donated funds, the site and remaining structures of Old Fort Union, together with such additional land, interests in land, and improvements thereon as the Secretary in his discretion may deem necessary to carry out the purposes of this section and section 450kk-1 of this title. Donated lands may be accepted subject to such reservations, terms, and conditions as may be satisfactory to the Secretary, including right of reversion to donor, or its successors and assigns, upon abandonment as a national monument, and reservation of mineral rights subject to condition that surface of donated lands may not be used or disturbed in connection therewith, without the consent of the Secretary.

(June 28, 1954, c. 401, § 1, 68 Stat. 298.)

HISTORICAL AND STATUTORY NOTES

Revision Notes and Legislative Reports
1954 Acts. Senate Report No. 1539, see 1954 U.S. Code Cong. and Adm. News, p. 2422.

LIBRARY REFERENCES

American Digest System
Armed Services ⬤54.
United States ⬤55.
Woods and Forests ⬤2.
Key Number System Topic Nos. 34, 393, 411.

§ 450kk-1. Establishment; publication in Federal Register; additional properties

Upon a determination of the Secretary of the Interior that sufficient land and other property have been acquired by the United

States for national-monument purposes, as provided in section 450kk of this title, such property shall be established as the "Fort Union National Monument" and thereafter shall be administered by the Secretary of the Interior in accordance with the laws and regulations applicable to national monuments. An order of the Secretary, constituting notice of such establishment, shall be published in the Federal Register.

Following establishment of the national monument, additional properties may be acquired as provided in section 450kk of this title, which properties, upon acquisition of title thereto by the United States, shall become a part of the national monument: *Provided,* That the total area of the national monument established pursuant to this section and section 450kk of this title shall not exceed one thousand acres, exclusive of such adjoining lands as may be covered by scenic easements.

(June 28, 1954, c. 401, § 2, 68 Stat. 299.)

HISTORICAL AND STATUTORY NOTES

Revision Notes and Legislative Reports
  1954 Acts. Senate Report No. 1539, see 1954 U.S. Code Cong. and Adm. News, p. 2422.

LIBRARY REFERENCES

American Digest System
  Armed Services ☞54.
  United States ☞57.
  Woods and Forests ☞8.
  Key Number System Topic Nos. 34, 393, 411.

§ 450*ll*. Booker T. Washington National Monument; acquisition of site

The Secretary of the Interior is authorized and directed to acquire, on behalf of the United States, by gift, purchase, or condemnation, all right, title, and interest in and to the real property located at Booker Washington Birthplace, Virginia.

(Apr. 2, 1956, c. 158, § 1, 70 Stat. 86.)

HISTORICAL AND STATUTORY NOTES

Short Title
  2002 Acts. Pub.L. 107–215, § 1, Aug. 21, 2002, 116 Stat. 1054, provided that: "This Act [enacting 16 U.S.C.A. § 450*ll*–3] may be cited as the 'Booker T. Washington National Monument Boundary Adjustment Act of 2002'."

Authorization of Appropriations
  Section 4 of Act Apr. 2, 1956, as amended by Pub.L. 92–272, Title II, § 201(2), Apr. 11, 1972, 86 Stat. 120, provided that: "There are authorized to be appropriated such sums as may be necessary to carry

out the provisions of this act [sections
450*ll* to 450*ll*–2 of this title]."

LIBRARY REFERENCES

American Digest System
  United States ☞55, 57.
  Key Number System Topic No. 393.

§ 450*ll*–1.   Establishment and supervision

The real property acquired under section 450*ll* of this title shall
constitute the Booker T. Washington National Monument and shall
be a public national memorial to Booker T. Washington, noted Negro
educator and apostle of good will. The Secretary of the Interior shall
have the supervision, management, and control of such national
monument, and shall maintain and preserve it in a suitable and
enduring manner which, in his judgment, will provide for the benefit
and enjoyment of the people of the United States.

(Apr. 2, 1956, c. 158, § 2, 70 Stat. 86.)

LIBRARY REFERENCES

American Digest System
  Woods and Forests ☞1, 5.
  Key Number System Topic No. 411.

§ 450*ll*–2.   Maintenance of museum; provision for parks, construction of roads and use of markers

The Secretary of the Interior is authorized to—

(1) maintain, either in an existing structure acquired under
section 450*ll* of this title or in a building constructed by him for
the purpose, a museum for relics and records pertaining to
Booker T. Washington, and for other articles of national and
patriotic interest, and to accept, on behalf of the United States,
for installation in such museum, articles which may be offered as
additions to the museum; and

(2) provide for public parks and recreational areas, construct
roads and mark with monuments, tablets, or otherwise, points of
interest, within the boundaries of the Booker T. Washington
National Monument.

(Apr. 2, 1956, c. 158, § 3, 70 Stat. 86.)

LIBRARY REFERENCES

American Digest System
  United States ☞57.
  Woods and Forests ☞5.
  Key Number System Topic Nos. 393, 411.

§ 450*ll*–3. Additional lands

(a) Lands added to monument

The boundary of the Booker T. Washington National Monument is modified to include the approximately 15 acres, as generally depicted on the map entitled 'Boundary Map, Booker T. Washington National Monument, Franklin County, Virginia', numbered BOWA 404/80,024, and dated February 2001. The map shall be on file and available for inspection in the appropriate offices of the National Park Service, Department of the Interior.

(b) Acquisition of additional lands

The Secretary of the Interior is authorized to acquire from willing owners the land or interests in land described in subsection (a) of this section by donation, purchase with donated or appropriated funds, or exchange.

(c) Administration of additional lands

Lands added to the Booker T. Washington National Monument by subsection (a) of this section shall be administered by the Secretary of the Interior as part of the monument in accordance with applicable laws and regulations.

(Apr. 2, 1956, c. 158, § 5, as added Aug. 21, 2002, Pub.L. 107–215, § 2, 116 Stat. 1054.)

HISTORICAL AND STATUTORY NOTES

Revision Notes and Legislative Reports

2002 Acts. House Report No. 107–223, see 2002 U.S. Code Cong. and Adm. News, p. 816.

LIBRARY REFERENCES

American Digest System

United States ⚷55.
Key Number System Topic No. 393.

§§ 450mm to 450mm–3. Repealed. Pub.L. 108–387, Title I, § 105(a), Oct. 30, 2004, 118 Stat. 2236

HISTORICAL AND STATUTORY NOTES

Section 450mm, Pub.L. 85–435, § 1, May 29, 1958, 72 Stat. 153, related to the establishment of Fort Clatsop National Memorial. See 16 U.S.C.A. § 410kkk–1 et seq.

Section 450mm–1, Pub.L. 85–435, § 2, May 29, 1958, 72 Stat. 153; Pub.L. 95–625, Title III, § 311, Nov. 10, 1978, 92 Stat. 3478; Pub.L. 107–221, § 3(a), Aug. 21, 2002, 116 Stat. 1333, related to the size of land designations and improvements.

Section 450mm–2, Pub.L. 85–435, § 3, May 29, 1958, 72 Stat. 153; Pub.L. 107–221, § 3(b), Aug. 21, 2002, 116 Stat. 1334, related to acquisition of lands.

Section 450mm–3, Pub.L. 85–435, § 4, May 29, 1958, 72 Stat. 153; Pub.L. 107–221, § 3(c), Aug. 21, 2002, 116 Stat. 1334, related to the effective date and administration of Fort Clatsop National Memorial.

Short Title

2002 Acts. Pub.L. 107–221, § 1, Aug. 21, 2002, 116 Stat. 1333, provided that: "This Act [amending 16 U.S.C.A. §§ 450mm–1 to 450mm–3 and enacting provisions set out as a note under 16 U.S.C.A. § 450mm–1] may be cited as the 'Fort Clatsop National Memorial Expansion Act of 2002'."

Congressional Findings

Pub.L. 107–221, § 2, Aug. 21, 2002, 116 Stat. 1333, provided that:

"The Congress finds the following:

"**(1)** Fort Clatsop National Memorial is the only unit of the National Park System solely dedicated to the Lewis and Clark Expedition.

"**(2)** In 1805, the members of the Lewis and Clark Expedition built Fort Clatsop at the mouth of the Columbia River near Astoria, Oregon, and they spent 106 days at the fort waiting for the end of winter and preparing for their journey home.

"**(3)** In 1958, Congress enacted Public Law 85–435 [Pub.L. 85–435, May 29, 1958, 72 Stat. 153, enacting this section and 16 U.S.C.A. §§ 450mm, 450mm–2, and 450mm–3] authorizing the establishment of Fort Clatsop National Memorial for the purpose of commemorating the culmination, and the winter encampment, of the Lewis and Clark Expedition following its successful crossing of the North American continent.

"**(4)** The 1995 General Management Plan for Fort Clatsop National Memorial, prepared with input from the local community, recommends the expansion of the memorial to include the trail used by expedition members to access the Pacific Ocean from the fort and the shore and forest lands surrounding the fort and trail to protect their natural settings.

"**(5)** Expansion of Fort Clatsop National Memorial requires Federal legislation because the size of the memorial is currently limited by statute to 130 acres.

"**(6)** Congressional action to allow for the expansion of Fort Clatsop National Memorial to include the trail to the Pacific Ocean would be timely and appropriate before the start of the bicentennial celebration of the Lewis and Clark Expedition planned to take place during the years 2004 through 2006."

§ 450nn.   General Grant National Memorial; establishment

The Secretary of the Interior is authorized and directed to accept, as a gift to the United States, title to the real property known as Grant's Tomb at Riverside Drive and West One Hundred and Twenty-Second Street in New York, New York, and thereafter to administer and maintain such real property as the General Grant National Memorial.

(Pub.L. 85–659, Aug. 14, 1958, 72 Stat. 614.)

LIBRARY REFERENCES

American Digest System

Armed Services ☞54.
Woods and Forests ☞1, 8.
Key Number System Topic Nos. 34, 411.

§ 450oo.   Grand Portage National Monument;   establishment;
effective date

For the purpose of preserving an area containing unique historical
values, there is authorized to be established, in the manner hereinafter provided, the Grand Portage National Monument in the State of
Minnesota which, subject to valid existing rights, shall comprise the
following described lands:

NORTHWEST COMPANY AREA

Tract numbered 1 beginning at a point about 28 feet from the
water line of Lake Superior and on the east boundary of the southwest quarter of the southeast quarter of section 4, said point marked
by a brass plug numbered I; thence northerly along said boundary
line a distance of 273.70 feet to a point marked by a brass plug
numbered II; thence in a westerly direction parallel to the south one-
sixteenth line of section 4 a distance of 1,320 feet to the intersection
of said line with the north-south quarter line of section 4, said point
of intersection being in the bed of a stream and witnessed by an iron
pipe located 60 feet southerly from said point and on the north-south
quarter line, and on the west bank of said stream; thence southerly
along said north-south quarter line a distance of 120 feet to the point
of intersection of said north-south quarter line and the south one-
sixteenth line of section 4 marked by an iron pipe set in concrete;
thence westerly along said one-sixteenth line a distance of 120 feet to
a point in path marked by brass plug numbered IV; thence southerly
in a direction parallel to the north-south quarter line of section 4 a
distance of 660 feet to an iron bolt in road intersection; thence
westerly parallel to the south one-sixteenth line of section 4 a
distance of 1,200 feet to the point of intersection of said line with the
west one-sixteenth line of said section 4 and marked by a brass plug
numbered VI; thence southerly along said west one-sixteenth line a
distance of 1,760 feet to a point marked by a brass plug numbered
VII; thence easterly along a line parallel to the north section line of
section 9 a distance of 486.21 feet to a point marked by an inclined
iron pipe, said point being the point where the said iron pipe enters
the concrete; thence along the said line extended a distance of
approximately 39 feet to the water's edge; thence along the shore
line of Lake Superior to the point where said shore line intersects the
east one-sixteenth line of section 4 extended; thence northerly along
said one-sixteenth line to place of beginning, all being located in
sections 4 and 9, township 63 north, range 6 east, in Grand Portage
Indian Reservation, State of Minnesota.   Right-of-way for existing

Bureau of Indian Affairs roads within the above described parcel of land is excluded therefrom.

Tract numbered 2 beginning at the point on the west one-sixteenth line of section 9 marked by brass plug numbered VII referred to in the description of tract numbered 1 above, thence westerly along a line parallel to the north section line of section 9 a distance of 275 feet to a point marked by an iron pipe; thence northerly along a line parallel to the west one-sixteenth line of section 9 a distance of 443.63 feet to a point marked by an iron pipe; thence easterly along a line parallel to the north section line of section 9 to the point of intersection of west one-sixteenth line of section 9; thence southerly along said one-sixteenth line to point of beginning, all lying in section 9 of township 63 north, range 6 east, in the Grand Portage Indian Reservation, State of Minnesota.

FORT CHARLOTTE AREA

The northeast quarter, section 29, township 64 north, range 5 east, or such lands within this quarter section as the Secretary of the Interior shall determine to be necessary for the protection and interpretation of the site of Fort Charlotte.

GRAND PORTAGE TRAIL SECTION

A strip of land 100 feet wide centering along the old Portage Trail beginning at the point where the trail intersects the present road to Grand Portage School, and continuing to the proposed United States Highway 61 right-of-way relocation in the northeast quarter of the northwest quarter, section 4, township 63 north, range 6 east, a strip of land 600 feet wide centering along the old Portage Trail as delineated on original General Land Office survey maps, from the north side of the proposed right-of-way to lands described at the Fort Charlotte site.

Establishment of the foregoing areas as the Grand Portage National Monument shall be effective when title to that portion of the aforesaid lands and interests in lands which is held in trust by the United States of America for the Minnesota Chippewa Tribe and the Grand Portage Band of Chippewa Indians, Minnesota, has been relinquished in accordance with section 450oo-1 of this title to the Secretary of the Interior for administration as a part of the Grand Portage National Monument. Notice of the establishment of the monument as authorized and prescribed by sections 450oo to 450oo-10 of this title shall be published in the Federal Register.

(Pub.L. 85–910, § 1, Sept. 2, 1958, 72 Stat. 1751.)

HISTORICAL AND STATUTORY NOTES

Revision Notes and Legislative Reports
1958 Acts. Senate Report No. 2475,
see 1958 U.S. Code Cong. and Adm.
News, p. 5224.

LIBRARY REFERENCES

American Digest System
   Armed Services ☞54.
   Woods and Forests ☞1, 8.
   Key Number System Topic Nos. 34, 411.

§ 450*oo*–1.   Acceptance of donations of land; instruments of relinquishment; life assignments

The Secretary of the Interior is authorized to accept, as a donation, the relinquishment of all right, title, and interest of the Minnesota Chippewa Tribe and the Grand Portage Band of Chippewa Indians, Minnesota, in and to any of the lands described in section 450*oo* of this title which is now held in trust by the United States of America for the said tribe or band; the executive committee of the Minnesota Chippewa Tribe and the tribal council of the Grand Portage Band of Chippewa Indians, Minnesota, are authorized to execute such instruments of relinquishment in favor of the United States; and acceptance of the relinquishment by the Secretary shall operate as a transfer of custody, control and administration of such properties for administration and as a part of the Grand Portage National Monument: *Provided*, That upon the acceptance of any donated lands and interests therein the Secretary shall recognize, honor, and respect, in accordance with the terms thereof, any existing life assignments on such properties.

(Pub.L. 85–910, § 2, Sept. 2, 1958, 72 Stat. 1752.)

HISTORICAL AND STATUTORY NOTES

Revision Notes and Legislative Reports
1958 Acts. Senate Report No. 2475,
see 1958 U.S. Code Cong. and Adm.
News, p. 5224.

LIBRARY REFERENCES

American Digest System
   Armed Services ☞54.
   United States ☞55.
   Woods and Forests ☞2.
   Key Number System Topic Nos. 34, 393, 411.

§ 450*oo*–2.   Procurement of other lands within monument

The Secretary of the Interior is authorized to procure any and all other lands or interests therein within the monument, including, but not limited to, any and all nontrust lands therein owned in fee simple by the Grand Portage Band of Chippewa Indians, Minnesota, and the council of said band is authorized to sell and convey such nontrust lands to the United States of America.

(Pub.L. 85–910, § 3, Sept. 2, 1958, 72 Stat. 1752.)

HISTORICAL AND STATUTORY NOTES

Revision Notes and Legislative Reports
   1958 Acts. Senate Report No. 2475, see 1958 U.S. Code Cong. and Adm. News, p. 5224.

LIBRARY REFERENCES

American Digest System
   Armed Services ☞54.
   United States ☞55.
   Woods and Forests ☞2.
   Key Number System Topic Nos. 34, 393, 411.

§ 450oo–3.   Visitor accommodations and services

The Secretary of the Interior, under regulations prescribed by him, shall grant recognized members of the Minnesota Chippewa Tribe the preferential privilege to provide those visitor accommodations and services, including guide services, which he deems are necessary within the monument.

(Pub.L. 85–910, § 4, Sept. 2, 1958, 72 Stat. 1753.)

HISTORICAL AND STATUTORY NOTES

Revision Notes and Legislative Reports
   1958 Acts. Senate Report No. 2475, see 1958 U.S. Code Cong. and Adm. News, p. 5224.

LIBRARY REFERENCES

American Digest System
   Armed Services ☞28, 54.
   United States ☞57.
   Key Number System Topic Nos. 34, 393.

§ 450oo–4.   Employment preferences

The Secretary of the Interior shall, insofar as practicable, give first preference to employment of recognized members of the Minnesota Chippewa Tribe in the performance of any construction, maintenance, or any other service within the monument for which they are qualified.

(Pub.L. 85–910, § 5, Sept. 2, 1958, 72 Stat. 1753.)

HISTORICAL AND STATUTORY NOTES

Revision Notes and Legislative Reports
  1958 Acts. Senate Report No. 2475,
see 1958 U.S. Code Cong. and Adm.
News, p. 5224.

LIBRARY REFERENCES

American Digest System
  Armed Services ⊙⇒54.
  United States ⊙⇒36.
  Key Number System Topic Nos. 34, 393.

§ 450oo–5. Production and sale of handicraft objects; noninterference with trade or business outside monument

The Secretary of the Interior shall encourage recognized members
of the Minnesota Chippewa Tribe in the production and sale of
handicraft objects within the monument. The administration of the
Grand Portage National Monument shall not in any manner interfere
with the operation or existence of any trade or business of said tribe
outside the boundaries of the national monument.

(Pub.L. 85–910, § 6, Sept. 2, 1958, 72 Stat. 1753.)

HISTORICAL AND STATUTORY NOTES

Revision Notes and Legislative Reports
  1958 Acts. Senate Report No. 2475,
see 1958 U.S. Code Cong. and Adm.
News, p. 5224.

LIBRARY REFERENCES

American Digest System
  Armed Services ⊙⇒54.
  United States ⊙⇒57.
  Key Number System Topic Nos. 34, 393.

§ 450oo–6. Traversing privileges; regulations

Recognized members of the Minnesota Chippewa Tribe shall not be
denied the privilege of traversing the area included within the Grand
Portage National Monument for the purposes of logging their land,
fishing, or boating, or as a means of access to their homes, businesses, or other areas of use and they shall have the right to traverse
such area in pursuit of their traditional rights to hunt and trap
outside the monument: *Provided*, That, in order to preserve and
interpret the historic features and attractions within the monument,
the Secretary may prescribe reasonable regulations under which the
monument may be traversed.

(Pub.L. 85–910, § 7, Sept. 2, 1958, 72 Stat. 1753.)

HISTORICAL AND STATUTORY NOTES

Revision Notes and Legislative Reports
   1958 Acts. Senate Report No. 2475,
see 1958 U.S. Code Cong. and Adm.
News, p. 5224.

LIBRARY REFERENCES

American Digest System
   Armed Services ⊙54.
   Woods and Forests ⊙5.
   Key Number System Topic Nos. 34, 411.

§ 450oo–7. Docking facilities

The Secretary of the Interior, subject to the availability of appropriated funds, shall construct and maintain docking facilities at the Northwest Company area for use in connection with the monument. Such facilities shall be available for use by the Minnesota Chippewa Tribe and its recognized members, without charge to them, under regulations to be prescribed by the Secretary.

(Pub.L. 85–910, § 8, Sept. 2, 1958, 72 Stat. 1753.)

HISTORICAL AND STATUTORY NOTES

Revision Notes and Legislative Reports
   1958 Acts. Senate Report No. 2475,
see 1958 U.S. Code Cong. and Adm.
News, p. 5224.

LIBRARY REFERENCES

American Digest System
   Armed Services ⊙54.
   United States ⊙57.
   Key Number System Topic Nos. 34, 393.

§ 450oo–8. Advisory assistance for developments upon adjacent lands

To the extent that appropriated funds and personnel are available therefor, the Secretary of the Interior shall provide consultative or advisory assistance to the Minnesota Chippewa Tribe and the Grand Portage Band of Chippewa Indians, Minnesota, in the planning of facilities or developments upon the lands adjacent to the monument.

(Pub.L. 85–910, § 9, Sept. 2, 1958, 72 Stat. 1753.)

HISTORICAL AND STATUTORY NOTES

Revision Notes and Legislative Reports
   1958 Acts. Senate Report No. 2475,
see 1958 U.S. Code Cong. and Adm.
News, p. 5224.

LIBRARY REFERENCES

American Digest System
   Armed Services ☞54.
   United States ☞57.
   Key Number System Topic Nos. 34, 393.

§ 450*oo*–9. Administration, protection, and development

When establishment of the monument has been effected, pursuant to sections 450*oo* to 450*oo*–10 of this title, the Secretary of the Interior shall administer, protect, and develop the monument in accordance with the provisions of sections 1, 2, 3, and 4 of this title, as amended.

(Pub.L. 85–910, § 10, Sept. 2, 1958, 72 Stat. 1753.)

HISTORICAL AND STATUTORY NOTES

Revision Notes and Legislative Reports
   1958 Acts. Senate Report No. 2475, see 1958 U.S. Code Cong. and Adm. News, p. 5224.

LIBRARY REFERENCES

American Digest System
   Armed Services ☞54.
   Woods and Forests ☞5.
   Key Number System Topic Nos. 34, 411.

§ 450*oo*–10. Reversion upon abandonment

In the event the Grand Portage National Monument is abandoned at any time after its establishment, title to the lands relinquished by the Minnesota Chippewa Tribe and the Grand Portage Band of Chippewa Indians, Minnesota, pursuant to section 450*oo*–1 of this title shall thereupon automatically revert to the Minnesota Chippewa Tribe and the Grand Portage Band of Chippewa Indians, Minnesota, their successors or assigns. In such event, the title will be taken in a fee simple status unless the United States holds other lands in trust for the Minnesota Chippewa Tribe or the Grand Portage Band of Chippewa Indians, Minnesota, in which event the title shall revert to the United States in trust for the Minnesota Chippewa Tribe or the Grand Portage Band of Chippewa Indians, Minnesota.

(Pub.L. 85–910, § 11, Sept. 2, 1958, 72 Stat. 1753.)

HISTORICAL AND STATUTORY NOTES

Revision Notes and Legislative Reports
   1958 Acts. Senate Report No. 2475, see 1958 U.S.Code Cong. and Adm.News, p. 5224.

LIBRARY REFERENCES

American Digest System
  Armed Services ☞54.
  United States ☞3.
  Woods and Forests ☞2.
  Key Number System Topic Nos. 34, 393, 411.

§ 450pp. Roger Williams National Memorial; acquisition of site

The Secretary of the Interior may acquire by gift, purchase with appropriated or donated funds, transfer from any Federal agency, exchange, or otherwise, not to exceed five acres of land (together with any buildings or other improvements thereon) and interests in land at the site of the old town spring, traditionally called Roger Williams Spring, in Providence, Rhode Island, for the purpose of establishing thereon a national memorial to Roger Williams in commemoration of his outstanding contributions to the development of the principles of freedom in this country: *Provided,* That property owned by the city of Providence or the Providence Redevelopment Agency may be acquired only with the consent of such owner.

(Pub.L. 89–293, § 1, Oct. 22, 1965, 79 Stat. 1069.)

LIBRARY REFERENCES

American Digest System
  Armed Services ☞54.
  United States ☞55.
  Woods and Forests ☞1, 8.
  Key Number System Topic Nos. 34, 393, 411.

§ 450pp–1. Establishment; notice of establishment; administration

The property acquired pursuant to section 450pp of this title shall be established as the Roger Williams National Memorial and the Secretary of the Interior shall publish notice of such establishment in the Federal Register. Such national Memorial shall be administered by the Secretary subject to the provisions of sections 1, 2, 3, and 4 of this title, as amended and supplemented, and sections 461 to 467 of this title.

(Pub.L. 89–293, § 2, Oct. 22, 1965, 79 Stat. 1069.)

LIBRARY REFERENCES

American Digest System
  Armed Services ☞54.
  Woods and Forests ☞5, 8.
  Key Number System Topic Nos. 34, 411.

§ 450pp–2. Cooperation with city of Providence and local historical and preservation societies

(a) Maintenance, operation, and development

The Secretary is authorized to cooperate with the city of Providence, local historical and preservation societies, and interested persons in the maintenance and operation of the Roger Williams National Memorial, and he may seek the assistance of and consult with such city, societies, and persons from time to time with respect to matters concerning the development and operation of the memorial.

(b) Acceptance of gifts

The Secretary may accept on behalf of the people of the United States gifts of historic objects and records pertaining to Roger Williams for appropriate display or other use in keeping with the commemoration of the founding of the principles of freedom in the United States and of the historical events that took place in the city of Providence in connection therewith.

(Pub.L. 89–293, § 3, Oct. 22, 1965, 79 Stat. 1070.)

LIBRARY REFERENCES

American Digest System
   Armed Services ☞54.
   Woods and Forests ☞8.
   Key Number System Topic Nos. 34, 411.

§ 450pp–3. Authorization of appropriations

There are hereby authorized to be appropriated not more than $146,000 for the acquisition of lands and interests in land and not more than $1,862,000 for the development of the Roger Williams National Memorial, as provided in sections 450pp to 450pp–3 of this title.

(Pub.L. 89–293, § 4, Oct. 22, 1965, 79 Stat. 1070; Pub.L. 96–607, Title I, § 101, Dec. 28, 1980, 94 Stat. 3539.)

HISTORICAL AND STATUTORY NOTES

Amendments
   1980 Amendments. Pub.L. 96–607 substituted "$146,000 for the acquisition of lands and interests in land and not more than $1,862,000" for "$700,000 for the acquisition of lands and interests in land and".

§§ 450qq to 450qq-4.   Omitted

HISTORICAL AND STATUTORY NOTES

Codifications

Sections, Pub.L. 90–606, § 1 to 5, Oct. 18, 1968, 82 Stat. 1188, 1189, provided for the Biscayne National Monument. The Monument was abolished and its lands, waters, and interests incorporated within and made part of the Biscayne National Park and funds of and authorizations of funds for the Monument made available for the Park pursuant to Pub.L. 96–287, Title I, § 103(b), June 28, 1980, 94 Stat. 600, classified to section 410gg–2(b) of this title.

Section 450qq, Pub.L. 90–606, § 1, Oct. 18, 1968, 82 Stat. 1188, authorized establishment of the Monument, made drawings of the Monument area available for public inspection in the offices of the National Park Service, authorized revision of boundaries, prescribed limitation of ninety-six thousand three hundred acres, and prohibited outward revision of the Monument or obstruction of prospective seaport channels. See section 410gg of this title.

Section 450qq–1, Pub.L. 90–606, § 2, Oct. 18, 1968, 82 Stat. 1188, provided for acquisition of property, authorized maximum of eighty acres for a mainland headquarters site and forty acres for a Key Largo visitor contact site, and authorized exchange of Federal for non-Federal property, including cash equalization payments. See section 410gg–1 of this title.

Section 450qq–2, Pub.L. 90–606, § 3, Oct. 18, 1968, 82 Stat. 1189, required the donation and transfer of State lands as condition for establishment of the Monument and Federal acquisition of other lands, and authorized land options for the Secretary and acquisitions to be made after State transfers.

Section 450qq–3, Pub.L. 90–606, § 4, Oct. 18, 1968, 82 Stat. 1189, provided for administration of the Monument and recognition of fishing rights under Florida law as otherwise regulated by the Secretary. See section 410gg–2 of this title.

Section 450qq–4, Pub.L. 90–606, § 5, Oct. 18, 1968, 82 Stat. 1189; Pub.L. 93–477, Title I, § 101(1), Oct. 26, 1974, 88 Stat. 1445; Pub.L. 95–625, Title I, § 101(4), Nov. 10, 1978, 92 Stat. 3470, authorized appropriation of $28,350,000 and $6,565,000 for land acquisition and development. See section 410gg–5 of this title.

§ 450rr.   R.M.S. Titanic; international maritime memorial; findings and purposes

(a) Findings

The Congress finds that—

(1) the R.M.S. Titanic, the ocean liner which sank on her maiden voyage after striking an iceberg on April 14, 1912, should be designated as an international maritime memorial to the men, women, and children who perished aboard her;

(2) the recent discovery of the R.M.S. Titanic, lying more than twelve thousand feet beneath the ocean surface, demonstrates the practical applications of ocean science and engineering;

(3) the R.M.S. Titanic, well preserved in the cold, oxygen-poor waters of the deep North Atlantic Ocean, is of major national and international cultural and historical significance, and merits appropriate international protection; and

(4) the R.M.S. Titanic represents a special opportunity for deep ocean scientific research and exploration.

(b) Purposes

The Congress declares that the purposes of sections 450rr to 450rr–6 of this title are—

(1) to encourage international efforts to designate the R.M.S. Titanic as an international maritime memorial to those who lost their lives aboard her in 1912;

(2) to direct the United States to enter into negotiations with other interested nations to establish an international agreement which will provide for the designation of the R.M.S. Titanic as an international maritime memorial, and protect the scientific, cultural, and historical significance of the R.M.S. Titanic;

(3) to encourage, in those negotiations or in other fora, the development and implementation of international guidelines for conducting research on, exploration of, and if appropriate, salvage of the R.M.S. Titanic; and

(4) to express the sense of the United States Congress that, pending such international agreement or guidelines, no person should physically alter, disturb, or salvage the R.M.S. Titanic in any research or exploratory activities which are conducted.

(Pub.L. 99–513, § 2, Oct. 21, 1986, 100 Stat. 2082.)

HISTORICAL AND STATUTORY NOTES

Short Titles

1986 Acts. Section 1 of Pub.L. 99–513, provided that: "This Act [enacting sections 450rr to 450rr–6 of this title] may be cited as the 'R.M.S. Titanic Maritime Memorial Act of 1986'."

LIBRARY REFERENCES

American Digest System
    Armed Services ☞54.
    Salvage ☞1.
    Shipping ☞3.5.
    Woods and Forests ☞1, 8.
    Key Number System Topic Nos. 34, 344, 354, 411.

Notes of Decisions

Injunctions 1
Practice and procedure 4
Recognition of agreements 2
Status of salvage award movant 3

1. Injunctions

The R.M.S. Titanic Maritime Memorial Act of 1986 did not preclude district court from exercising jurisdiction over wreck of the Titanic with respect to salvor's efforts to enjoin third parties from visiting the wreck and interfering with its salvage operations. R.M.S. Titanic, Inc. v. Haver, C.A.4 (Va.) 1999, 171 F.3d 943, certiorari denied 120 S.Ct. 74, 528 U.S. 825, 145 L.Ed.2d 63. Salvage ☞ 45

2. Recognition of agreements

"Procès–Verbal," memorializing agreement between salvador of Titanic shipwreck and French official that salvador had title to recovered artifacts, would not be recognized as authoritative by American court determining whether to grant salvage award; official had not made fact findings required under French law prior to awarding title, and recognition of agreement would be contrary to United States public policy, as embodied in statute, that artifacts raised from Titanic wreck should not be dispersed for private economic gain. R.M.S. Titanic, Inc. v. Wrecked and Abandoned Vessel, E.D.Va. 2004, 323 F.Supp.2d 724, stay granted in part 327 F.Supp.2d 664, affirmed in part, vacated in part and remanded 435 F.3d 521. International Law ☞ 10.9

3. Status of salvage award movant

Salvor-in-possession of historic shipwreck was precluded from arguing, on motion for salvage award, that it was owner of already-recovered artifacts under law of finds; salvager could not simultaneously claim both salvor and finder status with regard to same wreck, and was in any event estopped from contradicting its prior disclaimers, made to obtain salvor-in-possession status, of any intent to acquire title to artifacts. R.M.S. Titanic, Inc. v. Wrecked and Abandoned

Vessel, E.D.Va.2004, 323 F.Supp.2d 724, stay granted in part 327 F.Supp.2d 664, affirmed in part, vacated in part and remanded 435 F.3d 521. Salvage ☞ 43

4. Practice and procedure

United States' signature of an international agreement designating wreck of the Titanic an international memorial did not warrant continuance of salvage award hearing, on ground that it might put salvor-in-possession's continuing rights in question, where salvage award hearing concerned only amount of reward salvor should receive for its efforts in recovering artifacts from the Titanic wreck before United States signed agreement, and agreement had no bearing on award to which salvor was entitled for its past efforts. R.M.S. Titanic, Inc. v. Wrecked and Abandoned Vessel, E.D.Va. 2004, 327 F.Supp.2d 664. Salvage ☞ 49

§ 450rr–1. Definitions

For the purposes of sections 450rr to 450rr–6 of this title, the term—

(a) "Administrator" means the Administrator of the National Oceanic and Atmospheric Administration (NOAA);

(b) "person" means any individual (whether or not a citizen or national of the United States), any corporation, partnership, association, or other entity (whether or not organized or existing under the laws of any State), and any Federal, State, local, or foreign government or any entity of any such government;

(c) "R.M.S. Titanic" means the shipwrecked vessel R.M.S. Titanic, her cargo or other contents, including those items which are scattered on the ocean floor in her vicinity; and

(d) "Secretary" means the Secretary of State.

(Pub.L. 99–513, § 3, Oct. 21, 1986, 100 Stat. 2082.)

LIBRARY REFERENCES

American Digest System
    Armed Services ☞54.
    Salvage ☞1.
    Shipping ☞3.5.
    Key Number System Topic Nos. 34, 344, 354.

§ 450rr–2. Commendation

The Congress of the United States highly commends the members of the joint international expedition which discovered the R.M.S. Titanic.

(Pub.L. 99–513, § 4, Oct. 21, 1986, 100 Stat. 2083.)

§ 450rr–3. International guidelines

(a) The Administrator is directed to enter into consultations with the United Kingdom, France, Canada, and other interested nations to develop international guidelines for research on, exploration of, and if appropriate, salvage of the R.M.S. Titanic, which—

(1) are consistent with its national and international scientific, cultural, and historical significance and the purposes of sections 450rr to 450rr–6 of this title; and

(2) promote the safety of individuals involved in such operations.

(b) In carrying out subsection (a) of this section, the Administrator shall consult with the Secretary and shall promote full participation by other interested Federal agencies, academic and research institutions, and members of the public.

(Pub.L. 99–513, § 5, Oct. 21, 1986, 100 Stat. 2083.)

§ 450rr–4. International agreement

(a) Negotiations

The Secretary is directed to enter into negotiations with the United Kingdom, France, Canada, and other interested nations to develop an international agreement which provides for—

(1) the designation of the R.M.S. Titanic as an international maritime memorial; and

(2) research on, exploration of, and if appropriate, salvage of the R.M.S. Titanic consistent with the international guidelines developed pursuant to section 450rr–3 of this title and the purposes of sections 450rr to 450rr–6 of this title.

(b) Consultation with Administrator

In carrying out the requirements of subsection (a) of this section, the Secretary shall consult with the Administrator, who shall provide research and technical assistance to the Secretary.

(c) Reports to Congressional committees on progress of negotiations and consultations

The Secretary and the Administrator shall report semiannually to the Committee on Merchant Marine and Fisheries and the Committee on Foreign Affairs in the House of Representatives and to the Committee on Foreign Relations and the Committee on Commerce, Science, and Transportation in the Senate on the progress of the negotiations and consultations.

(d) Notification of agreement and recommendations to Congressional committees

Upon adoption of an international agreement as described in subsection (a) of this section, the Secretary shall provide notification of the agreement and recommendations for legislation to implement the agreement to the Committee on Merchant Marine and Fisheries and the Committee on Foreign Affairs in the House of Representatives and to the Committee on Foreign Relations and the Committee on Commerce, Science, and Transportation in the Senate.

(Pub.L. 99–513, § 6, Oct. 21, 1986, 100 Stat. 2083.)

HISTORICAL AND STATUTORY NOTES

Change of Name

Committee on Foreign Affairs of House of Representatives treated as referring to Committee on International Relations of House of Representatives by section 1(a) of Pub.L. 104–14, set out as a note preceding 2 U.S.C.A. § 21. Committee on International Relations of House of Representatives changed to Committee on Foreign Affairs of House of Representatives by House Resolution No. 6, One Hundred Tenth Congress, Jan. 5, 2007.

Abolition of House Committee on Merchant Marine and Fisheries

Committee on Merchant Marine and Fisheries of House of Representatives abolished and its jurisdiction transferred by House Resolution No. 6, One Hundred Fourth Congress, Jan. 4, 1995. For treatment of references to Committee on Merchant Marine and Fisheries, see section 1(b)(3) of Pub.L. 104–14, set out as a note preceding 2 U.S.C.A. § 21.

LIBRARY REFERENCES

American Digest System

Armed Services ⊜54.
Salvage ⊜1.
Shipping ⊜3.5.
Key Number System Topic Nos. 34, 344, 354.

§ 450rr–5.   Sense of Congress regarding conduct of future activities

It is the sense of Congress that research and limited exploration activities concerning the R.M.S. Titanic should continue for the purpose of enhancing public knowledge of its scientific, cultural, and historical significance: *Provided*, That, pending adoption of the international agreement described in section 450rr–4(a) of this title, or implementation of the international guidelines described in section 450rr–3 of this title, no person should conduct any such research or exploration activity which would physically alter, disturb, or salvage the R.M.S. Titanic.

(Pub.L. 99–513, § 7, Oct. 21, 1986, 100 Stat. 2084.)

LIBRARY REFERENCES

American Digest System
    Armed Services ☞54.
    Salvage ☞1.
    Shipping ☞3.5.
    Key Number System Topic Nos. 34, 344, 354.

§ 450rr–6. Disclaimer of extraterritorial sovereignty

By enactment of sections 450rr to 450rr–6 of this title, the United States does not assert sovereignty, or sovereign or exclusive rights or jurisdiction over, or the ownership of, any marine areas or the R.M.S. Titanic.

(Pub.L. 99–513, § 8, Oct. 21, 1986, 100 Stat. 2084.)

LIBRARY REFERENCES

American Digest System
    United States ☞3.
    Key Number System Topic No. 393.

Notes of Decisions

Jurisdiction   1

1. Jurisdiction

The R.M.S. Titanic Maritime Memorial Act of 1986 did not strip the federal courts of jurisdiction over wreck of the Titanic for purposes of recognizing, consistent with the jus gentium, a particular company as the wreck's exclusive salvor. R.M.S. Titanic, Inc. v. Haver, C.A.4 (Va.) 1999, 171 F.3d 943, certiorari denied 120 S.Ct. 74, 528 U.S. 825, 145 L.Ed.2d 63. Salvage ☞ 45

§ 450ss. Findings and purposes

Congress finds that—

    (1) few events in the past quarter-century have rocked Americans' perception of themselves and their institutions, and brought together the people of our Nation with greater intensity than the April 19, 1995, bombing of the Alfred P. Murrah Federal Building in downtown Oklahoma City;

    (2) the resulting deaths of 168 people, some of whom were children, immediately touched thousands of family members whose lives will forever bear scars of having those precious to them taken away so brutally;

(3) suffering with such families are countless survivors, including children, who struggle not only with the suffering around them, but their own physical and emotional injuries and with shaping a life beyond April 19;

(4) such losses and struggles arc personal and, since they resulted from so public an attack, they are also shared with a community, a Nation, and the world;

(5) the story of the bombing does not stop with the attack itself or with the many losses it caused. The responses of Oklahoma's public servants and private citizens, and those from throughout the Nation, remain as a testament to the sense of unity, compassion, even heroism, that characterized the rescue and recovery following the bombing;

(6) during the days immediately following the Oklahoma City bombing, Americans and people from around the world of all races, political philosophies, religions and walks of life responded with unprecedented solidarity and selflessness; and

(7) given the national and international impact and reaction, the Federal character of the site of the bombing, and the significant percentage of the victims and survivors who were Federal employees, the Oklahoma City Memorial will be established, designed, managed and maintained to educate present and future generations, through a public/private partnership, to work together efficiently and respectfully in developing a National Memorial relating to all aspects of the April 19, 1995, bombing in Oklahoma City.

(Pub.L. 105–58, § 2, Oct. 9, 1997, 111 Stat. 1261.)

HISTORICAL AND STATUTORY NOTES

Revision Notes and Legislative Reports
  1997 Acts. Senate Report No. 105–71 and Statement by President, see 1997 U.S. Code Cong. and Adm. News, p. 1799.

Short Title
  2004   Amendments. Pub.L.108–199, Div. F, Title V, § 544(a), Jan. 23, 2004, 118 Stat. 347, provided that: "This section [amending 16 U.S.C.A. §§ 450ss–1, 450ss–2, 450ss–3, and 450ss–5, repealing 16 U.S.C.A. §§ 450ss–4, 450ss–6, and

450ss–7, and enacting this note and provisions set out as notes under 16 U.S.C.A. §§ 450ss–3 and 450ss–4] may be cited as the 'Oklahoma City National Memorial Act Amendments of 2003'."

  1997 Acts. Pub.L. 105–58, § 1, Oct. 9, 1997, 111 Stat. 1261, provided: "This Act [enacting this section and sections 450ss–1 to 450ss–7 of this title] may be cited as the 'Oklahoma City National Memorial Act of 1997'."

LIBRARY REFERENCES

American Digest System
  United States ⊕57.
  Key Number System Topic No. 393.

§ 450ss–1. Definitions

In sections 450ss to 450ss–7 of this title:

(1) Foundation

The term "Foundation" means the Oklahoma City National Memorial Foundation, a not-for-profit corporation that is—

(A) described in section 501(c)(3) of Title 26;

(B) exempt from taxation under section 501(a) of such title; and

(C) dedicated to the support of the Memorial.

(2) Memorial

The term "Memorial" means the Oklahoma City National Memorial designated under section 450ss–2(a) of this title.

(3) Secretary

The term "Secretary" means the Secretary of the Interior.

(4) Trust

The term "Trust" means the Oklahoma City National Memorial Trust.

(Pub.L. 105–58, § 3, Oct. 9, 1997, 111 Stat. 1262; Pub.L. 108–199, Div. F, Title V, § 544(b), Jan. 23, 2004, 118 Stat. 347.)

HISTORICAL AND STATUTORY NOTES

Revision Notes and Legislative Reports

1997 Acts. Senate Report No. 105–71 and Statement by President, see 1997 U.S. Code Cong. and Adm. News, p. 1799.

2004 Acts. House Conference Report No. 108–401, see 2004 U.S. Code Cong. and Adm. News, p. 3.

Statement by President, see 2004 U.S. Code Cong. and Adm. News, p. S3.

References in Text

"Sections 450ss to 450ss–7 of this title", referred to in text, was in the original "This Act", meaning Pub.L. 105–58, Oct. 9, 1997, 111 Stat. 1261, known as the Oklahoma City National Memorial Act of 1997, which is classified to sections 450ss to 450ss–7 of this title.

Amendments

2004 Amendments. Par. (1). Pub.L. 108–199, Div. F, § 544(b)(1), (2), redesignated former par. (1) as (2) and inserted a new par. (1).

Par. (2). Pub.L. 108–199, Div. F, § 544(b)(1), redesignated former par. (1) as (2). Former par. (2) redesignated (3).

Par. (3). Pub.L. 108–199, Div. F, § 544(b)(1), redesignated former par. (2) as (3). Former par. (3) redesignated (4).

Par. (4). Pub.L. 108–199, Div. F, § 544(b)(1), redesignated former par. (3) as (4).

Pub.L. 108–199, Div. F, § 544(b)(3), in former par. (3), now redesignated (4), struck out " designated under section 450ss–3(a) of this title" following "Memorial Trust".

§ 450ss–2. Oklahoma City National Memorial

(a) In order to preserve for the benefit and inspiration of the people of the United States and the world, as a National Memorial certain lands located in Oklahoma City, Oklahoma, there is established as an affiliate of the National Park System the Oklahoma City National Memorial.

(b) Administration of Memorial

The Foundation shall administer the Memorial in accordance with sections 450ss to 450ss–7 of this title and the general objectives of the "Memorial Mission Statement", adopted March 26, 1996, by the Foundation.

(c) The Memorial area shall be compriscd of the lands, facilities and structures generally depicted on the map entitled "Oklahoma City National Memorial", numbered OCNM 001, and dated May 1997. The map shall be on file and available for public inspection in the appropriate office of the Foundation.

(Pub.L. 105–58, § 4, Oct. 9, 1997, 111 Stat. 1262; Pub.L. 108–199, Div. F, Title V, § 544(c), Jan. 23, 2004, 118 Stat. 347.)

HISTORICAL AND STATUTORY NOTES

Revision Notes and Legislative Reports

1997 Acts. Senate Report No. 105–71 and Statement by President, see 1997 U.S. Code Cong. and Adm. News, p. 1799.

2004 Acts. House Conference Report No. 108–401, see 2004 U.S. Code Cong. and Adm. News, p. 3.

Statement by President, see 2004 U.S. Code Cong. and Adm. News, p. S3.

References in Text

"Sections 450ss to 450ss–7 of this title", referred to in subsec. (b), was in the original "this Act", meaning the Oklahoma City National Memorial Act of 1997, Pub.L. 105–58, Oct. 9, 1997, 111 Stat. 1261, as amended, which is classified to 16 U.S.C.A. §§ 450ss to 450ss–7.

Amendments

2004 Amendments. Subsec. (a). Pub.L. 108–199, Div. F, § 544(c)(1), in the first sentence, substituted "an affiliate of the National Park System" for "a unit of the National Park System", and struck out the second sentence, which read: "The Memorial shall be administered by the Trust in cooperation with the Secretary and in accordance with the provisions of sections 450ss to 450ss–7 of this title, sections 1, 2, 3, and 4 of this title, and sections 461 to 467 of this title."

Subsec. (b). Pub.L. 108–199, Div. F, § 544(c)(2), (3), redesignated former subsec. (b) as (c) and inserted a new subsec. (b).

Subsec. (c). Pub.L. 108–199, Div. F, § 544(c)(2), (4), redesignated former subsec. (b) as (c) and, as so redesignated, rewrote the text thereof, which formerly read: "The Memorial area shall be comprised of the lands, facilities and structures generally depicted on the map entitled 'Oklahoma City National Memorial', numbered OCNM 001, and dated May 1997 (hereafter referred to in sections 450ss to 450ss–7 of this title as the 'map'):

"**(1)** Such map shall be on file and available for public inspection in the appropriate offices of the National Park Service and the Trust.

"**(2)** After advising the Committee on Energy and Natural Resources of the Senate and the Committee on Resources of the House of Representatives, in writing, the Trust, as established by section 450ss–3 of this title, in consultation with the Secretary, may make minor revisions of the boundaries of the Memorial when necessary by publication of a revised drawing or other boundary description in the Federal Register."

§ 450ss–3. Transfer of Memorial property, rights, authorities, and duties

(a) Transfer of Memorial property

(1) In general

Not later than 90 days after January 23, 2004, the Trust shall transfer to the Foundation—

    (A) all assets of the Trust, including all real and personal property of the Memorial, any appurtenances, buildings, facilities, monuments, contents, artifacts, contracts and contract rights, accounts, deposits, intangibles, trademarks, trade names, copyrights, all other intellectual property, all other real and personal property of every kind and character comprising the Memorial, and any amounts appropriated for the Trust;

    (B) any property owned by the Trust that is adjacent or related to the Memorial; and

    (C) all property maintained for the Memorial, together with all rights, authorities, and duties relating to the ownership, administration, operation, and management of the Memorial.

(2) Subsequent gifts

Any artifact, memorial, or other personal property that is received by, or is intended by any person to be given to, the Trust after the date of transfer of property under paragraph (1) shall be the property of the Foundation.

(b) Assumption of Trust obligations

Any obligations of the Trust relating to the Memorial that have been approved by the Trust before the date on which the property is transferred under subsection (a) of this section shall become the responsibility of the Foundation on the date of the transfer.

(c) Dissolution of Trust

Not later than 30 days after the transfer under subsection (a) of this section is completed—

    (1) the Trust shall be dissolved; and

    (2) the Trust shall notify the Secretary of the date of dissolution.

(d) Authority to enter into agreements

The Secretary, acting through the National Park Service, is authorized to enter into 1 or more cooperative agreements with the Foundation for the National Park Service to provide interpretive services related to the Memorial and such other assistance as may be agreed upon between the Secretary and the Foundation. The costs of the services and other agreed assistance shall be paid by the Secretary.

(e) General Services Administration authority

The Administrator of General Services shall provide, on a non-reimbursable basis, services necessary for the facilitation of the transfer of the Memorial to the Foundation.

(f) Limitation

Nothing in sections 450ss to 450ss-7 of this title shall prohibit the use of State and local law enforcement for the purposes of security related to the Memorial.

(Pub.L. 105-58, § 5, Oct. 9, 1997, 111 Stat. 1262; Pub.L. 108-199, Div. F, Title V, § 544(d), Jan. 23, 2004, 118 Stat. 347.)

HISTORICAL AND STATUTORY NOTES

Revision Notes and Legislative Reports
1997 Acts. Senate Report No. 105-71 and Statement by President, see 1997 U.S. Code Cong. and Adm. News, p. 1799.

2004 Acts. House Conference Report No. 108-401, see 2004 U.S. Code Cong. and Adm. News, p. 3.

Statement by President, see 2004 U.S. Code Cong. and Adm. News, p. S3.

References in Text
"Sections 450ss to 450ss-7 of this title", referred to in subsec. (f), was in the original "this Act", meaning the Oklahoma City National Memorial Act of 1997, Pub.L. 105-58, Oct. 9, 1997, 111 Stat. 1261, as amended, which is classified to 16 U.S.C.A. §§ 450ss to 450ss-7.

Amendments
2004 Amendments. Pub.L. 108-199, Div. F, § 544(d), rewrote this section, which formerly read:

"§ 450ss-3. Oklahoma City National Memorial Trust

"(a) Establishment

"There is established a wholly owned Government corporation to be known as the Oklahoma City National Memorial Trust.

"(b) Board of Directors

"(1) In general

"The powers and management of the Trust shall be vested in a board of Directors (hereinafter referred to as the "Board") consisting of the following 9 members:

"(A) The Secretary or the Secretary's designee.

"(B) Eight individuals, appointed by the President, from a list of recommendations submitted by the Governor of the State of Oklahoma; and a list of recommendations submitted by the Mayor of Oklahoma City, Oklahoma; and a list of recommendations submitted by the United States Senators from Oklahoma; and a list of recommendations submitted by United States Representatives from Oklahoma. The President shall make the appointments referred to in this subparagraph within 90 days after October 9, 1997.

"(2) Terms

"Members of the Board appointed under paragraph (1)(B) shall each serve for a term of 4 years, except that of the members first appointed, 2 shall serve for a term of 3 years; and 2 shall serve a term of 2 years. Any vacancy in the Board shall be filled in the same manner in which the original appointment was made, and any member appointed to fill a vacancy shall serve for the remainder of that term for which his or her predecessor was appointed. No appointed member may serve more than 8 years in consecutive terms.

"(3) Quorum

"Five members of the Board shall constitute a quorum for the conduct of business by the Board.

"(4) Organization and compensation

"The Board shall organize itself in such a manner as it deems most appropriate to effectively carry out the authorized activities of the Trust. Board members shall serve without pay, but may be reimbursed for the actual and necessary travel and subsistence expenses incurred by them in the performance of the duties of the Trust.

"(5) Liability of Directors

"Members of the Board of Directors shall not be considered Federal employees by virtue of their membership on the Board, except for purposes of the Federal Tort Claims Act and the Ethics in Government Act, and the provisions of chapter 11 of Title 18, United States Code.

"(6) Meetings

"The Board shall meet at least three times per year in Oklahoma City, Oklahoma and at least two of those meetings shall be opened to the public. Upon a majority vote, the Board may close any other meetings to the public. The Board shall establish procedures for providing public information and opportunities for public comment regarding operations maintenance and management of the Memorial; as well as, policy, planning and design issues.

"(7) Staff

"(A) Non-National Park Service staff

"The Trust is authorized to appoint and fix the compensation and duties of an executive director and such other officers and employees as it deems necessary without regard to the provisions of Title 5, United States Code, governing appointments in the competitive service, and may pay them without regard to the provisions of chapter 51, and subchapter III of chapter 53, Title 5, United States Code, relating to classification and General Schedule pay rates.

"(B) Interim Park Service staff

"At the request of the Trust, the Secretary shall provide for a period not to exceed 2 years, such personnel and technical expertise, as necessary, to provide assistance in the implementation of the provisions of sections 450ss to 450ss–7 of this title.

"(C) Park Service staff

"At the request of the Trust, the Secretary shall provide such uniformed personnel, on a reimbursable basis, to carry out day-to-day visitor service programs.

"(D) Other Federal employees

"At the request of the Trust, the Director of any other Federal agency may provide such personnel, on a reimbursable basis, to carry out day-to-day visitor service programs.

"(8) Necessary powers

"The Trust shall have all necessary and proper powers for the exercise of the authorities vested in it.

"(9) Taxes

"The Trust and all properties administered by the Trust shall be exempt from all taxes and special assessments of every kind by the State of Oklahoma, and its political subdivisions including the county of Oklahoma and the city of Oklahoma City.

"(10) Government corporation

"**(A)** The Trust shall be treated as a wholly owned Government corporation subject to chapter 91 of Title 31, United States Code (commonly referred to as the Government Corporation Control Act). Financial statements of the Trust shall be audited annually in accordance with section 9105 of Title 31 of the United States Code.

"**(B)** At the end of each calendar year, the Trust shall submit to the Committee on Energy and Natural Resources of the United States Senate and the Committee on Resources of the House of Representatives a comprehensive and detailed report of its operations, activities, and accomplishments for the prior fiscal year. The report also shall include a section that describes in general terms the Trust's goals for the current fiscal year."

Authorization of Secretary to Reimburse Previous Costs Paid by Foundation or Trust

Pub.L.108–199, Div. F, Title V, § 544(g), Jan. 23, 2004, 118 Stat. 348, provided that: "To the extent that funds are made available for the Trust, the Secretary of the Interior shall reimburse the Oklahoma City National Memorial Foundation for funds obligated or expended by the Oklahoma City National Memorial Foundation or the Oklahoma City Nation-al Memorial Trust to the Secretary of the Interior for interpretive services, security, and other costs and services related to the Oklahoma City National Memorial before the date of the enactment of this Act [Jan. 23, 2004]. The Oklahoma City National Memorial Foundation may use such reimbursed funds for the operation, maintenance, and permanent endowment of the Oklahoma City National Memorial."

§ 450ss–4. Repealed. Pub.L. 108–199, Div. F, Title V, § 544(e)(1), Jan. 23, 2004, 118 Stat. 348

HISTORICAL AND STATUTORY NOTES

Section, Pub.L. 105–58, § 6, Oct. 9, 1997, 111 Stat. 1264, related to duties and authorities of the Oklahoma City National Memorial Trust.

Effective Date of Repeal

Pub.L. 108–199, Div. F, Title V, § 544(e)(2), Jan. 23, 2004, 118 Stat. 348, provided that: "The repeal under this subsection [repealing this section] shall take effect upon the transfer of the Memorial property, rights, authorities, and duties pursuant to the amendments made by subsection (d) [Pub.L. 108–199, Div. F, Title V, § 544(d), Jan. 23, 2004, 118 Stat. 347, amending 16 U.S.C.A. § 430ss–3]."

§ 450ss–5. Limitations on funding

Authorization of Appropriations:[1]

(1) In general

In furtherance of the purposes of sections 450ss to 450ss–7 of this title, there is hereby authorized the sum of $5,000,000 for an endowment fund subject to paragraph (2), to remain available until expended.

(2) Matching requirement

Amounts appropriated in any fiscal year to carry out the provisions of sections 450ss to 450ss–7 may only be expended on a matching basis in a ratio of at least one non-Federal dollar to every Federal dollar. For the purposes of this provision, each non-Federal dollar donated to the Foundation for the creation, maintenance, operation, or endowment of the Memorial shall satisfy the matching dollar requirement without regard to the fiscal year in which such donation is made.

(Pub.L. 105–58, § 7, Oct. 9, 1997, 111 Stat. 1266; Pub.L. 108–199, Div. F, Title V, § 544(f), Jan. 23, 2004, 118 Stat. 348.)

[1] So in original. "Appropriations" probably should not be capitalized.

HISTORICAL AND STATUTORY NOTES

Revision Notes and Legislative Reports
1997 Acts. Senate Report No. 105–71 and Statement by President, see 1997 U.S. Code Cong. and Adm. News, p. 1799.

2004 Acts. House Conference Report No. 108–401, see 2004 U.S. Code Cong. and Adm. News, p. 3.

Statement by President, see 2004 U.S. Code Cong. and Adm. News, p. S3.

References in Text
"Sections 450ss to 450ss–7 of this title", referred to in text, was in the original "this Act", meaning the Oklahoma City National Memorial Act of 1997, Pub.L. 105–58, Oct. 9, 1997, 111 Stat.

1261, as amended, which is classified to 16 U.S.C.A. §§ 450ss to 450ss–7.

Amendments
2004 Amendments. Par. (1). Pub.L. 108–199, Div. F, § 544(f)(1), inserted "for an endowment fund subject to paragraph (2)" following "sum of $5,000,000".

Par. (2). Pub.L. 108–199, Div. F, § 544(f)(2), in the second sentence, substituted "donated to the Foundation for the creation, maintenance, operation, or endowment of the Memorial" for "donated to the Trust or to the Oklahoma City Memorial Foundation for the creation, maintenance, or operation of the Memorial".

§ 450ss–6. Repealed. Pub.L. 108–199, Div. F, Title V, § 544(h), Jan. 23, 2004, 118 Stat. 349

HISTORICAL AND STATUTORY NOTES

Section, Pub.L. 105–58, § 8, Oct. 9, 1997, 111 Stat. 1266, related to disposal of the site of the Alfred P. Murrah Federal Building to the memorial.

§ 450ss–7. Repealed. Pub.L. 108–199, Div. F, Title V, § 544(i), Jan. 23, 2004, 118 Stat. 349

HISTORICAL AND STATUTORY NOTES

Section, Pub.L. 105–58, § 9, Oct. 9, 1997, 111 Stat. 1266, related to the General Accounting Office [now Government Accountability Office] study of activities of the Trust and report of results to Congress.

SUBCHAPTER LXII—MISCELLANEOUS

§ 451. Repealed. Pub.L. 104–333, Div. I, Title VIII, § 801, Nov. 12, 1996, 110 Stat. 4186

HISTORICAL AND STATUTORY NOTES

Section, Acts Aug. 24, 1912, c. 355, § 1, 37 Stat. 460; July 1, 1918, c. 113, § 1, 40 Stat. 677; Feb. 13, 1940, c. 30, 54 Stat. 36, related to a limit on the cost of buildings in national parks.

§ 451a. Limitation on further extension or establishment of national parks in Wyoming

No further extension or establishment of national parks in Wyoming may be undertaken except by express authorization of Congress.

(Sept. 14, 1950, c. 950, § 1, 64 Stat. 849.)

HISTORICAL AND STATUTORY NOTES

Revision Notes and Legislative Reports
1950 Acts. House Report No. 2910, see 1950 U.S.Code Cong.Service, p. 3746.

Codifications
Section comprises only part of the last sentence of section 1 of Act Sept. 14, 1950. The remainder of section, except that part of the last sentence which re-

pealed sections 406 to 406d of this title, is set out as sections 406d–1 and 431a of this title.

Repeal of Inconsistent Laws
Repeal of laws inconsistent with Act Sept. 14, 1950, see note under section 406d–1 of this title.

CROSS REFERENCES

Grand Teton National Park in Wyoming, see 16 USCA § 406d–1 et seq.
National monuments in Wyoming, limitation on further extension or establishment, see 16 USCA § 431a.

LIBRARY REFERENCES

American Digest System
United States ☞3.
Woods and Forests ☞1, 2.
Key Number System Topic Nos. 393, 411.

§ 452. Revenues of national parks covered into Treasury; estimates for care of parks

All revenues of the national parks shall be covered into the Treasury to the credit of miscellaneous receipts, except in case of Hot Springs National Park such as may be necessary to pay obligations outstanding on June 30, 1922.

(June 12, 1917, c. 27, § 1, 40 Stat. 153; May 24, 1922, c. 199, 42 Stat. 590; Sept. 12, 1950, c. 946, Title III, § 301(95), 64 Stat. 844.)

HISTORICAL AND STATUTORY NOTES

Revision Notes and Legislative Reports
1950 Acts. House Report No. 2556 and Conference Report No. 3002, see 1950 U.S. Code Cong. Service, p. 3707.

Codifications
The words referring to Hot Springs National Park are taken from a part of the Department of the Interior Appropriation Act, 1923, May 24, 1922. In the original the provisions read as follows: "From and after July 1, 1922, all revenues of the Hot Springs National Park shall be covered into the Treasury to the credit of miscellaneous receipts, except such as

may be necessary to pay obligations outstanding on June 30, 1922".

Amendments
1950 Amendments. Act Sept. 12, 1950 repealed requirement that the Secretary of the Interior submit, annually, estimates of the amounts required for the care, maintenance, and development of the national parks.

Repeals
Act Sept. 12, 1950, c. 946, Title III, § 301(95), 64 Stat. 844, set out in the credit of this section, was repealed by Pub.L. 97–258, § 5(b), Sept. 13, 1982, 96 Stat. 1077.

CROSS REFERENCES

Disposition of revenue arising from licenses for occupancy and use of National Parks and Monuments, see 16 USCA § 810.

LIBRARY REFERENCES

American Digest System
United States ☞57.
Key Number System Topic No. 393.

Notes of Decisions

Special funds 1

_____

1. Special funds

The Secretary is not authorized, in view of the provision contained in this section requiring all revenues of the national parks to be covered into the Treasury, to include a proposed "waiver" provision in contracts with concessioners, which would provide for withholding part of their annual fees in a special fund held for the United States "to provide improvements or rehabilitations, and to develop or acquire additional facilities or properties," and it is, therefore, unnecessary to consider the legality of the proposed provision under § 484 of Title 31 and § 303b of Title 40.   41 Op.Atty.Gen. 127 (Jan. 27, 1953), 1953 WL 2796.

§ 452a. Acquisition of non-Federal land within existing boundaries of any National Park; donations; authorization of appropriations

In order to consolidate Federal land ownership within the existing boundaries of any National Park and to encourage the donation of funds for that purpose, the Secretary of the Interior is authorized to accept and to use in his discretion funds which may be donated subject to the condition that such donated funds are to be expended for purposes of this section by the Secretary only if Federal funds in an amount equal to the amount of such donated funds are appropriated for the purposes of this section.   There are authorized to be appropriated such funds as may be necessary to match funds that may be donated for such purposes: _Provided_, That the amount which may be appropriated annually for purposes of this section shall be limited to $500,000.

(Aug. 31, 1954, c. 1163, 68 Stat. 1037.)

HISTORICAL AND STATUTORY NOTES

Revision Notes and Legislative Reports
1954 Acts. Senate Report No. 2224, see 1954 U.S. Code Cong. and Adm. News, p. 3658.

Cape Hatteras National Seashore Recreational Area
Authority of the Secretary under this section extended to authorize acquisition of non–Federal land within boundaries of Cape Hatteras National Seashore Recreational Area, see sections 459a–6 to 459a–8 of this title.

CROSS REFERENCES

Cape Hatteras National Seashore Recreational Area, see 16 USCA § 459a–6.
Uniform application of this section to all areas of national park system when not in conflict with specific provisions applicable to an area, see 16 USCA § 1c.

LIBRARY REFERENCES

American Digest System
United States ☞55.
Key Number System Topic No. 393.

§ 453. Donations of land for park purposes near or adjacent to National Forest Reserve in North Carolina

The Secretary of the Interior is authorized to accept for park purposes any lands and rights-of-way, including the Grandfather Mountain, near or adjacent to the Government national forest in western North Carolina.

(June 12, 1917, c. 27, § 1, 40 Stat. 152.)

HISTORICAL AND STATUTORY NOTES

Codifications
"Government national forest" was substituted for "Government forest reserve" on authority of Act Mar. 4, 1907, c. 2907, 34 Stat. 1269, which provided that forest reserves shall hereafter be known as national forests.

CROSS REFERENCES

Acceptance of donations of property and money for purposes of national park and monument system, see 16 USCA § 6.

LIBRARY REFERENCES

American Digest System
United States ☞55.
Key Number System Topic No. 393.

§ 454. Repealed. Pub.L. 89–554, § 8(a), Sept. 6, 1966, 80 Stat. 642, 650

HISTORICAL AND STATUTORY NOTES

Section, Acts Aug. 24, 1912, c. 355, § 8, 37 Stat. 487; June 6, 1939, c. 185, 53 Stat. 810, authorized the superintendent, the acting superintendent, custodian, and principal clerks of the various national parks and other government reservations to administer oaths to expense accounts.

§ 455. Study of battlefields for commemorative purposes

The Secretary of the Army is authorized to have made studies and investigations and, where necessary, surveys of all battlefields within the continental limits of the United States whereon troops of the United States or of the original thirteen colonies have been engaged against a common enemy, with a view to preparing a general plan and such detailed projects as may be required for properly commemorating such battlefields or other adjacent points of historic and military interest.

(June 11, 1926, c. 555, § 1, 44 Stat. 726.)

HISTORICAL AND STATUTORY NOTES

Change of Name

The Department of War was designated the Department of the Army and the title of the Secretary of War was changed to Secretary of the Army by section 205(a) of Act July 26, 1947, c. 343, Title II, 61 Stat. 501. Section 205(a) of Act July 26, 1947, was repealed by section 53 of Act Aug. 10, 1956, c. 1041, 70A Stat. 641. Section 1 of Act Aug. 10, 1956, enacted "Title 10, Armed Forces" which in sections 3011 to 3013 continued the military Department of the Army under the administrative supervision of a Secretary of the Army.

LIBRARY REFERENCES

American Digest System

Armed Services ☞54.
Key Number System Topic No. 34.

§ 455a.   Report to Congress

Annually after December 1, 1926, the Secretary of the Army shall submit through the President to Congress a detailed report of progress made under sections 455 to 455c of this title, together with his recommendations for further operations.

(June 11, 1926, c. 555, § 2, 44 Stat. 727.)

HISTORICAL AND STATUTORY NOTES

Change of Name

The Department of War was designated the Department of the Army and the title of the Secretary of War was changed to Secretary of the Army by section 205(a) of Act July 26, 1947, c. 343, Title II, 61 Stat. 501. Section 205(a) of Act July 26, 1947, was repealed by section 53 of Act Aug. 10, 1956, c. 1041, 70A Stat. 641. Section 1 of Act Aug. 10, 1956, enacted "Title 10, Armed Forces" which in sections 3011 to 3013 continued the military Department of the Army under the administrative supervision of a Secretary of the Army.

Transfer of Functions

Administrative functions of certain national military parks and national monuments were transferred to the Department of the Interior by Ex.Ord. No. 6166, section 2, June 10, 1933, as amended by Ex.Ord. No. 6228, section 1, July 28, 1933, set out as a note under section 901 of Title 5, Government Organization and Employees.

National Park Service was substituted for Office of National Parks, Buildings, and Reservations referred to in Ex.Ord. No. 6166, § 2, June 10, 1933, by Act Mar. 2, 1934, c. 38, § 1, 48 Stat. 389.

LIBRARY REFERENCES

American Digest System

Armed Services ☞54.
Key Number System Topic No. 34.

§ 455b.   Inclusion of estimate of cost of projected surveys in appropriation estimates

The Secretary of the Army shall include annually in his Department of the Army appropriation estimates a list of the battlefields for which surveys or other field investigations are planned for the fiscal year in question, together with the estimated cost of making each survey or other field investigation.

(June 11, 1926, c. 555, § 3, 44 Stat. 727.)

HISTORICAL AND STATUTORY NOTES

Change of Name

The Department of War was designated the Department of the Army and the title of the Secretary of War was changed to Secretary of the Army by section 205(a) of Act July 26, 1947, c. 343, Title II, 61 Stat. 501. Section 205(a) of Act July 26, 1947, was repealed by section 53 of Act Aug. 10, 1956, c. 1041, 70A Stat. 641. Section 1 of Act Aug. 10, 1956, enacted "Title 10, Armed Forces" which in sections 3011 to 3013 continued the military Department of the Army under the administrative supervision of a Secretary of the Army.

Transfer of Functions

Administrative functions of certain national military parks and national monuments were transferred to the Department of the Interior by Ex.Ord. No. 6166, § 2, June 10, 1933, as amended by Ex. Ord. No. 6228, § 1, July 28, 1933, set out as a note under section 901 of Title 5, Government Organization and Employees.

National Park Service was substituted for Office of National Parks, Buildings, and Reservations referred to in Ex.Ord. No. 6166, § 2, June 10, 1933, by Act Mar. 2, 1934, c. 38, § 1, 48 Stat. 389.

LIBRARY REFERENCES

American Digest System

Armed Services ⊕54.
United States ⊕3.
Key Number System Topic Nos. 34, 393.

§ 455c. Purchase of real estate for military park

No real estate shall be purchased for military park purposes by the Government unless report thereon shall have been made by the Secretary of the Army through the President to Congress under the provisions of section 455a of this title.

(June 11, 1926, c. 555, § 4, 44 Stat. 727.)

HISTORICAL AND STATUTORY NOTES

Change of Name

The Department of War was designated the Department of the Army and the title of the Secretary of War was changed to Secretary of the Army by section 205(a) of Act July 26, 1947, c. 343, Title II, 61 Stat. 501. Section 205(a) of Act July 26, 1947, was repealed by section 53 of Act Aug. 10, 1956, c. 1041, 70A Stat. 641. Section 1 of Act Aug. 10, 1956, enacted "Title 10, Armed Forces" which in sections 3011 to 3013 continued the military Department of the Army under the administrative supervision of a Secretary of the Army.

Transfer of Functions

Administrative functions of certain national military parks and national monuments were transferred to the Department of the Interior by Ex.Ord. No. 6166, § 2, June 10, 1933, as amended by Ex. Ord. No. 6228, § 1, July 28, 1933, set out as a note under section 901 of Title 5, Government Organization and Employees.

National Park Service was substituted for Office of National Parks, Buildings, and Reservations referred to in Ex.Ord. No. 6166, § 2, June 10, 1933, by Act Mar. 2, 1934, c. 38, § 1, 48 Stat. 389.

Secretary of the Air Force

For transfer of certain functions relating to real property under the jurisdiction of the Department of the Air Force from the Secretary of the Army to the Secretary of the Air Force, see Secretary of Defense Transfer Order No. 14 [§ 2(4)], eff. July 1, 1948.

LIBRARY REFERENCES

American Digest System
Armed Services ☞54.
United States ☞55.
Woods and Forests ☞2.
Key Number System Topic Nos. 34, 393, 411.

§ 456. Expense of depositing money payable from appropriations

Appropriations made for the administration, protection and maintenance of the national parks and national monuments under the jurisdiction of the Secretary of the Interior shall be available for expense of depositing public money.

(May 10, 1926, c. 277, § 1, 44 Stat. 491.)

§ 456a. Collections and pay-roll deductions for meals and quarters

Cash collections and pay-roll deductions made for meals and quarters furnished by the National Park Service to employees of the Government in the field and to cooperating agencies may be credited as a reimbursement to the current appropriation for the administration of the park or monument in which the accommodations are furnished.

(May 9, 1935, c. 101, § 1, 49 Stat. 209.)

HISTORICAL AND STATUTORY NOTES

Codifications
Section is also set out as section 14b of this title.

Transfer of Functions
All functions of all other officers of the Department of the Interior and all functions of all agencies and employees of such Department were, with two exceptions, transferred to the Secretary of the Interior, with power vested in him to authorize their performance or the performance of any of his functions by any of such officers, agencies, and employees, by 1950 Reorg. Plan No. 3, §§ 1, 2, eff. May 24, 1950, 15 F.R. 3174, 64 Stat. 1262, set out in Appendix 1 to Title 5, Government Organization and Employees.

LIBRARY REFERENCES

American Digest System
United States ☞39(9).
Key Number System Topic No. 393.

§ 457. Action for death or personal injury within national park or other place under jurisdiction of United States; application of State laws

In the case of the death of any person by the neglect or wrongful act of another within a national park or other place subject to the exclusive jurisdiction of the United States, within the exterior boundaries of any State, such right of action shall exist as though the place were under the jurisdiction of the State within whose exterior boundaries such place may be; and in any action brought to recover on account of injuries sustained in any such place the rights of the parties shall be governed by the laws of the State within the exterior boundaries of which it may be.

(Feb. 1, 1928, c. 15, 45 Stat. 54.)

LIBRARY REFERENCES

American Digest System
>Federal Courts ☞428.
>United States ☞3, 127(1).
>Key Number System Topic Nos. 170B, 393.

Research References

ALR Library
>38 ALR 3rd 1247, Right of Member of Armed Forces to Recover from Manufacturer or Seller for Injury Caused by Defective Military Material, Equipment, Supplies, or Components Thereof.
>76 ALR 2nd 130, What Law Governs Liability of Manufacturer or Seller for Injury Caused by Product Sold.
>75 ALR 2nd 39, Privity of Contract as Essential to Recovery in Action Based on Theory Other Than Negligence, Against Manufacturer or Seller of Product Alleged to Have Caused Injury.
>73 ALR 2nd 1351, Place or Type of Motor Vehicle Accident as Affecting Applicability of Statute Providing for Constructive or Substituted Service Upon Nonresident Motorist.
>71 ALR 2nd 1296, Comment Note.--Action for Death Caused by Maritime Tort Within a State's Territorial Waters.
>14 ALR 2nd 992, What Actions Arise Under the Laws and Treaties of the United States So as to Vest Jurisdiction of Federal Courts.
>153 ALR 1050, Application of State Workmen's Compensation Act to Injury Occurring on Federal Property Within State or in Connection with Contracts in Relation to Such Property.
>143 ALR 1144, Conduct of Operator of Automobile at Railroad Crossing as Gross Negligence, Recklessness, Etc., Within Guest Statute.
>90 ALR 119, Extraterritorial Operation of Workmen's Compensation Statutes; Conflict of Laws.
>80 ALR 469, Applicability of Regulations or Rules Governing Vehicular Traffic to Driveways or Other Places Not Legal Highways.

Encyclopedias
>Am. Jur. 2d Death § 7, Statutes Applicable Where Wrong Is Committed in Place under Federal Jurisdiction.

Treatises and Practice Aids
>Federal Procedure, Lawyers Edition § 16:307, Choice of Law.
>Federal Procedure, Lawyers Edition § 66:483, Wrongful Death or Personal Injury Actions.
>Federal Procedure, Lawyers Edition § 66:484, Wrongful Death or Personal Injury Actions--What Law Applies.

Notes of Decisions

Generally 1	Construction 2
Admiralty 7	

1. Generally

This section envisions application of current substantive law of surrounding state in actions for death or personal injury occurring within federal enclave. Vasina v. Grumman Corp., C.A.2 (N.Y.) 1981, 644 F.2d 112.

2. Construction

Legislative establishment of policy which permits recovery for wrongful death is part of the law, to be given its appropriate weight not only in matters of statutory construction but also in those of decisional law. Moragne v. States Marine Lines, Inc., U.S.Fla.1970, 90 S.Ct. 1772, 398 U.S. 375, 26 L.Ed.2d 339, on remand 446 F.2d 906.   Death ☜ 11

In view of legislative history relative to this section governing wrongful death within a federal enclave, this section should be construed narrowly so as to provide no reference to state law, as a matter of federal law, for deciding issues of liability, nor to contain any implication as to applicable choice of law rules. Quadrini v. Sikorsky Aircraft Division, United Aircraft Corp., D.C.Conn.1977, 425 F.Supp. 81, on reconsideration 505 F.Supp. 1049.   United States ☜ 3

3. Construction with other laws

In suit brought under Federal Tort Claims Act section 1346(b) and 2401 of Title 28, arising from an accidental electrocution, this section providing that governing law in a suit to recover for the death of a person by the neglect or wrongful act of another within a federal enclave is that of the state within which the federal enclave is located as that state's law existed when the state ceded the property to the federal government was not applicable.   Morgan v. U.S., C.A.9 (Wash.) 1983, 709 F.2d 580.   United States ☜ 3;   United States ☜ 78(14)

Since Virginia, in ceding land to the United States which became the blue ridge parkway, retained "jurisdiction in all civil matters," federal question jurisdiction, relative to a fatal collision that occurred on the blue ridge parkway, did not exist either under section 1331 of Title 28 or under provision of this section that, on a federal reservation in which exclusive jurisdiction has been obtained by the United States, a state's civil statute becomes a law of the United States. Pratt v. Kelly, C.A.4 (Va.) 1978, 585 F.2d 692.   Federal Courts ☜ 193

4. Purpose

In view of legislative history relative to this section governing wrongful death within a federal enclave, provision that the "rights of the parties shall be governed by the laws of the State within the exterior boundaries of which it may be" was designated solely to make the survival statute of the jurisdiction surrounding the federal enclave applicable, for purpose of determining which parties may bring action, but was not intended to require application of the whole law or the substantive law of the place of injury in determining issues of liability.   Quadrini v. Sikorsky Aircraft Division, United Aircraft Corp., D.C.Conn.1977, 425 F.Supp. 81, on reconsideration 505 F.Supp. 1049.   United States ☜ 3

5. Law governing

The production of munitions for the Army was uniquely a federal interest, and therefore the National Parks Act would not allow munitions plant employees who suffered work-related hearing loss to assert a breach of plant operators' duty based on any state standard or regulation that was inconsistent with the operation of a federal munitions plant; legislative and executive branches were to determine what was and what was not consistent with the operation of the plant. Adams v. Alliant Techsystems Inc., W.D.Va.2002, 218 F.Supp.2d 792.   States ☜ 18.89;   War And National Emergency ☜ 1112

If federal jurisdiction over wrongful death action were grounded solely on diversity of citizenship, state law would apply and conflicts rule of the forum state would determine which state's substantive law would apply; however, where wrongful death claims also arose under this section, determination as to applicable substantive law required inquiry to determine what this section said or implied as to substantive law. Quadrini v. Sikorsky Aircraft Division, United Aircraft Corp., D.C.Conn.1977, 425 F.Supp. 81, on reconsideration 505 F.Supp. 1049. Federal Courts ☞ 409.1; Federal Courts ☞ 428

Law of state in which national park was situated would be applied in determining negligence, contributory negligence and assumption of risk in action against United States arising out of injury to park visitor by wild animal. Ashley v. U.S., D.C.Neb.1963, 215 F.Supp. 39, affirmed 326 F.2d 499. United States ☞ 78(14)

6. Federal common law

Virginia's personal injury law did not conflict with federal interest, as required for federal common law to displace state law in action brought by former munitions plant employees against plant operators, and thus operators were not entitled to sovereign immunity; although production of munitions was uniquely federal interest, operators did not demonstrate that duty of care owed to their employees conflicted with or burdened their federal regulatory or contractual obligations. Adams v. Alliant Techsystems, Inc., W.D.Va.2002, 201 F.Supp.2d 700, reconsideration denied 218 F.Supp.2d 792. Federal Courts ☞ 428; United States ☞ 125(24)

In absence of reason to believe that Congress intended, by enacting this section governing wrongful death within a federal enclave, to authorize federal court to fashion body of federal common law to govern substantive liability of parties and in view of fact that there is little, if any, federal interest to be served by providing national uniform rules of decision for suits arising out of wrongful deaths on federal enclaves, federal courts were not authorized to develop body of substantive common law to govern cases arising under this section. Quadrini v. Sikorsky Aircraft Division, United Aircraft Corp., D.C.Conn.1977, 425 F.Supp. 81, on reconsideration 505 F.Supp. 1049. United States ☞ 3

7. Admiralty

Congressional decision to place under state laws such areas as national parks, which are carved from existing state territories and are subject to no other general body of law, carries no implication of similar intent in vastly different realm of the admiralty. Moragne v. States Marine Lines, Inc., U.S.Fla.1970, 90 S.Ct. 1772, 398 U.S. 375, 26 L.Ed.2d 339, on remand 446 F.2d 906. Statutes ☞ 223.1

8. Laws of state within section

After effective date of state's cession to United States of land within Puget Sound Navy Yard, federal government's jurisdiction was exclusive, and laws subsequently enacted by state were ineffective in the navy yard, but Congress could, for such territory, adopt such later state legislation. Murray v. Joe Gerrick & Co., U.S.Wash.1934, 54 S.Ct. 432, 291 U.S. 315, 78 L.Ed. 821. United States ☞ 3

State law in effect at time of injury governs in suits brought under federal statute providing cause of action for wrongful death occurring on federal property, and not the state law in effect at time federal government acquired the relevant property. Ferebee v. Chevron Chemical Co., C.A.D.C.1984, 736 F.2d 1529, 237 U.S.App.D.C. 164, certiorari denied 105 S.Ct. 545, 469 U.S. 1062, 83 L.Ed.2d 432. United States ☞ 78(14)

Any duty or responsibility allocated to operators of federal munitions plant which was located on federal enclave, in facility use contract between government and plant operators, conclusively established that the duty or responsibility was consistent with the operation of the plant and, therefore, a suitable standard under the National Parks Act for determining plant operators' liability for negligence with respect to personal injuries sustained by plant employees; National Parks Act permitted application of state personal injury law to federal enclave only when not inconsistent with federal regulation or, in this case, operation of federal munitions plant, and duties set forth in contract signed by federal government could not be considered inconsistent with operation of plant. Adams v. Alliant Techsystems Inc., W.D.Va.2002, 218 F.Supp.2d 792. United States ☞ 3

Federal statute, which provides that state law shall apply to suit for death or injury of person within national park or other place within exclusive jurisdiction of United States, incorporated current Kansas law governing personal injury actions, and permitted driver, who was injured in federal military reservation in car accident, to incorporate failure to warn, products liability, and other theories that were not recognized in Kansas in 1872 when reservation was ceded to United States. Voelkel v. General Motors Corp., D.Kan.1994, 846 F.Supp. 1468, on reconsideration 846 F.Supp. 1482, affirmed 43 F.3d 1484. Federal Courts ⬤ 428

Federal Reservations Act required application of whole law, rather than just internal law, of state adjacent to federal enclave in which wrongful death allegedly occurred; thus, Louisiana choice of law rules applied in action against aircraft manufacturer by widow of Air Force sergeant who died in plane crash on Louisiana air base. Burgio v. McDonnell Douglas, Inc., E.D.N.Y.1990, 747 F.Supp. 865. United States ⬤ 78(14)

Where law which governed tort claims, in wrongful death action, was the tort law of North Carolina as it existed on Apr. 3, 1941, and where North Carolina did not recognize a cause of action in strict tort liability in 1941, plaintiffs failed to state a cause of action in strict tort liability against manufacturer of military helicopter which crashed within federal enclave in North Carolina, killing two marine corps officers. Quadrini v. Sikorsky Aircraft Division, United Aircraft Corp., D.C.Conn.1977, 425 F.Supp. 81, on reconsideration 505 F.Supp. 1049. Products Liability ⬤ 200; Products Liability ⬤ 113

In this section providing that right of action for death or personal injury within national park or other place subject to exclusive jurisdiction of United States, within exterior boundaries of state, shall exist as though the place were under the jurisdiction of such state and that "the rights of the parties shall be governed by the laws of the state", the quoted words relate to the substantive rights and not to the venue provisions. Reed v. Charizio, E.D.Va.1960, 183 F.Supp. 52. Federal Courts ⬤ 75

This section providing that rights of parties to action for wrongful death occurring in place subject to jurisdiction of United States shall be governed by "laws" of state within whose boundaries

such place is located uses quoted word as meaning existing law as declared from time to time by the state. Capetola v. Barclay-White Co., E.D.Pa.1943, 48 F.Supp. 797, affirmed 139 F.2d 556, certiorari denied 64 S.Ct. 939, 321 U.S. 799, 88 L.Ed. 1087. United States ⬤ 3

A recovery of damages for death occurring during the erection of a federal post office as result of a failure to plank over steel beams as required by former § 241, subd. 4, of McKinney's N.Y. Labor Law, which had been enacted prior to acquisition of the property by the federal government was authorized in absence of congressional action displacing the statute, since the common law and statutes in effect before the act of cession remained in force until displaced by Congress. Sadrakula v. James Stewart & Co., N.Y.A.D. 2 Dept.1938, 5 N.Y.S.2d 260, 254 A.D. 892, appeal denied 7 N.Y.S.2d 223, 255 A.D. 784, appeal denied 17 N.E.2d 684, 279 N.Y. 813, appeal denied 18 N.E.2d 314, 279 N.Y. 686, affirmed 20 N.E.2d 1015, 280 N.Y. 651, motion granted 21 N.E.2d 217, 280 N.Y. 730, affirmed 60 S.Ct. 431, 309 U.S. 94, 84 L.Ed. 596. United States ⬤ 3

9. Place of death or injury

Location of munitions plant on federal enclave would not shield plant operators from substantive tort claims of former plant employees, since state laws were adopted on such enclaves on continuing basis for wrongful death and personal injury actions. Adams v. Alliant Techsystems, Inc., W.D.Va.2002, 201 F.Supp.2d 700, reconsideration denied 218 F.Supp.2d 792. United States ⬤ 3

Statute providing for action in the case of death of a person within a national park or other place subject to exclusive jurisdiction of the United States did not apply to claims for death of servicemen in crash in Newfoundland while on route to Fort Campbell, Kentucky. In re Air Crash Disaster at Gander, Newfoundland on Dec. 12, 1985, W.D.Ky.1987, 660 F.Supp. 1202. United States ⬤ 3

10. Place within exterior boundaries of state

District of Columbia is not "within the exterior boundaries of any state" under this section. Watson v. Manhattan and Bronx Surface Transit Operating Authority, D.C.N.J.1980, 487 F.Supp. 1273. Death ⬤ 9

In action for injuries allegedly sustained by plaintiff, a Pennsylvania resident, as result of negligence of defendant, a Connecticut resident, in operation of defendant's automobile in which plaintiff was a passenger, on the Colonial National Parkway, which was owned and maintained by United States and which was located entirely in Virginia, the federal district court in Virginia had jurisdiction inasmuch as cause of action arose on a government reservation located entirely within Virginia, and moreover this section appeared to confer a right of action inasmuch as the parkway was situated within a national park; however, venue had not been acquired or waived even though service on defendant had been obtained pursuant to the Virginia nonresident motorist statute. Reed v. Charizio, E.D.Va.1960, 183 F.Supp. 52. Federal Courts ☞ 74; Federal Courts ☞ 95; Federal Courts ☞ 193

Under this section action brought to recover for injuries sustained in automobile collision occurring within confines of army air base, located in Ohio was governed by law of Ohio. Kitchens v. Duffield, Ohio App. 2 Dist.1947, 76 N.E.2d 101, 83 Ohio App. 41, 50 Ohio Law Abs. 161, 38 O.O. 142, affirmed 79 N.E.2d 906, 149 Ohio St. 500, 37 O.O. 200. Automobiles ☞ 229.5

In action by occupants against motorist for injuries sustained in accident in Yosemite National Park, the California guest law, West's Vehicle Code § 403, was operative in view of this section which provides that action for injuries sustained in national park shall be governed by laws of state wherein park is located. Whitmore v. French, Cal.1951, 235 P.2d 3, 37 Cal.2d 744. Automobiles ☞ 229.5

11. Federal prisoners

Law applicable to liability for injuries sustained by inmate in federal prison is law of state in which prison is located. Muniz v. U.S., S.D.N.Y.1968, 280 F.Supp. 542. United States ☞ 78(14)

12. Injuries

For purposes of statute providing that, in actions brought to recover for injuries sustained in a federal enclave, the rights of the parties shall be governed by the laws of the state within the exterior boundaries of which it may be, the term "injuries" refers only to physical injuries; in enacting statute, Congress meant to

provide relief for death or personal, i.e., physical, injuries caused by the neglect or wrongful act of another in a federal enclave. Kelly v. Lockheed Martin Services Group, D.Puerto Rico 1998, 25 F.Supp.2d 1. United States ☞ 3

13. Negligence

Failure of government to include in its pamphlet on bears in park an admonition to close automobile windows, which admonition was included in pamphlet issued after accident to plaintiff, an adult who was bitten by bear through open automobile window, was not negligence causing injury in view of fact that warning should have been unnecessary to person of plaintiff's age and maturity, and in view of fact that no one saw bear approach automobile before injury. Ashley v. U.S., D.C.Neb.1963, 215 F.Supp. 39, affirmed 326 F.2d 499. Animals ☞ 66.9

14. Malpractice

Georgia law was applied in shrimp boat captain's action under Federal Tort Claims Act, §§ 1346(b) and 2671 et seq. of Title 28, against United States based upon alleged malpractice of a doctor of the out-patient clinic of the United States Public Health Service Hospital in Savannah, Georgia. Watson v. U.S., C.A.5 (Fla.) 1965, 348 F.2d 913, certiorari denied 86 S.Ct. 544, 382 U.S. 976, 15 L.Ed.2d 467. United States ☞ 78(14)

15. Workers compensation

State workers' compensation claims are not personal injury claims, for purpose of statute conferring federal question jurisdiction upon personal injury claims arising on federal enclave. Adams v. Alliant Techsystems, Inc., W.D.Va. 2002, 201 F.Supp.2d 700, reconsideration denied 218 F.Supp.2d 792. Federal Courts ☞ 192

Employee of Pennsylvania contractor could not maintain action at common law for injuries sustained while temporarily engaged in construction work at Philadelphia Navy Yard, since Pennsylvania Workmen's Compensation Act, 77 P.S. §§ 1 et seq., provided exclusive remedy therefor. Capetola v. Barclay-White Co., E.D.Pa.1943, 48 F.Supp. 797, affirmed 139 F.2d 556, certiorari denied 64 S.Ct. 939, 321 U.S. 799, 88 L.Ed. 1087. Workers' Compensation ☞ 2084

Where employee entered employment within state, received instructions, supplies, and pay from employer's principal place of business within state, death of employee from injuries received in national park in another state while employee was engaged in transitory employment was compensable under state compensation law, as against contention that federal acts relating to injuries received in national park furnished sole remedy. Alexander v. Movietonews, N.Y.1937, 7 N.E.2d 712, 273 N.Y. 599. Workers' Compensation ⚖ 93

This section did not extend the California Compensation Act to the Yerba Buena Island, exclusive jurisdiction over which the state had ceded to the federal government, and hence insurance carrier against whom an award had been made under the Compensation Act for injuries sustained by a claimant on that island was not entitled to subrogation in compensation claimant's action against third persons whose negligence caused the claimant's injuries. Martin, Continental Cas. Co., Intervener, v. Clinton Const. Co., Cal.App. 1 Dist.1940, 105 P.2d 1029, 41 Cal.App.2d 35, rehearing denied 106 P.2d 629, 41 Cal.App.2d 35. United States ⚖ 3

Injury occurring within United States military reservation within state was not compensable under State Workmen's Compensation Act, where exclusive jurisdiction over reservation was ceded to United States, notwithstanding this section, which referred only to actions at law. Utley v. State Industrial Commission, Okla.1936, 55 P.2d 762, 176 Okla. 255. See, also, Utley v. State Industrial Commission, 1936, 55 P.2d 764, 176 Okl. 257.

16. Wrongful death

Under Hawaii choice-of-law principles, Hawaii law applied to wrongful death action brought against manufacturer of atomic simulator by parents of soldier who died after being injured when the simulator allegedly exploded a second time during demolition training on federal land on island of Hawaii. Jenkins v. Whittaker Corp., C.A.9 (Hawai'i) 1986, 785 F.2d 720, certiorari denied 107 S.Ct. 324, 479 U.S. 918, 93 L.Ed.2d 296. Death ⚖ 8

Where employee of repair company was killed, when gasoline exploded in a valve in a tanker in drydock in New York, employee's administratrix could not invoke the Death on the High Seas Act,

§§ 761 to 768 of Title 46, but since a ship in drydock is within admiralty jurisdiction, administratrix could sue under this section, and her recovery depended upon the Lord Campbell's Act, McKinney's N.Y. Decedent Estate Law, § 130. Puleo v. H.E. Moss & Co., C.C.A.2 (N.Y.) 1947, 159 F.2d 842, certiorari denied 67 S.Ct. 1733, 331 U.S. 847, 91 L.Ed. 1857, certiorari denied 67 S.Ct. 1736, 331 U.S. 847, 91 L.Ed. 1857. Admiralty ⚖ 21; Shipping ⚖ 73

Law of North Carolina, where army base was located, helicopter maintained and plaintiffs' decedents were stationed, applied to tort claims against manufacturer arising out of crash of helicopter on the base. Resnick v. Sikorsky Aircraft, a Div. of United Technologies Corp., D.Conn.1987, 660 F.Supp. 415. Products Liability ⚖ 105; Products Liability ⚖ 200

State substantive law that was in effect when state sovereignty was surrendered did not apply in wrongful death actions governed by this section relating to the availability of wrongful death actions on federally owned land. Vasina v. Grumman Corp., E.D.N.Y.1980, 492 F.Supp. 943, affirmed 644 F.2d 112. Death ⚖ 8

In wrongful death action against manufacturer of military helicopter which crashed within federal enclave in North Carolina, where inter alia, helicopter was in use at air station and the two decedents lived either on the enclave or in North Carolina, enclave was the location with the most significant relationship with the events and parties involved and, therefore, those claims which sounded in tort were governed by the law of the place of the crash, i.e., the federal enclave in North Carolina, Quadrini v. Sikorsky Aircraft Division, United Aircraft Corp., D.C.Conn.1977, 425 F.Supp. 81, on reconsideration 505 F.Supp. 1049. Death ⚖ 8

Though state law is inapplicable to maritime tort, not resulting in death, on navigable water, state may create right of action for death on such waters within its boundaries, at least where such right is not provided under federal law. Tardiff v. Bank Line, Ltd., E.D.La.1954, 127 F.Supp. 945. Admiralty ⚖ 21

Drowning of driver of automobile which had fallen into river while debarking from ferry would not have happened but for driver's negligence in approaching steel apron laid from ferry deck to landing barge at excessive speed with wheels cut sharply to the right, and driver was guilty of contributory negligence, which under law of Louisiana barred any recovery for his death under Louisiana wrongful death statute.   Byrd v. Napoleon Ave. Ferry Co., E.D.La.1954, 125 F.Supp. 573, affirmed 227 F.2d 958, certiorari denied 76 S.Ct. 783, 351 U.S. 925, 100 L.Ed. 1455.   Ferries ⟨key⟩ 32

17.   Jurisdiction

United States district court had jurisdiction over action between citizens of same state for personal injuries sustained in automobile accident on military reservation of Fort Leavenworth, a territory ceded by Kansas to United States, both under § 1331 of Title 28, giving jurisdiction in cases, arising under Constitution, laws and treaties of United States, and under this section.   Stokes v. Adair, C.A.4 (Va.) 1959, 265 F.2d 662, certiorari denied 80 S.Ct. 56, 361 U.S. 816, 4 L.Ed.2d 62.   Federal Courts ⟨key⟩ 192

Even if this section governing wrongful death within a federal enclave provided no clue as to the content or source of applicable substantive law, suit under this section would arise under federal law sufficiently to give rise to federal question jurisdiction.   Quadrini v. Sikorsky Aircraft Division, United Aircraft Corp., D.C.Conn.1977, 425 F.Supp. 81, on reconsideration 505 F.Supp. 1049.   Federal Courts ⟨key⟩ 192

Since federal law provides no cause of action for death as result of accident on vessel owned by non-resident of state while on navigable water therein, state may provide such right and a remedy for enforcement thereof by statute, so that federal court for Louisiana district obtained jurisdiction of defendant British corporation in action for death of Louisiana resident from injuries sustained on corporation's steamship at dock in Louisiana on service of summons on Louisiana Secretary of State under LSA–R.S. 13:3479, AND LSA–C.C. art. 2315.   Tardiff v. Bank Line, Ltd., E.D.La.1954, 127

F.Supp. 945.   Admiralty ⟨key⟩ 21;   Corporations ⟨key⟩ 668(14)

18.   Limitations

Virginia statute of limitations applied to personal injury claims brought by former munitions plant employees against plant operators, even though parties had entered agreement not to assert statute of limitations defense or other procedural bar not available in state court where suit had originally been filed, since their claims had arisen out of federal enclave subject to exclusive legislative jurisdiction of United States, and court was required to apply law of state surrounding enclave.   Adams v. Alliant Techsystems, Inc., W.D.Va.2002, 201 F.Supp.2d 700, reconsideration denied 218 F.Supp.2d 792.   Federal Courts ⟨key⟩ 423;   Limitation Of Actions ⟨key⟩ 15

19.   Removal of cases

An action based on violation of Missouri occupational disease statute and Missouri common-law duty to furnish an employee a safe place in which to work which resulted in an employee contracting lead poisoning while assisting in razing a federal building at Kansas City, Mo., which stood on land owned by the United States, did not "arise under laws of the United States" so as to authorize removal of the action from state to federal court, notwithstanding the laws of Missouri were by this section made applicable to the action.   Misner v. Cleveland Wrecking Co. of Cincinnati, W.D.Mo. 1938, 25 F.Supp. 763.   Removal Of Cases ⟨key⟩ 19(1)

20.   Persons entitled to maintain action

This section governing wrongful deaths within a federal enclave does not create a right in the decedent which could be enforced by plaintiff who could not bring suit under survival statute of jurisdiction surrounding the enclave but who would be a common-law heir of the decedent.   Quadrini v. Sikorsky Aircraft Division, United Aircraft Corp., D.C.Conn.1977, 425 F.Supp. 81, on reconsideration 505 F.Supp. 1049.   United States ⟨key⟩ 3

§ 458.   Travel expenses incident to study of battlefields;   payment

Mileage of officers of the Army and actual expenses of civilian employees traveling on duty in connection with the studies, surveys, and field investigations of battlefields shall be paid from the appropriations made from time to time to meet the expenses for these purposes.

(Mar. 8, 1928, c. 152, 45 Stat. 249.)

CROSS REFERENCES

Travel expenses of employees as covered by per diem allowance, see 5 USCA § 5702.

LIBRARY REFERENCES

American Digest System
  Armed Services ⊂54.
  United States ⊂39(9).
  Key Number System Topic Nos. 34, 393.

§ 458a. Mats for reproduction in magazines and newspapers of photographs of scenery

The Secretary of the Interior is authorized and directed to have prepared mats which may be used for the reproduction in magazines and newspapers of photographs of such of the scenery in the national parks as, in the opinion of the Secretary, would be of interest to the people of the United States and foreign nations. Any such mats may be furnished, without charge and under such regulations as the Secretary may prescribe, to the publishers of magazines, newspapers, and any other publications which may carry photographic reproductions.

(Aug. 27, 1940, c. 690, § 1, 54 Stat. 861.)

LIBRARY REFERENCES

American Digest System
  United States ⊂57.
  Key Number System Topic No. 393.

SUBCHAPTER LXIII—NATIONAL SEASHORE RECREATIONAL AREAS

§ 459. Cape Hatteras National Seashore Recreational Area; conditional establishment; acquisition of lands

When title to all the lands, except those within the limits of established villages, within boundaries to be designated by the Secretary of the Interior within the area of approximately one hundred square miles on the islands of Chicamacomico, Ocracoke, Bodie, Roanoke, and Collington, and the waters and the lands beneath the waters adjacent thereto shall have been vested in the United States, said area shall be, and is, established, dedicated, and set apart as a national seashore recreational area for the benefit and enjoyment of the people and shall be known as the Cape Hatteras National Seashore Recreational Area: *Provided*, That the United States shall not purchase by appropriation of public moneys any lands within the aforesaid area, but such lands shall be secured by the United States only by public or private donation.

(Aug. 17, 1937, c. 687, § 1, 50 Stat. 669; June 29, 1940, c. 459, § 1, 54 Stat. 702.)

HISTORICAL AND STATUTORY NOTES

Amendments
1940 Amendments. Act June 29, 1940 substituted "national seashore recreational area" for "national seashore" and "Cape Hatteras National Seashore Recreational Area" for "Cape Hatteras National Seashore".

LIBRARY REFERENCES

American Digest System
  United States ⟨key⟩55.
  Key Number System Topic No. 393.

Notes of Decisions

Condemnation proceedings   1
_____

1. Condemnation proceedings
   Under § 459 et seq. of this title relative to establishment of National Seashore Recreational Area in North Carolina, provisions relative to establishment of boundaries, right of authorized officer to purchase realty if prices are deemed reasonable, right of the Secretary of Interior to abandon project at his discretion 15 years after August, 1937, and the ultimate establishment of area, do not constitute conditions precedent to institution of condemnation proceedings. U.S. v. Souther-ly Portion of Bodie Island, N.C., E.D.N.C. 1953, 114 F.Supp. 427.   Eminent Domain ⟨key⟩ 169

   Statutes appropriating money and granting to Department of Conservation and Development power to condemn land in connection with preserving and rehabilitating certain shoreline did not grant authority for subsequent condemnation of land in order to convey it to United States for a national park. State v. Core Banks Club Properties, Inc., N.C.1969, 167 S.E.2d 385, 275 N.C. 328.   Eminent Domain ⟨key⟩ 41

§ 459a. Acceptance of donations; acquisition of property by purchase and condemnation

   The Secretary of the Interior is authorized to accept donations of land, interests in land, buildings, structures, and other property, within the boundaries of said national seashore recreational area as determined and fixed hereunder and donations of funds for the purchase and maintenance thereof, the title and evidence of title to lands acquired to be satisfactory to the Secretary of the Interior: *Provided*, That he may acquire on behalf of the United States under any donated funds by purchase, when purchasable at prices deemed by him reasonable, otherwise by condemnation under the provisions of section 3113 of Title 40, such tracts of land within the said national seashore recreational area as may be necessary for the completion thereof.

(Aug. 17, 1937, c. 687, § 2, 50 Stat. 669; June 29, 1940, c. 459, § 1, 54 Stat. 702.)

HISTORICAL AND STATUTORY NOTES

Codifications

In text, "section 3113 of Title 40" substituted for "sections 257 and 258 of Title 40", which originally read "the Act of August 1, 1888" on authority of Pub.L. 107–217, § 5(c), Aug. 21, 2002, 116 Stat. 1301, which is set out as a note preceding 40 U.S.C.A. § 101. Pub.L. 107–217, § 1, enacted Title 40 into positive law. The Act of August 1, 1888, is Act, Aug. 1, 1888, c. 728, 25 Stat. 357, which was classified to former 40 U.S.C.A. §§ 257 and 258, prior to being repealed by

Pub.L. 107–217, § 6(b), Aug. 21, 2002, 116 Stat. 1305, and its substance reenacted as 40 U.S.C.A. § 3113. Section 258 of Title 40 was previously omitted from the Code as superseded by Rule 71A, Federal Rules of Civil Procedure, Title 28.

Amendments

1940 Amendments. Act June 29, 1940 substituted "national seashore recreational area" for "national seashore" in two instances.

LIBRARY REFERENCES

American Digest System
    United States ⊗55.
    Key Number System Topic No. 393.

Research References

Treatises and Practice Aids
    Federal Procedure, Lawyers Edition § 14:262, Who May Condemn; Procedures Governing Condemnation.

§ 459a–1. Administration, protection, and development; commercial fishing by residents; hunting

The administration, protection, and development of the aforesaid national seashore recreational area shall be exercised under the direction of the Secretary of the Interior by the National Park Service, subject to the provisions of sections 1, 2, 3, and 4 of this title, as amended: *Provided*, That except as hereinafter provided nothing herein shall be construed to divest the jurisdiction of other agencies of the Government exercised on August 17, 1937, over Federal-owned lands within the area of the said Cape Hatteras National Seashore Recreational Area: *Provided further*, That the provisions of the Federal Power Act [16 USCA § 791a et seq.] shall not apply to this national seashore recreational area: *And provided further*, That the legal residents of villages referred to in section 459 of this title shall have the right to earn a livelihood by fishing within the boundaries to be designated by the Secretary of the Interior, subject to such rules and regulations as the said Secretary may deem necessary in order to protect the area for recreational use as provided for in sections 459 to 459a–3 of this title: *And provided further*,

That hunting shall be permitted, under such rules and regulations as may be prescribed by the Secretary of the Interior in conformity with the Migratory Bird Treaty Act of July 3, 1918 (40 Stat. 755) [16 U.S.C.A. § 703 et seq.], as follows: (a) Upon the waters of the sounds included within the national seashore recreational area, (b) in the area north of the Currituck County line, (c) on Ocracoke Island, and (d) within not more than two thousand acres of land in the remaining portion of said national seashore recreational area, as shall be designated by the Secretary of the Interior; except on lands and waters included in any existing or future wildlife or migratory bird refuge and adjacent closed waters.

(Aug. 17, 1937, c. 687, § 3, 50 Stat. 670; June 29, 1940, c. 459, §§ 1, 2, 54 Stat. 702.)

HISTORICAL AND STATUTORY NOTES

References in Text

The Federal Power Act, referred to in text, was in the original the "Act of June 10, 1920, known as the Federal Water Power Act," and was redesignated as the Federal Power Act by section 791a of this title. The Federal Power Act is Act June 10, 1920, c. 285, 41 Stat. 1063, as amended, and is classified generally to chapter 12 (section 791a et seq.) of this title. For complete classification of this Act to the Code, see section 791a of this title and Tables.

The Migratory Bird Treaty Act of July 3, 1918, referred to in text, is Act July 3, 1918, c. 128, 40 Stat. 755, as amended, which is classified generally to subchapter II (section 703 et seq.) of chapter 7 of this title. For complete classification of this Act to the Code, see section 710 of this title and Tables.

Amendments

1940 Amendments. Act June 29, 1940 substituted "national seashore recreational area" for "national seashore" wherever appearing and "Cape Hatteras National Seashore Recreational Area" for "Cape Hatteras National Seashore", and added last proviso in respect to hunting.

Transfer of Functions

All functions of all other officers of the Department of the Interior and all functions of all agencies and employees of such Department were, with two exceptions, transferred to the Secretary of the Interior, with power vested in him to authorize their performance or the performance of any of his functions by any of such officers, agencies, and employees, by 1950 Reorg. Plan No. 3, §§ 1, 2, eff. May 24, 1950, 15 F.R. 3174, 64 Stat. 1262, set out in Appendix 1 to Title 5, Government Organization and Employees.

LIBRARY REFERENCES

American Digest System
    Fish ⊛8.
    Game ⊛3.5.
    Key Number System Topic Nos. 176, 187.

Notes of Decisions

Commercial fishing rights   4
Discretion of Secretary   2
Duty of court   1
Findings by Secretary   3
Injunction   6

Parties   5

1. Duty of court

It was not the role of district court to substitute its judgment for that of the Secretary of Interior in deciding which regulations are necessary to administer the Cape Hatteras National Seashore Recreational Area in accordance with congressional mandate; rather, it was duty of the court, on challenge to Secretary's regulations governing commercial fishing activities, to insure that he gave due consideration to all factors which Congress directed him to consider in arriving at such decision. Peele v. Morton, E.D.N.C. 1975, 396 F.Supp. 584. Fish ⊕ 8

2. Discretion of Secretary

In prescribing rules and regulations necessary to protect Cape Hatteras National Seashore Recreational Area for recreational use the Secretary of Interior is to make specific findings as to impact of such regulations on ability of residents of the outer banks to continue to ply their fishing trade in the manner of their forefathers and to give such findings due consideration in the final decision; however, such duty does not detract from the Secretary's ultimate discretion to choose the course of action which he considers the most appropriate. Peele v. Morton, E.D.N.C.1975, 396 F.Supp. 584. Fish ⊕ 8

3. Findings by Secretary

Secretary of Interior's statement of findings in support of regulations restricting commercial fishermen from using seine nets on certain beaches within the Cape Hatteras National Seashore Recreational Area was incomplete and required a remand where findings were directed solely at determining proposed regulations' economic impact on villagers of the outer banks, i.e., there were no findings relating to the regulations' impact on the villagers' way of life as a cultural resource, and Secretary did not consider cumulative impact of all National Park Service regulations restricting villagers' ability to engage in their traditional occupation. Peele v. Morton, E.D.N.C.1975, 396 F.Supp. 584. Fish ⊕ 8

4. Commercial fishing rights

This section providing that residents of the Cape Hatteras National Seashore Recreational Area have the right to earn a livelihood by fishing within boundaries to be designated by Secretary of the Interior, subject to such rules and regulations as the Secretary may deem necessary to protect area for recreational use, does not amount to a congressional guarantee that the commercial fishermen of the outer banks will always have the unimpeded right to earn a livelihood by fishing in the manner of their forefathers nor does it authorize Secretary to completely ban commercial fishing; rather, Secretary must take account of residents' cultural heritage when deciding which regulations are necessary and proper for administration of the seashore. Peele v. Morton, E.D.N.C.1975, 396 F.Supp. 584. Fish ⊕ 8

5. Parties

Since ultimate disposition of dispute as to ban on certain commercial fishing activities in Cape Hatteras National Seashore Recreational Area would rest largely on result of further administrative proceedings and on application of appropriate legal standards to Secretary of Interior's findings of fact, congressman's application for leave to appear as amicus curiae would be denied. Peele v. Morton, E.D.N.C.1975, 396 F.Supp. 584. Amicus Curiae ⊕ 1

6. Injunction

Preliminary injunction delaying enforcement of regulations governing commercial fishing within Cape Hatteras National Seashore Recreational Area was not warranted where regulations would not become effective for several months, defects in Secretary of Interior's decision-making process were entirely procedural and the plaintiff, i.e., villagers of the outer banks, had not shown a strong likelihood that they would ultimately prevail on the merits. Peele v. Morton, E.D.N.C. 1975, 396 F.Supp. 584. Injunction ⊕ 138.48

§ 459a–2.   Preservation of natural features; acquisition of additional property; reversion of property on failure of conditions

Except for certain portions of the area, deemed to be especially adaptable for recreational uses, particularly swimming, boating, sailing, fishing, and other recreational activities of similar nature, which shall be developed for such uses as needed, the said area shall be permanently reserved as a primitive wilderness and no development of the project or plan for the convenience of visitors shall be undertaken which would be incompatible with the preservation of the unique flora and fauna or the physiographic conditions now prevailing in this area: *Provided,* That the Secretary of the Interior may, in his discretion, accept for administration, protection, and development by the National Park Service a minimum of ten thousand acres within the area described in section 459 of this title, including the existing Cape Hatteras State Park, and, in addition, any other portions of the area described in section 459 of this title if the State of North Carolina shall agree that if all the lands described in section 459 of this title shall not have been conveyed to the United States within fifteen years from August 17, 1937, the establishment of the aforesaid national seashore recreational area may, in the discretion of the said Secretary, be abandoned, and that, in the event of such abandonment, the said State will accept a reconveyance of title to all lands conveyed by it to the United States for said national seashore recreational area.   The lands donated to the United States for the purposes of sections 459 to 459a–3 of this title by parties other than said State shall revert in the event of the aforesaid abandonment to the donors, or their heirs, or other persons entitled thereto by law.

In the event of said abandonment, the Secretary of the Interior shall execute any suitable quitclaim deeds, or other writings entitled to record in the proper counties of North Carolina stating the fact of abandonment, whereupon title shall revert to those entitled thereto by law and no further conveyance or proof of reversion of title shall be required.

(Aug. 17, 1937, c. 687, § 4, 50 Stat. 670; June 29, 1940, c. 459, § 1, 54 Stat. 702; Mar. 6, 1946, c. 50, 60 Stat. 32.)

HISTORICAL AND STATUTORY NOTES

Revision Notes and Legislative Reports
    1946 Acts. House Report No. 1161, see 1946 U.S. Code Cong. Service, p. 1075.

Amendments
    1946 Amendments. Act Mar. 6, 1946 substituted "fifteen years" for "ten years" preceding "from August 17, 1937" in the proviso of the first sentence.
    1940 Amendments. Act June 29, 1940 substituted "national seashore recreational area" for "national seashore" wherever appearing.

Transfer of Functions
    All functions of all other officers of the Department of the Interior and all func-

tions of all agencies and employees of such Department were, with two exceptions, transferred to the Secretary of the Interior, with power vested in him to authorize their performance or the performance of any of his functions by any of such officers, agencies, and employees, by 1950 Reorg. Plan No. 3, §§ 1, 2, eff. May 24, 1950, 15 F.R. 3174, 64 Stat. 1262, set out in Appendix 1 to Title 5, Government Organization and Employees.

§ 459a–3. Migratory bird refuges not to be affected

Notwithstanding any other provisions of sections 459 to 459a–3 of this title, lands and waters on or after August 17, 1937, included in any migratory bird refuge under the jurisdiction of the Secretary of Agriculture, within the boundaries of the national seashore recreational area as designated by the Secretary of the Interior under section 459 of this title, shall continue as such refuge under the jurisdiction of the Secretary of Agriculture for the protection of migratory birds, but such lands and waters shall be a part of the aforesaid national seashore recreational area and shall be administered by the National Park Service for recreational uses not inconsistent with the purposes of such refuge under such rules and regulations as the Secretaries of the Interior and Agriculture may jointly approve. The proviso to section 459 of this title shall not limit the power of the Secretary of Agriculture to acquire lands for any migratory bird refuge by purchase with any funds made available therefor by applicable law.

(Aug. 17, 1937, c. 687, § 5, 50 Stat. 670; June 29, 1940, c. 459, § 1, 54 Stat. 702.)

HISTORICAL AND STATUTORY NOTES

Amendments
1940 Amendments. Act June 29, 1940 substituted "national seashore recreational area" for "national seashore" wherever appearing.

Transfer of Functions
All functions of all other officers of the Department of the Interior and all functions of all agencies and employees of such Department were, with two excep-

tions, transferred to the Secretary of the Interior, with power vested in him to authorize their performance or the performance of any of his functions by any of such officers, agencies, and employees, by 1950 Reorg. Plan No. 3, §§ 1, 2, eff. May 24, 1950, 15 F.R. 3174, 64 Stat. 1262, set out in Appendix 1 to Title 5, Government Organization and Employees.

§ 459a–4.   Omitted

HISTORICAL AND STATUTORY NOTES

Codifications

Section, Acts June 3, 1948, c. 393, 62 Stat. 301; June 30, 1949, c. 288, Title I, § 105(a), 63 Stat. 381, which transferred lands in Dare County, North Carolina, to the administrative jurisdiction of the Department of the Interior to be administered as a part of the Cape Hatteras National Seashore Recreational Area project, is omitted in view of Pub.L. 87–313, set out as a note under this section.

Disposal of Lands

Pub.L. 87–313, Sept. 26, 1961, 75 Stat. 675, provided: "That the tract of Federal property comprising eight and one-tenth acres of land situated in Dare County, North Carolina, approximately two miles north of Kitty Hawk, which was transferred to the administrative jurisdiction of the Department of the Interior by the Act of June 3, 1948 (62 Stat. 301; 16 U.S.C. 459a–4 [this section]), to be administered as a part of the Cape Hatteras National Seashore Recreational Area, may be disposed of by the Administrator of General Services in accordance with the provisions of the Federal Property and Administrative Services Act of 1949, as amended [40 U.S.C.A. § 471 et seq.]."

§ 459a–5.   Addition of lands; Naval Amphibious Training Station

There is transferred to the Secretary of the Interior without reimbursement or transfer of funds, administrative jurisdiction over an area of approximately twenty-one and eight-tenths acres of federally owned land, formerly designated as the Naval Amphibious Training Station, together with any improvements thereon which may exist at the time of the transfer, situated on Ocracoke Island within the village of Ocracoke, County of Hyde, in the State of North Carolina. The property so transferred shall be administered by the Department of the Interior and shall become a part of the Cape Hatteras National Seashore Recreational Area, when established.

(July 14, 1953, c. 191, 67 Stat. 148.)

LIBRARY REFERENCES

American Digest System

United States ☞55.
Key Number System Topic No. 393.

§ 459a–5a.   Addition of lands; Hatteras

The tracts of excess Federal lands and improvements thereon in the village of Hatteras, Dare County, North Carolina, bearing General Services Administration control numbers T–NC–442 and C–NC–444, comprising forty-three one-hundredths and one and five-tenths acres of land, respectively, the exact descriptions for which shall be determined by the Administrator of General Services, are transferred, without exchange of funds, to the administrative jurisdiction of the Secretary of the Interior to be administered as a part of the Cape Hatteras National Seashore Recreational Area, authorized by sections 459 to 459a–3 of this title, and shall be subject to all the laws and regulations applicable thereto.

(Pub.L. 85–540, July 18, 1958, 72 Stat. 398.)

LIBRARY REFERENCES

American Digest System

United States ⚷55.

Key Number System Topic No. 393.

§ 459a–6. Acquisition of non-Federal land within boundaries of recreational area

Section 452a of this title is amended to extend the authority of the Secretary of the Interior, contained therein, to the Cape Hatteras National Seashore Recreational Area.

(Aug. 6, 1956, c. 988, § 1, 70 Stat. 1066.)

HISTORICAL AND STATUTORY NOTES

Revision Notes and Legislative Reports

1956 Acts. House Report No. 2347, see 1956 U.S. Code Cong. and Adm. News, p. 4418.

LIBRARY REFERENCES

American Digest System

United States ⚷55.

Key Number System Topic No. 393.

§ 459a–7. Availability of appropriations

Any funds appropriated to the Department of the Interior for the acquisition of non-Federal lands within areas of the National Park System shall after August 6, 1956, be available for the acquisition of non-Federal lands within the Cape Hatteras National Seashore Recreational Area, and the appropriation of funds for the acquisition of such lands is authorized.

(Aug. 6, 1956, c. 988, § 2, 70 Stat. 1066.)

HISTORICAL AND STATUTORY NOTES

Revision Notes and Legislative Reports

1956 Acts. House Report No. 2347, see 1956 U.S. Code Cong. and Adm. News, p. 4418.

§ 459a–8. Limitation on expenditure

The total amount which may be expended for the land acquisition program at Cape Hatteras National Seashore Recreational Area, pursuant to the authorizations contained in sections 459a–6 to 459a–8 of this title, is expressly limited to $250,000.

(Aug. 6, 1956, c. 988, § 3, 70 Stat. 1066.)

HISTORICAL AND STATUTORY NOTES

Revision Notes and Legislative Reports
  1956 Acts. House Report No. 2347, see 1956 U.S. Code Cong. and Adm. News, p. 4418.

§ 459a–9. Conveyance of land for improvement with public health facility; reversion; consideration; status of property upon transfer of title

The Secretary of the Interior is authorized to convey the tract of land and improvements thereon situate in the village of Hatteras, Dare County, North Carolina, and administered as part of the Cape Hatteras National Seashore, formerly bearing General Services Administration excess property control number C-NC–444, comprising one and five-tenths acres, the exact description for which shall be determined by the Secretary, to the Board of Commissioners of Dare County, for purposes of providing thereon a public health facility: *Provided*, That title to the land and any improvements shall revert to the United States upon a finding and notification to the grantee by the Secretary that the property is used for purposes other than a public health facility. The conveyance herein authorized shall be without monetary consideration.

Upon the transfer of title to the grantee, the property herein conveyed shall cease to be a part of the Cape Hatteras National Seashore.

(Pub.L. 89–146, Aug. 28, 1965, 79 Stat. 583.)

HISTORICAL AND STATUTORY NOTES

Codifications
  Section is comprised of sections 1 and 2 of Pub.L. 89–146.

LIBRARY REFERENCES

American Digest System
    Armed Services ☜54.
    United States ☜57.
    Woods and Forests ☜4.
    Key Number System Topic Nos. 34, 393, 411.

§ 459a–10.　Transfer of Ocracoke Light Station to Secretary of the Interior

The Administrator of the General Services Administration shall transfer administrative jurisdiction over the Federal property consisting of approximately 2 acres, known as the Ocracoke Light Station, to the Secretary of the Interior, subject to such reservations, terms, and conditions as may be necessary for Coast Guard purposes. All property so transferred shall be included in and administered as part of the Cape Hatteras National Seashore.

(Pub.L. 105–383, Title IV, § 420, Nov. 13, 1998, 112 Stat. 3439.)

HISTORICAL AND STATUTORY NOTES

Revision Notes and Legislative Reports
1998 Acts. House Report No. 105–236, see 1998 U.S. Code Cong. and Adm. News, p. 794.

Transfer of Functions
For transfer of authorities, functions, personnel, and assets of the Coast Guard, including the authorities and functions of the Secretary of Transportation relating thereto, to the Department of Homeland Security, and for treatment of related references, see 6 U.S.C.A. §§ 468(b), 551(d), 552(d) and 557, and the Department of Homeland Security Reorganization Plan of November 25, 2002, as modified, set out as a note under 6 U.S.C.A. § 542.

LIBRARY REFERENCES

American Digest System
Woods and Forests ⬦4.
Key Number System Topic No. 411.

§ 459b.　Cape Cod National Seashore; description of area

(a) The area comprising that portion of the land and waters located in the towns of Provincetown, Truro, Wellfleet, Eastham, Orleans, and Chatham in the Commonwealth of Massachusetts, and described in subsection (b) of this section, is designated for establishment as Cape Cod National Seashore (hereinafter referred to as "the seashore").

(b) The area referred to in subsection (a) of this section is described as follows:

Beginning at a point in the Atlantic Ocean one-quarter of a mile due west of the mean low-water line of the Atlantic Ocean on Cape Cod at the westernmost extremity of Race Point, Provincetown, Massachusetts;

thence from the point of beginning along a line a quarter of a mile offshore of and parallel to the mean low-water line of the Atlantic Ocean, Cape Cod Bay, and Provincetown Harbor in generally southerly, easterly, and northerly directions rounding Long Point and then southwesterly to a point a quarter of a mile offshore of the mean low-water line on the harbor side of the dike depicted on the United States Geological Survey Province-town quadrangle sheet (1949) crossing an arm of the Province-town Harbor;

thence northerly, along a line a quarter of a mile offshore of and parallel to the low-water line at the dike to a point easterly of the point of intersection of the said dike with the boundary of the Province Lands Reservation as depicted on the said Province-town quadrangle sheet;

thence westerly to the said point of intersection of the dike and the Province Lands Reservation boundary;

thence along the boundaries of the Province Lands Reservation northwesterly, northeasterly, northerly, and easterly to the east-ernmost corner of the reservation being near United States Route 6;

thence leaving the said easternmost corner along an extension of the southerly reservation boundary line easterly to the north-erly right-of-way line of United States Route 6;

thence along the northerly right-of-way line of United States Route 6 in a general easterly direction crossing the Truro-Provincetown line and continuing in the town of Truro in a generally southeasterly direction to a point four-tenths of a mile southeasterly of the southerly right-of-way line of Highland Road;

thence easterly five-tenths of a mile to a point;

thence turning and running in a southeasterly direction paral-leling the general alinement of United States Route 6 and gener-ally distant therefrom five-tenths of a mile to a point approxi-mately 700 feet northwesterly of Long Nook Road;

thence southwesterly along a ridge generally paralleling the alinement of Long Nook Road and distant approximately 700 feet therefrom to a point two-tenths of a mile northeasterly of the northerly right-of-way line of United States Route 6;

thence southeasterly paralleling the general alinement of Unit-ed States Route 6 and generally distant two-tenths of a mile northeasterly thereof to a point 300 feet south of the southerly right-of-way line of Higgins Hollow Road;

thence in a general easterly direction paralleling the southerly alinement of Higgins Hollow Road and 300 feet distant southerly therefrom to a point five-tenths of a mile east of the easterly right-of-way line of said Route 6;

thence turning and running in a southeasterly and southerly direction paralleling the general alinement of United States Route 6 and distant five-tenths of a mile easterly therefrom to a point 300 feet north of the northerly right-of-way line of North Pamet Road;

thence in a generally southwesterly direction paralleling the general alinement of North Pamet Road and generally distant 300 feet northerly therefrom to a point approximately two-tenths of a mile east of the easterly right-of-way line of United States Route 6;

thence in a southerly direction paralleling the alinement of United States Route 6 and generally distant two-tenths of a mile easterly therefrom to a point three-tenths of a mile south of South Pamet Road;

thence west to the intersection of Old County Road and Mill Pond Road;

thence following the easterly right-of-way line of Old County Road southward to a point opposite the southerly right-of-way line of Ryder Beach Road at its intersection with Old County Road;

thence eastward to a point 300 feet east of the easterly right-of-way line of said Old County Road;

thence in a southerly direction paralleling Old County Road at a distance of 300 feet to the east of the easterly right-of-way line of said road to a point 600 feet south of the southerly right-of-way line of Prince Valley Road;

thence in a generally westerly direction, crossing Old County Road and the New York, New Haven, and Hartford Railroad right-of-way to the southern extremity of the town landing and beach in the Ryder Beach area, and continuing to a point in Cape Cod Bay a quarter of a mile offshore from the mean low-water line of Cape Cod Bay;

thence turning and running along a line a quarter of a mile offshore of and parallel to the mean low-water line of Cape Cod Bay in a general southerly and easterly direction rounding Jeremy Point and thence in a general northerly direction along a line a quarter of a mile offshore of and parallel to the mean low-water line on the westerly side of Wellfleet Harbor, to a point one quarter of a mile due north of the mean low-water line at the eastern tip of Great Island as depicted on the United States Geological Survey Wellfleet quadrangle sheet (1958);

thence north to the mean high-water line on the north shore of the Herring River estuary in the vicinity of its confluence with Wellfleet Harbor;

thence following the mean high-water line southwesterly, northwesterly, and northeasterly to the easterly right-of-way line of Chequesset Neck Road at its crossing of Herring River;

thence following the course of Herring River along the 20–foot contour line of the southeasterly shore thereof to a point near Mill Creek;

thence crossing Mill Creek in a northeasterly direction to the 20–foot contour level near to and northeast of the confluence of Mill Creek and Herring River;

thence following generally northerly and easterly along the easterly edge of the Herring River marshes on the 20–foot contour to a point north of which the easterly right-of-way line of a medium duty road, as depicted on said Wellfleet quadrangle sheet, crosses northward across a marshy stream near the juncture of said medium duty road with Bound Brook Island Road;

thence crossing said marshy stream along said easterly right-of-way line of said medium duty road, and continuing in a northerly direction to the 20–foot contour level on the north side of said marshy stream;

thence following the 20–foot contour line westward approximately 1,000 feet to its intersection with an unimproved dirt road, as depicted on said Wellfleet quadrangle sheet, leading from a point near the juncture of Bound Brook Island Road and the said medium duty road;

thence following said unimproved dirt road northwesterly for approximately 1,600 feet to the 20–foot contour line bordering the southerly edge of the Herring River marshes;

thence following said 20–foot contour line in an easterly direction to Route 6;

thence crossing Route 6 and continuing to a point on the easterly right-of-way line of a power transmission line as depicted on said Wellfleet quadrangle sheet;

thence in a general southerly direction along the said easterly right-of-way line of a power transmission line to the Eastham-Wellfleet town line;

thence southeasterly for a distance of approximately 5,200 feet to a point due north of the intersection of the easterly right-of-way line of Nauset Road with the northerly right-of-way line of Cable Road;

thence due south to the intersection of the said easterly right-of-way line of Nauset Road and the said northerly right-of-way line of Cable Road;

thence in a general southerly direction crossing Cable Road and along said easterly right-of-way line of Nauset Road to a point 500 feet north of the northerly right-of-way line of Doane Road and its intersection with Nauset Road;

thence west to a point 500 feet west of the westerly right-of-way line of Nauset Road;

thence southerly and westerly 500 feet from and parallel to the said right-of-way line of Nauset Road to the easterly right-of-way line of Salt Pond Road;

thence southerly along the easterly right-of-way line of said Salt Pond Road to its intersection with the southerly right-of-way line of Nauset Road;

thence westerly along the southerly right-of-way line of Nauset Road to its intersection with the easterly right-of-way line of United States Route 6;

thence southerly along the easterly right-of-way line of said Route 6 a distance of about four-tenths of a mile to the northerly boundary of the Eastham town hall property;

thence easterly to a point one-tenth of a mile from United States Route 6;

thence turning and running in a generally southerly direction paralleling the general alinement of United States Route 6 and generally distant therefrom one-tenth of a mile to a small stream approximately one-tenth of a mile beyond Governor Prence Road extended;

thence southeasterly along the said stream to the Orleans-Eastham town line;

thence along the Orleans-Eastham town line to the southerly tip of Stony Island;

thence generally southeasterly in the town of Orleans by Nauset Harbor Channel to a point due north of the northerly tip of Nauset Heights as depicted on United States Geological Survey Orleans quadrangle sheet (1946);

thence due south to the 20–foot contour line in Nauset Heights as delineated on the said Orleans quadrangle sheet;

thence generally southerly along the said 20–foot contour to a point about one-tenth of a mile northerly of Beach Road;

thence southwesterly along a line intersecting Beach Road at a point two-tenths of a mile easterly of the so-called Nauset Road leading northerly to Nauset Heights;

thence southerly to a head of a tributary to Little Pleasant Bay at the northerly tip of Pochet Neck as depicted on the said Orleans quadrangle sheet;

thence generally southerly along the thread of channel of the said tributary passing westerly and southwesterly around Pochet Island and thence southwesterly into Little Pleasant Bay passing to westerly of the northerly tip of Sampson Island, the westerly tip of Money Head, and the southwesterly tip of Hog Island following in general the centerline of Little Pleasant Bay to Pleasant Bay;

thence generally southeasterly in Pleasant Bay along a line passing midway between Sipson Island and Nauset Beach to a point on the Chatham-Orleans town line one-quarter of a mile westerly of the mean low-water line of Pleasant Bay on the westerly shore of Nauset Beach;

thence generally southerly in Pleasant Bay in the town of Chatham along a line a quarter of a mile offshore of and parallel to the said mean low-water line of Pleasant Bay on the westerly shore of Nauset Beach to a point a quarter of a mile south of the mean low-water line of the southern tip of Nauset Beach;

thence easterly rounding the southern tip of Nauset Beach along a line a quarter of a mile offshore of and parallel thereto;

thence generally northerly and northwesterly, and westerly along a line a quarter of a mile offshore of and parallel to the mean low-water line of the Atlantic Ocean on the easterly shore of Nauset Beach and on to the outer cape to the point of beginning.

(Pub.L. 87–126, § 1, Aug. 7, 1961, 75 Stat. 284.)

HISTORICAL AND STATUTORY NOTES

Revision Notes and Legislative Reports
  1961 Acts. Senate Report No. 428, see 1961 U.S. Code Cong. and Adm. News, p. 2212.

Separability of Provisions
  Pub.L. 87–126, § 10, Aug. 7, 1961, 75 Stat. 284, provided that: "If any provi-

sion of this Act [sections 459b to 459b–8 of this title] or the application of such provision to any person or circumstance is held invalid, the remainder of this Act [such sections] or the application of such provision to persons or circumstances other than those to which it is held invalid shall not be affected thereby."

CODE OF FEDERAL REGULATIONS

Zoning standards, see 36 CFR § 27.1 et seq.

LIBRARY REFERENCES

American Digest System
  Water Law ⊕2669.
  Key Number System Topic No. 405.

Research References

ALR Library
  144 ALR 486, Uses to Which Park Property May Be Devoted.

Notes of Decisions

Purpose   1

1. Purpose

Sections 459b to 459b–8 of this title were enacted by Congress in effort to strike balance between natural beauty and human element of Cape Cod while coping with congressional inability to enact zoning laws. U.S. v. Certain Lands in Truro, Barnstable County, Com. of Mass., D.C.Mass.1979, 476 F.Supp. 1031. Environmental Law ⚘ 125

§ 459b–1. Acquisition of property

(a) Authority of Secretary; manner and place; concurrence of State owner; transfer from Federal agency to administrative jurisdiction of Secretary

The Secretary of the Interior (hereinafter referred to as "Secretary") is authorized to acquire by purchase, gift, condemnation, transfer from any Federal agency, exchange, or otherwise, the land, waters, and other property, and improvements thereon and any interest therein, within the area which is described in section 459b of this title or which lies within the boundaries of the seashore as described pursuant to section 459b–2 of this title (both together hereinafter in sections 459b to 459b–8 of this title referred to as "such area"). Any property, or interest therein, owned by the Commonwealth of Massachusetts, by any of the towns referred to in section 459b of this title, or by any other political subdivision of said Commonwealth may be acquired only with the concurrence of such owner. Notwithstanding any other provision of law, any Federal property located within such area may, with the concurrence of the agency having custody thereof, be transferred without consideration to the administrative jurisdiction of the Secretary for use by him in carrying out the provisions of sections 459b to 459b–8 of this title.

(b) Use of funds; fair market value

The Secretary is authorized (1) to use donated and appropriated funds in making acquisitions under sections 459b to 459b–8 of this title, and (2) to pay therefor not more than the fair market value of any acquisitions which he makes by purchase under sections 459b to 459b–8 of this title.

(c) Exchange of property; cash equalization payments; reports to Congress

In exercising his authority to acquire property by exchange, the Secretary may accept title to any non-Federal property located within such area and convey to the grantor of such property any federally owned property under the jurisdiction of the Secretary within such area. The properties so exchanged shall be approximately equal in fair market value: *Provided*, That the Secretary may accept cash from or pay cash to the grantor in such an exchange in order to equalize the values of the properties exchanged.

The Secretary shall report to the Congress on every exchange carried out under authority of sections 459b to 459b–8 of this title within thirty days from its consummation, and each such report shall include a statement of the fair market values of the properties involved and of any cash equalization payment made or received.

(d) Exchange of property; addition to Cape Cod National Seashore

The Secretary may convey to the town of Provincetown, Massachusetts, a parcel of real property consisting of approximately 7.62 acres of Federal land within such area in exchange for approximately 11.157 acres of land outside of such area, as depicted on the map entitled "Cape Cod National Seashore Boundary Revision Map", dated May, 1997, and numbered 609/80,801, to allow for the establishment of a municipal facility to serve the town that is restricted to solid waste transfer and recycling facilities and for other municipal activities that are compatible with National Park Service laws and regulations.   Upon completion of the exchange, the Secretary shall modify the boundary of the Cape Cod National Seashore to include the land that has been added.

(e) "Fair market value" defined; appraisal

As used in sections 459b to 459b–8 of this title the term "fair market value" shall mean the fair market value as determined by the Secretary, who may in his discretion base his determination on an independent appraisal obtained by him.

(Pub.L. 87–126, § 2, Aug. 7, 1961, 75 Stat. 287; Pub.L. 105–280, § 1(a), Oct. 26, 1998, 112 Stat. 2694.)

HISTORICAL AND STATUTORY NOTES

Revision Notes and Legislative Reports
  1961 Acts. Senate Report No. 428, see 1961 U.S. Code Cong. and Adm. News, p. 2212.

Amendments
  1998 Amendments. Subsecs. (d), (e). Pub.L. 105–280, § 1(a)(1), (2) redesignated subsec. (d) as subsec. (e), and added new subsec. (d).

Termination of Reporting Requirements
  For termination of reporting provisions of subsec. (c) of this section, effective May 15, 2000, see Pub.L. 104–66, § 3003, as amended, set out as a note under 31 U.S.C.A. § 1113, and page 110 of House Document No. 103–7.

LIBRARY REFERENCES

American Digest System
  United States ⏦55.
  Key Number System Topic No. 393.

Notes of Decisions

Estoppel 1
Judicial review 2

_____

1. Estoppel

Fact that Director of Environmental Planning for Cape Cod National Seashore assured property owners that Seashore would exchange federal land for cottage which was endangered by erosion in 1978 did not estop government from subsequently denying its willingness to exchange property where owners knew that official did not have authority to bind government. Greenwald v. Olsen, D.C.Mass.1984, 583 F.Supp. 1002. Estoppel ⟜ 62.2(4)

2. Judicial review

This section grants Secretary of Interior almost unlimited discretion with regard to land exchanges and, therefore, district court is "without power" to subject such decision to judicial review. Greenwald v. Olsen, D.C.Mass.1984, 583 F.Supp. 1002. United States ⟜ 55

§ 459b–2. Establishment

(a) Notice in Federal Register

As soon as practicable after August 7, 1961, and following the acquisition by the Secretary of an acreage in the area described in section 459b of this title that is in the opinion of the Secretary efficiently administrable to carry out the purposes of sections 459b to 459b–8 of this title, the Secretary shall establish Cape Cod National Seashore by the publication of notice thereof in the Federal Register.

(b) Distribution of notice and map

Such notice referred to in subsection (a) of this section shall contain a detailed description of the boundaries of the seashore which shall encompass an area as nearly as practicable identical to the area described in section 459b of this title. The Secretary shall forthwith after the date of publication of such notice in the Federal Register (1) send a copy of such notice, together with a map showing such boundaries, by registered or certified mail to the Governor of the Commonwealth of Massachusetts and to the board of selectmen of each of the towns referred to in section 459b of this title; (2) cause a copy of such notice and map to be published in one or more newspapers which circulate in each of such towns; and (3) cause a certified copy of such notice, a copy of such map, and a copy of sections 459b to 459b–8 of this title to be recorded at the registry of deeds for Barnstable County, Massachusetts.

(Pub.L. 87–126, § 3, Aug. 7, 1961, 75 Stat. 288.)

HISTORICAL AND STATUTORY NOTES

Revision Notes and Legislative Reports
1961 Acts. Senate Report No. 428, see 1961 U.S. Code Cong. and Adm. News, p. 2212.

§ 459b–3. Acquisition by condemnation

(a) Right of use and occupancy for residential purposes for life or fixed term of years; exercise of right of election; impairment of interests of lienholders, etc.; right as running with land; transfer, assignment and termination of right; computation of compensation

(1) The beneficial owner or owners, not being a corporation, of a freehold interest in improved property which the Secretary acquires by condemnation may elect, as a condition to such acquisition, to retain the right of use and occupancy of the said property for noncommercial residential purposes for a term of twenty-five years, or for such lesser time as the said owner or owners may elect at the time of such acquisition.

(2) The beneficial owner or owners, not being a corporation, of a freehold estate in improved property which property the Secretary acquires by condemnation, who held, on September 1, 1959, with respect to such property, an estate of the same nature and quality, may elect, as an alternative and not in addition to whatever right of election he or they might have under paragraph (1) of this subsection, to retain the right of use and occupancy of the said property for noncommercial residential purposes (i) for a term limited by the nature and quality of his or their said estate, if his or their said estate is a life estate or an estate pur auter vie,[1] or (ii) for a term ending at the death of such owner or owners, or at the death of the survivor of them, if his or their said estate is an estate of fee simple.

(3) Where such property is held by a natural person or persons for his or their own life or lives or for the life or lives of another or others (such person or persons being hereinafter called "the life tenant"), with remainder in another or others, any right of election provided for in paragraph (2) of this subsection shall be exercised by the life tenant, and any right of election provided for in paragraph (1) of this subsection shall be exercised by the concurrence of the life tenant and the remainderman or remaindermen.

(4) The beneficial owner or owners of a term of years in improved property which the Secretary acquires by condemnation may elect, as a condition to such acquisition, to retain the right of use and occupancy of the said property for noncommercial residential purposes for a term not to exceed the remainder of his or their said term of years, or a term of twenty-five years, whichever shall be the lesser. The owner or owners of the freehold estate or estates in such property may, subject to the right provided for in the preceding sentence, exercise such right or rights of election as remain to them under paragraphs (1) and (2) of this subsection.

(5) No right of election accorded by paragraphs (1), (2), or (4) of this subsection shall be exercised to impair substantially the interests of holders of encumbrances, liens, assessments, or other charges upon or against the property.

(6) Any right or rights of use and occupancy retained pursuant to paragraphs (1), (2), and (4) of this subsection shall be held to run with the land, and may be freely transferred and assigned.

(7) In any case where a right of use and occupancy for life or for a fixed term of years is retained as provided in paragraph (1), (2), or (4) of this subsection, the compensation paid by the Secretary for the property shall not exceed the fair market value of the property on the date of its acquisition by the Secretary, less the fair market value on such date of the said right retained.

(8) The Secretary shall have authority to terminate any right of use and occupancy of property, retained as provided in paragraph (1), (2), or (4) of this subsection, at any time after the date when any use occurs with respect to such property which fails to conform or is in any manner opposed to or inconsistent with any applicable standard contained in regulations issued pursuant to section 459b–4 of this title and in effect on said date: *Provided*, That no use which is in conformity with the provisions of a zoning bylaw approved in accordance with said section 459b–4 which is in force and applicable to such property shall be held to fail to conform or be opposed to or inconsistent with any such standard. In the event that the Secretary exercises the authority conferred by this paragraph, he shall pay to the owner of the right so terminated an amount equal to the fair market value of the portion of said right which remained on the date of termination.

(b) Suspension of authority for one year and during existence of zoning regulations

(1) The Secretary's authority to acquire property by condemnation shall be suspended with respect to all improved property located within such area in all of the towns referred to in section 459b of this title for one year following August 7, 1961.

(2) Thereafter such authority shall be suspended with respect to all improved property located within such area in any one of such towns during all times when such town shall have in force and applicable to

such property a duly adopted, valid zoning bylaw approved by the Secretary in accordance with the provisions of section 459b–4 of this title.

(c) Suspension of authority respecting property used for commercial or industrial purposes

The Secretary's authority to acquire property by condemnation shall be suspended with respect to any particular property which is used for commercial or industrial purposes during any periods when such use is permitted by the Secretary and during the pendency of the first application for such permission made to the Secretary after August 7, 1961 provided such application is made not later than the date of establishment of the seashore.

(d) "Improved property" defined

The term "improved property," wherever used in sections 459b to 459b–8 of this title, shall mean a detached, one-family dwelling the construction of which was begun before September 1, 1959 (hereinafter referred to as "dwelling"), together with so much of the land on which the dwelling is situated, the said land being in the same ownership as the dwelling, as the Secretary shall designate to be reasonably necessary for the enjoyment of the dwelling for the sole purpose of noncommercial residential use, together with any structures accessory to the dwelling which are situated on the land so designated. The amount of the land so designated shall in every case be at least three acres in area, or all of such lesser amount as may be held in the same ownership as the dwelling, and in making such designation the Secretary shall take into account the manner of noncommercial residential use in which the dwelling and land have customarily been enjoyed: *Provided, however,* That the Secretary may exclude from the land so designated any beach or waters, together with so much of the land adjoining such beach or waters as the Secretary may deem necessary for public access thereto.

(e) Acquisition of clear, marketable and encumbrance-free title

Nothing in this section or elsewhere in sections 459b to 459b–8 of this title shall be construed to prohibit the use of condemnation as a means of acquiring a clear and marketable title, free of any and all encumbrances.

(Pub.L. 87–126, § 4, Aug. 7, 1961, 75 Stat. 288.)

1 So in original. Probably should be "pur autre vie".

HISTORICAL AND STATUTORY NOTES

Revision Notes and Legislative Reports
1961 Acts. Senate Report No. 428, see
1961 U.S. Code Cong. and Adm. News, p.
2212.

LIBRARY REFERENCES

American Digest System
     Eminent Domain ⟲5.
     United States ⟲55.
     Key Number System Topic Nos. 148, 393.

Research References

Treatises and Practice Aids
     Federal Procedure, Lawyers Edition § 14:263, "Improved Property" Exemption.

Notes of Decisions

Appraisal of property   1
Fair market value   2
Improved property   3
Trespass   4
Zoning   5

1. Appraisal of property

Property taken by government was not subject to being appraised in accordance with a 17-lot subdivision plan which expired because not perfected within seven years of approval, but was subject to being appraised on basis of town's ¾ acre zoning requirement, notwithstanding claim that landowner was unable to construct single-family dwellings in accordance with subdivision plan because of enactment of Cape Cod National Seashore Act, section 459b et seq. of this title, where government was not required under Act to take property if it was developed and, if it did decide to acquire property when it was developed, was required to give landowner fair market value of property in light of subdivision plan. U.S. v. 45.28 Acres of Land, More or Less, Situated in the Town of Truro and Wellfleet, D.C.Mass.1979, 483 F.Supp. 1099. Eminent Domain ⟲ 134

2. Fair market value

Although valid three-acre zoning provision was in effect in town during period before condemnation by federal Government, federal Government, which by federal action had caused zoning restriction to be imposed, would not be allowed to benefit from fluctuation in market value resulting therefrom, and thus general rule

that taker of property is required to pay only fair market value on date of taking subject to applicable zoning regulations would not be applied but, rather, fair market value of land would be determined pursuant to what zoning provision would have been in absence of federal intervention. U.S. v. Certain Lands in Truro, Barnstable County, Com. of Mass., D.C.Mass.1979, 476 F.Supp. 1031. Eminent Domain ⟲ 134

3. Improved property

Uninsulated wooden cottage which lacked any plumbing or electricity and which was occupied only during warmer months, did not qualify as "dwelling," and property on which it was located was not "improved property," within meaning of section of Cape Cod National Seashore Act suspending Secretary of Interior's authority to acquire "improved property" in Cape Code area by condemnation. U.S. v. Certain Land Located in County of Barnstable, C.A.1 (Mass.) 1989, 889 F.2d 352, certiorari denied 110 S.Ct. 1527, 494 U.S. 1057, 108 L.Ed.2d 766. Eminent Domain ⟲ 52

Structure which allegedly existed on property owner's Cape Cod land prior to 1959, the effective date of "improved property" exemption of the Cape Cod National Seashore Act was not "improved property" within meaning of the Act, where record indicated that structure was never served by utilities, had no waste disposal facilities, and that permits for such services or facilities were never obtained or issued. U.S. v. 7.92 Acres of Land, More or Less, Situated in Towns of

Provincetown and Truro, Barnstable County, Com. of Mass., C.A.1 (Mass.) 1985, 769 F.2d 4. Eminent Domain ⊸ 52

4. Trespass

United States was entitled to require defendants to remove themselves and their personal effects and properties from Cape Cod National Seashore, at their own expense, where the land upon which defendants' shacks were situated had been taken by Commonwealth of Massachusetts in 1956, and owners were required to remove structures within six months of date of recording of the taking instrument, since to extent that defendants did not comply with six-month removal requirement, or at some later time

erected, acquired, or occupied cottage on the land, nature of their property interests, if any, was personal property, and their presence on the land was in the nature of trespass. U.S. v. 733 Acres of Land, More or Less, Situated in Town of Truro, D.C.Mass.1982, 552 F.Supp. 1. Trespass ⊸ 11

5. Zoning

Power to enact zoning laws is vested in states and municipalities and not in federal government, and option of changing local zoning laws is not available to Congress of the United States. U.S. v. Certain Lands in Truro, Barnstable County, Com. of Mass., D.C.Mass.1979, 476 F.Supp. 1031. Zoning And Planning ⊸ 1017; Zoning And Planning ⊸ 1141

§ 459b–4. Zoning regulations

(a) Standards for approval; submission to Congress and municipalities; publication in Federal Register; approval of local bylaws; revocation of approval

As soon after August 7, 1961, as may be practicable, the Secretary shall issue regulations specifying standards for approval by him of zoning bylaws for purposes of section 459b–3 of this title. The Secretary may issue amended regulations specifying standards for approval by him of zoning bylaws whenever he shall consider such amended regulations to be desirable due to changed or unforeseen conditions.

All regulations and amended regulations proposed to be issued under authority of the two preceding sentences of this subsection shall be submitted to the Congress and to the towns named in section 459b of this title at least ninety calendar days (which ninety days, however, shall not include days on which either the House of Representatives or the Senate is not in session because of an adjournment of more than three calendar days to a day certain) before they become effective and the Secretary shall, before promulgating any such proposed regulations or amended regulations in final form, take due account of any suggestions for their modification which he may receive during said ninety-day period. All such regulations and amended regulations shall, both in their proposed form and in their final form, be published in the Federal Register.

The Secretary shall approve any zoning bylaw and any amendment to any approved zoning bylaws submitted to him which conforms to the standards contained in the regulations in effect at the time of the adoption by the town of such bylaw or such amendment unless before the time of adoption he has submitted to the Congress and the towns and published in the Federal Register as aforesaid proposed amended regulations with which the bylaw or amendment would not be in conformity, in which case he may withhold his approval pending completion of the review and final publication provided for in this subsection and shall thereafter approve the bylaw or amendment only if it is in conformity with the amended regulations in their final form. Such approval shall not be withdrawn or revoked, nor shall its effect be altered for purposes of section 459b–3 of this title by issuance of any such amended regulations after the date of such approval, so long as such bylaw or such amendment remains in effect as approved.

(b) Commercial and industrial use prohibition; acreage, frontage, setback and miscellaneous requirements

The standards specified in such regulations and amended regulations for approval of any zoning bylaw or zoning bylaw amendment shall contribute to the effect of (1) prohibiting the commercial and industrial use, other than any commercial or industrial use which is permitted by the Secretary, of all property within the boundaries of the seashore which is situated within the town adopting such bylaw; and (2) promoting the preservation and development, in accordance with the purposes of sections 459b to 459b–8 of this title, of the area comprising the seashore, by means of acreage, frontage, and setback requirements and other provisions which may be required by such regulations to be included in a zoning bylaw consistent with the laws of Massachusetts.

(c) Adverse provisions and absence of notice for variance as requiring disapproval of local bylaws

No zoning bylaw or amendment of a zoning bylaw shall be approved by the Secretary which (1) contains any provision which he may consider adverse to the preservation and development, in accordance with the purposes of sections 459b to 459b–8 of this title, of the area comprising the seashore, or (2) fails to have the effect of providing that the Secretary shall receive notice of any variance granted under and any exception made to the application of such bylaw or amendment.

(d) Termination of suspension of authority for acquisition by condemnation because of nonconforming variances and uses; agreements concerning exercise of authority

If any improved property with respect to which the Secretary's authority to acquire by condemnation has been suspended by reason of the adoption and approval, in accordance with the foregoing provisions of this section, of a zoning bylaw applicable to such property (hereinafter referred to as "such bylaw")—

(1) is made the subject of a variance under or an exception to such bylaw, which variance or exception fails to conform or is in any manner opposed to or inconsistent with any applicable standard contained in the regulations issued pursuant to this section and in effect at the time of the passage of such bylaw, or

(2) is property upon or with respect to which there occurs any use, commencing after the date of the publication by the Secretary of such regulations, which fails to conform or is in any manner opposed to or inconsistent with any applicable standard contained in such regulations (but no use which is in conformity with the provisions of such bylaw shall be held to fail to conform or be opposed to or inconsistent with any such standard),

the Secretary may, at any time and in his discretion, terminate the suspension of his authority to acquire such improved property by condemnation: *Provided, however*, That the Secretary may agree with the owner or owners of such property to refrain from the exercise of the said authority during such time and upon such terms and conditions as the Secretary may deem to be in the best interests of the development and preservation of the seashore.

(Pub.L. 87–126, § 5, Aug. 7, 1961, 75 Stat. 290.)

HISTORICAL AND STATUTORY NOTES

Revision Notes and Legislative Reports
  1961 Acts. Senate Report No. 428, see 1961 U.S. Code Cong. and Adm. News, p. 2212.

CODE OF FEDERAL REGULATIONS
  Zoning standards, see 36 CFR § 27.1 et seq.

LIBRARY REFERENCES
American Digest System
  Eminent Domain ☞5.
  Key Number System Topic No. 148.

§ 459b–5.   Certificate of suspension of authority for acquisition by condemnation

The Secretary shall furnish to any party in interest requesting the same, a certificate indicating, with respect to any property located within the seashore as to which the Secretary's authority to acquire such property by condemnation has been suspended in accordance with the provisions of sections 459b to 459b–8 of this title, that such authority has been so suspended and the reasons therefor.

(Pub.L. 87–126, § 6, Aug. 7, 1961, 75 Stat. 291.)

HISTORICAL AND STATUTORY NOTES

Revision Notes and Legislative Reports
1961 Acts. Senate Report No. 428, see
1961 U.S. Code Cong. and Adm. News, p.
2212.

LIBRARY REFERENCES

American Digest System
  Eminent Domain ☞5.
  Key Number System Topic No. 148.

§ 459b–6. Administration of acquired property

(a) Utilization of authority for conservation and management of natural resources

Except as otherwise provided in sections 459b to 459b–8 of this title, the property acquired by the Secretary under such sections shall be administered by the Secretary subject to the provisions of sections 1, 2, 3, and 4 of this title, as amended and supplemented, and in accordance with laws of general application relating to the national park system as defined by sections 1b to 1d of this title; except that authority otherwise available to the Secretary for the conservation and management of natural resources may be utilized to the extent he finds such authority will further the purposes of sections 459b to 459b–8 of this title.

(b) Preservation of seashore; incompatible visitor conveniences restricted; provisions for public enjoyment and understanding; developments for recreational activities; public use areas

(1) In order that the seashore shall be permanently preserved in its present state, no development or plan for the convenience of visitors shall be undertaken therein which would be incompatible with the preservation of the unique flora and fauna or the physiographic conditions now prevailing or with the preservation of such historic sites and structures as the Secretary may designate: *Provided,* That the Secretary may provide for the public enjoyment and understanding of the unique natural, historic, and scientific features of Cape Cod within the seashore by establishing such trails, observation points, and exhibits and providing such services as he may deem desirable for such public enjoyment and understanding: *Provided further,* That the Secretary may develop for appropriate public uses such portions of the seashore as he deems especially adaptable for camping, swimming, boating, sailing, hunting, fishing, the appreciation of historic sites and structures and natural features of Cape Cod, and other activities of similar nature.

416

(2) In developing the seashore the Secretary shall provide public use areas in such places and manner as he determines will not diminish for its owners or occupants the value or enjoyment of any improved property located within the seashore.

(c) Hunting and fishing regulations; navigation

The Secretary may permit hunting and fishing, including shellfishing, on lands and waters under his jurisdiction within the seashore in such areas and under such regulations as he may prescribe during open seasons prescribed by applicable local, State and Federal law. The Secretary shall consult with officials of the Commonwealth of Massachusetts and any political subdivision thereof who have jurisdiction of hunting and fishing, including shellfishing, prior to the issuance of any such regulations, and the Secretary is authorized to enter into cooperative arrangements with such officials regarding such hunting and fishing, including shellfishing, as he may deem desirable, except that the Secretary shall leave all aspects of the propagation and taking of shellfish to the towns referred to in section 459b of this title.

The Secretary shall not interfere with navigation of waters within the boundaries of the Cape Cod National Seashore by such means and in such areas as is now customary.

(Pub.L. 87–126, § 7, Aug. 7, 1961, 75 Stat. 291.)

HISTORICAL AND STATUTORY NOTES

Revision Notes and Legislative Reports
  1961 Acts. Senate Report No. 428, see 1961 U.S. Code Cong. and Adm. News, p. 2212.

CODE OF FEDERAL REGULATIONS

Special regulations for particular areas of system, see 36 CFR § 7.1 et seq.

LIBRARY REFERENCES

American Digest System
  Woods and Forests ⬤⧴5.
  Key Number System Topic No. 411.

Notes of Decisions

Appropriate public uses   1
Jurisdictional amount   3
Nude bathing   2

----

1. Appropriate public uses

  Secretary of the Interior's decision that restricted use of off-road vehicles permitted under National Park Service's 1985 management plan on Cape Cod National Seashore was appropriate public use of seashore, had rational basis and was not abuse of discretion, and decision to adopt 1985 plan would accordingly be upheld as providing for appropriate use of seashore within scope of Cape Cod National Seashore Act restrictions on seashore use. Conservation Law Foundation of

New England, Inc. v. Secretary of the Interior, C.A.1 (Mass.) 1989, 864 F.2d 954. United States ⇨ 57

In action seeking permanent injunction barring all off-road vehicle use on the Cape Code National Seashore until adoption of off-road vehicle management plan that adequately prevented both damage to seashore and interference with other recreational uses and that conformed to relevant statutes and executive orders, since it was arguable that National Park Service failed to consider adequately whether extensive off-road vehicle use of seashore, even if ecologically compatible, was an appropriate public use mandated by sections 459b–459b–8 of this title, district court would admit documentary evidence that bore on that issue. Conservation Law Foundation of New England, Inc. v. Clark, D.C.Mass.1984, 590 F.Supp. 1467. Environmental Law ⇨ 148

2. Nude bathing

Nude bathing at one of the more remote beaches at the Cape Cod Seashore National Park did not fall into the narrow category of claims involving freedom of choice with respect to certain basic matters of procreation, marriage and family life which the government may not invade absent compelling reason and without exhaustion of less restrictive alternatives. Williams v. Kleppe, C.A.1 (Mass.) 1976, 539 F.2d 803. Obscenity ⇨ 2.5; United States ⇨ 57

3. Jurisdictional amount

For purposes of satisfying jurisdictional amount in federal question suit seeking declaration of unconstitutionality of national park service regulation imposing total ban on nude bathing at Cape Cod Seashore National Park it could not be said that, applying conventional analysis, the claimed interest of one or more plaintiffs, some being residents of the Seashore area, might not exceed the jurisdictional amount; however, more realistically, court could rely on the extent of the claimed pecuniary burden on defendants were plaintiffs to prevail. Williams v. Kleppe, C.A.1 (Mass.) 1976, 539 F.2d 803. Federal Courts ⇨ 340.1

§ 459b–7. Cape Cod National Seashore Advisory Commission

(a) Establishment; termination

There is established a Cape Cod National Seashore Advisory Commission (hereinafter referred to as the "Commission"). The Commission shall terminate September 26, 2018.

(b) Membership; term

The Commission shall be composed of ten members each appointed for a term of two years by the Secretary as follows:

> **(1)** Six members to be appointed from recommendations made by each of the boards of selectmen of the towns referred to in section 459b of this title, one member from the recommendations made by each such board;

> **(2)** One member to be appointed from recommendations of the county commissioners of Barnstable County, Commonwealth of Massachusetts;

> **(3)** Two members to be appointed from recommendations of the Governor of the Commonwealth of Massachusetts; and

> **(4)** One member to be designated by the Secretary.

(c) Chairman; vacancies

The Secretary shall designate one member to be Chairman. Any vacancy in the Commission shall be filled in the same manner in which the original appointment was made.

(d) Compensation and expenses

A member of the Commission shall serve without compensation as such. The Secretary is authorized to pay the expenses reasonably incurred by the Commission in carrying out its responsibilities under sections 459b to 459b–8 of this title upon vouchers signed by the Chairman.

(e) Majority vote

The Commission established by this section shall act and advise by affirmative vote of a majority of the members thereof.

(f) Consultation of Secretary with Commission

The Secretary or his designee shall, from time to time, consult with the members of the Commission with respect to matters relating to the development of Cape Cod National Seashore and shall consult with the members with respect to carrying out the provisions of sections 459b–3 and 459b–4 of this title.

(g) Advice of Commission for commercial or industrial use permits and establishment of public use areas for recreational activities

No permit for the commercial or industrial use of property located within the seashore shall be issued by the Secretary, nor shall any public use area for recreational activity be established by the Secretary within the seashore, without the advice of the Commission, if such advice is submitted within a reasonable time after it is sought.

(h) Exemption from other provisions of law

(1) Any member of the Advisory Commission appointed under sections 459b to 459b–8 of this title shall be exempted, with respect to such appointment, from the operation of sections 281, 283, 284, and 1914 of Title 18 and section 190 of the Revised Statutes (5 U.S.C. 99) except as otherwise specified in paragraph (2) of this subsection.

(2) The exemption granted by paragraph (1) of this subsection shall not extend—

(i) to the receipt or payment of salary in connection with the appointee's Government service from any sources other than the private employer of the appointee at the time of his appointment; or

(ii) during the period of such appointment, and the further period of two years after the termination thereof, to the prosecution or participation in the prosecution, by any person so appointed, of any claim against the Government involving any matter concerning which the appointee had any responsibility arising out of his appointment during the period of such appointment.

(Pub.L. 87–126, § 8, Aug. 7, 1961, 75 Stat. 292; Pub.L. 99–420, Title II, § 201, Sept. 25, 1986, 100 Stat. 960; Pub.L. 105–280, § 1(b), Oct. 26, 1998, 112 Stat. 2694; Pub.L. 111–11, Title VII, § 7402, Mar. 30, 2009, 123 Stat. 1219.)

HISTORICAL AND STATUTORY NOTES

Revision Notes and Legislative Reports
    1961 Acts. Senate Report No. 428, see 1961 U.S. Code Cong. and Adm. News, p. 2212.

    1986 Acts. House Report No. 99–572, see 1986 U.S. Code Cong. and Adm. News, p. 2074.

    2009 Acts. Statement by President, see 2009 U.S. Code Cong. and Adm. News, p. S13.

References in Text
    Sections 281, 283, 284, and 1914 of Title 18, referred to in subsec. (h)(1), were repealed by Pub.L. 87–849, § 2, Oct. 23, 1962, 76 Stat. 1126, "Except as they [sections 281 and 283] may apply to retired officers of the armed forces of the United States)", and were supplanted by sections 203, 205, 207, and 209, respectively, of Title 18, Crimes and Criminal Procedure.

    Section 190 of the Revised Statutes, referred to in subsec. (h)(1), was repealed by Pub.L. 87–849, § 3, Oct. 23, 1962, 76 Stat. 1126. See section 207 of Title 18.

Amendments
    2009   Amendments. Subsec.   (a). Pub.L. 111–11, § 7402, in the second sentence, struck out "2008" and inserted "2018".

    1998   Amendments. Subsec.   (a). Pub.L. 105–280, § 1(b), substituted "The Commission shall terminate September 26, 2008" for "Said Commission shall terminate 30 years after the date the seashore is established under section 459b–2 of this title.".

    1986   Amendments. Subsec.   (a). Pub.L. 99–420 substituted "30 years" for "ten years".

Effective and Applicability Provisions
    2009 Acts. Pub.L. 111–11, Title VII, § 7402, Mar. 30, 2009, 123 Stat. 1219, provided in part that amendment by Pub.L. 111–11, § 7402, is "[e]ffective September 26, 2008".

Reestablishment and Extension of Commission
    Pub.L. 99–349, Title I, c. VII, July 2, 1986, 100 Stat. 731, provided: "That the Cape Cod National Seashore Advisory Commission established under section 8(a) of the Act of August 7, 1961 (Public Law 87–126; 75 Stat. 292) [subsec. (a) of this section] is reestablished and extended through February 28, 1996[.]"

LIBRARY REFERENCES

American Digest System
    Woods and Forests ⊂=7.
    Key Number System Topic No. 411.

§ 459b–8. Authorization of appropriations

There are authorized to be appropriated such sums as may be necessary to carry out the provisions of sections 459b to 459b–8 of this title; except that no more than $42,917,575 shall be appropriated for the acquisition of land and waters and improvements thereon, and interests therein, and incidental costs relating thereto, in accordance with the provisions of such sections.

(Pub.L. 87–126, § 9, Aug. 7, 1961, 75 Stat. 293; Pub.L. 91–252, May 14, 1970, 84 Stat. 216; Pub.L. 98–141, § 3, Oct. 31, 1983, 97 Stat. 909.)

HISTORICAL AND STATUTORY NOTES

Revision Notes and Legislative Reports
  1961 Acts. Senate Report No. 428, see 1961 U.S. Code Cong. and Adm. News, p. 2212.
  1970 Acts. House Report No. 91–902, see 1970 U.S. Code Cong. and Adm. News, p. 3035.
  1983 Acts. Senate Report No. 98–141, see 1983 U.S. Code Cong. and Adm. News, p. 1308.

Amendments
  1983 Amendments. Pub.L. 98–141 substituted "$42,917,575" for "$33,500,000".
  1970 Amendments. Pub.L. 91–252 substituted "$33,500,000" for "$16,000,000".

§ 459c. Point Reyes National Seashore; purposes; authorization for establishment

In order to save and preserve, for purposes of public recreation, benefit, and inspiration, a portion of the diminishing seashore of the United States that remains undeveloped, the Secretary of the Interior (hereinafter referred to as the "Secretary") is authorized to take appropriate action in the public interest toward the establishment of the national seashore set forth in section 459c–1 of this title.

(Pub.L. 87–657, § 1, Sept. 13, 1962, 76 Stat. 538.)

HISTORICAL AND STATUTORY NOTES

Revision Notes and Legislative Reports
  1962 Acts. House Report No. 1628, see 1962 U.S. Code Cong. and Adm. News, p. 2500.

LIBRARY REFERENCES

American Digest System
  Water Law ⚮2669.
  Key Number System Topic No. 405.

§ 459c–1. Description of area

(a) Boundary map; availability; publication in Federal Register

The Point Reyes National Seashore shall consist of the lands, waters, and submerged lands generally depicted on the map entitled "Boundary Map, Point Reyes National Seashore", numbered 612–80,008–E and dated May 1978, plus those areas depicted on the map entitled "Point Reyes and GGNRA Amendments, dated October 25, 1979".

The map referred to in this section shall be on file and available for public inspection in the Offices of the National Park Service, Department of the Interior, Washington, District of Columbia. After advising the Committee on Natural Resources of the United States House of Representatives and the Committee on Energy and Natural Resources of the United States Senate in writing, the Secretary may make minor revisions of the boundaries of the Point Reyes National Seashore when necessary by publication of a revised drawing or other boundary description in the Federal Register.

(b) Bear Valley Ranch right-of-way

The area referred to in subsection (a) of this section shall also include a right-of-way to the aforesaid tract in the general vicinity of the northwesterly portion of the property known as "Bear Valley Ranch", to be selected by the Secretary, of not more than four hundred feet in width, together with such adjoining lands as would be deprived of access by reason of the acquisition of such right-of-way.

(Pub.L. 87–657, § 2, Sept. 13, 1962, 76 Stat. 538; Pub.L. 89–666, § 1(a), Oct. 15, 1966, 80 Stat. 919; Pub.L. 93–550, Title II, § 201, Dec. 26, 1974, 88 Stat. 1744; Pub.L. 95–625, Title III, § 318(a), Nov. 10, 1978, 92 Stat. 3486; Pub.L. 96–199, Title I, § 101(a)(1), Mar. 5, 1980, 94 Stat. 67; Pub.L. 103–437, § 6(d)(16), Nov. 2, 1994, 108 Stat. 4584.)

HISTORICAL AND STATUTORY NOTES

Revision Notes and Legislative Reports
 1962 Acts. House Report No. 1628, see 1962 U.S. Code Cong. and Adm. News, p. 2500.

 1966 Acts. House Report No. 2067, see 1966 U.S. Code Cong. and Adm. News, p. 3320.

 1974 Acts. Senate Report No. 93–1221, see 1974 U.S. Code Cong. and Adm. News, p. 6646.

 1980 Acts. Senate Report No. 96–484, see 1980 U.S. Code Cong. and Adm. News, p. 133.

 1994 Acts. House Report No. 103–779, see 1994 U.S. Code Cong. and Adm. News, p. 3639.

References in Text
 Sections 20 to 20g of this title, referred to in text, were repealed by Pub.L. 105–391, Title IV, § 415(a), Nov. 13, 1998, 112 Stat. 3515.

Amendments
 1994 Amendments. Subsec. (a). Pub.L. 103–437, § 6(d)(16), substituted reference to Committee on Natural Resources of the House of Representatives for reference to Committee on Interior and Insular Affairs of the House of Representatives.

 1980 Amendments. Subsec. (a). Pub.L. 96–199 added ", plus those areas depict-ed on the map entitled 'Point Reyes and GGNRA Amendments, dated October 25, 1979'" following "dated May 1978".

 1978 Amendments. Subsec. (a). Pub.L. 95–625 substituted as a description of the area the lands generally depicted on Boundary Map numbered 612–80,008–E and dated May 1978 for prior such depiction on Boundary Map numbered 612–80,008–B, and dated August 1974; included submerged lands in the description; made the map specifically available in the Washington, District of Columbia, Office; and authorized minor revisions of boundaries and publication thereof in the Federal Register after advising Congressional committees.

 1974 Amendments. Subsec. (a). Pub.L. 93–550 substituted as a boundary description Boundary Map No. 612–80,008–B, and dated August 1974, on file in the office of the National Park Service Department of Interior, for a boundary map designated NS–PR–7001, dated June 1, 1960, on file with the Director of the National Park Service, Washington, D.C., and all measurements relating thereto.

 1966 Amendments. Subsec. (b). Pub.L. 89–666 inserted "to the aforesaid tract in the general vicinity of the northwesterly portion of the property known as 'Bear Valley Ranch' following right-of-way", deleted "from the intersection of Sir Francis Drake Boulevard and Haggerty Gulch" following "aforesaid tract" and included such adjoining lands as would be deprived of access by reason of the right-of-way.

Change of Name

Committee on Natural Resources of House of Representatives treated as referring to Committee on Resources of House of Representatives by section 1(a) of Pub.L. 104–14, set out as a note preceding 2 U.S.C.A. § 21. Committee on Resources of House of Representatives changed to Committee on Natural Resources of House of Representatives by House Resolution No. 6, One Hundred Tenth Congress, Jan. 5, 2007.

LIBRARY REFERENCES

American Digest System
Water Law ⬤2669.
Key Number System Topic No. 405.

Notes of Decisions

Authority of Secretary 3
Delegation of authority 2
Easements 5
Power of Secretary 4
Purpose 1
Selection of right-of-way 6

1. Purpose

The intent of Congress when referring to map in subsec. (a) of this section, stating that the area of national seashore park was described by reference to map and had certain metes and bounds description, but not in separate subdivision dealing separately with access corridor to be selected by Secretary outside the seashore area proper was only to exemplify mapwise the seashore area proper as described by metes and bounds, not to bind the Secretary to that map in selection of the outside access corridor. U.S. v. 121 Acres of Land, More or Less, in Marin County, State of Cal., N.D.Cal.1967, 263 F.Supp. 737. Eminent Domain ⬤ 57

2. Delegation of authority

This section providing that national seashore area shall include right-of-way, to be selected by Secretary, of not more than 400 feet in width to the tract from specified boulevard intersection was reasonable delegation of selection of access corridor to Secretary under the evident guiding standard that it be an access corridor to connect northern boundary of national seashore area with boulevard substantially in the vicinity of the intersection. U.S. v. 121 Acres of Land, More or Less, in Marin County, State of Cal., N.D.Cal.1967, 263 F.Supp. 737. Eminent Domain ⬤ 6.1

3. Authority of Secretary

400-foot right-of-way which reached boulevard indirectly and substantially by road intersecting the boulevard at point only a few hundred feet from boulevard intersection named within this section providing that national seashore area shall include right-of-way, to be selected by Secretary, to the tract from the boulevard intersection with another thoroughfare was within authority granted by this section. U.S. v. 121 Acres of Land, More or Less, in Marin County, State of Cal., N.D.Cal.1967, 263 F.Supp. 737. Eminent Domain ⬤ 55

4. Power of Secretary

In view of authorization under this section for decision of Secretary to take condemnees' parcels in connection with right-of-way the Secretary was empowered to select between national seashore area and a certain intersection, his taking thereof was not arbitrary, capricious, or in bad faith. U.S. v. 121 Acres of Land, More or Less, in Marin County, State of Cal., N.D.Cal.1967, 263 F.Supp. 737. Eminent Domain ⬤ 58

5. Easements

Right-of-way within this section providing that national seashore area shall include right-of-way, to be selected by Secretary, of not more than 400 feet in width to the tract from intersection referred to a strip of land, an access corridor, and did not authorize merely the acquisition of easement as opposed to fee estate. U.S. v. 121 Acres of Land, More or Less, in Marin County, State of Cal., N.D.Cal. 1967, 263 F.Supp. 737. Eminent Domain ⬤ 58

6. Selection of right-of-way

Subsec. (b) of this section providing that national seashore area shall include a right-of-way, to be selected by Secretary, of not more than 400 feet in width to the tract from a specified intersection permitted the Secretary to route the right-of-way in any direction he might select, including that through condemnee's parcels. U.S. v. 121 Acres of Land, More or Less, in Marin County, State of Cal., N.D.Cal.1967, 263 F.Supp. 737. Eminent Domain ⊕ 57

§ 459c–2. Acquisition of property

(a) Authority of Secretary; manner and place; concurrence of State owner; transfer from Federal agency to administrative jurisdiction of Secretary; liability of United States under contracts contingent on appropriations

The Secretary is authorized to acquire, and it is the intent of Congress that he shall acquire as rapidly as appropriated funds become available for this purpose or as such acquisition can be accomplished by donation or with donated funds or by transfer, exchange, or otherwise the lands, waters, and other property, and improvements thereon and any interest therein, within the areas described in section 459c–1 of this title or which lie within the boundaries of the seashore as established under section 459c–4 of this title (hereinafter referred to as "such area"). Any property, or interest therein, owned by a State or political subdivision thereof may be acquired only with the concurrence of such owner. Notwithstanding any other provision of law, any Federal property located within such area may, with the concurrence of the agency having custody thereof, be transferred without consideration to the administrative jurisdiction of the Secretary for use by him in carrying out the provisions of sections 459c to 459c–7 of this title. In exercising his authority to acquire property in accordance with the provisions of this subsection, the Secretary may enter into contracts requiring the expenditure, when appropriated, of funds authorized by section 459c–7 of this title, but the liability of the United States under any such contract shall be contingent on the appropriation of funds sufficient to fulfill the obligations thereby incurred.

(b) Payment for acquisition; fair market value

The Secretary is authorized to pay for any acquisitions which he makes by purchase under sections 459c to 459c–7 of this title their fair market value, as determined by the Secretary, who may in his discretion base his determination on an independent appraisal obtained by him.

(c) Exchange of property; cash equalization payments

In exercising his authority to acquire property by exchange, the Secretary may accept title to any non-Federal property located within such area and convey to the grantor of such property any federally owned property under the jurisdiction of the Secretary within California and adjacent States, notwithstanding any other provision of law. The properties so exchanged shall be approximately equal in fair market value, provided that the Secretary may accept cash from or pay cash to the grantor in such an exchange in order to equalize the values of the properties exchanged.

(Pub.L. 87–657, § 3, Sept. 13, 1962, 76 Stat. 539; Pub.L. 91–223, § 2(a), Apr. 3, 1970, 84 Stat. 90.)

HISTORICAL AND STATUTORY NOTES

Revision Notes and Legislative Reports
  1962 Acts. House Report No. 1628, see 1962 U.S. Code Cong. and Adm. News, p. 2500.
  1970 Acts. Senate Report No. 91–738, see 1970 U.S. Code Cong. and Adm. News, p. 2681.

References in Text
  Section 459c–3, included within "sections 459c to 459c–7" referred to in sub-

secs. (a) and (b), was repealed by Pub.L. 91–223, § 2(b), Apr. 3, 1970, 84 Stat. 90.

Amendments
  1970 Amendments. Pub.L. 91–223 substituted introductory "The" for "Except as provided in section 459c–3 of this title, the".

LIBRARY REFERENCES

American Digest System
  United States ☞55.
  Key Number System Topic No. 393.

Notes of Decisions

Authorization to acquire   1
Fair market value   2

mented 459 F.2d 504, 198 Ct.Cl. 506. Eminent Domain ☞ 320

1. Authorization to acquire
  In light of legislative history of Point Reyes National Seashore, declaration by Congress that it was going to acquire land resulted in acquisition of inchoate interest at once, to be perfected later. Drakes Bay Land Co. v. U.S., Ct.Cl.1970, 424 F.2d 574, 191 Ct.Cl. 389, supple-

2. Fair market value
  Residual land or economic analysis approach is a proper approach in determining market value of a tract of land whose highest and best use is for subdivision and sale of lots. Drakes Bay Land Co. v. U.S., Ct.Cl.1972, 459 F.2d 504, 198 Ct.Cl. 506. Eminent Domain ☞ 134

§ 459c–3. Repealed. Pub.L. 91–223, § 2(b), Apr. 3, 1970, 84 Stat. 90

HISTORICAL AND STATUTORY NOTES

  Section, Pub.L. 87–657, § 4, Sept. 13, 1962, 76 Stat. 540, provided conditions for exercise of eminent domain within

pastoral zone and defined the term "ranching and dairying purposes".

§ 459c–4. Point Reyes National Seashore

(a) Establishment; notice in Federal Register

As soon as practicable after September 13, 1962, and following the acquisition by the Secretary of an acreage in the area described in section 459c–1 of this title, that is in the opinion of the Secretary efficiently administrable to carry out the purposes of sections 459c to 459c–7 of this title, the Secretary shall establish Point Reyes National Seashore by the publication of notice thereof in the Federal Register.

(b) Distribution of notice and map

Such notice referred to in subsection (a) of this section shall contain a detailed description of the boundaries of the seashore which shall encompass an area as nearly as practicable identical to the area described in section 459c–1 of this title. The Secretary shall forthwith after the date of publication of such notice in the Federal Register (1) send a copy of such notice, together with a map showing such boundaries, by registered or certified mail to the Governor of the State and to the governing body of each of the political subdivisions involved; (2) cause a copy of such notice and map to be published in one or more newspapers which circulate in each of the localities; and (3) cause a certified copy of such notice, a copy of such map, and a copy of sections 459c to 459c–7 of this title to be recorded at the registry of deeds for the county involved.

(Pub.L. 87–657, § 4, formerly § 5, Sept. 13, 1962, 76 Stat. 540, renumbered Pub.L. 91–223, § 2(c), Apr. 3, 1970, 84 Stat. 90.)

HISTORICAL AND STATUTORY NOTES

Revision Notes and Legislative Reports
  1962 Acts. House Report No. 1628, see 1962 U.S. Code Cong. and Adm. News, p. 2500.
  1970 Acts. Senate Report No. 91–738, see 1970 U.S. Code Cong. and Adm. News, p. 2681.

References in Text
  Section 459c–3, included within "sections 459c to 459c–7" referred to in text, was repealed by Pub.L. 91–223, § 2(b), Apr. 3, 1970, 84 Stat. 90.

Amended Description of Boundaries of Point Reyes National Seashore; Publication in Federal Register
  Pub.L. 93–550, Title II, § 202, Dec. 26, 1974, 88 Stat. 1744, provided that: "The Secretary of the Interior shall, as soon as practicable after the date of enactment of this title [Dec. 26, 1974], publish an amended description of the boundaries of the Point Reyes National Seashore in the Federal Register, and thereafter he shall take such action with regard to such amended description and the map referred to in section 201 of this title [amending section 459c–1 of this title] as is required in the second sentence of subsection (b) of section 4 of the act of September 13, 1962, as amended [subsec. (b) of this section]."

LIBRARY REFERENCES

American Digest System
  Water Law ☞2669.
  Key Number System Topic No. 405.

§ 459c–5. Owner's reservation of right of use and occupancy for fixed term of years or life

(a) Election of term; fair market value; termination; notification; lease of Federal lands: restrictive covenants, offer to prior owner or leaseholder

Except for property which the Secretary specifically determines is needed for interpretive or resources management purposes of the seashore, the owner of improved property or of agricultural property on the date of its acquisition by the Secretary under sections 459c to 459c–7 of this title may, as a condition of such acquisition, retain for himself and his or her heirs and assigns a right of use and occupancy for a definite term of not more than twenty-five years, or, in lieu thereof, for a term ending at the death of the owner or the death of his or her spouse, whichever is later. The owner shall elect the term to be reserved. Unless the property is wholly or partly donated to the United States, the Secretary shall pay to the owner the fair market value of the property on the date of acquisition minus the fair market value on that date of the right retained by the owner. A right retained pursuant to this section shall be subject to termination by the Secretary upon his or her determination that it is being exercised in a manner inconsistent with the purposes of sections 459c to 459c–7 of this title, and it shall terminate by operation of law upon the Secretary's notifying the holder of the right of such determination and tendering to him or her an amount equal to the fair market value of that portion of the right which remains unexpired. Where appropriate in the discretion of the Secretary, he or she may lease federally owned land (or any interest therein) which has been acquired by the Secretary under sections 459c to 459c–7 of this title, and which was agricultural land prior to its acquisition. Such lease shall be subject to such restrictive covenants as may be necessary to carry out the purposes of sections 459c to 459c–7 of this title. Any land to be leased by the Secretary under this section shall be offered first for such lease to the person who owned such land or was a leaseholder thereon immediately before its acquisition by the United States.

(b) "Improved and agricultural property" defined

As used in sections 459c to 459c–7 of this title, the term "improved property" shall mean a private noncommercial dwelling, including the land on which it is situated, whose construction was begun before September 1, 1959, or, in the case of areas added by action of the Ninety-fifth Congress, May 1, 1978, or, in the case of areas added by action of the Ninety-sixth Congress, May 1, 1979, and structures accessory thereto (hereinafter in this subsection referred to as "dwelling"), together with such amount and locus of the property adjoining and in the same ownership as such dwelling as the Secretary designates to be reasonably necessary for the enjoyment of such dwelling for the sole purpose of noncommercial residential use and occupancy. In making such designation the Secretary shall take into account the manner of noncommercial residential use and occupancy in which the dwelling and such adjoining property has usually been enjoyed by its owner or occupant. The term "agricultural property" as used in sections 459c to 459c–7 of this title means lands which were in regular use for, or were being converted to agricultural, ranching, or dairying purposes as of May 1, 1978, or, in the case of areas added by action of the Ninety-sixth Congress, May 1, 1979, together with residential and other structures related to the above uses of the property that were in existence or under construction as of May 1, 1978.

(c) Payment deferral; scheduling; interest rate

In acquiring those lands authorized by the Ninety-fifth Congress for the purposes of sections 459c to 459c–7 of this title, the Secretary may, when agreed upon by the landowner involved, defer payment or schedule payments over a period of ten years and pay interest on the unpaid balance at a rate not exceeding that paid by the Treasury of the United States for borrowing purposes.

(d) Lands donated by State of California

The Secretary is authorized to accept and manage in accordance with sections 459c to 459c–7 of this title, any lands and improvements within or adjacent to the seashore which are donated by the State of California or its political subdivisions. He is directed to accept any such lands offered for donation which comprise the Tomales Bay State Park, or lie between said park and Fish Hatchery Creek. The boundaries of the seashore shall be changed to include any such donated lands.

(e) Fee or admission charge prohibited

Notwithstanding any other provision of law, no fee or admission charge may be levied for admission of the general public to the seashore.

(Pub.L. 87–657, § 5, formerly § 6, Sept. 13, 1962, 76 Stat. 541; renumbered § 5, Pub.L. 91–223, § 2(c), Apr. 3, 1970, 84 Stat. 90, and amended Pub.L. 95–625, Title III, § 318(b) to (d), Nov. 10, 1978, 92 Stat. 3487; Pub.L. 96–199, Title I, § 101(a)(2) to (4), Mar. 5, 1980, 94 Stat. 67.)

HISTORICAL AND STATUTORY NOTES

Revision Notes and Legislative Reports

1962 Acts. House Report No. 1628, see 1962 U.S. Code Cong. and Adm. News, p. 2500.

1970 Acts. Senate Report No. 91–738, see 1970 U.S. Code Cong. and Adm. News, p. 2681.

1980 Acts. Senate Report No. 96–484, see 1980 U.S. Code Cong. and Adm. News, p. 133.

References in Text

Section 459c–3 of this title, included within the reference in text to sections 459c to 459c–7 of this title, was repealed by Pub.L. 91–223, § 2(b), Apr. 3, 1970, 84 Stat. 90.

Amendments

1980 Amendments. Subsec. (a). Pub.L. 96–199, § 101(a)(2), substituted "Except for property which the Secretary specifically determines is needed for interpretive or resources management purposes, the" for "The" at the beginning of the subsection.

Subsec. (b). Pub.L. 96–199, § 101(a)(3), added ", or, in the case of areas added by action of the Ninety-sixth Congress, May 1, 1979" following "May 1, 1978" and added "that were in exis-

tence or under construction as of May 1, 1978" following "related to the above uses of the property".

Subsecs. (d), (e). Pub.L. 96–199, § 101(a)(4), added subsecs. (d) and (e).

1978 Amendments. Subsec. (a). Pub.L. 95–625, § 318(b), extended provision to agricultural property; provided for: retention rights of heirs and assigns, retention rights for term of twenty-five years or for term ending with death of owner or spouse, whichever was later, as elected by owner, which provision previously authorized retention for term of fifty years, termination of right of retention and notice thereof, and for lease of federally owned lands, subject to restrictive covenants, with first offer to prior owner or leaseholder; and included clause relating to donation of property to the United States.

Subsec. (b). Pub.L. 95–625, § 318(c), defined "improved property" to include private dwelling, the construction of which was begun, in the case of areas added by action of the Ninety-fifth Congress, before May 1, 1978, and included definition of "agricultural property".

Subsec. (c). Pub.L. 95–625, § 318(d), added subsec. (c).

LIBRARY REFERENCES

American Digest System

Public Lands ☞49.

Key Number System Topic No. 317.

§ 459c–6. Administration of property

(a) Protection, restoration, and preservation of natural environment

Except as otherwise provided in sections 459c to 459c–7 of this title, the property acquired by the Secretary under such sections shall be administered by the Secretary without impairment of its natural values, in a manner which provides for such recreational, educational, historic preservation, interpretation, and scientific research opportunities as are consistent with, based upon, and supportive of the maximum protection, restoration, and preservation of the natural environment within the area, subject to the provisions of sections 1, 2, 3, and 4 of this title, as amended and supplemented, and in accordance with other laws of general application relating to the national park system as defined by sections 1b to 1d of this title, except that authority otherwise available to the Secretary for the conservation and management of natural resources may be utilized to the extent he finds such authority will further the purposes of sections 459c to 459c–7 of this title.

(b) Hunting and fishing regulations

The Secretary may permit hunting and fishing on lands and waters under his jurisdiction within the seashore in such areas and under such regulations as he may prescribe during open seasons prescribed by applicable local, State, and Federal law. The Secretary shall consult with officials of the State of California and any political subdivision thereof who have jurisdiction of hunting and fishing prior to the issuance of any such regulations, and the Secretary is authorized to enter into cooperative agreements with such officials regarding such hunting and fishing as he may deem desirable.

(Pub.L. 87–657, § 6, formerly § 7, Sept. 13, 1962, 76 Stat. 541; renumbered § 6, Pub.L. 91–223, § 2(c), Apr. 3, 1970, 84 Stat. 90, and amended Pub.L. 94–544, § 4(a), Oct. 18, 1976, 90 Stat. 2515; Pub.L. 94–567, § 7(a), Oct. 20, 1976, 90 Stat. 2695.)

HISTORICAL AND STATUTORY NOTES

Revision Notes and Legislative Reports
  1962 Acts. House Report No. 1628, see 1962 U.S. Code Cong. and Adm. News, p. 2500.
  1970 Acts. Senate Report No. 91–738, see 1970 U.S. Code Cong. and Adm. News, p. 2681.
  1976 Acts. House Report No. 94–1680, see 1976 U.S.Code Cong. and Adm.News, p. 5593.

References in Text
  Section 459c–3 of this title, included within the reference in subsec. (a) to sections 459c to 459c–7 of this title, was repealed by Pub.L. 91–223, § 2(b), Apr. 3, 1970, 84 Stat. 90.

Codifications
  Section 7(a) of Pub.L. 94–567 enacted the identical amendment to subsec. (a) of this section as section 4(a) of Pub.L. 94–544.

Amendments
  1976 Amendments. Subsec. (a). Pub.L. 94–544 inserted provision which directed the Secretary to administer the property acquired in such a manner so as to provide recreational, educational, historic preservation, interpretation, and scientific research opportunities consistent with the maximum protection, restoration, and preservation of the environment.

LIBRARY REFERENCES

American Digest System
  Fish ⚎8.
  Game ⚎3.5.
  United States ⚎57.
  Woods and Forests ⚎5.
  Key Number System Topic Nos. 176, 187, 393, 411.

§ 459c–6a. The Clem Miller Environmental Education Center; designation

The Secretary shall designate the principal environmental education center within the seashore as "The Clem Miller Environmental

Education Center'', in commemoration of the vision and leadership which the late Representative Clem Miller gave to the creation and protection of Point Reyes National Seashore.

(Pub.L. 87–657, § 7, as added Pub.L. 94–544, § 4(b), Oct. 18, 1976, 90 Stat. 2515, and amended Pub.L. 94–567, § 7(b), Oct. 20, 1976, 90 Stat. 2695.)

HISTORICAL AND STATUTORY NOTES

Revision Notes and Legislative Reports
   1976 Acts. House Report No. 94–1680, see 1976 U.S. Code Cong. and Adm. News, p. 5593.

Codifications
   Section 7(b) of Pub.L. 94–567 enacted the identical section as section 4(b) of Pub.L. 94–544.

LIBRARY REFERENCES

American Digest System
   Water Law ☞2645.
   Key Number System Topic No. 405.

§ 459c–6b.   Cooperation with utilities district; land use and occupancy; terms and conditions

The Secretary shall cooperate with the Bolinas Public Utilities District to protect and enhance the watershed values within the seashore. The Secretary may, at his or her discretion, permit the use and occupancy of lands added to the seashore by action of the Ninety-fifth Congress by the utilities district for water supply purposes, subject to such terms and conditions as the Secretary deems are consistent with the purposes of sections 459c to 459c–7 of this title.

(Pub.L. 87–657, § 8, as added Pub.L. 95–625, Title III, § 318(e), Nov. 10, 1978, 92 Stat. 3487.)

HISTORICAL AND STATUTORY NOTES

Revision Notes and Legislative Reports
   1962 Acts. House Report No. 1628, see 1962 U.S. Code Cong. and Adm. News, p. 2500.

References in Text
   Section 459c–3 of this title, included within the reference in text to sections

459c to 459c–7 of this title, was repealed by Pub.L. 91–223, § 2(b), Apr. 3, 1970, 84 Stat. 90.

LIBRARY REFERENCES

American Digest System
   United States ☞57.
   Key Number System Topic No. 393.

§ 459c–7.   Authorization of appropriations; restriction on use of land

There are authorized to be appropriated such sums as may be necessary to carry out the provisions of sections 459c to 459c–7 of this title, except that no more than $57,500,000 shall be appropriated for the acquisition of land and waters and improvements thereon, and interests therein, and incidental costs relating thereto, in accordance with the provisions of such sections: *Provided,* That no freehold, leasehold, or lesser interest in any lands hereafter acquired within the boundaries of the Point Reyes National Seashore shall be conveyed for residential or commercial purposes except for public accommodations, facilities, and services provided pursuant to sections 20 to 20g and 462(h) of this title. In addition to the sums heretofore authorized by this section, there is further authorized to be appropriated $5,000,000 for the acquisition of lands or interests therein.

(Pub.L. 87–657, § 9, formerly § 8, Sept. 13, 1962, 76 Stat. 541; Pub.L. 89–666, § 1(b), Oct. 15, 1966, 80 Stat. 919; renumbered § 7 and amended Pub.L. 91–223, §§ 1, 2(c), Apr. 3, 1970, 84 Stat. 90; renumbered § 8, Pub.L. 94–544, § 4(b), Oct. 18, 1976, 90 Stat. 2515; renumbered § 8, Pub.L. 94–567, § 7(b), Oct. 20, 1976, 90 Stat. 2695; renumbered § 9 and amended Pub.L. 95–625, Title III, § 318(e), (f), Nov. 10, 1978, 92 Stat. 3487; Pub.L. 96–199, Title I, § 101(a)(5), Mar. 5, 1980, 94 Stat. 67.)

HISTORICAL AND STATUTORY NOTES

Revision Notes and Legislative Reports

1962 Acts. House Report No. 1628, see 1962 U.S. Code Cong. and Adm. News, p. 2500.

1966 Acts. House Report No. 2067, see 1966 U.S. Code Cong. and Adm. News, p. 3320.

1970 Acts. Senate Report No. 91–738, see 1970 U.S. Code Cong. and Adm. News, p. 2681.

1976 Acts. House Report No. 94–1680, see 1976 U.S. Code Cong. and Adm. News, p. 5593.

1980 Acts. Senate Report No. 96–484, see 1980 U.S. Code Cong. and Adm. News, p. 133.

References in Text

Section 459c–3 of this title, included within the reference in text to sections 459c to 459c–7 of this title, was repealed by Pub.L. 91–223, § 2(b), Apr. 3, 1970, 84 Stat. 90.

Sums "heretofore" authorized by this section, referred to in text, means sums authorized by this section prior to the enactment on Mar. 5, 1980, of Pub.L. 96–199, which added the authorization for a $5,000,000 appropriation for the acquisition of lands or interest in lands.

Codifications

Section 7(b) of Pub.L. 94–567 made the identical change in the credit as did section 4(b) of Pub.L. 94–544.

Amendments

1980 Amendments. Pub.L. 96–199 added provisions authorizing an appropriation of $5,000,000 for the acquisition of lands or interests therein.

1970 Amendments. Pub.L. 91–223, § 1, substituted "$57,500,000" for "$19,135,000", restricted conveyances of any interest in any lands acquired after April 3, 1970, only for public accommodations, facilities, and services under provisions for concessions in areas administered by National Park Service.

1966 Amendments. Pub.L. 89–666 substituted "$19,135,000" for "$14,000,000".

LIBRARY REFERENCES

American Digest System

United States ⟊57.
Key Number System Topic No. 393.

§ 459d. Padre Island National Seashore; description of land and waters

In order to save and preserve, for purposes of public recreation, benefit, and inspiration, a portion of the diminishing seashore of the United States that remains undeveloped, the Secretary of the Interior shall take appropriate action in the public interest toward the establishment of the following described lands and waters as the Padre Island National Seashore: Beginning at a point one statute mile northerly of North Bird Island on the easterly line of the Intracoastal Waterway; thence due east to a point on Padre Island one statute mile west of the mean high water line of the Gulf of Mexico; thence southwesterly paralleling the said mean high water line of the Gulf of Mexico a distance of about three and five-tenths statute miles; thence due east to the two-fathom line on the east side of Padre Island as depicted on National Ocean Survey chart numbered 1286; thence along the said two-fathom line on the east side of Padre Island as depicted on National Ocean Survey charts numbered 1286, 1287, and 1288 to the Willacy–Cameron County line extended; thence westerly along said county line to a point 1,500 feet west of the mean high water line of the Gulf of Mexico as that line was determined by the survey of J.S. Boyles and is depicted on sections 9 and 10 of the map entitled "Survey of Padre Island made for the office of the Attorney General of the State of Texas", dated August 7 to 11, 1941, and August 11, 13, and 14, 1941, respectively; thence northerly along a line parallel to said survey line of J.S. Boyles and distant therefrom 1,500 feet west to a point on the centerline of the Port Mansfield Channel; thence westerly along said centerline to a point three statute miles west of the said two-fathom line; thence northerly parallel with said two-fathom line to 27 degrees 20 minutes north latitude; thence westerly along said latitude to the easterly line of the Intracoastal Waterway; thence northerly following the easterly line of the Intracoastal Waterway as indicated by channel markers in the Laguna Madre to the point of beginning.

(Pub.L. 87–712, § 1, Sept. 28, 1962, 76 Stat. 650.)

HISTORICAL AND STATUTORY NOTES

Revision Notes and Legislative Reports
  1962 Acts. House Report No. 2179, see 1962 U.S. Code Cong. and Adm. News, p. 2714.

Change of Name
  The Coast and Geodetic Survey was consolidated with the National Weather Bureau in 1965 to form the Environmental Science Services Administration by Reorg. Plan No. 2 of 1965, eff. July 13,

1965, 30 F.R. 8819, 79 Stat. 1318. The Environmental Science Services Administration was abolished in 1970 and its personnel, property, records, etc., were transferred to the National Oceanic and Atmospheric Administration by Reorg. Plan No. 4 of 1970, eff. Oct. 3, 1970, 35 F.R. 15627, 84 Stat. 2090. By order of the Acting Associate Administrator of the National Oceanic and Atmospheric Administration, 35 F.R. 19249, Dec. 19,

1970, the Coast and Geodetic Survey was redesignated the National Ocean Survey.

See notes under sections 311 and 1511 of Title 15, Commerce and Trade.

LIBRARY REFERENCES

American Digest System
     Water Law ⬤2645.
     Key Number System Topic No. 405.

Notes of Decisions

Preemption   1
Right of action   2

Mines And Minerals ⬤ 92.8; States ⬤ 18.59

2. Right of action

Although National Park Service organic statute and Padre Island National Seashore Enabling Legislation did not provide directly for judicial review of National Park Service regulations governing access to mineral rights through national parks, and neither statute created private right of action, owner of mineral estate under park could challenge Service's authority under Administrative Procedure Act (APA) and thereby trigger federal question jurisdiction. Dunn-McCampbell Royalty Interest, Inc. v. National Park Service, C.A.5 (Tex.) 1997, 112 F.3d 1283, rehearing and suggestion for rehearing en banc denied 124 F.3d 195. Action ⬤ 3; Mines And Minerals ⬤ 92.21

1. Preemption

Federal statutory authority to regulate and manage federal surface lands on national seashore, and National Park Service's regulations implementing that authority, preempted Texas law as it governed mineral developer's right to use federal surface; both federal regulatory scheme and Texas law addressed same subject matter and activity, and were in direct conflict with respect to mineral developer's use of federal lands. Dunn McCampbell Royalty Interest, Inc. v. National Park Service, S.D.Tex.1995, 964 F.Supp. 1125, affirmed 112 F.3d 1283, rehearing and suggestion for rehearing en banc denied 124 F.3d 195.

§ 459d–1. Acquisition of property

(a) Authority of Secretary; manner and place; concurrence of State owner; transfer from Federal agency to administrative jurisdiction of Secretary

The Secretary of the Interior (hereinafter referred to as the "Secretary") is authorized to acquire by donation, purchase with donated or appropriated funds, condemnation, transfer from any Federal agency, exchange, or otherwise, the land, waters, and other property, and improvements thereon and any interest therein, within the areas described in section 459d of this title or which lie within the boundaries of the seashore as established under section 459d–2 of this title (hereinafter referred to as "such area"). Any property, or interest therein, owned by the State of Texas or political subdivision thereof may be acquired only with the concurrence of such owner. Notwithstanding any other provision of law, any Federal property located within such area may, with the concurrence of the agency having custody thereof, be transferred without consideration to the administrative jurisdiction of the Secretary for use by him in carrying out the provisions of sections 459d to 459d–7 of this title.

(b) Fair market value; appraisal

The Secretary is authorized to pay for any acquisitions which he makes by purchase under sections 459d to 459d–7 of this title their fair market value, as determined by the Secretary, who may in his discretion base his determination on an independent appraisal obtained by him.

(c) Exchange of property; cash equalization payments

In exercising his authority to acquire property by exchange, the Secretary may accept title to any non-Federal property located within such area and convey to the grantor of such property any federally owned property under the jurisdiction of the Secretary within such area. The properties so exchanged shall be approximately equal in fair market value: *Provided,* That the Secretary may accept cash from or pay cash to the grantor in such an exchange in order to equalize the values of the properties exchanged.

(Pub.L. 87–712, § 2, Sept. 28, 1962, 76 Stat. 650.)

HISTORICAL AND STATUTORY NOTES

Revision Notes and Legislative Reports
  1962 Acts. House Report No. 2179, see 1962 U.S. Code Cong. and Adm. News, p. 2714.

Revision of Boundaries; Addition and Deletion of Acreage
  Pub.L. 94–578, Title I, § 101(13), Oct. 21, 1976, 90 Stat. 2733, as amended Pub.L. 96–199, Title I, § 111, Mar. 5, 1980, 94 Stat. 70, provided in part that: "The Secretary of the Interior is author-

ized to revise the boundary of the seashore [Padre Island National Seashore, Texas] to add approximately two hundred and seventy-four acres and to delete approximately two thousand acres, and sections 302 and 303 of the Act of April 11, 1972 (86 Stat. 120, 121) [Pub.L. 92–272, Title III, §§ 302, 303, Apr. 11, 1972, 86 Stat. 121, which sections were not classified to the Code], shall apply to the boundary revision authorized herein."

LIBRARY REFERENCES

American Digest System
  United States ☞55.
  Key Number System Topic No. 393.

§ 459d–2. Establishment

(a) Notice in Federal Register

As soon as practicable after September 28, 1962 and following the acquisition by the Secretary of an acreage in the area described in section 459d of this title, that is in the opinion of the Secretary efficiently administrable to carry out the purposes of sections 459d to 459d–7 of this title, the Secretary shall establish the area as a national seashore by the publication of notice thereof in the Federal Register.

(b) Distribution of notice and map

Such notice referred to in subsection (a) of this section shall contain a detailed description of the boundaries of the seashore which shall encompass an area as nearly as practicable identical to the area described in section 459d of this title. The Secretary shall forthwith after the date of publication of such notice in the Federal Register (1) send a copy of such notice, together with a map showing such boundaries, by registered or certified mail to the Governor of the State and to the governing body of each of the political subdivisions involved; (2) cause a copy of such notice and map to be published in one or more newspapers which circulate in each of the localities; and (3) cause a certified copy of such notice, a copy of such map, and a copy of sections 459d to 459d–7 of this title to be recorded at the registry of deeds for the county involved.

(Pub.L. 87–712, § 3, Sept. 28, 1962, 76 Stat. 651.)

HISTORICAL AND STATUTORY NOTES

Revision Notes and Legislative Reports
 1962 Acts. House Report No. 2179, see 1962 U.S. Code Cong. and Adm. News, p. 2714.

LIBRARY REFERENCES

American Digest System
 Water Law ☞2645.
 Key Number System Topic No. 405.

§ 459d–3. Reservation of oil, gas, and other minerals

(a) When acquiring land, waters, or interests therein, the Secretary shall permit a reservation by the grantor of all or any part of the oil and gas minerals in such land or waters and of other minerals therein which can be removed by similar means, with the right of occupation and use of so much of the surface of the land or waters as may be required for all purposes reasonably incident to the mining or removal of such from beneath the surface of these lands and waters and the lands and waters adjacent thereto, under such regulations as may be prescribed by the Secretary with respect to such mining or removal.

(b) Any acquisition hereunder shall exclude and shall not diminish any right of occupation or use of the surface under grants, leases, or easements existing on April 11, 1961, which are reasonably necessary for the exploration, development, production, storing, processing, or transporting of oil and gas minerals that are removed from outside the boundaries of the national seashore and the Secretary may grant additional rights of occupation or use of the surface for the purposes aforesaid upon the terms and under such regulations as may be prescribed by him.

(Pub.L. 87–712, § 4, Sept. 28, 1962, 76 Stat. 651.)

HISTORICAL AND STATUTORY NOTES

Revision Notes and Legislative Reports
1962 Acts. House Report No. 2179, see
1962 U.S. Code Cong. and Adm. News, p.
2714.

LIBRARY REFERENCES

American Digest System
   Mines and Minerals ⊕2.
   Key Number System Topic No. 260.

§ **459d–4.** **Administration; utilization of authority for conservation and management of natural resources**

Except as otherwise provided in sections 459d to 459d–7 of this title, the property acquired by the Secretary under such sections shall be administered by the Secretary, subject to the provisions of sections 1, 2, 3, and 4 of this title, as amended and supplemented, and in accordance with other laws of general application relating to the areas administered and supervised by the Secretary through the National Park Service; except that authority otherwise available to the Secretary for the conservation and management of natural resources may be utilized to the extent he finds such authority will further the purposes of sections 459d to 459d–7 of this title.

(Pub.L. 87–712, § 5, Sept. 28, 1962, 76 Stat. 652.)

HISTORICAL AND STATUTORY NOTES

Revision Notes and Legislative Reports
1962 Acts. House Report No. 2179, see
1962 U.S. Code Cong. and Adm. News, p.
2714.

LIBRARY REFERENCES

American Digest System
   Woods and Forests ⊕5.
   Key Number System Topic No. 411.

Notes of Decisions

Jurisdiction 2
Property acquired by Secretary 1
———————

1. Property acquired by Secretary
   Federal regulation of plaintiffs' mineral estate on national seashore was not precluded under Padre Enabling Act, despite claim that estate did not constitute property acquired by Secretary of Interior; "property acquired" language in Act related to federally-owned surface estate on national seashore. Dunn McCampbell

Royalty Interest, Inc. v. National Park Service, S.D.Tex.1995, 964 F.Supp. 1125, affirmed 112 F.3d 1283, rehearing and suggestion for rehearing en banc denied 124 F.3d 195. Mines And Minerals ⊕ 92.5(1)

2. Jurisdiction
   Sole avenue to federal courts for "facial" challenge to validity of National Park Service regulations concerning national seashore is through Administrative Procedure Act (APA) rather than through

Padre Island National Seashore (PINS)   National Park Service, N.D.Tex.1997, 982
enabling statute. Austral Oil Co., Inc. v.   F.Supp. 1238. United States ☞ 57

§ 459d–5. Roadways to access highways from mainland

The Secretary may provide for roadways from the north and south
boundaries of such public recreation area to the access highways
from the mainland to Padre Island.

(Pub.L. 87–712, § 6, Sept. 28, 1962, 76 Stat. 652.)

HISTORICAL AND STATUTORY NOTES

Revision Notes and Legislative Reports
  1962 Acts. House Report No. 2179, see
1962 U.S. Code Cong. and Adm. News, p.
2714.

LIBRARY REFERENCES

American Digest System
  United States ☞57.
  Key Number System Topic No. 393.

§ 459d–6. Aerial gunnery and bombing range agreements of Secretary of the Interior and Secretary of the Navy

The Secretary of the Interior shall enter into such administrative
agreements with the Secretary of the Navy as the Secretary of the
Navy may deem necessary to assure that the Secretary of the Interior
will not exercise any authority granted by sections 459d to 459d–7 of
this title so as to interfere with the use by the Department of the Navy
of any aerial gunnery or bombing range located in the vicinity of
Padre Island.

(Pub.L. 87–712, § 7, Sept. 28, 1962, 76 Stat. 652.)

HISTORICAL AND STATUTORY NOTES

Revision Notes and Legislative Reports
  1962 Acts. House Report No. 2179, see
1962 U.S. Code Cong. and Adm. News, p.
2714.

LIBRARY REFERENCES

American Digest System
  United States ☞57.
  Key Number System Topic No. 393.

§ 459d–7. Authorization of appropriations

There are authorized to be appropriated such sums as may be
necessary to carry out the provisions of sections 459d to 459d–7 of

this title; except that no more than $5,350,000 shall be appropriated for the acquisition of land and waters and improvements thereon, and interests therein, and incidental costs relating thereto, in accordance with the provisions of such sections.

(Pub.L. 87–712, § 8, Sept. 28, 1962, 76 Stat. 652; Pub.L. 94–578, Title I, § 101(13), Oct. 21, 1976, 90 Stat. 2733.)

HISTORICAL AND STATUTORY NOTES

Revision Notes and Legislative Reports
  1962 Acts. House Report No. 2179, see 1962 U.S. Code Cong. and Adm. News, p. 2714.

Codifications
  Section 101(13) of Pub.L. 94–578, cited as a credit to this section, as amended by

Pub.L. 96–199, Title I, § 111, Mar. 5, 1980, 94 Stat. 70, is also set out in part as a note under section 459d–1 of this title.

Amendments
  1976 Amendments. Pub.L. 94–578 substituted "$5,350,000" for "$5,000,000".

§ 459e. Fire Island National Seashore

(a) Purposes; authorization for establishment

For the purpose of conserving and preserving for the use of future generations certain relatively unspoiled and undeveloped beaches, dunes, and other natural features within Suffolk County, New York, which possess high values to the Nation as examples of unspoiled areas of great natural beauty in close proximity to large concentrations of urban population, the Secretary of the Interior is authorized to establish an area to be known as the "Fire Island National Seashore".

(b) Boundaries

The boundaries of the national seashore shall extend from the easterly boundary of the main unit of Robert Moses State Park eastward to Moriches Inlet and shall include not only Fire Island proper, but also such islands and marshlands in the Great South Bay, Bellport Bay, and Moriches Bay adjacent to Fire Island as Sexton Island, West Island, Hollins Island, Ridge Island, Pelican Island, Pattersquash Island, and Reeves Island and such other small and adjacent islands, marshlands, and wetlands as would lend themselves to contiguity and reasonable administration within the national seashore and, in addition, the waters surrounding said area to distances of one thousand feet in the Atlantic Ocean and up to four thousand feet in Great South Bay and Moriches Bay and, in addition, mainland terminal and headquarters sites, not to exceed a total of twelve acres, on the Patchogue River within Suffolk County, New York, all as delineated on a map identified as "Fire Island National Seashore", numbered OGP–0004, dated May 1978. The Secretary shall publish said map in the Federal Register, and it may also be examined in the offices of the Department of the Interior.

(Pub.L. 88–587, § 1, Sept. 11, 1964, 78 Stat. 928; Pub.L. 95–625, Title III, § 322(a), Nov. 10, 1978, 92 Stat. 3488.)

HISTORICAL AND STATUTORY NOTES

Revision Notes and Legislative Reports
  1964 Acts. Senate Report No. 1300, see 1964 U.S. Code Cong. and Adm. News, p. 3710.

Amendments
  1978 Amendments. Subsec. (b). Pub.L. 95–625 inserted phrase "the main unit of" preceding "Robert Moses State Park", included in the boundaries the mainland terminal and headquarters sites, not to exceed a total of twelve acres, on the Patchogue River within Suffolk County, New York, and substituted map numbered OGP–0004, dated May 1978 for OGP–0002, dated June 1964 and requirement of publishing the map in the

Federal Register for prior provision for filing the map with the Federal Register.

Short Title
  1984 Amendments. Pub.L. 98–482, § 1, Oct. 17, 1984, 98 Stat. 2255, provided: "That this Act [amending sections 459e–1 and 459e–2 of this title] may be cited as the 'Fire Island National Seashore Amendments Act of 1984'."

  1964 Acts. Pub.L. 88–587, Sept. 11, 1964, 78 Stat. 928, which enacted this section and sections 459e–1 through 459e–9 of this title, is known as the Fire Island National Seashore Act.

LIBRARY REFERENCES

American Digest System
  Water Law ☜2645.
  Key Number System Topic No. 405.

§ 459e–1. Acquisition of property

(a) Authority of Secretary; manner and place; concurrence of State owner; transfer from Federal agency to administrative jurisdiction of Secretary; liability of United States under contracts contingent on appropriations

The Secretary is authorized to acquire, and it is the intent of Congress that he shall acquire as appropriated funds become available for the purpose or as such acquisition can be accomplished by donation or with donated funds or by transfer, exchange, or otherwise, the lands, waters, and other property, and improvements thereon and any interest therein, within the boundaries of the seashore as established under section 459e of this title. Any property or interest therein owned by the State of New York, by Suffolk County, or by any other political subdivision of said State may be acquired only with the concurrence of such owner. Notwithstanding any other provision of law, any Federal property located within such area may, with the concurrence of the agency having custody thereof, be transferred without consideration to the administrative jurisdiction of the Secretary for use by him in carrying out the provisions of sections 459e to 459e–9 of this title. In exercising his authority to acquire property in accordance with the provisions of this subsection, the Secretary may enter into contracts requiring the expenditure, when appropriated, of funds authorized by sections 459e to 459e–9 of this title, but the liability of the United States under any such contract shall be contingent on the appropriation of funds sufficient to fulfill the obligations thereby incurred.

(b) Establishment; notice in Federal Register

When the Secretary determines that lands and waters or interests therein have been acquired by the United States in sufficient quantity to provide an administrative unit, he shall declare the establishment of the Fire Island National Seashore by publication of notice in the Federal Register.

(c) Fair market value

The Secretary shall pay not more than the fair market value, as determined by him, for any land or interest therein acquired by purchase.

(d) Exchange of property; cash equalization payments

When acquiring land by exchange the Secretary may accept title to any nonfederally owned land located within the boundaries of the national seashore and convey to the grantor any federally owned land under the jurisdiction of the Secretary. The lands so exchanged shall be approximately equal in fair market value, but the Secretary may accept cash from or pay cash to the grantor in order to equalize the values of the lands exchanged.

(e) Limitation of condemnation power during existence of zoning ordinance; Davis Park-Smith Point County Park area exception; beneficial owner's election of alternatives as condition for acquisition

With one exception the Secretary shall not acquire any privately owned improved property or interests therein within the boundaries of the seashore or any property or interests therein within the communities delineated on the boundary map mentioned in section 459e of this title, except beach or waters and adjoining land within such communities which the Secretary determines are needed for public access to the beach, without the consent of the owners so long as the appropriate local zoning agency shall have in force and applicable to such property a duly adopted, valid, zoning ordinance that is satisfactory to the Secretary. The sole exception to this limitation on the power of the Secretary to condemn improved property where appropriate zoning ordinances exist shall be in the approximately eight-mile area from the easterly boundary of the Brookhaven town park at Davis Park, in the town of Brookhaven, to the westerly boundary of the Smith Point County Park. In this area

441

only, when the Secretary deems it advisable for carrying out the purposes of sections 459e to 459e–9 of this title or to improve the contiguity of the park land and ease its administration, the Secretary may acquire any land or improvements therein by condemnation. In every case in which the Secretary exercises this right of condemnation of improved property the beneficial owner or owners (not being a corporation) of any improved property so condemned, provided he, she, or they held the same or a greater estate in the property on July 1, 1963, may elect as a condition of such acquisition by the Secretary any one of the following three alternatives:

(1) that the Secretary shall take the said property in fee simple absolute and pay the fair market value thereof as of the date of such taking;

(2) that the owner or owners shall retain a life estate in said property, measured on the life of the sole owner or on the life of any one person among multiple owners (notice of the person so designated to be filed in writing with the Secretary within six months after the taking) or on the life of the survivor in title of any estate held on July 1, 1963, as a tenancy by the entirety. The price in such case shall be diminished by the actuarial fair market value of the life estate retained, determined on the basis of standard actuarial methods;

(3) that the owner or owners shall retain an estate for twenty-five years. The price in this case shall likewise be diminished by the value of the estate retained.

(f) "Improved property" defined

The term "improved property" as used in sections 459e to 459e–9 of this title shall mean any building, the construction of which was begun before July 1, 1963, and such amount of land, not in excess of two acres in the case of a residence or ten acres in the case of a commercial or industrial use, on which the building is situated as the Secretary considers reasonably necessary to the use of the building: *Provided*, That the Secretary may exclude from improved properties any beach or waters, together with so much of the land adjoining such beach or waters as he deems necessary for public access thereto.

(g) Undeveloped tracts and property; suspension of condemnation authority; natural state

The authority of the Secretary to condemn undeveloped tracts within the Dune District as depicted on map entitled "Fire Island National Seashore" numbered OGP–0004 dated May, 1978, is suspended so long as the owner or owners of the undeveloped property therein maintain the property in its natural state. Undeveloped property within the Dune District that is acquired by the Secretary shall remain in its natural state.

(h) Sale of property acquired by condemnation; excepted properties; proceeds available for acquisition of property

(1)(A) The Secretary shall sell any property described in subparagraph (B) of this paragraph acquired by condemnation under sections 459e to 459e–9 of this title to the highest bidder; except that—

(i) no property shall be sold at less than its fair market value; and

(ii) no property shall be sold unless it is sold subject to covenants or other restrictions that will ensure that the use of such property conforms—

(I) to the standards specified in regulations issued under section 459e–2(a) of this title which are in effect at the time of such sale, and

(II) to any approved zoning ordinance or amendment thereof to which such property is subject.

(B) The property referred to in subparagraph (A) of this paragraph is any property within the boundaries of the national seashore as delineated on the map mentioned in section 459e of this title except—

(i) property within the Dune district referred to in subsection (g) of this section;

(ii) beach or waters and adjoining land within the exempt communities referred to in the first sentence of subsection (e) of this section; and

(iii) property within the eight-mile area described in the second sentence of subsection (e) of this section; and

(iv) any property acquired prior to October 1, 1982, that the Secretary determines should be retained to further the purpose of sections 459e to 459e–9 of this title.

(2) Notwithstanding any other provision of law, all moneys received from sales under paragraph (1) of this subsection may be retained and shall be available to the Secretary, without further appropriation, only for purposes of acquiring property under sections 459e to 459e–9 of this title.

(i) Injunctive relief; termination

(1) Upon or after the commencement of any action for condemnation with respect to any property under sections 459c to 459e–9 of this title, the Secretary, through the Attorney General of the United States, may apply to the United States District Court for the Eastern

District of New York for a temporary restraining order or injunction to prevent any use of, or construction upon, such property that—

(A) fails, or would result in a failure of such property, to conform to the standards specified in regulations issued under section 459e–2(a) of this title in effect at the time such use or construction began; or

(B) in the case of undeveloped tracts in the Dune district referred to in subsection (g) of this section, would result in such undeveloped property not being maintained in its natural state.

(2) Any temporary restraining order or injunction issued pursuant to such an application shall terminate in accordance with the provisions of section 459e–2(g) of this title.

(Pub.L. 88–587, § 2, Sept. 11, 1964, 78 Stat. 929; Pub.L. 95–625, Title III, § 322(b), Nov. 10, 1978, 92 Stat. 3489; Pub.L. 98–482, § 2, Oct. 17, 1984, 98 Stat. 2255.)

HISTORICAL AND STATUTORY NOTES

Revision Notes and Legislative Reports
1964 Acts. Senate Report No. 1300, see 1964 U.S. Code Cong. and Adm. News, p. 3710.

1984 Acts. House Report No. 98–1065, see 1984 U.S. Code Cong. and Adm. News, p. 3844.

References in Text
Section 459e–8, included within the reference in subsecs. (a), (e), (f), (h), and (i) to "sections 459e to 459e–9", was omitted from the Code.

Amendments
1984 Amendments. Subsecs. (h), (i). Pub.L. 98–482 added subsecs. (h) and (i).

1978 Amendments. Subsec. (g). Pub.L. 95–625 added subsec. (g).

LIBRARY REFERENCES

American Digest System
United States ☞55.
Key Number System Topic No. 393.

Notes of Decisions

Absence of funds as termination of authority 4
Arbitrary and capricious takings 7
Consent to condemnation 3
Constitutionality 1
Cross-claims 8
Grounds for condemnation 2
Injunctions 9
Zoning ordinances suitable to Secretary 5
Zoning powers of local government 6

---

1. Constitutionality
Vesting, under subsecs. (e) and (f) of this section, of discretion in Secretary to decide whether local zoning ordinances are "satisfactory" and to determine what acreage adjacent to residence is "reasonably necessary to use of the building," for purposes of determining what will be considered "improved" property under this section, did not constitute unconstitutional delegation of congressional authority depriving parcel owner, who sought to construct residence on parcel, of due process. U.S. v. 0.16 of an Acre of Land, More or Less, Situated in Suffolk County, State of N.Y., E.D.N.Y.1981, 517 F.Supp. 1115. Constitutional Law ☞ 2411; Constitutional Law ☞ 4076; Eminent Domain ☞ 3

2. Grounds for condemnation
Taking of privately owned parcel on which owner sought to construct resi-

dence was not invalid on basis that taking was not for congressionally authorized purpose of conserving and preserving relatively unspoiled and undeveloped beaches, dunes, and other natural features pursuant to section 459e et seq. of this title, absent showing by owner that his parcel bore no discernable relation to protecting beaches, dunes, and other natural features of the seashore. U.S. v. 0.16 of an Acre of Land, More or Less, Situated in Suffolk County, State of N.Y., E.D.N.Y. 1981, 517 F.Supp. 1115. Eminent Domain ☞ 41

3. Consent to condemnation

Where subsec. (e) of this section requires consent of landowners prior to condemnation of portion of realty, and landowners relied on $600,000 offer for entire realty in giving consent conditional on condemnation proceedings against entire realty, landowners could not withdraw consent after jury award of $375,000 in absence of agreement that only difference between Government's offer and landowner's higher appraisal would be litigated particularly where there was no dispute as to value of that portion of realty as to which consent was necessary. U.S. v. Two Tracts of Land in Town of Brookhaven, Suffolk County, State of N.Y., C.A.2 (N.Y.) 1969, 412 F.2d 347, certiorari denied 90 S.Ct. 222, 396 U.S. 906, 24 L.Ed.2d 183. Eminent Domain ☞ 169

4. Absence of funds as termination of authority

Absent any remaining funds for condemnation, the statutory scheme devised by Congress, to wit, section 459e et seq. of this title, left the Secretary powerless to arrest the allegedly destructive development of Fire Island; and the federal courts could not, by a grant of injunctive relief, arm the Secretary with "go-ahead" power when Congress saw fit not to do so. Biderman v. Morton, C.A.2 (N.Y.) 1974, 497 F.2d 1141. Environmental Law ☞ 700

5. Zoning ordinances suitable to Secretary

Where owner of parcel within Fire Island National Seashore applied to town board for variance from zoning ordinance setback requirements, subsec. (e) of this section suspending authority of Secretary to acquire property within towns in the area that have adopted zon-

ing ordinances suitable to the Secretary automatically ceased under section 459e-2(e) of this title that governed variances and Secretary had power to condemn the parcel. U.S. v. 0.16 of an Acre of Land, More or Less, Situated in Suffolk County, State of N.Y., E.D.N.Y.1981, 517 F.Supp. 1115. Eminent Domain ☞ 45

6. Zoning powers of local government

Section 459e et seq. of this title does not prohibit any zoning action by the various local governments located on the seashore. Biderman v. Morton, C.A.2 (N.Y.) 1974, 497 F.2d 1141. Zoning And Planning ☞ 1017

7. Arbitrary and capricious takings

Acquisition by Secretary of privately owned parcel on which owner sought to construct residence was not invalid as being arbitrary, capricious, and in bad faith, even though parcel was within developed community and even though other plots of size and location similar to subject parcel contained residences, where subject parcel was only parcel both located on seashore and located on border of federal lands. U.S. v. 0.16 of an Acre of Land, More or Less, Situated in Suffolk County, State of N.Y., E.D.N.Y. 1981, 517 F.Supp. 1115. Eminent Domain ☞ 45

8. Cross-claims

Where federal government joined town as codefendant in condemnation proceeding under §§ 459e to 459e-7 and 459e-9 of this title only to determine and extinguish any claims town might have against subject property and condemnees sought by cross-claim against town to recover damages from town for its failure to construct highway bisecting condemned tracts, and cross-claim would unnecessarily prolong trial and would cause jury to be misled and confused, permission to file cross-claim would be denied. U.S. v. Eight Tracts of Land in Town of Brookhaven, Suffolk County, State of N.Y., E.D.N.Y.1967, 270 F.Supp. 160. Federal Civil Procedure ☞ 786

9. Injunctions

In suit seeking a preliminary injunction to restrain the issuance of construction permits and the granting of zoning variances on Fire Island pending the completion of an environmental impact statement, injunctive relief against the named

445

federal defendants was inappropriate under the circumstances, including the fact
that congressional funding of section
459e et seq. of this title had been essen-
tially exhausted; furthermore, relief
against the municipal defendants was
barred by the failure of plaintiffs to identify a discernible basis for the exercise of
federal injunctive power over those non-
federal officials. Biderman v. Morton,
C.A.2 (N.Y.) 1974, 497 F.2d 1141. Environmental Law ☞ 701

§ 459e–2. Zoning regulations

(a) Amendment; standards for approval of ordinances

In order to carry out the provisions of section 459e–1 of this title,
the Secretary shall issue regulations, which may be amended from
time to time, specifying standards that are consistent with the purposes of sections 459e to 459e–9 of this title for zoning ordinances
which must meet his approval.

(b) Commercial or industrial use prohibition; size, location or use restrictions for commercial, residential, and other structures; reconciliation of population density with protection of natural resources

The standards specified in such regulations shall have the object of
(1) prohibiting new commercial or industrial uses, other than commercial or industrial uses which the Secretary considers are consistent with the purposes of sections 459e to 459e–9 of this title, of all
property within the national seashore, and (2) promoting the protection and development for purposes of sections 459e to 459e–9 of this
title of the land within the national seashore by means of limitations
or restrictions on the size, location or use of any commercial,
residential, and other structures. In accomplishing these objectives,
such standards shall seek to reconcile the population density of the
seashore on October 17, 1984, with the protection of the natural
resources of the Seashore [1] consistent with the purposes for which it
has been established as provided by sections 459e to 459e–9 of this
title.

(c) Approval of ordinances

Following issuance of such regulations the Secretary shall approve
any zoning ordinance or any amendment to any approved zoning
ordinance submitted to him that conforms to the standards contained
in the regulations in effect at the time of adoption of the ordinance or
amendment. Such approval shall remain effective for so long as
such ordinance or amendment remains in effect as approved.

(d) Adverse provisions and absence of notice for variance as requiring disapproval of ordinances

No zoning ordinance or amendment thereof shall be approved by
the Secretary which (1) contains any provisions that he considers

adverse to the protection and development, in accordance with the purposes of sections 459e to 459e–9 of this title, of the area comprising the national seashore; or (2) fails to have the effect of providing that the Secretary shall receive notice of any variance granted under, or any exception made to, the application of such ordinance or amendment.

(e) Termination of suspension of authority for acquisition by condemnation because of nonconforming variances and uses

In the case of any property, including improved property but excluding undeveloped property in the Dune district referred to in section 459e–1(g) of this title, with respect to which the Secretary's authority to acquire by condemnation has been suspended under sections 459e to 459e–9 of this title if—

(1) such property is, after October 17, 1984, made the subject of a variance under, or becomes for any reason an exception to, any applicable zoning ordinance approved under this section; and

(2) such variance or exception results, or will result, in such property being used in a manner that fails to conform to any applicable standard contained in regulations of the Secretary issued pursuant to this section and in effect at the time such variance or exception took effect;

then the suspension of the Secretary's authority to acquire such property by condemnation shall automatically cease.

(f) Certificate of suspension of authority for acquisition by condemnation

The Secretary shall furnish to any party in interest upon request a certificate indicating the property with respect to which the Secretary's authority to acquire by condemnation is suspended.

(g) Injunctive relief; termination

Notwithstanding any other provision of sections 459e to 459e–9 of this title, the Secretary of the Interior, acting through the Attorney General of the United States, may apply to the United States District Court for the Eastern District of New York for a temporary restraining order or injunction to prohibit the use of, including construction upon, any property within the seashore in a manner that—

(1) will cause or is likely to cause significant harm to the natural resources of the seashore, or

(2) is inconsistent with the purposes for which the seashore was established.

Except to the extent the Court may deem necessary in extraordinary circumstances, no such order or injunction shall continue in effect for more than one hundred and eighty days. During the period of such order or injunction, the Secretary shall diligently and in good faith negotiate with the owner of the property to assure that following termination of the order or injunction, the inconsistent use is abated or the significant harm to the natural resources is mitigated.

(Pub.L. 88–587, § 3, Sept. 11, 1964, 78 Stat. 930; Pub.L. 98–482, §§ 3–5, Oct. 17, 1984, 98 Stat. 2256.)

[1] So in original. Probably should be "seashore".

HISTORICAL AND STATUTORY NOTES

Revision Notes and Legislative Reports
  1964 Acts. Senate Report No. 1300, see 1964 U.S. Code Cong. and Adm. News, p. 3710.
  1984 Acts. House Report No. 98–1065, see 1984 U.S. Code Cong. and Adm. News, p. 3844.

References in Text
  Section 459e–8, included within the reference in subsecs. (a), (b), (d), (e), and (g) to "sections 459e to 459e–9", was omitted from the Code.

Amendments
  1984   Amendments. Subsec.   (b). Pub.L. 98–482, § 4, substituted "by means of limitations or restrictions on the size, location or use of any commercial, residential, and other structures" for "by means of acreage, frontage, and setback requirements" and required the standards to seek reconciliation of the population density of the Seashore on Oct. 17, 1984, with the protection of the natural resources of the Seashore.

  Subsec. (e). Pub.L. 98–482, § 3, in revising the provisions, incorporated existing text in provisions designated pars. (1) and (2), made the provisions applicable to any property, and excluded undeveloped property in the Dune district.

  Subsec. (g). Pub.L. 98–482, § 5, added subsec. (g).

CODE OF FEDERAL REGULATIONS

Zoning standards, see 36 CFR § 28.1 et seq.

LIBRARY REFERENCES

American Digest System
  Eminent Domain ⊕5.
  Key Number System Topic No. 148.

Notes of Decisions

Commercial or business signs 1

---

1. Commercial or business signs
  Village ordinance which was enacted to conform to regulations promulgated by the Secretary under authority of §§ 459e to 459e–7 and 459e–9 of this title and which prohibited commercial or business signs exceeding four square feet in area and provided penal sanctions was a valid and permissible exercise of the police power, in the name of aesthetics, in light of the special cultural values and natural resources of the area, despite contention that, as applied to drugstore in which first aid was administered on occasion, the ordinance contravened health and safety considerations with respect to a service in the public interest. People v. Goodman, N.Y.1972, 290 N.E.2d 139, 338 N.Y.S.2d 97, 31 N.Y.2d 262, reargument denied 296 N.E.2d 459, 343 N.Y.S.2d 1026, 32 N.Y.2d 705. Zoning And Planning ⊕ 1111

§ 459e–3.   Retention by owner of right of use and occupancy of improved property for residential purposes

(a) Time limit; value of reserved right

Owners of improved property acquired by the Secretary may reserve for themselves and their successors or assigns a right of use and occupancy of the improved property for noncommercial residential purposes for a term that is not more than twenty-five years. The value of the reserved right shall be deducted from the fair market value paid for the property.

(b) Termination of right; compensation

A right of use and occupancy reserved pursuant to this section shall be subject to termination by the Secretary upon his determination that the use and occupancy is not consistent with an applicable zoning ordinance approved by the Secretary in accordance with the provisions of section 459e–2 of this title, and upon tender to the owner of the right an amount equal to the fair market value of that portion of the right which remains unexpired on the date of termination.

(Pub.L. 88–587, § 4, Sept. 11, 1964, 78 Stat. 931.)

HISTORICAL AND STATUTORY NOTES

Revision Notes and Legislative Reports
1964 Acts. Senate Report No. 1300, see 1964 U.S. Code Cong. and Adm. News, p. 3710.

LIBRARY REFERENCES

American Digest System
United States ☞57.
Key Number System Topic No. 393.

Notes of Decisions

Easements   2
Nature of rights retained   1

1. Nature of rights retained
Where condemnees exercised election under this section to retain an estate for 25 years in parcels condemned, condemnees had right to challenge condemnor's taking of tracts on theory that condemnee had retained only right of use and occupancy for 25 years. U.S. v. Eight Tracts of Land in Town of Brookhaven, Suffolk County, State of N.Y., E.D.N.Y.1967, 270 F.Supp. 160. Eminent Domain ☞ 319

2. Easements
Condemnee exercising election under this section to retain 25-year estate was not entitled to grant of easement or rights over other adjoining property condemned or to be condemned, although failure to grant such rights appertaining to the retained estate would increase amount of compensation payable. U.S. v. Eight Tracts of Land in Town of Brookhaven, Suffolk County, State of N.Y., E.D.N.Y. 1967, 270 F.Supp. 160. Eminent Domain ☞ 319

§ 459e–4. Hunting and fishing regulations

The Secretary shall permit hunting, fishing, and shellfishing on lands and waters under his administrative jurisdiction within the Fire Island National Seashore in accordance with the laws of New York and the United States of America, except that the Secretary may designate zones where, and establish periods when, no hunting shall be permitted for reasons of public safety, administration, or public use and enjoyment. Any regulations of the Secretary under this section shall be issued after consultation with the Conservation Department of the State of New York.

(Pub.L. 88–587, § 5, Sept. 11, 1964, 78 Stat. 931.)

HISTORICAL AND STATUTORY NOTES

Revision Notes and Legislative Reports
 1964 Acts. Senate Report No. 1300, see 1964 U.S. Code Cong. and Adm. News, p. 3710.

LIBRARY REFERENCES

American Digest System
 Fish ☞8.
 Game ☞3.5.
 Key Number System Topic Nos. 176, 187.

§ 459e–5. Acceptance of donations

The Secretary may accept and use for purposes of sections 459e to 459e–9 of this title any real or personal property or moneys that may be donated for such purposes.

(Pub.L. 88–587, § 6, Sept. 11, 1964, 78 Stat. 931.)

HISTORICAL AND STATUTORY NOTES

Revision Notes and Legislative Reports
 1964 Acts. Senate Report No. 1300, see 1964 U.S. Code Cong. and Adm. News, p. 3710.

References in Text
 Section 459e–8, included within the reference in text to "sections 459e to 459e–9", was omitted from the Code.

LIBRARY REFERENCES

American Digest System
 United States ☞55.
 Key Number System Topic No. 393.

§ 459e–6. Administration, protection, and development

(a) Conservation of natural resources of Seashore; preservation and access to Sunken Forest Preserve

The Secretary shall administer and protect the Fire Island National Seashore with the primary aim of conserving the natural resources located there. The area known as the Sunken Forest Preserve shall be preserved from bay to ocean in as nearly its present state as possible, without developing roads therein, but continuing the present access by those trails already existing and limiting new access to similar trails limited in number to those necessary to allow visitors to explore and appreciate this section of the seashore.

(b) Access to Davis Park–Smith Point County Park area

Access to that section of the seashore lying between the easterly boundary of the Ocean Ridge portion of Davis Park and the westerly boundary of the Smith Point County Park shall be provided by ferries and footpaths only, and no roads shall be constructed in this section except such minimum roads as may be necessary for park maintenance vehicles. No development or plan for the convenience of visitors shall be undertaken therein which would be incompatible with the preservation of the flora and fauna or the physiographic conditions now prevailing, and every effort shall be exerted to maintain and preserve this section of the seashore as well as that set forth in the preceding paragraph in as nearly their present state and condition as possible.

(c) Utilization of authority for conservation and development of natural resources; user fees

In administering, protecting, and developing the entire Fire Island National Seashore, the Secretary shall be guided by the provisions of sections 459e to 459e–9 of this title and the applicable provisions of the laws relating to the national park system, and the Secretary may utilize any other statutory authority available to him for the conservation and development of natural resources to the extent he finds that such authority will further the purposes of sections 459e to 459e–9 of this title. Appropriate user fees may be collected notwithstanding any limitation on such authority by any provision of law.

(Pub.L. 88–587, § 7, Sept. 11, 1964, 78 Stat. 931; Pub.L. 95–625, Title III, § 322(c), Nov. 10, 1978, 92 Stat. 3489.)

HISTORICAL AND STATUTORY NOTES

Revision Notes and Legislative Reports
 1964 Acts. Senate Report No. 1300, see 1964 U.S. Code Cong. and Adm. News, p. 3710.

References in Text
 Section 459e–8, included within the reference in subsec. (c) to "sections 459e to 459e–9", was omitted from the Code.

Amendments
 1978 Amendments. Subsec. (b). Pub.L. 95–625 substituted "Ocean Ridge portion of Davis Park" for "Brookhaven town park at Davis Park".

CODE OF FEDERAL REGULATIONS

Special regulations for particular areas of system, see 36 CFR § 7.1 et seq.

LIBRARY REFERENCES

American Digest System
  Woods and Forests ⊕5.
  Key Number System Topic No. 411.

§ 459e–7. Shore erosion control or beach protection measures; Fire Island inlet

(a) Authority of Chief of Engineers

The authority of the Chief of Engineers, Department of the Army, to undertake or contribute to shore erosion control or beach protection measures on lands within the Fire Island National Seashore shall be exercised in accordance with a plan that is mutually acceptable to the Secretary of the Interior and the Secretary of the Army and that is consistent with the purposes of sections 459e to 459e–9 of this title.

(b) Land contribution

The Secretary shall also contribute the necessary land which may be required at any future date for the construction of one new inlet across Fire Island in such location as may be feasible in accordance with plans for such an inlet which are mutually acceptable to the Secretary of the Interior and the Secretary of the Army and that is consistent with the purposes of sections 459e to 459e–9 of this title.

(Pub.L. 88–587, § 8, Sept. 11, 1964, 78 Stat. 932.)

HISTORICAL AND STATUTORY NOTES

Revision Notes and Legislative Reports
  1964 Acts. Senate Report No. 1300, see 1964 U.S. Code Cong. and Adm. News, p. 3710.

References in Text
  Section 459e–8, included within the reference in subsecs. (a) and (b) to "sections 459e to 459e–9", was omitted from the Code.

LIBRARY REFERENCES

American Digest System
  Water Law ⊕2645.
  Key Number System Topic No. 405.

Notes of Decisions

Duty of government   1

---

1. Duty of government
  Area landowners did not establish that federal and state agencies and officials had duty under Endangered Species Act (ESA), Fire Island National Seashore Act (FINSA), National Park Service Act, Water Resources Development Act, or § 1983 to adopt proposed interim measure to combat island's shore erosion problem or to otherwise act in manner that would likely redress landowners' alleged injuries from shore erosion on island, and therefore landowners lacked

constitutional standing to sue agencies and officials to enforce such laws; to the extent that statutes required action, they also accorded agencies and officials considerable discretion.   New York Coastal Partnership, Inc. v. U.S. Dept. of Interior, C.A.2 (N.Y.) 2003, 341 F.3d 112, certiorari denied 126 S.Ct. 352, 546 U.S. 820, 163 L.Ed.2d 61.   Environmental Law ☞ 656

§ 459e–8.   Omitted

HISTORICAL AND STATUTORY NOTES

Codifications
Section, Pub.L. 88–587, § 9, Sept. 11, 1964, 78 Stat. 932, which provided for the creation of a Fire Island National Seashore Advisory Commission, has been omitted as executed in view of a provision of subsec. (a) that the Commission terminate on Sept. 11, 1974, or on the declaration of the establishment of the Fire Island National Seashore, whichever occurs first.

§ 459e–9.   Authorization of appropriations

There is hereby authorized to be appropriated not more than $23,000,000 for the acquisition of lands and interests in land pursuant to sections 459e to 459e–9 of this title, and, after December 23, 1980, not more than $500,000 for development.

(Pub.L. 88–587, § 10, Sept. 11, 1964, 78 Stat. 933; Pub.L. 94–578, Title I, § 101(5), Oct. 21, 1976, 90 Stat. 2732; Pub.L. 95–625, Title III, § 322(d), Nov. 10, 1978, 92 Stat. 3489; Pub.L. 96–585, § 1(e), Dec. 23, 1980, 94 Stat. 3379.)

HISTORICAL AND STATUTORY NOTES

Revision Notes and Legislative Reports
1964 Acts. Senate Report No. 1300, see 1964 U.S. Code Cong. and Adm. News, p. 3710.

References in Text
Section 459e–8, included within the reference in text to "sections 459e to 459e–9", was omitted from the Code.

Amendments
1980 Amendments. Pub.L. 96–585 added provision authorizing $500,000 appropriation for development.

1978 Amendments. Pub.L. 95–625 substituted   "$23,000,000"   for "$18,000,000".

1976 Amendments. Pub.L. 94–578 substituted   "$18,000,000"   for "$16,000,000".

§ 459e–10.   Authority to accept donation of William Floyd Estate

The Secretary of the Interior is authorized to accept the donation of approximately six hundred and eleven acres of lands, submerged lands, islands, and marshlands or interests therein, known as the William Floyd Estate, located in the town of Brookhaven, county of Suffolk, and State of New York, delineated on a certain map entitled "Map of the Fire Island National Seashore, Including the William

Floyd Estate", numbered OGP–0003, dated May 1965, which map or a true copy thereof shall be filed with the Federal Register and may be examined in the offices of the Department of the Interior. Such donation may be accepted subject to such terms, covenants, and conditions as the Secretary finds will be in the public interest.

(Pub.L. 89–244, § 1, Oct. 9, 1965, 79 Stat. 967.)

LIBRARY REFERENCES

American Digest System
   United States ⊙▪55.
   Key Number System Topic No. 393.

§ 459e–11.　Authority to accept donation of main dwelling on William Floyd Estate; lease-back of donated property

The Secretary is also authorized to accept the donation of the main dwelling on said lands, which was the birthplace and residence of General William Floyd (a signer of the Declaration of Independence) and the furnishings therein and any outbuildings, subject to like terms, covenants, and conditions. The Secretary is authorized to lease said lands, dwellings, and outbuildings to the grantors thereof for a term of not more than twenty-five years, at $1 per annum, and during the period of the leasehold the Secretary may provide protective custody for such property.

(Pub.L. 89–244, § 2, Oct. 9, 1965, 79 Stat. 967.)

LIBRARY REFERENCES

American Digest System
   United States ⊙▪55.
   Key Number System Topic No. 393.

§ 459e–12.　Administration of property of William Floyd Estate; detached unit

Upon expiration or surrender of the aforesaid lease the property shall become a detached unit of the Fire Island National Seashore, and shall be administered, protected, and developed in accordance with the laws applicable thereto subject, with respect to said main dwelling and the furnishings therein, to such terms, covenants, and conditions which the Secretary shall have accepted and approved upon the donation thereof as in the public interest.

(Pub.L. 89–244, § 3, Oct. 9, 1965, 79 Stat. 967.)

LIBRARY REFERENCES

American Digest System
  Woods and Forests ⊗5.
  Key Number System Topic No. 411.

§ 459f. Assateague Island National Seashore; purposes; description of area

For the purpose of protecting and developing Assateague Island in the States of Maryland and Virginia and certain adjacent waters and small marsh islands for public outdoor recreation use and enjoyment, the Assateague Island National Seashore (hereinafter referred to as the "seashore") shall be established and administered in accordance with the provisions of sections 459f to 459f–11 of this title. The seashore shall comprise the area within Assateague Island and the small marsh islands adjacent thereto, together with the adjacent water areas not more than one-half mile beyond the mean high waterline of the land portions as generally depicted on a map identified as "Proposed Assateague Island National Seashore, Boundary Map, NS–AI–7100A, November, 1964", which map shall be on file and available for public inspection in the offices of the Department of the Interior.

(Pub.L. 89–195, § 1, Sept. 21, 1965, 79 Stat. 824.)

HISTORICAL AND STATUTORY NOTES

References in Text
  Sections 459f–6 and 459f–8, included within the reference in text to "sections 459f to 459f–11", were repealed by Pub.L. 94–578, Title III, § 301, Oct. 21, 1976, 90 Stat. 2733.

LIBRARY REFERENCES

American Digest System
  Armed Services ⊗54.
  United States ⊗57.
  Key Number System Topic Nos. 34, 393.

Research References

ALR Library
  136 ALR 379, Deed as Conveying Fee or Easement.
  98 ALR 640, Right of Owner of Dominant Estate to Have Compensation for Taking of Easement by Eminent Domain Determined with Reference to Land and Improvements Held in the Dominant Estate.

§ 459f–1. Acquisition of property

(a) Authority of Secretary; manner and place; fair market value; concurrence of State owner; transfer from Federal agency to administrative jurisdiction of Secretary

Within the boundaries of the seashore, the Secretary of the Interior (hereinafter referred to as the "Secretary") is authorized to acquire

lands, waters, and other property, or any interest therein, by donation, purchase with donated or appropriated funds, exchange, or in
such other method as he may find to be in the public interest. The
Secretary is authorized to include within the boundaries of the
seashore, not to exceed 112 acres of land or interests therein on the
mainland in Worcester County, Maryland. In the case of acquisition
by negotiated purchase, the property owners shall be paid the fair
market value by the Secretary. Any property or interests therein
owned by the States of Maryland or Virginia shall be acquired only
with the concurrence of such owner. Notwithstanding any other
provision of law, any Federal property located within the boundaries
of the seashore may, with the concurrence of the agency having
custody thereof, be transferred without consideration to the administrative jurisdiction of the Secretary for purposes of the seashore.

**(b) Exchange of property; cash equalization payments; scenic ease-
ment donation**

When acquiring lands by exchange, the Secretary may accept title
to any non–Federal property within the boundaries of the seashore
and convey to the grantor of such property any federally owned
property under the jurisdiction of the Secretary which the Secretary
classifies suitable for exchange or other disposal, and which is
located in Maryland or Virginia. The properties so exchanged shall
be approximately equal in fair market value, but the Secretary may
accept cash from or pay cash to the grantor in order to equalize the
values of the properties exchanged. Notwithstanding the acreage
limitation set forth in sections 459f to 459f–11 of this title, the
Secretary is authorized to accept the donation of a scenic easement
covering the parcel of land adjacent to the seashore and known as
the "Woodcock Property".

**(c) Bridge acquisition; amount of compensation; payment terms
and conditions**

The Secretary is authorized to acquire all of the right, title, or
interest of the Chincoteague–Assateague Bridge and Beach Authority,
a political subdivision of the State of Virginia, in the bridge constructed by such authority across the Assateague Channel, together
with all lands or interests therein, roads, parking lots, buildings, or
other real or personal property of such authority, and to compensate
the authority in such amount as will permit it to meet its valid
outstanding obligations at the time of such acquisition. Payments by
the Secretary shall be on such terms and conditions as he shall
consider to be in the public interest. Any of the aforesaid property
outside the boundaries of the national seashore, upon acquisition by
the Secretary, shall be subject to his administration for purposes of
the seashore.

(d) Owner's reservation of right of use and occupancy for residential or hunting purposes for term of years; adjustment of compensation; rules and regulations for appearance of buildings; "improved property" defined

Owners of improved property acquired by the Secretary may reserve for themselves and their successors or assigns a right of use and occupancy of the improved property for noncommercial residential purposes or for hunting purposes, as hereinafter provided, for a term that is not more than twenty-five years. In such cases, the Secretary shall pay to the owner of the property the fair market value thereof less the fair market value of the right retained by such owner: *Provided*, That such use and occupancy shall be subject to general rules and regulations established by the Secretary with respect to the outward appearance of any buildings on the lands involved. The term "improved property" as used in sections 459f to 459f–11 of this title shall mean (1) any single-family residence the construction of which was begun before January 1, 1964, and such amount of land, not in excess of three acres, on which the building is situated as the Secretary considers reasonably necessary to the noncommercial residential use of the building, and (2) any property fronting on the Chincoteague Bay or Sinepuxent Bay, including the offshore bay islands adjacent thereto, that is used chiefly for hunting and continues in such use: *Provided*, That the Secretary may exclude from improved properties any marsh, beach, or waters, together with so much of the land adjoining such marsh, beach, or waters as he deems necessary for public use or public access thereto.

(Pub.L. 89–195, § 2, Sept. 21, 1965, 79 Stat. 824; Pub.L. 101–512, Title I, Nov. 5, 1990, 104 Stat. 1924; Pub.L. 102–320, § 1(1) to (4), July 10, 1992, 106 Stat. 321.)

HISTORICAL AND STATUTORY NOTES

References in Text

Sections 459f–6 and 459f–8, included within the reference in subsecs. (b) and (d) to "sections 459f to 459f–11", were repealed by Pub.L. 94–578, Title III, § 301, Oct. 21, 1976, 90 Stat. 2733.

Codifications

Amendment by Pub.L. 101–512, Title I, Nov. 5, 1990, 104 Stat. 1924, was executed to subsecs. (a) and (b) of this section, as the probable intent of Congress, notwithstanding directory language to amend section 459 of this title.

Amendments

1992 Amendments. Subsec. (a). Pub.L. 102–320, § 1(1), (2), substituted provisions authorizing inclusion within seashore boundaries of 112 acres on mainland in Worcester County, Maryland, for provisions authorizing acquisition of a maximum of 16 acres in such county for an administrative site, and substituted provisions authorizing transfer of Federal property within boundaries of seashore to jurisdiction of Secretary, for provisions authorizing transfer of Federal property within boundaries of seashore and a maximum of 16 acres in mainland Worcester County, Maryland, to jurisdiction of Secretary.

Subsec. (b). Pub.L. 102–320, § 1(3), (4), substituted provision making any non-Federal property within boundaries of seashore subject to acquisition by exchange, for provision making any non-Federal property within boundaries of seashore and not more than 10 acres of non-Federal property on mainland in Worcester County, Maryland, subject to acquisition by exchange, and authorized Secretary to accept donation of easement covering parcel of land known as the "Woodcock Property".

1990 Amendments. Subsecs. (a), (b). Pub.L. 101–512 substituted "sixteen acres" for "ten acres". See Codifications note under this section.

LIBRARY REFERENCES

American Digest System
United States ☞55.
Key Number System Topic No. 393.

Notes of Decisions

Manner of recovery of value   1
Persons entitled to condemnation award   2
Presumptions   3

1. Manner of recovery of value

Where plats, advertisements and deeds gave to owner of each lot purchased from developers an implied easement, appurtenant to his lot, to use as private beach 14 miles of beach on Assateague Island value of that easement was reflected in value of each individual lot and owner was entitled to recover that value either by award in condemnation case or by sale to government which was establishing national park on the whole of the island. U.S. v. Certain Land in County of Worcester, State of Md., D.C.Md.1970, 311 F.Supp. 1039, adhered to 324 F.Supp. 1170. Eminent Domain ☞ 85

2. Persons entitled to condemnation award

Deeds from developers of Assateague Island to organization of lot purchasers conveying land in fee simple to be held by grantee as community ocean beach property for benefit of all existing and future owners of record of properties situated on island did not create a specific trust but conveyed whatever interest developers owned in property conveyed to be used for corporate purposes and, upon condemnation of the beach land, the organization and not the developers were entitled to any award for such property. U.S. v. Certain Land in County of Worcester, State of Md., D.C.Md.1970, 311 F.Supp. 1039, adhered to 324 F.Supp. 1170. Eminent Domain ☞ 152(1); Trusts ☞ 30.5(1)

3. Presumptions

Designation of streets on plats and sale and conveyance of lots by reference to such plats raises presumption of offer to dedicate streets to the public. U.S. v. Certain Land in County of Worcester, State of Md., D.C.Md.1970, 311 F.Supp. 1039, adhered to 324 F.Supp. 1170. Dedication ☞ 41

§ 459f–2. Compensation for bridge construction costs; acquisition of land for park purposes

(a) Bridge construction costs; compensation of State; limitation of amount

If the bridge from Sandy Point to Assateague Island is operated by the State of Maryland as a toll-free facility, the Secretary is authorized and directed to compensate said State in the amount of two-thirds of the cost of constructing the bridge, including the cost of bridge approaches, engineering, and all other related costs, but the total amount of such compensation shall be not more than $1,000,000; and he is authorized to enter into agreements with the State of Maryland relating to the use and management of the bridge.

(b) Acquisition or lease of Federal lands for State park purposes; terms and conditions; reversion upon noncompliance; consideration for lease; amount of payment for conveyance of title and improvements; limitation of reimbursement for beach protection

The State of Maryland shall have the right to acquire or lease from the United States such lands, or interests therein, on the island north of the area now used as a State park as the State may from time to time determine to be needed for State park purposes, and the Secretary is authorized and directed to convey or lease such lands, or interests therein, to the State for such purposes upon terms and conditions which he deems will assure its public use in harmony with the purposes of sections 459f to 459f–11 of this title. In the event any of such terms and conditions are not complied with, all the property, or any portion thereof, shall, at the option of the Secretary, revert to the United States in its then existing condition. Any lease hereunder shall be for such consideration as the Secretary deems equitable; and any conveyance of title to land hereunder may be made only upon payment by the State of such amounts of money as were expended by the United States to acquire such land, or interests therein, and upon payments of such amounts as will reimburse the United States for the cost of any improvements placed thereon by the United States, including the cost to it of beach protection: *Provided,* That reimbursement for beach protection shall not exceed 30 per centum, as determined by the Secretary, of the total cost of the United States of such protection work.

(Pub.L. 89–195, § 3, Sept. 21, 1965, 79 Stat. 825.)

HISTORICAL AND STATUTORY NOTES

References in Text

Sections 459f–6 and 459f–8, included within the reference in subsec. (b) to "sections 459f to 459f–11" were repealed by Pub.L. 94–578, Title III, § 301, Oct. 21, 1976, 90 Stat. 2733.

LIBRARY REFERENCES

American Digest System

United States ☞57.

Key Number System Topic No. 393.

§ 459f–3. Establishment of Seashore; notice in Federal Register

When the Secretary determines that land, water areas, or interests therein within the area generally depicted on the map referred to in section 459f of this title are owned or have been acquired by the United States in sufficient quantities to provide an administrable unit, he shall declare the establishment of the Assateague Island

National Seashore by publication of notice thereof in the Federal Register. Such notice shall contain a refined description or map of the boundaries of the seashore as the Secretary may find desirable, and the exterior boundaries shall encompass an area as nearly as practicable identical to the area described in section 459f of this title.

(Pub.L. 89–195, § 4, Sept. 21, 1965, 79 Stat. 825.)

LIBRARY REFERENCES

American Digest System
  Water Law ⊗═2645.
  Key Number System Topic No. 405.

§ 459f–4. Hunting and fishing provisions

The Secretary shall permit hunting and fishing on land and waters under his control within the seashore in accordance with the appropriate State laws, to the extent applicable, except that the Secretary may designate zones where, and establish periods when, no hunting or fishing shall be permitted for reasons of public safety, administration, fish or wildlife management or public use and enjoyment: *Provided*, That nothing in sections 459f to 459f–11 of this title shall limit or interfere with the authority of the States to permit or to regulate shellfishing in any waters included in the national seashore: *Provided further*, That nothing in said sections shall add to or limit the authority of the Federal Government in its administration of Federal laws regulating migratory waterfowl. Except in emergencies, any regulations of the Secretary pursuant to this section shall be put into effect only after consultation with the appropriate State agency responsible for hunting and fishing activities. The provisions of this section shall not apply to the Chincoteague National Wildlife Refuge.

(Pub.L. 89–195, § 5, Sept. 21, 1965, 79 Stat. 826.)

HISTORICAL AND STATUTORY NOTES

References in Text
  Sections 459f–6 and 459f–8, included within the reference in text to "sections 459f to 459f–11", were repealed by Pub.L. 94–578, Title III, § 301, Oct. 21, 1976, 90 Stat. 2733.

LIBRARY REFERENCES

American Digest System
  Fish ⊗═8.
  Game ⊗═3.5.
  Key Number System Topic Nos. 176, 187.

§ 459f–5. Administration of Seashore

(a) Public outdoor recreation and enjoyment; utilization of other authorities

Except as provided in subsection (b) of this section, the Secretary shall administer the Assateague Island National Seashore for general purposes of public outdoor recreation, including conservation of natural features contributing to public enjoyment. In the administration of the seashore and the administrative site the Secretary may utilize such statutory authorities relating to areas administered and supervised by the Secretary through the National Park Service and such statutory authority otherwise available to him for the conservation and management of natural resources as he deems appropriate to carry out the purposes of sections 459f to 459f–11 of this title.

(b) Refuge land and waters; application of national wildlife refuge provisions; public recreation uses in accordance with provisions for national conservation recreational areas

Notwithstanding any other provision of sections 459f to 459f–11 of this title, land and waters in the Chincoteague National Wildlife Refuge, which are a part of the seashore, shall be administered for refuge purposes under laws and regulations applicable to national wildlife refuges, including administration for public recreation uses in accordance with the provisions of the Act of September 28, 1962 (Public Law 87–714; 76 Stat. 653 [16 U.S.C.A. § 460k et seq.]).

(c) Cooperative agreements and technical assistance to protect seashore resources

The Secretary is authorized to enter into cooperative agreements with local, State, and Federal agencies and with educational institutions and nonprofit entities to coordinate research designed to ensure full protection of the natural and cultural resources of the seashore, consistent with the purposes for which the seashore was established, and other applicable law. The Secretary is also authorized to provide technical assistance to local, State, and Federal agencies and to educational institutions and non-profit entities in order to further such purposes. The Secretary shall submit a report every two years to the Congress on the results of the coordinated research program authorized by this section and plans to implement the recommendations arising from such research.

(Pub.L. 89–195, § 6, Sept. 21, 1965, 79 Stat. 826; Pub.L. 102–320, § 1(5), July 10, 1992, 106 Stat. 322.)

HISTORICAL AND STATUTORY NOTES

References in Text

Sections 459f–6 and 459f–8, included within the reference in subsecs. (a) and (b) to "sections 459f to 459f–11", were repealed by Pub.L. 94–578, Title III, § 301, Oct. 21, 1976, 90 Stat. 2733.

The Act of September 28, 1962, referred to in subsec. (b), popularly known as the Refuge Recreation Act, is classified generally to subchapter LXVIII (section 460k et seq.) of this chapter.

Amendments

1992 Amendments. Subsec. (c). Pub.L. 102–320, § 1(5), added subsec. (c).

Designation of Herbert H. Bateman Education and Administrative Center

Pub.L. 106–480, §§ 1, 2, Nov. 9, 2000, 114 Stat. 2186, provided that:

"**Sec. 1. Designation.**

"A building proposed to be located within the boundaries of the Chincoteague National Wildlife Refuge, on Assateague Island, Virginia, shall be known and designated as the 'Herbert H. Bateman Education and Administrative Center.

"**Sec. 2. References.**

"Any reference in a law, map, regulation, document, paper, or other record of the United States to the building referred to in section 1 [of this note] shall be deemed to be a reference to the 'Herbert

H. Bateman Education and Administrative Center'."

Pub.L. 106–369, § 8, Oct. 27, 2000, 114 Stat. 1419, provided that:

"**(a) In general.**—A building proposed to be located within the boundaries of the Chincoteague National Wildlife Refuge, on Assateague Island, Virginia, shall be known and designated as the 'Herbert H. Bateman Education and Administrative Center'.

"**(b) References.**—Any reference in a law, map, regulation, document, paper, or other record of the United States to the building referred to in subsection (a) shall be deemed to be a reference to the Herbert H. Bateman Education and Administrative Center."

Chincoteague National Wildlife Refuge; Establishment of Herbert H. Bateman Educational and Administrative Center

Pub.L. 106–291, Title I, § 141, Oct. 11, 2000, 114 Stat. 949, provided that: "The building housing the visitors center within the boundaries of the Chincoteague National Wildlife Refuge on Assateague Island, Virginia, shall be known and designated as the 'Herbert H. Bateman Educational and Administrative Center' and shall hereafter be referred to in any law, map, regulation, document, paper, or other record of the United States as the 'Herbert H. Bateman Educational and Administrative Center'."

CODE OF FEDERAL REGULATIONS

Special regulations for particular areas of system, see 36 CFR § 7.1 et seq.

LIBRARY REFERENCES

American Digest System

Woods and Forests ⊗5.
Key Number System Topic No. 411.

§ 459f–6. Repealed. Pub.L. 94–578, Title III, § 301, Oct. 21, 1976, 90 Stat. 2733

HISTORICAL AND STATUTORY NOTES

Section, Pub.L. 89–195, § 7, Sept. 21, 1965, 79 Stat. 826, made provision for the construction of overnight and other public accommodation facilities, land selection and land fill, concession facilities, and the promulgation of rules and regulations covering those areas by the Secretary of the Interior. See section 459f–11 of this title.

§ 459f–7.   Beach erosion control and hurricane protection

The Secretary of the Interior and the Secretary of the Army shall cooperate in the study and formulation of plans for beach erosion control and hurricane protection of the seashore; and any such protective works that are undertaken by the Chief of Engineers, Department of the Army, shall be carried out in accordance with a plan that is acceptable to the Secretary of the Interior and is consistent with the purposes of sections 459f to 459f–11 of this title.

(Pub.L. 89–195, § 8, Sept. 21, 1965, 79 Stat. 827.)

HISTORICAL AND STATUTORY NOTES

References in Text
Sections 459f–6 and 459f–8, included within the reference in text to "sections 459f to 459f–11", were repealed by Pub.L. 94–578, Title III, § 301, Oct. 21, 1976, 90 Stat. 2733.

LIBRARY REFERENCES

American Digest System
United States ⊗57.
Key Number System Topic No. 393.

§ 459f–8.   Repealed.   Pub.L. 94–578, Title III, § 301, Oct. 21, 1976, 90 Stat. 2733

HISTORICAL AND STATUTORY NOTES

Section, Pub.L. 89–195, § 9, Sept. 21, 1965, 79 Stat. 827, authorized and directed the Secretary of the Interior to construct and maintain a road from the Chincoteague-Assateague Island Bridge to an area in the wildlife refuge that he deemed appropriate for recreation purposes and to acquire the necessary lands and rights-of-way for a road from the Chincoteague-Assateague Island Bridge to the Sandy Point-Assateague Bridge. See section 459f–11 of this title.

§ 459f–9.   Public utility facilities; purchase of facilities without value to utility; amount of payment

The Secretary of the Interior is authorized to purchase from a public utility any facilities of that utility which are no longer of value to it as a result of the establishment of the Assateague Island National Seashore and shall pay for such facilities an amount equal to the cost of constructing such facilities less depreciation.

(Pub.L. 89–195, § 10, Sept. 21, 1965, 79 Stat. 827.)

LIBRARY REFERENCES

American Digest System
United States ⊗57.
Key Number System Topic No. 393.

§ 459f–10. Authorization of appropriations

There are hereby authorized to be appropriated the sum of not more than $22,400,000 (including such sums, together with interest, as may be necessary to satisfy final judgments rendered against the United States) for the acquisition of lands and interests in land and such sums as may be necessary for the development of the area authorized under sections 459f to 459f–11 of this title.

(Pub.L. 89–195, § 11, Sept. 21, 1965, 79 Stat. 827; Pub.L. 92–272, Title I, § 101(1), Apr. 11, 1972, 86 Stat. 120; Pub.L. 94–578, Title I, § 101(2), Oct. 21, 1976, 90 Stat. 2732.)

HISTORICAL AND STATUTORY NOTES

References in Text

Sections 459f–6 and 459f–8, included within the reference in text to "sections 459f to 459f–11", were repealed by Pub.L. 94–578, Title III, § 301, Oct. 21, 1976, 90 Stat. 2733.

Amendments

1976 Amendments. Pub.L. 94–578 substituted "$22,400,000" for "$21,050,000".

1972 Amendments. Pub.L. 92–272 substituted "$21,050,000 (including such sums, together with interest, as may be necessary to satisfy final judgments rendered against the United States)" for "$16,250,000".

§ 459f–11. Comprehensive plan for protection, management, and use of seashore

(a) Contents; transmittal to Congressional committees

Within two years of October 21, 1976, the Secretary shall develop and transmit to the Committees on Interior and Insular Affairs of the Senate and the House of Representatives a comprehensive plan for the protection, management, and use of the seashore, to include but not be limited to the following considerations:

(1) measures for the full protection and management of the natural resources and natural ecosystems of the seashore;

(2) present and proposed uses of the seashore and the lands and waters adjacent or related thereto, the uses of which would reasonably be expected to influence the administration, use, and environmental quality of the seashore;

(3) plans for the development of facilities necessary and appropriate for visitor use and enjoyment of the seashore, with identification of resource and user carrying capacities, along with the anticipated costs for all proposed development;

(4) plans for visitor transportation systems integrated and coordinated with lands and facilities adjacent to, but outside of, the seashore; and

(5) plans for fostering the development of cooperative agreements and land and resource use patterns outside the seashore which would be compatible with the protection and management of the seashore.

(b) Consultation by other Federal agencies with Secretary

Notwithstanding any other provision of law, no Federal loan, grant, license, or other form of assistance for any project which, in the opinion of the Secretary would significantly adversely affect the administration, use, and environmental quality of the seashore shall be made, issued, or approved by the head of any Federal agency without first consulting with the Secretary to determine whether or not such project is consistent with the plan developed pursuant to this section and allowing him at least thirty days to comment in writing on such proposed action.

(Pub.L. 89–195, § 12, as added Pub.L. 94–578, Title III, § 301, Oct. 21, 1976, 90 Stat. 2733.)

HISTORICAL AND STATUTORY NOTES

Change of Name

Committee on Interior and Insular Affairs of the House of Representatives changed to Committee on Natural Resources of the House of Representatives on Jan. 5, 1993, by House Resolution No. 5, One Hundred Third Congress. Committee on Natural Resources of House of Representatives treated as referring to Committee on Resources of House of Representatives by section 1(a) of Pub.L. 104–14, set out as a note preceding 2 U.S.C.A. 21. Committee on Resources of House of Representatives changed to Committee on Natural Resources of House of Representatives by House Resolution No. 6, One Hundred Tenth Congress, Jan. 5, 2007.

LIBRARY REFERENCES

American Digest System
Water Law ⬯2645.
Key Number System Topic No. 405.

§ 459g. Cape Lookout National Seashore; purposes; authorization for establishment; description of area

In order to preserve for public use and enjoyment an area in the State of North Carolina possessing outstanding natural and recreational values, there is hereby authorized to be established the Cape Lookout National Seashore (hereinafter referred to as "seashore"), which shall comprise the lands and adjoining marshlands and waters on the outer banks of Carteret County, North Carolina, between Ocracoke Inlet and Beaufort Inlet, as generally depicted on the map entitled "Boundary Map, Cape Lookout National Seashore", dated March 1974, and numbered 623–20,009, which is on file in the Office of the National Park Service, Department of the Interior.

(Pub.L. 89–366, § 1, Mar. 10, 1966, 80 Stat. 33; Pub.L. 93–477, Title IV, § 406(1), Oct. 26, 1974, 88 Stat. 1448.)

HISTORICAL AND STATUTORY NOTES

Revision Notes and Legislative Reports
  1966 Acts. House Report No. 1278, see 1966 U.S. Code Cong. and Adm. News, p. 1925.

Amendments
  1974 Amendments. Pub.L. 93–477 substituted " 'Boundary, Map, Cape Lookout

National Seashore,' dated March 1974, and numbered 623–20,009" for " 'Proposed Boundaries—Proposed Cape Lookout National Seashore', dated April 1964, and numbered NS–CL–7101–B", and deleted proviso relating to certain property not to be included in seashore.

LIBRARY REFERENCES

American Digest System
  Water Law ⚖2519, 2645.
  Key Number System Topic No. 405.

§ 459g–1.   Acquisition of property

(a) Transfer from Federal agency to administrative jurisdiction of Secretary; non-Federal lands

Notwithstanding any other provision of law, Federal property located within the boundaries of the Cape Lookout National Seashore may, with the concurrence of the agency having custody thereof, be transferred to the administrative jurisdiction of the Secretary of the Interior for the purposes of the seashore. Such transfer shall be made without transfer of funds. Lands owned by the State of North Carolina or any political subdivision thereof may be acquired only by donation, but the Secretary may, subject to the provisions of section 459g–6 of this title, acquire any other non-Federal lands, marshlands, waters, or interests therein which are located within the boundaries of the seashore by donation, purchase with donated or appropriated funds, or exchange. Notwithstanding any other provision of law, the Secretary may accept any lands donated by the State of North Carolina subject to a provision for reversion to the State conditioned upon continued use of the property for national seashore purposes. Land donated by the State of North Carolina pursuant to this subsection shall constitute consideration for the transfer by the United States of 1.5 acres of land that is to be used as a site for a public health facility in the village of Hatteras, Dare County, North Carolina.

(b) Exchange of property; cash equalization payments

When acquiring lands by exchange, the Secretary may accept title to any non-Federal property within the boundaries of the seashore and convey to the grantor of such property any federally owned property in the State of North Carolina under his jurisdiction which he classifies as proper for exchange or other disposition. Failing to effectuate an exchange of properties of approximately equal fair market value, the Secretary may accept cash from or pay cash to the grantor in such an exchange in order to equalize the values of the properties exchanged.

(c) Owner's reservation of right of use and occupancy for residential purposes for life or fixed term of years; exclusion of property necessary for public use and access; election of term

Any person who on January 1, 1966, owned property which on July 1, 1963, was developed and used for noncommercial residential purposes may reserve for himself and his assigns, as a condition to the purchase or acquisition by exchange of such property by the Secretary, a right of use and occupancy of the residence and not in excess of three acres of land on which the residence is situated, for noncommercial residential purposes for a term ending at the death of the owner, or the death of his spouse, or the death of either of them, or, in lieu thereof, for a definite term not to exceed twenty-five years: *Provided,* That the Secretary may exclude from such reserved property any marsh, beach, or waters, together with so much of the land adjoining such marsh, beach, or waters as he deems necessary for public access thereto. The owner shall elect the term of the right to be reserved. The Secretary is authorized to accept donations of property for purposes of the seashore in which a right of use and occupancy for noncommercial residential purposes is reserved for the period stated in this subsection if the land on which the residence is situated and to which the right attaches is not in excess of three acres and there is excluded from the reserved property such marsh, beach, or waters and adjoining land as the Secretary deems necessary for public use and access thereto.

(d) Termination of use and occupancy inconsistent with statutory purposes and upon tender of sum for unexpired right

A right of use and occupancy reserved in lands that are donated or otherwise acquired pursuant to this section shall be subject to termination by the Secretary upon his determination that such use and occupancy is being exercised in a manner not consistent with the purposes of sections 459g to 459g–7 of this title and upon tender to the holder of the right of an amount equal to the fair market value of that portion of the right which remains unexpired on the date of termination.

(e) Administrative site; landing dock and related approach or access facilities

The Secretary of the Interior is authorized to purchase with donated or appropriated funds, or acquire by exchange, not to exceed one hundred acres of lands or interests in lands at or near Beaufort,

North Carolina, as an administrative site, and for a landing dock and related facilities that may be used to provide a suitable approach or access to the seashore.

(Pub.L. 89–366, § 2, Mar. 10, 1966, 80 Stat. 34; Pub.L. 93–477, Title IV, § 406(2), Oct. 26, 1974, 88 Stat. 1448.)

HISTORICAL AND STATUTORY NOTES

Revision Notes and Legislative Reports
  1966 Acts. House Report No. 1278, see 1966 U.S. Code Cong. and Adm. News, p. 1925.

Amendments
  1974 Amendments. Subsec. (a). Pub.L. 93–477 substituted provisions relating to acquisition by donation of lands owned by the State of North Carolina and acquisition by donation, purchase or exchange of non-Federal lands, marshlands, etc., and acceptance of lands donated by North Carolina, for provisions relating to acquisition of non-Federal lands, marshlands, etc., by donation only and acquisition by exchange lands comprising the Shackleford Banks.

LIBRARY REFERENCES

American Digest System
  United States ☞55.
  Key Number System Topic No. 393.

§ 459g–2. Establishment; notice in Federal Register; copies to Congress

When title to lands and interests in lands in an amount sufficient to constitute an efficiently administerable [1] unit for the purposes of sections 459g to 459g–7 of this title is vested in the United States, the Secretary shall declare the establishment of the seashore by publication of notice thereof in the Federal Register. Such notice shall contain a refined description or map of the boundaries of the seashore as the Secretary may find desirable and such exterior boundaries shall encompass, as nearly as possible, the area generally described in section 459g of this title. Copies of said description or map shall be furnished to the Speaker of the House and the President of the Senate not less than thirty days prior to publication in the Federal Register. Following such establishment, and subject to the limitations and conditions prescribed in sections 459g to 459g–7 of this title, the Secretary may, subject to the provisions of section 459g–1 of this title, acquire the remainder of the lands and interests in lands within the boundaries of the seashore.

(Pub.L. 89–366, § 3, Mar. 10, 1966, 80 Stat. 35; Pub.L. 93–477, Title IV, § 406(3), Oct. 26, 1974, 88 Stat. 1448.)

[1] So in original. Probably should be "administrable".

HISTORICAL AND STATUTORY NOTES

Revision Notes and Legislative Reports
  1966 Acts. House Report No. 1278, see 1966 U.S. Code Cong. and Adm. News, p. 1925.

Amendments
  1974 Amendments. Pub.L. 93–477 substituted "in an amount sufficient to constitute an efficiently administerable unit for the purposes of sections 459g to 459g–7 of this title" for "which under section 459g–1(a) of this title may be acquired for the purposes of the seashore by donation only", and "establishment of the seashore by publication" for "establishment of the Cape Lookout National Seashore by publication".

LIBRARY REFERENCES

American Digest System
  Water Law ⊙2519, 2645.
  Key Number System Topic No. 405.

§ 459g–3.   Hunting and fishing provisions

The Secretary shall permit hunting and fishing, including shellfishing, on lands, marshlands, and waters under his jurisdiction within the Cape Lookout National Seashore in accordance with the laws of the State of North Carolina and the United States, to the extent applicable, except that the Secretary may designate zones where, and establish periods when, no hunting or fishing shall be permitted for reasons of public safety, administration, fish or wildlife management, or public use and enjoyment. Except in emergencies, any rules and regulations of the Secretary pursuant to this section shall be put into effect only after consultation with the North Carolina Wildlife Resources Commission and the North Carolina Department of Conservation and Development.

(Pub.L. 89–366, § 4, Mar. 10, 1966, 80 Stat. 35.)

HISTORICAL AND STATUTORY NOTES

Revision Notes and Legislative Reports
  1966 Acts. House Report No. 1278, see 1966 U.S. Code Cong. and Adm. News, p. 1925.

LIBRARY REFERENCES

American Digest System
  Fish ⊙8.
  Game ⊙3.5.
  Key Number System Topic Nos. 176, 187.

§ 459g–4.   Administration; public outdoor recreation and enjoyment; utilization of authorities for conservation and development of natural resources

(a) The Secretary shall administer the Cape Lookout National Seashore for the general purposes of public outdoor recreation, including conservation of natural features contributing to public enjoyment. In the administration of the seashore and the administrative site, the Secretary may utilize such statutory authorities relating to areas administered and supervised by the Secretary through the National Park Service and such statutory authorities otherwise available to him for the conservation and management of natural resources as he deems appropriate to carry out the purposes of sections 459g to 459g–7 of this title.

(b)(1) The Secretary, in accordance with this subsection, shall allow a herd of not less than 110 free roaming horses, with a target population of between 120 and 130 free roaming horses, in Cape Lookout National Seashore (hereinafter referred to as the "Seashore"): *Provided*, That nothing in this section shall be construed to preclude the Secretary from implementing or enforcing the provisions of paragraph (3).

(2) Within 180 days after July 16, 1998, the Secretary shall enter into an agreement with the Foundation for Shackleford Horses (a nonprofit corporation established under the laws of the State of North Carolina), or another qualified nonprofit entity, to provide for management of free roaming horses in the seashore. The agreement shall—

(A) provide for cost-effective management of the horses while ensuring that natural resources within the seashore are not adversely impacted; and

(B) allow the authorized entity to adopt any of those horses that the Secretary removes from the seashore.

(3) The Secretary shall not remove, assist in, or permit the removal of any free roaming horses from Federal lands within the boundaries of the seashore—

(A) unless the entity with whom the Secretary has entered into the agreement under paragraph (2), following notice and a 90–day response period, fails to meet the terms and conditions of the agreement; or

(B) unless removal is carried out as part of a plan to maintain the viability of the herd; or

(C) except in the case of an emergency, or to protect public health and safety.

(4) The Secretary shall annually monitor, assess, and make available to the public findings regarding the population, structure, and health of the free roaming horses in the national seashore.

(5) Nothing in this subsection shall be construed to require the Secretary to replace horses or otherwise increase the number of horses within the boundaries of the seashore where the herd numbers fall below 110 as a result of natural causes, including, but not limited to, disease or natural disasters.

(6) Nothing in this subsection shall be construed as creating liability for the United States for any damages caused by the free roaming horses to property located inside or outside the boundaries of the seashore.

(Pub.L. 89–366, § 5, Mar. 10, 1966, 80 Stat. 35; Pub.L. 105–202, § 2, July 16, 1998, 112 Stat. 676; Pub.L. 105–229, § 1, Aug. 13, 1998, 112 Stat. 1517; Pub.L. 109–117, § 1, Dec. 1, 2005, 119 Stat. 2526.)

HISTORICAL AND STATUTORY NOTES

Revision Notes and Legislative Reports
  1966 Acts. House Report No. 1278, see 1966 U.S. Code Cong. and Adm. News, p. 1925.

References in Text
  "180 days after July 16, 1998," referred to in subsec. (b)(2), originally read, "180 days after enactment of this subsection", meaning 180 days after the date of enactment of Pub.L. 105–202, which enacted subsec. (b) on July 16, 1998. See Codifications and 1998 and 2005 Amendments notes set out under this section.

Codifications
  Pub.L. 105–229 replicated prior amendment made to this section by section 2 of Pub.L. 105–202. Pub.L 109–117, § 1(b), repealed the duplicative amendment made to this section by Pub.L. 105–229. See References in Text and 1998 Amendments notes set out under this section.

Amendments
  2005 Amendments. Pub.L. 109–117, § 1(b), repealed duplicative amendments made by Pub.L. 105–229, requiring no change in text. See Codifications note and 1998 Amendments notes set out under this section.

Subsec. (b)(1). Pub.L. 109–117, § 1(a)(1), struck out "100 free roaming horses" and inserted "not less than 110 free roaming horses, with a target population of between 120 and 130 free roaming horses,".

Subsec. (b)(3)(B). Pub.L. 109–117, § 1(a)(2), rewrote subpar. (B), which formerly read: "unless the number of free roaming horses on Federal lands within Cape Lookout National Seashore exceeds 110; or".

Subsec. (b)(5). Pub.L. 109–117, § 1(a)(3), struck out "100" and inserted "110".

  1998 Amendments. Pub.L. 105–229, § 1, replicated prior amendment by Pub.L. 105–202 by designating existing provisions as subsec. (a) and adding subsec. (b). In subsec. (b)(2), Pub.L. 105–229 substituted "180 days after enactment of this subsection" for "180 days after July 16, 1998". See References in Text and Codifications notes set out under this section.

  Pub.L. 105–202, § 2, designated existing provisions as subsec. (a) and added subsec. (b).

LIBRARY REFERENCES

American Digest System
  Woods and Forests ⟨=5.
  Key Number System Topic No. 411.

§ 459g–5. Shore erosion control or beach protection measures

The authority of the Chief of Engineers, Department of the Army, to undertake or contribute to shore erosion control or beach protection measures within the Cape Lookout National Seashore shall be exercised in accordance with a plan that is mutually acceptable to the Secretary of the Interior and the Secretary of the Army, and that is consistent with the purposes of sections 459g to 459g–7 of this title.

(Pub.L. 89–366, § 6, Mar. 10, 1966, 80 Stat. 35.)

HISTORICAL AND STATUTORY NOTES

Revision Notes and Legislative Reports
  1966 Acts. House Report No. 1278, see 1966 U.S. Code Cong. and Adm. News, p. 1925.

LIBRARY REFERENCES

American Digest System
  United States ⟋57.
  Key Number System Topic No. 393.

§ 459g–6. Preservation and designation as wilderness; review of area by Secretary; report to President

On or before January 1, 1978, the Secretary shall review the area within the seashore and shall report to the President, in accordance with section 1132(c) and (d) of this title, his recommendations as to the suitability or nonsuitability of any area within the seashore for preservation as wilderness, and any designation of any such areas as a wilderness shall be accomplished in accordance with section 1132(c) and (d) of this title.

(Pub.L. 89–366, § 7, Mar. 10, 1966, 80 Stat. 35; Pub.L. 93–477, Title IV, § 406(4), Oct. 26, 1974, 88 Stat. 1449.)

HISTORICAL AND STATUTORY NOTES

Revision Notes and Legislative Reports
  1966 Acts. House Report No. 1278, see 1966 U.S. Code Cong. and Adm. News, p. 1925.

Amendments
  1974 Amendments. Pub.L. 93–477 substituted provisions authorizing review of area and report to the President by the Secretary with regard to suitability of area for preservation as wilderness for provisions authorizing appropriations.

LIBRARY REFERENCES

American Digest System
  United States ⟋57.
  Key Number System Topic No. 393.

§ 459g–7. Authorization of appropriations; master plan to Congressional committees; time; contents

There are hereby authorized to be appropriated such sums as may be necessary to carry out the purposes of sections 459g to 459g–7 of this title, not to exceed $13,903,000 for acquisition of lands and interests therein, of which no more than $1,000,000 may be expended for acquisition of lands owned by Core Banks Club Properties, Incorporated. For development of essential public facilities there are authorized to be appropriated not more than $2,935,000. On or before January 1, 1978, the Secretary shall develop and transmit to the Committees on Interior and Insular Affairs of the United States Congress a final master plan for the full development of the seashore consistent with the preservation objectives of sections 459g to 459g–7 of this title, indicating—

(1) the facilities needed to accommodate the health, safety and recreation needs of the visiting public;

(2) the location and estimated cost of all facilities; and

(3) the projected need for any additional facilities within the seashore.

(Pub.L. 89–366, § 8, as added Pub.L. 93–477, Title IV, § 406(5), Oct. 26, 1974, 88 Stat. 1449, and amended Pub.L. 98–141, § 4, Oct. 31, 1983, 97 Stat. 909.)

HISTORICAL AND STATUTORY NOTES

Revision Notes and Legislative Reports
  1966 Acts. House Report No. 1278, see 1966 U.S. Code Cong. and Adm. News, p. 1925.

  1983 Acts. Senate Report No. 98–141, see 1983 U.S. Code Cong. and Adm. News, p. 1308.

Amendments
  1983 Amendments. Pub.L. 98–141 substituted "$13,903,000" for "$7,903,000".

Change of Name
  Committee on Interior and Insular Affairs of the House of Representatives changed to Committee on Natural Resources of the House of Representatives on Jan. 5, 1993, by House Resolution No. 5, One Hundred Third Congress. Committee on Natural Resources of House of Representatives treated as referring to Committee on Resources of House of Representatives by section 1(a) of Pub.L. 104–14, set out as a note preceding 2 U.S.C.A. § 21. Committee on Resources of House of Representatives changed to Committee on Natural Resources of House of Representatives by House Resolution No. 6, One Hundred Tenth Congress, Jan. 5, 2007.

§ 459h. Gulf Islands National Seashore

(a) Establishment

In order to preserve for public use and enjoyment certain areas possessing outstanding natural, historic, and recreational values, the Secretary of the Interior (hereinafter referred to as the "Secretary") may establish and administer the Gulf Islands National Seashore (hereinafter referred to as the "seashore").

(b) Composition

(1) In general

The seashore shall comprise the areas described in paragraphs (2) and (3).

(2) Areas included in boundary plan numbered NS–GI–7100J

The areas described in this paragraph are the following gulf coast islands and mainland areas, together with adjacent water areas as generally depicted on the drawing entitled "Proposed Boundary Plan, Proposed Gulf Islands National Seashore," numbered NS–GI–7100J, and dated December 1970:

(A) Ship, Petit Bois, and Horn Islands in Mississippi;

(B) the eastern portion of Perdido Key in Florida;

(C) Santa Rosa Island in Florida;

(D) the Naval Live Oaks Reservation in Florida;

(E) Fort Pickens and the Fort Pickens State Park in Florida; and

(F) a tract of land in the Pensacola Naval Air Station in Florida that includes the Coast Guard Station and Lighthouse, Fort San Carlos, Fort Barrancas, and Fort Redoubt and sufficient surrounding land for proper administration and protection of the historic resources.

(3) Cat Island

Upon its acquisition by the Secretary, the area described in this paragraph is the parcel consisting of approximately 2,000 acres of land on Cat Island, Mississippi, as generally depicted on the map entitled "Boundary Map, Gulf Islands National Seashore, Cat Island, Mississippi", numbered 635/80085, and dated November 9, 1999 (referred to in sections 459h to 459h–10 of this title as the "Cat Island Map").

(4) Availability of Map

The Cat Island Map shall be on file and available for public inspection in the appropriate offices of the National Park Service.

(Pub.L. 91–660, § 1, Jan. 8, 1971, 84 Stat. 1967; Pub.L. 106–554, § 1(a)(4) [Div. B, Title I, § 137(a)], Dec. 21, 2000, 114 Stat. 2763, 2763A–231.)

HISTORICAL AND STATUTORY NOTES

Revision Notes and Legislative Reports
1971 Acts. Senate Report No. 91–1514, see 1970 U.S. Code Cong. and Adm. News, p. 5955.

2000 Acts. House Report No. 106–645 and Statement by President, see 2000 U.S. Code Cong. and Adm. News, p. 2459.

References in Text
Sections 459h to 459h–10 of this title, referred to in subsec. (b)(3), was in the original "this title", and was translated as reading "this Act", meaning Pub.L. 91–660, which enacted sections 459h to 459h–10 of this title, to reflect the probable intent of Congress, because Pub.L. 91–660 does not contain titles.

Amendments
2000 Amendments. Pub.L. 106–554, § 1(a)(4) [Div. B, Title I, § 137(a)], rewrote the section. Prior to amendment, the section read:

474

"§ 459h. Gulf Islands National Seashore; purposes; authorization for establishment; boundaries

"In order to preserve for public use and enjoyment certain areas possessing outstanding natural, historic, and recreational values, the Secretary of the Interior (hereinafter referred to as the "Secretary") may establish and administer the Gulf Islands National Seashore (hereinafter referred to as the "seashore"). The seashore shall comprise the following gulf coast islands and mainland areas, together with adjacent water areas as generally depicted on the drawing entitled "Proposed Boundary Plan, Proposed Gulf Islands National Seashore," numbered NS–GI–7100J, and dated December 1970:

"(1) Ship, Petit Bois, and Horn Islands in Mississippi;

"(2) the eastern portion of Perdido Key in Florida;

"(3) Santa Rosa Island in Florida;

"(4) the Naval Live Oaks Reservation in Florida;

"(5) Fort Pickens and the Fort Pickens State Park in Florida; and

"(6) a tract of land in the Pensacola Naval Air Station in Florida that includes the Coast Guard Station and Lighthouse, Fort San Carlos, Fort Barrancas, and Fort Redoubt and sufficient surrounding land for proper administration and protection of the historic resources."

LIBRARY REFERENCES

American Digest System
    Water Law ☞2519, 2645.
    Key Number System Topic No. 405.

§ 459h–1. Acquisition of property

(a) Authority of Secretary; concurrence of State owner; administrative site and related facilities; transfer from Federal agency to administrative jurisdiction of Secretary

Within the boundaries of the seashore, the Secretary may acquire submerged land, land, waters, and interests therein by donation, purchase with donated or appropriated funds, or exchange, except that property owned by a State or any political subdivision thereof may be acquired only with the consent of the owner. The Secretary may acquire by any of the above methods not more than four hundred acres of land or interests therein outside of the seashore boundaries on the mainland in the vicinity of Biloxi-Gulfport, Mississippi, for an administrative site and related facilities for access to the seashore. With the concurrence of the agency having custody thereof, any Federal property within the seashore and mainland site may be transferred without consideration to the administrative jurisdiction of the Secretary for the purposes of the seashore.

(b) Improved residential property owner's reservation of right of use and occupancy for residential purposes for life or fixed term of years; election by owner; transfer or assignment of right; adjustment of compensation

With respect to improved residential property acquired for the purposes of sections 459h to 459h–10 of this title, which is beneficially owned by a natural person and which the Secretary of the Interior determines can be continued in that use for a limited period of time without undue interference with the administration, development, or public use of the seashore, the owner thereof may on the date of its acquisition by the Secretary retain a right of use and occupancy of the property for noncommercial residential purposes for a term, as the owner may elect, ending either (1) at the death of the owner or his spouse, whichever occurs later, or (2) not more than twenty-five years from the date of acquisition. Any right so retained may during its existence be transferred or assigned. The Secretary shall pay to the owner the fair market value of the property on the date of such acquisition, less their fair market value on such date of the right retained by the owner.

(c) "Improved residential property" defined

As used in sections 459h to 459h–10 of this title, "improved residential property" means a single-family year-round dwelling, the construction of which began before January 1, 1967, and which serves as the owner's permanent place of abode at the time of its acquisition by the United States, together with not more than three acres of land on which the dwelling and appurtenant buildings are located that the Secretary finds is reasonably necessary for the owner's continued use and occupancy of the dwelling: *Provided*, That the Secretary may exclude from improved residential property any marsh, beach, or waters and adjoining land that the Secretary deems is necessary for public access to such marsh, beach, or waters.

(d) Termination of use and occupancy inconsistent with statutory purposes and upon tender of sum for unexpired right

The Secretary may terminate a right of use and occupancy retained pursuant to this section upon his determination that such use and occupancy is being exercised in a manner not consistent with the purposes of sections 459h to 459h–10 of this title, and upon tender to the holder of the right an amount equal to the fair market value of that portion of the right which remains unexpired on the date of termination.

(e) Acquisition authority

(1) In general

The Secretary may acquire, from a willing seller only—

(A) all land comprising the parcel described in subsection (b)(3) that is above the mean line of ordinary high tide, lying and being situated in Harrison County, Mississippi;

(B) an easement over the approximately 150–acre parcel depicted as the "Boddie Family Tract" on the Cat Island Map for the purpose of implementing an agreement with the owners of the parcel concerning the development and use of the parcel; and

(C)(i) land and interests in land on Cat Island outside the 2,000–acre area depicted on the Cat Island Map; and

(ii) submerged land that lies within 1 mile seaward of Cat Island (referred to in sections 459h to 459h–10 of this title as the "buffer zone"), except that submerged land owned by the State of Mississippi (or a subdivision of the State) may be acquired only by donation.

(2) Administration

(A) In general

Land and interests in land acquired under this subsection shall be administered by the Secretary, acting through the Director of the National Park Service.

(B) Buffer zone

Nothing in sections 459h to 459h–10 of this title or any other provision of law shall require the State of Mississippi to convey to the Secretary any right, title, or interest in or to the buffer zone as a condition for the establishment of the buffer zone.

(3) Modification of boundary

The boundary of the seashore shall be modified to reflect the acquisition of land under this subsection only after completion of the acquisition.

(Pub.L. 91–660, § 2, Jan. 8, 1971, 84 Stat. 1967; Pub.L. 92–275, § 1(1), Apr. 20, 1972, 86 Stat. 123; Pub.L. 106–554, § 1(a)(4) [Div. B, Title I, § 137(b)], Dec. 21, 2000, 114 Stat. 2763, 2763A–231.)

HISTORICAL AND STATUTORY NOTES

Revision Notes and Legislative Reports

1971 Acts. Senate Report No. 91–1514, see 1970 U.S. Code Cong. and Adm. News, p. 5955.

1972 Acts. House Report No. 92–986, see 1972 U.S. Code Cong. and Adm. News, p. 2234.

2000 Acts. House Report No. 106–645 and Statement by President, see 2000 U.S. Code Cong. and Adm. News, p. 2459.

References in Text

Subsection (b)(3), referred to in subsec. (e)(1)(A), probably means subsection (b)(3) of section 459h of this title. Sub-

section (b) of this section does not contain a par. (3).

Sections 459h to 459h–10 of this title, referred to in subsec. (e)(1)(C)(ii), (2)(B), was in the original "this title", and was translated as reading "this Act", meaning Pub.L. 91–660, which enacted sections 459h to 459h–10 of this title, to reflect the probable intent of Congress, because Pub.L. 91–660 does not contain titles.

Amendments

2000 Amendments. Subsec. (a). Pub.L. 106–554, § 1(a)(4) [Div. B, Title I, § 137(b)(1)], substituted "submerged land, land," for "lands" after "Secretary may acquire".

Subsec. (e). Pub.L. 106–554, § 1(a)(4) [Div. B, Title I, § 137(b)(2)], added subsec. (e).

1972 Amendments. Subsec. (a). Pub.L. 92–275 increased amount of property authorized to be acquired from one hundred thirty-five to four hundred acres.

LIBRARY REFERENCES

American Digest System
United States ☜55.
Key Number System Topic No. 393.

§ 459h–2. Designation of hunting and fishing zones; regulation of maritime activities

(a) In general

The Secretary shall permit hunting and fishing on lands and waters within the seashore in accordance with applicable Federal and States laws: *Provided*, That he may designate zones where, and establish periods when, no hunting or fishing will be permitted for reasons of public safety, administration, fish or wildlife management, or public use and enjoyment. Except in emergencies, any regulations issued by the Secretary pursuant to this section shall be put into effect only after consultation with the appropriate State agencies responsible for hunting and fishing activities.

(b) No authority to regulate maritime activities

Nothing in sections 459h to 459h–10 of this title or any other provision of law shall affect any right of the State of Mississippi, or give the Secretary any authority, to regulate maritime activities, including nonseashore fishing activities (including shrimping), in any area that, on December 21, 2000, is outside the designated boundary of the seashore (including the buffer zone).

(Pub.L. 91–660, § 3, Jan. 8, 1971, 84 Stat. 1968; Pub.L. 106–554, § 1(a)(4) [Div. B, Title I, § 137(c)], Dec. 21, 2000, 114 Stat. 2763, 2763A–232.)

HISTORICAL AND STATUTORY NOTES

Revision Notes and Legislative Reports
1971 Acts. Senate Report No. 91–1514, see 1970 U.S. Code Cong. and Adm. News, p. 5955.

2000 Acts. House Report No. 106–645 and Statement by President, see 2000 U.S. Code Cong. and Adm. News, p. 2459.

Amendments
2000 Amendments. Subsec. (a). Pub.L. 106–554, § 1(a)(4) [Div. B, Title I, § 137(c)(1)], designated the existing text as subsec. (a) and inserted the subsec. (a) heading.

Subsec. (b). Pub.L. 106–554, § 1(a)(4) [Div. B, Title I, § 137(c)(2)], added subsec. (b).

LIBRARY REFERENCES

American Digest System
Fish ☜8.

Game ☞3.5.
Key Number System Topic Nos. 176, 187.

§ 459h–3. Rights-of-way or easements for transportation of oil and gas minerals

Any acquisition of lands, waters, or interests therein shall not diminish any existing rights-of-way or easements which are necessary for the transportation of oil and gas minerals through the seashore which oil and gas minerals are removed from outside the boundaries thereof; and, the Secretary, subject to appropriate regulations for the protection of the natural and recreational values for which the seashore is established, shall permit such additional rights-of-way or easements as he deems necessary and proper.

(Pub.L. 91–660, § 4, Jan. 8, 1971, 84 Stat. 1968.)

HISTORICAL AND STATUTORY NOTES

Revision Notes and Legislative Reports
  1971 Acts. Senate Report No. 91–1514,
see 1970 U.S. Code Cong. and Adm.
News, p. 5955.

LIBRARY REFERENCES

American Digest System
  Public Lands ☞49.
  Key Number System Topic No. 317.

§ 459h–4. Administration of seashore; conservation and management of wildlife and natural resources; authority to designate areas as national historic sites; agreements

(a) In general

Except as otherwise provided in sections 459h to 459h–10 of this title, the Secretary shall administer the seashore in accordance with sections 1, 2, 3, and 4 of this title, as amended and supplemented.   In the administration of the seashore the Secretary may utilize such statutory authorities available to him for the conservation and management of wildlife and natural resources as he deems appropriate to carry out the purposes of sections 459h to 459h–10 of this title.   With respect to Fort Redoubt, Fort San Carlos, Fort Barrancas at Pensacola Naval Air Station, Fort Pickens on Santa Rosa Island, and Fort McRee on Perdido Key, Florida, and Fort Massachusetts on Ship Island, Mississippi, together with such adjacent lands as the Secretary may designate, the Secretary shall administer such lands so as to recognize, preserve, and interpret their national historical significance in accordance with sections 461 to 467 of this title, and he may designate them as national historic sites.

(b) Agreements

  (1) In general

  The Secretary may enter into agreements—

    (A) with the State of Mississippi for the purposes of managing resources and providing law enforcement assistance, subject to authorization by State law, and emergency services on or within any land on Cat Island and any water and submerged land within the buffer zone; and

    (B) with the owners of the approximately 150–acre parcel depicted as the 'Boddie Family Tract' on the Cat Island Map concerning the development and use of the land.

  (2) No authority to enforce certain regulations

  Nothing in this subsection authorizes the Secretary to enforce Federal regulations outside the land area within the designated boundary of the seashore.

(Pub.L. 91–660, § 5, Jan. 8, 1971, 84 Stat. 1968; Pub.L. 106–554, § 1(a)(4) [Div. B, Title I, § 137(d)], Dec. 21, 2000, 114 Stat. 2763, 2763A–232.)

HISTORICAL AND STATUTORY NOTES

Revision Notes and Legislative Reports
  1971 Acts. Senate Report No. 91–1514, see 1970 U.S. Code Cong. and Adm. News, p. 5955.

  2000 Acts. House Report No. 106–645 and Statement by President, see 2000 U.S. Code Cong. and Adm. News, p. 2459.

Amendments
  2000 Amendments. Subsec. (a). Pub.L. 106–554, § 1(a)(4) [Div. B, Title I, § 137(d)(1)], designated the existing text as subsec. (a) and inserted the subsec. (a) heading.

  Subsec. (b). Pub.L. 106–554, § 1(a)(4) [Div. B, Title I, § 137(d)(2)], added subsec. (b).

LIBRARY REFERENCES

American Digest System
  Woods and Forests ⟬5.
  Key Number System Topic No. 411.

§ 459h–5. Beach erosion control and hurricane protection; study and formulation of plans; activities by Chief of Engineers, Department of Army

The Secretary of the Interior and the Secretary of the Army may cooperate in the study and formulation of plans for beach erosion control and hurricane protection of the seashore. Any such protective works or spoil deposit activities undertaken by the Chief of Engineers, Department of the Army, shall be carried out within the seashore in accordance with a plan that is acceptable to the Secretary of the Interior and that is consistent with the purposes of sections 459h to 459h–10 of this title.

(Pub.L. 91–660, § 6, Jan. 8, 1971, 84 Stat. 1969.)

HISTORICAL AND STATUTORY NOTES

Revision Notes and Legislative Reports
1971 Acts. Senate Report No. 91–1514, see 1970 U.S. Code Cong. and Adm. News, p. 5955.

LIBRARY REFERENCES

American Digest System
    United States ⊸57.
    Key Number System Topic No. 393.

§ 459h–6. Transfer of Horn Island and Petit Bois National Wildlife Refuges from National Wildlife Refuge System; administration

(a) There are hereby transferred from the National Wildlife Refuge System to the seashore the Horn Island and Petit Bois National Wildlife Refuges to be administered in accordance with the provisions of sections 459h to 459h–10 of this title.

(b) If any of the Federal land on Santa Rosa or Okaloosa Island, Florida, under the jurisdiction of the Department of Defense is ever excess to the needs of the Armed Forces, the Secretary of Defense shall transfer the excess land to the administrative jurisdiction of the Secretary of the Interior, subject to the terms and conditions acceptable to the Secretary of the Interior and the Secretary of Defense. The Secretary of the Interior shall administer the transferred land as part of the seashore in accordance with the provisions of sections 459h to 459h–10 of this title.

(Pub.L. 91–660, § 7, Jan. 8, 1971, 84 Stat. 1969; Pub.L. 109–163, Div. B, Title XXVIII, § 2872(b), Jan. 6, 2006, 119 Stat. 3535.)

HISTORICAL AND STATUTORY NOTES

Revision Notes and Legislative Reports
    1971 Acts. Senate Report No. 91–1514, see 1970 U.S. Code Cong. and Adm. News, p. 5955.
    2006 Acts. House Conference Report No. 109–360, see 2005 U.S. Code Cong. and Adm. News, p. 1678.
    Statement by President, see 2005 U.S. Code Cong. and Adm. News, p. S54.

References in Text
    Sections 459h to 459h–10 of this title, referred to in text, originally read "this Act", meaning Pub.L. 91–660, January 8, 1971, 84 Stat. 1967, as amended, which enacted this section and 16 U.S.C.A. §§ 459h, 459h–1 to 459h–5, 459h–7 to 459h–10.

Amendments

2006 Amendments. Subsec. (a). Pub.L. 109–163, § 2872(b)(1), inserted the subsec. (a) identifier.

Subsec. (b). Pub.L. 109–163, § 2872(b)(2), added subsec. (b).

Transfer of Excess Department of Defense Property on Santa Rosa and Okaloosa Island, Florida, to Gulf Islands National Seashore

Pub.L. 109–163, Div. B, Title XXVIII, § 2872(a), Jan. 6, 2006, 119 Stat. 3534, provided that:

"**(a) Findings.**—Congress finds the following:

"**(1)** Public Law 91–660 of the 91st Congress [Gulf Islands National Seashore Act, Pub.L. 91–660, Jan. 8, 1971, 84 Stat. 1967, which is principally classified to this section and 16 U.S.C.A. §§ 459h, 459h–1 to 459h–5, 459h–7 to 459h–10; for complete classification, see Tables] established the Gulf Islands National Seashore in the States of Florida and Mississippi.

"**(2)** The original boundaries of the Gulf Islands National Seashore encompassed certain Federal land used by the Air Force and the Navy, and the use of such land was still required by the Armed Forces when the seashore was established.

"**(3)** Senate Report 91–1514 of the 91th Congress addressed the relationship between these military lands and the Gulf Islands National Seashore as follows: 'While the military use of these lands is presently required, they remain virtually free of adverse development and they are included in the boundaries of the seashore so that they can be wholly or partially transferred to the Department of the Interior when they become excess to the needs of the Air Force.'.

"**(4)** Although section 2(a) of Public Law 91–660 (16 U.S.C. 459h–1(a)) authorized the eventual transfer of Federal land within the boundaries of the Gulf Islands National Seashore from the Department of Defense to the Secretary of the Interior, an amendment mandating the transfer of excess Department of Defense land on Santa Rosa and Okaloosa Island, Florida, to the Secretary of the Interior is required to ensure that the purposes of the Gulf Islands National Seashore are fulfilled."

LIBRARY REFERENCES

American Digest System

Woods and Forests ⚬—4, 8.
Key Number System Topic No. 411.

§ 459h–7. Preservation of any area as wilderness; study and report to President; procedure for designation of any area as a wilderness

Within four years from January 8, 1971, the Secretary of the Interior shall review the area within the Gulf Islands National Seashore and shall report to the President, in accordance with subsections (c) and (d) of section 1132 of this title, and recommend as to the suitability or nonsuitability of any area within the seashore for preservation as wilderness, and any designation of any such area as a wilderness shall be accomplished in accordance with said subsections.

(Pub.L. 91–660, § 8, Jan. 8, 1971, 84 Stat. 1969.)

§ 459h–8. Authority of Department of Army or Chief of Engineers over navigation or related matters

No provision of sections 459h to 459h–10 of this title, or of any other Act made applicable thereby, shall be construed to affect, supersede, or modify any authority of the Department of the Army or the Chief of Engineers, with respect to navigation or related matters except as specifically provided in section 459h–5 of this title.

(Pub.L. 91–660, § 9, Jan. 8, 1971, 84 Stat. 1969.)

§ 459h–9. Gulf Islands National Seashore Advisory Commission; establishment; termination; membership; term; Chairman; compensation and payment of expenses; consultation by Secretary

There is hereby established a Gulf Islands National Seashore Advisory Commission. The Commission shall terminate ten years after the date the seashore is established pursuant to sections 459h to 459h–10 of this title. The Commission shall be composed of three members from each county in which the seashore is located, each appointed for a term of two years by the Secretary as follows:

(1) one member to be appointed from recommendations made by the county commissioners in the respective counties;

(2) one member to be appointed from recommendations made by the Governor of the State from each county; and

(3) one member to be designated by the Secretary from each county.

Provided, That two members shall be appointed to the Advisory Commission in each instance in counties whose population exceeds one hundred thousand.

The Secretary shall designate one member to be Chairman. Any vacancy in the Commission shall be filled in the same manner in which the original appointment was made.

Members of the Commission shall serve without compensation as such. The Secretary is authorized to pay the expenses reasonably incurred by the Commission in carrying out its responsibilities under sections 459h to 459h–10 of this title on vouchers signed by the Chairman.

The Secretary or his designee shall, from time to time, consult with the Commission with respect to the matters relating to the development of the Gulf Islands National Seashore.

(Pub.L. 91–660, § 10, Jan. 8, 1971, 84 Stat. 1969.)

HISTORICAL AND STATUTORY NOTES

Revision Notes and Legislative Reports
 1971 Acts. Senate Report No. 91–1514, see 1970 U.S. Code Cong. and Adm. News, p. 5955.

Termination of Advisory Commissions
 Advisory Commissions in existence on January 5, 1973, to terminate not later than the expiration of the two-year period following January 5, 1973, unless, in the case of a commission established by the President or an officer of the Federal Government, such commission is renewed by appropriate action prior to the expiration of such two-year period, or in the case of a commission established by the Congress, its duration is otherwise provided for by law, see sections 3(2) and 14 of Pub.L. 92–463, Oct. 6, 1972, 86 Stat. 770, 776, set out in Appendix 2 to Title 5, Government Organization and Employees.

LIBRARY REFERENCES

American Digest System
 Woods and Forests ☞7.
 Key Number System Topic No. 411.

§ 459h–10. Authorization of appropriations

(a) In general

There are authorized to be appropriated not more than $22,162,000 for the acquisition of lands and interests in lands and not more than $24,224,000 for development.

(b) Authorization for acquisition of land

In addition to the funds authorized by subsection (a) of this section, there are authorized to be appropriated such sums as are necessary to acquire land and submerged land on and adjacent to Cat Island, Mississippi.

(Pub.L. 91–660, § 11, Jan. 8, 1971, 84 Stat. 1970; Pub.L. 92–275, § 1(2), Apr. 20, 1972, 86 Stat. 123; Pub.L. 94–578, Title I, § 101(6), Oct. 21, 1976, 90 Stat. 2732; Pub.L. 95–625, Title I, § 101(13), Nov. 10, 1978, 92 Stat. 3471; Pub.L. 106–554, § 1(a)(4) [Div. B, Title I, § 137(e)], Dec. 21, 2000, 114 Stat. 2763, 2763A–232.)

HISTORICAL AND STATUTORY NOTES

Revision Notes and Legislative Reports

1971 Acts. Senate Report No. 91–1514, see 1970 U.S. Code Cong. and Adm. News, p. 5955.

1972 Acts. House Report No. 92–986, see 1972 U.S. Code Cong. and Adm. News, p. 2234.

2000 Acts. House Report No. 106–645 and Statement by President, see 2000 U.S. Code Cong. and Adm. News, p. 2459.

Amendments

2000 Amendments. Subsec. (a). Pub.L. 106–554, § 1(a)(4) [Div. B, Title I, § 137(e)(1)], designated the existing text as subsec. (a) and inserted the subsec. (a) heading.

Subsec. (b). Pub.L. 106–554, § 1(a)(4) [Div. B, Title I, § 137(e)(2)], added subsec. (b).

1978 Amendments. Pub.L. 95–625 substituted "$24,224,000 for development." for "$17,774,000 (June 1970 prices) for development, plus or minus such amounts, if any, as may be justified by reason of ordinary fluctuations in construction costs as indicated by engineering cost indices applicable to the types of construction involved herein."

1976 Amendments. Pub.L. 94–578 substituted "$22,162,000" for "$3,462,000".

1972 Amendments. Pub.L. 92–275 increased appropriations authorization for lands and land interests from $3,120,000 to $3,462,000 and for development from $14,779,000 (1970 prices) to $17,774,000 (June 1970 prices).

§ 459i. Cumberland Island National Seashore; establishment; boundary revisions: notification of Congressional committees, publication in Federal Register

In order to provide for public outdoor recreation use and enjoyment of certain significant shoreline lands and waters of the United States, and to preserve related scenic, scientific, and historical values, there is established in the State of Georgia the Cumberland Island National Seashore (hereinafter referred to as the "seashore") consisting of the area generally depicted on the drawing entitled "Boundary Map, Cumberland Island National Seashore", numbered CUIS 40,000E, and dated January 1978, which shall be on file and available for public inspection in the offices of the National Park Service, Department of the Interior. The Secretary of the Interior (hereinafter referred to as the "Secretary") may after notifying the Committee on Energy and Natural Resources of the Senate and the Committee on Natural Resources of the House of Representatives in writing, make minor adjustments in the boundary of the seashore from time to time by publication of a revised drawing or other boundary description in the Federal Register, but the total acreage within the boundaries shall not exceed forty thousand five hundred acres.

(Pub.L. 92–536, § 1, Oct. 23, 1972, 86 Stat. 1066; Pub.L. 95–625, Title III, § 323, Nov. 10, 1978, 92 Stat. 3489; Pub.L. 98–170, Nov. 29, 1983, 97 Stat. 1116; Pub.L. 103–437, § 6(*l*), Nov. 2, 1994, 108 Stat. 4586.)

HISTORICAL AND STATUTORY NOTES

Revision Notes and Legislative Reports

    1972 Acts. House Report No. 92–1405, see 1972 U.S. Code Cong. and Adm. News, p. 4296.

    1994 Acts. House Report No. 103–779, see 1994 U.S. Code Cong. and Adm. News, p. 3639.

Amendments

    1994 Amendments. Pub.L. 103–437, § 6(*l*), substituted "Committee on Energy and Natural Resources of the Senate and the Committee on Natural Resources of the House of Representatives" for "Committees on Interior and Insular Affairs of the United States House of Representatives and United States Senate".

    1983 Amendments. Pub.L. 98–170 substituted "CUIS 40,000E" for "CUIS 40,000D".

    1978 Amendments. Pub.L. 95–625 substituted reference to Boundary Map "numbered CUIS 40,000D, and dated January 1978" for "numbered CUIS–40,000B, and dated June 1971".

Short Title

    2004 Amendments. Pub.L. 108–447, Div. E, Title I, § 145(c), Dec. 8, 2004, 118 Stat. 3074, provided that: "This section [amending 16 U.S.C.A. § 459i–5 and provisions listed in a table under 16 U.S.C.A. § 1132] may be cited as the 'Cumberland Island Wilderness Boundary Adjustment Act of 2004'."

Change of Name

    Committee on Interior and Insular Affairs of the House of Representatives changed to Committee on Natural Resources of the House of Representatives on Jan. 5, 1993, by House Resolution No. 5, One Hundred Third Congress. Committee on Natural Resources of House of Representatives treated as referring to Committee on Resources of House of Representatives by section 1(a) of Pub.L. 104–14, set out as a note preceding 2 U.S.C.A. § 21. Committee on Resources of House of Representatives changed to Committee on Natural Resources of House of Representatives by House Resolution No. 6, One Hundred Tenth Congress, Jan. 5, 2007.

LIBRARY REFERENCES

American Digest System

    Water Law ⟲2519, 2645.

    Key Number System Topic No. 405.

§ 459i–1. Acquisition of lands; authority of Secretary; mainland lands for access to seashore administrative and visitor facilities; State lands; transfer from Federal agency to administrative jurisdiction of Secretary

Within the boundaries of the seashore, the Secretary may acquire lands, waters, and interests therein by purchase, donation, transfer from any Federal agency, or exchange. The Secretary may also acquire not to exceed one hundred acres of lands or interests in lands on the mainland to provide access to the administrative and visitor facilities for the seashore. Any lands or interests therein owned by the State of Georgia, or any political subdivision thereof may be acquired only by donation. Notwithstanding any other provision of law, any Federal property located within the boundaries of the seashore may, with the concurrence of the agency having custody thereof, be transferred without transfer of funds to the administrative jurisdiction of the Secretary for the purposes of the seashore.

(Pub.L. 92–536, § 2, Oct. 23, 1972, 86 Stat. 1066.)

HISTORICAL AND STATUTORY NOTES

Revision Notes and Legislative Reports
  1972 Acts. House Report No. 92–1405, scc 1972 U.S. Code Cong. and Adm. News, p. 4296.

LIBRARY REFERENCES

American Digest System
  United States ⊙=55.
  Key Number System Topic No. 393.

§ 459i–2. Cumberland Island Parkway; right-of-way; administration; regulations

For the purpose of providing access from Interstate 95 to the mainland administrative and visitor facilities of the seashore, the Secretary may designate as the Cumberland Island Parkway a right-of-way, together with adjacent or related sites for public noncommercial recreational use and for interpretation of scenic and historic values, of not more than one thousand acres of lands, waters, and interests therein. The Secretary is authorized to acquire only by donation those lands and interests therein, and other property comprising such right-of-way and adjacent or related sites as he may designate pursuant to sections 459i to 459i–9 of this title for the development, hereby authorized, of a roadway of parkway standards, including necessary bridges, spurs, connecting roads, access roads, and other facilities, and for the development and interpretation of recreation areas and historic sites in connection therewith. Lands acquired for the parkway shall be administered as a part of the seashore, subject to all laws and regulations applicable thereto, and subject to such special regulations as the Secretary may promulgate for the parkway.

(Pub.L. 92–536, § 3, Oct. 23, 1972, 86 Stat. 1066.)

HISTORICAL AND STATUTORY NOTES

Revision Notes and Legislative Reports
  1972 Acts. House Report No. 92–1405, see 1972 U.S. Code Cong. and Adm. News, p. 4296.

§ 459i–3. Acquisition of property

(a) Private right of use and occupancy for residential purposes for fixed term of years or for life; election by owner; exception of property for visitor facilities or administration of seashore; compensation; contemporaneous restriction on development of public use facilities; lands, waters, and interests from National Park Foundation

With the exception of any property deemed necessary by the Secretary for visitor facilities or administration of the seashore, any owner or owners of improved property on the date of its acquisition by the Secretary may, as a condition of such acquisition, retain for themselves and their successors or assigns a right of use and occupancy of the property for noncommercial residential purposes, for twenty-five years, or, in lieu thereof, for a term ending at the death of the owner or his spouse, whichever is later. The owner shall elect the term to be reserved. The Secretary shall pay to the owner the fair market value of the property on the date of such acquisition less the fair market value on such date of the right retained by the owner: *Provided, however,* That, in addition, for so long as a right of use and occupancy remains in effect by the donors of land of one hundred acres or more, the Secretary shall not, with respect to such lands, develop any public use facilities except for trails, road access, and utilities: *Provided further,* That when acquiring lands, waters, and interests therein from the National Park Foundation, its successors and assigns, the Secretary shall acquire such lands, waters, and interests subject to the written terms and conditions contained in those transactions, including but not limited to options, entered into by the National Park Foundation prior to January 1, 1973, and that such previous written rights and interests shall prevail over provisions of this subsection.

(b) Commercial use prohibition; termination of use and occupancy upon tender of compensation

A right of use and occupancy retained or enjoyed pursuant to this section may be terminated with respect to the entire property by the Secretary upon his determination that the property or any portion thereof has ceased to be used for noncommercial residential purposes and upon tender to the holder of a right an amount equal to the fair market value, as of the date of tender, of that portion of the right which remains unexpired on the date of termination.

(c) "Improved property" defined

The term "improved property", as used in this section shall mean a detached, noncommercial residential dwelling, the construction of which was begun before February 1, 1970 (hereinafter referred to as "dwelling"), together with so much of the land on which the dwelling is situated, the said land being in the same ownership as the dwelling, as the Secretary shall designate to be reasonably necessary for the enjoyment of the dwelling for the sole purpose of noncommercial residential use, together with any structures accessory to the dwelling which are situated on the land so designated.

(d) Little Cumberland Island; acquisition restrictions

(1) In order to provide an opportunity for the establishment of a natural and scenic preserve by voluntary private action of certain owners of lands within the seashore, and notwithstanding anything to the contrary herein contained, no lands or interests in lands shall be acquired on Little Cumberland Island without the consent of the owner, for a period of one year from October 23, 1972, except as specifically otherwise provided herein.

(2) In the event that the owners of land on Little Cumberland Island enter into an irrevocable trust or some other irrevocable agreement for the preservation of the resources of Little Cumberland Island which, in the judgment of the Secretary, assures the protection of the resources in a manner consistent with the purposes for which the seashore is established, the authority of the Secretary to acquire such lands shall be suspended for such time as the trust is in effect and the lands are used and occupied in accordance therewith.

(3) If, at any time during the one-year period following October 23, 1972, the Secretary determines that any lands on Little Cumberland Island are threatened with development, or other uses, inconsistent with the establishment or continuation of the trust herein referred to, then the Secretary may acquire such lands, or interests therein, by any of the methods provided for in section 459i–1 of this title.

(Pub.L. 92–536, § 4, Oct. 23, 1972, 86 Stat. 1066.)

HISTORICAL AND STATUTORY NOTES

Revision Notes and Legislative Reports
  1972 Acts. House Report No. 92–1405, see 1972 U.S. Code Cong. and Adm. News, p. 4296.

LIBRARY REFERENCES

American Digest System
    United States ☞55.
    Key Number System Topic No. 393.

Notes of Decisions

Admissibility of evidence 2
Publication of rights 1

1. Publication of rights

Landowners, defendants in condemnation proceeding, by claiming that they had made offer to donate the land demonstrated their awareness of their rights under this section authorizing donation with reservation of life estate, and having shown awareness of rights could claim no injuries from any failure of government to publicize such rights. U.S. v. 34.60 Acres of Land, More or Less, in Camden County, C.A.5 (Ga.) 1981, 642 F.2d 788, certiorari denied 102 S.Ct. 125, 454 U.S.

830, 70 L.Ed.2d 107. Eminent Domain ☞ 171

2. Admissibility of evidence

In condemnation suit, wherein landowners contended that they had offered to donate their property under this section, reserving life estate, but were improperly refused, evidence of negative fact that National Park Foundation had no record whatsoever of any offer, written or oral, from landowners would have been admissible at trial. U.S. v. 34.60 Acres of Land, More or Less, in Camden County, C.A.5 (Ga.) 1981, 642 F.2d 788, certiorari denied 102 S.Ct. 125, 454 U.S. 830, 70 L.Ed.2d 107. Evidence ☞ 351

§ 459i–4. Hunting and fishing

The Secretary shall permit hunting, fishing, and trapping on lands and waters under his jurisdiction within the boundaries of the seashore in accordance with the appropriate laws of Georgia and the United States to the extent applicable, except that he may designate zones where, and establish periods when, no hunting, fishing, or trapping shall be permitted for reasons of public safety, administration, fish and wildlife management, or public use and enjoyment. Except in emergencies, any regulations prescribing any such restrictions shall be put into effect only after consultation with the appropriate State agency responsible for hunting, fishing, and trapping activities.

(Pub.L. 92–536, § 5, Oct. 23, 1972, 86 Stat. 1068.)

HISTORICAL AND STATUTORY NOTES

Revision Notes and Legislative Reports
1972 Acts. House Report No. 92–1405, see 1972 U.S. Code Cong. and Adm. News, p. 4296.

LIBRARY REFERENCES

American Digest System
    Fish ☞8.
    Game ☞3.5.
    Key Number System Topic Nos. 176, 187.

§ 459i–5. Administration, protection, and development

(a) Applicability of provisions; utilization of statutory authorities

The seashore shall be administered, protected, and developed in accordance with the provisions of sections 1, 2, 3, and 4 of this title, as amended and supplemented, except that any other statutory authority available to the Secretary for the conservation and management of natural resources may be utilized to the extent he finds such authority will further the purposes of sections 459i to 459i–9 of this title.

(b) Preservation in primitive state; recreational activities exception

Except for certain portions of the seashore deemed to be especially adaptable for recreational uses, particularly swimming, boating, fishing, hiking, horseback riding, and other recreational activities of similar nature, which shall be developed for such uses as needed, the seashore shall be permanently preserved in its primitive state, and, except as provided in subsection (c) of this section, no development of the project or plan for the convenience of visitors shall be undertaken which would be incompatible with the preservation of the unique flora and fauna or the physiographic conditions not [1] prevailing, nor shall any road or causeway connecting Cumberland Island to the mainland be constructed.

(c) Tours of the seashore

Notwithstanding subsection (b) of this section, the Secretary may enter into not more than 3 concession contracts, as the Secretary determines appropriate, for the provision of tours for visitors to the seashore that are consistent with—

(1) sections 459i to 459i–9 of this title;

(2) the Wilderness Act (16 U.S.C. 1131 et seq.); and

(3) Public Law 97–250 (96 Stat. 709).

(Pub.L. 92–536, § 6, Oct. 23, 1972, 86 Stat. 1068; Pub.L. 108–447, Div. E, Title I, § 145(b), Dec. 8, 2004, 118 Stat. 3073.)

[1] So in original.

HISTORICAL AND STATUTORY NOTES

Revision Notes and Legislative Reports

1972 Acts. House Report No. 92–1405, see 1972 U.S. Code Cong. and Adm. News, p. 4296.

2004 Acts. House Conference Report No. 108–792, see 2004 U.S. Code Cong. and Adm. News, p. 2577.

Statement by President, see 2004 U.S. Code Cong. and Adm. News, p. S46.

References in Text

The Wilderness Act, referred to in subsec. (c)(2), is Pub.L. 88–577, Sept. 3, 1964, 78 Stat. 890, which enacted chapter 23 of this title, 16 U.S.C.A. § 1131 et seq.

Public Law 97–250, referred to in subsec. (c)(3), is Pub.L. 97–250, Sept. 8, 1982, 96 Stat. 709, which enacted 16 U.S.C.A. § 122a, amended 16 U.S.C.A.

§ 121, and enacted provisions set out as notes under 16 U.S.C.A. §§ 121 and 1132.

Amendments
2004 Amendments. Subsec. (b). Pub.L. 108–447, Div. E, § 145(b)(1), sub-

stituted "and, except as provided in subsection (c) of this section, no development of the project" for "and no development of the project".

Subsec. (c). Pub.L. 108–447, Div. E, § 145(b)(2), added subsec. (c).

LIBRARY REFERENCES

American Digest System
Woods and Forests ⊕5.
Key Number System Topic No. 411.

§ 459i–6. State and local jurisdiction

Nothing in sections 459i to 459i–9 of this title shall deprive the State of Georgia or any political subdivision thereof of its civil or criminal jurisdiction over persons found, acts performed, and offenses committed within the boundaries of the seashore, or of its right to tax persons, corporations, franchises, or other non-Federal property on lands included therein.

(Pub.L. 92–536, § 7, Oct. 23, 1972, 86 Stat. 1068.)

HISTORICAL AND STATUTORY NOTES

Revision Notes and Legislative Reports
1972 Acts. House Report No. 92–1405, see 1972 U.S. Code Cong. and Adm. News, p. 4296.

LIBRARY REFERENCES

American Digest System
United States ⊕3.
Key Number System Topic No. 393.

Notes of Decisions

Taxation of life estates 1

1. Taxation of life estates

Property owners, who had conveyed their property by deed to the United States "in fee simple," reserving to themselves "a term of years ending upon the death of both the owners," had retained a life estate and were subject to real prop-

erty taxes, even though the deed conveying the property to the United States contained restrictions preventing changes in structure, use or maintenance incompatible with the announced purpose of creating and maintaining a national park or nature preserve on the property. Henderson v. Tax Assessors, Camden County, Ga.App.1980, 275 S.E.2d 78, 156 Ga.App. 590. Taxation ⊕ 2188

§ 459i–7. Water resource developments

The authority of the Secretary of the Army to undertake or contribute to water resource developments, including shore erosion control, beach protection and navigation improvements on land and/or waters within the Cumberland Island National Seashore shall be exercised in accordance with plans which are mutually acceptable to the Secretary of the Interior and the Secretary of the Army and which are consistent with both the purpose of sections 459i to 459i–9 of this title and the purpose of existing statutes dealing with water and related land resource development.

(Pub.L. 92–536, § 8, Oct. 23, 1972, 86 Stat. 1068.)

HISTORICAL AND STATUTORY NOTES

Revision Notes and Legislative Reports
   1972 Acts. House Report No. 92–1405,
see 1972 U.S.Code Cong. and Adm.News,
p. 4296.

LIBRARY REFERENCES

American Digest System
   Water Law ⟜2519, 2645.
   Key Number System Topic No. 405.

§ 459i–8.   Report to President

Within three years from October 23, 1972, the Secretary of the Interior shall report to the President, in accordance with section 1132(c) and (d) of this title, his recommendations as to the suitability or nonsuitability of any area within the national seashore for preservation as wilderness, and any designation of any such area as a wilderness shall be accomplished in accordance with said section 1132(c) and (d) of this title.

(Pub.L. 92–536, § 9, Oct. 23, 1972, 86 Stat. 1068.)

HISTORICAL AND STATUTORY NOTES

Revision Notes and Legislative Reports
   1972 Acts. House Report No. 92–1405,
see 1972 U.S.Code Cong. and Adm.News,
p. 4296.

LIBRARY REFERENCES

American Digest System
   Woods and Forests ⟜5.
   Key Number System Topic No. 411.

§ 459i–9.   Authorization of appropriations

There are authorized to be appropriated not to exceed $28,500,000 for the acquisition of lands and interests in lands and not to exceed $27,840,000 for development of the seashore.

(Pub.L. 92–536, § 10, Oct. 23, 1972, 86 Stat. 1068; Pub.L. 95–625, Title II, § 201(3), Nov. 10, 1978, 92 Stat. 3473.)

HISTORICAL AND STATUTORY NOTES

Revision Notes and Legislative Reports
1972 Acts. House Report No. 92–1405, see 1972 U.S.Code Cong. and Adm.News, p. 4296.

Amendments
1978 Amendments. Pub.L. 95–625 increased land acquisition appropriations

authorization to $28,500,000 from $10,500,000.

§ 459j. Canaveral National Seashore; establishment; boundary; boundary revisions; limitation on area

In order to preserve and protect the outstanding natural, scenic, scientific, ecologic, and historic values of certain lands, shoreline, and waters of the State of Florida, and to provide for public outdoor recreation use and enjoyment of the same, there is hereby established the Canaveral National Seashore (hereinafter referred to as the "seashore"), as generally depicted on the map entitled "Boundary Map, Canaveral National Seashore", dated August 1974 and numbered NS–CAN–40,000A. Such seashore shall comprise approximately sixty-seven thousand five hundred acres within the area more particularly described by a line beginning at the intersection of State Highway 3 and State Road 402, thence generally easterly following State Road 402 to a point one-half mile offshore in the Atlantic Ocean, thence northwesterly along a line which is at each point one-half mile distant from the high water mark to Bethune Beach, thence inland in a generally westerly direction through Turner Flats and Shipyard Canal, thence northwesterly to the Intracoastal Waterway, thence southerly along the Intracoastal Waterway to the boundary of the Kennedy Space Center, thence southwesterly to United States Highway 1, thence southerly along State Highway 3 to the point of beginning. The boundary map shall be on file and available for public inspection in the offices of the United States Fish and Wildlife Service and National Park Service, Department of the Interior, Washington, District of Columbia. After advising the Committee on Energy and Natural Resources of the Senate and the Committee on Natural Resources of the House of Representatives, in writing, at least sixty days prior to making any boundary revisions, the Secretary may from time to time make minor revisions in the boundaries of the seashore by publication of a revised map or other boundary description in the Federal Register: *Provided*, That the total acreage included within the boundaries shall not exceed that enumerated in this section.

(Pub.L. 93–626, § 1, Jan. 3, 1975, 88 Stat. 2121; Pub.L. 103–437, § 6(a)(4), Nov. 2, 1994, 108 Stat. 4583.)

HISTORICAL AND STATUTORY NOTES

Revision Notes and Legislative Reports
   1975 Acts. Senate Report No. 93–1333, see 1974 U.S.Code Cong. and Adm.News, p. 7520.
   1994 Acts. House Report No. 103–779, see 1994 U.S. Code Cong. and Adm. News, p. 3639.

Amendments
   1994 Amendments. Pub.L. 103–437, § 6(a)(4), substituted "Committee on Energy and Natural Resources of the Senate and the Committee on Natural Resources of the House of Representatives" for "Committees on Interior and Insular Affairs of the United States Congress".

Change of Name
   Committee on Interior and Insular Affairs of the House of Representatives

changed to Committee on Natural Resources of the House of Representatives on Jan. 5, 1993, by House Resolution No. 5, One Hundred Third Congress. Committee on Natural Resources of House of Representatives treated as referring to Committee on Resources of House of Representatives by section 1(a) of Pub.L. 104–14, set out as a note preceding 2 U.S.C.A. § 21. Committee on Resources of House of Representatives changed to Committee on Natural Resources of House of Representatives by House Resolution No. 6, One Hundred Tenth Congress, Jan. 5, 2007.

LIBRARY REFERENCES

American Digest System
   Water Law ⊸2519, 2645.
   Key Number System Topic No. 405.

§ 459j–1. Acquisition of property; donation and development of State lands; transfer from Federal agency to administrative jurisdiction of Secretary; written cooperative agreement with National Aeronautics and Space Administration; construction and development; report to Congressional committees

Within the boundaries of the seashore, the Secretary may acquire lands, waters, and interests therein by donation, purchase with donated or appropriated funds, exchange, or transfer. Any property owned by the State of Florida or any political subdivision thereof may be acquired only by donation. It is the intent and purpose of sections 459j to 459j–8 of this title that the Secretary shall have sole authority to develop and improve those State owned lands donated now and in the future in accordance with the intent and purposes of sections 459j to 459j–8 of this title. Notwithstanding any other provision of law, any federally owned property within the boundaries of the seashore may, with the concurrence of the agency having custody thereof, be transferred without consideration to the administrative jurisdiction of the Secretary of the Interior and he may develop and administer such lands in a manner consistent with the purposes of sections 459j to 459j–8 of this title. In accepting lands transferred by the National Aeronautics and Space Administration pursuant to sections 459j to 459j–8 of this title, the Secretary shall enter into a written cooperative agreement with the Administrator to assure the use of such lands in a manner which is deemed consistent with the public safety and with the needs of the space and defense programs of the Nation: *Provided*, That no new construction or development shall be permitted within the seashore, except for the construction of such facilities as the Secretary deems necessary for the health and safety of the visiting public or for the proper administration of the seashore: *Provided further*, That after January 3, 1975, the Secretary of the Interior, in cooperation with the Administrator of the National Aeronautics and Space Administration, shall submit to the Committees on Natural Resources and on Science, Space, and Technology of the House of Representatives and to the Committees on Energy and Natural Resources and on Commerce, Science, and Transportation of the Senate a report of all land transfers made by the National Aeronautics and Space Administration to the Department of the Interior under sections 459j to 459j–8 of this title.

(Pub.L. 93–626, § 2, Jan. 3, 1975, 88 Stat. 2122; Pub.L. 103–437, § 6(*o*), Nov. 2, 1994, 108 Stat. 4586.)

HISTORICAL AND STATUTORY NOTES

Revision Notes and Legislative Reports

1975 Acts. Senate Report No. 93–1333, see 1974 U.S.Code Cong. and Adm.News, p. 7520.

1994 Acts. House Report No. 103–779, see 1994 U.S. Code Cong. and Adm. News, p. 3639.

Amendments

1994 Amendments. Pub.L. 103–437, § 6(*o*), substituted "Committees on Natural Resources and on Science, Space, and Technology of the House of Representatives and to the Committees on Energy and Natural Resources and on Commerce, Science, and Transportation of the Senate" for "Committees on Interior and Insular Affairs of the Congress and to the Committee on Science and Astronautics of the House of Representatives and to the Committee on Aeronautical and Space Sciences of the Senate".

Change of Name

Committee on Natural Resources of House of Representatives treated as referring to Committee on Resources of House of Representatives by section 1(a) of Pub.L. 104–14, set out as a note preceding 2 U.S.C.A. § 21. Committee on Resources of House of Representatives changed to Committee on Natural Re-

sources of House of Representatives by House Resolution No. 6, One Hundred Tenth Congress, Jan. 5, 2007.

Committee on Science, Space, and Technology of House of Representatives treated as referring to Committee on Science of House of Representatives by section 1(a) of Pub.L. 104–14, set out as a note preceding 2 U.S.C.A. § 21. Committee on Science of House of Representatives changed to Committee on Science and Technology of House of Representatives by House Resolution No. 6, One Hundred Tenth Congress, Jan. 5, 2007.

Additions to Seashore

Pub.L. 100–564, §§ 1, 3, Oct. 31, 1988, 102 Stat. 2831, directed Secretary of Interior to acquire approximately 25 acres of land in State of Florida known as Seminole Rest and approximately 10 acres of land known as Stuckey's, both areas depicted on a map entitled "Additions to Canaveral National Seashore", and to file such map with the Committee on Interior and Insular Affairs [now Committee on Resources] of the House of Representatives, and the Committee on Energy and Natural Resources of the Senate, and authorized appropriations to carry out such acquisitions.

§ 459j–2.   Improved property

(a) Owner's reservation of right of use and occupancy for residential purposes for life or fixed term of years; exception of property for visitor facilities, access to, or administration of seashore; compensation

Except for property deemed necessary by the Secretary for visitor facilities, or for access to or administration of the seashore, any owner or owners of improved property on the date of its acquisition by the Secretary may, as a condition of such acquisition, retain for themselves and their successors or assigns a right of use and occupancy of the improved property for noncommercial residential purposes for a definite term not to exceed twenty-five years, or in lieu thereof, for a term ending at the death of the owner, or the death of his spouse, whichever is the later. The owner shall elect the term to be reserved. Unless the property is wholly or partially donated to the United States, the Secretary shall pay to the owner the fair market value of the property on the date of such acquisition less the fair market value on such date of the right retained by the owner.

(b) Termination of use and occupancy upon inconsistent use; tender of compensation

The Secretary may terminate a right of use and occupancy retained pursuant to this section upon his determination that such use and occupancy is being exercised in a manner not consistent with the purposes of sections 459j to 459j–8 of this title, and upon tender to the holder of the right of an amount equal to the fair market value of that portion of the right which remains unexpired on the date of termination.

(c) "Improved property" defined

The term "improved property", as used in this section shall mean a detached, noncommercial residential dwelling, the construction of which was begun before January 1, 1971 (hereafter referred to as "dwelling"), together with so much of the land on which the dwelling is situated, the said land being in the same ownership as the dwelling, as the Secretary shall designate to be reasonably necessary for the enjoyment of the dwelling for the sole purpose of noncommercial residential use, together with any structures, necessary to the dwelling which are situated on the land so designated.

(d) Condemnation as means for acquiring clear and marketable title

Except as otherwise provided, the Secretary shall have the authority to use condemnation as a means of acquiring a clear and marketable title, free of any and all encumbrances.

(Pub.L. 93–626, § 3, Jan. 3, 1975, 88 Stat. 2123.)

HISTORICAL AND STATUTORY NOTES

Revision Notes and Legislative Reports
1975 Acts. Senate Report No. 93–1333,
see 1974 U.S.Code Cong. and Adm.News,
p. 7520.

LIBRARY REFERENCES

American Digest System
United States ☞3.
Key Number System Topic No. 393.

§ 459j–3. Designation of hunting, fishing and trapping zones; regulations; consultation with appropriate State agencies

The Secretary shall permit hunting, fishing, and trapping on lands and waters under his jurisdiction within the boundaries of the seashore in accordance with the appropriate laws of the State of Florida and the United States to the extent applicable, except that he may designate zones where, and establish periods when, no hunting, fishing, or trapping shall be permitted for reasons of public safety, administration, fish and wildlife management, public use and enjoyment, protection of the resource, or competing public use. Except in emergencies, any regulations prescribing any such restrictions shall be put into effect only after consultation with the appropriate State agency responsible for hunting, fishing, and trapping activities.

(Pub.L. 93–626, § 4, Jan. 3, 1975, 88 Stat. 2123.)

HISTORICAL AND STATUTORY NOTES

Revision Notes and Legislative Reports
1975 Acts. Senate Report No. 93–1333,
see 1974 U.S.Code Cong. and Adm.News,
p. 7520.

LIBRARY REFERENCES

American Digest System
Fish ☞8.
Game ☞3.5.
Key Number System Topic Nos. 176, 187.

§ 459j–4.   Administration, protection, and development

(a) Conservation and management of natural resources

The seashore shall be administered, protected, and developed in accordance with the provisions of sections 1, 2, 3, and 4 of this title, as amended and supplemented, except that any other statutory authority available to the Secretary for the conservation management of natural resources may be utilized to the extent he finds such authority will further the purposes of sections 459j to 459j–8 of this title.

(b) Administration of lands in Merritt Island National Wildlife Refuge

Notwithstanding any other provisions of sections 459j to 459j–8 of this title, lands and waters in the Merritt Island National Wildlife Refuge as described in subsection (c) (2) of this section which are part of the seashore shall be administered for refuge purposes through the United States Fish and Wildlife Service pursuant to the National Wildlife Refuge System Administration Act, as amended (80 Stat. 926; 16 U.S.C. 668dd–668ee), except that the Secretary may utilize such additional authority as may be available to him for the conservation and management of wildlife and natural resources, the development of outdoor recreation opportunities, and interpretive education as he deems appropriate, consistent with the preservation of natural and wildlife values.

(c) Division of management authority between National Park Service and United States Fish and Wildlife Service

The Secretary shall cause to be issued a well defined division of management authority between the National Park Service and the United States Fish and Wildlife Service. It is the intent and purpose of sections 459j to 459j–8 of this title that such management authority, generally, shall be as follows:

(1) The National Park Service shall administer those lands and waters described as follows: beginning at the intersection of State Highway 3 and State Road 402; thence easterly along State Road 402 and continuing easterly in a straight line to a point one-half mile offshore in the Atlantic Ocean, following the southern boundary of the seashore created in section 1; thence northwesterly along the boundary of the seashore created in section 1, which line is at each point one-half mile distance from the high water mark, to Bethune Beach; thence inland in a generally westerly direction through Turner Flats and Shipyard Canal; thence northwesterly to the Intracoastal Waterway; thence southerly along the Intracoastal Waterway to the bound-

ary of the Kennedy Space Center; then southwesterly to United States Highway 1; thence southerly along State Highway 3 to the northern boundary of H. M. Gomez Grant; thence easterly along the northern boundary of H. M. Gomez Grant and continuing easterly in a straight line to a point of intersection with the line between the marsh and the dunes; thence southerly along the line between the marsh and the dunes to a point approximately one-half mile north of the southern boundary of the seashore created in section 1; thence westerly in a straight line to connect with and to follow the Government Railroad to its intersection with State Highway 3; thence southerly along State Highway 3 to the point of beginning. The portion of land bounded by the northern boundary of the H. M. Gomez Grant is hereby transferred to the Secretary of the Interior and may be used for the purpose of establishing such facilities as are needed for the administration of the seashore, for the construction of the principal visitor center which shall be designated as the "Spessard L. Holland Visitor Center", and for a central access to the seashore: *Provided, however,* That the Secretary of the Interior, upon the request of the Administrator of the National Aeronautics and Space Administration, shall close this area or any part thereof to the public when necessary for space operations. In administering the shoreline and adjacent lands the Secretary shall retain such lands in their natural and primitive condition, shall prohibit vehicular traffic on the beach except for administrative purposes, and shall develop only those facilities which he deems essential for public health and safety.

(2) The United States Fish and Wildlife Service shall administer the remaining lands described in section 459j of this title.

(Pub.L. 93–626, § 5, Jan. 3, 1975, 88 Stat. 2123.)

HISTORICAL AND STATUTORY NOTES

Revision Notes and Legislative Reports

1975 Acts. Senate Report No. 93–1333, see 1974 U.S. Code Cong. and Adm. News, p. 7520.

References in Text

The National Wildlife Refuge System Administration Act, as amended, referred to in subsec. (b), consists of sections 4 and 5 of Pub.L. 89–669, Oct. 15, 1966, 80 Stat. 927, as amended, and is classified to sections 668dd, 668ee of this title. For further details, see Short Title note set out under section 668dd of this title.

Canaveral National Seashore in Brevard County, Florida

Pub.L. 108–108, Title I, § 126, Nov. 10, 2003, 117 Stat. 1269, provided that:

"None of the funds made available in this or any other Act for any fiscal year may be used to designate, or to post any sign designating, any portion of Canaveral National Seashore in Brevard County, Florida, as a clothing-optional area or as an area in which public nudity is permitted, if such designation would be contrary to county ordinance."

Similar provisions were contained in the following prior appropriations Acts:

Pub.L. 108–7, Div. F, Title I, § 128, Feb. 20, 2003, 117 Stat. 242.

Pub.L. 107–63, Title III, § 313, Nov. 5, 2001, 115 Stat. 467.

Pub.L. 106–291, Title III, § 316, Oct. 11, 2000, 114 Stat. 989.

Pub.L. 106–113, Div. B, § 1000(a)(3) [Title III, § 317], Nov. 29, 1999, 113 Stat. 1535, 1501A–192.

Pub.L. 105–277, Div. A, § 101(e) [Title III, § 318], Oct. 21, 1998, 112 Stat. 2681–289.

Pub.L. 105–83, Title III, § 328, Nov. 14, 1997, 111 Stat. 1600.

LIBRARY REFERENCES

American Digest System
  Woods and Forests ⟜5.
  Key Number System Topic No. 411.

§ 459j–5.   Canaveral National Seashore Advisory Commission

(a) Establishment; duties; termination; membership; term of members; appointment; Chairman

There is hereby established the Canaveral National Seashore Advisory Commission which shall consult and advise with the Secretary on all matters of planning, development, and operation of the seashore and shall provide such other advice and assistance as may be useful in carrying out the purposes of sections 459j to 459j–8 of this title. The Commission shall terminate ten years after the date the seashore is established pursuant to sections 459j to 459j–8 of this title, unless extended by the Congress. The Commission shall be composed of six members who shall serve for terms of two years. Members shall be appointed by the Secretary, one of whom he shall designate as Chairman, in the following manner:

(1) one member from each county in which the seashore is located, to be selected from recommendations made by the county commission in each county;

(2) two members representing the State of Florida who shall be selected from recommendations made by the Governor of Florida; and

(3) two members representing the general public: *Provided,* That one member shall be appointed from each county in which the seashore is located.

(b) Meetings; vacancies

After the Secretary designates the member to be Chairman, the Commission may meet as often as necessary at the call of the Chairman or of the Secretary, or upon petition of a majority of the members of the Commission. Any vacancy in the Commission shall be filled in the same manner as the original appointment was made.

(c) Compensation; payment of expenses upon vouchers

Members of the Commission shall serve without compensation, as such, but the Secretary may pay, upon vouchers signed by the

Chairman, the expenses reasonably incurred by the Commission and its members in carrying out their responsibilities under this section.

(Pub.L. 93–626, § 6, Jan. 3, 1975, 88 Stat. 2124; Pub.L. 94–398, Sept. 4, 1976, 90 Stat. 1204.)

HISTORICAL AND STATUTORY NOTES

Revision Notes and Legislative Reports
  1975 Acts. Senate Report No. 93–1333, see 1974 U.S.Code Cong. and Adm.News, p. 7520.

  1976 Acts. Senate Report No. 94–1157, see 1976 U.S.Code Cong. and Adm.News, p. 2126.

Amendments
  1976 Amendments. Subsec. (a). Pub.L. 94–398 substituted "six members" for "five members" in introductory provisions and substituted "two" for "one" and added requirement relating to residency of each member in cl. (3).

LIBRARY REFERENCES

American Digest System
  Woods and Forests ⬤➡1, 7, 8.
  Key Number System Topic No. 411.

§ 459j–6.   Transfer of lands for use as administrative and visitor facilities to Secretary of the Interior; use of portion of John F. Kennedy Space Center; transfer of excess land within seashore to Secretary of the Interior

On January 3, 1975, those lands to be used for the administrative and visitor facilities described in section 459j–4(c)(1) of this title shall be transferred by sections 459j to 459j–8 of this title to the Secretary of the Interior and those portions of the John F. Kennedy Space Center falling within the boundaries of the seashore as defined in section 459j of this title shall become a part of the seashore, and within ninety days thereafter, the Administrator, National Aeronautics and Space Administration, shall grant to the Secretary for carrying out the intent and purpose of sections 459j to 459j–8 of this title such use of said portions as the Administrator determines is not inconsistent with public safety and the needs of the space and defense programs of the Nation. Notwithstanding any other provision of law, any lands within the seashore which the Administrator determines to be excess to the needs of such agency shall be transferred to the Secretary of the Interior for administration in accordance with the provisions of sections 459j to 459j–8 of this title: *Provided*, That any portions of the John F. Kennedy Space Center within the seashore not transferred to the Secretary shall remain under the control and jurisdiction of the Administrator.

(Pub.L. 93–626, § 7, Jan. 3, 1975, 88 Stat. 2125.)

HISTORICAL AND STATUTORY NOTES

Revision Notes and Legislative Reports
   1975 Acts. Senate Report No. 93–1333,
see 1974 U.S.Code Cong. and Adm.News,
p. 7520.

LIBRARY REFERENCES

American Digest System
   United States ☞57.
   Woods and Forests ☞4.
   Key Number System Topic Nos. 393, 411.

§ 459j–7.   Report to President

Within three years from January 3, 1975, the Secretary shall review the area within the seashore and shall report to the President, in accordance with section 1132(c) and (d) of this title, his recommendations as to the suitability or nonsuitability of any area within the seashore for preservation as wilderness, and any designation of any such areas as a wilderness shall be accomplished in accordance with section 1132(c) and (d) of this title.

(Pub.L. 93–626, § 8, Jan. 3, 1975, 88 Stat. 2125.)

HISTORICAL AND STATUTORY NOTES

Revision Notes and Legislative Reports
   1975 Acts. Senate Report No. 93–1333,
see 1974 U.S.Code Cong. and Adm.News,
p. 7520.

§ 459j–8.   Authorization of appropriations; reports to Congressional committees

(a) Acquisition of lands and interests in lands

There are hereby authorized to be appropriated such sums as may be necessary to carry out the purposes of sections 459j to 459j–8 of this title, but not more than $7,941,000 for the acquisition of lands and interests in lands. In order to avoid excessive costs resulting from delays in the acquisition program, the Secretary shall make every reasonable effort to promptly acquire the privately owned lands within the seashore. Until all such lands are acquired, he shall report, in writing on June 30 of each year to the Committee on Energy and Natural Resources of the Senate and the Committee on Natural Resources of the House of Representatives, the following information:

   (1) the amount of land acquired during the current fiscal year and the amount expended therefor;

   (2) the amount of land remaining to be acquired; and

(3) the amount of land programed for acquisition in the ensuing fiscal year and the estimated cost thereof.

(b) Development of essential public facilities

For the development of essential public facilities there are authorized to be appropriated $2.6 million in addition to the sums previously appropriated.

(Pub.L. 93–626, § 9, Jan. 3, 1975, 88 Stat. 2125; Pub.L. 100–564, § 2, Oct. 31, 1988, 102 Stat. 2831; Pub.L. 103–437, § 6(m), Nov. 2, 1994, 108 Stat. 4586.)

HISTORICAL AND STATUTORY NOTES

Revision Notes and Legislative Reports

1975 Acts. Senate Report No. 93–1333, see 1974 U.S.Code Cong. and Adm.News, p. 7520.

1994 Acts. House Report No. 103–779, see 1994 U.S. Code Cong. and Adm. News, p. 3639.

Amendments

1994 Amendments. Subsec. (a). Pub.L. 103–437, § 6(m)(1), substituted "Committee on Energy and Natural Resources of the Senate and the Committee on Natural Resources of the House of Representatives" for "Committees on Interior and Insular Affairs of the United States Congress".

Subsec. (b). Pub.L. 103–437, § 6(m)(2), struck out provisions which directed Secretary, within 3 years from Jan. 3, 1975, to develop and transmit to Congressional committees, a final master plan for development of Canaveral National Seashore.

1988 Amendments. Subsec. (b). Pub.L. 100–564 substituted "$2.6 million in addition to the sums previously appropriated" for "not more than $500,000".

Change of Name

Committee on Natural Resources of House of Representatives treated as referring to Committee on Resources of House of Representatives by section 1(a) of Pub.L. 104–14, set out as a note preceding 2 U.S.C.A. § 21. Committee on Resources of House of Representatives changed to Committee on Natural Resources of House of Representatives by House Resolution No. 6, One Hundred Tenth Congress, Jan. 5, 2007.

SUBCHAPTER LXIV—RECREATIONAL DEMONSTRATION PROJECTS

§ 459r.　Disposition of recreational demonstration projects

Except as provided in section 459s of this title, the Secretary of the Interior is authorized, with the approval of the President, to convey or lease to the States or to the political subdivisions thereof, without consideration, any or all of the recreational demonstration projects and lands, improvements, and equipment comprised within such projects transferred to him by Executive Order Numbered 7496, dated November 14, 1936, or any parts of such projects, when in his judgment such grantees or lessees are adequately prepared to administer, operate, and maintain such project areas for public park, recreational, and conservation purposes, or he may, with the approval of the President, transfer to other Federal agencies any of the aforesaid recreational demonstration areas that may be of use to such agencies.

(June 6, 1942, c. 380, § 1, 56 Stat. 326.)

HISTORICAL AND STATUTORY NOTES

Delegation of Functions

For delegation to the Secretary of the Interior of authority vested in the President by this section, see Ex. Ord. No. 10752, Feb. 12, 1958, 23 F.R. 973, set out as a note following section 715j of Title 15, Commerce and Trade.

Silver Creek Project

Act July 30, 1947, c. 351, 61 Stat. 519, provided: "That, in order to carry out the purposes of the act of June 6, 1942 [56 Stat. 326; sections 459r to 459t of this title], relating to the disposition of recreational demonstration areas, and to effectuate the transfer to the State of Oregon, pursuant to that act, of the Silver Creek recreational demonstration project, the following-described revested Oregon and California Railroad grant lands shall hereafter be administered as a part of the Silver Creek recreational demonstration project and shall be subject to all of the provisions of the aforesaid Act of June 6, 1942:

"**WILLAMETTE MERIDIAN**. "Township 8 south, range 1 east:

"Section 13, east half southeast quarter and southeast quarter northeast quarter;

"Section 25, all;

"Section 35, north half northeast quarter northeast quarter and north

half south half northeast quarter northeast quarter;

"Township 8 south, range 2 east;

"Section 17, south half southwest quarter and northwest quarter southwest quarter;

"Section 19, lots 3, 4, and northeast quarter;

"Section 29, west half; and

"Section 31, north half;

comprising one thousand seven hundred and ninety-one and ninety-three one-hundredths acres.

"**SEC. 2.** The following-described lands also shall become a part of the Silver Creek recreational demonstration project and shall be subject to the provisions of the act of June 6, 1942, upon acquisition of title thereto by the Oregon and California Revested Lands Administration:

"**WILLAMETTE MERIDIAN**. "Township 8 south, range 1 east: Section 36, northeast quarter, northeast quarter northwest quarter, north half southeast quarter northwest quarter, north half south half southeast quarter northwest quarter, north half northwest quarter northwest quarter, and north half south half northwest quarter northwest quarter; comprising two hundred and sixty acres"

EXECUTIVE ORDERS
EXECUTIVE ORDER NO. 7496

Nov. 14, 1936, 1 F.R. 1946

TRANSFER OF RECREATIONAL DEMONSTRATION PROJECTS

By virtue of and pursuant to the authority vested in me by Title II of the National Industrial Recovery Act (48 Stat. 200), (title 15, sections 701 to 712) the Emergency Relief Appropriation Act of 1935 (49 Stat. 115), and the Emergency Relief Appropriation Act of 1936 (Public No. 739, 74th Congress), (title 15, ch. 16 note) I hereby order as follows:

1. There is transferred from the Resettlement Administration to the Secretary of the Interior (a) all the real and personal property or any interest therein, together with all contracts, options, rights and interests, books, papers, memoranda, records, etc., acquired by the Resettlement Administration in connection with the recreational demonstration projects set forth in the attached schedule with

funds appropriated or made available to carry out the provisions of the National Industrial Recovery Act by the Fourth Deficiency Act, fiscal year 1933 (48 Stat. 274, 275), and by the Emergency Appropriation Act, fiscal year 1935 (48 Stat. 1055), and with funds appropriated by the Emergency Relief Appropriation Act of 1935 (49 Stat. 115), and by the Emergency Relief Appropriation Act of 1936 (Public No. 739, 74th Congress), (title 15, ch. 16 note) and (b) all personnel, whether in the District of Columbia or elsewhere, now employed in connection with the acquisition of land for those recreational demonstration projects, together with all administration personnel records pertaining to the employees transferred, and to those employees engaged in development activities as of July 31, 1936, who were released by the Resettlement Administration on that date to permit the Department of the Interior to enter them on its rolls as of Aug. 1.

2. There is transferred and allocated to the Secretary of the Interior all balances of appropriations heretofore made available to or allotted for expenditure by the Resettlement Administration both for acquiring land for the recreational demonstration projects set forth in the attached schedule and for developing those projects, under the said National Industrial Recovery Act, Fourth Deficiency Act, fiscal year 1933, Emergency Appropriation Act, fiscal year 1935, Emergency Relief Appropriation Act of 1935, and Emergency Relief Appropriation Act of 1936, to be used for the purposes for which such funds were made available or allotted to the Resettlement Administration. The Secretary of the Interior shall assume all outstanding obligations, commitments, and encumbrances heretofore incurred by the Resettlement Administration in connection with the said projects.

3. The Secretary of the Interior is authorized, through the National Park Service, to complete and administer the projects transferred to him by this Executive Order and to exercise with respect to any real or personal property or any interest therein, contracts, options, rights and interests, books, papers, memoranda, and records acquired in connection with such projects, all the powers and functions given to the Resettlement Administration in connection therewith by Executive Orders Nos. 7027 and 7028 of Apr. 30, 1935, and Apr. 30, 1935, respectively.

4. The Secretary of the Interior is authorized to prescribe such rules and regulations as may be necessary to carry out the administrative functions transferred and delegated to him by this Executive Order.

Schedule of Recreational Demonstration Projects

OP No.	RA No.	Name
65–11–24	LD–ME–2	Camden Hills
56–143	LP–ME–2	Camden Hills
65–11–25	LD–ME–3	Acadia
56–144	LP–ME–3	Acadia
65–25–340	LD–MD–4	Catoctin
56–147	LP–MD–4	Catoctin
65–13–145	LD–NH–1	Bear Brook
56–183	LP–NH–1	Bear Brook
65–23–3466	LD–PA–6	Racoon Creek
56–232	LP–PA–6	Racoon Creek
65–23–3467	LD–PA–7	French Creek
56–233	LP–PA–7	French Creek
65–23–3468	LD–PA–8	Laurel Hill
56–234	LP–PA–8	Laurel Hill
65–23–3469	LD–PA–11	Blue Knob
56–235	LP–PA–11	Blue Knob
65–23–3470	LD–PA–12	Hickory Run
56–236	LP–PA–12	Hickory Run
65–16–365	LD–RI–2	Beach Pond
56–238	LP–RI–2	Beach Pond
65–51–3019	LD–MI–4	Waterloo
56–152	LP–MI–4	Waterloo
65–51–3020	LD–MI–6	Yankee Springs
56–153	LP–MI–6	Yankee Springs
65–71–4637	LD–MN–7	St. Croix
56–160	LP–MN–7	St. Croix
65–54–1683	LD–IL–5	Pere Marquette
56–126	LP–IL–5	Pere Marquette
65–52–2067	LD–IN–5	Versailles
56–129	LP–IN–5	Versailles
65–52–2068	LD–IN–6	Winemac
56–130	LP–IN–6	Winemac
65–55–2838	LD–MO–6	Lake of the Ozarks
56–167	LP–MO–6	Lake of the Ozarks
65–55–2839	LD–MO–7	Cuivre River
56–168	LP–MO–7	Cuivre River
65–55–2840	LD–MO–8	Montserrat
56–169	LP–MO–8	Montserrat
65–43–1491	LD–KY–4	Otter Creek
56–136	LP–KY–4	Otter Creek
65–32–1133	LD–NC–8	Crabtree Creek
56–203	LP–NC–8	Crabtree Creek
65–32–1134	LD–NC–11	Appalachian National Parkway (Blue Ridge Parkway)
56–204	LP–NC–11	Appalachian National Parkway (Blue Ridge Parkway)
65–44–1315	LD–TN–11	Montgomery Bell
56–266	LP–TN–11	Montgomery Bell
65–44–1316	LD–TN–12	Shelby Forest Park
56–267	LP–TN–12	Shelby Forest Park
65–44–1317	LD–TN–13	Falls Creek Falls
56–268	LP–TN–13	Falls Creek Falls
65–31–1155	LD–VA–5	Swift Creek
56–277	LP–VA–5	Swift Creek
65–31–1156	LD–VA–6	Chopawamsic
56–278	LP–VA–6	Chopawamsic
65–31–1158	LD–VA–7	Shenandoah National Park
56–279	LP–VA–7	Shenandoah National Park
65–31–1516	LD–VA–8	Appalachian National Park

OP No.	RA No.	Name
56–280.........	LP-VA–8	....Appalachian National Park
65-31–1157	..... LD-VA–9	....Bull Run
56–281.........	LP-VA–9	....Bull Run
65-31–1159	..... LD-VA–13	...Waysides
56–282.........	LP-VA–13	...Waysides
65-61–1184	..... LD-AL–11	...Oak Mountain
56–96.........	LP-AL–11	...Oak Mountain
65-34–3167	..... LD-GA–9	....Hard Labor Creek
56–120.........	LP-GA–9	....Hard Labor Creek
65-34–3168	..... LD-GA–11	...Alex Stephens Memorial
56–121.........	LP-GA–11	...Alex Stephens Memorial
65-34–3169	..... LD-GA–12	...Pine Mountain
56–122.........	LP-GA–12	...Pine Mountain
65-33–1838	..... LD-SC–7	....Cheraw
56–243.........	LP SC–7	....Cheraw
65-33–1839	..... LD-SC–8	....Kings Mountain
56–244.........	LP-SC–8	....Kings Mountain

OP No.	RA No.	Name
65-33–1840	..... LD-SC–12	...Waysides
56–245.........	LP-SC–12	...Waysides
65-73–221	..... LD-ND–12	..Roosevelt Park
56–216.........	LP-ND–12	..Roosevelt Park
65-74–1475	..... LD-SD–14	..Badlands
56–259.........	LP-SD–14	..Badlands
65-74–1476	..... LD-SD–15	..Custer Park
56–260.........	LP-SD–15	..Custer Park
65-65–695	..... LD-OK–9	..Lake Murray
56–225.........	LP-OK–9	....Lake Murray
65-03–1801	..... LD-CF–5	....Mendocino Woodlands
56–104.........	LP-CF–5	....Mendocino Woodlands
65-83–245	..... LD-WY–2	..Lake Guernsey
56–297.........	LP-WY–2	....Lake Guernsey
65-94–677	..... LD-OR–4	..Silver Creek
56–299.........	LP-OR–4	....Silver Creek
65-85–932	..... LD-NM–14	..White Sands
56–197.........	LP-NM–14	..White Sands

LIBRARY REFERENCES

American Digest System

United States ⟨⟩57.

Woods and Forests ⟨⟩4.

Key Number System Topic Nos. 393, 411.

§ 459s.   Lands for certain projects added to certain projects

After June 6, 1942, the lands acquired for the Acadia, French Creek, Shenandoah, and White Sands recreational demonstration projects shall be added to and become a part of Acadia National Park, Hopewell Village National Historic Site, Shenandoah National Park, and White Sands National Monument, in the order named above, subject to all laws, rules, and regulations applicable to the respective areas to which such recreational demonstration projects are added.

(June 6, 1942, c. 380, § 2, 56 Stat. 327.)

HISTORICAL AND STATUTORY NOTES

Codifications

Proviso directing the Secretary of the Interior to file with the National Archives within six months after June 6, 1942, a map of each recreational demonstration project enumerated in the section has been omitted.

Catocin Recreational Demonstration Area

Act Aug. 24, 1954, c. 903, 68 Stat. 791, provided: "That the Secretary of the Interior, for the purpose of consolidating Federal holdings of land acquired for the Catoctin recreational demonstration area, Frederick County, Maryland, is hereby empowered, in his discretion, to obtain for the United States land and interests in lands held in private ownership within the established watersheds and boundaries of said recreational demonstration area by accepting from the owners of such privately owned land complete relinquishment thereof, and the Secretary may grant to such owners in exchange therefor, in each instance, federally owned lands of approximately equal value now a part of the Catoctin recreational demonstration area, that he considers are not essential for the administration, control, and operation of the aforesaid recreational demonstration area. Any land acquired by the United States pursuant to this authorization shall become a part of the Catoctin recreational demonstration area upon the vesting of title in the Unit-

507

ed States, and shall be subject to the laws applicable thereto."

Silver Creek Recreational Demonstration Project

Act June 9, 1947, c. 100, 61 Stat. 129, provided:

"That for the purpose of consolidating Federal holdings of lands acquired for the Silver Creek recreational demonstration project, in the State of Oregon, the Secretary of the Interior is hereby authorized to exchange any such lands for other lands of approximately equal value when in his opinion such action is in the interest of the United States, the title to any lands acquired hereunder to be satisfactory to the Attorney General. Upon the vesting of title thereto in the United States, any lands acquired pursuant to this authorization shall become a part of the Silver Creek recreational demonstration project, and shall be subject to the laws applicable thereto.

"**Sec. 2.** Upon the conveyance of the Silver Creek recreational demonstration project to the State of Oregon, or political subdivision thereof, pursuant to the Act of June 6, 1942 (56 Stat. 326 [sections 459r to 459t of this title]), the Secretary of the Interior may authorize the grantee to exchange or otherwise dispose of any lands so conveyed in order to acquire other lands of approximately equal value for the purpose of consolidating the holdings of the grantee, the title to lands so acquired to be satisfactory to the Attorney General. For the aforesaid purpose the Secretary is authorized to execute a release, as to the particular lands involved, of any condition providing for a reversion

of title to the United States, that may be contained in the conveyance by the United States to said grantee. No such release shall be executed, however, unless the grantee shall agree, in form satisfactory to the Secretary, that the lands to be acquired by it shall be subject to the conditions contained in the original conveyance from the United States, except that, in lieu of a provision for reversion, the grantee shall agree to convey said lands to the United States upon a finding by the Secretary in accordance with the procedure provided in said Act of June 6, 1942, that the grantee has not complied with such conditions during a period of more than three years. Lands so conveyed to the United States shall be subject to administration or disposition in like manner as recreational demonstration project lands that revert to the United States under the terms of the aforesaid Act."

Hopewell Village Boundary Revision

Act July 24, 1946, c. 604, 60 Stat. 655, provided: "That the Secretary of the Interior is hereby authorized to withdraw from the Hopewell Village National Historic Site, Pennsylvania, all or any part of the lands added to the Hopewell Village National Historic Site by the Act approved June 6, 1942, entitled 'An Act to authorize the disposition of recreational demonstration projects, and for other purposes [sections 459r to 459t of this title]', which in his opinion are not required for historic-site purposes. Any lands so withdrawn shall revert to the status of a recreational demonstration area."

LIBRARY REFERENCES

American Digest System
    United States ☞57.
    Woods and Forests ☞2.
    Key Number System Topic Nos. 393, 411.

§ 459t. Secretary of the Interior authorized to execute deeds and leases for project lands; inclusion of conditional covenants

The Secretary of the Interior is authorized to execute on behalf of the United States all necessary deeds and leases to effect the purposes of sections 459r to 459t of this title. Every such deed or lease shall contain the express condition that the grantee or lessee shall use the property exclusively for public park, recreational, and conservation purposes, and the further express condition that the United States assumes no obligation for the maintenance or operation of the property after the acceptance of such deed or during the term of such lease, and may contain such other conditions not inconsistent with such express conditions as may be agreed upon by the Secretary and the grantee or lessee: *Provided*, That the title and right to possession of any lands so conveyed or leased, together with the improvements thereon, shall revert to the United States upon a finding by the Secretary, after notice to such grantee or lessee and after an opportunity for a hearing, that the grantee or lessee has not complied with such conditions during a period of more than three years, which finding shall be final and conclusive, and such lands and improvements thereon, upon such reversion to the United States, shall be returned to the jurisdiction of the Department of the Interior and upon determination of the Secretary may be considered as surplus real property to be disposed of in accordance with section 1303 of Title 40.

(June 6, 1942, c. 380, § 3, 56 Stat. 327.)

HISTORICAL AND STATUTORY NOTES

Codifications

In text, "section 1303 of Title 40" substituted for "sections 304a to 304e of Title 40", which originally read "the Act of August 27, 1935 (49 U.S.C. 885)", on authority of Pub.L. 107–217, § 5(c), Aug. 21, 2002, 116 Stat. 1301, which is set out as a note preceding 40 U.S.C.A. § 101. Pub.L. 107–217, § 1, enacted Title 40 into positive law. The Act of August 27, 1935, is Act Aug. 27, 1935, c. 744, 49 Stat. 885, as amended, which was classified to former 40 U.S.C.A. §§ 304a to 304e prior to being repealed by Pub.L. 107–217, § 6(b), Aug. 21, 2002, 116 Stat. 1310, and its substance reenacted as 40 U.S.C.A. § 1303.

LIBRARY REFERENCES

American Digest System
    United States ☞57.
    Key Number System Topic No. 393.

§ 459u. Exchange of recreational demonstration project lands by grantee

In order to facilitate the administration of former recreational demonstration project lands and to consolidate the holdings of the grantees to whom such lands have been or may be granted pursuant to sections 459r to 459t of this title, the Secretary of the Interior may authorize any such grantee to exchange or otherwise dispose of any lands or interests in lands conveyed to it in order to acquire other lands or interests therein of approximately equal value.

For the aforesaid purpose, the Secretary is authorized to execute a release, as to the particular lands involved, of any condition providing for a reversion of title to the United States, that may be contained in the conveyance by the United States to said grantee. No such release shall be executed, however, unless the grantee shall agree, in form satisfactory to the Secretary, that the lands to be acquired by it shall be subject to the conditions contained in the original conveyance from the United States, except that in lieu of a provision for reversion, the grantee shall agree to convey said lands to the United States upon a finding by the Secretary in accordance with the procedure provided in said sections, that the grantee has not complied with such conditions during a period of more than three years. Lands so conveyed to the United States shall be subject to administration or disposition in like manner as recreational demonstration project lands that revert to the United States under the terms of the aforesaid sections.

(Aug. 3, 1950, c. 522, 64 Stat. 399.)

HISTORICAL AND STATUTORY NOTES

Revision Notes and Legislative Reports
  1950 Acts. Senate Report No. 1934, see 1950 U.S.Code Cong. Service, p. 2883.

LIBRARY REFERENCES

American Digest System
  United States ⊕55.
  Woods and Forests ⊕4.
  Key Number System Topic Nos. 393, 411.

SUBCHAPTER LXV—NATIONAL PARKWAYS

§ 460. Natchez Trace Parkway

All lands and easements heretofore and hereafter conveyed to the United States by the States of Mississippi, Alabama, and Tennessee for the right-of-way for the projected parkway between Natchez, Mississippi, and Nashville, Tennessee, together with sites acquired or to be acquired for recreational areas in connection therewith, and a right-of-way for said parkway of a width sufficient to include the highway and all bridges, ditches, cuts, and fills appurtenant thereto, but not exceeding a maximum of two hundred feet through Government-owned lands (except that where small parcels of Government-owned lands would otherwise be isolated, or where topographic conditions or scenic requirements are such that bridges, ditches, cuts, fills, parking overlooks, and landscape development could not reasonably be confined to a width of two hundred feet, the said maximum may be increased to such width as may be necessary, with the written approval of the department or agency having jurisdiction over such lands) as designated on maps heretofore or hereafter approved by the Secretary of the Interior, shall be known as the Natchez Trace Parkway and shall be administered and maintained by the Secretary of the Interior through the National Park Service, subject to the provisions of sections 1, 2, 3, and 4 of this title, the provisions of which sections, as amended and supplemented, are extended over and made applicable to said parkway: *Provided*, That the Secretary of Agriculture is authorized, with the concurrence of the Secretary of the Interior, to connect with said parkway such roads and trails as may be necessary for the protection, administration, or utilization of adjacent and nearby national forests and the resources thereof: *And provided further*, That the Forest Service and the National Park Service shall, insofar as practicable, coordinate and correlate such recreational developments as each may plan, construct, or permit to be constructed, on lands within their respective jurisdictions, which, by mutual agreement, should be given special treatment for recreational purposes.

(May 18, 1938, c. 251, § 1, 52 Stat. 407.)

HISTORICAL AND STATUTORY NOTES

Transfer of Functions

All functions of all other officers of the Department of the Interior and all functions of all agencies and employees of such Department were, with two exceptions, transferred to the Secretary of the Interior, with power vested in him to authorize their performance or the performance of any of his functions by any of such officers, agencies, and employees, by 1950 Reorg. Plan No. 3, §§ 1, 2, eff. May 24, 1950, 15 F.R. 3174, 64 Stat. 1262, set out in Appendix 1 to Title 5, Government Organization and Employees.

All functions of the Administrator of General Services were transferred to the Secretary of Commerce by 1949 Reorg. Plan No. 7, § 2, eff. Aug. 20, 1949, 14 F.R. 5228, 63 Stat. 1070, set out in Appendix 1 to Title 5.

All functions, powers, and duties of the Secretary of Commerce and other officers and offices of the Department of Commerce relating generally to highways under Reorg. Plan No. 7 of 1949 were transferred to and vested in the Secretary of Transportation by Pub.L. 89–670, Oct. 15, 1966, 80 Stat. 931. Reorg. Plan No. 7 of 1949 was amended by section 2(b) of Pub.L. 97–449, Jan. 12, 1983, 96 Stat. 2439, to reflect such transfer.

All functions of the Federal Works Agency and of all agencies thereof, together with all functions of the Federal Works Administrator were transferred to the Administrator of General Services by § 103(a) of the Federal Property and Administrative Services Act of 1949, Act June 30, 1949, c. 288, Title I, 63 Stat. 380. Both the Federal Works Agency and the office of Federal Works Administrator were abolished by § 103(b) of that Act, which was repealed by Pub.L. 107–217, § 6(b), Aug. 21, 2002, 116 Stat. 1313; see now generally 40 U.S.C.A. § 303(b).

Effective Date of Transfer of Functions

Transfer of functions by Act June 30, 1949, as effective July 1, 1949, see § 605, formerly § 505, of Act June 30, 1949, c. 288, 63 Stat. 403, renumbered by Act Sept. 5, 1950, c. 849, § 6(a), (b), 64 Stat. 583.

Boundary Adjustment and Land Acquisition

Pub.L. 106–527, Nov. 22, 2000, 114 Stat. 2515, provided that:

"**Section 1.   Definitions.**

"In this Act [this note]:

"**(1) Parkway.**—The term 'Parkway' means the Natchez Trace Parkway, Mississippi.

"**(2) Secretary.**—The term 'Secretary' means the Secretary of the Interior.

"**Sec. 2. Boundary adjustment and land acquisition.**

"**(a) In general.**—The Secretary shall adjust the boundary of the Parkway to include approximately—

"**(1)** 150 acres of land, as generally depicted on the map entitled 'Alternative Alignments/Area', numbered 604–20062A and dated May 1998; and

"**(2)** 80 acres of land, as generally depicted on the map entitled 'Emerald Mound Development Concept Plan', numbered 604–20042E and dated August 1987.

"**(b) Maps.**—The maps referred to in subsection (a) shall be on file and available for public inspection in the office of the Director of the National Park Service.

"**(c) Acquisition.**—The Secretary may acquire the land described in subsection (a) by donation, purchase with donated or appropriated funds, or exchange (including exchange with the State of Mississippi, local governments, and private persons).

"**(d) Administration.**—Land acquired under this section shall be administered by the Secretary as part of the Parkway.

"**Sec. 3. Authorization of leasing.**

"The Secretary, acting through the Superintendent of the Parkway, may lease land within the boundary of the Parkway to the city of Natchez, Mississippi, for any purpose compatible with the Parkway.

"**Sec. 4. Authorization of appropriations.**

"There are authorized to be appropriated such sums as are necessary to carry out this Act [this note]."

Relocation of Portions of Parkway

Pub.L. 85–746, Aug. 25, 1958, 72 Stat. 839, provided:

"That the Secretary of the Interior is authorized to enter into an agreement with the Pearl River Valley Water Supply District which shall provide for the district, upon terms and conditions which the Secretary determines are in the public interest, to relocate those portions of sections 3–O and 3–N of the Natchez Trace Parkway in Madison County, Mississippi, required in connection with the Pearl River Reservoir.

"**Sec. 2.** To cooperate in the relocation, the Secretary of the Interior is authorized to transfer to the Pearl River Valley Water Supply District the aforesaid portions of the existing Natchez Trace Parkway lands and roadway in exchange for the contemporaneous transfer to the United States of relocated parkway lands and roadway situated and constructed in accordance with the terms and conditions of the agreement authorized by the first section of this Act: Provided, That such exchange shall be made on the basis of approximately equal values.

"**Sec. 3.** The Secretary of the Interior is authorized to accept and to use until expended without additional authority any funds provided by the district for the purpose of this Act pursuant to agreement with the Secretary of the Interior, and any such funds shall be placed in a separate account in the Treasury which shall be available for such purpose."

Lands in French Camp

The Secretary of the Interior was authorized to relinquish or modify certain restrictions upon the use of privately owned lands in the village of French Camp along the Natchez Trace Parkway by Act Jan. 7, 1941, c. 939, 54 Stat. 1227.

LAW REVIEW AND JOURNAL COMMENTARIES

Consorting with forests: Rethinking our relationship to natural resources and how we should value their loss. Katharine K. Baker, 22 Ecology L.Q. 677 (1995).

LIBRARY REFERENCES

American Digest System
     Public Lands ⟐49.
     Key Number System Topic No. 317.

Research References

ALR Library

76 ALR, Fed. 279, Necessity and Sufficiency of Environmental Impact Statements under § 102(2)(C) of National Environmental Policy Act of 1969 (42 U.S.C.A. § 4332(2)(C)) in Cases Involving Projects Relating to Acquisition, Construction, Alteration, or Disposition of Government Facilities.

33 ALR, Fed. 9, Uniform Relocation Assistance and Real Property Acquisition Policies Act of 1970 (42 U.S.C.A. §§ 4601-4655).

32 ALR, Fed. 332, Validity, Construction, and Application of Endangered Species Act of 1973 (16 U.S.C.A. §§ 1531-1543).

47 ALR 2nd 381, Right of Public to Fish in Stream Notwithstanding Objection by Riparian Owner.

§ 460–1.   Inclusion of Ackia Battleground National Monument and Meriwether Lewis National Monument

To facilitate the administration of two areas of the national park system, known as Ackia Battleground National Monument, Mississippi, and Meriwether Lewis National Monument, Tennessee, those areas are included in the Natchez Trace Parkway, which they adjoin; and they shall be administered as a part of the parkway. In order to provide continued recognition of the significance of these portions of the parkway, the Secretary of the Interior shall provide them with appropriate designations in accordance with the historical events which occurred on them.

(Pub.L. 87–131, Aug. 10, 1961, 75 Stat. 335.)

LIBRARY REFERENCES

American Digest System

Armed Services ☞54.
Key Number System Topic No. 34.

§ 460a.   Licenses or permits for right-of-way over parkway lands

In the administration of the Natchez Trace Parkway, the Secretary of the Interior may issue revocable licenses or permits for rights-of-way over, across, and upon parkway lands, or for the use of parkway lands by the owners or lessees of adjacent lands, for such purposes and under such nondiscriminatory terms, regulations, and conditions as he may determine to be not inconsistent with the use of such lands for parkway purposes.

(May 18, 1938, c. 251, § 2, 52 Stat. 408.)

CODE OF FEDERAL REGULATIONS

Special regulations for particular areas of system, see 36 CFR § 7.1 et seq.

§ 460a–1. Acceptance of lands conveyed for Blue Ridge or Natchez Trace Parkways

The Secretary of the Interior is authorized, in his discretion, to approve and accept, on behalf of the United States, title to any lands and interests in land heretofore or hereafter conveyed to the United States for the purposes of the Blue Ridge or the Natchez Trace Parkways, or for recreational areas in connection therewith.

(June 30, 1936, c. 883, § 3, as added June 8, 1940, c. 277, § 3, 54 Stat. 250.)

§ 460a–2. Blue Ridge Parkway; establishment; administration and maintenance

All lands and easements heretofore or hereafter conveyed to the United States by the States of Virginia and North Carolina for the right-of-way for the projected parkway between the Shenandoah and Great Smoky Mountains National Parks, together with sites acquired or to be acquired for recreational areas in connection therewith, and a right-of-way for said parkway of a width sufficient to include the highway and all bridges, ditches, cuts, and fills appurtenant thereto, but not exceeding a maximum of two hundred feet through Government-owned lands (except that where small parcels of Government-owned lands would otherwise be isolated, or where topographic conditions or scenic requirements are such that bridges, ditches, cuts, fills, parking overlooks, landscape development, recreational and other facilities requisite to public use of said parkway could not reasonably be confined to a width of two hundred feet, the said maximum may be increased to such width as may be necessary, with the written approval of the department or agency having jurisdiction over such lands) as designated on maps heretofore or hereafter approved by the Secretary of the Interior, shall be known as the Blue Ridge Parkway and shall be administered and maintained by the Secretary of the Interior through the National Park Service, subject to the provisions of sections 1, 2, 3, and 4 of this title, the provisions of which sections, as amended and supplemented, are extended over and made applicable to said parkway: *Provided,* That the Secretary of Agriculture is authorized, with the concurrence of the Secretary of the Interior, to connect with the parkway such roads and trails as may be necessary for the protection, administration, or utilization of adjacent and nearby national forests and the resources thereof: *And provided further*, That the Forest Service and the National Park Service shall, insofar as practicable, coordinate and correlate such recreational development as each may plan, construct, or permit to be constructed, on lands within their respective jurisdictions which, by mutual agreement, should be given special treatment for recreational purposes.

(June 30, 1936, c. 883, § 1, 49 Stat. 2041; June 8, 1940, c. 277, § 1, 54 Stat. 249.)

HISTORICAL AND STATUTORY NOTES

Amendments

1940 Amendments. Act June 8, 1940 added the exceptions set out in the text in parenthesis.

Transfer of Functions

All functions of all other officers of the Department of the Interior and all functions of all agencies and employees of such Department were, with two exceptions, transferred to the Secretary of the Interior, with power vested in him to authorize their performance or the performance of any of his functions by any of such officers, agencies, and employees, by 1950 Reorg. Plan No. 3, §§ 1, 2, eff. May 24, 1950, 15 F.R. 3174, 64 Stat. 1262, set out in Appendix 1 to Title 5, Government Organizations and Employees.

All functions of the Administrator of General Services were transferred to the Secretary of Commerce by 1949 Reorg. Plan No. 7, § 2, eff. Aug. 20, 1949, 14 F.R. 5228, 63 Stat. 1070. See Appendix 1 to Title 5.

All functions, powers, and duties of the Secretary of Commerce and other officers and offices of the Department of Commerce relating generally to highways under Reorg. Plan No. 7 of 1949 were transferred to and vested in the Secretary of Transportation by Pub.L. 89–670, § 6(a)(1)(M), Oct. 15, 1966, 80 Stat. 938. Reorg. Plan No. 7 of 1949 was amended by section 2(b) of Pub.L. 97–449, Jan. 12, 1983, 96 Stat. 2439, to reflect such transfer.

All functions of the Federal Works Agency and of all agencies thereof, together with all functions of the Federal Works Administrator were transferred to the Administrator of General Services by § 103(a) of the Federal Property and Administrative Services Act of 1949, Act June 30, 1949, c. 288, Title I, 63 Stat. 380. Both the Federal Works Agency and the office of Federal Works Administrator were abolished by § 103(b) of that Act, which was repealed by Pub.L. 107–217, § 6(b), Aug. 21, 2002, 116 Stat. 1313; see now generally 40 U.S.C.A. § 303(b).

Effective Date of Transfer of Functions

Transfer of functions by Act June 30, 1949, as effective July 1, 1949, see § 605, formerly § 505, of Act June 30, 1949, c. 288, 63 Stat. 403, renumbered by Act Sept. 5, 1950, c. 849, § 6(a), (b), 64 Stat. 583.

CROSS REFERENCES

Acceptance of lands conveyed for purposes of Blue Ridge Parkway, see 16 USCA § 460a–1.

CODE OF FEDERAL REGULATIONS

Special regulations for particular areas of system, see 36 CFR § 7.1 et seq.

§ 460a–3. Licenses or permits to owners of adjacent lands

In the administration of the Blue Ridge Parkway, the Secretary of the Interior may issue revocable licenses or permits for rights-of-way over, across, and upon parkway lands, or for the use of parkway lands by the owners or lessees of adjacent lands, for such purposes and under such nondiscriminatory terms, regulations, and conditions as he may determine to be not inconsistent with the use of such lands for parkway purposes.

(June 30, 1936, c. 883, § 2, as added June 8, 1940, c. 277, § 2, 54 Stat. 250.)

§ 460a–4. Transfer of jurisdiction to Secretary of Agriculture; national forest lands

When in his judgment the public interest will be served thereby, the Secretary of the Interior is authorized, upon concurrence of the Secretary of Agriculture, to transfer to the jurisdiction of the Secretary of Agriculture for national forest purposes lands or interests in lands acquired for or in connection with the Blue Ridge Parkway. Lands transferred under this section shall become national forest lands subject to all laws, rules, and regulations applicable to lands acquired pursuant to the Weeks Law of March 1, 1911 (36 Stat. 961), as amended.

(May 13, 1952, c. 263, 66 Stat. 69.)

HISTORICAL AND STATUTORY NOTES

References in Text
    The Weeks Law of March 1, 1911 (36 Stat. 961), as amended, referred to in text, is Act Mar. 1, 1911, c. 186, 36 Stat. 961, as amended, which is classified to sections 480, 500, 515 to 519, 521, 552 and 563 of this title. For complete classification of this Act to the Code, see Short Title note set out under section 552 of this title and Tables.

CROSS REFERENCES

Blue Ridge Parkway extension; jurisdiction of Secretary of Interior, see 16 USCA § 460a–9.

LIBRARY REFERENCES

American Digest System
United States ⊜57.
Key Number System Topic No. 393.

§ 460a–5. Acquisition of land contiguous to Blue Ridge or Natchez Trace Parkways

In order to consolidate, on the Blue Ridge Parkway and the Natchez Trace Parkway, the land forming each such parkway, to adjust ownership lines, and to eliminate hazardous crossings of and accesses to these parkways, the Secretary of the Interior is authorized to acquire, by purchase or exchange, land and interests in land contiguous to the parkways. In consummating exchanges under this section, the Secretary may transfer parkway land, interests therein, and easements: *Provided*, That the property rights so exchanged shall be approximately equal in value.

(Pub.L. 87–76, June 30, 1961, 75 Stat. 196.)

HISTORICAL AND STATUTORY NOTES

Blue Ridge Parkway and Town of Blowing Rock Land Exchange Act of 2009
Pub.L. 111–167, §§ 1 to 3, May 24, 2010, 124 Stat. 1188, provided that:

"Sec. 1. Short Title.

"This Act [enacting this note] may be cited as the 'Blue Ridge Parkway and Town of Blowing Rock Land Exchange Act of 2009'.

"Sec. 2. Definitions.

"In this Act [this note]:

"**(1) Secretary.**—The term 'Secretary' means the Secretary of the Interior.

"**(2) Town.**—The term 'Town' means the Town of Blowing Rock in the State of North Carolina.

"**(3) Map.**—The term 'map' means the National Park Service map titled 'Blue Ridge Parkway, Proposed Land Exchange with Town of Blowing Rock', numbered '601/90,000A', and dated 'April, 2008'.

"**(4) Exchange.**—The term 'exchange' means the exchange of land authorized by section 3(a) [this note].

"Sec. 3. Land Exchange.

"**(a) In general.**—Subject to subsection (d), the Secretary may exchange approximately 20 acres of land within the boundary of the Blue Ridge Parkway that are

generally depicted on the map as 'Blowing Rock Reservoir', for approximately 192 acres of land owned by the Town that are generally depicted on the map as 'Town of Blowing Rock Exchange Lands'.

"**(b) Map availability.**—The map shall be on file and available for public inspection in the appropriate offices of the National Park Service.

"**(c) Timing.**—The Secretary shall seek to complete the land exchange not later than three years after the date of the enactment of this Act [May 24, 2010].

"**(d) Applicable laws; terms and conditions.**—The exchange shall be subject to—

"**(1)** laws, regulations, and policies applicable to exchanges of land administered by the National Park Service, including those concerning land appraisals, equalization of values, and environmental compliance; and

"**(2)** such terms and conditions as the Secretary considers appropriate.

"**(e) Equalization of values.**—If the lands proposed for exchange are found to be not equal in value, the equalization of values may be achieved by adjusting the acreage amounts identified in subsection (a).

"**(f) Boundary adjustment.**—Upon completion of the exchange, the Secretary shall adjust the boundary of the Blue Ridge Parkway to reflect the exchanged lands.

"(g) **Administration.**—Lands acquired by the Secretary through the exchange shall be administered as part of the Blue Ridge Parkway in accordance with all applicable laws and regulations.

"(h) **Future disposition of property.**—If the Town desires to dispose of the reservoir property that is the subject of the exchange, the Secretary shall have the right of first refusal to acquire the property for the Blue Ridge Parkway."

Eastern Band of Cherokee Indians Land Exchange Act of 2003

Pub.L. 108–108, Title I, § 138, Nov. 10, 2003, 117 Stat. 1271, provided that:

"(a) **Short title.**—This section [this note] may be cited as the 'Eastern Band of Cherokee Indians Land Exchange Act of 2003'.

"(b) **Findings and purposes.**—

"(1) **Findings.**—Congress finds the following:

"(A) Since time immemorial, the ancestors of the Eastern Band of Cherokee Indians have lived in the Great Smoky Mountains of North Carolina. The Eastern Band's ancestral homeland includes substantial parts of seven eastern States and the land that now constitutes the Great Smoky Mountains National Park.

"(B) The Eastern Band has proposed a land exchange with the National Park Service and has spent over $1,500,000 for studies to thoroughly inventory the environmental and cultural resources of the proposed land exchange parcels.

"(C) Such land exchange would benefit the American public by enabling the National Park Service to acquire the Yellow Face tract, comprising 218 acres of land adjacent to the Blue Ridge Parkway.

"(D) Acquisition of the Yellow Face tract for protection by the National Park Service would serve the public interest by preserving important views for Blue Ridge Parkway visitors, preserving habitat for endangered species and threatened species including the northern flying squirrel and the rock gnome lichen, preserving valuable high altitude wetland seeps, and preserving the property from rapidly advancing residential development.

"(E) The proposed land exchange would also benefit the Eastern Band by allowing it to acquire the Ravensford tract, comprising 143 acres adjacent to the Tribe's trust territory in Cherokee, North Carolina, and currently within the Great Smoky Mountains National Park and Blue Ridge Parkway. The Ravensford tract is part of the Tribe's ancestral homeland as evidenced by archaeological finds dating back no less than 6,000 years.

"(F) The Eastern Band has a critical need to replace the current Cherokee Elementary School, which was built by the Department of the Interior over 40 years ago with a capacity of 480 students. The school now hosts 794 students in dilapidated buildings and mobile classrooms at a dangerous highway intersection in downtown Cherokee, North Carolina.

"(G) The Eastern Band ultimately intends to build a new three-school campus to serve as an environmental, cultural, and educational 'village,' where Cherokee language and culture can be taught alongside the standard curriculum.

"(H) The land exchange and construction of this educational village will benefit the American public by preserving Cherokee traditions and fostering a vibrant, modern, and well-educated Indian nation.

"(I) The land exchange will also reunify tribal reservation lands now separated between the Big Cove Community and the balance of the Qualla Boundary, reestablishing the territorial integrity of the Eastern Band.

"(J) The Ravensford tract contains no threatened species or endangered species listed pursuant to the Endangered Species Act of 1973 [Pub.L. 93–205, Dec. 28, 1973, 87 Stat. 884; which is classified principally to 16 U.S.C.A. § 1531 et seq.]. The 218–acre Yellow Face tract has a number of listed threatened species and endangered species and a higher appraised value than the 143–acre Ravensford tract.

"**(K)** The American public will benefit from the Eastern Band's commitment to mitigate any impacts on natural and cultural resources on the Ravensford tract, by among other things reducing the requested acreage from 168 to 143 acres.

"**(L)** The Congress and the Department of the Interior have approved land exchanges in the past when the benefits to the public and requesting party are clear, as they are in this case.

"**(2) Purposes.**—The purposes of this section [this note] are the following:

"**(A)** To acquire the Yellow Face tract for protection by the National Park Service, in order to preserve the Waterrock Knob area's spectacular views, endangered species and high altitude wetland seeps from encroachment by housing development, for the benefit and enjoyment of the American public.

"**(B)** To transfer the Ravensford tract, to be held in trust by the United States for the benefit of the Eastern Band of Cherokee Indians, in order to provide for an education facility that promotes the cultural integrity of the Eastern Band and to reunify two Cherokee communities that were historically contiguous, while mitigating any impacts on natural and cultural resources on the tract.

"**(C)** To promote cooperative activities and partnerships between the Eastern band and the National Park Service within the Eastern Band's ancestral homelands.

"**(c) Land exchange.**—

"**(1) In general.**—The Secretary of the Interior ('Secretary') shall exchange the Ravensford tract, currently in the Great Smoky Mountains National Park and the Blue Ridge Parkway, for the Yellow Face tract adjacent to the Waterrock Knob Visitor Center on the Blue Ridge Parkway.

"**(2) Treatment of exchanged lands.**—Effective upon receipt by the Secretary of a deed or deeds satisfactory to the Secretary for the lands comprising the Yellow Face tract (as described in subsection (3)) to the United States, all right, title, and interest of the United States in and to the Ravensford tract (as described in subsection (4)),

including all improvements and appurtenances, are declared to be held in trust by the United States for the benefit of the Eastern Band of Cherokee Indians as part of the Cherokee Indian Reservation.

"**(3) Yellow Face tract.**—The Yellow Face tract shall contain Parcels 88 and 89 of the Hornbuckle Tract, Yellow Face Section, Qualla Township, Jackson County, North Carolina, which consist altogether of approximately 218 acres and are depicted as the 'Yellow Face Tract' on the map entitled 'Land Exchange Between the National Park Service and the Eastern Band of Cherokee Indians,' numbered 133/80020A, and dated November 2002. The map shall be on file and available for public inspection in the appropriate offices of the National Park Service and the Bureau of Indian Affairs. Upon completion of the land exchange, the Secretary shall adjust the boundary of the Blue Ridge Parkway to include such lands and shall manage the lands as part of the parkway.

"**(4) Ravensford tract.**—The lands declared by subsection (2) to be held in trust for the Eastern Band of Cherokee Indians shall consist of approximately 143 acres depicted as the 'Ravensford Tract' on the map identified in subsection (3). Upon completion of the land exchange, the Secretary shall adjust the boundaries of Great Smoky Mountains National Park and the Blue Ridge Parkway to exclude such lands.

"**(5) Legal descriptions.**—Not later than 1 year after the date of enactment of this section [Nov. 10, 2003], the Secretary of the Interior shall file a legal description of the areas described in subsections (3) and (4) with the Committee on Resources [now Natural Resources] of the House of Representatives and the Committee on Indian Affairs and the Committee on Energy and Natural Resources of the Senate. Such legal descriptions shall have the same force and effect as if the information contained in the description were included in those subsections except that the Secretary may correct clerical and typographical errors in such legal descriptions. The legal descriptions shall be on file and available for public inspection in the offices of the National Park Service and the Bureau of Indian Affairs.

"(d) Implementation process.—

"(1) Government-to-government agreements.—In order to fulfill the purposes of this section [this note] and to establish cooperative partnerships for purposes of this section [this note] the Director of the National Park Service and the Eastern Band of Cherokee Indians shall enter into government-to-government consultations and shall develop protocols to review planned construction on the Ravensford tract. The Director of the National Park Service is authorized to enter into cooperative agreements with the Eastern Band for the purpose of providing training, management, protection, preservation, and interpretation of the natural and cultural resources on the Ravensford tract.

"(2) Construction standards.— Recognizing the mutual interests and responsibilities of the Eastern Band of Cherokee Indians and the National Park Service for the conservation and protection of the resources on the Ravensford tract, the National Park Service and the Eastern Band shall develop mutually agreed upon standards for size, impact, and design of construction consistent with the purposes of this section [this note] on the Ravensford tract. The standards shall be consistent with the Eastern Band's need to develop educational facilities and support infrastructure adequate for current and future generations and shall otherwise minimize or mitigate any adverse impacts on natural or cultural resources. The standards shall be based on recognized best practices for environmental sustainability and shall be reviewed periodically and revised as necessary. Development of the tract shall be limited to a road and utility corridor, an educational campus, and the infrastructure necessary to support such development. No new structures shall be constructed on the part of the Ravensford tract depicted as the 'No New Construction' area on the map referred to in subsection (c)(3), which is generally the area north of the point where Big Cove Road crosses the Raven Fork River. All development on the Ravensford tract shall be conducted in a manner consistent with this section and such development standards.

"(e) Gaming prohibition.—Gaming as defined and regulated by the Indian Gaming Regulatory Act (25 U.S.C. 2701 et seq.) [Pub.L. 100–497, Oct. 17, 1988, 102 Stat. 2467] shall be prohibited on the Ravensford tract."

LIBRARY REFERENCES

American Digest System
    United States ☞55.
    Key Number System Topic No. 393.

Notes of Decisions

Public uses   1

_____

1. Public uses
    Proposed taking for recreational uses of land adjoining Blue Ridge Parkway through eminent domain was within purpose of this section authorizing acquisition of land contiguous to Parkway and permitting condemnation when necessary or advantageous to procure real estate for public uses. U.S. v. 365.0 Acres of Land, More or Less, in Augusta County, Com. of Va., C.A.4 (Va.) 1970, 428 F.2d 459. Eminent Domain ☞ 17

§ 460a–6.   Blue Ridge Parkway extension; acceptance of lands; public use, administration, and maintenance areas; survey location of parkway extension crossing national forest land; transfer from Federal agency to administrative jurisdiction of Secretary of the Interior; national forest uses following transfer within national forest

The Secretary of the Interior is authorized to accept, on behalf of the United States, donations of land and interests in land in the States of North Carolina and Georgia, to construct thereon an extension of the Blue Ridge Parkway from the vicinity of Beech Gap, North Carolina, to the vicinity of Kennesaw Mountain National Battlefield Park north of Atlanta and Marietta, Georgia, and to provide public use, administration, and maintenance areas in connection therewith.   The lands accepted for the parkway extension may vary in width but shall average not more than one hundred and twenty-five acres per mile in fee simple plus not more than twenty-five acres per mile in scenic easements.   The survey location and width of any portion of the parkway extension that crosses national forest land shall be jointly determined by the Secretary of the Interior and the Secretary of Agriculture.   Where the parkway extension designated by the Secretary of the Interior traverses Federal lands, the head of the department or agency having jurisdiction over such lands is authorized to transfer to the Secretary of the Interior the part of the Federal lands mutually agreed upon as necessary for the construction, maintenance, and administration of the parkway extension and public use thereof, without transfer of funds.   Any such transfer within a national forest shall not preclude any national forest use that is compatible with parkway use and that is agreed upon by the Secretary of the Interior and the Secretary of Agriculture.

(Pub.L. 90–555, § 1, Oct. 9, 1968, 82 Stat. 967.)

LIBRARY REFERENCES

American Digest System
   United States ☞55.
   Key Number System Topic No. 393.

§ 460a–7. Coordination of recreational development on parkway and national forest lands; administration of forest land recreational facilities and access road development by Secretary of Agriculture; forest road and Appalachian Trail relocation and reconstruction and alternative forest road provision by Secretary of the Interior

To effectuate the recommendations in the report to the Congress on the North Carolina–Georgia extension of the Blue Ridge Parkway, made pursuant to the Act of August 10, 1961 (75 Stat. 337)—

(1) The Secretary of the Interior and the Secretary of Agriculture shall, insofar as practicable, coordinate and correlate recreational development on lands within the parkway and adjacent or related national forest lands: *Provided*, That within national forest boundaries recreational developments and facilities on Federal lands other than those actually within the national parkway shall be administered by the Secretary of Agriculture;

(2) Upon the request of the Secretary of Agriculture, the Secretary of the Interior shall relocate and reconstruct any national forest roads that may be disturbed by the parkway extension, or provide alternative roads that are necessary to the protection, administration, or utilization of the national forests, and shall allow access to areas to be developed by the Secretary of Agriculture on adjacent national forest lands unless to do so will materially impair the primary purposes of the parkway;

(3) The Secretary of the Interior may relocate and reconstruct portions of the Appalachian Trail, including trail shelters, that may be disturbed by the parkway extension and such relocation and reconstruction may be performed (A) on non-Federal lands when the Appalachian Trail Conference obtains the consent of the owner to the use of the lands for the purpose and agrees to assume maintenance thereof, and (B) upon national forest lands with the approval of the Secretary of Agriculture.

(Pub.L. 90–555, § 2, Oct. 9, 1968, 82 Stat. 968.)

HISTORICAL AND STATUTORY NOTES

References in Text

The Act of Aug. 10, 1961 (75 Stat. 337), referred to in text, is Pub.L. 87–135, which authorized an appropriation of $35,000 for a survey of a proposed national parkway from the Blue Ridge Parkway at Tennessee Bald or Beech Gap southwest and running into the State of Georgia, and was not classified to the Code.

LIBRARY REFERENCES

American Digest System

Public Lands ☜49.
Woods and Forests ☜5.
Key Number System Topic Nos. 317, 411.

§ 460a–8.   Licenses or permits for rights-of-way over parkway lands

The Secretary of the Interior may issue revocable licenses or permits for rights-of-way over, across, and upon parkway lands, or for the use of parkway lands by the owners or lessees of adjacent lands, or for such purposes and under such terms and conditions as he may determine to be consistent with the use of such lands for parkway purposes.

(Pub.L. 90–555, § 3, Oct. 9, 1968, 82 Stat. 968.)

LIBRARY REFERENCES

American Digest System
  Public Lands ☞49.
  Key Number System Topic No. 317.

§ 460a–9.   Part of Blue Ridge Parkway; administration and maintenance of parkway extension

The parkway extension herein authorized shall be a part of the Blue Ridge Parkway and shall be administered and maintained by the Secretary of the Interior in accordance with the laws and regulations applicable thereto, including section 460a–4 of this title.

(Pub.L. 90–555, § 4, Oct. 9, 1968, 82 Stat. 968.)

LIBRARY REFERENCES

American Digest System
  Woods and Forests ☞5.
  Key Number System Topic No. 411.

§ 460a–10.   Transfer of national forest lands to Secretary of Agriculture

With the concurrence of the Secretary of Agriculture the Secretary of the Interior may transfer to the Secretary of Agriculture for national forest purposes lands or interests in lands within national forests acquired for, or in connection with, the parkway extension.

(Pub.L. 90–555, § 5, Oct. 9, 1968, 82 Stat. 968.)

LIBRARY REFERENCES

American Digest System
  United States ☞57.
  Key Number System Topic No. 393.

§ 460a–11. Authorization of appropriations

There is hereby authorized to be appropriated, for construction of the Blue Ridge Parkway extension, not more than $87,536,000, plus or minus such amounts, if any, as may be justified by reason of fluctuations in construction costs as indicated by engineering cost indices applicable to the type of construction involved herein.

(Pub.L. 90–555, § 6, Oct. 9, 1968, 82 Stat. 968.)

§§ 460b, 460c. Repealed. Pub.L. 85–767, § 2 [19, 21, 23, 33], Aug. 27, 1958, 72 Stat. 919

HISTORICAL AND STATUTORY NOTES

Section 460b, Acts June 16, 1936, c. 582, § 5, 49 Stat. 1520; June 8, 1938, c. 328, § 8, 52 Stat. 635; Sept. 5, 1940, c. 715, § 9, 54 Stat. 870, related to determination of location of parkways upon public lands, national forests, or other Federal reservations.

Section 460c, Act Sept. 7, 1950, c. 912, § 4(b), 64 Stat. 787, related to administration of parkway appropriations.

SUBCHAPTER LXVI—PUBLIC PARK AND RECREATIONAL FACILITIES AT WATER RESOURCE DEVELOPMENT PROJECTS

§ 460d. Construction and operation of public parks and recreational facilities in water resource development projects; lease of lands; preference for use; penalty; application of section 3401 of Title 18; citations and arrests with and without process; limitations; disposition of receipts

The Chief of Engineers, under the supervision of the Secretary of the Army, is authorized to construct, maintain, and operate public park and recreational facilities at water resource development projects under the control of the Department of the Army, to permit the construction of such facilities by local interests (particularly those to be operated and maintained by such interests), and to permit the maintenance and operation of such facilities by local interests. The Secretary of the Army is also authorized to grant leases of lands, including structures or facilities thereon, at water resource development projects for such periods, and upon such terms and for such purposes as he may deem reasonable in the public interest: *Provided,* That leases to nonprofit organizations for park or recreational purposes may be granted at reduced or nominal considerations in recognition of the public service to be rendered in utilizing the leased premises: *Provided further,* That preference shall be given to federally recognized Indian tribes and Federal, State, or local governmental agencies, and licenses or leases where appropriate, may be granted without monetary considerations, to such Indian tribes or agencies for the use of all or any portion of a project area for any public purpose, when the Secretary of the Army determines such action to be in the public interest, and for such periods of time and upon such conditions as he may find advisable: *And provided further*, That in any such lease or license to a federally recognized Indian tribe [1] Federal, State, or local governmental agency which involves lands to be utilized for the development and conservation of fish and wildlife, forests, and other natural resources, the licensee or lessee may be authorized to cut timber and harvest crops as may be necessary to further such beneficial uses and to collect and utilize the proceeds of any sales of timber and crops in the development, conservation, maintenance, and utilization of such lands. Any balance of proceeds not so utilized shall be paid to the United States at such time or times as the Secretary of the Army may determine appropriate. The water areas of all such projects shall be open to public use generally for boating, swimming, bathing, fishing, and other recreational purposes, and ready access to and exit from such areas along the shores of such projects shall be maintained for general public use, when such use is determined by the Secretary of the Army not to be contrary to the public interest, all under such rules and regulations as the Secretary of the Army may deem necessary, including but not limited to prohibitions of dumping and unauthorized disposal in any manner of refuse, garbage, rubbish, trash, debris, or litter of any kind at such water resource development projects, either into the waters of such projects or onto any land federally owned and administered by the Chief of Engineers. Any violation of such rules and regulations shall be punished by a fine of not more than $500 or imprisonment for not more than six months, or both. Any persons charged with the violation of such rules and regulations may be tried and sentenced in accordance with the provisions of section 3401 of Title 18. All persons designated by the Chief of Engineers for that purpose shall have the authority to issue a citation for violation of the regulations adopted by the Secretary of the Army, requiring the appearance of any person charged with violation to appear before the United States magistrate judge, within whose jurisdiction the water resource development project is located, for trial; and upon sworn information of any competent person any United States magistrate judge in the proper jurisdiction shall issue process for the arrest of any person charged with the violation of said regulations; but nothing herein contained shall be construed as preventing the arrest by any officer of the United States, without process, of any person taken in the act of violating said regulations. No use of any area to which this section applies shall be permitted which is inconsistent with the laws for the protection of fish and game of the State in which such area is situated. All moneys received by the United States for leases or privileges shall be deposited in the Treasury of the United States as miscellaneous receipts.

(Dec. 22, 1944, c. 665, § 4, 58 Stat. 889; July 24, 1946, c. 596, § 4, 60 Stat. 642; Sept. 3, 1954, c. 1264, Title II, § 209, 68 Stat. 1266; Oct. 23, 1962, Pub.L. 87–874, Title II, § 207, 76 Stat. 1195; Sept. 3, 1964, Pub.L. 88–578, § 2(a), 78 Stat. 899; Dec. 31, 1970, Pub.L. 91–611, Title II, § 234, 84 Stat. 1833; Dec. 1, 1990, Pub.L. 101–650, Title III, § 321, 104 Stat. 5117; Nov. 8, 2007, Pub.L. 110–114, Title II, § 2026, 121 Stat. 1079.)

¹ So in original.

HISTORICAL AND STATUTORY NOTES

Revision Notes and Legislative Reports

2007 Acts. House Conference Report No. 110–280, see 2007 U.S. Code Cong. and Adm. News, p. 320.

1944 Acts. House Report No. 1309, see 1944 U.S.Code Cong.Service, p. 1349.

1964 Acts. Senate Report No. 1364 and Conference Report No. 1847, see 1964 U.S.Code Cong. and Adm.News, p. 3633.

Amendments

2007 Amendments. Pub.L. 110–114, § 2026(1), inserted "federally recognized Indian tribes and" before "Federal, State, or local governmental agencies,".

Pub.L. 110–114, § 2026(2), inserted "Indian tribes or" after "without monetary considerations, to such".

Pub.L. 110–114, § 2026(3), inserted "federally recognized Indian tribe" after "That in any such lease or license to a".

1970 Amendments. Pub.L. 91–611 provided that the rules and regulations should include but not be limited to prohibitions of dumping and unauthorized disposal of refuse, garbage, rubbish, trash, debris, or litter of any kind at water resource development projects, prescribed penalty for violation of the rules and regulations, provided for trial and sentence in accordance with section 3401 of Title 18, authorized issuance of citation for violation of the regulations, provided for issuance of process for arrest of any violators, and recognized the authority of Federal officer without process to arrest any person taken in act of violating the regulations.

1964 Amendments. Pub.L. 88–578 struck out ", without charge," following "The water areas of all such projects shall be open to public use generally".

1962 Amendments. Pub.L. 87–874 substituted references to water resource development projects for references to reservoir areas wherever appearing, and authorized the Chief of Engineers to permit the construction, maintenance, and operation of facilities by local interests.

1954 Amendments. Act Sept. 3, 1954 amended section generally, and, among other changes, inserted "for park or recreational purposes" in first proviso, inserted "or leases where appropriate" in second proviso, and inserted third proviso permitting lessees and licensees to cut timber and harvest crops in certain cases and containing provisions with respect to the collection, utilization, and disposition of the proceeds from the sale of timber and crops.

1946 Amendments. Act July 24, 1946 inserted first proviso dealing with leases to nonprofit organizations.

Effective and Applicability Provisions

1964 Acts. Amendment by Pub.L. 88–578 effective Jan. 1, 1965, see section 1(a) of Pub.L. 88–578, set out in part as a note under section 460*l*–4 of this title.

Change of Name

The Department of War was designated the Department of the Army and the title of the Secretary of War was changed to Secretary of the Army by section 205(a) of Act July 26, 1947, c. 343, Title II, 61 Stat. 501. Section 205(a) of Act July 26, 1947, was repealed by section 53 of Act Aug. 10, 1956, c. 1041, 70A Stat. 641. Section 1 of Act Aug. 10, 1956, enacted "Title 10, Armed Forces" which in sections 3010 to 3013 continued the military Department of the Army under the administrative supervision of a Secretary of the Army.

"United States magistrate judge" substituted for "United States magistrate" wherever appearing in text pursuant to section 321 of Pub.L. 101–650, set out as a note under section 631 of Title 28, Judiciary and Judicial Procedure.

Transfer of Functions

For transfer of certain functions relating to real property under the jurisdiction of the Air Force, and certain functions relating to construction of buildings and facilities in so far as they may pertain to the Department of the Air Force, from the Secretary of the Army to the Secretary of the Air Force, see Secretary of Defense Transfer Order Nos. 14, eff. July 1, 1948; 18, eff. July 7, 1948; and 40 [App.B (66)], July 22, 1949.

Recreation Policy

Pub.L. 104–303, Title II, § 208(a), Oct. 12, 1996, 110 Stat. 3680, provided that:

"**(1) In general.**—The Secretary shall provide increased emphasis on, and opportunities for recreation at, water resources projects operated, maintained, or constructed by the Corps of Engineers.

"**(2) Report.**—Not later than 2 years after the date of the enactment of this Act [Oct. 12, 1996], the Secretary shall transmit to Congress a report on specific measures taken to implement this subsection."

Cabin Site Leases

Pub.L. 99–662, Title XI, § 1134(a)–(c), Nov. 17, 1986, 100 Stat. 4250, provided that:

"**(a)** On and after December 31, 1989, the Secretary shall continue in effect any lease or assignment thereof to which this section applies, until such time as such lease is terminated by the leaseholder, any successors or assigns of the leaseholder, or by the Secretary under subsection (b) of this section. Any such continuation beyond the date of expiration of such lease as in effect on December 31, 1989, shall be at fair market rentals and on such other reasonable terms and conditions not inconsistent with this section as the Secretary deems necessary. No continuation shall be made beyond such date unless the leaseholder agrees (1) to hold the United States harmless from any claim for damages or injury to persons or property arising from occupancy of or through the use of the property subject to such lease, and (2) to not unreasonably expand existing improvements.

"**(b)(1)** On and after December 31, 1989, the Secretary and any other officer or employee of the United States shall not terminate a lease to which this section applies, except as provided in paragraph (2) of this subsection.

"**(2)** On and after December 31, 1989, the Secretary may terminate a lease to which this section applies only if—

"**(A)** the property covered by the lease is needed for immediate use for public park purposes or other higher public use or for a navigation or flood control project; or

"**(B)** the leaseholder substantially violates a provision of such lease.

"**(c)** Subsections (a) and (b) of this section apply to (1) any cottage site lease of property, which lease was entered into by the Secretary of the Army pursuant to section 4 of the Act entitled 'An Act authorizing the construction of certain public works on rivers and harbors for flood control, and for other purposes', approved December 22, 1944 (58 Stat. 889; 16 U.S.C. 460d) [this section] and is in effect on December 31, 1989, and (2) any assignment of such a lease."

Prohibition on Orders to Remove Houseboats, etc., From Reservoirs or Projects Administered by Secretary of the Army

Pub.L. 99–662, Title XI, § 1134(d), Nov. 17, 1986, 100 Stat. 4251, as amended Pub.L. 101–640, Title III, § 320, Nov. 28, 1990, 104 Stat. 4643, provided that: "On or after December 31, 1989, no houseboat, boathouse, floating cabin, sleeping facilities at marinas, or lawfully installed dock or cabin or trailer and appurtenant structures shall be required to be removed from any Federal water resources reservoir or lake project administered by the Secretary on which it was located on the date of enactment of this Act [Nov. 17, 1986], if (1) such property is maintained in usable and safe condition, (2) such property does not occasion a threat to life or property, and (3) the holder of the lease, permit, or license is in substantial compliance with the existing lease or license, except where necessary for immediate use for public purposes or other higher public use or for a navigation or flood control project."

Pub.L. 97–140, § 6, Dec. 29, 1981, 95 Stat. 1718, provided that: "Notwithstanding any other provision of law, no houseboat, floating cabin, marina (including any with sleeping facilities), or lawfully installed dock or cabin and appurtenant structures shall be required to be removed before December 31, 1989, from any Federal water resources reservoir or lake project administered by the Secretary of the Army, acting through the Chief of Engineers, on which it was located on the date of enactment of this Act, if such property is maintained in usable condi-tion, and, in the judgment of the Chief of Engineers, does not occasion a threat to life or property."

Similar provisions were contained in Pub.L. 97–128, § 8, Dec. 29, 1981, 95 Stat. 1685.

Section as Unaffected by Submerged Lands Act

Provisions of this section as not amended, modified or repealed by the Submerged Lands Act, see section 1303 of Title 43, Public Lands.

CROSS REFERENCES

Non–Federal interests not required to assume operation and maintenance of recreational facility as condition to new construction, see 33 USCA § 2297.

CODE OF FEDERAL REGULATIONS

Nondiscrimination in federally-assisted programs, see 36 CFR § 312.1 et seq.
Public use of development projects, see 36 CFR § 327.0 et seq.

LAW REVIEW AND JOURNAL COMMENTARIES

South Dakota v. Bourland: Another Supreme Court move away from recognition of tribal sovereignty.   25 Envtl.L. 209 (1995).
The Missouri River and adaptive management: Protecting ecological function and legal process.   John H. Davidson and Thomas Earl Geu, 80 Neb. L.Rev. 816 (2001).

LIBRARY REFERENCES

American Digest System
United States ⊜57, 81.
Key Number System Topic No. 393.

Research References

ALR Library
32 ALR, Fed. 332, Validity, Construction, and Application of Endangered Species Act of 1973 (16 U.S.C.A. §§ 1531-1543).
47 ALR 2nd 381, Right of Public to Fish in Stream Notwithstanding Objection by Riparian Owner.
129 ALR 1163, Lease by Municipality of Property Intended for Use and Benefit of Public as Affecting Its Duty and Responsibility in Respect of the Manner and Conditions of Operation and Maintenance of the Property by the Lessee.
Encyclopedias
24 Am. Jur. Proof of Facts 3d 543, Zoning--Invalidity of Single-Family Zoning Ordinance.

Notes of Decisions

Authority of Secretary 2	**State regulation and control 3**
Indian treaty rights 8	**Tribal regulatory authority 6**
Injunction 10	**Uses inconsistent with state fish and game laws 5**
Jurisdiction 9	
Leases and licenses 7	
Questions for Congress 1	

Water resource development projects 4

___

1. Questions for Congress

It is for Congress, not the Army Corps of Engineers, to decide the purposes for which private property can be taken under eminent domain. U.S. v. 2,606.84 Acres of Land in Tarrant County, Tex., N.D.Tex.1969, 309 F.Supp. 887, reversed on other grounds 432 F.2d 1286, certiorari denied 91 S.Ct. 1368, 402 U.S. 916, 28 L.Ed.2d 658, rehearing denied 91 S.Ct. 2203, 403 U.S. 912, 29 L.Ed.2d 690. Eminent Domain ☞ 7

2. Authority of Secretary

The Secretary of the Army had authority under this section, to grant leases of lands, including structures or facilities thereon, situated within the Bull Shoals Reservoir area, and the Chief of Engineers, under the supervision of the Secretary, had authority to permit the construction, maintenance and operation of recreational facilities in the Reservoir area. U.S. v. Weaver, W.D.Ark.1954, 124 F.Supp. 517. United States ☞ 57

3. State regulation and control

Regulatory authority of Army Corps of Engineers, under Flood Control Act, over areas taken from Lower Brule Sioux Reservation to build dam and reservoir did not preempt state regulation of hunting or fishing by nonmembers on taken lands, in light of statutory language recognizing state fish and game laws and provisions for application of state law in Corps' regulations governing public use of taken lands and waters. Lower Brule Sioux Tribe v. State of S.D., C.A.8 (S.D.) 1997, 104 F.3d 1017, rehearing and suggestion for rehearing en banc denied, certiorari denied 118 S.Ct. 64, 522 U.S. 816, 139 L.Ed.2d 26. Indians ☞ 353; Indians ☞ 363

4. Water resource development projects

Army Corps of Engineers' conclusion that water areas of lakeshore property subleased to quasi-public operator of group camp "remain[ed] open to public use generally," as required by Flood Control Act, was based on permissible construction of Act, even though lease allowed operator to impose reasonable restrictions, such as limiting access to campers, program participants, or groups who had reserved use of area; just because water areas were no longer

open to unrestricted public use did not mean that water areas are closed to public use. Liddle v. Corps of Engineers of U.S. Army, M.D.Tenn.1997, 981 F.Supp. 544. United States ☞ 57

The Chesapeake and Delaware Canal Inland Waterway from the Delaware River to the Chesapeake Bay is a "water resource development" within meaning of this section as amended in 1962, and land taken in connection therewith may be used for the construction of recreational facilities and ready access to and exit from such facilities maintained for the general public use. U.S. v. 0.01 Acre of Land, More or Less, in Cecil County, State of Md., D.C.Md.1970, 310 F.Supp. 1379. Eminent Domain ☞ 318

5. Uses inconsistent with state fish and game laws

This section, authorizing Missouri River flood control project, that no use of any area to which applicable section applied was to be inconsistent with laws for protection of fish and game of the state in which such area was situated did not authorize South Dakota to apply its laws to hunting and fishing activities by members of Lower Brule Sioux Tribe members within those areas of reservation taken for the Fort Randall and Big Bend projects and language meant only that Secretary of the Army could not promulgate regulations which contravened state conservation laws within public park and recreation facilities. Lower Brule Sioux Tribe v. State of S.D., C.A.8 (S.D.) 1983, 711 F.2d 809, certiorari denied 104 S.Ct. 707, 464 U.S. 1042, 79 L.Ed.2d 171. Indians ☞ 353; Indians ☞ 363

6. Tribal regulatory authority

District court did not err in finding that non-Indian conduct on land within Indian reservation which had been taken by government for construction of dam and reservoir neither threatened nor had direct effect on political integrity, economic security, or health or welfare of tribe, and tribe did not retain jurisdiction over non-Indians in taken lands, notwithstanding fact that non-Indian hunters and fishers had harassed cattle owned by Indians grazing on land, failed to close pasture gates, let down wires on fences, and through hunting on land reduced amount of deer available to tribal members. State of S.D. v. Bourland, C.A.8 (S.D.)

1994, 39 F.3d 868. Indians ☞ 223; Indians ☞ 352; Indians ☞ 362

7. Leases and licenses

Zoning ordinance designating, as single family residential district, the site of proposed recreational vehicle park on land leased by United States directly conflicted with government's approval of park, and thus was preempted by federal law. Crystal Bay Marina v. Sweeden, N.D.Okla.1996, 939 F.Supp. 839. Zoning And Planning ☞ 1028

In action to enjoin violation of regulations promulgated by the Secretary of the Army governing operation of commercial boats on government reservoir, evidence established that defendant by general supervision and direction of the business of renting boats, had been and was indirectly causing boats to be placed upon and operated upon waters of reservoir for a fee or profit, without being authorized to do so by lease, license or concession contract with the Department of the Army, in violation of regulation. U.S. v. Weaver, W.D.Ark.1954, 124 F.Supp. 517. Injunction ☞ 128(8)

The public interest cannot be fulfilled in a government-owned recreation area by allowing those who apply first for a property lease for a specified term to thereafter invoke due process principles and maintain an interest in such property, judicially enforceable in a civil rights action, perpetually or for as long as they desire. Cubellis v. Costar, W.D.Pa.1974, 65 F.R.D. 49. Civil Rights ☞ 1071

Park district, which executed agreement permitting persons to operate concession within certain area, could not convey any greater interest than district had under license, which had been granted to district by United States and permitted district to use area for public park and recreational purposes; thus, though such agreement was referred to as a "lease," it was only a concession agreement, which was in effect a license, and any right acquired by licensees was not a property right requiring just compensation to licensees for its taking when State Park Service eliminated roadway leading from state part area to licensees' resort. Lee v. North Dakota Park Service, N.D. 1977, 262 N.W.2d 467. Eminent Domain ☞ 83; Licenses ☞ 44(2)

8. Indian treaty rights

Flood Control Act and Cheyenne River Act abrogated Cheyenne River Sioux Tribe's rights under Fort Laramie Treaty to regulate non-Indian hunting and fishing on land taken by United States for dam and reservoir project; Flood Control Act opened lands taken for dam and reservoir project for general recreational use of public, and Cheyenne River Act declared that sum paid to Tribe for former trust land taken for project was final and complete settlement of all claims, rights, and demands. South Dakota v. Bourland, U.S.S.D.1993, 113 S.Ct. 2309, 508 U.S. 679, 124 L.Ed.2d 606, on remand 997 F.2d 512, on remand 39 F.3d 868. Indians ☞ 352; Indians ☞ 362

This section which authorized establishment of comprehensive flood control plan along the Missouri River, did not abrogate any treaty rights of the Lower Brule Tribe or its members. Lower Brule Sioux Tribe v. State of S.D., C.A.8 (S.D.) 1983, 711 F.2d 809, certiorari denied 104 S.Ct. 707, 464 U.S. 1042, 79 L.Ed.2d 171. Indians ☞ 123

Congress eliminated power of Lower Brule Sioux Tribe to exclude non-Indians from reservation lands taken for dam-building project, as Flood Control Act of 1944 opened taken lands for general recreational use of public, thus abrogating any original treaty right to regulate non-Indian hunting and fishing within federal taken areas. Lower Brule Sioux Tribe v. State of S.D., D.S.D.1996, 917 F.Supp. 1434, affirmed 104 F.3d 1017, rehearing and suggestion for rehearing en banc denied, certiorari denied 118 S.Ct. 64, 522 U.S. 816, 139 L.Ed.2d 26. Indians ☞ 352; Indians ☞ 362

Federal statute [16 U.S.C.A. § 460d], authorizing recreational facilities at Army Corps of Engineers' reservoirs and water resource projects and giving general approval to implementation of designated plans for Missouri River Basin Program, did not grant authority to United States to condemn, without approval of Secretary of the Interior, certain Winnebago treaty lands along eastern bank of Missouri River. Bear v. U.S., D.C.Neb.1985, 611 F.Supp. 589, affirmed 810 F.2d 153. Eminent Domain ☞ 45

9. Jurisdiction

United States District Court for the Western District of Arkansas had jurisdiction of the subject-matter and parties to action by the United States against citizens and residents of the district to enjoin alleged violation of regulations promulgated by the Secretary of the Army governing operation of commercial boats on Bull Shoals Reservoir. U.S. v. Weaver, W.D.Ark.1954, 124 F.Supp. 517. Federal Courts ☞ 71; Federal Courts ☞ 194

10. Injunction

Injunction requiring removal of private dock from public recreation area was appropriate remedy for abuse of discretion by Army Corps of Engineers in permitting construction of the dock in violation of applicable regulations governing management of public recreation area and transfer of ownership to holder of 30-year commercial concession lease from the Corps was not an adequate remedy as adjacent landowner's view from her property, which view was restricted by dock construction, weighed more heavily than hardship caused by removal. Matthews v. U.S., C.A.11 (Ga.) 1983, 713 F.2d 677. Water Law ☞ 1253

In action by United States against county judges to require them to reinstate or pay for reinstallation of barricade placed across road in public park by Army Corps of Engineers and or-

dered removed by judges, issuance of preliminary injunction requiring judges to reinstate barricade was not abuse of discretion, in light of probability that Government would succeed on merits, fact that threat of trespass upon Government property by and through uncontrolled means of access to subject roadway demonstrated substantial injury to Government warranting restoration of status quo, and fact that harm to local public was minimal pending final resolution of controversy since access to barricaded area was otherwise available by lengthier route. U.S. v. Gannaway, C.A.8 (Mo.) 1976, 536 F.2d 784. Injunction ☞ 135

An individual, who had been and was indirectly causing boats to be placed upon and operated upon waters of government reservoir for a fee or profit without a lease, license or concession contract with the Department of the Army, as required by regulations promulgated by the Secretary of the Army, should be enjoined and restrained from renting boats and, either directly or indirectly, personally or through an agent, transporting such boats to or from waters of the reservoir. U.S. v. Weaver, W.D.Ark.1954, 124 F.Supp. 517. Injunction ☞ 92

§ 460d–1. Rentals or other considerations in leases for construction, maintenance, and operation of commercial recreational facilities; adjustment by Chief of Engineers

The Chief of Engineers, under the supervision of the Secretary of the Army, is authorized to amend any lease entered into providing for the construction, maintenance, and operation of commercial recreational facilities at a water resource development project under the jurisdiction of the Secretary of the Army so as to provide for the adjustment, either by increase or decrease, from time to time during the term of such lease of the amount of rental or other consideration payable to the United States under such lease, when and to the extent he determines such adjustment or extension to be necessary or advisable in the public interest. No adjustment shall be made under the authority of this section so as to increase or decrease the amount of rental or other consideration payable under such lease for any period prior to the date of such adjustment.

(Pub.L. 87–236, Sept. 14, 1961, 75 Stat. 509; Pub.L. 89–298, Title II, § 215, Oct. 27, 1965, 79 Stat. 1088.)

531

Amendments
  1965 Amendments. Pub.L. 89–298 deleted "before November 1, 1956," following "lease entered into".

American Digest System
  United States ⊕57.
  Key Number System Topic No. 393.

§ 460d–2. Adjustment by Secretary of Agriculture

The Secretary of Agriculture is authorized to amend any lease entered into with respect to lands under the jurisdiction of the Forest Service providing for the construction, maintenance, and operation of commercial recreational facilities at a Federal reservoir project so as to provide for the adjustment, either by increase or decrease, from time to time during the term of such lease of the amount of rental or other consideration payable to the United States under such lease, when and to the extent he determines such adjustment to be necessary or advisable in the public interest. No adjustment shall be made under the authority of this section so as to increase or decrease the amount of rental or other consideration payable under such lease for any period prior to the date of such adjustment.

(Pub.L. 87–411, Mar. 3, 1962, 76 Stat. 20.)

American Digest System
  United States ⊕57.
  Key Number System Topic No. 393.

§ 460d–3. Recreational user fees

(a) Prohibition on admissions fees

No entrance or admission fees shall be collected after March 31, 1970, by any officer or employee of the United States at public recreation areas located at lakes and reservoirs under the jurisdiction of the Corps of Engineers, United States Army.

(b) Fees for use of developed recreation sites and facilities

(1) Establishment and collection

Notwithstanding section 460l–6a(b) of this title, the Secretary of the Army is authorized, subject to paragraphs (2) and (3), to establish and collect fees for the use of developed recreation sites and facilities, including campsites, swimming beaches, and boat launching ramps but excluding a site or facility which includes only a boat launch ramp and a courtesy dock.

(2) Exemption of certain facilities

The Secretary shall not establish or collect fees under this subsection for the use or provision of drinking water, wayside exhibits, roads, scenic drives, overlook sites, picnic tables, toilet facilities, surface water areas, undeveloped or lightly developed shoreland, or general visitor information.

(3) Per vehicle limit

The fee under this subsection for use of a site or facility (other than an overnight camping site or facility or any other site or facility at which a fee is charged for use of the site or facility as of August 10, 1993) for persons entering the site or facility by private, noncommercial vehicle transporting not more than 8 persons (including the driver) shall not exceed $3 per day per vehicle. Such maximum amount may be adjusted annually by the Secretary for changes in the Consumer Price Index of All Urban Consumers published by the Bureau of Labor Statistics of the Department of Labor.

(4) Deposit into Treasury account

All fees collected under this subsection shall be deposited into the Treasury account for the Corps of Engineers established by section 460*l*–6a(i) of this title and, subject to the availability of appropriations, shall be used for the purposes specified in section 460*l*–6a(i)(3) of this title at the water resources development project at which the fees were collected.

(Pub.L. 90–483, Title II, § 210, Aug. 13, 1968, 82 Stat. 746; Pub.L. 103–66, Title V, § 5001(a), Aug. 10, 1993, 107 Stat. 378; Pub.L. 104–303, Title II, § 208(b)(1), Oct. 12, 1996, 110 Stat. 3680.)

HISTORICAL AND STATUTORY NOTES

Revision Notes and Legislative Reports
1993 Acts. House Report No. 103–111 and House Conference Report No. 103–213, see 1993 U.S. Code Cong. and Adm. News, p. 378.

References in Text
Section 460l–6a(b), (i)(3), of this title, referred to in subsec. (b)(1), (4), was repealed by Pub.L. 108–447, Div. J, Title VIII, § 813(a), Dec. 8, 2004, 118 Stat. 3390, as amended by Pub.L. 109–54, Title I, § 132(a), Aug. 2, 2005, 119 Stat. 526.

Amendments
1996 Amendments. Subsec. (b)(4). Pub.L. 104–303, § 208(b)(1), added provisions relating to use of funds.

1993 Amendments. Catchline. Pub.L. 103–66, § 5001(a)(1), enacted section catchline "Recreational user fees".

Subsec. (a). Pub.L. 103–66, § 5001(a)(1), designated existing text as subsec. (a).

Pub.L. 103–66, § 5001(a)(2), struck out provision directing the collection of user fees at highly developed facilities requiring personnel and not at undeveloped or lightly developed areas.

Subsec. (b). Pub.L. 103–66, § 5001(a)(3), added subsec. (b).

Alternative to Annual Passes

Pub.L. 104–303, Title II, § 208(c), Oct. 12, 1996, 110 Stat. 3680, as amended Pub.L. 106–53, Title II, § 218, Aug. 17, 1999, 113 Stat. 294, provided that:

"**(1) In general.**—The Secretary shall evaluate the feasibility of implementing an alternative to the $25 annual pass that the Secretary currently offers to users of recreation facilities at water resources projects of the Corps of Engineers.

"**(2) Annual pass.**—The evaluation under paragraph (1) shall include the establishment on a test basis of an annual pass that costs $10 or less for the use of recreation facilities, including facilities at Raystown Lake, Pennsylvania.

"**(3) Report.**—Not later than December 31, 1999, the Secretary shall transmit to Congress a report on the results of the evaluation carried out under this subsection, together with recommendations concerning whether annual passes for individual projects should be offered on a nationwide basis.

"**(4) Expiration of authority.**—The authority to establish an annual pass under paragraph (2) shall expire on the [sic] December 31, 2003."

LIBRARY REFERENCES

American Digest System

United States ⬤⇒57.
Key Number System Topic No. 393.

Notes of Decisions

Fees charged by lessees   1

_____

1. Fees charged by lessees

Following changes effected by Omnibus Budget Reconciliation Act of 1993, Flood Control Act did not limit ability of Army Corps of Engineers to permit its lessees to charge user fees for boat launching that Corps deemed reasonable in public interest; while boat owners claimed that latter Act's express reference to maximum $3 fee that could be charged by Corps itself meant either that no fees would be charged by lessees or that lessees were limited to $3 maximum, Corps reasonably interpreted Act to place no limit on fees that could be charged at lessee-operated facilities provided that fees were reasonable and in public interest as determined by Corps. Center Hill Defense Fund v. U.S. Army Corps of Engineers, Nashville Dist., M.D.Tenn.1995, 886 F.Supp. 1389. Wharves ⬤⇒ 9

§ 460d–3a. Contracts to provide visitor reservation services

The Secretary of the Army may, under such terms and conditions as the Secretary deems appropriate, contract with any public or private entity to provide visitor reservation services. Any such contract in effect on or after October 1, 2004, may provide that the contractor shall be permitted to deduct a commission to be fixed by the Secretary from the amount charged the public for providing such services and to remit the net proceeds therefrom to the contracting agency.

(Pub.L. 110–161, Div. C, Title I, § 121, Dec. 26, 2007, 121 Stat. 1946.)

HISTORICAL AND STATUTORY NOTES

Revision Notes and Legislative Reports
2007 Acts. House Report No. 110–197, see 2007 U.S. Code Cong. and Adm. News, p. 661.

Statement by President, see 2007 U.S. Code Cong. and Adm. News, p. S34.

SUBCHAPTER LXVII—COTTAGE SITE DEVELOPMENTS AND USES IN RESERVOIR AREAS

§ 460e.   Authorization for sale of public lands; rights of lessee

Whenever the Secretary of the Army determines that any Government-owned lands other than lands withdrawn or reserved from the public domain within reservoir areas under his control (1) are not required for project purposes or for public recreational use, and (2) are being used for or are available for cottage site development and use, he is authorized to offer such lands, or any part thereof, for sale for such purposes in accordance with the provisions of this subchapter: *Provided, however,* That any lands held under lease for cottage site purposes on August 6, 1956 shall not be offered for sale to anyone other than the lessee until after sixty days from the date of the written notice to the lessee as provided in section 460f of this title, or the termination or expiration date of such lease, whichever is later, and the lessee shall have the right during such period to purchase any lands leased to him which the Secretary determines are available for sale.

(Aug. 6, 1956, c. 987, § 1, 70 Stat. 1065.)

HISTORICAL AND STATUTORY NOTES

Revision Notes and Legislative Reports
1956 Acts. Senate Report No. 2789, see 1956 U.S.Code Cong. and Adm.News, p. 4416.

LIBRARY REFERENCES

American Digest System
United States ⊕57.
Key Number System Topic No. 393.

Research References

Treatises and Practice Aids
Federal Procedure, Lawyers Edition § 66:176, Notice of Availability.

§ 460f.   Notice and method of sale; price; conveyance

(a) Public notice

Public notice of the availability of the lands for sale for cottage site development and use shall be given in such manner as the Secretary of the Army may by regulation prescribe, including publication within the vicinity of the lands available for sale: *Provided, however,* That notice to lessees of cottage sites shall be given in writing within 90 days after publication of such regulations in the Federal Register and the notice shall state the appraised fair market value of the land available for sale to such lessee.

(b) Method of sale

The sale of lands for cottage site development and use shall be accomplished by any method which the Secretary of the Army determines to be in the public interest, including public auction, seal bids, and by negotiation with lessees and with others after competitive bidding.

(c) Price

The price to be paid for any lands sold for cottage site development and use pursuant to the provisions of this subchapter shall be not less than the appraised fair market value thereof as determined by the Secretary of the Army.

(d) Conveyance

The Secretary of the Army is authorized to convey by quitclaim deed all the right, title, and interest of the United States in and to the lands sold for cottage site development and use pursuant to the provisions of this subchapter, the conveyance to be on condition that the property conveyed shall be used for cottage site purposes only, and in the event of use for any other purposes, title to the land and improvements shall revert to and vest in the United States; and subject to such other conditions, reservations, and restrictions as the Secretary may determine to be necessary for the management and operation of the reservoir, or for the protection of lessees or owners of cottage sites within the area.

(Aug. 6, 1956, c. 987, § 2, 70 Stat. 1065.)

HISTORICAL AND STATUTORY NOTES

Revision Notes and Legislative Reports
  1956 Acts. Senate Report No. 2789, see 1956 U.S.Code Cong. and Adm.News, p. 4416.

CODE OF FEDERAL REGULATIONS

Procedure for sale of lands, see 33 CFR §§ 211.71 to 211.81.

LIBRARY REFERENCES

American Digest System
  United States ⚖58(1).
  Key Number System Topic No. 393.

Research References

Treatises and Practice Aids
Federal Procedure, Lawyers Edition § 66:176, Notice of Availability.
Federal Procedure, Lawyers Edition § 66:177, Manner of Sale.

§ 460g.   Transfer to State, etc., for roadway purposes

The Secretary of the Army may, by quitclaim deed, deed of easement, or otherwise, transfer to the State in which lands sold for
cottage site development and use pursuant to this subchapter are
located, or to any political subdivision thereof, or to any organization
consisting of not less than 50 per centum of the owners of cottage
sites in the area, without monetary consideration, any lands being
used or to be used for roads primarily to serve the cottage site areas:
Provided, however, That the deed or other instrument transferring
such land shall specifically provide for appropriate use and maintenance of the property by the State, political subdivision, or organization, and any deed conveying title to such lands for roadway purposes shall contain the condition and limitation that in the event the
land conveyed shall fail or cease to be used for roadway purposes the
same shall immediately revert to and vest in the United States.

(Aug. 6, 1956, c. 987, § 3, 70 Stat. 1065.)

HISTORICAL AND STATUTORY NOTES

Revision Notes and Legislative Reports
1956 Acts. Senate Report No. 2789,
see 1956 U.S.Code Cong. and Adm.News,
p. 4416.

LIBRARY REFERENCES

American Digest System
United States ☞58(1).
Key Number System Topic No. 393.

§ 460h.   Costs of surveys or relocation of boundaries

The costs of any surveys or the relocation of boundary markers
necessary as an incident of a conveyance or other property transfer
under this subchapter shall be borne by the grantee.

(Aug. 6, 1956, c. 987, § 4, 70 Stat. 1066.)

HISTORICAL AND STATUTORY NOTES

Revision Notes and Legislative Reports
1956 Acts. Senate Report No. 2789,
see 1956 U.S.Code Cong. and Adm.News,
p. 4416.

American Digest System
United States ☞3.
Key Number System Topic No. 393.

§ 460i. Delegation of powers; regulations

The Secretary of the Army may delegate any authority conferred upon him by this subchapter to any officer or employee of the Department of the Army. Any such officer or employee shall exercise the authority so delegated under rules and regulations approved by the Secretary.

(Aug. 6, 1956, c. 987, § 5, 70 Stat. 1066.)

HISTORICAL AND STATUTORY NOTES

Revision Notes and Legislative Reports
 1956 Acts. Senate Report No. 2789,
see 1956 U.S.Code Cong. and Adm.News,
p. 4416.

§ 460j. Disposition of proceeds

The proceeds from any sale made under this subchapter shall be covered into the Treasury of the United States as miscellaneous receipts.

(Aug. 6, 1956, c. 987, § 6, 70 Stat. 1066.)

HISTORICAL AND STATUTORY NOTES

Revision Notes and Legislative Reports
 1956 Acts. Senate Report No. 2789,
see 1956 U.S.Code Cong. and Adm.News,
p. 4416.

LIBRARY REFERENCES

American Digest System
United States ☞81.
Key Number System Topic No. 393.

SUBCHAPTER LXVIII—NATIONAL CONSERVATION RECREATIONAL AREAS

CROSS REFERENCES

Public recreation uses in—
Chincoteague National Wildlife Refuge, see 16 USCA § 459f–5.
National Wildlife Refuge System, see 16 USCA § 668dd.

§ 460k.   **Public recreation use of fish and wildlife conservation areas; compatibility with conservation purposes; appropriate incidental or secondary use; consistency with other Federal operations and primary objectives of particular areas; curtailment; forms of recreation not directly related to primary purposes of individual areas; repeal or amendment of provisions for particular areas**

In recognition of mounting public demands for recreational opportunities on areas within the National Wildlife Refuge System, national fish hatcheries, and other conservation areas administered by the Secretary of the Interior for fish and wildlife purposes; and in recognition also of the resulting imperative need, if such recreational opportunities are provided, to assure that any present or future recreational use will be compatible with, and will not prevent accomplishment of, the primary purposes for which the said conservation areas were acquired or established, the Secretary of the Interior is authorized, as an appropriate incidental or secondary use, to administer such areas or parts thereof for public recreation when in his judgment public recreation can be an appropriate incidental or secondary use: *Provided*, That such public recreation use shall be permitted only to the extent that is practicable and not inconsistent with other previously authorized Federal operations or with the primary objectives for which each particular area is established: *Provided further*, That in order to insure accomplishment of such primary objectives, the Secretary, after consideration of all authorized uses, purposes, and other pertinent factors relating to individual areas, shall curtail public recreation use generally or certain types of public recreation use within individual areas or in portions thereof whenever he considers such action to be necessary: *And provided further*, That none of the aforesaid refuges, hatcheries, game ranges, and other conservation areas shall be used during any fiscal year for those forms of recreation that are not directly related to the primary purposes and functions of the individual areas until the Secretary shall have determined—

(a) that such recreational use will not interfere with the primary purposes for which the areas were established, and

(b) that funds are available for the development, operation, and maintenance of these permitted forms of recreation. This section shall not be construed to repeal or amend previous enactments relating to particular areas.

(Pub.L. 87–714, § 1, Sept. 28, 1962, 76 Stat. 653; Pub.L. 89–669, § 9, Oct. 15, 1966, 80 Stat. 930.)

HISTORICAL AND STATUTORY NOTES

Revision Notes and Legislative Reports
1962 Acts. Senate Report No. 1858, see 1962 U.S.Code Cong. and Adm.News, p. 2723.

1966 Acts. Senate Report No. 1453 and Conference Report No. 2205, see 1966 U.S.Code Cong. and Adm.News, p. 3342.

Amendments
1966 Amendments. Pub.L. 89–669 substituted "areas within the National Wild-

life Refuge System" for "national wildlife refuges, game ranges," in the introductory text.

Short Title
1962 Acts. Pub.L. 87–714, Sept. 28, 1962, 76 Stat. 653, is popularly known as the "Refuge Recreation Act".

CODE OF FEDERAL REGULATIONS

Fish hatchery areas,
Hunting and fishing activities, see 50 CFR § 71.1 et seq.
Management, see 50 CFR § 70.1 et seq.
Hunting, provisions applicable, see 50 CFR § 32.1 et seq.
Land use management, see 50 CFR § 29.1 et seq.
Wildlife species management, see 50 CFR § 31.1 et seq.

LIBRARY REFERENCES

American Digest System
Fish ⬩8.
Game ⬩3.5.
Key Number System Topic Nos. 176, 187.

Research References

ALR Library
32 ALR, Fed. 332, Validity, Construction, and Application of Endangered Species Act of 1973 (16 U.S.C.A. §§ 1531-1543).
169 ALR 851, Right to Intervene in Suit to Determine Validity or Construction of Law or Governmental Regulations.

Notes of Decisions

Easement with limited public access   1
Exclusive concession contract   2
Fines   3

---

1. Easement with limited public access

Fish and Wildlife Service's acquisition of conservation easement on wetlands habitat did not violate Fish and Wildlife Act or Refuge Recreation Act, even if restrictions limited public access to land that had been privately owned. Sabine River Authority v. U.S. Dept. of Interior, E.D.Tex.1990, 745 F.Supp. 388, affirmed 951 F.2d 669, rehearing denied, certiorari denied, certiorari denied 113 S.Ct. 75, 506 U.S. 823, 121 L.Ed.2d 40. Environmental Law ⬩ 135; Environmental Law ⬩ 525

2. Exclusive concession contract

Exclusive concession contract between United States of America, United States

Fish and Wildlife Service, Department of Interior, and corporation which provided recreational facilities, granting corporation exclusive right to operate recreational facilities in designated area was valid and precluded any other person from operating a concession in geographical area covered by contract. Loxahatchee Recreation, Inc. v. Harrison, Fla.App. 4 Dist. 1979, 367 So.2d 237. United States ⬩ 66

3. Fines

Fine of $200 and a special assessment would be imposed at sentencing of defendant convicted of trespass on a national wildlife refuge with a motor vehicle, where presentence investigation report (PSR) showed that motor vehicle traffic impacted the refuge by disrupting sediment cycles, causing erosion, and destroying vegetation and plant life,

including threatened species. U.S. v.
Sanderlin, E.D.N.C.2007, 491 F.Supp.2d
542. Costs ⚬⛥ 292; Fines ⚬⛥ 1.5

§ 460k–1. Acquisition of lands for recreational development; funds

The Secretary is authorized to acquire areas of land, or interests therein, which are suitable for—

(1) incidental fish and wildlife-oriented recreational development,

(2) the protection of natural resources,

(3) the conservation of endangered species or threatened species listed by the Secretary pursuant to section 1533 of this title, or

(4) carrying out two or more of the purposes set forth in paragraphs (1) through (3) of this section, and are adjacent to, or within, the said conservation areas, except that the acquisition of any land or interest therein pursuant to this section shall be accomplished only with such funds as may be appropriated therefor by the Congress or donated for such purposes, but such property shall not be acquired with funds obtained from the sale of Federal migratory bird hunting stamps.

Lands acquired pursuant to this section shall become a part of the particular conservation area to which they are adjacent.

(Pub.L. 87–714, § 2, Sept. 28, 1962, 76 Stat. 653; Pub.L. 92–534, Oct. 23, 1972, 86 Stat. 1063; Pub.L. 93–205, § 13(d), Dec. 28, 1973, 87 Stat. 902.)

HISTORICAL AND STATUTORY NOTES

Revision Notes and Legislative Reports
1962 Acts. Senate Report No. 1858, see 1962 U.S.Code Cong. and Adm.News, p. 2723.

1972 Acts. Senate Report No. 92–1291, see 1972 U.S.Code Cong. and Adm.News, p. 4281.

1973 Acts. Senate Report No. 93–307 and Conference Report No. 93–740, see 1973 U.S.Code Cong. and Adm.News, p. 2989.

Amendments
1973 Amendments. Pub.L. 93–205 inserted references to the acquisition of interests in land the conservation of endangered species or threatened species listed by the Secretary pursuant to section 1533 of this title.

1972 Amendments. Pub.L. 92–534 substituted provisions authorizing the Secretary to acquire lands suitable for fish and wildlife oriented recreational development, or for the protection of natural resources and adjacent to conservation areas, for provisions authorizing the Secretary to acquire limited areas of land for recreational development adjacent to conservation areas in existence or approved by the Migratory Bird Conservation Commission as of September 28, 1962.

Effective and Applicability Provisions
1973 Acts. Amendment by Pub.L. 93–205 effective Dec. 28, 1973, see section 16 of Pub.L. 93–205, set out as a note under section 1531 of this title.

LIBRARY REFERENCES

American Digest System
    United States ⊜55.
    Key Number System Topic No. 393.

Research References

ALR Library
    32 ALR, Fed. 332, Validity, Construction, and Application of Endangered Species
    Act of 1973 (16 U.S.C.A. §§ 1531-1543).

§ 460k–2. Cooperation with agencies, organizations and individuals; acceptance of donations; restrictive covenants

In furtherance of the purposes of this subchapter, the Secretary is authorized to cooperate with public and private agencies, organizations, and individuals, and he may accept and use, without further authorization, donations of funds and real and personal property. Such acceptance may be accomplished under the terms and conditions of restrictive covenants imposed by donors when such covenants are deemed by the Secretary to be compatible with the purposes of the wildlife refuges, games ranges, fish hatcheries, and other fish and wildlife conservation areas.

(Pub.L. 87–714, § 3, Sept. 28, 1962, 76 Stat. 653.)

HISTORICAL AND STATUTORY NOTES

Revision Notes and Legislative Reports
    1962 Acts. Senate Report No. 1858,
see 1962 U.S.Code Cong. and Adm.News,
p. 2723.

LIBRARY REFERENCES

American Digest System
    United States ⊜57.
    Key Number System Topic No. 393.

§ 460k–3. Charges and fees; permits; regulations; penalties; enforcement

The Secretary may establish reasonable charges and fees and issue permits for public use of national wildlife refuges, game ranges, national fish hatcheries, and other conservation areas administered by the Department of the Interior for fish and wildlife purposes. The Secretary may issue regulations to carry out the purposes of this subchapter. A violation of such regulations shall be a misdemeanor with maximum penalties of imprisonment for not more than six months, or a fine of not more than $500, or both. The provisions of this subchapter and any such regulation shall be enforced by any officer or employee of the United States Fish and Wildlife Service designated by the Secretary of the Interior.

(Pub.L. 87–714, § 4, Sept. 28, 1962, 76 Stat. 654; Pub.L. 95–616, § 3(e), Nov. 8, 1978, 92 Stat. 3111; Pub.L. 98–473, Title II, § 221, Oct. 12, 1984, 98 Stat. 2028.)

HISTORICAL AND STATUTORY NOTES

Revision Notes and Legislative Reports
1962 Acts. Senate Report No. 1858, see 1962 U.S.Code Cong. and Adm.News, p. 2723.

1978 Acts. Senate Report No. 95–1175 and House Conference Report No. 95–1730, see 1978 U.S. Code Cong. and Adm. News, p. 7641.

1984 Acts. House Report No. 98–1030 and House Conference Report No. 98–1159, see 1984 U.S.Code Cong. and Adm.News, p. 3182.

Amendments
1984 Amendments. Pub.L. 98–473 substituted "misdemeanor" for "petty offense (18 U.S.C. 1)".

1978 Amendments. Pub.L. 95–616 provided for designation of enforcement personnel.

Effective and Applicability Provisions
1984 Acts. Amendment by Pub.L. 98–473, effective Nov. 1, 1987, and applicable only to offenses committed after the taking effect of such amendment, see section 235(a)(1) of Pub.L. 98–473, set out as a note under section 3551 of this title.

LIBRARY REFERENCES

American Digest System
Fish ☞8.
Game ☞3.5.
United States ☞57.
Woods and Forests ☞5.
Key Number System Topic Nos. 176, 187, 393, 411.

Notes of Decisions

Validity of regulations 1

———

1. Validity of regulations
Special federal regulations would violate standard of sections 460k to 460k–4 of this title inasmuch as degree and manner of boating use which they would permit was not incidental or secondary use, was inconsistent, and would interfere with the refuge's primary purpose. Defenders of Wildlife v. Andrus, D.C.D.C. 1978, 455 F.Supp. 446. Environmental Law ☞ 525

§ 460k–4. Authorization of appropriations

There is authorized to be appropriated such funds as may be necessary to carry out the purposes of this subchapter, including the construction and maintenance of public recreational facilities.

(Pub.L. 87–714, § 5, Sept. 28, 1962, 76 Stat. 654.)

HISTORICAL AND STATUTORY NOTES

Revision Notes and Legislative Reports
1962 Acts. Senate Report No. 1858,
see 1962 U.S.Code Cong. and Adm.News,
p. 2723.

Research References

ALR Library
    32 ALR, Fed. 332, Validity, Construction, and Application of Endangered Species
        Act of 1973 (16 U.S.C.A. §§ 1531-1543).

SUBCHAPTER LXIX—OUTDOOR RECREATION PROGRAMS

PART A—COORDINATION OF PROGRAMS

§ 460*l*.   Congressional findings and declaration of policy

The Congress finds and declares it to be desirable that all American
people of present and future generations be assured adequate outdoor recreation resources, and that it is desirable for all levels of
government and private interests to take prompt and coordinated
action to the extent practicable without diminishing or affecting their
respective powers and functions to conserve, develop, and utilize
such resources for the benefit and enjoyment of the American people.

(Pub.L. 88–29, § 1, May 28, 1963, 77 Stat. 49.)

HISTORICAL AND STATUTORY NOTES

Revision Notes and Legislative Reports
    1963 Acts. Senate Report No. 11 and
Conference Report No. 303, see 1963
U.S.Code Cong. and Adm.News, p. 664.

Environmental Quality Council
    For functions of the Environmental
Quality Council concerning outdoor recreation, see sections 102 and 103 of Ex.
Ord. No. 11472, May 29, 1969, 34 F.R.
8693, set out as a note under section
4321 of Title 42, The Public Health and
Welfare.

CODE OF FEDERAL REGULATIONS

Nondiscrimination in federally-assisted programs, see 43 CFR § 17.1 et seq. and
    Appendices.

LIBRARY REFERENCES

American Digest System
    Woods and Forests ⬅1.
    Key Number System Topic No. 411.

Research References

ALR Library
    121 ALR 12, Right to Abandon and Effect of Abandonment of Eminent Domain
        Proceedings.

§ 460*l*–1.   Powers and duties of Secretary of the Interior

In order to carry out the purposes of this part, the Secretary of the Interior is authorized to perform the following functions and activities:

(a) Inventory and evaluation of needs and resources

Prepare and maintain a continuing inventory and evaluation of outdoor recreation needs and resources of the United States.

(b) Classification of resources

Prepare a system for classification of outdoor recreation resources to assist in the effective and beneficial use and management of such resources.

(c) Nationwide plan; contents; problems, solutions and actions; initial plan; revisions of plan; transmittal to Congress and Governors

Formulate and maintain a comprehensive nationwide outdoor recreation plan, taking into consideration the plans of the various Federal agencies, States, and their political subdivisions. The plan shall set forth the needs and demands of the public for outdoor recreation and the current and foreseeable availability in the future of outdoor recreation resources to meet those needs. The plan shall identify critical outdoor recreation problems, recommend solutions, and recommend desirable actions to be taken at each level of government and by private interests. The Secretary shall transmit the initial plan, which shall be prepared as soon as practicable within five years on and after May 28, 1963, to the President for transmittal to the Congress. Future revisions of the plan shall be similarly transmitted at succeeding five-year intervals. When a plan or revision is transmitted to the Congress, the Secretary shall transmit copies to the Governors of the several States.

(d) Technical assistance and advice; cooperation with States and private interests

Provide technical assistance and advice to and cooperate with States, political subdivisions, and private interests, including nonprofit organizations, with respect to outdoor recreation.

(e) Interstate and regional cooperation

Encourage interstate and regional cooperation in the planning, acquisition, and development of outdoor recreation resources.

(f) Research and education

(1) Sponsor, engage in, and assist in research relating to outdoor recreation, directly or by contract or cooperative agreements, and make payments for such purposes without regard to the limitations of section 3324(a) and (b) of Title 31 concerning advances of funds when he considers such action in the public interest, (2) undertake studies and assemble information concerning outdoor recreation, directly or by contract or cooperative agreement, and disseminate such information without regard to the provisions of section 3204 of Title 39, and (3) cooperate with educational institutions and others in order to assist in establishing education programs and activities and to encourage public use and benefits from outdoor recreation.

(g) Federal interdepartmental cooperation; coordination of Federal plans and activities; expenditures; reimbursement

(1) Cooperate with and provide technical assistance to Federal departments and agencies and obtain from them information, data, reports, advice, and assistance that are needed and can reasonably be furnished in carrying out the purposes of this part, and (2) promote coordination of Federal plans and activities generally relating to outdoor recreation. Any department or agency furnishing advice or assistance hereunder may expend its own funds for such purposes, with or without reimbursement, as may be agreed to by that agency.

(h) Donations

Accept and use donations of money, property, personal services, or facilities for the purposes of this part.

(Pub.L. 88–29, § 2, May 28, 1963, 77 Stat. 49; Pub.L. 91–375, § 6(h), Aug. 12, 1970, 84 Stat. 776; Pub.L. 97–258, § 4(b), Sept. 13, 1982, 96 Stat. 1067.)

HISTORICAL AND STATUTORY NOTES

Revision Notes and Legislative Reports
1982 Acts. House Report No. 97–651, see 1982 U.S.Code Cong. and Adm.News, p. 1895.

Codifications
In subsec. (f), "section 3324(a) and (b) of Title 31" was substituted for "section 3648 of the Revised Statutes (31 U.S.C. 529)" on authority of Pub.L. 97–258, § 4(b), Sept. 13, 1982, 96 Stat. 1067, the first section of which enacted Title 31, Money and Finance.

Amendments
1970 Amendments. Subsec. (f). Pub.L. 91–375 substituted "section 3204 of Title 39" for "section 4154 of Title 39".

Effective and Applicability Provisions
1970 Acts. Amendment by Pub.L. 91–375 effective within 1 year after Aug. 12, 1970, on date established therefor by the Board of Governors of the United States Postal Service and published by it in the Federal Register, see section 15(a) of Pub.L. 91–375, set out as a note preceding section 101 of Title 39, Postal Service.

Study Regarding Improved Outdoor Recreational Access for Persons With Disabilities
Pub.L. 105–359, § 1, Nov. 10, 1998, 112 Stat. 3275, provided that:

"**(a) Study required.**—The Secretary of Agriculture and the Secretary of the Interior shall jointly conduct a study regarding ways to improve the access for persons with disabilities to outdoor recreational opportunities (such as fishing, hunting, trapping, wildlife viewing, hiking, boating, and camping) made available to the public on the Federal lands described in subsection (b).

"(b) Covered Federal lands.—The Federal lands referred to in subsection (a) are the following:

"**(1)** National Forest System lands.

"**(2)** Units of the National Park System.

"**(3)** Areas in the National Wildlife Refuge System.

"**(4)** Lands administered by the Bureau of Land Management.

"**(c) Report on study.**—Not later than 18 months after the date of the enactment of this Act [Nov. 10, 1998], the Secretaries shall submit to Congress a report containing the results of the study."

Termination of Reporting Requirements

For termination, effective May 15, 2000, of provisions in subsec. (c) of this section relating to transmittal to Congress, at five-year intervals, of revisions of nationwide outdoor recreation plan, see Pub.L. 104–66, § 3003, as amended, set out as a note under 31 U.S.C.A. § 1113, and page 112 of House Document No. 103–7.

Connecticut River National Recreation Area Feasibility Study

Pub.L. 89–616, Oct. 3, 1966, 80 Stat. 867, directed the Secretary of the Interior to study, investigate, and formulate recommendations on the feasibility and desirability of establishing all or parts of the Connecticut River Valley from its source to its mouth, in the States of Connecticut, Massachusetts, Vermont, and New Hampshire, as a Connecticut River National Recreation Area and to submit to the President, within two years after Oct. 3, 1966, a report of his findings and recommendations, with the President to submit to the Congress such recommendations, including legislation, as he deemed appropriate.

LIBRARY REFERENCES

American Digest System
   United States ☞57.
   Key Number System Topic No. 393.

§ 460*l*–2. Consultations of Secretary of the Interior with administrative officers; execution of administrative responsibilities in conformity with nationwide plan

In order further to carry out the policy declared in section 460*l* of this title, the heads of Federal departments and independent agencies having administrative responsibility over activities or resources the conduct or use of which is pertinent to fulfillment of that policy shall, either individually or as a group, (a) consult with and be consulted by the Secretary from time to time both with respect to their conduct of those activities and their use of those resources and with respect to the activities which the Secretary of the Interior carries on under authority of this part which are pertinent to their work, and (b) carry out such responsibilities in general conformance with the nationwide plan authorized under section 460*l*–1(c) of this title.

(Pub.L. 88–29, § 3, May 28, 1963, 77 Stat. 50.)

HISTORICAL AND STATUTORY NOTES

Revision Notes and Legislative Reports
1963 Acts. Senate Report No. 11 and Conference Report No. 303, see 1963 U.S.Code Cong. and Adm.News, p. 664.

CROSS REFERENCES

Project reports; views of Secretary of Interior, see 16 USCA § 460l–17.

LIBRARY REFERENCES

American Digest System
United States ☞57.
Key Number System Topic No. 393.

§ 460l–3. Definitions

As used in this part, the term "United States" shall include the District of Columbia and the terms "United States" and "States" may, to the extent practicable, include the Commonwealth of Puerto Rico, the Virgin Islands, Guam, American Samoa, the Trust Territory of the Pacific Islands, and the Commonwealth of the Northern Mariana Islands.

(Pub.L. 88–29, § 4, May 28, 1963, 77 Stat. 50; Pub.L. 96–205, Title VI, § 608(c), Mar. 12, 1980, 94 Stat. 92.)

HISTORICAL AND STATUTORY NOTES

Revision Notes and Legislative Reports
  1963 Acts. Senate Report No. 11 and Conference Report No. 303, see 1963 U.S.Code Cong. and Adm.News, p. 664.

  1980 Acts. Senate Report No. 96–467, see 1980 U.S.Code Cong. and Adm.News, p. 135.

Amendments
  1980 Amendments. Pub.L. 96–205 added references to the Trust Territory of the

Pacific Islands and the Commonwealth of the Northern Mariana Islands.

Termination of Trust Territory of the Pacific Islands
  For termination of Trust Territory of the Pacific Islands, see note set out preceding section 1681 of Title 48.

PART B—LAND AND WATER CONSERVATION FUND

CROSS REFERENCES

Application of §§ 460l–4 to 4605l–11 of this title to all areas of national park system to extent not in conflict with specific provisions applicable to an area, see 16 USCA § 1c.
Authorization of appropriations for acquisition of lands in,
  Chattahoochee River National Recreation Area, see 16 USCA § 460ii–4.
  Columbia River Gorge National Scenic Area, see 16 USCA § 544n.
  King Range National Conservation Area, see 16 USCA § 460y–9.
  Manassas National Battlefield Park, see 16 USCA § 429b–4.
  National trails system, see 16 USCA § 1249.
  Northern Minnesota, see 16 USCA § 577h.
Ceiling on appropriations, see 43 USCA § 1457a.
Comprehensive water resources planning; coordination with comprehensive statewide development planning, see 42 USCA § 1962c–2.

Consideration in proposals for financial assistance of needs and opportunities for,
  Establishing recreation and historic trails, see 16 USCA § 1247.
  Establishing State and local wild, scenic and recreational river areas, see 16
    USCA § 1282.
  Protecting and restoring estuaries, see 16 USCA § 1225.
Consistency of public water-based fish and wildlife or recreational development
    with existing comprehensive statewide outdoor recreation plans, see 7
    USCA § 1011.
Endangered species; acquisition of land for implementation of conservation
    program, see 16 USCA § 1534.
Grants,
  Historic preservation, see 16 USCA § 470b.
  Ice Age National Scientific Reserve, see 16 USCA § 469h.
  Pinelands National Reserve, see 16 USCA § 471i.
  Water resources projects, see 16 USCA § 1278.
Land use plans; coordination with statewide outdoor recreation plans, see 43
    USCA § 1712.
Limitations on Federal expenditures affecting,
  Coastal Barrier Resources System, see 16 USCA § 3505.
  Colorado River Floodway, see 43 USCA § 1600e.
  Columbia River Gorge National Scenic Area, see 16 USCA § 544l.
National trails system; "without expense to the United States" defined, see 16
    USCA § 1251.
State recreational boating safety programs, see 46 USCA § 13101.
Transfer of functions from Secretary of Interior to Secretary of Housing and
    Urban Development, see 42 USCA § 3534.
Transfer of funds from Highway Trust Fund, see 26 USCA § 9503.
Virgin Islands National Park; authorization of appropriations for grant to Territo-
    ry of the Virgin Islands, see 16 USCA § 398f.
Wild, scenic, or recreational rivers; administration by State or political subdivi-
    sion without expense to United States, see 16 USCA § 1273.

§ 460*l*–4. Land and water conservation provisions; statement of purposes

The purposes of this part are to assist in preserving, developing, and assuring accessibility to all citizens of the United States of America of present and future generations and visitors who are lawfully present within the boundaries of the United States of America such quality and quantity of outdoor recreation resources as may be available and are necessary and desirable for individual active participation in such recreation and to strengthen the health and vitality of the citizens of the United States by (1) providing funds for and authorizing Federal assistance to the States in planning, acquisition, and development of needed land and water areas and facilities and (2) providing funds for the Federal acquisition and development of certain lands and other areas.

(Pub.L. 88–578, Title I, § 1(b), Sept. 3, 1964, 78 Stat. 897.)

HISTORICAL AND STATUTORY NOTES

Revision Notes and Legislative Reports
  1964 Acts. Senate Report No. 1364
and Conference Report No. 1847, see

1964 U.S.Code Cong. and Adm.News, p.
3633.

Effective and Applicability Provisions

1964 Acts. Section 1(a) of Pub.L. 88–578 provided in part that: "This Act [see Short Title note under this section] shall become effective on Jan. 1, 1965."

Short Title

1964 Acts. Section 1(a) of Pub.L. 88–578 provided in part that: "This Act [enacting this part, amending section 460d of this title, repealing section 14 of this title, and amending provisions set out as a note under section 120 of Title 23, Highways] may be cited as the 'Land and Water Conservation Fund Act of 1965'."

Transfer of Functions

The enforcement functions of the Secretary of Agriculture or other appropriate officer or entity in the Department of Agriculture, insofar as they involve lands and programs under the jurisdiction of that Department, related to compliance with system activities requiring coordination and approval under general authorities of sections 460*l*–4 to 460*l*–11 of this title and the enforcement functions of the Secretary of the Interior or other appropriate official or entity in the Department of the Interior related to compliance with rights-of-way across recreation lands as they relate to pre-construction, construc-

tion, and initial operation of an approved transportation system for the transport of Canadian natural gas and Alaskan natural gas as such terms are defined in the Alaskan Natural Gas Transportation Act of 1976, section 719 et seq. of Title 15, Commerce and Trade, were transferred to the Federal Inspector for the Alaska Natural Gas Transportation System, effective July 1, 1979, until the first anniversary of the date of initial operation of the Alaska Natural Gas Transportation System, pursuant to sections 102(f) and 203(a) of 1979 Reorg. Plan No. 1, June 12, 1979, 44 F.R. 33665, 33666, 93 Stat. 1373, set out in Appendix 1 to Title 5, Government Organization and Employees.

Survey of Entrance and User Fees

Pub.L. 91–308, § 4, July 7, 1970, 84 Stat. 410, directed the Secretary of the Interior to complete a survey as to the policy to be implemented with regard to entrance and user fees and report his findings to the Senate and House Committees on Interior and Insular Affairs [now the Committee on Energy and Natural Resources of the Senate and the Committee on Resources of the House of Representatives] on or before Feb. 1, 1971.

CROSS REFERENCES

Uniform application of §§ 460*l*–4 to 460*l*–11 of this title to all areas of national park system when not in conflict with specific provisions applicable to an area, see 16 USCA § 1c.

CODE OF FEDERAL REGULATIONS

Nondiscrimination in federally-assisted programs, see 43 CFR § 17.1 et seq. and Appendices.

LAW REVIEW AND JOURNAL COMMENTARIES

Land conservation and restoration: Moving to the landscape level. David J. Hayes, 21 Va. Envtl. L.J. 115 (2002).

LIBRARY REFERENCES

American Digest System

United States ⊙57.
Key Number System Topic No. 393.

Research References

ALR Library

32 ALR, Fed. 332, Validity, Construction, and Application of Endangered Species Act of 1973 (16 U.S.C.A. §§ 1531-1543).

§ **460*l*–5.** Land and water conservation fund; establishment; covering certain revenues and collections into fund

During the period ending September 30, 2015, there shall be covered into the land and water conservation fund in the Treasury of the United States, which fund is hereby established and is hereinafter referred to as the "fund", the following revenues and collections:

(a) Surplus property sales

All proceeds (except so much thereof as may be otherwise obligated, credited, or paid under authority of those provisions of law set forth in section 572(a) or 574(a)–(c) of Title 40 or the Independent Offices Appropriation Act, 1963 (76 Stat. 725) or in any later appropriation Act) hereafter received from any disposal of surplus real property and related personal property under the Federal Property and Administrative Services Act of 1949, as amended, notwithstanding any provision of law that such proceeds shall be credited to miscellaneous receipts of the Treasury. Nothing in this part shall affect existing laws or regulations concerning disposal of real or personal surplus property to schools, hospitals, and States and their political subdivisions.

(b) Motorboat fuels tax

The amounts provided for in section 460*l*–11 of this title.

(c) Other revenues

(1) In addition to the sum of the revenues and collections estimated by the Secretary of the Interior to be covered into the fund pursuant to this section, as amended, there are authorized to be appropriated annually to the fund out of any money in the Treasury not otherwise appropriated such amounts as are necessary to make the income of the fund not less than $300,000,000 for fiscal year 1977, and $900,000,000 for fiscal year 1978 and for each fiscal year thereafter through September 30, 2015.

(2) To the extent that any such sums so appropriated are not sufficient to make the total annual income of the fund equivalent to the amounts provided in clause (1), an amount sufficient to cover the remainder thereof shall be credited to the fund from revenues due and payable to the United States for deposit in the Treasury as miscellaneous receipts under the Outer Continental Shelf Lands Act, as amended (43 U.S.C. 1331 et seq.): *Provided*, That notwithstanding the provisions of section 460*l*–6 of this title, moneys covered into the fund under this paragraph shall remain in the fund until appropriated by the Congress to carry out the purpose of this part.

(Pub.L. 88–578, Title I, § 2, Sept. 3, 1964, 78 Stat. 897; Pub.L. 89–72, § 11; July 9, 1965, 79 Stat. 218; Pub.L. 90–401, §§ 1(a), 2, July 15, 1968, 82 Stat. 354, 355; Pub.L. 91–308, § 2, July 7, 1970, 84 Stat. 410; Pub.L. 91–485, § 1, Oct. 22, 1970, 84 Stat. 1084; Pub.L. 94–273, § 2(7), Apr. 21, 1976, 90 Stat. 375; Pub.L. 94–422, Title I, § 101(1), Sept. 28, 1976, 90 Stat. 1313; Pub.L. 95–42, § 1(1), June 10, 1977, 91 Stat. 210; Pub.L. 100–203, Title V, § 5201(f)(1), Dec. 22, 1987, 101 Stat. 1330–267.)

HISTORICAL AND STATUTORY NOTES

Revision Notes and Legislative Reports

1964 Acts. Senate Report No. 1364 and Conference Report No. 1847, see 1964 U.S.Code Cong. and Adm.News, p. 3633.

1965 Acts. House Report No. 254 and Conference Report No. 538, see 1965 U.S.Code Cong. and Adm.News, p. 1864.

1968 Acts. Senate Report No. 1071 and Conference Report No. 1598, see 1968 U.S.Code Cong. and Adm.News, p. 2613.

1970 Acts. House Report No. 91–1000, see 1970 U.S.Code Cong. and Adm.News, p. 3402.

House Report No. 91–1225, see 1970 U.S.Code Cong. and Adm.News, p. 4300.

1976 Acts. Senate Report No. 94–367 and House Conference Report No. 94–1468, see 1976 U.S.Code Cong. and Adm.News, p. 2442.

House Report No. 94–1000, see 1976 U.S.Code Cong. and Adm.News, p. 690.

1977 Acts. Senate Report No. 95–162, see 1977 U.S.Code Cong. and Adm.News, p. 322.

1987 Acts. House Report No. 100–391 (Parts I and II) and House Conference Report No. 100–495, see 1987 U.S.Code Cong. and Adm.News, p. 2313–1.

References in Text

The Independent Offices Appropriation Act, 1963 (76 Stat. 725), referred to in subsec. (a), probably means the provisions of section 101 of Pub.L. 87–741 appearing under the heading "Operating Expenses, Utilization and Disposal Service", which provisions were not classified to the Code.

The Federal Property and Administrative Services Act of 1949, referred to in subsec. (a), is Act June 30, 1949, c. 288, 63 Stat. 377, as amended, Title III of

which is currently classified to subchapter IV of chapter 4 of Title 41, 41 U.S.C.A. § 251 et seq., and the remainder of which was formerly classified to chapter 10 of former Title 40, 40 U.S.C.A. § 471 et seq., prior to being repealed by Pub.L. 107–217, § 6(b), Aug. 21, 2002, 116 Stat. 1313; see now generally chapter 1 of Title 40, 40 U.S.C.A. § 101 et seq.

The Outer Continental Shelf Lands Act, referred to in subsec. (c)(2), is Act Aug. 7, 1953, c. 345, 67 Stat. 462, as amended, which is classified generally to subchapter III (section 1331 et seq.) of chapter 29 of Title 43, Public Lands. For complete classification of this Act to the Code, see Short Title note set out under section 1331 of Title 43 and Tables.

Codifications

"Section 572(a) or 574(a)–(c) of Title 40" substituted in subsec. (a) for "section 485(b)(e), Title 40, United States Code," on authority of Pub.L. 107–217, § 5(c), Aug. 21, 2002, 116 Stat. 1303, the first section of which enacted Title 40.

In subsec. (a), "sections 572 and 574 of Title 40" substituted for "section 485(b) (e), Title 40", which probably should have read "section 485(b) to (e), title 40" as originally enacted, on authority of Pub.L. 107–217, § 5(c), Aug. 21, 2002, 116 Stat. 1301, which is set out as a note preceding 40 U.S.C.A. § 101. Pub.L. 107–217, § 1, enacted Title 40 into positive law. Former 40 U.S.C.A. § 485 was enacted as part of the Federal Property and Administrative Services Act of 1949 by Act June 30, 1949, c. 288, Title II, § 204, 63 Stat. 388, as amended, which was repealed by Pub.L. 107–217, § 6(a), Aug. 21, 2002, 116 Stat. 1313. The substance of former 40 U.S.C.A. § 485(b) to (e) was reenacted in 40 U.S.C.A. §§ 572 and 574.

Amendments

1987 Amendments. Pub.L. 100–203, § 5201(f)(1)(A), substituted "2015" for "1989" in introductory provisions.

Subsec. (c)(1). Pub.L. 100–203, § 5201(f)(1)(B), substituted "2015" for "1989".

1977 Amendments. Subsec. (c)(1). Pub.L. 95–42 substituted "and $900,000,000 for fiscal year 1978" for "$600,000,000 for fiscal year 1978, $750,000,000 for fiscal year 1979, and $900,000,000 for fiscal year 1980".

1976 Amendments. Pub.L. 94–422 struck out in provisions preceding subsec. (a) ", and during such additional period as may be required to repay any advances made pursuant to section 460*l*–7(b) of this title" following "September 30, 1989".

Pub.L. 94–273 substituted "September" for "June" in provisions preceding subsec. (a).

Subsec. (a). Pub.L. 94–422 reenacted subsec. without change except for reference to section 485(b)(e) which as originally enacted read "section 485(b)–(e)".

Subsec. (b). Pub.L. 94–422 reenacted subsec. (b) without change.

Subsec. (c)(1). Pub.L. 94–422 substituted "$300,000,000 for fiscal year 1977, $600,000,000 for fiscal year 1978, $750,000,000 for fiscal year 1979, and $900,000,000 for fiscal year 1980 and for each fiscal year thereafter through September 30, 1989," for "$200,000,000 for each of the fiscal years 1968, 1969, and 1970, and not less than $300,000,000 for each fiscal year thereafter through September 30, 1989.".

Pub.L. 94–273 substituted "September" for "June".

Subsec. (c)(2). Pub.L. 94–422 substituted "equivalent to the amounts" for "amount to $200,000,000 or $300,000,000 for each of such fiscal years, as".

1970 Amendments. Subsec. (a)(i). Pub.L. 91–308 substituted "not more than $10" for "not more than $7". See 1968 Amendments Note under this section.

Subsec. (c)(1). Pub.L. 91–485, § 1(a) substituted "fiscal years 1968, 1969, and 1970, and not less than $300,000,000 for each fiscal year thereafter through June 30, 1989." for "five fiscal years beginning July 1, 1968, and ending June 30, 1973".

Subsec. (c)(2). Pub.L. 91–485, § 1(b), substituted "$200,000,000 or $300,000,000 for each of such fiscal years, as provided in cl. (1)," for "$200,000,000 for each of such fiscal years,".

1968 Amendments. Subsec. (a). Pub.L. 90–401, § 1(a), redesignated former subsec. (b) as subsec. (a). Former subsec. (a), except for the fourth paragraph thereof, established a system of admission and user fees for all Federal recreation areas and was eliminated. The fourth paragraph covering the repeal of provisions prohibiting the collection of recreation fees and user charges was redesignated as section 10 of Pub.L. 88–587 and is set out as section 460*l*–10c.

Subsec. (b). Pub.L. 90–401, § 1(a), redesignated former subsec. (c) as subsec. (b). Former subsec. (b) redesignated (a).

Subsec. (c). Pub.L. 90–401, § 2, added subsec. (c). Former subsec. (c) redesignated (b).

1965 Amendments. Subsec. (a). Pub.L. 89–72 substituted "notwithstanding any other provision of law:" for "notwithstanding any provision of law that such proceeds shall be credited to miscellaneous receipts of the Treasury:" and "or affect any contract heretofore entered into by the United States that provides that such revenues collected at particular Federal areas shall be credited to specific purposes" for "or any provision of law that provides that any fees or charges collected at particular Federal areas shall be used for or credited to specific purposes or special funds as authorized by that provision of law".

Effective and Applicability Provisions

1968 Acts. Pub.L. 90–401, § 1(d), July 15, 1968, 82 Stat. 355, as amended Pub.L. 91–308, § 1, July 7, 1970, 84 Stat. 410, provided that: "The provisions of subsections (a) and (c) of this section [striking out, except for fourth par., former subsec. (a) of this section which had set out a system of admission and user fees for all Federal recreation areas, transferring former fourth par. to section 460*l*–10c of this title, redesignating former subsecs. (b) and (c) as subsecs. (a) and (b) respectively and striking out reference to admission fees in section 460*l*–9(a) of this title] shall be effective December 31, 1971. Until that date reve-

553

nues derived from the subsection (a) that is repealed by this section shall continue to be covered into the fund."

1965 Acts. Section effective Jan. 1, 1965, see note set out under section 460*l*-4 of this title.

Elimination of System of Admission and User Fees for Federal Recreation Areas Pub.L. 90–401, § 1(b), July 15, 1968, 82 Stat. 354, relating to admission and user fees for Federal recreation areas and facilities, was repealed by Pub.L. 92–347, § 1, July 11, 1972, 86 Stat. 459.

EXECUTIVE ORDERS
EXECUTIVE ORDER NO. 11200
Feb. 26, 1965, 30 F.R. 2645
ESTABLISHMENT OF RECREATION USER FEES

WHEREAS it is desirable that all American people of present and future generations be assured adequate outdoor recreation resources, and it is desirable for all levels of government and private interests to take prompt and coordinated action to the extent practicable without diminishing or affecting their respective powers and functions to conserve, develop, and utilize such resources for the benefit and enjoyment of the American people; and

WHEREAS these resources are to a considerable extent located on lands administered by the Federal Government through the National Park Service, the Bureau of Land Management, the Bureau of Sport Fisheries and Wildlife, the Bureau of Reclamation, the Forest Service, the Corps of Engineers, the Tennessee Valley Authority, and the United States Section of the International Boundary and Water Commission (United States and Mexico); and

WHEREAS the Act of May 28, 1963, 77 Stat. 49 [sections 460*l* to 460*l*-3 of this title], vested the Secretary of the Interior with legal authority to promote coordination of Federal plans and activities generally relating to outdoor recreation; and

WHEREAS it is fair and equitable that the users of certain recreation areas and facilities managed by such agencies pay a reasonable fee for the recreation benefits received; and

WHEREAS it is desirable to establish uniformity of practices among such Federal agencies regarding recreation user fees and related matters; and

WHEREAS the Congress, recognizing the need for urgent and effective action in this regard, enacted the Land and Water Conservation Fund Act of 1965, Public Law 88–578; 78 Stat. 897 (hereafter in this order referred to as "the Act") [sections 460*l*-4 to 460*l*-11 of this title];

NOW, THEREFORE, by virtue of the authority vested in me by the Act, by Section 301 of Title 3 of the United States Code [section 301 of Title 3, the President], and as President of the United States, it is ordered as follows:

Section 1. Designation of areas for 1965. **(a)** All areas administered by the National Park Service, Bureau of Land Management, Bureau of Sport Fisheries and Wildlife, Bureau of Reclamation, Forest Service, Corps of Engineers, Tennessee Valley Authority and the United States Section of the International Boundary and Water Commission (United States and Mexico), at which entrance, admission, or other recreation user fees (hereafter in this order referred to as "recreation user fees") were collected directly by those Federal agencies during any part of 1964 are hereby designated, pursuant to section 2(a) of the Act [subsec. (a) of this section], as areas at which recreation user fees shall be charged during 1965.

(b) The Secretary of the Interior, the Secretary of Agriculture, the Secretary of Defense, the Board of Directors of the Tennessee Valley Authority, and the Commissioner, United States Section of the International Boundary and Water Commission (United States and Mexico), or their designees, shall, by April 1, 1965, designate any additional areas under their respective jurisdictions at which recreation user fees are to be charged during 1965.

(c) Recreation user fees for such areas shall be prescribed as provided in section 5 of this Order.

Sec. 2. Designation of areas for years after 1965. (a) Subject to the provisions of subsection (b) of this section, the areas designated by Section 1(a), or pursuant to Section 1(b), of this Order are hereby designated as areas for which recreation user fees shall be charged for years after 1965.

(b) The officials described in Section 1(b) of this Order shall, before January 1, 1966, and at least annually thereafter, review all areas then under their respective jurisdictions, including those described in subsection (a) of this section, to determine (1) whether any additional areas should, in accordance with the designation criteria prescribed by Section 3 of this Order (or under those designation criteria as revised by the Secretary of the Interior pursuant to Section 6(c) of this Order), be designated as areas for which recreation user fees shall be charged, or (2) whether the recreation user fee for any area theretofore designated should be increased, reduced, or eliminated under the designation criteria then in effect.

(c)(1) Whenever, in accordance with subsection (b) of this section, it is determined that the recreation user fee for an area should be reduced or eliminated, such action shall be taken forthwith.

(2) Whenever, in accordance with subsection (b) of this section, it is determined that a recreation user fee should be charged with respect to an area with respect to which no such fee has theretofore been charged, such new fee shall be charged only after the posting requirements of Section 4 of this Order have been satisfied.

Sec. 3. Criteria for designation of areas. (a) Areas shall, in accordance with Section 1(b) and Section 2(b) of this Order and to the extent permitted by the Act, be designated as areas at which recreation user fees shall be charged if the following conditions are found to exist concurrently:

(1) The area is administered by any of the eight agencies specified in Section 1(a) of this Order;

(2) The area is administered primarily for scenic, scientific, historical, cultural, or recreational purposes;

(3) The area has recreation facilities or services provided at Federal expense; and

(4) The nature of the area is such that fee collection is administratively and economically practical.

(b) Areas designated as those at which recreation user fees shall be charged shall hereafter in this Order be referred to as "designated areas."

Sec. 4. Posting of designated areas. The heads of administering agencies and departments shall provide for the posting of signs at all designated areas such as will clearly notify the visiting public that recreation user fees are charged therein. All areas designated pursuant to Sections 1 and 2 of this Order shall be so posted prior to the beginning of the recreation season or as soon as practicable following designation. No recreation user fee established pursuant to this Order shall be effective with respect to any designated area until that designated area has been posted.

Sec. 5. Establishment of fees. (a) Each official described in section 1(b) of this Order shall, subject to the criteria prescribed by the Secretary of the Interior, establish a recreation user fee for each designated area administered under his jurisdiction by selecting from a schedule of fees, prescribed by the Secretary of the Interior pursuant to Section 6 of this Order, the fee which is appropriate for each such designated area under criteria prescribed by the Secretary pursuant to that section. Each such official shall also specify which designated areas shall be excluded from the coverage of the annual fee described in section 2(a)(1) of the Act [subsec. (a)(i) of this section] and which, as a result of that exclusion will be subject to the fee described in section 2(a)(iii) of the Act. The range of recreation user fees to be charged and the criteria for their selection shall be established under the procedures prescribed by section 6 of this Order.

(b) The Secretary of the Interior shall prescribe the procedures for the production, distribution, and sale of the Land and Water Conservation Fund Sticker, which shall be issued to those individuals who elect to pay the annual fee. The Secretary of the Interior shall also prescribe the manner in which the Sticker shall be displayed. The conditions under which it may be used shall be determined under the procedures prescribed by section 6 of this Order.

Sec. 6. Coordination. **(a)** The Secretary of the Interior shall, after consultation with the heads of other affected departments and agencies, adopt such coordination measures as are necessary to carry out the purposes of Sections 2(a) and 4(a) of the Act [subsec. (a) of this section and 460*l*–7(a) of this title] and the provisions of this order.

(b)(1) In order that the purposes of the Act and of this Order may be effectuated without delay, the Secretary of the Interior shall, subject to the limitations imposed by the Act and without regard to the other provisions of this section, forthwith issue a schedule of recreation user fees and criteria to be used in determining which such fees shall be charged with respect to each of the designated areas.

(2) Subject to the limitations imposed by the Act and subject to the provisions of subsections (a), (c), and (d) of this section, the Secretary of the Interior may, from time to time, amend or replace the schedule of fees and the criteria prescribed by him pursuant to subsection (b)(1) of this section.

(c) Subject to the limits set forth in the Act, the measures which the Secretary of the Interior may adopt pursuant to subsection (a) of this section may include, but are not limited to, the following—

(1) Initial preparation and coordination of the comprehensive statement of estimated requirements during the ensuing fiscal year for appropriations from the Land and Water Conservation Fund, as required by Section 4(a) of the Act [section 460*l*–7(a) of this title].

(2) Development of such additional procedures and interpretive materials as are necessary to facilitate the implementation of this Order and related provisions of the Act.

(3) Review and revision, if needed, of the criteria for designation set forth in Section 3 of this Order.

(d) Except with respect to the schedule of fees and the criteria prescribed by the Secretary pursuant to subsection (b)(1) of this section, measures and regulations adopted by the Secretary pursuant to this Order shall not become effective until 30 days after they are presented for the consideration of the other officials described in Section 1(b). Any such official who does not concur in any such measure or regulation may, within that 30-day period, refer the matter to the Recreation Advisory Council established under Executive Order No. 11017 [set out as a note under section 17k of this title] for resolution. If a proposed measure is referred to the Council for resolution, it shall not become effective until approved by the Council. With the approval of all other officials described in Section 1(b) of this Order, the provisions of this subsection may be waived with respect to any specific measure or regulation adopted by the Secretary of the Interior pursuant to this order so that any such measure or regulation may be made effective before the expiration of the 30-day waiting period prescribed by the first sentence of this subsection.

Sec. 7. Review of contracts. The officials described in Section 1(b) of this Order shall, within a reasonable time, review all existing contracts and other arrangements between their respective agencies and any non–Federal public entity which relate to non–Federal management of Federally-owned outdoor recreation areas. Special attention shall be given to any provision in any such contract or other arrangement which prohibits or discourages in any way such non–Federal public entity from charging recreation user fees. Unless otherwise prohibited by law, each such restrictive provision shall be the subject of renegotiation designed to accomplish a modification thereof that will permit the charging of recreation user fees.

Sec. 8. Regulations. The Secretary of the Interior is authorized to issue such regulations as may be necessary to carry out his functions under this Order.

LYNDON B. JOHNSON

CROSS REFERENCES

Allocation of funds; amounts credited to special account, see 16 USCA § 460*l*–7.
Matching Federal grants under Urban Park and Recreation Recovery Program, see 16 USCA § 2508.
Proceeds from sales of rights-of-way retained by United States, see 16 USCA § 1248.

Uniform application of Pub.L. 90–401, July 15, 1968, classified to this section and §§ 460*l*–7, 460*l*–9, 460*l*–10a to 460*l*–10c, and 460*l*–22 of this title, to all areas of national park system when not in conflict with specific provisions applicable to an area, see 16 USCA § 1c.

Use of fund moneys for publicity purposes, see 16 USCA § 460*l*–10.

LIBRARY REFERENCES

American Digest System
United States ⊚57, 81.
Key Number System Topic No. 393.

Notes of Decisions

Persons entitled to maintain action   1

___

1. Persons entitled to maintain action
Although conservation and environmental groups as plaintiffs alleged violation of subsec. (a) of this section, they failed to allege the threatened or actual injury resulting from the violation necessary to establish standing, in that, inter alia, it was speculative at best to predict

that defendants' failure to pay proceeds from real property sales into the Fund had reduced or was likely to reduce amount of congressional appropriations for federal or state conservation projects, and there was also a want of allegations tending to show that court order would increase appropriation for conservation programs. Conservation Law Foundation of New England, Inc. v. Harper, D.C.Mass.1984, 587 F.Supp. 357.

§ 460*l*–5a. Repealed. Pub.L. 100–203, Title V, § 5201(d)(1), Dec. 22, 1987, 101 Stat. 1330–266

HISTORICAL AND STATUTORY NOTES

Section, Pub.L. 96–514, Title I, § 100, Dec. 12, 1980, 94 Stat. 2960, provided for revenues received from recreation fee collections by Federal agencies to be paid into the Land and Water Conservation Fund and to be available for appropriation for any and all authorized purposes.

Recreation Use Fees Collected and Deposited in United States Treasury by Corps of Engineers
Pub.L. 97–88, Title I, § 100, Dec. 4, 1981, 95 Stat. 1136, which related to

special recreation use fees collected by, and deposited in the Treasury by the Corps of Engineers, was repealed by Pub.L. 100–203, Title V, § 5201(d)(3), Dec. 22, 1987, 101 Stat. 1330–267.

§ 460*l*–6. Appropriations for expenditure of land and water conservation fund moneys; transfers to miscellaneous receipts of Treasury

Moneys covered into the fund shall be available for expenditure for the purposes of this part only when appropriated therefor. Such appropriations may be made without fiscal-year limitation. Moneys made available for obligation or expenditure from the fund or from the special account established under section 460*l*–6a(i)(1) of this title may be obligated or expended only as provided in this part.

(Pub.L. 88–578, Title I, § 3, Sept. 3, 1964, 78 Stat. 899; Pub.L. 100–203, Title V, § 5201(f)(2), Dec. 22, 1987, 101 Stat. 1330–267.)

HISTORICAL AND STATUTORY NOTES

Revision Notes and Legislative Reports
    1964 Acts. Senate Report No. 1364 and Conference Report No. 1847, see 1964 U.S.Code Cong. and Adm.News, p. 3633.

    1987 Acts. House Report No. 100–391 (Parts I and II) and House Conference Report No. 100–495, 1987 U.S.Code Cong. and Adm.News, p. 2313–1.

Amendments
    1987 Amendments. Pub.L. 100–203 amended last sentence generally. Prior to amendment, last sentence read as follows: "Moneys covered into this fund not subsequently authorized by the Congress for expenditures within two fiscal years following the fiscal year in which such moneys had been credited to the fund, shall be transferred to miscellaneous receipts of the Treasury."

Effective and Applicability Provisions
    1965 Acts. Section effective Jan. 1, 1965, see note set out under section 460*l*–4 of this title.

CROSS REFERENCES

Authorization of appropriations for, options to acquire lands and waters in national park system, see 16 USCA § 460*l*–10b.

Moneys covered into fund from miscellaneous receipts of the Treasury; retention in fund until appropriated by Congress, see 16 USCA § 460*l*–5.

§ 460*l*–6a. Admission and special recreation use fees

(a) to (g) Repealed. Pub.L. 108–447, Div. J, Title VIII, § 813(a), Dec. 8, 2004, 118 Stat. 3390

(h) Repealed. Pub.L. 104–66, Title I, § 1081(f), Dec. 21, 1995, 109 Stat. 721

(i) Covering of fees collected into special account for agency established in Treasury

    (1)(A), (B) Repealed. Pub.L. 108–447, Div. J, Title VIII, § 813(a), Dec. 8, 2004, 118 Stat. 3390, as amended Pub.L. 109–54, Title I, § 132(a), Aug. 2, 2005, 119 Stat. 526

    (C) Units at which entrance fees or admissions fees cannot be collected

        (i) Withholding of amounts

        Notwithstanding section 107 of the Department of the Interior and Related Agencies Appropriations Act, 1998 (16 U.S.C. 460*l*–6a note; Public Law 105–83), the Secretary of the Interior shall withhold from the special account under section 6806(a) of this title 100 percent of the fees and charges collected in connection with any unit of the National Park System at which entrance fees or admission fees cannot be collected by reason of deed restrictions.

        (ii) Use of amounts

        Amounts withheld under clause (i) shall be retained by the Secretary and shall be available, without further Act of appropriation, for expenditure by the Secretary for the unit with respect to which the amounts were collected for the purposes of enhancing the quality of the visitor experience, protection of resources, repair and maintenance, interpretation, signage, habitat or facility enhancement, resource preservation, annual operation (including fee collection), maintenance, and law enforcement.

(2) to (4) Repealed.   Pub.L. 108–447, Div. J, Title VIII, § 813(a), Dec. 8, 2004, 118 Stat. 3390, as amended Pub.L. 109–54, Title I, § 132(a), Aug. 2, 2005, 119 Stat. 526

(j) Funds available to National Park Service; required allocations; computations; unexpended funds

(1) 10 percent of the funds made available to the Director of the National Park Service under subsection (i) of this section in each fiscal year shall be allocated among units of the National Park System on the basis of need in a manner to be determined by the Director.

(2) 40 percent of the funds made available to the Director of the National Park Service under subsection (i) of this section in each fiscal year shall be allocated among units of the National Park System in accordance with paragraph (3) of this subsection and 50 percent shall be allocated in accordance with paragraph (4) of this subsection.

(3) The amount allocated to each unit under this paragraph for each fiscal year shall be a fraction of the total allocation to all units under this paragraph. The fraction for each unit shall be determined by dividing the operating expenses at that unit during the prior fiscal year by the total operating expenses at all units during the prior fiscal year.

(4) The amount allocated to each unit under this paragraph for each fiscal year shall be a fraction of the total allocation to all units under this paragraph. The fraction for each unit shall be determined by dividing the user fees and admission fees collected under this section at that unit during the prior fiscal year by the total of user fees and admission fees collected under this section at all units during the prior fiscal year.

(5) Amounts allocated under this subsection to any unit for any fiscal year and not expended in that fiscal year shall remain available for expenditure at that unit until expended.

(k) Selling of permits and collection of fees by volunteers at designated areas; collecting agency duties; surety bonds; selling of annual admission permits by public and private entities under arrangements with collecting agency head

When authorized by the head of the collecting agency, volunteers at designated areas may sell permits and collect fees authorized or established pursuant to this section. The head of such agency shall ensure that such volunteers have adequate training regarding—

(1) the sale of permits and the collection of fees,

(2) the purposes and resources of the areas in which they are assigned, and

(3) the provision of assistance and information to visitors to the designated area.

The Secretary shall require a surety bond for any such volunteer performing services under this subsection. Funds available to the collecting agency may be used to cover the cost of any such surety bond. The head of the collecting agency may enter into arrangements with qualified public or private entities pursuant to which such entities may sell (without cost to the United States) annual admission permits (including Golden Eagle Passports) at any appropriate location. Such arrangements shall require each such entity to reimburse the United States for the full amount to be received from the sale of such permits at or before the agency delivers the permits to such entity for sale.

(*l*) Charge for transportation provided by National Park Service for viewing National Park System units; charge in lieu of admission fee; maximum charge; apportionment and expenditure of charges

(1) Where the National Park Service provides transportation to view all or a portion of any unit of the National Park System, the Director may impose a charge for such service in lieu of an admission fee under this section. The charge imposed under this paragraph shall not exceed the maximum admission fee under subsection (a) of this section.

(2) Notwithstanding any other provision of law, half of the charges imposed under paragraph (1) shall be retained by the unit of the National Park System at which the service was provided. The remainder shall be covered into the special account referred to in subsection (i) of this section in the same manner as receipts from fees collected pursuant to this section. Fifty percent of the amount retained shall be expended only for maintenance of transportation systems at the unit where the charge was imposed. The remaining 50 percent of the retained amount shall be expended only for activities related to resource protection at such units.

(m) Admission fee at National Park System units where primary public access is provided by concessioner; maximum fee

Where the primary public access to a unit of the National Park System is provided by a concessioner, the Secretary may charge an admission fee at such units only to the extent that the total of the fee charged by the concessioner for access to the unit and the admission fee does not exceed the maximum amount of the admission fee which could otherwise be imposed under subsection (a) of this section.

(n) Commercial tour use fees

(1) In the case of each unit of the National Park System for which an admission fee is charged under this section, the Secretary of the Interior shall establish, by October 1, 1993, a commercial tour use fee to be imposed on each vehicle entering the unit for the purpose of providing commercial tour services within the unit. Fee revenue derived from such commercial tour use fees shall be deposited into the special account established under subsection (i) of this section.

(2) The Secretary shall establish the amount of fee per entry as follows:

(A) $25 per vehicle with a passenger capacity of 25 persons or less, and

(B) $50 per vehicle with a passenger capacity of more than 25 persons.

(3) The Secretary may periodically make reasonable adjustments to the commercial tour use fee imposed under this subsection.

(4) The commercial tour use fee imposed under this subsection shall not apply to either of the following:

(A) Any vehicle transporting organized school groups or outings conducted for educational purposes by schools or other bona fide educational institutions.

(B) Any vehicle entering a park system unit pursuant to a contract issued under the Act of October 9, 1965 (16 U.S.C. 20 to 20g) entitled "An Act relating to the establishment of concession policies in the areas administered by the National Park Service and for other purposes."

(5)(A) The provisions of this subsection shall apply to aircraft entering the airspace of units of the National Park System identified in section 2(b) and section 3 of Public Law 100–91 for the specific purpose of providing commercial tour services within the airspace of such units.

(B) The provisions of this subsection shall also apply to aircraft entering the airspace of other units of the National Park System for the specific purpose of providing commercial tour services if the Secretary determines that the level of such services is equal to or greater than the level at those units of the National Park System specified in subparagraph (A).

(Pub.L. 88–578, Title I, § 4, as added Pub.L. 92–347, § 2, July 11, 1972, 86 Stat. 459, and amended Pub.L. 93–81, §§ 1, 2, Aug. 1, 1973, 87 Stat. 178, 179; Pub.L. 93–303, § 1, June 7, 1974, 88 Stat. 192; Pub.L. 96–344, § 9, Sept. 8, 1980, 94 Stat. 1135; Pub.L. 100–203, Title V, § 5201(a) to (c), Dec. 22, 1987, 101 Stat. 1330–263, 1330–264; Pub.L. 101–650, Title III, § 321, Dec. 1, 1990, 104 Stat. 5117; Pub.L. 103–66, Title V, § 5001(b), Title X, §§ 10001, 10002, Aug. 10, 1993, 107 Stat. 379, 402, 403; Pub.L. 103–437, § 6(p)(1), Nov. 2, 1994, 108 Stat. 4586; Pub.L. 104–66, Title I, § 1081(f), Dec. 21, 1995, 109 Stat. 721; Pub.L. 105–327, § 1, Oct. 30, 1998, 112 Stat. 3055; Pub.L. 108–447, Div. J, Title VIII, § 813(a), Dec. 8, 2004, 118 Stat. 3390; Pub.L. 109–54, Title I, § 132(a), (b), Aug. 2, 2005, 119 Stat. 526.)

HISTORICAL AND STATUTORY NOTES

Revision Notes and Legislative Reports
1964 Acts. Senate Report No. 1364 and Conference Report No. 1847, see 1964 U.S. Code Cong. and Adm. News, p. 3633.

1972 Acts. House Report No. 92–742 and Conference Report No. 92–1164, see 1972 U.S. Code Cong. and Adm. News, p. 2823.

1973 Acts. Senate Report No. 93–250 and Senate Report No. 93–312, see 1973 U.S. Code Cong. and Adm. News, p. 1683.

1974 Acts. House Report No. 93–1076, see 1974 U.S. Code Cong. and Adm. News, p. 3257.

1987 Acts. House Report No. 100–391(Parts I and II) and House Conference Report No. 100–495, 1987 U.S. Code Cong. and Adm. News, p. 2313–1.

1990 Acts. Senate Report No. 101–416, see 1990 U.S. Code Cong. and Adm. News, p. 6802.

1993 Acts. House Report No. 103–111 and House Conference Report No. 103–213, see 1993 U.S. Code Cong. and Adm. News, p. 378.

1994 Acts. House Report No. 103–779, see 1994 U.S. Code Cong. and Adm. News, p. 3639.

1995 Acts. House Report No. 104–327, see 1995 U.S. Code Cong. and Adm. News, p. 674.

2004 Acts. House Conference Report No. 108–792, see 2004 U.S. Code Cong. and Adm. News, p. 2577.

Statement by President, see 2004 U.S. Code Cong. and Adm. News, p. S46.

2005 Acts. House Conference Report No. 109–188, see 2005 U.S. Code Cong. and Adm. News, p. 381.

Statement by President, see 2005 U.S. Code Cong. and Adm. News, p. S15.

References in Text
The Act of October 9, 1965 (16 U.S.C. 20 to 20g) entitled "An Act relating to the establishment of concession policies in the areas administered by the National Park Service and for other purposes", referred to in subsec. (n)(4)(B), is Pub.L. 89–249, Oct. 9, 1965, 79 Stat. 969, which is classified principally to subchapter IV (section 20 et seq.) of this chapter. For complete classification of this Act to the Code, see Short Title note set out under section 20 of this title and Tables.

Amendments
2005 Amendments. Subsec. (i)(1)(C). Pub.L. 109–54, § 132(a), amended Pub.L. 108–447, § 813(a), by inserting an exception for par. (1)(C) in the repeal of subsec. (i), resulting in the restoration of par. (1)(C).

Subsec. (i)(1)(C)(i). Pub.L. 109–54, § 132(b)(1), struck out "Notwithstanding subparagraph (A), section 315(c) of section 101(c) of the Omnibus Consolidated Recessions and Appropriations Act of 1996 (16 U.S.C. 460*l*–6a note; Public Law 104–134), or section 107" and inserted "Notwithstanding section 107".

Pub.L. 109–54, § 132(b)(2), struck out "account under subparagraph (A)" and inserted "account under section 807(a) of the Federal Lands Recreation Enhancement Act (16 U.S.C. 6806(a))".

2004 Amendments. Subsecs. (a) to (g). Pub.L. 108–447, Div. J, § 813(a), repealed subsecs. (a) to (g), which related to admission and use fee authorities.

Subsec. (i). Pub.L. 108–447, Div. J, § 813(a), as amended by Pub.L. 109–54, § 132(a), repealed subsec. (i), which related to the covering of fees collected into special accounts, except for par. (1)(C).

1998 Amendments. Subsec. (i)(1)(C). Pub.L. 105–327, § 1, added subpar. (C).

1995 Amendments. Subsec. (h). Pub.L. 104–66, § 1081(f), struck out subsec. (h), which required Bureau of Outdoor Recreation to transmit periodic reports to Congress, no later than Mar. 31 annually, relating to fee collection areas.

1994 Amendments. Subsec. (h). Pub.L. 103–437, § 6(p)(1), substituted "Committee on Natural Resources of the House of Representatives and the Committee on Energy and Natural Resources of the Senate" for "Committees on Interior and Insular Affairs of the United States House of Representatives and United States Senate".

1993 Amendments. Subsec. (a)(1)(A). Pub.L. 103–66, § 10002(d), designated existing text as cl. (i) and added cl. (ii).

Pub.L. 103–66, § 10002(e), in cl. (i) substituted provision stating that annual permit shall be valid for 12 months from date of payment, for provision stating that annual permit shall be valid during calendar year of payment.

Subsec. (a). Pub.L. 103–66, § 10001(a)(1), authorized admission fees at National Conservation Areas, National Monuments, National Volcanic Monuments, National Scenic Areas, and no more than 21 areas of concentrated public use.

Pub.L. 103–66, § 10001(a)(2), added provision defining "area of concentrated public use".

Subsec. (a)(4). Pub.L. 103–66, § 10001(b), substituted "for a one-time charge of $10," for "without charge,".

Subsec. (b). Pub.L. 103–66, § 5001(b), struck out provision requiring at least one primitive campground where no charge is imposed at each lake or reservoir under jurisdiction of Army Corps of Engineers where camping is permitted.

Pub.L. 103–66, § 10002(a)(2), made amendment identical to that made by

Pub.L. 103–66, § 5001(b), thus requiring no change to text.

Subsec. (i)(1). Pub.L. 103–66, § 10002(b), designated existing text as par. (1) and added par. (2).

Subsec. (n). Pub.L. 103–66, § 1002(c), added subsec. (n).

1987 Amendments. Subsec. (a)(1)(A), (B). Pub.L. 100–203, § 5201(a)(1), (2), designated existing provisions as subpar. (A) and, in subpar. (A) as so designated, increased Golden Eagle Passport fee from $10 per year to $25 per year, and added subpar. (B).

Subsec. (a)(2). Pub.L. 100–203, § 5201(a)(3), authorized single visit permit fees of $5 per private, noncommercial vehicle and $3 per person entering by means other than private noncommercial vehicle, which amounts shall apply to all designated areas.

Subsec. (a)(3). Pub.L. 100–203, § 5201(a)(4), added provision prohibiting the charging of admission fees at National Park System units providing significant outdoor recreation opportunities in urban environments and to which access is publicly available.

Subsec. (a)(6) to (12). Pub.L. 100–203, § 5201(a)(5), added pars. (6) through (12).

Subsec. (f). Pub.L. 100–203, § 5201(b), struck out provisions requiring that fees collected by Federal agencies be covered into a special account to be administered in conjunction with but separate from the Land and Water Conservation Fund, and providing that such revenues be available for outdoor recreation functions of the agencies by which the fees were collected, with proviso limiting the amount which may be appropriated for the enhancement of the fee collection system established by this section.

Subsecs. (i) to (m). Pub.L. 100–203, § 5201(c), added subsecs. (i) through (m).

1980 Amendments. Subsec. (a)(2). Pub.L. 96–344, § 9(1), substituted provision defining "single visit" as a more or less continuous stay within a designated area and providing that payment of a single visit admission authorizes exits from and reentries to a single designated area for a period of from one to fifteen days, such period to be determined by the administrating Secretary, for provision defining "single visit" as the length of time a visitor remained within the exterior boundary of a designated fee area beginning from the first day he entered until he left, except that on the same day the admission fee was paid, the visitor could leave and reenter without paying an additional admission fee.

Subsec. (a)(5). Pub.L. 96–344, § 9(2), added par. (5).

Subsec. (b). Pub.L. 96–344, § 9(3), inserted '', or permittee under paragraph (5) of subsection (a) of this section,'' following "Passport permittee".

1974 Amendments. Subsec. (a). Pub.L. 93–303, § 1(b), inserted "which are operated and maintained by a Federal agency and" following "areas".

Subsec. (a)(1). Pub.L. 93–303, § 1(c), among other changes, substituted "The permittee" for "Any person purchasing the annual permit", inserted provisions authorizing the permittee and his spouse, children, and parents accompanying him to enter an area where entry is by any means other than private, noncommercial vehicles, changed provisions which relate to the purchase of the annual permit to allow its sale at any designated area instead of through the offices of the Secretary of the Interior and the Secretary of Agriculture, through all post offices of the first- and second-class, and at such other offices as the Postmaster General directed, and eliminated provisions which empowered the Secretary of the Interior to transfer to the Postal Service from the permit receipts such funds as are adequate to reimburse the Postal Service for the cost of the service.

Subsec. (a)(2). Pub.L. 93–303, § 1(d), eliminated "or who enter such an area by means other than by private, noncommercial vehicle" which followed "annual permit" in the first sentence. See subsec. (a)(1) of this section.

Subsec. (a)(4). Pub.L. 93–303, § 1(e), substituted "a lifetime admission permit" for "an annual entrance permit", limited the issuance of this permit to citizens of, or persons domiciled in the United States, and inserted provisions to allow the permittee and his spouse and children accompanying him to enter an area which entry is by any means other than private, noncommercial vehicle.

Subsec. (b). Pub.L. 93–303, § 1(f), (g), among other changes, substituted "daily recreation use fee" for "special recre-

ation use fees", authorized a fee for boat launching facilities where specialized facilities or services such as mechanical or hydraulic boat lifts or facilities are provided, required the Corps of Engineers to provide at least one primitive campground where no charge shall be imposed at each lake or reservoir under its jurisdiction, incorporated provisions formerly in subsec. (b)(1) allowing any Golden Age Passport permittee to utilize the recreation facilities at a rate of 50 per centum of the established use fee, eliminated the remainder of former subsec. (b)(1) which related to determination of daily use fees for overnight occupancy, and redesignated former subsec. (b)(2) as (c).

Subsec. (c). Pub.L. 93–303, § 1(g), redesignated former subsec. (b)(2) as (c). Former subsec. (c) redesignated (d).

Subsec. (d). Pub.L. 93–303, § 1(g), (h), redesignated former subsec. (c) as (d), and substituted therein "a fee has been established pursuant to this section" for "an admission fee or special recreation use fee has been established".

Subsec. (e). Pub.L. 93–303, § 1(g), (i), redesignated former subsec. (d) as (e), and substituted therein "collection of any fee established pursuant to this section" for "collection of any entrance fee and/or special recreation use fee, as the case may be".

Subsec. (f). Pub.L. 93–303, § 1(g), (j), redesignated former subsec. (e) as (f), and inserted provisions therein empowering the head of any Federal agency to contract with any public or private entity to provide visitor reservation services.

Subsecs. (g), (h). Pub.L. 93–303, § 1(g), redesignated former subsecs. (f) and (g) as (g) and (h), respectively.

1973 Amendments. Subsec. (a)(2). Pub.L. 93–81, § 2, added the definition of "single visit".

Subsec. (b). Pub.L. 93–81, § 1, added in the opening paragraph the proviso that there shall be no charge for the day use or recreational use of facilities such as picnic areas, boat ramps, where no mechanical or hydraulic equipment is provided, drinking water, wayside exhibits, roads, trails, overlook sites, visitors' centers, scenic drives and toilet facilities and that no fee be charged for access to or use of campground not having flush restrooms, showers, access and circulatory roads, sanitary disposal stations, visitor protection control, designated tent or trailer spaces, refuse containers and potable water.

Effective and Applicability Provisions

2005 Acts. Pub.L. 109–54, Title I, § 132(c), Aug. 2, 2005, 119 Stat. 526, provided that: "Except as provided in this section, section 4(i)(1)(C) of the Land and Water Conservation Fund Act of 1965 (16 U.S.C. 460l–6a(i)(1)(C) [subsec. (i)(1)(C) of this section]) shall be applied and administered as if section 813(a) of the Federal Lands Recreation Enhancement Act (16 U.S.C. 6812(a) [repealing subsecs. (a) to (i) of this section]) (and the amendments made by that section) had not been enacted."

Change of Name

"United States magistrate judge" substituted for "United States magistrate" in subsec. (e) pursuant to section 321 of Pub.L. 101–650, set out as a note under section 631 of Title 28, Judiciary and Judicial Procedure.

Transfer of Functions

Enforcement functions of Secretary or other official in Department of Interior related to compliance with rights-of-way across recreation lands issued under this part and such functions of Secretary or other official in Department of Agriculture, insofar as they involve lands and programs under jurisdiction of that Department, related to compliance with this part with respect to pre-construction, construction, and initial operation of transportation system for Canadian and Alaskan natural gas were transferred to the Federal Inspector, Office of Federal Inspector for the Alaska Natural Gas Transportation System, until the first anniversary of date of initial operation of the Alaska Natural Gas Transportation System, see Reorg. Plan No. 1 of 1979, §§ 102(e), (f), 203(a), 44 F.R. 33663, 33666, 93 Stat. 1373, 1376, effective July 1, 1979, set out in Appendix 1 to Title 5, Government Organization and Employees.

Construction

Pub.L. 109–54, Title I, § 132(d), Aug. 2, 2005, 119 Stat. 526, provided that: "This section and the amendments made by this section [amending Pub.L. 108–447, Div. J, Title VIII, § 813(a), Dec. 8, 2004, 118 Stat. 3377, which amended this section and 16 U.S.C.A. § 6812] take effect as of December 8, 2004."

Limitations on Recreation Fee Demonstration Program

Pub.L. 108–447, Div. E, Title III, § 319, Dec. 8, 2004, 118 Stat. 3097, provided that: "A project undertaken by the Forest Service under the Recreation Fee Demonstration Program as authorized by section 315 of the Department of the Interior and Related Agencies Appropriations Act for Fiscal Year 1996 [Pub.L. 104–134, Title I, § 101(c) [Title III, § 315], Apr. 26, 1996, 110 Stat. 1321–200, set out as a note under this section], as amended, shall not result in—

"**(1)** displacement of the holder of an authorization to provide commercial recreation services on Federal lands. Prior to initiating any project, the Secretary shall consult with potentially affected holders to determine what impacts the project may have on the holders. Any modifications to the authorization shall be made within the terms and conditions of the authorization and authorities of the impacted agency; and

"**(2)** The return of a commercial recreation service to the Secretary for operation when such services have been provided in the past by a private sector provider, except when—

"**(A)** the private sector provider fails to bid on such opportunities;

"**(B)** the private sector provider terminates its relationship with the agency; or

"**(C)** the agency revokes the permit for non-compliance with the terms and conditions of the authorization.

In such cases, the agency may use the Recreation Fee Demonstration Program to provide for operations until a subsequent operator can be found through the offering of a new prospectus."

Similar provisions were contained in the following prior Appropriations Acts:

Pub.L. 108–108, Title III, § 319, Nov. 10, 2003, 117 Stat. 1306.

Pub.L. 108–7, Div. F, Title III, § 319, Feb. 20, 2003, 117 Stat. 274.

Pub.L. 107–63, Title III, § 325, Nov. 5, 2001, 115 Stat. 470.

Pub.L. 106–291, Title III, § 334, Oct. 11, 2000, 114 Stat. 997.

Pub.L. 106–113, Div. B, § 1000(a)(3) [Title III, § 344], Nov. 29, 1999, 113 Stat. 1535, 1501A–203.

Repeal of Superseded Admission and Use Fee Authorities

Pub.L. 108–447, Div. J, Title VIII, § 813(a), which repealed subsecs. (a) to (g) and (i) of this section, provided in part that "the Secretary may continue to issue Golden Eagle Passports, Golden Age Passports, and Golden Access Passports under [this] section until the date the notice required by section 5(a)(3) [16 U.S.C.A. § 6804(a)(3)] is published in the Federal Register regarding the establishment of the National Parks and Federal Recreational Lands Pass"; see 16 U.S.C.A. § 6812(a).

National Park Service Entrance and Recreational Use Fees

Pub.L. 106–176, Title III, § 310, Mar. 10, 2000, 114 Stat. 34, provided that:

"(a) The Secretary of the Interior is authorized to retain and expend revenues from entrance and recreation use fees at units of the National Park System where such fees are collected under section 4 of the Land and Water Conservation Fund Act of 1965 (16 U.S.C. 460l–6a) [this section], notwithstanding the provisions of section 4(i) of such Act [subsec. (i) of this section]. Fees shall be retained and expended in the same manner and for the same purposes as provided under the Recreational Fee Demonstration Program (section 315 of Public Law 104–134, as amended (16 U.S.C. 460l–6a note).

"(b) Nothing in this section shall affect the collection of fees at units of the National Park System designated as fee demonstration projects under the Recreational Fee Demonstration Program.

"(c) The authorities in this section shall expire upon the termination of the Recreational Fee Demonstration Program."

Recreation User Fees

Pub.L. 106–53, Title II, § 225, Aug. 17, 1999, 113 Stat. 297, provided that:

"(a) **Withholding of amounts.—**

"(1) **In general.—**During fiscal years 1999 through 2002, the Secretary may withhold from the special account established under section 4(i)(1)(A) of the Land and Water Conservation Fund Act of 1965 (16 U.S.C. 460l–6a(i)(1)(A)) 100 percent of the amount of receipts above a baseline of $34,000,000 per each fiscal year received from fees imposed at recreation sites under the administra-

tive jurisdiction of the Department of the Army under section 4(b) of that Act(16 U.S.C. 460l–6a(b)).

"(2) **Use.—**The amounts withheld shall be retained by the Secretary and shall be available, without further Act of appropriation, for expenditure by the Secretary in accordance with subsection (b).

"(3) **Availability.—**The amounts withheld shall remain available until September 30, 2005.

"(b) **Use of amounts withheld.—**In order to increase the quality of the visitor experience at public recreational areas and to enhance the protection of resources, the amounts withheld under subsection (a) may be used only for—

"(1) repair and maintenance projects (including projects relating to health and safety);

"(2) interpretation;

"(3) signage;

"(4) habitat or facility enhancement;

"(5) resource preservation;

"(6) annual operation (including fee collection);

"(7) maintenance; and

"(8) law enforcement related to public use.

"(c)**Availability.—**Each amount withheld by the Secretary shall be available for expenditure, without further Act of appropriation, at the specific project from which the amount, above baseline, is collected."

Recreational Fee Demonstration Program

Pub.L. 105–83, Title I, § 107, Nov. 14, 1997, 111 Stat. 1561, provided that: "In fiscal year 1998 and thereafter, for those years in which the recreation fee demonstration program authorized in Public Law 104–134 [section 315 of Pub.L. 104–134, set out in a note under this section] is in effect, the fee collection support authority provided in 16 U.S.C. 460l–6(i)(1)(B) [subsec. (i)(1)(B) of this section] applies only to parks not included in the fee demonstration program, and that the amount retained under this authority to cover fee collection costs will not exceed those costs at the non-demonstration parks, or 15 percent of all fees collected at non-demonstration parks in a fiscal year whichever is less. Fee collection costs for parks included in the fee demonstration program will be covered by the fees retained at those parks."

Pub.L. 104–134, Title I, § 101(c) [Title III, § 315], Apr. 26, 1996, 110 Stat. 1321–200; renumbered Title I, Pub.L. 104–140, § 1(a), May 2, 1996, 110 Stat. 1327, and amended Pub.L. 104–208, Div. A, Title I, § 101(d) [Title I, Title III, § 319], Sept. 30, 1996, 110 Stat. 3009–181, 3009–223; Pub.L. 105–18, Title II, § 5001, June 12, 1997, 111 Stat. 181; Pub.L. 105–83, Title III, § 320, Nov. 14, 1997, 111 Stat. 1596; Pub.L. 105–277, Div. A, § 101(e) [Title III, § 327], Oct. 21, 1998, 112 Stat. 2681–291; Pub.L. 106–291, Title III, § 336, Oct. 11, 2000, 114 Stat. 997; Pub.L. 107–63, Title III, § 312, Nov. 5, 2001, 115 Stat. 466; Pub.L. 108–108, Title III, § 332, Nov. 10, 2003, 117 Stat. 1309; Pub.L. 108–447, Div. E, Title III, § 331, Dec. 8, 2004, 118 Stat. 3099, establishing pilot programs to demonstrate feasibility of user-generated cost recovery for recreation areas and habitat enhancement projects, was repealed by Pub.L. 108–447, Div. J, Title VIII, § 813(b), Dec. 8, 2004, 118 Stat. 3390.

Study to Assess Traffic Congestion and Overcrowding at Certain Park System Units

Pub.L. 100–203, Title V, § 5201(e), Dec. 22, 1987, 110 Stat. 1330–267, directed the Secretary of the Interior to assess the extent to which traffic congestion and overcrowding occurs at certain park system units during times of seasonally high usage and to conduct a study of (A) the feasibility of reducing vehicular traffic within the national park system units through fee reductions for visitors traveling by bus and through other means which could shift visitation from automobile to buses, and (B) the feasibility of encouraging more even seasonal distribution of visitation, with the study to include a pilot project to be carried out in Yosemite National Park, and a report containing the results of the study to be transmitted to the Committee on Interior and Insular Affairs of the House of Representatives and to the Committee on Energy and Natural Resources of the Senate within 3 years of Dec. 22, 1987.

Prohibition on Entrance Fee at Statue of Liberty National Monument

Pub.L. 100–55, June 19, 1987, 101 Stat. 371, provided: "That, notwithstanding any other provision of law, after the date of enactment of this Act [June 19, 1987], the Secretary of the Interior shall not charge any entrance or admission fee at the Statue of Liberty National Monument, New Jersey and New York."

Establishment and Collection of Use or Royalty Fees for Manufacture, Reproduction, or Use of "Golden Eagle Insignia"

Pub.L. 92–347, § 3(a), July 11, 1972, 86 Stat. 459, provided that: "The Secretary of the Interior may establish and collect use or royalty fees for the manufacture, reproduction, or use of 'The Golden Eagle Insignia', originated by the Department of the Interior and announced in the December 3, 1970, issue of the Federal Register (35 Federal Register 18376) as the official symbol for Federal recreation areas designated for recreation fee collection. Any fees collected pursuant to this subsection shall be covered into the Land and Water Conservation Fund."

Termination of Rights in "Golden Eagle Insignia"

Pub.L. 92–347, § 3(d), July 11, 1972, 86 Stat. 462, provided that: "The rights in 'The Golden Eagle Insignia' under this Act [which enacted this section and section 715 of Title 18, enacted notes set out hereunder and repealed note set out under section 460*l*–5 of this title], shall terminate if the use by the Secretary of the Interior of 'The Golden Eagle Insignia' is abandoned. Nonuse for a continuous period of two years shall constitute abandonment."

CROSS REFERENCES

Interpretive shuttle transportation service; Harpers Ferry National Historical Park, see 16 USCA § 450bb–2.

Limitations on obligations or expenditures of moneys from special account, 16 USCA § 460*l*–6.

Tallgrass Prairie National Preserve unit of National Park System, see 16 USCA § 698u–3.

CODE OF FEDERAL REGULATIONS

Applicability and scope of provisions, see 36 CFR § 1.1 et seq.
Criminal law enforcement, see 43 CFR § 9260.0–1 et seq.
Public use of development projects, see 36 CFR § 327.0 et seq.
Recreation fees, see 36 CFR § 71.1 et seq.

LAW REVIEW AND JOURNAL COMMENTARIES

Federal user fees: A legal and economic analysis. Clayton P. Gillette and Thomas
    D. Hopkins, 67 B.U.L.Rev. 840 (1987).

LIBRARY REFERENCES

American Digest System
    United States ⬅57.
    Key Number System Topic No. 393.

Research References

ALR Library
    38 ALR 3rd 1070, Validity, Construction, and Application of Statutes Making
    Public Proceedings Open to the Public.

Notes of Decisions

Available funds   2
Equal protection   1
Recreational activity   3

1. Equal protection

Recreational Fee Program authorizing the Forest Service to collect user fees for admission to national forest area did not violate equal protection, on theory it discriminated against people of low income and that an administrative pass exemption for non-recreational activities within the program area discriminated against people who did not live or work in the vicinity of the area. U.S. v. Morow, E.D.Cal.2002, 185 F.Supp.2d 1135. Constitutional Law ⬅ 3216; Woods And Forests ⬅ 8; Constitutional Law ⬅ 3521

2. Available funds

Interior Department was precluded by moratorium clause in Congress' 1999 appropriations bill from funding, though Indian Self-Determination and Education Assistance Act, certain purportedly "residual" functions of Citizen Potawatomi Nation, inasmuch as Congress had specified that provision of funds under Act was subject to availability of appropriations. Citizen Potawatomi Nation v. Norton, C.A.10 (Okla.) 2001, 248 F.3d 993, modified on rehearing 257 F.3d 1158. Indians ⬅ 139

3. Recreational activity

Climber who hiked into recreational fee area in national forest and who camped within the area overnight was engaged in recreational activity so as to require payment of user fee under the Recreational Fee Program, notwithstanding his contention that he entered fee area for the purpose of engaging in some type of religious ritual, and that hiking and climbing activities were collateral. U.S. v. Morow, E.D.Cal.2002, 185 F.Supp.2d 1135. Woods And Forests ⬅ 8

§ 460*l*–6b. Repealed. Pub.L. 100–203, Title V, § 5201(d)(2), Dec. 22, 1987, 101 Stat. 1330–267

HISTORICAL AND STATUTORY NOTES

Section, Pub.L. 96–87, Title IV, § 402, Oct. 12, 1979, 93 Stat. 666; Pub.L. 96–487, Title II, § 202(3)(a), Dec. 2, 1980, 94 Stat. 2382, prohibited entrance or admission fees in excess of amounts in effect January 1, 1979 to any unit of the

National Park System and user fees for
transportation services and facilities in
Denali National Park, Alaska.

§ 460*l*–6c.   Admission, entrance, and recreation fees

(a) Definitions

As used in this section:

(1) Area of concentrated public use

The term "area of concentrated public use" means an area
administered by the Secretary that meets each of the following
criteria:

(A) The area is managed primarily for outdoor recreation
purposes.

(B) Facilities and services necessary to accommodate
heavy public use are provided in the area.

(C) The area contains at least 1 major recreation attrac-
tion.

(D) Public access to the area is provided in such a manner that admission fees can be efficiently collected at 1 or
more centralized locations.

(2) Boat launching facility

The term "boat launching facility" includes any boat launching
facility, regardless of whether specialized facilities or services,
such as mechanical or hydraulic boat lifts or facilities, are
provided.

(3) Campground

The term "campground" means any campground where a
majority of the following amenities are provided, as determined
by the Secretary:

(A) Tent or trailer spaces.

(B) Drinking water.

(C) an access road.

(D) Refuse containers.

(E) Toilet facilities.

(F) The personal collection of recreation use fees by an
employee or agent of the Secretary.

(G) Reasonable visitor protection.

(H) If campfires are permitted in the campground, simple
devices for containing the fires.

(4) Secretary

The term "Secretary" means the Secretary of Agriculture.

(b) Authority to impose fees

The Secretary may charge—

(1) admission or entrance fees at national monuments, national volcanic monuments, national scenic areas, and areas of concentrated public use administered by the Secretary; and

(2) recreation use fees at lands administered by the Secretary in connection with the use of specialized outdoor recreation sites, equipment, services, and facilities, including visitors' centers, picnic tables, boat launching facilities, and campgrounds.

(c) Amount of fees

The amount of the admission, entrance, and recreation fees authorized to be imposed under this section shall be determined by the Secretary.

(Pub.L. 103–66, Title I, § 1401, Aug. 10, 1993, 107 Stat. 331.)

HISTORICAL AND STATUTORY NOTES

Revision Notes and Legislative Reports
  1993 Acts. House Report No. 103–111 and House Conference Report No. 103–213, see 1993 U.S. Code Cong. and Adm. News, p. 378.

Codifications
  Section was enacted as part of the Agricultural Reconciliation Act of 1993 and not part of the Land and Water Conservation Fund Act of 1965 which enacted this part.

LIBRARY REFERENCES

American Digest System
  United States ⊂⇒57.
  Key Number System Topic No. 393.

§ 460*l*–6d. Commercial filming

(a) Commercial filming fee

The Secretary of the Interior and the Secretary of Agriculture (hereafter individually referred to as the "Secretary" with respect to lands under their respective jurisdiction) shall require a permit and shall establish a reasonable fee for commercial filming activities or similar projects on Federal lands administered by the Secretary. Such fee shall provide a fair return to the United States and shall be based upon the following criteria:

(1) The number of days the filming activity or similar project takes place on Federal land under the Secretary's jurisdiction.

(2) The size of the film crew present on Federal land under the Secretary's jurisdiction.

(3) The amount and type of equipment present.

The Secretary may include other factors in determining an appropriate fee as the Secretary deems necessary.

(b) Recovery of costs

The Secretary shall also collect any costs incurred as a result of filming activities or similar project, including but not limited to administrative and personnel costs. All costs recovered shall be in addition to the fee assessed in subsection (a) of this section.

(c) Still photography

(1) Except as provided in paragraph (2), the Secretary shall not require a permit nor assess a fee for still photography on lands administered by the Secretary if such photography takes place where members of the public are generally allowed. The Secretary may require a permit, fee, or both, if such photography takes place at other locations where members of the public are generally not allowed, or where additional administrative costs are likely.

(2) The Secretary shall require and shall establish a reasonable fee for still photography that uses models or props which are not a part of the site's natural or cultural resources or administrative facilities.

(d) Protection of resources

The Secretary shall not permit any filming, still photography or other related activity if the Secretary determines—

(1) there is a likelihood of resource damage;

(2) there would be an unreasonable disruption of the public's use and enjoyment of the site; or

(3) that the activity poses health or safety risks to the public.

(e) Use of proceeds

(1) All fees collected under this section shall be available for expenditure by the Secretary, without further appropriation, in accordance with the formula and purposes established for the Recreational Fee Demonstration Program (Public Law 104–134). All fees collected shall remain available until expended.

(2) All costs recovered under this section shall be available for expenditure by the Secretary, without further appropriation, at the site where collected. All costs recovered shall remain available until expended.

(f) Processing of permit applications

The Secretary shall establish a process to ensure that permit applicants for commercial filming, still photography, or other activity are responded to in a timely manner.

(Pub.L. 106–206, § 1, May 26, 2000, 114 Stat. 314.)

HISTORICAL AND STATUTORY NOTES

References in Text

"This section", referred to in subsec. (e), originally read "this Act", meaning Pub.L. 106–206, May 26, 2000, 114 Stat. 314, which enacted this section.

The Recreational Fee Demonstration Program (Pub.L. 104–134), referred to in subsec. (e)(1), is Pub.L. 104–434, Title I, § 101(c) [Title III, § 315], April 26, 1996, 110 Stat. 1321–156, 1321–200, as amend-

ed, which was set out as a note under 16 U.S.C.A. § 460l–6a, prior to repeal by Pub.L. 108–447, Div. J, Title VIII, § 813(b), Dec. 8, 2004, 118 Stat. 3390.

Codifications

Section was enacted as Pub.L. 106–206 and not as part of the Land and Conservation Fund Act of 1965 which was enacted in this part.

§ 460*l*–7.   Allocation of land and water conservation fund for State and Federal purposes

There shall be submitted with the annual budget of the United States a comprehensive statement of estimated requirements during the ensuing fiscal year for appropriations from the fund. Not less than 40 per centum of such appropriations shall be available for Federal purposes. Those appropriations from the fund up to and including $600,000,000 in fiscal year 1978 and up to and including $750,000,000 in fiscal year 1979 shall continue to be allocated in accordance with this section. There shall be credited to a special account within the fund $300,000,000 in fiscal year 1978 and $150,000,000 in fiscal year 1979 from the amounts authorized by section 460*l*–5 of this title. Amounts credited to this account shall remain in the account until appropriated. Appropriations from the special account shall be available only with respect to areas existing and authorizations enacted prior to the convening of the Ninety-fifth Congress, for acquisition of lands, waters, or interests in lands or waters within the exterior boundaries, as aforesaid, of—

(1) the national park system;

(2) national scenic trails;

(3) the national wilderness preservation system;

(4) federally administered components of the National Wild and Scenic Rivers System; and

(5) national recreation areas administered by the Secretary of Agriculture.

(Pub.L. 88–578, Title I, § 5, formerly § 4, Sept. 3, 1964, 78 Stat. 900; Pub.L. 90–401, § 3, July 15, 1968, 82 Stat. 355, renumbered § 5, Pub.L. 92–347, § 2, July 11, 1972, 86 Stat. 459, and amended Pub.L. 94–273, § 3(4), Apr. 21, 1976, 90 Stat. 376; Pub.L. 94–422, Title I, § 101(2), Sept. 28, 1976, 90 Stat. 1314; Pub.L. 95–42, § 1(2), June 10, 1977, 91 Stat. 210.)

HISTORICAL AND STATUTORY NOTES

Revision Notes and Legislative Reports

1964 Acts. Senate Report No. 1364 and Conference Report No. 1847, see 1964 U.S.Code Cong. and Adm.News, p. 3633.

1968 Acts. Senate Report No. 1071 and Conference Report No. 1598, see 1968 U.S.Code Cong. and Adm.News, p. 2613.

1972 Acts. House Report No. 92–742 and Conference Report No. 92–1164, see 1972 U.S.Code Cong. and Adm.News, p. 2823.

1976 Acts. House Report No. 94–1000, see 1976 U.S.Code Cong. and Adm.News, p. 690.

Senate Report No. 94–367 and House Conference Report No. 94–1468, see 1976 U.S.Code Cong. and Adm.News, p. 2442.

1977 Acts. Senate Report No. 95–162, see 1977 U.S.Code Cong. and Adm.News, p. 322.

References in Text

The convening of the Ninety-fifth Congress, referred to in text, took place on Jan. 4, 1977.

Amendments

1977 Amendments. Pub.L. 95–42 provided that appropriations from the fund up to and including $600,000,000 in fiscal year 1978 and up to and including $750,000,000 in fiscal year 1979 continue to be allocated in accordance with this section, that there be credited to a special account within the fund $300,000,000 in fiscal year 1978 and $150,000,000 in fiscal year 1979 from the amounts authorized by section 460l–5 of this title, that amounts credited to this account remain in the account until appropriated, and that appropriations from the special account be available only with respect to areas existing and authorizations enacted prior to the convening of the Ninety-fifth Congress, for acquisition of lands, waters, or interests in lands or waters within the exterior boundaries of the national park system, national scenic trails, the national wilderness preservation system, federally administered components of the National Wild and Scenic Rivers System, and national recreation areas administered by the Secretary of Agriculture.

1976 Amendments. Pub.L. 94–422 revised former subsec. (a), dropping subsec. (a) designation and eliminating provisions relating to the authority of the President to vary percentages of the fund to be made available to the States and Federal government, and struck out former subsec. (b) relating to advance appropriations to be allocated for State and Federal purposes and the schedule and procedure for repayment of such appropriations.

Subsec. (b). Pub.L. 94–273 substituted "October" for "July" wherever appearing therein.

1968 Amendments. Subsec. (b). Pub.L. 90–401 substituted "until the end of fiscal year 1969" for "for a total of eight years" in the provision spelling out the term during which the advance appropriations are authorized from moneys in the Treasury not otherwise appropriated in amounts averaging not more than $60,000,000 for each fiscal year.

Effective and Applicability Provisions

1965 Acts. Section effective Jan. 1, 1965, see note set out under section 460l–4 of this title.

CROSS REFERENCES

Acquisition of lands—

   Hassel Island, Virgin Islands National Park, see 16 USCA § 398f.

   National trails system, see 16 USCA § 1249.

Just compensation to owner of real property; Redwood National Park, see 16 USCA § 79c.

LIBRARY REFERENCES

American Digest System

   United States ☞57.

   Key Number System Topic No. 393.

§ 460*l*–8. Financial assistance to States

(a) Authority of Secretary of the Interior; payments to carry out purposes of land and water conservation provisions

The Secretary of the Interior (hereinafter referred to as the "Secretary") is authorized to provide financial assistance to the States from moneys available for State purposes. Payments may be made to the States by the Secretary as hereafter provided, subject to such terms and conditions as he considers appropriate and in the public interest to carry out the purposes of this part, for outdoor recreation: (1) planning, (2) acquisition of land, waters, or interests in land or waters, or (3) development.

(b) Apportionment among States; finality of administrative determination; formula; notification; reapportionment of unobligated amounts; definition of State

Sums appropriated and available for State purposes for each fiscal year shall be apportioned among the several States by the Secretary, whose determination shall be final, in accordance with the following formula:

    (1) Forty per centum of the first $225,000,000; thirty per centum of the next $275,000,000; and twenty per centum of all additional appropriations shall be apportioned equally among the several States; and

    (2) At any time, the remaining appropriation shall be apportioned on the basis of need to individual States by the Secretary in such amounts as in his judgment will best accomplish the purposes of this part. The determination of need shall include among other things a consideration of the proportion which the population of each State bears to the total population of the United States and of the use of outdoor recreation resources of individual States by persons from outside the State as well as a consideration of the Federal resources and programs in the particular States.

    (3) The total allocation to an individual State under paragraphs (1) and (2) of this subsection shall not exceed 10 per centum of the total amount allocated to the several States in any one year.

    (4) The Secretary shall notify each State of its apportionments; and the amounts thereof shall be available thereafter for payment to such State for planning, acquisition, or development projects as hereafter prescribed. Any amount of any apportionment that has not been paid or obligated by the Secretary during the fiscal year in which such notification is given and for two fiscal years thereafter shall be reapportioned by the Secretary in accordance with paragraph (2) of this subsection, without regard to the 10 per centum limitation to an individual State specified in this subsection.

(5) For the purposes of paragraph (1) of this subsection, the District of Columbia, Puerto Rico, the Virgin Islands, Guam, American Samoa, and the Commonwealth of the Northern Mariana Islands (when such islands achieve Commonwealth status) shall be treated collectively as one State, and shall receive shares of such apportionment in proportion to their populations. The above listed areas shall be treated as States for all other purposes of sections 460*l*–4 to 460*l*–6a and 460*l*–7 to 460*l*–10e of this title.

(c) Matching requirements

Payments to any State shall cover not more than 50 per centum of the cost of planning, acquisition, or development projects that are undertaken by the State. The remaining share of the cost shall be borne by the State in a manner and with such funds or services as shall be satisfactory to the Secretary. No payment may be made to any State for or on account of any cost or obligation incurred or any service rendered prior to September 3, 1964.

(d) Comprehensive State plan; necessity; adequacy; contents; correlation with other plans; factors for formulation of Housing and Home Finance Agency financed plans; planning projects; wetlands consideration; wetlands priority plan

A comprehensive statewide outdoor recreation plan shall be required prior to the consideration by the Secretary of financial assistance for acquisition or development projects. The plan shall be adequate if, in the judgment of the Secretary, it encompasses and will promote the purposes of this part: *Provided*, That no plan shall be approved unless the Governor of the respective State certifies that ample opportunity for public participation in plan development and revision has been accorded. The Secretary shall develop, in consultation with others, criteria for public participation, which criteria shall constitute the basis for the certification by the Governor. The plan shall contain—

(1) the name of the State agency that will have authority to represent and act for the State in dealing with the Secretary for purposes of this part;

(2) an evaluation of the demand for and supply of outdoor recreation resources and facilities in the State;

(3) a program for the implementation of the plan; and

(4) other necessary information, as may be determined by the Secretary.

The plan shall take into account relevant Federal resources and programs and shall be correlated so far as practicable with other State, regional, and local plans. Where there exists or is in preparation for any particular State a comprehensive plan financed in part with funds supplied by the Housing and Home Finance Agency, any statewide outdoor recreation plan prepared for purposes of this part shall be based upon the same population, growth, and other pertinent factors as are used in formulating the Housing and Home Finance Agency financed plans.

The Secretary may provide financial assistance to any State for projects for the preparation of a comprehensive statewide outdoor recreation plan when such plan is not otherwise available or for the maintenance of such plan.

For fiscal year 1988 and thereafter each comprehensive statewide outdoor recreation plan shall specifically address wetlands within that State as an important outdoor recreation resource as a prerequisite to approval, except that a revised comprehensive statewide outdoor recreation plan shall not be required by the Secretary, if a State submits, and the Secretary, acting through the Director of the National Park Service, approves, as a part of and as an addendum to the existing comprehensive statewide outdoor recreation plan, a wetlands priority plan developed in consultation with the State agency with responsibility for fish and wildlife resources and consistent with the national wetlands priority conservation plan developed under section 3921 of this title or, if such national plan has not been completed, consistent with the provisions of that section [1]

(e) Projects for land and water acquisition; development

In addition to assistance for planning projects, the Secretary may provide financial assistance to any State for the following types of projects or combinations thereof if they are in accordance with the State comprehensive plan:

> **(1)** For the acquisition of land, waters, or interests in land or waters, or wetland areas and interests therein as identified in the wetlands provisions of the comprehensive plan (other than land, waters, or interests in land or waters acquired from the United States for less than fair market value), but not including incidental costs relating to acquisition.
>
> Whenever a State provides that the owner of a single-family residence may, at his option, elect to retain a right of use and occupancy for not less than six months from the date of acquisition of such residence and such owner elects to retain such a right, such owner shall be deemed to have waived any benefits under sections 4623, 4624, 4625, and 4626 of Title 42 and for the

purposes of those sections such owner shall not be considered a displaced person as defined in section 4601(6) of Title 42.

(2) For development of basic outdoor recreation facilities to serve the general public, including the development of Federal lands under lease to States for terms of twenty-five years or more: *Provided,* That no assistance shall be available under this part to enclose or shelter facilities normally used for outdoor recreation activities, but the Secretary may permit local funding, and after September 28, 1976, not to exceed 10 per centum of the total amount allocated to a State in any one year to be used for sheltered facilities for swimming pools and ice skating rinks in areas where the Secretary determines that the severity of climatic conditions and the increased public use thereby made possible justifies the construction of such facilities.

(f) Requirements for project approval; conditions; progress payments; payments to Governors or State officials or agencies; State transfer of funds to public agencies; conversion of property to other uses; reports to Secretary; accounting; records; audit; discrimination prohibited

(1) Payments may be made to States by the Secretary only for those planning, acquisition, or development projects that are approved by him. No payment may be made by the Secretary for or on account of any project with respect to which financial assistance has been given or promised under any other Federal program or activity, and no financial assistance may be given under any other Federal program or activity for or on account of any project with respect to which such assistance has been given or promised under this part. The Secretary may make payments from time to time in keeping with the rate of progress toward the satisfactory completion of individual projects: *Provided,* That the approval of all projects and all payments, or any commitments relating thereto, shall be withheld until the Secretary receives appropriate written assurance from the State that the State has the ability and intention to finance its share of the cost of the particular project, and to operate and maintain by acceptable standards, at State expense, the particular properties or facilities acquired or developed for public outdoor recreation use.

(2) Payments for all projects shall be made by the Secretary to the Governor of the State or to a State official or agency designated by the Governor or by State law having authority and responsibility to accept and to administer funds paid hereunder for approved projects. If consistent with an approved project, funds may be transferred by the State to a political subdivision or other appropriate public agency.

(3) No property acquired or developed with assistance under this section shall, without the approval of the Secretary, be converted to other than public outdoor recreation uses. The Secretary shall approve such conversion only if he finds it to be in accord with the then existing comprehensive statewide outdoor recreation plan and only upon such conditions as he deems necessary to assure the substitution of other recreation properties of at least equal fair market value and of reasonably equivalent usefulness and location.[2]: *Provided*, That wetland areas and interests therein as identified in the wetlands provisions of the comprehensive plan and proposed to be acquired as suitable replacement property within that same State that is otherwise acceptable to the Secretary, acting through the Director of the National Park Service, shall be considered to be of reasonably equivalent usefulness with the property proposed for conversion.

(4) No payment shall be made to any State until the State has agreed to (1) provide such reports to the Secretary, in such form and containing such information, as may be reasonably necessary to enable the Secretary to perform his duties under this part, and (2) provide such fiscal control and fund accounting procedures as may be necessary to assure proper disbursement and accounting for Federal funds paid to the State under this part.

(5) Each recipient of assistance under this part shall keep such records as the Secretary shall prescribe, including records which fully disclose the amount and the disposition by such recipient of the proceeds of such assistance, the total cost of the project or undertaking in connection with which such assistance is given or used, and the amount and nature of that portion of the cost of the project or undertaking supplied by other sources, and such other records as will facilitate an effective audit.

(6) The Secretary, and the Comptroller General of the United States, or any of their duly authorized representatives, shall have access for the purpose of audit and examination to any books, documents, papers, and records of the recipient that are pertinent to assistance received under this part.

(7) Repealed. Pub.L. 104–333, Div. I, Title VIII, § 814(d)(1)(H), Nov. 12, 1996, 110 Stat. 4196

(8) With respect to property acquired or developed with assistance from the fund, discrimination on the basis of residence, including preferential reservation or membership systems, is prohibited except to the extent that reasonable differences in admission and other fees may be maintained on the basis of residence.

(g) Coordination with Federal agencies

In order to assure consistency in policies and actions under this part with other related Federal programs and activities (including those conducted pursuant to Title VII of the Housing Act of 1961 [42 U.S.C.A. § 1500 et seq.] and section 701 of the Housing Act of 1954 [40 U.S.C.A. § 461]) and to assure coordination of the planning, acquisition, and development assistance to States under this section with other related Federal programs and activities, the President may issue such regulations with respect thereto as he deems desirable and such assistance may be provided only in accordance with such regulations.

(h) Capital improvement and other projects to reduce crime

(1) Availability of funds

In addition to assistance for planning projects, and in addition to the projects identified in subsection (e) of this section, and from amounts appropriated out of the Violent Crime Reduction Trust Fund, the Secretary may provide financial assistance to the States, not to exceed $15,000,000, for projects or combinations thereof for the purpose of making capital improvements and other measures to increase safety in urban parks and recreation areas, including funds to—

(A) increase lighting within or adjacent to public parks and recreation areas;

(B) provide emergency phone lines to contact law enforcement or security personnel in areas within or adjacent to public parks and recreation areas;

(C) increase security personnel within or adjacent to public parks and recreation areas; and

(D) fund any other project intended to increase the security and safety of public parks and recreation areas.

(2) Eligibility

In addition to the requirements for project approval imposed by this section, eligibility for assistance under this subsection shall be dependent upon a showing of need. In providing funds under this subsection, the Secretary shall give priority to projects proposed for urban parks and recreation areas with the highest rates of crime and, in particular, to urban parks and recreation areas with the highest rates of sexual assault.

(3) Federal share

Notwithstanding subsection (c) of this section, the Secretary may provide 70 percent improvement grants for projects undertaken by any State for the purposes described in this subsection, and the remaining share of the cost shall be borne by the State.

(Pub.L. 88–578, Title I, § 6, formerly § 5, Sept. 3, 1964, 78 Stat. 900, renumbered § 6, Pub.L. 92–347, § 2, July 11, 1972, 86 Stat. 459, and amended Pub.L. 93–303, § 2, June 7, 1974, 88 Stat. 194; Pub.L. 94–422, Title I, § 101(3), Sept. 28, 1976, 90 Stat. 1314; Pub.L. 95–625, Title VI, § 606, Nov. 10, 1978, 92 Stat. 3519; Pub.L. 99–645, Title III, § 303, Nov. 10, 1986, 100 Stat. 3587; Pub.L. 103–322, Title IV, § 40133, Sept. 13, 1994, 108 Stat. 1918; Pub.L. 103–437, § 6(p)(2), Nov. 2, 1994, 108 Stat. 4586; Pub.L. 104–333, Div. I, Title VIII, § 814(d)(1)(H), Nov. 12, 1996, 110 Stat. 4196.)

¹ So in original. Probably should be followed by a period.
² So in original. The period probably should not appear.

HISTORICAL AND STATUTORY NOTES

Revision Notes and Legislative Reports
1964 Acts. Senate Report No. 1364 and Conference Report No. 1847, see 1964 U.S. Code Cong. and Adm. News, p. 3633.

1972 Acts. House Report No. 92–742 and Conference Report No. 92–1164, see 1972 U.S. Code Cong. and Adm. News, p. 2823.

1974 Acts. House Report No. 93–1076, see 1974 U.S. Code Cong. and Adm. News, p. 3257.

1976 Acts. Senate Report No. 94–367 and House Conference Report No. 94–1468, see 1976 U.S. Code Cong. and Adm. News, p. 2442.

1986 Acts. Senate Report No. 99–445, see 1986 U.S. Code Cong. and Adm. News, p. 6113.

1994 Acts. House Report Nos. 103–324 and 103–489, and House Conference Report No. 103–711, see 1994 U.S. Code Cong. and Adm. News, p. 1801.

House Report No. 103–779, see 1994 U.S. Code Cong. and Adm. News, p. 3639.

References in Text
Title VII of the Housing Act of 1961, referred to in subsec. (g), is Title VII of Pub.L. 87–70, June 30, 1961, 75 Stat. 183, which was classified generally to chapter 8C (section 1500 et seq.) of Title 42, The Public Health and Welfare, and was omitted pursuant to section 5316 of Title 42 which terminated the authority to make grants or loans under such chapter after Jan. 1, 1975. For complete classification of this Act to the Code, see Short Title of 1961 Amendment note set out

under section 1701 of Title 12, Banks and Banking.

Section 461 of Title 40, referred to in Subsec. (g), was repealed by Pub.L. 97–35, Title III, § 313(b), Aug. 13, 1981, 95 Stat. 398.

Amendments
1996 Amendments. Subsec. (f)(7). Pub.L. 104–333, § 814(d)(1)(H), struck out par. (7) relating to annual State evaluations, lists of funded projects, and reports.

1994 Amendments. Subsec. (f)(7). Pub.L. 103–437, § 6(p)(2), substituted "Committee on Natural Resources of the House of Representatives and the Committee on Energy and Natural Resources of the Senate" for "Committees on Interior and Insular Affairs of the United States Congress".

Subsec. (h). Pub.L. 103–322, § 40133, added subsec. (h).

1986 Amendments. Subsec. (d). Pub.L. 99–645, § 303(1), added provision requiring that for fiscal year 1988 and thereafter, each comprehensive statewide outdoor recreation plan shall specifically address wetlands within that State as an important outdoor recreation resource as a prerequisite to approval or, alternatively, that a State submit a wetlands priority plan developed in consultation with the responsible State agency and approved by the Secretary, acting through the Director of the National Park Service, as part of and as an addendum to the existing comprehensive statewide outdoor recreation plan.

Subsec. (e)(1). Pub.L. 99–645, § 303(2), added provision relating to wetlands areas and interests therein as identified in the wetlands provisions of the comprehensive plan.

Subsec. (f)(3).   Pub.L. 99–645, § 303, added provision that wetland areas and interests therein as identified in the wetlands provisions of the comprehensive plan and proposed to be acquired as suitable replacement property within that same State that is otherwise acceptable to the Secretary, acting through the Director of the National Park Service, shall be considered to be of reasonably equivalent usefulness with the property proposed for conversion.

1978   Amendments. Subsec.   (f)(7). Pub.L. 95–625 provided in the first sentence for transmission of grant program evaluations ", so as to be received by the Secretary no later than December 31," and in the third sentence for reports to Congressional Committees "by no later than March 1 of each year".

1976 Amendments. Subsec. (a). Pub.L. 94–422 reenacted subsec. (a) without change.

Subsec. (b)(1).   Pub.L. 94–422 substituted "Forty per centum of the first $225,000,000; thirty per centum of the next $275,000,000; and twenty per centum of all additional appropriations" for "two-fifths".

Subsec. (b)(2).   Pub.L. 94–422 substituted "At any time, the remaining appropriation" for "three-fifths".

Subsec. (b)(3).   Pub.L. 94–422 designated as subsec. (b)(3) the first paragraph following subsec. (b)(2), and as so designated, substituted "10 per centum" for "7 per centum".

Subsec. (b)(4).   Pub.L. 94–422 designated as subsec. (b)(4) the second paragraph following subsec. (b)(2), and as so designated, substituted "in accordance with paragraph (2) of this subsection, without regard to the 10 per centum limitation to an individual State specified in this subsection" for "in accordance with paragraph (2) of this subsection".

Subsec. (b)(5).   Pub.L. 94–422 designated as subsec. (b)(5) the third paragraph following subsec. (b)(2), and as so designated, added Northern Mariana Islands to those areas to be treated and provision that such areas be treated collectively as one State for purposes of subsec. (b)(1) and substituted requirement that a State shall receive shares of apportionment in proportion to their population for requirement that the State's population shall be included as part of the total population in computing apportionment under subsec. (b)(2).

Subsec. (c).   Pub.L. 94–422 reenacted subsec. (c) without change.

Subsec. (d).   Pub.L.   94–422   added proviso that no plan shall be approved unless certified by the Governor that public participation in plan development and revision has been accorded and that the Secretary shall develop criteria for public participation to form basis of certification by Governor.

Subsec. (e)(2).   Pub.L. 94–422 added proviso that no assistance shall be available under sections 460*l*–4 to 460*l*–11 of this title to enclose or shelter facilities normally used for outdoor recreation activities and authorized Secretary to permit local funding after Sept. 28, 1976 not to exceed 10 per cent of total amount allocated to States.

Subsec. (f).   Pub.L. 94–422 designated existing six paragraphs as pars. (1) to (6), respectively, and added pars. (7) and (8).

Subsec. (g).   Pub.L. 94–422 reenacted subsec. (g) without change.

1974   Amendments. Subsec.   (e)(1). Pub.L. 93–303 inserted sentence relating to waiver of benefits by an owner of a single-family residence who elects to retain a right of use and occupancy for not less than six months from the date of acquisition of the residence.

Effective and Applicability Provisions
1965 Acts. Section effective Jan. 1, 1965, see note set out under section 460*l*–4 of this title.

EXECUTIVE ORDERS

EXECUTIVE ORDER NO. 11237

Ex. Ord. No. 11237, July 27, 1965, 30 F.R. 9433, which related to coordination of planning and acquisition of land under outdoor recreation and open space programs, was revoked by Ex. Ord. No. 12553, Feb. 25, 1986, 51 F.R. 7237.

CROSS REFERENCES

Areawide development project defined, see 42 USCA § 3338.

Project reports; conformity of proposed recreation and fish and wildlife development with State comprehensive plan, see 16 USCA § 460*l*–17.

Utilization of statewide comprehensive outdoor recreation plans for—

State and local projects regarding wild, scenic, and recreational river areas, see 16 USCA § 1282.

Volunteer planning, development, maintenance, and management of trails in national trails system, see 16 USCA § 1250.

LIBRARY REFERENCES

American Digest System

United States ⇔82(1).

Key Number System Topic No. 393.

Notes of Decisions

Conversion to other than recreation uses
1

Discrimination on basis of residence   2

Environmental impact statement   3

Liability of federal government   6

Persons entitled to maintain action   5

Ripeness for judicial review   4

---

1. Conversion to other than recreation uses

Proposed test drilling in state park aimed at determining feasibility of commercial diamond mining did not constitute "conversion" under Federal Land and Water Conservation Fund Act; exploratory drilling would not limit public use of park, except for ten- to twelve-week period when 5,000 square foot region would be cordoned off; moreover, no permanent damage would come to land and supply of minerals available to public visitors would not be depleted. Sierra Club v. Davies, C.A.8 (Ark.) 1992, 955 F.2d 1188. Mines And Minerals ⇔ 4

Where property acquired through purchase of conservation easement was right to prevent further development of land underlying easement, and by proposed amendment, holder of fee would be permitted to engage in precisely such development, changing both character of land and population having access to it, change constituted "conversion to other than public outdoor recreation uses" within meaning of Land and Water Conservation Fund Act. Friends of Shawangunks, Inc. v. Clark, C.A.2 (N.Y.) 1985, 754 F.2d 446. Environmental Law ⇔ 43

2. Discrimination on basis of residence

Where there was no showing that funds allocated pursuant to this section funds had been used to acquire or develop property involved and where differential in mooring fees, as between residents and nonresidents of Hawaii, was not unreasonable, Hawaii Rev.Stat. § 266–21.1(c)(1) according disparate treatment to residents and nonresidents did not violate subsec. *l*–8(f)(8) or this section. Hawaii Boating Ass'n v. Water Transp. Facilities Division, Dept. of Transp., State of Hawaii, C.A.9 (Hawai'i) 1981, 651 F.2d 661. Wharves ⇔ 3

Fact that redevelopment authority, which sought confirmation of its title to certain land next to river and determination of extent of existing public rights in alleged ways to waterfront, had accepted grant from Bureau of Outdoor Recreation of United States Department of Interior did not have to transform town ways into highways, despite contention that otherwise there would be violation of prohibition of "discrimination on the basis of residence" contained in subsec. (f)(8) of this section applicable to projects funded by such grants, and thus fact that town order, which discontinued all public rights in all ways lying within land in question, was adopted without complying with statutory notice requirements applicable to highways did not mean that such order was invalid. Newburyport Redevelopment Authority v. Com., Mass.App. Ct.1980, 401 N.E.2d 118, 9 Mass.App.Ct. 206. Highways ⇔ 18; Highways ⇔ 77(3)

3. Environmental impact statement

Highway project, across a state park which was established with grant of substantial federal funds, was federal action subject to environmental impact statement requirements of National Environmental Policy Act, because of inevitability of need for at least one federal approval. Maryland Conservation Council, Inc. v. Gilchrist, C.A.4 (Md.) 1986, 808 F.2d 1039. Environmental Law ☞ 595(7)

4. Ripeness for judicial review

Action to enjoin construction of private marina in state park facing the Statue of Liberty was not ripe for judicial review absent final decision by the National Park Service on whether construction of the marina in park purchased and approved with federal government assistance would be unauthorized conversion within meaning of the Land and Water Conservation Fund Act, despite informal determination that there was no conversion; matter would not be ripe for judicial review until agency determination, whether labeled "final" or "preliminary," was about to result in concrete action. City of Jersey City v. Hodel, D.N.J.1989, 714 F.Supp. 126. Administrative Law And Procedure ☞ 704; Environmental Law ☞ 662

5. Persons entitled to maintain action

Plaintiffs did not have standing to bring action in federal court to set aside approval of federal funds for the purpose of developing state outdoor recreational park where the injury alleged, that the development of the land would deplete state funds available for development of parks in other areas of the state, was not the result of any action by the Secretary. Johnson v. Morton, C.A.5 (Tex.) 1972, 456 F.2d 68, certiorari denied 93 S.Ct. 114, 409 U.S. 887, 34 L.Ed.2d 144. Federal Civil Procedure ☞ 111

6. Liability of federal government

Where disappointed bidder for construction contract on regional park project submitted its bid not to federal agency, but to municipality in charge of constructing park, and there was no contractual or regulatory provision making municipality agent of federal government, federal government could not be sued for alleged wrongful denial of bid, merely because project was funded and sponsored by Bureau of Outdoor Recreation and Housing and Urban Development Department. Cofan Associates, Inc. v. U.S., Cl.Ct.1983, 4 Cl.Ct. 85.

§ 460*l*-9. Allocation of land and water conservation fund moneys for Federal purposes

(a) Allowable purposes and subpurposes; acquisition of land and waters and interests therein; offset for specified capital costs

Moneys appropriated from the fund for Federal purposes shall, unless otherwise allotted in the appropriation Act making them available, be allotted by the President to the following purposes and subpurposes:

(1) For the acquisition of land, waters, or interests in land or waters as follows:

National Park System; recreation areas—Within the exterior boundaries of areas of the National Park System now or hereafter authorized or established and of areas now or hereafter authorized to be administered by the Secretary of the Interior for outdoor recreation purposes.

National Forest System—Inholdings within (a) wilderness areas of the National Forest System, and (b) other areas of national forests as the boundaries of those forests exist on the effective date of this Act, or purchase units approved by the National

Forest Reservation Commission subsequent to the date of this Act, all of which other areas are primarily of value for outdoor recreation purposes: *Provided*, That lands outside of but adjacent to an existing national forest boundary, not to exceed three thousand acres in the case of any one forest, which would comprise an integral part of a forest recreational management area may also be acquired with moneys appropriated from this fund: *Provided further*, That except for areas specifically authorized by Act of Congress, not more than 15 per centum of the acreage added to the National Forest System pursuant to this section shall be west of the 100th meridian.

National Wildlife Refuge System—Acquisition for (a) endangered species and threatened species authorized under section 1534(a) of this title; (b) areas authorized by section 460k–1 of this title; (c) national wildlife refuge areas under section 742f(a)(4) of this title and wetlands acquired under section 3922 of this title; (d) any areas authorized for the National Wildlife Refuge System by specific Acts.

(2) For payment into miscellaneous receipts of the Treasury as a partial offset for those capital costs, if any, of Federal water development projects hereafter authorized to be constructed by or pursuant to an Act of Congress which are allocated to public recreation and the enhancement of fish and wildlife values and financed through appropriations to water resource agencies.

(3) Appropriations allotted for the acquisition of land, waters, or interests in land or waters as set forth under the headings "National Park System; Recreation Areas" and "National Forest System" in paragraph (1) of this subsection shall be available therefor notwithstanding any statutory ceiling on such appropriations contained in any other provision of law enacted prior to the convening of the Ninety-fifth Congress or, in the case of national recreation areas, prior to the convening of the Ninety-sixth Congress; except that for any such area expenditures may not exceed a statutory ceiling during any one fiscal year by 10 per centum of such ceiling or $1,000,000, whichever is greater.

(b) Acquisition restrictions

Appropriations from the fund pursuant to this section shall not be used for acquisition unless such acquisition is otherwise authorized by law: *Provided, however*, That appropriations from the fund may be used for preacquisition work in instances where authorization is imminent and where substantial monetary savings could be realized.

(c) Boundary changes; donations; authority of Secretary

(1) Whenever the Secretary of the Interior determines that to do so will contribute to, and is necessary for, the proper preservation, protection, interpretation, or management of an area of the national park system, he may, following timely notice in writing to the Committee on Resources of the House of Representatives and to the Committee on Energy and Natural Resources of the Senate of his intention to do so, and by publication of a revised boundary map or other description in the Federal Register, (i) make minor revisions of the boundary of the area, and moneys appropriated from the fund shall be available for acquisition of any lands, waters, and interests therein added to the area by such boundary revision subject to such statutory limitations, if any, on methods of acquisition and appropriations thereof as may be specifically applicable to such area; and (ii) acquire by donation, purchase with donated funds, transfer from any other Federal agency, or exchange, lands, waters, or interests therein adjacent to such area, except that in exercising his authority under this clause (ii) the Secretary may not alienate property administered as part of the national park system in order to acquire lands by exchange, the Secretary may not acquire property without the consent of the owner, and the Secretary may acquire property owned by a State or political subdivision thereof only by donation. Prior to making a determination under this subsection, the Secretary shall consult with the duly elected governing body of the county, city, town, or other jurisdiction or jurisdictions having primary taxing authority over the land or interest to be acquired as to the impacts of such proposed action, and he shall also take such steps as he may deem appropriate to advance local public awareness of the proposed action. Lands, waters, and interests therein acquired in accordance with this subsection shall be administered as part of the area to which they are added, subject to the laws and regulations applicable thereto.

(2) For the purposes of clause (i) of paragraph (1), in all cases except the case of technical boundary revisions (resulting from such causes as survey error or changed road alignments), the authority of the Secretary under such clause (i) shall apply only if each of the following conditions is met:

   (A) The sum of the total acreage of lands, waters, and interests therein to be added to the area and the total such acreage to be deleted from the area is not more than 5 percent of the total Federal acreage authorized to be included in the area and is less than 200 acres in size.

585

(B) The acquisition, if any, is not a major Federal action significantly affecting the quality of the human environment, as determined by the Secretary.

(C) The sum of the total appraised value of the lands, waters, and interests therein to be added to the area and the total appraised value of the lands, waters, and interests therein to be deleted from the area does not exceed $750,000.

(D) The proposed boundary revision is not an element of a more comprehensive boundary modification proposal.

(E) The proposed boundary has been subject to a public review and comment period.

(F) The Director of the National Park Service obtains written consent for the boundary modification from all property owners whose lands, waters, or interests therein, or a portion of whose lands, waters, or interests therein, will be added to or deleted from the area by the boundary modification.

(G) The lands abut other Federal lands administered by the Director of the National Park Service.

Minor boundary revisions involving only deletions of acreage owned by the Federal Government and administered by the National Park Service may be made only by Act of Congress.

(Pub.L. 88–578, Title I, § 7, formerly § 6, Sept. 3, 1964, 78 Stat. 903; Pub.L. 90–401, § 1(c), July 15, 1968, 82 Stat. 355; renumbered § 7, Pub.L. 92–347, § 2, July 11, 1972, 86 Stat. 459, and amended Pub.L. 93–205, § 13(c), Dec. 28, 1973, 87 Stat. 902; Pub.L. 94–422, Title I, § 101(4), Sept. 28, 1976, 90 Stat. 1317; Pub.L. 95–42, § 1(3)–(5), June 10, 1977, 91 Stat. 210, 211; Pub.L. 96–203, § 2, Mar. 10, 1980, 94 Stat. 81; Pub.L. 99–645, Title III, § 302, Nov. 10, 1986, 100 Stat. 3587; Pub.L. 103–437, § 6(p)(3), Nov. 2, 1994, 108 Stat. 4586; Pub.L. 104–333, Div. I, Title VIII, § 814(b), (d)(2)(C), Nov. 12, 1996, 110 Stat. 4194, 4196; Pub.L. 106–176, Title I, §§ 120(b), 129, Mar. 10, 2000, 114 Stat. 28, 30.)

HISTORICAL AND STATUTORY NOTES

Revision Notes and Legislative Reports

  1964 Acts. Senate Report No. 1364 and Conference Report No. 1847, see 1964 U.S.Code Cong. and Adm.News, p. 3633.

  1968 Acts. Senate Report No. 1071 and Conference Report No. 1598, see 1968 U.S.Code Cong. and Adm.News, p. 2613.

  1972 Acts. House Report No. 92–742 and Conference Report No. 92–1164, see 1972 U.S.Code Cong. and Adm.News, p. 2823.

  1973 Acts. Senate Report No. 93–307 and Conference Report No. 93–740, see 1973 U.S.Code Cong. and Adm.News, p. 2989.

  1976 Acts. Senate Report No. 94–367 and House Conference Report No. 94–1468, see 1976 U.S.Code Cong. and Adm. News, p. 2442.

  1977 Acts. Senate Report No. 95–162, see 1977 U.S.Code Cong. and Adm.News, p. 322.

  1986 Acts. Senate Report No. 99–445, see 1986 U.S.Code Cong. and Adm.News, p. 6113.

  1994 Acts. House Report No. 103–779, see 1994 U.S. Code Cong. and Adm. News, p. 3639.

2000 Acts. House Report No. 106–17, see 2000 U.S. Code Cong. and Adm. News, p. 22.

References in Text

Effective date of this Act, referred to in subsec. (a)(1), means effective date of Pub.L. 88–578, which was Jan. 1, 1965. See Effective and Applicability Provisions note set out under section 460*l*–4 of this title.

The convening of the Ninety-fifth Congress, referred to in subsec. (a)(3), took place on Jan. 4, 1977.

The convening of the Ninety-sixth Congress, referred to in subsec. (a)(3), took place on Jan. 15, 1979.

Codifications

Amendment to section 814(b)(2)(G) of Pub.L. 104–333 by Pub.L. 106–176, Title I, § 129, Mar. 10, 2000, 114 Stat. 30, was executed to subsec. (c)(2)(G) of this section as the probable intent of Congress. There is no section 814(b)(2)(G) in Pub.L. 104–333, and section 814(b)(2)(B) of Pub.L. 104–333 amended subsec. (c) of this section by adding par. (2), including subpar. (G).

Amendments

2000 Amendments. Subsec. (c)(2)(C). Pub.L. 106–276, § 120(b)(1), struck out "lands, water, and interest therein" and inserted "lands, waters, and interests therein".

Subsec. (c)(2)(F). Pub.L. 106–176, § 120(b)(2), struck out "lands, water, or interests therein, or a portion of whose lands, water, or interests therein," and inserting "lands, waters, or interests therein, or a portion of whose lands, waters, or interests therein,".

Subsec. (c)(2)(G). Pub.L. 106–176, § 129, struck out "are adjacent to" and inserted "abut". See Codifications note above.

1996 Amendments. Subsec. (a)(3). Pub.L. 104–333, § 814(d)(2)(C), struck out provision relating to notice by Secretary to Committees before spending funds exceeding ceiling by at least $1 million.

Subsec. (c)(1). Pub.L. 104–333, § 814(b), designated existing provisions as par. (1), and as so designated substituted "Committee on Resources" for "Committee on Natural Resources" and struck out provision relating to authority applying only to boundaries established in or after 1965.

Subsec. (c)(2). Pub.L. 104–333, § 814(b)(2)(B), added par. (2).

1994 Amendments. Subsecs. (a)(3), (c). Pub.L. 103–437, § 6(p)(3), substituted "Committee on Natural Resources of the House of Representatives" for "Committee on Interior and Insular Affairs of the House of Representatives".

1986 Amendments. Subsec. (a)(1). Pub.L. 99–645, in provisions relating to the National Wildlife Refuge System, substituted "national wildlife refuge areas under section 742f(a)(4) of this title and wetlands acquired under section 3922 of this title" for "national wildlife refuge areas under section 742f(a)(5) of this title except migratory waterfowl areas which are authorized to be acquired by the Migratory Bird Conservation Act of 1929, as amended".

1980 Amendments. Subsec. (a)(3). Pub.L. 96–203, § 2(1), added provisions relating to applicability to national recreation areas.

Subsec. (c). Pub.L. 96–203, § 2(2), substituted "apply only to those boundaries established subsequent to January 1, 1965;" for "expire ten years from the date of enactment of the authorizing legislation establishing such boundaries;".

1977 Amendments. Subsec. (a)(3). Pub.L. 95–42, § 1(3), added par. (3).

Subsec. (b). Pub.L. 95–42, § 1(4), added proviso that appropriations from the fund may be used for preacquisition work in instances where authorization is imminent and where substantial monetary savings could be realized.

Subsec. (c). Pub.L. 95–42, § 1(5), added subsec. (c).

1976 Amendments. Subsec. (a)(1). Pub.L. 94–422 in paragraph designated "National Forest System" inserted "or purchased units approved by the National Forest Reservation Commission, subsequent to September 3, 1965, all of" following "January 1, 1965," and substituted "three thousand" for "five hundred" and incorporated provisions contained in paragraphs designated "Endangered Species and Threatened Species" and "Recreation at refuges" into paragraph designated "National Wildlife Refuge System" adding references to section 742f(a)(5) of this title, the Migratory Bird Conservation Act of 1929, and areas authorized for the National Wildlife Refuge System by specific Acts.

Subsec. (b). Pub.L. 94–422 reenacted subsec. (b) without change.

1973 Amendments. Subsec. (a)(1). Pub.L. 93–205 substituted reference to "Endangered species and threatened species" followed by a definition covering "lands, waters, or interests therein, the acquisition of which is authorized under section 1534(a) of this title, needed for the purpose of conserving endangered or threatened species of fish or wildlife or plants" for a reference to "Threatened species" followed by a definition covering "any national area which may be authorized for the preservation of species of fish or wildlife that are threatened with extinction".

1968 Amendments. Subsec. (a). Pub.L. 90–401 struck out "in substantially the same proportion as the number of visitor-days in areas and projects hereinafter described for which admission fees are charged under section 460l–5 of this title" following "purposes and subpurposes" in the material preceding par. (1).

Effective and Applicability Provisions
1973 Acts. Amendment by Pub.L. 93–205 effective Dec. 28, 1973, see section 16 of Pub.L. 93–205, set out as an Effective and Applicability Provisions note under section 1531 of this title.

1968 Acts. Amendment by Pub.L. 90–401 effective Dec. 31, 1971, with the revenues until Dec. 31, 1971, derived from the subsection (a) of section 460l–5 which was repealed by Pub.L. 90–401, to continue to be covered into the land and water conservation fund, see section 1(d) of Pub.L. 90–401, as amended by section 1 of Pub.L. 91–308, set out as a note under section 460l–5 of this title.

1965 Acts. Section effective Jan. 1, 1965, see note set out under section 460l–4 of this title.

Change of Name
Committee on Resources of House of Representatives changed to Committee on Natural Resources of House of Representatives by House Resolution No. 6, One Hundred Tenth Congress, Jan. 5, 2007.

CROSS REFERENCES

Acquisition of lands and waters,
Flaming Gorge National Recreation Area, see 16 USCA § 460v–7.
Ouachita National Forest, see 16 USCA § 460vv–18.
Siuslaw National Forest, see 16 USCA § 541e.
Boundary modification deemed boundary in existence as of January 1, 1965, for—
Hiawatha National Forest, modified to include Grand Island National Recreation Area, see 16 USCA § 460aaa–1.
Monongahela National Forest, modified to include Spruce Knob–Seneca Rocks National Recreation Area, see 16 USCA § 460p–2.
Mount Hood or Gifford Pinchot National Forests, modified to include Columbia River Gorge National Scenic Area, see 16 USCA § 544g.
Snoqualmie National Forest and Gifford Pinchot National Forest, see 16 USCA § 110c.
Inyo National Forest, boundary of as modified in 1984 to include Mono Basin Scenic Area to be treated for purposes of subsec. (a)(1) of this section as if it were the boundary on Jan. 1, 1964, see 16 USCA § 543a.
Manassas National Battlefield Park; changes in boundary prohibited, see 16 USCA § 429b.
Nonreimbursable project costs allocated to recreation and fish and wildlife enhancement, see 16 USCA § 460l–17.
Revisions in boundary of,
Everglades National Park, see 16 USCA § 410r–6.
Natchez National Historical Park, see 16 USCA § 410oo–1.
National Park of American Samoa, see 16 USCA § 410qq–1.
Pecos National Historical Park, see 16 USCA § 410rr–1.
San Francisco Maritime National Historical Park, see 16 USCA § 410nn.
Timucuan Ecological and Historic Preserve, see 16 USCA § 698n.
Statutory ceiling on appropriations,
Chattahoochee River National Recreation Area, see 16 USCA § 460ii–4.

Statutory ceiling on appropriations,—Cont'd
Voyageurs National Park, see 16 USCA § 160k.

LIBRARY REFERENCES

American Digest System
United States ⊗55.
Key Number System Topic No. 393.

Notes of Decisions

Acquisition restrictions 3
Condemnation authority 2
Congressional intent 1
Exchange restrictions 4

1. Congressional intent

The acquisition of private lands within the boundaries of national parks has long been favored by the Congress as reflected by its contingent appropriations for acquisition of such inholdings. U.S. v. 0.37 Acres of Land, More or Less in Flathead County, State of Mont., D.C.Mont.1976, 414 F.Supp. 470. Eminent Domain ⊗ 45

2. Condemnation authority

Authority to condemn private lands in Glacier National Park is provided by this chapter creating a fund out of which lands within exterior boundaries of national parks may be acquired. U.S. v. 0.37 Acres of Land, More or Less in Flathead County, State of Mont., D.C.Mont. 1976, 414 F.Supp. 470. Eminent Domain ⊗ 45

3. Acquisition restrictions

This section providing that appropriations from fund utilized to acquire lands within exterior boundaries of national parks shall not be used for purpose of

acquisition unless acquisition is otherwise authorized by law does no more than state that a congressional intent to acquire must be found before land and water conservation funds may be spent for acquisition. U.S. v. 0.37 Acres of Land, More or Less in Flathead County, State of Mont., D.C.Mont.1976, 414 F.Supp. 470. United States ⊗ 85

4. Exchange restrictions

Proposed exchange whereby National Park Service planned to exchange Park Service property, a restrictive height easement, on a parcel of land on waterfront in Georgetown section of District of Columbia, for, inter alia, public access easement on west bank of Rock Creek, violated express caveat of section of Land and Water Conservation Fund Act [16 U.S.C.A. § 460*l*–9(c)(ii)] that no Park Service property be exchanged to acquire land adjacent to a national park, since Rock Creek National Park property is immediately adjacent to proposed public access easement. Committee of 100 on Federal City v. Hodel, D.C.D.C.1985, 611 F.Supp. 547, reversed on other grounds 777 F.2d 711, 250 U.S.App.D.C. 52. United States ⊗ 55; United States ⊗ 58(3)

§ 460*l*–10. Availability of land and water conservation fund for publicity purposes; standardized temporary signing; standards and guidelines

Moneys derived from the sources listed in section 460*l*–5 of this title shall not be available for publicity purposes: *Provided, however,* That in each case where significant acquisition or development is initiated, appropriate standardized temporary signing shall be located on or near the affected site, to the extent feasible, so as to indicate the action taken is a product of funding made available through the Land and Water Conservation Fund. Such signing may indicate the per centum and dollar amounts financed by Federal and non-Federal funds, and that the source of the funding includes moneys derived from Outer Continental Shelf receipts. The Secretary shall prescribe standards and guidelines for the usage of such signing to assure consistency of design and application.

(Pub.L. 88–578, Title I, § 8, formerly § 7, Sept. 3, 1964, 78 Stat. 903, renumbered § 8, Pub.L. 92–347, § 2, July 11, 1972, 86 Stat. 459, and amended Pub.L. 94–422, Title I, § 101(5), Sept. 28, 1976, 90 Stat. 1318.)

HISTORICAL AND STATUTORY NOTES

Revision Notes and Legislative Reports
　1964 Acts. Senate Report No. 1364 and Conference Report No. 1847, see 1964 U.S.Code Cong. and Adm.News, p. 3633.

　1972 Acts. House Report No. 92–742 and Conference Report No. 92–1164, see 1972 U.S.Code Cong. and Adm.News, p. 2823.

　1976 Acts. Senate Report No. 94–367 and House Conference Report No. 94–1468, see 1976 U.S.Code Cong. and Adm.News, p. 2442.

Amendments
　1976 Amendments. Pub.L. 94–422 added proviso that temporary standardized signs shall be placed at or near any acquisition or development project undertaken through use of the fund and that the Secretary is to determine the standards and guidelines of such signing.

Effective and Applicability Provisions
　1965 Acts. Section effective Jan. 1, 1965, see note set out under section 460*l*–4 of this title.

LIBRARY REFERENCES

American Digest System
　United States ☞57.
　Key Number System Topic No. 393.

§ 460*l*–10a.　Contracts for acquisition of lands and waters

Not to exceed $30,000,000 of the money authorized to be appropriated from the fund by section 460*l*–6 of this title may be obligated by contract during each fiscal year for the acquisition of lands, waters, or interests therein within areas specified in section 460*l*–9(a)(1) of this title. Any such contract may be executed by the head of the department concerned, within limitations prescribed by the Secretary of the Interior. Any such contract so entered into shall be deemed a contractual obligation of the United States and shall be liquidated with money appropriated from the fund specifically for liquidation of such contract obligation. No contract may be entered into for the acquisition of property pursuant to this section unless such acquisition is otherwise authorized by Federal law.

(Pub.L. 88–578, Title I, § 9, formerly § 8, as added Pub.L. 90–401, § 4, July 15, 1968, 82 Stat. 355, and amended Pub.L. 91–308, § 3, July 7, 1970, 84 Stat. 410; renumbered § 9, Pub.L. 92–347, § 2, July 11, 1972, 86 Stat. 459, and amended Pub.L. 93–303, § 3, June 7, 1974, 88 Stat. 194.)

HISTORICAL AND STATUTORY NOTES

Revision Notes and Legislative Reports
1964 Acts. Senate Report No. 1364 and Conference Report No. 1847, see 1964 U.S. Code Cong. and Adm. News, p. 3633.

1968 Acts. Senate Report No. 1071 and Conference Report No. 1598, see 1968 U.S. Code Cong. and Adm. News, p. 2613.

1970 Acts. House Report No. 91–1000, see 1970 U.S. Code Cong. and Adm. News, p. 3402.

1972 Acts. House Report No. 92–742 and Conference Report No. 92–1164, see 1972 U.S. Code Cong. and Adm. News, p. 2823.

1974 Acts. House Report No. 93–1076, see 1974 U.S. Code Cong. and Adm. News, p. 3257.

Amendments
1974 Amendments. Pub.L. 93–303 substituted "section 7(a)(1)" for "section 6(a)(1)", which, for purposes of codification, is translated as "section 460*l*–9(a)(1)."

1970 Amendments. Pub.L. 91–308 substituted "fiscal year" for "of fiscal years 1969 and 1970".

Rescission of Contract Authority
Provisions rescinding contract authority provided for specific fiscal years by this section were contained in the following Appropriation Acts:

2009—Pub.L. 111–88, Div. A, Title I, Oct. 30, 2009, 123 Stat. 2912.

Pub.L. 111–8, Div. E, Title I, Mar. 11, 2009, 123 Stat. 709.

2007—Pub.L. 110–161, Div. F, Title I, Dec. 26, 2007, 121 Stat. 2106.

2006—Pub.L. 109–289, Div. B, Title II, § 20504, as added Pub.L. 110–5, § 2, Feb. 15, 2007, 121 Stat. 26.

Pub.L. 109–54, Title I, Aug. 2, 2005, 119 Stat. 509.

2005—Pub.L. 108–447, Div. E, Title I, Dec. 8, 2004, 118 Stat. 3050.

2004—Pub.L. 108–108, Title I, Nov. 10, 2003, 117 Stat. 1251.

2003—Pub.L. 108–7, Div. F, Title I, Feb. 20, 2003, 117 Stat. 226.

2002—Pub.L. 107–63, Title I, Nov. 5, 2001, 115 Stat. 425.

2001—Pub.L. 106–291, Title I, Oct. 11, 2000, 114 Stat. 930.

2000—Pub.L. 106–113, Div. B, § 1000(a)(3) [Title I], Nov. 29, 1999, 113 Stat. 1535, 1501A–143.

1999—Pub.L. 105–277, Div. A, § 101(e) [Title I], Oct. 21, 1998, 112 Stat. 2681–240.

1998—Pub.L. 105–83, Title I, Nov. 14, 1997, 111 Stat. 1550.

1997—Pub.L. 104–208, Div. A, Title I, § 101(d) [Title I], Sept. 30, 1996, 110 Stat. 3009–188.

1996—Pub.L. 104–134, Title I, § 101(c) [Title I], Apr. 26, 1996, 110 Stat.1321–163; renumbered Title I Pub.L. 104–140, § 1(a), May 2, 1996, 110 Stat. 1327.

1995—Pub.L. 103–332, Title I, Sept. 30, 1994, 108 Stat. 2506.

1994—Pub.L. 103–138, Title I, Nov. 11, 1993, 107 Stat. 1386.

1993—Pub.L. 102–381, Title I, Oct. 5, 1992, 106 Stat. 1383.

1992—Pub.L. 102–154, Title I, Nov. 13, 1991, 105 Stat. 998.

1991—Pub.L. 101–512, Title I, Nov. 5, 1990, 104 Stat. 1922.

1990—Pub.L. 101–121, Title I, Oct. 23, 1989, 103 Stat. 708.

1989—Pub.L. 100–446, Title I, Sept. 27, 1988, 102 Stat. 1781.

1988—Pub.L. 100–202, § 101(g) [Title I], Dec. 22, 1987, 101 Stat. 1329–222; Pub.L. 100–71, Title I, July 11, 1987, 101 Stat. 414.

1987—Pub.L. 99–349, Title I, c. VII, July 2, 1986, 100 Stat. 731.

CROSS REFERENCES

Contracts for providing interpretive shuttle transportation service in Harpers Ferry National Historical Park, see 16 USCA § 450bb–2.

§ 460*l*–10b. Contracts for options to acquire lands and waters in national park system

The Secretary of the Interior may enter into contracts for options to acquire lands, waters, or interests therein within the exterior boundaries of any area the acquisition of which is authorized by law for inclusion in the national park system. The minimum period of any such option shall be two years, and any sums expended for the purchase thereof shall be credited to the purchase price of said area. Not to exceed $500,000 of the sum authorized to be appropriated from the fund by section 460*l*–6 of this title may be expended by the Secretary in any one fiscal year for such options.

(Pub.L. 88–578, Title I, § 10, formerly § 9, as added Pub.L. 90–401, § 4, July 15, 1968, 82 Stat. 355, and renumbered Pub.L. 92–347, § 2, July 11, 1972, 86 Stat. 459.)

HISTORICAL AND STATUTORY NOTES

Revision Notes and Legislative Reports
    1964 Acts. Senate Report No. 1364 and Conference Report No. 1847, see 1964 U.S.Code Cong. and Adm.News, p. 3633.
    1968 Acts. Senate Report No. 1071 and Conference Report No. 1598, see

1968 U.S.Code Cong. and Adm.News, p. 2613.

    1972 Acts. House Report No. 92–742 and Conference Report No. 92–1164, see 1972 U.S.Code Cong. and Adm.News p. 2823.

§ 460*l*–10c. Repeal of provisions prohibiting collection of recreation fees or user charges

All other provisions of law that prohibit the collection of entrance, admission, or other recreation user fees or charges authorized by this part or that restrict the expenditure of funds if such fees or charges are collected are hereby also repealed: *Provided*, That no provision of any law or treaty which extends to any person or class of persons a right of free access to the shoreline of any reservoir or other body of water, or to hunting and fishing along or on such shoreline, shall be affected by this repealer.

(Pub.L. 88–578, Title I, § 11, formerly § 2(a) (in part), Sept. 3, 1964, 78 Stat. 899; renumbered § 10, Pub.L. 90–401, § 1(a), July 15, 1968, 82 Stat. 354; renumbered § 11, Pub.L. 92–347, § 2, July 11, 1972, 86 Stat. 459.)

HISTORICAL AND STATUTORY NOTES

Revision Notes and Legislative Reports

1964 Acts. Senate Report No. 1364 and Conference Report No. 1847, see 1964 U.S.Code Cong. and Adm.News, p. 3633.

1968 Acts. Senate Report No. 1071 and Conference Report No. 1598, see 1968 U.S.Code Cong. and Adm.News, p. 2613.

1972 Acts. House Report No. 92–742 and Conference Report No. 92–1164, see 1972 U.S.Code Cong. and Adm.News, p. 2823.

Codifications

In addition to the text set out in the section above, the original contained provisions directing the repeal of section 14 of this title and the deletion of '', without charge,'' in the sentence of section 460d of this title beginning ''The water areas of all such projects shall be open to public use generally''. The repeals and deletions called for by those provisions were executed as thus directed so that those provisions have been omitted from the text as executed.

Section formerly constituted the fourth paragraph of section 2(a) of Pub.L. 88–578 which was classified to section 460*l*–5(a) of this title. The paragraph was lifted out of section 2(a) and redesignated section 10 by section 1(a) of Pub.L. 90–401, which, for purposes of classification, resulted in the designation of the paragraph as section 460*l*–10c of this title [this section].

Effective and Applicability Provisions

1968 Acts. Transfer of the provisions of this section from section 460*l*–5(a) of this title to this section effective Dec. 31, 1971, see section 1(d) of Pub.L. 90–401, as amended by section 1 of Pub.L. 91–308, set out as an Effective Date of 1968 Amendments note under section 460*l*–5 of this title.

1965 Acts. Section effective Jan. 1, 1965, see note set out under section 460*l*–4 of this title.

§ 460*l*–10d. Review and report; submittal to Congressional committees; contents

Within one year of September 28, 1976, the Secretary is authorized and directed to submit to the Committees on Interior and Insular Affairs of the Senate and House of Representatives a comprehensive review and report on the needs, problems, and opportunities associated with urban recreation in highly populated regions, including the resources potentially available for meeting such needs. The report shall include site specific analyses and alternatives, in a selection of geographic environments representative of the Nation as a whole, including, but not limited to, information on needs, local capabilities for action, major site opportunities, trends, and a full range of options and alternatives as to possible solutions and courses of action designed to preserve remaining open space, ameliorate recreational deficiency, and enhance recreational opportunity for urban populations, together with an analysis of the capability of the Federal Government to provide urban-oriented environmental education programs (including, but not limited to, cultural programs in the arts and crafts) within such options. The Secretary shall consult with, and request the views of, the affected cities, counties, and States on the alternatives and courses of action identified.

(Pub.L. 88–578, Title I, § 12, as added Pub.L. 94–422, Title I, § 101(6), Sept. 28, 1976, 90 Stat. 1318.)

HISTORICAL AND STATUTORY NOTES

Revision Notes and Legislative Reports
  1964 Acts. Senate Report No. 1364 and Conference Report No. 1847, see 1964 U.S.Code Cong. and Adm.News, p. 3633.

  1976 Acts. Senate Report No. 94–367 and House Conference Report No. 94–1468, see 1976 U.S.Code Cong. and Adm.News, p. 2442.

Change of Name
  Committee on Interior and Insular Affairs of the House of Representatives changed to Committee on Natural Resources of the House of Representatives on Jan. 5, 1993, by House Resolution No. 5, One Hundred Third Congress. Committee on Natural Resources of House of Representatives treated as referring to Committee on Resources of House of Representatives by section 1(a) of Pub.L. 104–14, set out as a note preceding 2 U.S.C.A. § 21. Committee on Resources of House of Representatives changed to Committee on Natural Resources of House of Representatives by House Resolution No. 6, One Hundred Tenth Congress, Jan. 5, 2007.

LIBRARY REFERENCES

American Digest System
  United States ⬤⇒57.
  Key Number System Topic No. 393.

§ 460*l*–10e. Advisory Commission on water-based recreation

(a) Appointment; report

The President shall appoint an advisory commission to review the opportunities for enhanced opportunities for water-based recreation which shall submit a report to the President and to the Committee on Energy and Natural Resources of the Senate and to the Committee on Transportation and Infrastructure and the Committee on Resources of the House of Representatives within one year from November 12, 1996.

(b) Members

The members of the Commission shall include—

(1) the Secretary of the Interior, or his designee;

(2) the Secretary of the Army, or his designee;

(3) the Chairman of the Tennessee Valley Authority, or his designee;

(4) the Secretary of Agriculture, or his designee;

(5) a person nominated by the National Governor's Association; and

(6) four persons familiar with the interests of the recreation and tourism industry, conservation and recreation use, Indian tribes, and local governments, at least one of whom shall be familiar with the economics and financing of recreation-related infrastructure.

(c) Chairman; vacancies; administration

The President shall appoint one member to serve as Chairman. Any vacancy on the Commission shall be filled in the same manner as the original appointment. Members of the Commission shall serve without compensation but shall be reimbursed for travel, subsistence, and other necessary expenses incurred by them in the performance of their duties. The Secretary of the Interior shall provide all financial, administrative, and staffing requirements for the Commission, including office space, furnishings, and equipment. The heads of other Federal agencies are authorized, at the request of the Commission, to provide such information or personnel, to the extent permitted by law and within the limits of available funds, to the Commission as may be useful to accomplish the purposes of this section.

(d) Hearings

The Commission may hold such hearings, sit and act at such times and places, take such testimony, and receive such evidence as it deems advisable: *Provided,* That, to the maximum extent possible, the Commission shall use existing data and research. The Commission is authorized to use the United States mail in the same manner and upon the same conditions as other departments and agencies of the United States.

(e) Contents of report

The report shall review the extent of water-related recreation at Federal man-made lakes and reservoirs and shall develop alternatives to enhance the opportunities for such use by the public. In developing the report, the Commission shall—

> **(1)** review the extent to which recreation components identified in specific authorizations associated with individual Federal man-made lakes and reservoirs have been accomplished;
>
> **(2)** evaluate the feasibility of enhancing recreation opportunities at federally managed lakes and reservoirs under existing statutes;
>
> **(3)** consider legislative changes that would enhance recreation opportunities consistent with and subject to the achievement of the authorized purposes of Federal water projects; and
>
> **(4)** make recommendations on alternatives for enhanced recreation opportunities including, but not limited to, the establishment of a National Recreation Lake System under which specific lakes would receive national designation and which would be managed through innovative partnership-based agreements be-

tween Federal agencies, State and local units of government, and the private sector.

Any such alternatives shall be consistent with and subject to the authorized purposes for any man-made lakes and reservoirs and shall emphasize private sector initiatives in concert with State and local units of government.

(Pub.L. 88–578, Title I, § 13, as added Pub.L. 104–333, Div. I, Title X, § 1021(b), Nov. 12, 1996, 110 Stat. 4210, and amended Pub.L. 105–83, Title V, § 505, Nov. 14, 1997, 111 Stat. 1617; Pub.L. 106–176, Title I, §§ 123(b), Mar. 10, 2000, 114 Stat. 29.)

HISTORICAL AND STATUTORY NOTES

Revision Notes and Legislative Reports
1997 Acts. House Report No. 105–163 and Statement by President, see 1997 U.S. Code Cong. and Adm. News, p. 2183.

2000 Acts. House Report No. 106–17, see 2000 U.S. Code Cong. and Adm. News, p. 22.

Amendments
2000 Amendments. Subsec. (b)(6). Pub.L. 106–176, § 123(b)(1), struck out "recreation related infrastructure." and inserted "recreation-related infrastructure."

Subsec. (e). Pub.L. 106–176, § 123(b)(2)(A), (C), struck out "water related recreation" and inserted "water-related recreation" in the first sentence, and struck out "manmade lakes" each place it appeared and inserted "man-made lakes".

Subsec. (e)(2). Pub.L. 106–176, § 123(b)(2)(B), struck out "at federally-managed lakes" and inserted "at federally managed lakes".

1997 Amendments. Pub.L. 105–83, § 505, made technical amendments to ensure proper sequence, and therefore required no change in text.

Change of Name
Committee on Resources of House of Representatives changed to Committee on Natural Resources of House of Repre-

sentatives by House Resolution No. 6, One Hundred Tenth Congress, Jan. 5, 2007.

Recreational Opportunities at Federally Managed Man-made Lakes and Reservoirs
Pub.L. 104–333, Div. I, Title X, § 1021(a), Nov. 12, 1996, 110 Stat. 4210, as amended Pub.L. 106–176, Title I, § 123(a), Mar. 10, 2000, 114 Stat. 29, provided that: "The Congress finds that the Federal Government, under the authority of the Reclamation Act [June 7, 1902, c. 1093, 32 Stat. 388, as amended; see Tables for complete classification] and other statutes, has developed man-made lakes and reservoirs that have become a powerful magnet for diverse recreational activities and that such activities contribute to the well-being of families and individuals and the economic viability of local communities. The Congress further finds that in order to further the purposes of the Land and Water Conservation Fund, the President should appoint an advisory commission to review the current and anticipated demand for recreational opportunities at federally managed man-made lakes and reservoirs through creative partnerships involving Federal, State, and local governments and the private sector and to develop alternatives for enhanced recreational use of such facilities."

LIBRARY REFERENCES

American Digest System
United States ⊜35.
Key Number System Topic No. 393.

§ 460*l*–11.   Transfers to and from land and water conservation fund

(a) Motorboat fuel taxes from highway trust fund into conservation fund

There shall be set aside in the land and water conservation fund in the Treasury of the United States provided for in sections 460*l*–4 to 460*l*–6a and 460*l*–7 to 460*l*–10e of this title the amounts specified in section 9503(c)(4)(B) of Title 26 (relating to special motor fuels and gasoline used in motorboats).

(b) Refunds of gasoline taxes for certain nonhighway purposes or used by local transit systems and motorboat fuel taxes from conservation fund into general fund of Treasury

There shall be paid from time to time from the land and water conservation fund into the general fund of the Treasury amounts estimated by the Secretary of the Treasury as equivalent to—

(1) the amounts paid before October 1, 2012, under section 6421 of Title 26 (relating to amounts paid in respect of gasoline used for certain nonhighway purposes or by local transit systems) with respect to gasoline used after December 31, 1964, in motorboats, on the basis of claims filed for periods ending before October 1, 2011; and

(2) 80 percent of the floor stocks refunds made before October 1, 2012, under section 6412(a)(2) of Title 26 with respect to gasoline to be used in motorboats.

(Pub.L. 88–578, Title II, § 201, Sept. 3, 1964, 78 Stat. 904; Pub.L. 91–605, Title III, § 302, Dec. 31, 1970, 84 Stat. 1743; Pub.L. 94–273, § 3(4), Apr. 21, 1976, 90 Stat. 376; Pub.L. 94–280, Title III, § 302, May 5, 1976, 90 Stat. 456; Pub.L. 95–599, Title V, § 503(b), Nov. 6, 1978, 92 Stat. 2757; Pub.L. 97–424, Title V, § 531(c), Jan. 6, 1983, 96 Stat. 2191; Pub.L. 99–514, § 2, Title XVIII, § 1875(e), Oct. 22, 1986, 100 Stat. 2095, 2897; Pub.L. 100–17, Title V, § 503(c), Apr. 2, 1987, 101 Stat. 258; Pub.L. 101–508, Title XI, § 11211(g)(2), Nov. 5, 1990, 104 Stat. 1388–427; Pub.L. 102–240, Title VIII, § 8002(d)(2)(B), Dec. 18, 1991, 105 Stat. 2204; Pub.L. 105–178, Title IX, § 9002(c)(2)(B), June 9, 1998, 112 Stat. 500; Pub.L. 109–59, Title XI, § 11101(c)(2)(B), Aug. 10, 2005, 119 Stat. 1944.)

HISTORICAL AND STATUTORY NOTES

Revision Notes and Legislative Reports
1964 Acts. Senate Report No. 1364 and Conference Report No. 1847, see 1964 U.S.Code Cong. and Adm.News, p. 3633.

1970 Acts. House Report No. 91–1554 and Conference Report No. 91–1780, see 1970 U.S.Code Cong. and Adm.News p. 5392.

1976 Acts. House Report No. 94–1000, see 1976 U.S.Code Cong. and Adm.News, p. 690.

House Report No. 94–716 and House Conference Report No. 94–1017, see 1976 U.S.Code Cong. and Adm.News, p. 798.

1978 Acts. House Report No. 95–1485 and House Conference Report No.

95–1797, see 1978 U.S.Code Cong. and Adm.News, p. 6575.

1983 Acts. House Report No. 97–555 and House Conference Report 97–987, see 1982 U.S.Code Cong. and Adm.News, p. 3639.

1986 Acts. House Conference Report No. 99–841 and Statement by President, see 1986 U.S.Code Cong. and Adm.News, p. 4075.

1987 Acts. Senate Report No. 100–4 and House Conference Report No. 100–27, see 1987 U.S.Code Cong. and Adm.News, p. 66.

1990 Acts. House Report No. 101–881, House Conference Report No. 101–964, and President's Signing Statement, see 1990 U.S.Code Cong. and Adm.News, p. 2017.

1991 Acts. House Report No. 102–171 (I & II) and House Conference Report No. 102–404, see 1991 U.S.Code Cong. and Adm.News, p. 1526.

1998 Acts. House Conference Report No. 105–550 and Statement by President, see 1998 U.S. Code Cong. and Adm. News, p. 64.

2005 Acts. House Conference Report No. 109–203, see 2005 U.S. Code Cong. and Adm. News, p. 452.

Statement by President, see 2005 U.S. Code Cong. and Adm. News, p. S24.

Amendments
2005 Amendments. Subsec. (b)(1). Pub.L. 109–59, § 11101(c)(2)(B)(i), (ii), struck out "2003" and inserted "2011", and struck out "2004" and inserted "2012".

Subsec. (b)(2). Pub.L. 109–59, § 11101(c)(2)(B)(ii), struck out "2004" and inserted "2012".

1998 Amendments. Subsec. (b). Pub.L. 105–178, § 9002(c)(2)(B), substituted "2003" for "1997" in par. (1) and substituted "2004" for "1998" each place it appeared.

1991 Amendments. Subsec. (b). Pub.L. 102–240 substituted reference to 1997 for reference to 1995 and reference to 1998 for reference to 1996 wherever appearing.

1990 Amendments. Subsec. (b). Pub.L. 101–508 substituted "1995" for "1993" in par. (1) and "1996" for "1994" in pars. (1) and (2).

1987 Amendments. Subsec. (b). Pub.L. 100–17 substituted "1994" for "1989" wherever appearing, and substituted "1993" for "1988" in cl. (1).

1986 Amendments. Subsec. (a). Pub.L. 99–514, § 2, substituted "Internal Revenue Code of 1986" for "Internal Revenue Code of 1954", which for purposes of codification was translated as "Title 26" thus requiring no change in text.

Pub.L. 99–514, § 1875(e), substituted "section 9503(c)(4)(B) of Title 26" for "section 209(f)(5) of the Highway Revenue Act of 1956".

Subsec. (b)(1). Pub.L. 99–514, § 2, substituted "Internal Revenue Code of 1986" for "Internal Revenue Code of 1954", which for purposes of codification was translated as "Title 26" thus requiring no change in text.

1983 Amendments. Subsec. (b). Pub.L. 97–424, § 531(c)(1), substituted "1989" for "1985" wherever appearing.

Subsec. (b)(1). Pub.L. 97–424, § 531(c)(2), substituted "1988" for "1984".

1978 Amendments. Subsec. (b). Pub.L. 95–599 substituted "1984" for "1979" and "1985" for "1980" wherever appearing.

1976 Amendments. Subsec. (b). Pub.L. 94–280 substituted "1979" for "1977" and "1980" for "1978" in two places.

Pub.L. 94–273 substituted "October" for "July" wherever appearing.

1970 Amendments. Subsec. (b). Pub.L. 91–605 substituted "1977" for "1972" and substituted in two places "1978" for "1973".

Effective and Applicability Provisions
2005 Acts. Amendments by Pub.L. 109–59, § 11101, effective Aug. 10, 2005, see Pub.L. 109–59, § 11101(e), set out as a note under 26 U.S.C.A. § 4041.

1986 Acts. Amendment by sections 1801 to 1880 of Pub.L. 99–514 effective as if included in the provision of the Tax Reform Act of 1984, Pub.L. 98–369, to which such amendment relates, except as otherwise provided, see section 1881 of Pub.L. 99–514, set out as a note under section 48 of Title 26, Internal Revenue Code.

1983 Acts. Amendment by section 531(c) of Pub.L. 97–424, amending subsec. (b) of this section, effective Jan. 1,

1983, see section 531(e) of Pub.L. 97–424, set out as an Effective Date; Savings Provision note under section 9503 of Title 26, Internal Revenue Code.

1965 Acts. Section effective Jan. 1, 1965, see note set out under section 460*l*–4 of this title.

Plan Amendments Not Required Until January 1, 1989

For provisions directing that if any amendments made by subtitle A or subtitle C of Title XI [sections 1101–1147 and 1171–1177] of Title XVIII [sections 1800–1899A] of Pub.L. 99–514 require an amendment to any plan, such plan amendment shall not be required to be made before the first plan year beginning on or after Jan. 1, 1989, see section 1140 of Pub.L. 99–514, as amended, set out as a note under section 401 of Title 26, Internal Revenue Code.

CROSS REFERENCES

Revenues and collections covered into land and water conservation fund, see 16 USCA § 460*l*–5.

LIBRARY REFERENCES

American Digest System
United States ⬒81.
Key Number System Topic No. 393.

Research References

ALR Library
32 ALR, Fed. 332, Validity, Construction, and Application of Endangered Species Act of 1973 (16 U.S.C.A. §§ 1531-1543).

Part C—Water Resources Projects

CROSS REFERENCES

Colorado River Basin projects; conservation and development of fish and wildlife resources and enhancement of recreation opportunities, see 43 USCA § 1527.
Operation and maintenance of recreational facilities at water resources projects, see 33 USCA § 2297.
Reimbursement of costs allocated to recreation and fish and wildlife enhancement—
Lower Colorado River Basin Development Fund, see 43 USCA § 1541.
Modification of structure of dams, see 43 USCA § 508.

§ 460*l*–12. Recreation and fish and wildlife benefits of Federal multiple-purpose water resources projects; Congressional declaration of policy

It is the policy of the Congress and the intent of this part that (a) in investigating and planning any Federal navigation, flood control, reclamation, hydroelectric, or multiple-purpose water resource project, full consideration shall be given to the opportunities, if any, which the project affords for outdoor recreation and for fish and wildlife enhancement and that, wherever any such project can reasonably serve either or both of these purposes consistently with the provisions of this part, it shall be constructed, operated, and maintained accordingly; (b) planning with respect to the development of the recreation potential of any such project shall be based on the coordination of the recreational use of the project area with the use of existing and planned Federal, State, or local public recreation developments; and (c) project construction agencies shall encourage non-Federal public bodies to administer project land and water areas for recreation and fish and wildlife enhancement purposes and operate, maintain, and replace facilities provided for those purposes unless such areas or facilities are included or proposed for inclusion within a national recreation area, or are appropriate for administration by a Federal agency as a part of the national forest system, as a part of the public lands classified for retention in Federal ownership, or in connection with an authorized Federal program for the conservation and development of fish and wildlife.

(Pub.L. 89–72, § 1, July 9, 1965, 79 Stat. 213.)

HISTORICAL AND STATUTORY NOTES

Revision Notes and Legislative Reports
  1965 Acts. House Report No. 254 and Conference Report No. 538, see 1965 U.S.Code Cong. and Adm.News, p. 1864.

References in Text
  This part, referred to in text, was, in the original, "this Act," meaning Pub.L. 89–72, which, in addition to enacting sections 460*l*–12 to 460*l*–21 of this title also

amended sections 460*l*–5(a) and 662(d) of this title.

Short Title
  1965 Acts. Pub.L. 89–72, § 12, July 9, 1965, 79 Stat. 218, provided: "This Act [enacting sections 460*l*–12 to 460*l*–21 of this title and amending sections 460*l*–5(a) and 662(d) of this title], may be cited as the 'Federal Water Project Recreation Act'."

LIBRARY REFERENCES

American Digest System
  Fish ☞8.
  Game ☞3.5.
  Key Number System Topic Nos. 176, 187.

Notes of Decisions

Construction with other laws 1
Water storage 2

1. Construction with other laws

  Army Corps of Engineers was not illegally constructing the Meramec Park Reservoir, on ground that it had not requested and received assurances from the State of Missouri that it would share in the cost of recreational development, as required by the Federal Water Project Recreation Act, sections 460*l*–12 to 460*l*–21 of this title, since the reservoir, which was first authorized by the Flood Control Act of 1938, Act June 28, 1938, c. 795, 52 Stat. 1215, is not covered by the

Federal Water Project Recreation Act. Sierra Club v. Froehlke, E.D.Mo.1975, 392 F.Supp. 130, affirmed 534 F.2d 1289. Water Law ☞ 2869

2. Water storage

  This section authorizing consideration of opportunities for recreation and wildlife enhancement, assuming it applied to waters in the San Juan-Chama Project, did not suggest that specific limitations on use of project water should be ignored in favor of recreation or wildlife and did not authorize storage solely for recreational purposes. Jicarilla Apache Tribe v. U.S., C.A.10 (N.M.) 1981, 657 F.2d 1126. Water Law ☞ 2351

§ 460*l*–13.   Non-Federal administration of project land and water areas

(a) Allocation of costs

If, before authorization of a project, non-Federal public bodies indicate their intent in writing to agree to administer project land and water areas for recreation or fish and wildlife enhancement or for both of these purposes pursuant to the plan for the development of the project approved by the head of the agency having administrative jurisdiction over it and to bear not less than one-half the separable costs of the project allocated to recreation, and to bear one-quarter of such costs allocated to fish and wildlife enhancement, and not less than one–half the costs of operation, maintenance, and replacement incurred therefor—

    (1) the benefits of the project to said purpose or purposes shall be taken into account in determining the economic benefits of the project;

    (2) costs shall be allocated to said purpose or purposes and to other purposes in a manner which will insure that all project purposes share equitably in the advantages of multiple-purpose construction: *Provided*, That the costs allocated to recreation or fish and wildlife enhancement shall not exceed the lesser of the benefits from those functions or the costs of providing recreation or fish and wildlife enhancement benefits or reasonably equivalent use and location by the least costly alternative means; and

    (3) not more than one-half the separable costs of the project allocated to recreation and exactly three-quarters of such costs allocated to fish and wildlife enhancement and all the joint costs of the project allocated to recreation and fish and wildlife enhancement shall be borne by the United States and be nonreimbursable.

Projects authorized during the calendar year 1965 may include recreation and fish and wildlife enhancement on the foregoing basis without the required indication of intent. Execution of an agreement as aforesaid shall be a prerequisite to commencement of construction of any project to which this subsection is applicable.

(b) Non–Federal share of costs

The non-Federal share of the separable costs of the project allocated to recreation and fish and wildlife enhancement shall be borne by non-Federal interests, under either or both of the following methods as may be determined appropriate by the head of the Federal agency having jurisdiction over the project: (1) payment, or provision of lands, interests therein, or facilities for the project; or (2) repayment, with interest at a rate comparable to that for other interest-bearing functions of Federal water resource projects, within fifty years of first use of project recreation or fish and wildlife enhancement facilities: *Provided,* That the source of repayment may be limited to entrance and user fees or charges collected at the project by non-Federal interests if the fee schedule and the portion of fees dedicated to repayment are established on a basis calculated to achieve repayment as aforesaid and are made subject to review and renegotiation at intervals of not more than five years.

(Pub.L. 89–72, § 2, July 9, 1965, 79 Stat. 214; Pub.L. 93–251, Title I, § 77(a)(1), (2), Mar. 7, 1974, 88 Stat. 33; Pub.L. 102–575, Title XXVIII, § 2804(a), Oct. 30, 1992, 106 Stat. 4691.)

HISTORICAL AND STATUTORY NOTES

Revision Notes and Legislative Reports

1965 Acts. House Report No. 254 and Conference Report No. 538, see 1965 U.S.Code Cong. and Adm.News, p. 1864.

1992 Acts. Senate Report No. 102–267 and House Conference Report No. 102–1016, see 1992 U.S. Code Cong. and Adm. News, p. 4041.

Amendments

1992 Amendments. Subsec. (a). Pub.L. 102–575, Title XXVIII, § 2804(a), in matter preceding par. (1), directed non–Federal public bodies to agree in writing to bear not less than one–half the costs of operation, maintenance, and replacement of a project, rather than all the costs of operation, maintenance, and replacement of a project.

1974 Amendments. Subsec. (a). Pub.L. 93–251 substituted in text preceding item (1) "separable costs of the project allocated to recreation, and to bear one-quarter of such costs allocated to fish and wildlife enhancement" for "separable costs of the project allocated to either or both of said purposes, as the case may be" and in item (3) "separable costs of the project allocated to recreation and exactly three-quarters of such costs allocated to fish and wildlife enhancement" for "separable costs", respectively.

Effective and Applicability Provisions

1974 Acts. Pub.L. 93–251, Title I, § 77(b), Mar. 7, 1974, 88 Stat. 33, provided that: "The amendments made by this section [to subsec. (a) of this section and section 460*l*–14(b)(1) of this title] shall apply to all projects the construction of which is not substantially completed on the date of enactment of this Act [Mar. 7, 1974]."

Cost Sharing Requirements

Pub.L. 93–251, Title I, § 77(c), Mar. 7, 1974, 88 Stat. 33, provided that: "In the case of any project (1) authorized subject to specific cost-sharing requirements which were based on the same percentages as those established in the Federal Water Project Recreation Act [section 460*l*–12 et seq. of this title], and (2) construction of which is not substantially completed on the date of enactment of this Act [Mar. 7, 1974], the cost-sharing requirements for such project shall be the same percentages as are established by the amendments made by subsection (a) of this section [to subsec. (a) of this section and section 460*l*–14(b)(1) of this title] for projects which are subject to the Federal Water Project Recreation Act [section 460*l*–12 et seq. of this title]."

LIBRARY REFERENCES

American Digest System
    United States ☞57.
    Key Number System Topic No. 393.

§ 460*l*–14. Facilities or project modifications to be provided without written indication of intent

(a) Other project purposes as justification; public health and safety requirement of minimum facilities at access points; basis for calculation of benefits; nonreimbursable costs

No facilities or project modifications which will furnish recreation or fish and wildlife enhancement benefits shall be provided in the absence of the indication of intent with respect thereto specified in section 460*l*–13(a) of this title unless (1) such facilities or modifications serve other project purposes and are justified thereby without regard to such incidental recreation or fish and wildlife enhancement benefits as they may have or (2) they are minimum facilities which are required for the public health and safety and are located at access points provided by roads existing at the time of project construction or constructed for the administration and management of the project. Calculation of the recreation and fish and wildlife enhancement benefits in any such case shall be based on the number of visitor-days anticipated in the absence of recreation and fish and wildlife enhancement facilities or modifications except as hereinbefore provided and on the value per visitor-day of the project without such facilities or modifications. Project costs allocated to recreation and fish and wildlife enhancement on this basis shall be nonreimbursable.

(b) Preservation of recreation and fish and wildlife enhancement potential; execution of agreements within ten year period; disposition of lands in absence of such agreements, prohibition against uses conflicting with project purposes, and preference to uses promoting and not detracting from such potential

Notwithstanding the absence of an indication of intent as specified in section 460*l*–13(a) of this title, lands may be provided in connection with project construction to preserve the recreation and fish and wildlife enhancement potential of the project:

(1) If non–Federal public bodies execute an agreement after initial operation of the project (which agreement shall provide that the non–Federal public bodies will administer project land and water areas for recreation or fish and wildlife enhancement or both pursuant to the plan for the development of the project approved by the head of the agency having administrative jurisdiction over it and will bear not less than one-half the costs of lands, facilities, and project modifications provided for recreation, and will bear one-quarter of such costs for fish and wildlife enhancement, and not less than one-half the costs of planning studies, and the costs of operation, maintenance, and

replacement attributable thereto) the remainder of the costs of lands, facilities, and project modifications provided pursuant to this paragraph shall be nonreimbursable. Such agreement and subsequent development, however, shall not be the basis for any reallocation of joint costs of the project to recreation or fish and wildlife enhancement.

(2) If, within ten years after initial operation of the project, there is not an executed agreement as specified in paragraph (1) of this subsection, the head of the agency having jurisdiction over the project may utilize the lands for any lawful purpose within the jurisdiction of his agency, or may offer the land for sale to its immediate prior owner or his immediate heirs at its appraised fair market value as approved by the head of the agency at the time of offer or, if a firm agreement by said owner or his immediate heirs is not executed within ninety days of the date of the offer, may transfer custody of the lands to another Federal agency for use for any lawful purpose within the jurisdiction of that agency, or may lease the lands to a non–Federal public body, or may transfer the lands to the Administrator of General Services for disposition in accordance with the surplus property laws of the United States. In no case shall the lands be used or made available for use for any purpose in conflict with the purposes for which the project was constructed, and in every case except that of an offer to purchase made, as hereinbefore provided, by the prior owner or his heirs preference shall be given to uses which will preserve and promote the recreation and fish and wildlife enhancement potential of the project or, in the absence thereof, will not detract from that potential.

(c) Expansion or modification of existing facilities

(1) Any recreation facility constructed under this part may be expanded or modified if—

    (A) the facility is inadequate to meet recreational demands; and

    (B) a non–Federal public body executes an agreement which provides that such public body—

        (i) will administer the expanded or modified facilities pursuant to a plan for development for the project that is approved by the agency with administrative jurisdiction over the project; and

        (ii) will bear not less than one-half of the planning and capital costs of such expansion or modification and not less than one-half of the costs of the operation, maintenance, and replacement attributable to the expansion of the facility.

(2) The Federal share of the cost of expanding or modifying a recreational facility described in paragraph (1) may not exceed 50 percent of the total cost of expanding or modifying the facility.

(Pub.L. 89–72, § 3, July 9, 1965, 79 Stat. 214; Pub.L. 93–251, Title I, § 77(a)(3), Mar. 7, 1974, 88 Stat. 33; Pub.L. 102–575, Title XXVIII, § 2804(b), (d), Oct. 30, 1992, 106 Stat. 4691.)

HISTORICAL AND STATUTORY NOTES

Revision Notes and Legislative Reports
   1965 Acts. House Report No. 254 and Conference Report No. 538, see 1965 U.S.Code Cong. and Adm.News, p. 1864.

   1992 Acts. Senate Report No. 102–267 and House Conference Report No. 102–1016, see 1992 U.S. Code Cong. and Adm. News, p. 4041.

References in Text
   The surplus property laws of the United States, referred to in subsec. (b)(2), are principally classified to chapter 1 of Title 40, 40 U.S.C.A. § 101 et seq.

   This part, referred to in subsec. (c)(1), was, in the original, "this Act" meaning Pub.L. 89–72, which, in addition to enacting sections 460*l*–12 to 460*l*–21 of this title also amended sections 460*l*–5(a) and 662(d) of this title.

Amendments
   1992 Amendments. Subsec. (b)(1). Pub.L. 102–575, Title XXVIII, § 2804(b), substituted provisions relating to non–Federal public bodies executing an agreement after initial operation of project which shall include provisions for

such bodies to bear not less than one-half the costs of planning studies, and the costs of operation, maintenance, and re-placement attributable thereto, for provi-sions relating to such bodies executing an agreement within ten years after ini-tial operation of project which shall in-clude provisions for such bodies to bear all costs of operation, maintenance, and replacement attributable thereto.

   Subsec. (c).   Pub.L. 102–575, Title XXVIII, § 2804(d), added subsec. (c).

   1974 Amendments. Subsec. (b)(1). Pub.L. 93–251 substituted "modifications provided for recreation, and will bear one-quarter of such costs for fish and wildlife enhancement" for "modifications provided for either or both of those pur-poses, as the case may be".

Effective and Applicability Provisions
   1974 Acts. Amendment by Pub.L. 93–251 applicable to all projects the con-struction of which was not substantially completed on Mar. 7, 1974, see section 77(b) of Pub.L. 93–251, set out as a note under section 460*l*–13 of this title.

LIBRARY REFERENCES

American Digest System
   United States ☞57.
   Key Number System Topic No. 393.

Notes of Decisions

1.   Retroactive effect
   Federal Water Project Recreation Act (FWPRA) provision, that land acquired by condemnation for purposes of water pro-ject could be reoffered to original owner, did not apply to project commenced be-fore its effective date.   Uithoven v. Stone, N.D.Miss.1995, 906 F.Supp. 369, af-firmed 96 F.3d 1445, certiorari denied

117 S.Ct. 948, 519 U.S. 1111, 136 L.Ed.2d 836.   Eminent Domain ☞ 27

2.   Construction with other laws
   Government could use condemned land for wildlife mitigation purposes without violating provision of Federal Water Pro-ject Recreation Act (FWPRA) allowing for utilization of land for any "lawful pur-pose," even though it was claimed that such use violated Water Resources Devel-opment Act ((WRDA); WRDA prohibited using property condemned "under this paragraph" for wildlife mitigation, but

did not prevent use of property previously condemned via other legislation for that purpose. Uithoven v. Stone, N.D.Miss. 1995, 906 F.Supp. 369, affirmed 96 F.3d

1445, certiorari denied 117 S.Ct. 948, 519 U.S. 1111, 136 L.Ed.2d 836. Eminent Domain ⚭ 17; Eminent Domain ⚭ 27

§ 460*l*–15. Lease of facilities and lands to non–Federal public bodies

At projects, the construction of which has commenced or been completed as of July 9, 1965, where non–Federal public bodies agree to administer project land and water areas for recreation and fish and wildlife enhancement purposes and to bear the [1] not less than one-half the costs of operation, maintenance, and replacement of existing facilities serving those purposes, such facilities and appropriate project lands may be leased to non–Federal public bodies.

(Pub.L. 89–72, § 4, July 9, 1965, 79 Stat. 215; Pub.L. 102–575, Title XXVIII, § 2804(c), Oct. 30, 1992, 106 Stat. 4691.)

[1] So in original. The word "the" is probably not necessary.

HISTORICAL AND STATUTORY NOTES

Revision Notes and Legislative Reports
  1965 Acts. House Report No. 254 and Conference Report No. 538, see 1965 U.S.Code Cong. and Adm.News, p. 1864.

  1992 Acts. Senate Report No. 102–267 and House Conference Report No. 102–1016, see 1992 U.S. Code Cong. and Adm. News, p. 4041.

Amendments
  1992 Amendments. Pub.L. 102–575, Title XXVIII, § 2804(c), substituted "bear the [sic] not less than one-half the costs of operation, maintenance, and replacement of existing facilities" for "bear the costs of operation, maintenance, and replacement of existing facilities".

LIBRARY REFERENCES

American Digest System
  United States ⚭57.
  Key Number System Topic No. 393.

§ 460*l*–16. Postauthorization development of projects without allocation or reallocation of costs

Nothing herein shall be construed as preventing or discouraging postauthorization development of any project for recreation or fish and wildlife enhancement or both by non-Federal public bodies pursuant to agreement with the head of the Federal agency having jurisdiction over the project. Such development shall not be the basis for any allocation or reallocation of project costs to recreation or fish and wildlife enhancement.

(Pub.L. 89–72, § 5, July 9, 1965, 79 Stat. 215.)

HISTORICAL AND STATUTORY NOTES

Revision Notes and Legislative Reports
1965 Acts. House Report No. 254 and
Conference Report No. 538, see 1965
U.S.Code Cong. and Adm.News, p. 1864.

LIBRARY REFERENCES

American Digest System
   United States ☞57.
   Key Number System Topic No. 393.

§ 460*l*–17. Miscellaneous provisions

(a) Project reports; outdoor recreation views; conformity to State comprehensive plan

The views of the Secretary of the Interior developed in accordance with section 460*l*–2 of this title, with respect to the outdoor recreation aspects shall be set forth in any report of any project or appropriate unit thereof within the purview of this part. Such views shall include a report on the extent to which the proposed recreation and fish and wildlife development conforms to and is in accord with the State comprehensive plan developed pursuant to section 460*l*–8(d) of this title.

(b) Omitted

(c) Migratory waterfowl refuges at Federal projects; expenditure limitation for acquisition of lands

Expenditures for lands or interests in lands hereafter acquired by project construction agencies for the establishment of migratory waterfowl refuges recommended by the Secretary of the Interior at Federal water resource projects, when such lands or interests in lands would not have been acquired but for the establishment of a migratory waterfowl refuge at the project, shall not exceed $28,000,000: *Provided*, That the aforementioned expenditure limitation in this subsection shall not apply to the costs of mitigating damages to migratory waterfowl caused by such water resource project.

(d) Nonapplication to certain projects

This part shall not apply to the Tennessee Valley Authority, but the Authority is authorized to recognize and provide for recreational and other public uses at any dams and reservoirs heretofore or hereafter constructed in a manner consistent with the promotion of navigation, flood control, and the generation of electrical energy, as otherwise required by law, nor to projects constructed under authority of the Small Reclamation Projects Act, as amended [43 U.S.C.A. § 422a et seq.], or under authority of the Watershed Protection and Flood Prevention Act, as amended [16 U.S.C.A. § 1001 et seq.].

(e) Nonapplication to certain other projects

Sections 460*l*–13, 460*l*–14, 460*l*–15, and 460*l*–16 of this title shall not apply to nonreservoir local flood control projects, beach erosion control projects, small boat harbor projects, hurricane protection projects, or to project areas or facilities authorized by law for inclusion within a national recreation area or appropriate for administration by a Federal agency as a part of the national forest system, as a part of the public lands classified for retention in Federal ownership, or in connection with an authorized Federal program for the conservation and development of fish and wildlife.

(f) Interpretation of "nonreimbursable"

As used in this part, the term "nonreimbursable" shall not be construed to prohibit the imposition of entrance, admission, and other recreation user fees or charges.

(g) Nonapplication of section 460*l*–9(a)(2) to nonreimbursable costs of the United States

Section 460*l*–9(a)(2) of this title shall not apply to costs allocated to recreation and fish and wildlife enhancement which are borne by the United States as a nonreimbursable project cost pursuant to section 460*l*–13(a) or section 460*l*–14(b)(1) of this title.

(h) Deposits in Treasury as miscellaneous receipts; deposits of revenue from conveyance of certain lands in Land and Water Conservation Fund

All payments and repayment by non–Federal public bodies under the provisions of this part shall be deposited in the Treasury as miscellaneous receipts, and revenue from the conveyance by deed, lease, or otherwise, of lands under section 460*l*–14(b)(2) of this title shall be deposited in the Land and Water Conservation Fund.

(Pub.L. 89–72, § 6, July 9, 1965, 79 Stat. 216; Pub.L. 94–576, Oct. 21, 1976, 90 Stat. 2728.)

HISTORICAL AND STATUTORY NOTES

Revision Notes and Legislative Reports
 1965 Acts. House Report No. 254 and Conference Report No. 538, see 1965 U.S.Code Cong. and Adm.News, p. 1864.
 1976 Acts. Senate Report No. 94–1353, see 1976 U.S.Code Cong. and Adm.News, p. 6160.

References in Text
 This part, referred to in text, was, in the original, this Act, meaning Pub.L.

89–72, which, in addition to enacting sections 460*l*–12 to 460*l*–21 of this title, also amended sections 460*l*–5(a) and 662(d) of this title.

 The Small Reclamation Projects Act, as amended, referred to in subsec. (d), is classified to sections 422a et seq. of Title 43, Public Lands. For complete classification of this Act to the Code, see section 422k of Title 43 and Tables.

The Watershed Protection and Flood Prevention Act, as amended, referred to in subsec. (d), is Act Aug. 4, 1954, c. 656, 68 Stat. 666, as amended, which is classified generally to chapter 18 (section 1001 et seq.) of this title. For complete classification of this Act to the Code, see Short Title note set out under section 1001 of this title and Tables.

Codifications
Subsec. (b) section 6 of Pub.L. 89–72 amended section 662(d) of this title.

Amendments
1976 Amendments. Subsec. (d). Pub.L. 94–576 authorized recreational and other public uses at dams and reservoirs consistent with promotion of navigation, flood control, and generation of electrical energy.

LIBRARY REFERENCES

American Digest System
United States ⊕57.
Key Number System Topic No. 393.

§ 460l–18. Authority of Secretary of the Interior

(a) Provision of facilities, acquisition of lands, and provision for public use and enjoyment of project lands, facilities, and water areas in coordination with other project purposes; execution of agreements before providing lands, facilities, and project modifications

The Secretary is authorized, in conjunction with any reservoir heretofore constructed by him pursuant to the Federal reclamation laws or any reservoir which is otherwise under his control, except reservoirs within national wildlife refuges, to investigate, plan, construct, operate and maintain, or otherwise provide for public outdoor recreation and fish and wildlife enhancement facilities, to acquire or otherwise make available such adjacent lands or interests therein as are necessary for public outdoor recreation or fish and wildlife use, and to provide for public use and enjoyment of project lands, facilities, and water areas in a manner coordinated with the other project purposes.   Lands, facilities and project modifications for the purposes of this subsection may be provided only after an agreement in accordance with subsection (b) or (c) of section 460l–14 of this title has been executed.

(b) Agreements with government agencies to promote development and operation of lands or facilities for recreation and fish and wildlife enhancement purposes

The Secretary of the Interior is authorized to enter into agreements with Federal agencies or State or local public bodies for the administration of project land and water areas and the operation, maintenance, and replacement of facilities and to transfer project lands or facilities to Federal agencies or State or local public bodies by lease agreement or exchange upon such terms and conditions as will best promote the development and operation of such lands or facilities in the public interest for recreation and fish and wildlife enhancement purposes.

(c) Transfer of lands; consent of other Federal agencies to use of lands for recreation or fish and wildlife purposes; transfers to Secretary of Agriculture of forest lands; continuing administration of lands and waters for other project purposes; prohibition against limitation of authority under existing provisions of law

No lands under the jurisdiction of any other Federal agency may be included for or devoted to recreation or fish and wildlife purposes under the authority of this section without the consent of the head of such agency; and the head of any such agency is authorized to transfer any such lands to the jurisdiction of the Secretary of the Interior for purposes of this section. The Secretary of the Interior is authorized to transfer jurisdiction over project lands within or adjacent to the exterior boundaries of national forests and facilities thereon to the Secretary of Agriculture for recreation and other national forest system purposes; and such transfer shall be made in each case in which the project reservoir area is located wholly within the exterior boundaries of a national forest unless the Secretaries of Agriculture and Interior jointly determine otherwise. Where any project lands are transferred hereunder to the jurisdiction of the Secretary of Agriculture, the lands involved shall become national forest lands: *Provided*, That the lands and waters within the flow lines of any reservoir or otherwise needed or used for the operation of the project for other purposes shall continue to be administered by the Secretary of the Interior to the extent he determines to be necessary for such operation. Nothing herein shall limit the authority of the Secretary of the Interior granted by existing provisions of law relating to recreation or fish and wildlife development in connection with water resource projects or to disposition of public lands for such purposes.

(Pub.L. 89–72, § 7, July 9, 1965, 79 Stat. 216; Pub.L. 102–377, Title II, § 206, Oct. 2, 1992, 106 Stat. 1332; Pub.L. 102–575, Title XXVIII, § 2804(e), Oct. 30, 1992, 106 Stat. 4692.)

HISTORICAL AND STATUTORY NOTES

Revision Notes and Legislative Reports
  1965 Acts. House Report No. 254 and Conference Report No. 538, see 1965 U.S.Code Cong. and Adm.News, p. 1864.

  1992 Acts. Senate Report No. 102–267 and House Conference Report No. 102–1016, see 1992 U.S. Code Cong. and Adm. News, p. 4041.

References in Text
  The Federal reclamation laws, referred to in subsec. (a), are classified generally to chapter 12 (section 371 et seq.) of Title 43, Public Lands.

Codifications
  Amendment by section 2804(e)(1) of Pub.L. 102–575, directing, in subsec. (a),

the deletion of the proviso in the first sentence and the insertion of a period after "purposes", could not be executed since an identical amendment by section 206 of Pub.L. 102–377 was already executed.

Amendments
   1992   Amendments. Subsec.   (a).
Pub.L.   102–575,   Title   XXVIII,

§ 2804(e)(2), substituted "subsection (b) or (c) of section 460l–14 of this title" for "section 460l–14(b) of this title".

Pub.L. 102–377 deleted proviso relating to a $100,000 per project limitation.

LIBRARY REFERENCES

American Digest System
   United States ☞57.
   Key Number System Topic No. 393.

§ 460*l*–19.   Feasibility reports

Effective on and after July 1, 1966, neither the Secretary of the Interior nor any bureau nor any person acting under his authority shall engage in the preparation of any feasibility report under reclamation law with respect to any water resource project unless the preparation of such feasibility report has been specifically authorized by law, any other provision of law to the contrary notwithstanding.

(Pub.L. 89–72, § 8, July 9, 1965, 79 Stat. 217.)

HISTORICAL AND STATUTORY NOTES

Revision Notes and Legislative Reports
   1965 Acts. House Report No. 254 and Conference Report No. 538, see 1965 U.S. Code Cong. and Adm. News, p. 1864.

References in Text
   Reclamation law, referred to in text, is classified generally to chapter 12 (section 371 et seq.) of Title 43, Public Lands.

§ 460*l*–20.   Construction of projects under certain laws with allocations to recreation and fish and wildlife enhancement exceeding allocations to other functions unauthorized; exception

Nothing contained in this part shall be taken to authorize or to sanction the construction under the Federal reclamation laws or under any Rivers and Harbors or Flood Control Act of any project in which the sum of the allocations to recreation and fish and wildlife enhancement exceeds the sum of the allocations to irrigation, hydroelectric power, municipal, domestic and industrial water supply, navigation, and flood control, except that this section shall not apply to any such project for the enhancement of anadromous fisheries, shrimp, or for the conservation of migratory birds protected by treaty, when each of the other functions of such a project has, of itself, a favorable benefit-cost ratio.

(Pub.L. 89–72, § 9, July 9, 1965, 79 Stat. 217.)

611

HISTORICAL AND STATUTORY NOTES

Revision Notes and Legislative Reports

1965 Acts. House Report No. 254 and Conference Report No. 538, see 1965 U.S. Code Cong. and Adm. News, p. 1864.

References in Text

This part, referred to in text, was, in the original, this Act, meaning Pub.L. 89–72, which, in addition to enacting the sections 460*l*–12 to 460*l*–21 of this title, also amended sections 460*l*–5(a) and 662(d) of this title.

The Federal reclamation laws, referred to in text, are classified generally to chapter 12 (section 371 et seq.) of Title 43, Public Lands.

Rivers and Harbors or Flood Control Act, referred to in text, is classified principally to Title 33, Navigation and Navigable Waters.

LIBRARY REFERENCES

American Digest System

United States ⚷57.
Key Number System Topic No. 393.

§ 460*l*–21. Definitions

As used in this part:

(a) The term "project" shall mean a project or any appropriate unit thereof.

(b) The term "separable costs," as applied to any project purpose, means the difference between the capital cost of the entire multiple-purpose project and the capital cost of the project with the purpose omitted.

(c) The term "joint costs" means the difference between the capital cost of the entire multiple-purpose project and the sum of the separable costs for all project purposes.

(d) The term "feasibility report" shall mean any report of the scope required by the Congress when formally considering authorization of the project of which the report treats.

(e) The term "capital cost" includes interest during construction, wherever appropriate.

(Pub.L. 89–72, § 10, July 9, 1965, 79 Stat. 218.)

HISTORICAL AND STATUTORY NOTES

Revision Notes and Legislative Reports

1965 Acts. House Report No. 254 and Conference Report No. 538, see 1965 U.S. Code Cong. and Adm. News, p. 1864.

References in Text

This part, referred to in text, was, in the original, this Act, meaning Pub.L. 89–72, which, in addition to enacting enumerated sections 460*l*–12 to 460*l*–21 of this title, also amended sections 460*l*–5(a) and 662(d) of this title.

PART D—LAND TRANSFERS

§ 460*l*–22. Conveyance of property and interests in property in national park system and miscellaneous areas

(a) Freehold and leasehold interests; competitive bidding

With respect to any property acquired by the Secretary of the Interior within a unit of the national park system or miscellaneous area, except property within national parks, or within national monuments of scientific significance, the Secretary may convey a freehold or leasehold interest therein, subject to such terms and conditions as will assure the use of the property in a manner which is, in the judgment of the Secretary, consistent with the purpose for which the area was authorized by the Congress.   In any case in which the Secretary exercises his discretion to convey such interest, he shall do so to the highest bidder, in accordance with such regulations as the Secretary may prescribe, but such conveyance shall be at not less than the fair market value of the interest, as determined by the Secretary; except that if any such conveyance is proposed within two years after the property to be conveyed is acquired by the Secretary, he shall allow the last owner or owners of record of such property thirty days following the date on which they are notified by the Secretary in writing that such property is to be conveyed within which to notify the Secretary that such owners wish to acquire such interest.   Upon receiving such timely request, the Secretary shall convey such interest to such person or persons, in accordance with such regulations as the Secretary may prescribe, upon payment or agreement to pay an amount equal to the highest bid price.

(b) Exchange of lands; other disposal; equal land values

The Secretary of the Interior is authorized to accept title to any non-Federal property or interest therein within a unit of the National Park System or miscellaneous area under his administration, and in exchange therefor he may convey to the grantor of such property or interest any Federally-owned property or interest therein under his jurisdiction which he determines is suitable for exchange or other disposal and which is located in the same State as the non-Federal property to be acquired: *Provided, however,* That timber lands subject to harvest under a sustained yield program shall not be so exchanged.   Upon request of a State or a political subdivision thereof, or of a party in interest, prior to such exchange the Secretary or his designee shall hold a public hearing in the area where the lands to be exchanged are located. The values of the properties so exchanged either shall be approximately equal, or if they are not approximately equal, the values shall be equalized by the payment of cash to the grantor from funds appropriated for the acquisition of land for the area, or to the Secretary as the circumstances require.

(c) Solid waste disposal operations prohibited; exceptions; regulations

In order to protect the air, land, water, and natural and cultural values of the National Park System and the property of the United States therein, no solid waste disposal site (including any site for the disposal of domestic or industrial solid wastes) may be operated within the boundary of any unit of the National Park System, other than—

(1) a site which was operating as of September 1, 1984, or

(2) a site used only for disposal of wastes generated within that unit of the park system so long as such site will not degrade any of the natural or cultural resources of such park unit.

The Secretary of the Interior shall promulgate regulations to carry out the provisions of this subsection, including reasonable regulations to mitigate the adverse effects of solid waste disposal sites in operation as of September 1, 1984, upon property of the United States.

(d) Proceeds credited to land and water conservation fund

The proceeds received from any conveyance under this section shall be credited to the land and water conservation fund in the Treasury of the United States.

(Pub.L. 90–401, § 5, July 15, 1968, 82 Stat. 356; Pub.L. 98–506, § 2, Oct. 19, 1984, 98 Stat. 2338.)

HISTORICAL AND STATUTORY NOTES

Revision Notes and Legislative Reports
1968 Acts. Senate Report No. 1071 and Conference Report No. 1598, see 1968 U.S. Code Cong. and Adm. News, p. 2613.

Amendments
1984 Amendments. Subsec. (c). Pub.L. 98–506 added subsec. (c). Former subsec. (c) redesignated (d).

Subsec. (d). Pub.L. 98–506 redesignated former subsec. (c) as (d).

CROSS REFERENCES

Gettysburg National Military Park; conveyance of freehold and leasehold interests, see 16 USCA § 430g–5.
Jefferson National Expansion Memorial, transfers of land owned by United States, consistency with requirements of this section, see 16 USCA § 450jj–4.

Kalaupapa National Historical Park; exchange of lands, see 16 USCA § 410jj–3.

Klondike Gold Rush National Historical Park; cooperation by Secretary of Interior with Federal, State, and local agencies relating to use, development, or disposal of lands, see 16 USCA § 410bb–1.

National Park Service administrative reform and exemption from leasing requirements, see 16 USCA § 17o.

Uniform application of this section to all areas of national park system when not in conflict with specific provisions applicable to an area, see 16 USCA § 1c.

CODE OF FEDERAL REGULATIONS

Authority and procedure, see 36 CFR § 17.1 et seq.

LIBRARY REFERENCES

American Digest System
  Public Lands ⊂⊃49.
  United States ⊂⊃58(1).
  Key Number System Topic Nos. 317, 393.

Research References

Forms
  Federal Procedural Forms § 55:95, Conveyance of Leasehold or Freehold Interests.

Notes of Decisions

Construction with other laws   1
Exchange of lands   2

---

1.   Construction with other laws

The language of section 396e of this title providing that "Notwithstanding any other provision of law" did not repeal by implication the provisions of subsec. (b) of this section restricting the land available for exchange transactions in the National Park System to land located in the same State as the non-Federal property. 1982 (Counsel–Inf.Op.) 6 O.L.C. 251.

2.   Exchange of lands

Determination by National Park Service that properties involved in exchange of national park property for other property which was within national park and was adjacent to another national park were of approximately equal value was not rendered unreasonable by statement of person representing Service at public hearing on the proposed exchange, indicating that Service believed proposed exchange was in the public interest, in that statement made no reference whatsoever to equal value issue, and final decision on that issue appeared to be product of reasonable review of differing appraisals. Committee of 100 on Federal City v. Hodel, C.A.D.C.1985, 777 F.2d 711, 250 U.S.App.D.C. 52.   United States ⊂⊃ 58(3)

National Park Service had authority to execute agreement pursuant to which parties who proposed to construct observation tower adjacent to Gettysburg National Cemetery were to build tower on site other than site originally selected and right-of-way over federal land to alternative site would be granted.   Com. of Pennsylvania v. Morton, D.C.D.C.1974, 381 F.Supp. 293.   United States ⊂⊃ 57

PART E—RECLAMATION RECREATION MANAGEMENT

§ 460*l*–31.   Findings

The Congress finds and declares the following:

(1) There is a Federal responsibility to provide opportunities for public recreation at Federal water projects.

(2) Some provisions of the Federal Water Project Recreation Act [16 U.S.C.A. § 460*l*–12 et seq.] are outdated because of increases in demand for outdoor recreation and changes in the economic climate for recreation managing entities.

(3) Provisions of such Act relating to non-Federal responsibility for all costs of operation, maintenance, and replacement of recreation facilities result in an unfair burden, especially in cases where the facilities are old or underdesigned.

(4) Provisions of such Act that limit the Federal share of recreation facility development at water projects completed before 1965 to $100,000 preclude a responsible Federal share in providing adequate opportunities for safe outdoor recreation.

(5) There should be Federal authority to expand existing recreation facilities to meet public demand, in partnership with non-Federal interests.

(6) Nothing in this part changes the responsibility of the Bureau to meet the purposes for which Federal Reclamation projects were initially authorized and constructed.

(7) It is therefore in the best interest of the people of this Nation to amend the Federal Water Project Recreation Act [16 U.S.C.A. § 460*l*–12 et seq.] to remove outdated restrictions and authorize the Secretary of the Interior to undertake specific measures for the management of Reclamation lands.

(Pub.L. 102–575, Title XXVIII, § 2802, Oct. 30, 1992, 106 Stat. 4690.)

HISTORICAL AND STATUTORY NOTES

Revision Notes and Legislative Reports
  1992 Acts. Senate Report No. 102–267 and House Conference Report No. 102–1016, see 1992 U.S. Code Cong. and Adm. News, p. 4041.

References in Text
  The Federal Water Project Recreation Act, referred to in pars. (2) and (7), is Pub.L. 89–72, July 9, 1965, 79 Stat. 213, as amended, which enacted Part C (section 460*l*–12 et seq.) of this subchapter. For complete classification of this Act to the Code, see Short Title note set out under section 460*l*–12 of this title and Tables.

Short Title
  1992 Acts. Pub.L. 102–575, Title XVIII, § 2801, Oct. 30, 1992, 106 Stat. 4690, provided that: "This title [enacting this part and amending sections 460*l*–13 to 460*l*–15 and 460*l*–18 of this title] may be cited as the 'Reclamation Recreation Management Act of 1992'."

LIBRARY REFERENCES

American Digest System
  Water Law ⊗⇒2690.
  Key Number System Topic No. 405.

§ 460*l*–32. Definitions

For the purposes of this part:

  (1) The term "Reclamation lands" means real property administered by the Secretary, acting through the Commissioner of

Reclamation, and includes all acquired and withdrawn lands and water areas under jurisdiction of the Bureau.

(2) The term "Reclamation program" means any activity authorized under the Federal reclamation laws (the Act of June 17, 1902 (32 Stat. 388, chapter 1093; 43 U.S.C. 371)),[1] and Acts supplementary thereto and amendatory thereof).

(3) The term "Reclamation project" means any water supply or water delivery project constructed or administered by the Bureau of Reclamation under the Federal reclamation laws (the Act of June 17, 1902 (32 Stat. 388, chapter 1093; 43 U.S.C. 371), and Acts supplementary thereto and amendatory thereof).

(4) The term "Secretary" means the Secretary of the Interior.

(Pub.L. 102–575, Title XXVIII, § 2803, Oct. 30, 1992, 106 Stat. 4691.)

[1] So in original. There should probably be only a single closing parenthesis.

HISTORICAL AND STATUTORY NOTES

Revision Notes and Legislative Reports
1992 Acts. Senate Report No. 102–267 and House Conference Report No. 102–1016, see 1992 U.S. Code Cong. and Adm. News, p. 4041.

References in Text
The Federal reclamation laws, referred to in pars. (2) and (3), are comprised of Act June 17, 1902, c. 1093, 32 Stat. 388, popularly known as the Reclamation Act, and Acts amendatory thereof and supplementary thereto, which are classified generally to chapter 12 (section 371 et seq.) of Title 43, Public Lands. For complete

classification of Act June 17, 1902 to the Code, see Short Title note set out under section 371 of Title 43 and Tables.

References in Text
Act of June 17, 1902, referred to in pars. (2) and (3), is Act June 17, 1902, ch. 1093, 32 Stat. 388, popularly known as the Reclamation Act, which is classified generally to chapter 12 of Title 43, 43 U.S.C.A. § 371 et seq. However, section 371 of Title 43 is Act Dec. 5, 1924, c. 4, § 4, subsec. A, 43 Stat. 701. For complete classification, see Short Title note set out under 43 U.S.C.A. § 371 and Tables.

§ 460*l*–33. Management of reclamation lands

(a) Administration

(1) Upon a determination that any such fee, charge, or commission is reasonable and appropriate, the Secretary acting through the Commissioner of Reclamation, is authorized to establish—

(A) filing fees for applications and other documents concerning entry upon and use of Reclamation lands;

(B) recreation user fees; and

(C) charges or commissions for the use of Reclamation lands.

(2) The Secretary, acting through the Commissioner of Reclamation, shall promulgate such regulations as the Secretary determines to be necessary—

(A) to carry out the provisions of this section and section 460*l*–34 of this title;

(B) to ensure the protection, comfort, and well–being of the public (including the protection of public safety) with respect to the use of Reclamation lands; and

(C) to ensure the protection of resource values.

(b) Inventory

The Secretary, acting through the Commissioner of Reclamation, is authorized to—

(1) prepare and maintain on a continuing basis an inventory of resources and uses made of Reclamation lands and resources, keep records of such inventory, and make such records available to the public; and

(2) ascertain the boundaries of Reclamation lands and provide a means for public identification (including, where appropriate, providing signs and maps).

(c) Planning

(1)[1]**(A)** The Secretary, acting through the Commissioner of Reclamation, is authorized to develop, maintain, and revise resource management plans for Reclamation lands.

(B) Each plan described in subparagraph (A)—

(i) shall be consistent with applicable laws (including any applicable statute, regulation, or Executive order);

(ii) shall be developed in consultation with—

(I) such heads of Federal and non-Federal departments or agencies as the Secretary determines to be appropriate; and

(II) the authorized beneficiaries (as determined by the Secretary) of any Reclamation project included in the plan; and

(iii) shall be developed with appropriate public participation.

(C) Each plan described in subparagraph (A) shall provide for the development, use, conservation, protection, enhancement, and management of resources of Reclamation lands in a manner that is compatible with the authorized purposes of the Reclamation project associated with the Reclamation lands.

(d) Nonreimbursable funds

Funds expended by the Secretary in carrying out the provisions of this part shall be nonreimbursable under the Federal reclamation laws (the Act of June 17, 1902 (32 Stat. 388, chapter 1093; 43 U.S.C. 371), and Acts supplementary thereto and amendatory thereof).

(Pub.L. 102–575, Title XXVIII, § 2805, Oct. 30, 1992, 106 Stat. 4692.)

[1] So in original. No par. (2) was enacted.

HISTORICAL AND STATUTORY NOTES

Revision Notes and Legislative Reports
1992 Acts. Senate Report No. 102–267 and House Conference Report No. 102–1016, see 1992 U.S. Code Cong. and Adm. News, p. 4041.

References in Text
The Federal reclamation laws, referred to in subsec. (d), are comprised of Act June 17, 1902, c. 1093, 32 Stat. 388, popularly known as the Reclamation Act, and Acts amendatory thereof and supplementary thereto, which are classified generally to chapter 12 (section 371 et seq.) of Title 43, Public Lands. For complete classification of Act June 17, 1902 to the

Code, see Short Title note set out under section 371 of Title 43 and Tables.

References in Text
Act of June 17, 1902, referred to in subsec. (d), is Act June 17, 1902, ch. 1093, 32 Stat. 388, popularly known as the Reclamation Act, which is classified generally to chapter 12 of Title 43, 43 U.S.C.A. § 371 et seq. However, section 371 of Title 43 is Act Dec. 5, 1924, c. 4, § 4, subsec. A, 43 Stat. 701. For complete classification, see Short Title note set out under 43 U.S.C.A. § 371 and Tables.

LIBRARY REFERENCES

American Digest System
Woods and Forests ⚭5.
Key Number System Topic No. 411.

§ 460*l*–34. Protection of authorized purposes of reclamation projects

(a) Nothing in this part shall be construed to change, modify, or expand the authorized purposes of any Reclamation project.

(b) The expansion or modification of a recreational facility constructed under this part shall not increase the capital repayment responsibilities or operation and maintenance expenses of the beneficiaries of authorized purposes of the associated Reclamation project. The term "beneficiaries" does not include those entities who sign agreements or enter into contracts for recreation facilities pursuant to the Federal Water Project Recreation Act [16 U.S.C.A. § 460*l*–12 et seq.].

(Pub.L. 102–575, Title XXVIII, § 2806, Oct. 30, 1992, 106 Stat. 4693.)

HISTORICAL AND STATUTORY NOTES

Revision Notes and Legislative Reports
1992 Acts. Senate Report No. 102–267 and House Conference Report No. 102–1016, see 1992 U.S. Code Cong. and Adm. News, p. 4041.

References in Text
The Federal Water Project Recreation Act, referred to in subsec. (b), is Pub.L.

89–72, July 9, 1965, 79 Stat. 213, as amended, which is generally classified to sections 460*l*–12 to 460*l*–21 of this title. For complete classification of this Act to the Code, see Short Title note set out under section 460*l*–12 of this title and Tables.

LIBRARY REFERENCES

American Digest System
Woods and Forests ⚭5.
Key Number System Topic No. 411.

SUBCHAPTER LXX—OZARK NATIONAL SCENIC RIVERWAYS

§ 460m. Establishment

For the purpose of conserving and interpreting unique scenic and other natural values and objects of historic interest, including preservation of portions of the Current River and the Jacks Fork River in Missouri as free-flowing streams, preservation of springs and caves, management of wildlife, and provisions for use and enjoyment of the outdoor recreation resources thereof by the people of the United States, the Secretary of the Interior (hereinafter referred to as the "Secretary") shall designate for establishment as the Ozark National Scenic Riverways the area (hereinafter referred to as "such area") generally depicted on map numbered NR OZA 7002 entitled "Proposed Ozark National Rivers" dated December 1963 which map is on file for public inspection in the office of the National Park Service, Department of the Interior: *Provided,* That the area so designated shall not include more than sixty-five thousand acres of land now in private ownership and that no lands shall be designated within two miles of the present boundaries of the municipalities of Eminence and Van Buren, Missouri. The Secretary, with the concurrence of the State, shall designate for inclusion in the Ozark National Scenic Riverways, the lands composing Big Springs, Alley Springs, and Round Spring State Parks, and the Secretary is hereby directed to negotiate with the State for the donation and the inclusion of such park lands in the Ozark National Scenic Riverways.

(Pub.L. 88–492, § 1, Aug. 27, 1964, 78 Stat. 608.)

HISTORICAL AND STATUTORY NOTES

Revision Notes and Legislative Reports
  1964 Acts. House Report No. 1241, see 1964 U.S.Code Cong. and Adm.News, p. 3157.

LIBRARY REFERENCES

American Digest System
  Water Law ☞2519.
  Key Number System Topic No. 405.

Research References

ALR Library
  144 ALR 486, Uses to Which Park Property May Be Devoted.

§ 460m–1. Acquisition of lands, easements, etc.; exchange of lands; consent of State; reversion to State; administrative jurisdiction of Federal lands or waters

The Secretary may, within the area designated or altered pursuant to section 460m–3 of this title, acquire lands and interests therein, including scenic easements, by such means as he may deem to be in the public interest: *Provided,* That scenic easements may only be acquired with the consent of the owner of the lands or waters thereof: *And provided further,* That any parcel of land containing not more than five hundred acres, which borders either the Current River or the Jacks Fork River, and which is being primarily used for agricultural purposes, shall be acquired by the Secretary in its entirety unless the owner of any such parcel consents to the acquisition of a part thereof. Property so acquired which lies outside the boundary generally depicted on the map referred to in section 460m of this title may be exchanged by the Secretary for any land of approximately equal value within the boundaries. Lands and waters owned by the State of Missouri within such area may be acquired with the consent of the State and, notwithstanding any other provision of law, subject to provision for reversion to such State conditioned upon continued use of the property for National Scenic Riverway. Federally owned lands or waters lying within such area shall, upon establishment of the area pursuant to section 460m–3 of this title, be transferred to the administrative jurisdiction of the Secretary, without transfer of funds, for administration as part of the Ozark National Scenic Riverways.

(Pub.L. 88–492, § 2, Aug. 27, 1964, 78 Stat. 608; Pub.L. 92–272, Title IV, § 401, Apr. 11, 1972, 86 Stat. 122.)

HISTORICAL AND STATUTORY NOTES

Revision Notes and Legislative Reports
  1964 Acts. House Report No. 1241, see 1964 U.S.Code Cong. and Adm.News, p. 3157.

Amendments
  1972 Amendments. Pub.L. 92–272 substituted provisions authorizing lands and waters owned by the State of Missouri to be acquired with the consent of the State, subject to reversion to such State conditioned upon the continued use of the property for the National Scenic Riverway, for provisions authorizing lands and waters owned by the State of Missouri to be acquired only with the consent of the State.

LIBRARY REFERENCES

American Digest System
  United States ⊂⊃55.
  Key Number System Topic No. 393.

§ 460m–2. Reservation of use and occupancy of improved property for noncommercial residential purposes; term; valuation

Any owner or owners, including beneficial owners (hereinafter in this section referred to as "owner"), of improved property on the date of its acquisition by the Secretary may, as a condition to such acquisition, retain the right of use and occupancy of the improved property for noncommercial residential purposes for a term ending at the death of such owner, or the death of his spouse, or at the death of the survivor of either of them. The owner shall elect the term to be reserved. The Secretary shall pay to the owner the fair market value of the property on the date of such acquisition less the fair market value on such date of the right retained by the owner. (Pub.L. 88–492, § 3, Aug. 27, 1964, 78 Stat. 608.)

HISTORICAL AND STATUTORY NOTES

Revision Notes and Legislative Reports
   1964 Acts. House Report No. 1241, see 1964 U.S.Code Cong. and Adm.News, p. 3157.

LIBRARY REFERENCES

American Digest System
   United States ☞57.
   Key Number System Topic No. 393.

§ 460m–3. Establishment; notice in Federal Register; alteration of boundaries; acreage limitation

When the Secretary determines that lands and waters, or interests therein, have been acquired by the United States in sufficient quantity to provide an administrable unit, he shall declare establishment of the Ozark National Scenic Riverways by publication of notice in the Federal Register. The Secretary may thereafter alter such boundaries from time to time, except that the total acreage in the Ozark National Scenic Riverways shall not exceed sixty-five thousand acres, exclusive of land donated by the State of Missouri or its political subdivisions and of federally owned land transferred pursuant to section 460m–1 of this title.

(Pub.L. 88–492, § 4, Aug. 27, 1964, 78 Stat. 609.)

HISTORICAL AND STATUTORY NOTES

Revision Notes and Legislative Reports
   1964 Acts. House Report No. 1241, see 1964 U.S.Code Cong. and Adm.News, p. 3157.

CODE OF FEDERAL REGULATIONS

National Park Service, general provisions, see 36 CFR § 1.1 et seq.

LIBRARY REFERENCES

American Digest System
   United States ☞57.
   Key Number System Topic No. 393.

§ 460m–4.   Cooperative land development programs; hunting and fishing

(a) Development of comprehensive plans

In furtherance of the purposes of this subchapter, the Secretary is authorized to cooperate with the State of Missouri, its political subdivisions, and other Federal agencies and organizations in formulating comprehensive plans for the Ozark National Scenic Riverways and for the related watershed of the Current and Jacks Fork Rivers in Missouri, and to enter into agreements for the implementation of such plans. Such plans may provide for land use and development programs, for preservation and enhancement of the natural beauty of the landscape, and for conservation of outdoor resources in the watersheds of the Current and Jacks Fork Rivers.

(b) Establishment of hunting and fishing zones and periods

The Secretary shall permit hunting and fishing on lands and waters under his jurisdiction within the Ozark National Scenic Riverways area in accordance with applicable Federal and State laws. The Secretary may designate zones where, and establish periods when, no hunting shall be permitted, for reasons of public safety, administration, or public use and enjoyment and shall issue regulations after consultation with the Conservation Commission of the State of Missouri.

(Pub.L. 88–492, § 5, Aug. 27, 1964, 78 Stat. 609.)

HISTORICAL AND STATUTORY NOTES

Revision Notes and Legislative Reports
1964 Acts. House Report No. 1241, see 1964 U.S.Code Cong. and Adm.News, p. 3157.

LIBRARY REFERENCES

American Digest System
Fish ⬥8.
Game ⬥3.5.
Key Number System Topic Nos. 176, 187.

§ 460m–5.   Administration

The Ozark National Scenic Riverways shall be administered in accordance with the provisions of sections 1, 2, 3, and 4 of this title, as amended and supplemented, and in accordance with other laws of general application relating to the areas administered and supervised by the Secretary through the National Park Service; except that authority otherwise available to the Secretary for the conservation and management of natural resources may be utilized to the extent he finds such authority will further the purposes of this subchapter.

(Pub.L. 88–492, § 6, Aug. 27, 1964, 78 Stat. 609.)

HISTORICAL AND STATUTORY NOTES

Revision Notes and Legislative Reports
1964 Acts. House Report No. 1241, see 1964 U.S.Code Cong. and Adm.News, p. 3157.

CODE OF FEDERAL REGULATIONS

Special regulations for particular areas of system, see 36 CFR § 7.1 et seq.

LIBRARY REFERENCES

American Digest System
Woods and Forests ⬅5.
Key Number System Topic No. 411.

Notes of Decisions

Estoppel　2
Miscellaneous rules and regulations　3
Power to regulate　1

1.　Power to regulate

United States acted within its constitutional authority in attempting to regulate the business activities of members of an association of canoe rental businesses as they affect the Ozark National Scenic Riverways, even though the members themselves might never enter federally owned property, but strictly keep to state or county roads and rights-of-way within the Riverways. Free Enterprise Canoe Renters Ass'n of Missouri v. Watt, C.A.8 (Mo.) 1983, 711 F.2d 852. United States ⬅ 57

2.　Estoppel

In regard to National Park Service regulation prohibiting the delivery or retrieval within the boundaries of Ozark National Scenic Riverways of rented watercraft without a permit, the Park Service was not estopped to enforce the regulation against plaintiffs, members of an association of canoe rental businesses, because of plaintiffs' alleged reliance on Williams II; plaintiffs' reliance was not justified by the Park Service's conduct, and plaintiffs failed to show reasonable reliance on an official statement of the law later determined to be invalid. Free Enterprise Canoe Renters Ass'n of Missouri v. Watt, C.A.8 (Mo.) 1983, 711 F.2d 852. Estoppel ⬅ 62.2(4)

3.　Miscellaneous rules and regulations

National Park Service regulation prohibiting activities associated with commercial rental of canoes within boundaries of Ozark National Scenic Riverways unless businesses obtained a permit from the Service was reasonably related to congressional purpose of conserving and interpreting unique scenic and other natural values. Free Enterprise Canoe Renters Ass'n of Missouri v. Watt, E.D.Mo. 1982, 549 F.Supp. 252, affirmed 711 F.2d 852. United States ⬅ 57

§ 460m–6.　Free-roaming horses

(a) In general

The Secretary, in accordance with this section, shall allow free-roaming horses in the Ozark National Scenic Riverways. Within 180 days after November 12, 1996, the Secretary shall enter into an agreement with the Missouri Wild Horse League or another qualified nonprofit entity to provide for management of free-roaming horses. The agreement shall provide for cost-effective management of the horses and limit Federal expenditures to the costs of monitoring the agreement. The Secretary shall issue permits for adequate pastures to accommodate the historic population level of the free-roaming horse herd, which shall be not less than the number of horses in existence on November 12, 1996, nor more than 50.

(b) Removal of horses

The Secretary may not remove, or assist in, or permit the removal of any free-roaming horses from Federal lands within the boundary of the Ozark National Scenic Riverways unless—

(1) the entity with whom the Secretary has entered into the agreement under subsection (a) of this section, following notice and a 90–day response period, substantially fails to meet the terms and conditions of the agreement;

(2) the number of free-roaming horses exceeds 50; or

(3) in the case of an emergency or to protect public health and safety, as defined in the agreement.

(c) Construction; liability of United States

Nothing in this section shall be construed as creating liability for the United States for any damages caused by the free-roaming horses to property located inside or outside the boundaries of the Ozark National Scenic Riverways.

(Pub.L. 88–492, § 7, Aug. 27, 1964, 78 Stat. 609; Pub.L. 104–333, Div. I, Title VIII, § 803(b), Nov. 12, 1996, 110 Stat. 4186.)

HISTORICAL AND STATUTORY NOTES

Revision Notes and Legislative Reports
  1964 Acts. House Report No. 1241, see 1964 U.S.Code Cong. and Adm.News, p. 3157.

References in Text
  November 12, 1996, referred to in subsec. (a), was in the original "enactment of this section" and "date of enactment of this section", respectively, and was translated as November 12, 1996, the date of

approval of Pub.L. 104–333, which amended this section generally, as the probable intent of Congress.

Amendments
  1996 Amendments. Pub.L. 104–333, § 803(b), substituted provisions relating to free-roaming horses for provisions relating to Ozark National Scenic Riverways Commission.

LIBRARY REFERENCES

American Digest System
  Woods and Forests ⊱5, 7.
  Key Number System Topic No. 411.

§ 460m–7. Authorization of appropriations

There are hereby authorized to be appropriated such sums (but not more than $10,804,000 for the acquisition of lands or interests in lands) as are necessary to carry out the purposes of this subchapter.

(Pub.L. 88–492, § 8, Aug. 27, 1964, 78 Stat. 610; Pub.L. 92–272, Title I, § 101(7), Apr. 11, 1972, 86 Stat. 120.)

HISTORICAL AND STATUTORY NOTES

Revision Notes and Legislative Reports
1964 Acts. House Report No. 1241, see 1964 U.S.Code Cong. and Adm.News, p. 3157.

Amendments
1972 Amendments. Pub.L. 92–272 increased the maximum amount authorized

to be appropriated for the acquisition of lands or interests in lands from not more than $7,000,000 to not more than $10,804,000.

SUBCHAPTER LXXI—BUFFALO NATIONAL RIVER

§ 460m–8. Establishment

For the purposes of conserving and interpreting an area containing unique scenic and scientific features, and preserving as a free-flowing stream an important segment of the Buffalo River in Arkansas for the benefit and enjoyment of present and future generations, the Secretary of the Interior (hereinafter referred to as the "Secretary") may establish and administer the Buffalo National River. The boundaries of the national river shall be as generally depicted on the drawing entitled "Proposed Buffalo National River" numbered NR–BUF–7103 and dated December 1967, which shall be on file and available for public inspection in the offices of the National Park Service, Department of the Interior. The Secretary is authorized to make minor revisions of the boundaries of the national river when necessary, after advising the Committee on Natural Resources of the House of Representatives and the Committee on Energy and Natural Resources of the Senate in writing, but the total acreage within such boundaries shall not exceed ninety-five thousand seven hundred and thirty acres.

(Pub.L. 92–237, § 1, Mar. 1, 1972, 86 Stat. 44; Pub.L. 103–437, § 6(n)(1), Nov. 2, 1994, 108 Stat. 4586.)

HISTORICAL AND STATUTORY NOTES

Revision Notes and Legislative Reports
1972 Acts. Senate Report No. 92–130, see 1972 U.S.Code Cong. and Adm.News, p. 1969.

1994 Acts. House Report No. 103–779, see 1994 U.S. Code Cong. and Adm. News, p. 3639.

Amendments
1994 Amendments. Pub.L. 103–437, § 6(n)(1), substituted "Committee on Natural Resources of the House of Representatives and the Committee on Energy and Natural Resources of the Senate" for "Committees on Interior and Insular Af-

fairs of the United States House of Representatives and the United States Senate".

Change of Name
Committee on Natural Resources of House of Representatives treated as referring to Committee on Resources of House of Representatives by section 1(a) of Pub.L. 104–14, set out as a note preceding 2 U.S.C.A. § 21. Committee on Resources of House of Representatives changed to Committee on Natural Resources of House of Representatives by House Resolution No. 6, One Hundred Tenth Congress, Jan. 5, 2007.

LIBRARY REFERENCES

American Digest System
   Water Law ⊕2519, 2519.
   Key Number System Topic No. 405.

Notes of Decisions

Admissibility of evidence   2
Mining claims   1
Mootness   3

___

1. Mining claims

Plaintiff's mining claim on land within national river established by Congress were invalid since sections 460m–8 to 460m–14 of this title establishing river made it part of the National Park System, and since such provisions implicitly withdrew the lands in question from mineral entry and location. Brown v. U.S. Dept. of Interior, C.A.8 (Ark.) 1982, 679 F.2d 747. Mines And Minerals ⊕ 9

2. Admissibility of evidence

It was not abuse of discretion to admit testimony about executory sales contract concerning property government acquired to maintain scenic beauty of river, even though contract was executed seven years after Congress' enactment of legislation including property within project area. U.S. v. 428.02 Acres of Land, More or Less, Situate in Newton and Searcy Counties, Ark., C.A.8 (Ark.) 1982, 687 F.2d 266. Evidence ⊕ 555.6(2)

3. Mootness

Army Corps of Engineers's voluntary revocation of permit to build dam on creek mooted action by river advocacy groups alleging that issuance of permit without approval of Secretary of Interior violated statute governing water projects on protected river; federal agency, rather than private party, revoked permit, Corps had not announced intention to reissue permit, Ozark Society v. Melcher, E.D.Ark.2003, 248 F.Supp.2d 810. Federal Courts ⊕ 13.25

§ 460m–9. Acquisition of lands and waters

(a) Donation, purchase, and exchange; reimbursement of State of Arkansas

Within the boundaries of the Buffalo National River, the Secretary may acquire lands and waters or interests therein by donation, purchase or exchange, except that lands owned by the State of Arkansas or a political subdivision thereof may be acquired only by donation: *Provided*, That the Secretary may, with funds appropriated for development of the area, reimburse such State for its share of the cost of facilities developed on State park lands if such facilities were developed in a manner approved by the Secretary and if the development of such facilities commenced subsequent to March 1, 1972: *Provided further*, That such reimbursement shall not exceed a total of $375,000. When an individual tract of land is only partly within the boundaries of the national river, the Secretary may acquire all of the tract by any of the above methods in order to avoid the payment of severance costs. Land so acquired outside of the boundaries of the national river may be exchanged by the Secretary for non-Federal lands within the national river boundaries, and any portion of the land not utilized for such exchanges may be disposed of in accordance with the provisions of the Federal Property and Administrative Services Act of 1949, as amended. With the concurrence of the agency having custody thereof, any Federal property within the boundaries of the national river may be transferred without consideration to the administrative jurisdiction of the Secretary for administration as part of the national river.

(b) Retention of rights

Except for property which the Secretary determines to be necessary for the purposes of administration, development, access or public use, an owner or owners (hereafter referred to as "owner") of any improved property which is used solely for noncommercial residential purposes on the date of its acquisition by the Secretary or any owner of lands used solely for agricultural purposes (including, but not limited to, grazing) may retain, as a condition of the acquisition of such property or lands, a right of use and occupancy of such property for such residential or agricultural purposes. The term of the right retained shall expire upon the death of the owner or the death of his spouse, whichever occurs later, or in lieu thereof, after a definite term which shall not exceed twenty-five years after the date of acquisition. The owner shall elect, at the time of conveyance, the term of the right reserved. The Secretary shall pay the owner the fair market value of the property on the date of such acquisition, less the fair market value of the term retained by the owner. Such right may, during its existence, be conveyed or transferred, but all rights of use and occupancy shall be subject to such terms and conditions as the Secretary deems appropriate to assure the use of such property in accordance with the purposes of this subchapter. Upon a determination that the property, or any portion thereof, has ceased to be used in accordance with such terms and conditions, the Secretary may terminate the right of use and occupancy by tendering to the holder of such right an amount equal to the fair market value, as of the date of the tender, of that portion of the right which remains unexpired on the date of termination.

(c) "Improved property" defined

As used in this section the term "improved property" means a detached year-round one-family dwelling which serves as the owner's permanent place of abode at the time of acquisition, and construction of which was begun before September 3, 1969, together with so much of the land on which the dwelling is situated, the said land being in the same ownership as the dwelling, as the Secretary shall designate to be reasonably necessary for the enjoyment of the dwelling for the sole purpose of noncommercial residential use.

(Pub.L. 92–237, § 2, Mar. 1, 1972, 86 Stat. 44.)

HISTORICAL AND STATUTORY NOTES

Revision Notes and Legislative Reports
  1972 Acts. Senate Report No. 92–130, see 1972 U.S.Code Cong. and Adm.News, p. 1969.

References in Text
  The Federal Property and Administrative Services Act of 1949, referred to in subsec. (a), is Act June 30, 1949, c. 288, 63 Stat. 377, as amended, Title III of which is currently classified to subchapter IV of chapter 4 of Title 41, 41 U.S.C.A. § 251 et seq., and the remainder of which was formerly classified to chapter 10 of former Title 40, 40 U.S.C.A. § 471 et seq., prior to being repealed by Pub.L. 107–217, § 6(b), Aug. 21, 2002, 116 Stat. 1313; see now generally chapter 1 of Title 40, 40 U.S.C.A. § 101 et seq.

LIBRARY REFERENCES

American Digest System
  United States ☞55.
  Key Number System Topic No. 393.

§ 460m–10. Hunting and fishing; rules and regulations

The Secretary shall permit hunting and fishing on lands and waters under his jurisdiction within the boundaries of the Buffalo National River in accordance with applicable Federal and State laws, except that he may designate zones where and establish periods when, no hunting or fishing shall be permitted for reasons of public safety, administration, fish or wildlife management, or public use and enjoyment.   Except in emergencies, any rules and regulations of the Secretary pursuant to this section shall be put into effect only after consultation with the Arkansas Fish and Game Commission.

(Pub.L. 92–237, § 3, Mar. 1, 1972, 86 Stat. 45.)

HISTORICAL AND STATUTORY NOTES

Revision Notes and Legislative Reports
  1972 Acts. Senate Report No. 92–130, see 1972 U.S.Code Cong. and Adm.News, p. 1969.

LIBRARY REFERENCES

American Digest System
  Fish ☞8.
  Game ☞3.5.
  Key Number System Topic Nos. 176, 187.

§ 460m–11. Water resource projects

The Federal Energy Regulatory Commission shall not license the construction of any dam, water conduit, reservoir, powerhouse, transmission line, or other project works under the Federal Power Act (41 Stat. 1063), as amended (16 U.S.C. 791a et seq.), on or directly affecting the Buffalo National River and no department or agency of the United States shall assist by loan, grant, license, or otherwise in the construction of any water resources project that would have a direct and adverse effect on the values for which such river is established, as determined by the Secretary. Nothing contained in the foregoing sentence, however, shall preclude licensing of, or assistance to, developments below or above the Buffalo National River or on any stream tributary thereto which will not invade the area or unreasonably diminish the scenic, recreational, and fish and wildlife values present in the area on March 1, 1972. No department or agency of the United States shall recommend authorization of any water resources project that would have a direct and adverse effect on the values for which such river is established, as determined by the Secretary, nor shall such department or agency request appropriations to begin construction on any such project, whether heretofore or hereafter authorized, without, at least sixty days in advance, (i) advising the Secretary, in writing, of its intention so to do and (ii) reporting to the Committee on Natural Resources of the House of Representatives and the Committee on Energy and Natural Resources of the Senate, respectively, the nature of the project involved and the manner in which such project would conflict with the purposes of this subchapter or would affect the national river and the values to be protected by it under this subchapter.

(Pub.L. 92–237, § 4, Mar. 1, 1972, 86 Stat. 45; Pub.L. 95–91, Title IV, § 402(a)(1)(A), Aug. 4, 1977, 91 Stat. 583; Pub.L. 103–437, § 6(n)(1), Nov. 2, 1994, 108 Stat. 4586.)

HISTORICAL AND STATUTORY NOTES

Revision Notes and Legislative Reports

1972 Acts. Senate Report No. 92–130, see 1972 U.S.Code Cong. and Adm.News, p. 1969.

1977 Acts. Senate Report No. 95–164 and House Conference Report No. 95–539, see 1977 U.S.Code Cong. and Adm.News, p. 854.

1994 Acts. House Report No. 103–779, see 1994 U.S. Code Cong. and Adm. News, p. 3639.

References in Text

The Federal Power Act, referred to in text, is Act June 10, 1920, c. 285, 41 Stat. 1063, which is classified to section 791a et seq. of this title. For complete classification of this Act to the Code, see section 791a of this title and Tables.

Amendments

1994 Amendments. Pub.L. 103–437, § 6(n)(1), substituted "Committee on Natural Resources of the House of Representatives and the Committee on Energy and Natural Resources of the Senate" for

"Committees on Interior and Insular Affairs of the United States House of Representatives and the United States Senate".

Change of Name

Committee on Natural Resources of House of Representatives treated as referring to Committee on Resources of House of Representatives by section 1(a) of Pub.L. 104–14, set out as a note preceding 2 U.S.C.A. § 21. Committee on Resources of House of Representatives changed to Committee on Natural Resources of House of Representatives by House Resolution No. 6, One Hundred Tenth Congress, Jan. 5, 2007.

Transfer of Functions

"Federal Energy Regulatory Commission" was substituted for "Federal Power Commission" in text on authority of Pub.L. 95–91, Title IV, § 402(a)(1)(A), Aug. 4, 1977, 91 Stat. 583, see section 7172(a)(1)(A) of Title 42, The Public Health and Welfare.

The Federal Power Commission was terminated and its functions, personnel, property, funds, etc., were transferred to the Secretary of Energy (except for certain functions which were transferred to the Federal Energy Regulatory Commission) by sections 7151(b), 7171(a), 7172(a), 7291, and 7293 of Title 42.

LIBRARY REFERENCES

American Digest System

United States ⚷57.
Key Number System Topic No. 393.

§ 460m–12. Administration, protection, and development

The Secretary shall administer, protect, and develop the Buffalo National River in accordance with the provisions of sections 1, 2, 3, and 4 of this title, as amended and supplemented; except that any other statutory authority available to the Secretary for the conservation and management of natural resources may be utilized to the extent he finds such authority will further the purposes of this subchapter.

(Pub.L. 92–237, § 5, Mar. 1, 1972, 86 Stat. 45.)

HISTORICAL AND STATUTORY NOTES

Revision Notes and Legislative Reports

1972 Acts. Senate Report No. 92–130, see 1972 U.S.Code Cong. and Adm.News, p. 1969.

LIBRARY REFERENCES

American Digest System

Woods and Forests ⚷5.
Key Number System Topic No. 411.

§ 460m–13. Suitability for preservation as a wilderness; area review and report to President

Within three years from March 1, 1972, the Secretary shall review the area within the boundaries of the national river and shall report to the President, in accordance with section 1132(c) and (d) of this title, his recommendation as to the suitability or nonsuitability of any area within the national river for preservation as a wilderness, and any designation of any such area as a wilderness, shall be accomplished in accordance with said section 1132(c) and (d) of this title.

(Pub.L. 92–237, § 6, Mar. 1, 1972, 86 Stat. 46.)

HISTORICAL AND STATUTORY NOTES

Revision Notes and Legislative Reports
1972 Acts. Senate Report No. 92–130,
see 1972 U.S.Code Cong. and Adm.News,
p. 1969.

CODE OF FEDERAL REGULATIONS

National Park Service, general provisions, see 36 CFR § 1.1 et seq.

LIBRARY REFERENCES

American Digest System
   Water Law ⚯2519.
   Key Number System Topic No. 405.

§ 460m–14. Authorization of appropriations

For the acquisition of lands and interests in lands, there are authorized to be appropriated not more than $39,948,000. For development of the national river, there are authorized to be appropriated not to exceed $9,371,000.

(Pub.L. 92–237, § 7, Mar. 1, 1972, 86 Stat. 46; Pub.L. 94–578, Title I, § 101(3), Title III, § 310, Oct. 21, 1976, 90 Stat. 2732, 2736; Pub.L. 95–625, Title II, § 201(2), Nov. 10, 1978, 92 Stat. 3473.)

HISTORICAL AND STATUTORY NOTES

Revision Notes and Legislative Reports
   1972 Acts. Senate Report No. 92–130,
see 1972 U.S.Code Cong. and Adm.News,
p. 1969.

Amendments
   1978 Amendments. Pub.L. 95–625 increased land acquisition appropriations authorization to $39,948,000 from $30,071,500.

   1976 Amendments. Pub.L. 94–578, § 101(3), substituted "$30,071,500" for "$16,115,000".

Pub.L. 94–578, § 310, substituted "For development of the national river, there are authorized to be appropriated not to exceed $9,371,000" for "For development of the national river, there are authorized to be appropriated not more than $283,000 in fiscal year 1974; $2,923,000 in fiscal year 1975; $3,643,000 in fiscal year 1976; $1,262,000 in fiscal year 1977; and $1,260,000 in fiscal year 1978. The sums appropriated each year shall remain available until expended".

SUBCHAPTER LXXI–A—NEW RIVER GORGE NATIONAL RIVER

§ 460m–15. Establishment; administration, protection, and development; utilization of other authorities; boundary description, availability for public inspection

For the purpose of conserving and interpreting outstanding natural, scenic, and historic values and objects in and around the New River Gorge and preserving as a free-flowing stream an important segment of the New River in West Virginia for the benefit and enjoyment of present and future generations, the Secretary of the

Interior (hereinafter referred to as the "Secretary") shall establish and administer the New River Gorge National River. The Secretary shall administer, protect, and develop the national river in accordance with the provisions of sections 1, 2, 3, and 4 of this title, as amended and supplemented; except that any other statutory authority available to the Secretary for the preservation and management of natural resources may be utilized to the extent he finds such authority will further the purposes of this subchapter. The boundaries of the national river shall be as generally depicted on the drawing entitled "Proposed New River Gorge National River" numbered NERI 80,034, dated May 2001, which shall be on file and available for public inspection in the offices of the National Park Service, Department of the Interior.

(Pub.L. 95–625, Title XI, § 1101, Nov. 10, 1978, 92 Stat. 3544; Pub.L. 100–534, Title I, § 101, Oct. 26, 1988, 102 Stat. 2700; Pub.L. 104–333, Div. I, Title IV, § 406(a)(1), Nov. 12, 1996, 110 Stat. 4149; Pub.L. 107–356, § 2(a), Dec. 17, 2002, 116 Stat. 3013.)

HISTORICAL AND STATUTORY NOTES

Revision Notes and Legislative Reports
  1988 Acts. Senate Report No. 100–481, see 1988 U.S.Code Cong. and Adm.News, p. 3574.
  2002 Acts. House Report No. 107–509, see 2002 U.S. Code Cong. and Adm. News, p. 1987.

Amendments
  2002 Amendments. Pub.L. 107–356, § 2(a), struck out "NERI–80,028A, dated March 1996" and inserted "NERI–80,034, dated May 2001".
  1996 Amendments. Pub.L. 104–333, § 406(a)(1), substituted "NERI–80,028A, dated March 1996" for "NERI–80,023, dated January 1987".
  1988 Amendments. Pub.L. 100–534 substituted "NERI–80,023, dated January 1987" for "NERI–20,002, dated July 1978".

Short Title
  2002 Amendments. Pub.L. 107–356, § 1, Dec. 17, 2002, 116 Stat. 3013, provided that: "This Act [amending this section and enacting provisions set out as a note under this section] may be cited as the 'New River Boundary Act of 2002'."
  1988 Amendments. Pub.L. 100–534, § 1, Oct. 26, 1988, 102 Stat. 2699, provided that: "This Act [enacting sections 460m–26 to 460m–29 and 460ww to 460ww–5 of this title, amending this section and section 1274 of this title and

enacting provisions set out as notes under this section and section 1274 of this title] may be cited as the 'West Virginia National Interest River Conservation Act of 1987'."

Boundary Modification—Land Exchange
  Pub.L. 107–356, § 2(b), Dec. 17, 2002, 116 Stat. 3013, provided that:

  "**(1) In general.**—The Secretary of the Interior shall complete a fee simple land exchange in the vicinity of Beauty Mountain, Fayette County, West Virginia, to acquire a tract of land identified as NERI Tract Number 150–07 that lies adjacent to the boundary of the New River Gorge National River in exchange for a tract of land identified as NERI Tract Number 150–08 located within such boundary.

  "**(2) Treatment of exchanged lands.**—Upon the completion of such land exchange—

    "**(A)** the land acquired by the United States in the exchange shall be included in the boundaries, and administered as part, of the New River Gorge National River; and

    "**(B)** the land conveyed by the United States in the exchange shall be excluded from the boundaries, and shall not be administered as part, of the New River Gorge National River."

New, Gauley, Meadow, and Bluestone Rivers; Congressional Findings and Purpose

Pub.L. 100–534, § 2, Oct. 26, 1988, 102 Stat. 2699, provided that:

"(a) **Findings.**—The Congress finds that—

"(1) The outstanding natural, scenic, cultural and recreational values of the segment of the New River in West Virginia within the boundaries of the New River Gorge National River have been preserved and enhanced by its inclusion in the National Park System.

"(2) The establishment of the New River Gorge National River has provided the basis for increased recreation and tourism activities in southern West Virginia due to its nationally recognized status and has greatly contributed to the regional economy.

"(3) Certain boundary modifications to the New River Gorge National River are necessary to further protect the scenic resources within the river's visual corridor and to provide for better management of the national park unit.

"(4) Several tributaries of the New River in West Virginia also possess remarkable and outstanding features of national significance. The segment of the Gauley River below Summersville Dam has gained national recognition as a premier whitewater recreation resource. The lower section of the Bluestone River and the lower section of the Meadow River possess remarkable and outstanding natural, scenic, and recreational values due to their predominantly undeveloped condition.

"(5) Portions of several of the New River tributaries, including segments of the Gauley River, the Meadow River, and the Bluestone River are suitable for inclusion in the National Park System or the National Wild and Scenic Rivers System.

"(6) It is in the national interest to preserve the natural condition of certain segments of the New, Gauley, Meadow, and Bluestone Rivers in West Virginia and to enhance recreational opportunities available on the free-flowing segments.

"(b) **Purpose.**—The purpose of this Act [enacting sections 460m–26 to 460m–29 and 460ww to 460ww–5 of this title, amending this section and section 1274 of this title, and enacting provisions set out as notes under this section and section 1274 of this title] is to provide for the protection and enhancement of the natural, scenic, cultural, and recreational values on certain free-flowing segments of the New, Gauley, Meadow, and Bluestone Rivers in the State of West Virginia for the benefit and enjoyment of present and future generations."

Coordination Among Recreational Resources

Pub.L. 100–534, Title IV, § 401, Oct. 26, 1988, 102 Stat. 2707, provided that: "Subject to existing authority, the Secretary of the Interior shall cooperate with, and assist, any regional authority comprised of representatives of West Virginia State authorities and local government authorities in or any combination of the foregoing Nicholas, Fayette, Raleigh, Summers, Greenbrier, and Mercer Counties, West Virginia, for the purposes of providing for coordinated development and promotion of recreation resources of regional or national significance which are located in southern West Virginia and management by State or Federal agencies, including State, local and National Park System units, State and National Forest System units, and historic sites."

Special Provisions

Pub.L. 100–534, Title IV, § 402, Oct. 26, 1988, 102 Stat. 2707, provided that: "Subject to his responsibilities to protect the natural resources of the National Park System, the Secretary of the Interior shall enter into a cooperative agreement with the State of West Virginia providing for the State's regulation, in accordance with State law, of persons providing commercial recreational watercraft services on units of the National Park System and components of the National Wild and Scenic Rivers System subject to this Act [see Short Title of 1988 Amendments note under this section]."

Consolidated Management

Pub.L. 100–534, Title IV, § 404, Oct. 26, 1988, 102 Stat. 2708, provided that: "In order to achieve the maximum economy and efficiency of operations in the administration of the National Park System units established or expanded pursuant to this Act [see Short Title of 1988 Amendments note under this section], the Secretary shall consolidate offices and personnel administering all such units to the extent practicable and shall utilize the existing facilities of the New River Gorge National River to the extent practicable."

New Spending Authority
Pub.L. 100–534, Title IV, § 405, Oct. 26, 1988, 102 Stat. 2708, provided that:

"Any new spending authority which is provided under this Act [see Short Title of 1988 Amendments note under this section] shall be effective for any fiscal year only to the extent or in such amounts as provided in appropriation Acts."

CODE OF FEDERAL REGULATIONS

National Park Service, general provisions, see 36 CFR § 1.1 et seq.

LIBRARY REFERENCES

American Digest System
Water Law ⊸2519.
Key Number System Topic No. 405.

§ 460m–16. Acquisition of property

(a) Authority of Secretary; manner; donation of State lands; improved and unimproved properties

Within the boundaries of the New River Gorge National River, the Secretary may acquire lands and waters or interests therein by donation, purchase with donated or appropriated funds, transfer, or exchange. Lands owned by the State of West Virginia or a political subdivision thereof may be acquired by donation only. In addition, the Secretary may acquire by any of the foregoing methods not to exceed ten acres outside the boundaries of the national river for an administrative headquarters site, and funds appropriated for land acquisition shall be available for the acquisition of the administrative headquarters site. The authority of the Secretary to condemn in fee, improved properties as defined in subsection (c) of this section shall not be invoked as long as the owner of such improved property holds and uses it in a manner compatible with the purposes of this subchapter. The Secretary may acquire any such improved property without the consent of the owner whenever he finds that such property has undergone, since January 1, 1978, or is imminently about to undergo, changes in land use which are incompatible with the purposes of the national river. The Secretary may acquire less than fee interest in any improved or unimproved property within the boundaries of the national river.

(b) Non-federally owned lands; cooperative agreements affecting properties of historical significance

On non-federally owned lands within the national river boundaries, the Secretary is authorized to enter into cooperative agreements with organizations or individuals to mark or interpret properties of significance to the history of the Gorge area.

(c) "Improved property" defined

For the purposes of this Act, the term "improved property" means (i) a detached single family dwelling, the construction of which was begun before January 1, 1977 (hereafter referred to as "dwelling"), together with so much of the land on which the dwelling is situated, the said land being in the same ownership as the dwelling, as the Secretary shall designate to be reasonably necessary for the enjoyment of the dwelling for the sole purpose of noncommercial residential use, together with any structures necessary to the dwelling which are situated on the land so designated, or (ii) property developed for agricultural uses, together with any structures accessory thereto which were so used on or before January 1, 1977, or (iii) commercial and small business properties which were so used on or before January 1, 1977, the purpose of which is determined by the Secretary to contribute to visitor use and enjoyment of the national river. In determining when and to what extent a property is to be considered an "improved property", the Secretary shall take into consideration the manner of use of such buildings and lands prior to January 1, 1977, and shall designate such lands as are reasonably necessary for the continued enjoyment of the property in the same manner and to the same extent as existed prior to such date.

(d) Owner's reservation of right of use and occupancy for fixed term of years or for life; election by owner; fair market value; termination; notification

The owner of an improved property, as defined in this subchapter, on the date of its acquisition, as a condition of such acquisition, may retain for himself, his heirs and assigns, a right of use and occupancy of the improved property for noncommercial residential, or agricultural purposes, or the continuation of existing commercial operations, as the case may be, for a definite term of not more than twenty-five years, or, in lieu thereof, for a term ending at the death of the owner or the death of his spouse, whichever is later. The owner shall elect the term to be reserved. Unless the property is wholly or partially donated, the Secretary shall pay to the owner the fair market value of the property on the date of its acquisition, less the fair market value of the property on that date of the right retained by the owner. A right retained by the owner pursuant to this section shall be subject to termination by the Secretary upon his determination that it is being exercised in a manner inconsistent with the purposes of this subchapter, and it shall terminate by operation of law upon notification by the Secretary to the holder of the right of such determination and tendering to him the amount equal to the fair market value of that portion which remains unexpired.

(Pub.L. 95–625, Title XI, § 1102, Nov. 10, 1978, 92 Stat. 3545; Pub.L. 99–500, § 101(h), [Title I, § 116(a)], Oct. 18, 1986, 100 Stat. 1783–242, 1783–266; Pub.L. 99–590, Title X, § 1001, Oct. 30, 1986, 100 Stat. 3339; Pub.L. 99–591, § 101(h), [Title I, § 116(a)], Oct. 30, 1986, 100 Stat. 3341–266.)

HISTORICAL AND STATUTORY NOTES

Revision Notes and Legislative Reports
   1986 Acts. Statement by President, see 1986 U.S.Code Cong. and Adm.News, p. 5627.

References in Text
   This Act, referred to in subsec. (c), means Pub.L. 95–625, Nov. 10, 1978, 94 Stat. 3467, known as the National Parks and Recreation Act of 1978. For classification of such Act in the Code, see Short Title of 1978 Amendments note under section 1 of this title and Tables.

Codifications
   Pub.L. 99–591 is a corrected version of Pub.L. 99–500.

Amendments
   1986   Amendments. Subsec.   (a). Pub.L. 99–500, Pub.L. 99–590, and Pub.L. 99–591, amended subsec. (a), identically inserting provisions authorizing the Secretary to acquire not to exceed ten acres outside the boundaries of the national river for an administrative headquarters site and providing that funds appropriated for land acquisition be available for acquisition of the administrative headquarters site.

LIBRARY REFERENCES

American Digest System
   United States ☞55.
   Key Number System Topic No. 393.

§ 460m–17. Lands and areas plan; submission to Congressional committees

Within two years from November 10, 1978, the Secretary shall submit, in writing, to the House Committee on Interior and Insular Affairs, the Senate Committee on Energy and Natural Resources and the Committees on Appropriations of the United States Congress, a detailed plan which shall indicate—

(i) the lands and areas which he deems essential to the protection and public enjoyment of the natural, scenic, and historic values and objects of this national river;

(ii) the lands which he has previously acquired by purchase, donation, exchange, or transfer for the purpose of this national river;

(iii) the annual acquisition program (including the level of funding) which he recommends for the ensuing four fiscal years; and

(iv) the feasibility and suitability of including within the boundaries of the national river, the section of the New River from Fayetteville to Gauley Bridge, and reasons therefor.

(Pub.L. 95–625, Title XI, § 1103, Nov. 10, 1978, 92 Stat. 3546.)

HISTORICAL AND STATUTORY NOTES

Change of Name

Committee on Interior and Insular Affairs of the House of Representatives changed to Committee on Natural Resources of the House of Representatives on Jan. 5, 1993, by House Resolution No. 5, One Hundred Third Congress. Committee on Natural Resources of House of Representatives treated as referring to Committee on Resources of House of Representatives by section 1(a) of Pub.L. 104–14, set out as a note preceding 2 U.S.C.A. § 21. Committee on Resources of House of Representatives changed to Committee on Natural Resources of House of Representatives by House Resolution No. 6, One Hundred Tenth Congress, Jan. 5, 2007.

LIBRARY REFERENCES

American Digest System

United States ⊕57.
Key Number System Topic No. 393.

§ 460m–18. Zoning laws and ordinances; establishment; assistance; restrictions; variances

The Secretary shall on his own initiative, or at the request of any local government having jurisdiction over land located in or adjacent to the Gorge area, assist and consult with the appropriate officials and employees of such local government in establishing zoning laws or ordinances which will assist in achieving the purposes of this subchapter. In providing assistance pursuant to this section, the Secretary shall endeavor to obtain provisions in such zoning laws or ordinances which—

(1) have the effect of restricting incompatible commercial and industrial use of all real property in or adjacent to the Gorge area;

(2) aid in preserving the character of the Gorge area by appropriate restrictions on the use of real property in the vicinity, including, but not limited to, restrictions upon building and construction of all types; signs and billboards; the burning of cover; cutting of timber; removal of topsoil, sand, or gravel; dumping, storage, or piling of refuse; or any other use which would detract from the esthetic character of the Gorge area; and

(3) have the effect of providing that the Secretary shall receive advance notice of any hearing for the purpose of granting a variance and any variance granted under, and of any exception made to, the application of such law or ordinance.

(Pub.L. 95–625, Title XI, § 1104, Nov. 10, 1978, 92 Stat. 3546.)

§ 460m–19. Mineral lands

(a) Mining; prohibition and limitation

Notwithstanding any other provision of law, no surface mining of any kind shall be permitted on federally owned lands within the boundary of the national river where the subsurface estate is not federally owned. Underground mining on such lands may be permitted by the Secretary only if—

(1) the mining operation will have no significant adverse impact on the public use and enjoyment of the national river;

(2) the mining operation will disturb the minimum amount of surface necessary to extract the mineral; and

(3) the surface is not significantly disturbed, unless there is no technologically feasible alternative.

(b) Timber harvesting

The harvesting of timber on federally owned lands within the national river boundary is prohibited, except insofar as it is necessary for the Secretary to remove trees for river access, historic sites, primitive campgrounds, scenic vistas, or as may be necessary from time to time for reasons of public health and safety.

(c) Civil action; jurisdiction; recovery

The owner of a mineral estate subject to this section who believes he has suffered a loss by operation of this section, may bring an action only in a United States district court to recover just compensation, which shall be awarded if the court finds that such loss constitutes a taking of property compensable under the Constitution.

(Pub.L. 95–625, Title XI, § 1105, Nov. 10, 1978, 92 Stat. 3546.)

§ 460m–20. Hunting and fishing zones; designation; rules and regulations, consultation

The Secretary shall permit hunting and fishing on lands and waters under his jurisdiction within the boundaries of the New River Gorge

National River in accordance with applicable Federal and State laws, and he may designate zones where, and establish periods when, no hunting or fishing shall be permitted for reasons of public safety, administration, fish or wildlife management, or public use and enjoyment.   Except in emergencies, any rules and regulations of the Secretary pursuant to this section shall be put into effect only after consultation with the appropriate State agency responsible for hunting and fishing activities.   The Secretary shall permit the State of West Virginia to undertake fish stocking activities carried out by the State, in consultation with the Secretary, on waters within the boundaries of the national river.   Nothing in this Act shall be construed as affecting the jurisdiction of the State of West Virginia with respect to fish and wildlife.

(Pub.L. 95–625, Title XI, § 1106, Nov. 10, 1978, 92 Stat. 3547; Pub.L. 104–333, Div. I, Title IV, § 406(a)(2), Nov. 12, 1996, 110 Stat. 4149; Pub.L. 111–11, Title VII, § 7115, Mar. 30, 2009, 123 Stat. 1202.)

HISTORICAL AND STATUTORY NOTES

Revision Notes and Legislative Reports

2009 Acts. Statement by President, see 2009 U.S. Code Cong. and Adm. News, p. S13.

References in Text

This Act, referred to in text, means Pub.L. 95–625, Nov. 10, 1978, 92 Stat. 3467, as amended, known as the National Parks and Recreation Act of 1978.   For classification of such Act to the Code, see Short Title of 1978 Amendment note under section 1 of this title and Tables.

Amendments

2009 Amendments. Pub.L. 111–11, § 7115, which directed substitution of "shall" for "may" in first sentence, was executed by substituting "shall" for "may" the first time appearing, which was preceding "permit hunting and fishing".

1996 Amendments. Pub.L. 104–333, § 406(a)(2), added provision relating to West Virginia.

New River Gorge National River

Pub.L. 108–108, Title I, § 150, Nov. 10, 2003, 117 Stat. 1281, provided that: "The National Park Service shall issue a special regulation concerning continued hunting at New River Gorge National River in compliance with the requirements of the Administrative Procedures Act [Act June 11, 1946, c. 324, 60 Stat. 237; see Tables for complete classification], with opportunity for public comment, and shall also comply with the National Environmental Policy Act [Pub.L. 91–190, Jan. 1, 1970, 83 Sat. 852, which is classified principally to 42 U.S.C.A. § 4321 et seq.] as appropriate.   Notwithstanding any other provision of law, the September 25, 2003 interim final rule authorizing continued hunting at New River Gorge National River shall be in effect until the final special regulation supercedes it."

LIBRARY REFERENCES

American Digest System
  Fish ⬒8.
  Game ⬒3.5.
  Key Number System Topic Nos. 176, 187.

§ 460m–21. Project work prohibition; advisement to Secretary; report to Congress

The Federal Energy Regulatory Commission shall not license the construction of any dam, water conduit, reservoir, powerhouse, transmission line, or other project works under the Federal Power Act (41 Stat. 1063) as amended (16 U.S.C. 791a et seq.), on or directly affecting the New River Gorge National River, and no department or agency of the United States shall assist by loan, grant, license, or otherwise in the construction of any water resources project that would have a direct and adverse effect on the values for which such river was established, as determined by the Secretary. Nothing contained in the foregoing sentence, however, shall preclude licensing of, or assistance to, developments below or above the New River Gorge National River or on any stream tributary thereto which will not invade the area or diminish the scenic, recreation, and fish and wildlife values present in the area on November 10, 1978. No department or agency of the United States shall recommend authorization of any water resources project that would have a direct and adverse effect on the values for which such river was established, as determined by the Secretary, or request appropriations to begin construction on any such project whether heretofore or hereafter authorized, without advising the Secretary in writing of its intention to do so at least sixty days in advance, and without specifically reporting to the Congress in writing at the time it makes its recommendation or request in what respect construction of such project would be in conflict with the purposes of this section and would effect [1] the national river and the values to be protected by it under this section.

(Pub.L. 95–625, Title XI, § 1107, Nov. 10, 1978, 92 Stat. 3547.)

[1] So original. Probably should be "affect".

HISTORICAL AND STATUTORY NOTES

References in Text

The Federal Power Act (41 Stat. 1063) as amended (16 U.S.C. 791a et seq.), referred to in text, is Act June 10, 1920, c. 285, 41 Stat. 1063, as amended, which is classified generally to chapter 12 (section 791a et seq.) of this title. For complete classification of this Act to the Code, see section 791a of this title and Tables.

LIBRARY REFERENCES

American Digest System

United States ⚖57.

Key Number System Topic No. 393.

§ 460m–22. General management plan; submission to Congressional committees

Within three years from November 10, 1978, the Secretary shall develop and transmit to the Senate Committee on Energy and Natural Resources and the House Committee on Interior and Insular Affairs, a general management plan for the protection and development of the national river consistent with the purposes of this subchapter, indicating—

(1) measures for the preservation of the area's resources;

(2) indications of types and general intensities of development (including visitor circulation and transportation patterns, systems and modes) associated with public enjoyment and use of the area, including general locations, timing of implementation, and anticipated costs;

(3) identification of and implementation commitments for visitor carrying capacities for all areas of the unit; and

(4) indications of potential modifications to the external boundaries of the unit, and the reasons therefor.

(Pub.L. 95–625, Title XI, § 1109, Nov. 10, 1978, 92 Stat. 3548.)

HISTORICAL AND STATUTORY NOTES

Change of Name

Committee on Interior and Insular Affairs of the House of Representatives changed to Committee on Natural Resources of the House of Representatives on Jan. 5, 1993, by House Resolution No. 5, One Hundred Third Congress. Committee on Natural Resources of House of Representatives treated as referring to Committee on Resources of House of Representatives by section 1(a) of Pub.L. 104–14, set out as a note preceding 2 U.S.C.A. § 21. Committee on Resources of House of Representatives changed to Committee on Natural Resources of House of Representatives by House Resolution No. 6, One Hundred Tenth Congress, Jan. 5, 2007.

LIBRARY REFERENCES

American Digest System
Water Law ⬤⇒2519.
Key Number System Topic No. 405.

§ 460m–23.   Cooperation

The Secretary of the Army shall cooperate with the Secretary of the Interior concerning the water requirements of the national river. The Secretary of the Army shall provide for release of water from the Bluestone Lake project consistent with that project's purposes and activities in sufficient quantity and in such manner to facilitate protection of biological resources and recreational use of the national river.

(Pub.L. 95–625, Title XI, § 1110, Nov. 10, 1978, 92 Stat. 3548.)

CROSS REFERENCES

Flow management of Bluestone Lake project, see 16 USCA § 460m–28.

LIBRARY REFERENCES

American Digest System
United States ⬤⇒57.
Key Number System Topic No. 393.

§ 460m–24.   Class I or class II redesignation for clean air purposes

For the purposes of part C of the Clean Air Act [42 U.S.C.A. § 7470 et seq.], the State may redesignate the national river only as class I or class II.

(Pub.L. 95–625, Title XI, § 1111, Nov. 10, 1978, 92 Stat. 3548.)

HISTORICAL AND STATUTORY NOTES

References in Text

The Clean Air Act, referred to in text, is Act July 14, 1955, c. 360, as amended generally by Pub.L. 88–206, Dec. 17, 1963, 77 Stat. 392, and later by Pub.L. 95–95, Aug. 7, 1977, 91 Stat. 685. The Clean Air Act was originally classified to chapter 15B (section 1857 et seq.) of Title 42, The Public Health and Welfare. On enactment of Pub.L. 95–95, the Act was reclassified to chapter 85 (section 7401 et seq.) of Title 42. Part C of the Clean Air Act is classified generally to part C (section 7470 et seq.) of subchapter I of chapter 85 of Title 42. For complete classification of this Act to the Code, see Short Title note set out under section 7401 of Title 42 and Tables.

LIBRARY REFERENCES

American Digest System

Water Law ☞2519.

Key Number System Topic No. 405.

§ 460m–25.   Authorization of appropriations

There are hereby authorized to be appropriated such sums as may be necessary for the purposes of this subchapter, but not to exceed $20,000,000 for the acquisition of lands and interests in lands, and not to exceed $3,000,000 for development.

(Pub.L. 95–625, Title XI, § 1112, Nov. 10, 1978, 92 Stat. 3548; Pub.L. 99–500, § 101(h), [Title I, § 116(b)], Oct. 18, 1986, 100 Stat. 1783–242, 1783–266, Pub.L. 99–590, Title X, § 1002, Oct. 30, 1986, 100 Stat. 3340; Pub.L. 99–591, § 101(h), [Title I, § 116(b)], Oct. 30, 1986, 100 Stat. 3341–266.)

HISTORICAL AND STATUTORY NOTES

Revision Notes and Legislative Reports

1986 Acts. Statement by President, see 1986 U.S.Code Cong. and Adm.News, p. 5627.

Codifications

Pub.L. 99–591 is a corrected version of Pub.L. 99–500.

Amendments

1986 Amendments. Pub.L. 99–500, Pub.L. 99–590, and Pub.L. 99–591 amended section identically, substituting "$3,000,000" for "$500,000".

§ 460m–26.   Cooperative agreements with State

In administering the national river, the Secretary is authorized to enter into cooperative agreements with the State of West Virginia, or any political subdivision thereof, for the rendering, on a reimbursable or non-reimbursable basis, of rescue, fire fighting, and law enforcement services and cooperative assistance by nearby law enforcement and fire preventive agencies.

(Pub.L. 95–625, Title XI, § 1113, as added Pub.L. 100–534, Title I, § 102, Oct. 26, 1988, 102 Stat. 2700.)

HISTORICAL AND STATUTORY NOTES

Revision Notes and Legislative Reports
  1988 Acts. Senate Report No. 100–481, see 1988 U.S.Code Cong. and Adm.News, p. 3574.

LIBRARY REFERENCES

American Digest System
  States ⊕4.19.
  Key Number System Topic No. 360.

§ 460m–27. Improvement of access at Cunard

(a) Development and improvement

The Secretary shall expeditiously acquire such lands, and undertake such developments and improvements, as may be necessary to provide for commercial and noncommercial access to the river near Cunard. No restriction shall be imposed on such access based on the time of day, except to the extent required to protect public health and safety.

(b) Interim measures

Pending completion of the developments and improvements referred to in subsection (a) of this section, the Secretary shall permit the motorized towing of whitewater rafts in the section of the national river between Thurmond and Cunard when the volume of flow in the river is less than three thousand cubic feet per second.

(Pub.L. 95–625, Title XI, § 1114, as added Pub.L. 100–534, Title I, § 103, Oct. 26, 1988, 102 Stat. 2700.)

HISTORICAL AND STATUTORY NOTES

Revision Notes and Legislative Reports
  1988 Acts. Senate Report No. 100–481, see 1988 U.S.Code Cong. and Adm.News, p. 3574.

LIBRARY REFERENCES

American Digest System
  United States ⊕57.
  Key Number System Topic No. 393.

§ 460m–28.   Flow management

(a) Findings

The Congress finds that adjustments of flows from Bluestone Lake project during periods of low flow are necessary to respond to the congressional mandate contained in section 460m–23 of this title and that such adjustments could enhance the quality of the recreational experience in the segments of the river below the lake during those periods as well as protect the biological resources of the river.

(b) Report to Congress required

The Secretary of the Army, in conjunction with the Secretary of the Interior, shall conduct a study and prepare a report under this section. The report shall be submitted to the Committee on Energy and Natural Resources of the United States Senate and the Committee on Interior and Insular Affairs of the United States House of Representatives not later than December 31, 1989. Before submission of the report to these Committees, a draft of the report shall be made available for public comment. The final report shall include the comments submitted by the Secretary of the Interior and the public, together with the response of the Secretary of the Army to those comments.

(c) Contents of study

The study under this section shall examine the feasibility of adjusting the timing of daily releases from Bluestone Lake project during periods when flows from the lake are less than three thousand cubic feet per second. The purpose of such adjustment shall be to improve recreation (including, but not limited to, fishing and whitewater recreation) in the New River Gorge National River. Any such adjustments in the timing of flows which are proposed in such report shall be consistent with other project purposes and shall not have significant adverse effects on fishing or on any other form of recreation in Bluestone Lake or in any segment of the river below Bluestone Lake. The study shall assess the effects of such flow adjustments on the quality of recreation on the river in the segments of the river between Hinton and Thurmond and between Thurmond and the downstream boundary of the New River Gorge National River, taking into account the levels of recreational visitation in each of such segments.

(d) Test procedures

As part of the study under this section, the Secretary of the Army shall conduct test releases from Bluestone Lake project during twenty-four-hour periods during the summer of 1989 when flows are less than three thousand cubic feet per second from the project. All such adjustments shall conform to the criteria specified in subsection (c) of this section. The tests shall provide adjustments in the timing of daily flows from Bluestone Lake project which permit flows higher than the twenty-four-hour average to reach downstream recreational segments of the river during morning and afternoon hours. The tests shall develop specific data on the effects of flow adjustments on the speed of the current and on water surface levels in those segments. No test shall be conducted when flows from the lake are less than one thousand seven hundred cubic feet per second and no test shall reduce flows below that level.

(Pub.L. 95–625, Title XI, § 1115, as added Pub.L. 100–534, Title I, § 104, Oct. 26, 1988, 102 Stat. 2701.)

HISTORICAL AND STATUTORY NOTES

Revision Notes and Legislative Reports
  1988 Acts. Senate Report No. 100–481, see 1988 U.S.Code Cong. and Adm.News, p. 3574.

Change of Name
  Committee on Interior and Insular Affairs of the House of Representatives changed to Committee on Natural Resources of the House of Representatives on Jan. 5, 1993, by House Resolution No. 5, One Hundred Third Congress. Committee on Natural Resources of House of Representatives treated as referring to Committee on Resources of House of Representatives by section 1(a) of Pub.L. 104–14, set out as a note preceding 2 U.S.C.A. § 21. Committee on Resources of House of Representatives changed to Committee on Natural Resources of House of Representatives by House Resolution No. 6, One Hundred Tenth Congress, Jan. 5, 2007.

LIBRARY REFERENCES

American Digest System
  Water Law ⊛2519.
  Key Number System Topic No. 405.

§ 460m–29. Glade Creek visitor facility

In order to provide for public use and enjoyment of the scenic and natural resources of the New River Gorge National River and in order to provide public information to visitors with respect to the national river and associated State parklands, the Secretary is authorized and directed to construct a scenic overlook and visitor information facility at a suitable location accessible from Interstate 64 in the vicinity of Glade Creek within the boundary of the national river. There is authorized to be appropriated such sums as may be necessary to carry out construction (including all related planning and design) of the scenic overlook and visitor information facility.

(Pub.L. 95–625, Title XI, § 1116, as added Pub.L. 100–534, Title I, § 105, Oct. 26, 1988, 102 Stat. 2702.)

HISTORICAL AND STATUTORY NOTES

Revision Notes and Legislative Reports
  1988 Acts. Senate Report No. 100–481,
see 1988 U.S.Code Cong. and Adm.News,
p. 3574.

LIBRARY REFERENCES

American Digest System
  Water Law ☞2519.
  Key Number System Topic No. 405.

§ 460m–29a.   New River Gorge and Gauley River Visitor Center

The Secretary of the Interior is authorized to construct a visitor
center and such other related facilities as may be deemed necessary
to facilitate visitor understanding and enjoyment of the New River
Gorge National River and the Gauley River National Recreation Area
in the vicinity of the confluence of the New and Gauley Rivers. Such
center and related facilities are authorized to be constructed at a site
outside of the boundary of the New River Gorge National River or
Gauley River National Recreation Area unless a suitable site is
available within the boundaries of either unit.

(Pub.L. 104–333, Div. I, Title IV, § 406(b), Nov. 12, 1996, 110 Stat. 4150.)

HISTORICAL AND STATUTORY NOTES

Codifications

Section was enacted as part of the Omnibus Parks and Public Lands Management Act of 1996 [Pub.L. 104–333] and not as part of Title XI of Pub.L. 95–625, the National Parks and Recreation Act of 1978, which enacted this subchapter.

New River Visitor Center

Pub.L. 105–178, Title I, § 1214(c), June 9, 1998, 112 Stat. 205 provided that:

"(1) In general.—The Secretary shall allocate to the Secretary of the Interior amounts made available by this subsection for the planning, design, and construction of a visitor center, and such other related facilities as may be necessary, to facilitate visitor understanding and enjoyment of the scenic, historic, cultural, and recreational resources of the New River Gorge National River in the State of West Virginia. The center and related facilities shall be located at a site for which title is held by the United States in the vicinity of the I–64 Sandstone intersection.

"(2) Authorization of appropriations.— There are authorized to be appropriated out of the Highway Trust Fund (other than the Mass Transit Account) to carry out this subsection $1,300,000 for fiscal year 1998, $1,200,000 for fiscal year 1999, and $9,900,000 for fiscal year 2000.

"(3) Applicability of Title 23.—Funds authorized by this subsection shall be available for obligation in the same manner as if such funds were apportioned under chapter 1 of title 23, United States Code [section 101 et seq. of Title 23]; except that such funds shall remain available until expended."

LIBRARY REFERENCES

American Digest System
  United States ☞57.
  Key Number System Topic No. 393.

§ 460m–30. Applicable provisions of other law

(a) Cooperative agreements

The provisions of section 460ww–1(e)(1) of this title shall apply to the New River Gorge National River in the same manner and to the same extent as such provisions apply to the Gauley River National Recreation Area.

(b) Remnant lands

The provisions of the second sentence of section 460ww–2(a) of this title shall apply to tracts of land partially within the boundaries of the New River Gorge National River in the same manner and to the same extent as such provisions apply to tracts of land only partially within the Gauley River National Recreation Area.

(Pub.L. 95–625, Title XI, § 1117, as added Pub.L. 104–333, Div. I, Title IV, § 406(a)(3), Nov. 12, 1996, 110 Stat. 4150.)

SUBCHAPTER LXXII—LAKE MEAD NATIONAL RECREATION AREA

§ 460n. Administration

In recognition of the national significance of the Lake Mead National Recreation Area, in the States of Arizona and Nevada, and in order to establish a more adequate basis for effective administration of such area for the public benefit, the Secretary of the Interior hereafter may exercise the functions and carry out the activities prescribed by this subchapter.

(Pub.L. 88–639, § 1, Oct. 8, 1964, 78 Stat. 1039.)

HISTORICAL AND STATUTORY NOTES

Revision Notes and Legislative Reports
  1964 Acts. House Report No. 1039, see
1964 U.S.Code Cong. and Adm.News, p.
3918.

LIBRARY REFERENCES

American Digest System
  Woods and Forests ⊕5.
  Key Number System Topic No. 411.

§ 460n–1. Boundaries of area; filing of map with Federal Register; revision; donations of land; property acquisition and exclusion

Lake Mead National Recreation Area shall comprise that particular land and water area which is shown on a certain map, identified as "boundary map, RA–LM–7060–B, revised July 17, 1963", which is on file and which shall be available for public inspection in the office of the National Park Service of the Department of the Interior. An exact copy of such map shall be filed with the Federal Register within thirty days following October 8, 1964, and an exact copy thereof shall be available also for public inspection in the headquarters office of the superintendent of the said Lake Mead National Recreation Area.

The Secretary of the Interior is authorized to revise the boundaries of such national recreation area, subject to the requirement that the total acreage of that area, as revised, shall be no greater than the present acreage thereof. In the event of such boundary revision, maps of the recreation area, as revised, shall be prepared by the Department of the Interior, and shall be filed in the same manner, and shall be available for public inspection also in accordance with the aforesaid procedures and requirements relating to the filing and availability of maps. The Secretary may accept donations of land and interests in land within the exterior boundaries of such area, or such property may be procured by the Secretary in such manner as he shall consider to be in the public interest.

In exercising his authority to acquire property by exchange, the Secretary may accept title to any non–Federal property located within the boundaries of the recreation area and convey to the grantor of such property any federally owned property under the jurisdiction of the Secretary, notwithstanding any other provision of law. The properties so exchanged shall be approximately equal in fair market value: *Provided*, That the Secretary may accept cash from or pay cash to the grantor in such an exchange in order to equalize the values of the properties exchanged.

Establishment or revision of the boundaries of the said national recreation area, as herein prescribed, shall not affect adversely any valid rights in the area, nor shall it affect the validity of withdrawals heretofore made for reclamation or power purposes. All lands in the recreation area which have been withdrawn or acquired by the United States for reclamation purposes shall remain subject to the primary use thereof for reclamation and power purposes so long as they are withdrawn or needed for such purposes. There shall be excluded from the said national recreation area by the Secretary of the Interior any property for management or protection by the Bureau of Reclamation, which would be subject otherwise to inclusion in the said recreation area, and which the Secretary of the Interior considers in the national interest should be excluded therefrom.

(Pub.L. 88–639, § 2, Oct. 8, 1964, 78 Stat. 1039.)

HISTORICAL AND STATUTORY NOTES

Revision Notes and Legislative Reports
  1964 Acts. House Report No. 1039, see 1964 U.S.Code Cong. and Adm.News, p. 3918.

Transfer of Administrative Jurisdiction to National Park Service
  Pub.L. 107–282, Title III, § 302, Nov. 6, 2002, 116 Stat. 2006, provided that:

  "**(a) In general.**—Administrative jurisdiction over the parcel of land described in subsection (b) is transferred from the Bureau of Land Management to the Na-

tional Park Service for inclusion in the Lake Mead National Recreation Area.

  "**(b) Description of land.**—The parcel of land referred to in subsection (a) is the approximately 10 acres of Bureau of Land Management land, as depicted on the map entitled 'Eldorado/Spirit Mountain' and dated October 1, 2002.

  "**(c) Use of land.**—The parcel of land described in subsection (b) shall be used by the National Park Service for administrative facilities."

CROSS REFERENCES

Authorization of appropriations, see 16 USCA § 460n–9.

LIBRARY REFERENCES

American Digest System
  Water Law ⚬═2519.
  Key Number System Topic No. 405.

§ 460n–2.   Hualapai Indian lands; inclusion within area; mineral rights; leases and permits; hunting and fishing rights

The authorities granted by this subchapter shall be subject to the following exceptions and qualifications when exercised with respect to any tribal or allotted lands of the Hualapai Indians that may be included within the exterior boundaries of the Lake Mead National Recreation Area:

  (a) The inclusion of Indian lands within the exterior boundaries of the area shall not be effective until approved by the Hualapai Tribal Council.

  (b) Mineral developments or use of the Indian lands shall be permitted only in accordance with the laws that relate to Indian lands.

  (c) Leases and permits for general recreational use, business sites, home sites, vacation cabin sites, and grazing shall be executed in accordance with the laws relating to leases of Indian lands, provided that all development and improvement leases so granted shall conform to the development program and standards prescribed for the Lake Mead National Recreation Area.

  (d) Nothing in this subchapter shall deprive the members of the Hualapai Tribe of hunting and fishing privileges presently exercised by them, nor diminish those rights and privileges of that part of the reservation which is included in the Lake Mead Recreation Area.

(Pub.L. 88–639, § 3, Oct. 8, 1964, 78 Stat. 1039.)

HISTORICAL AND STATUTORY NOTES

Revision Notes and Legislative Reports
 1964 Acts. House Report No. 1039, see
1964 U.S.Code Cong. and Adm.News, p.
3918.

LIBRARY REFERENCES

American Digest System
 Armed Services ⚘54.
 Indians ⚘150.
 Key Number System Topic Nos. 34, 209.

§ 460n–3. Purposes and uses of area

(a) Public recreation, benefit, and use

Lake Mead National Recreation Area shall be administered by the Secretary of the Interior for general purposes of public recreation, benefit, and use, and in a manner that will preserve, develop, and enhance, so far as practicable, the recreation potential, and in a manner that will preserve the scenic, historic, scientific, and other important features of the area, consistently with applicable reservations and limitations relating to such area and with other authorized uses of the lands and properties within such area.

(b) Specific activities

In carrying out the functions prescribed by this subchapter, in addition to other related activities that may be permitted hereunder, the Secretary may provide for the following activities, subject to such limitations, conditions, or regulations as he may prescribe, and to such extent as will not be inconsistent with either the recreational use or the primary use of that portion of the area heretofore withdrawn for reclamation purposes:

 (1) General recreation use, such as bathing, boating, camping, and picnicking;

 (2) Grazing;

 (3) Mineral leasing;

 (4) Vacation cabin site use, in accordance with existing policies of the Department of the Interior relating to such use, or as such policies may be revised hereafter by the Secretary.

(Pub.L. 88–639, § 4, Oct. 8, 1964, 78 Stat. 1040.)

HISTORICAL AND STATUTORY NOTES

Revision Notes and Legislative Reports
  1964 Acts. House Report No. 1039, see
1964 U.S.Code Cong. and Adm.News, p.
3918.

LIBRARY REFERENCES

American Digest System
  Public Lands ☞17.
  United States ☞57.
  Key Number System Topic Nos. 317, 393.

Notes of Decisions

Construction with other laws   1

___

1. Construction with other laws
  Since Congress had given Secretary of
Interior authority to lease all materials at

Lake Mead National Recreation Area,
Atomic Energy Act of 1954, section 2011
et seq. of Title 42, was not applicable to
that area. Sierra Club v. Watt, D.C.Utah
1983, 566 F.Supp. 380. Mines And Minerals ☞ 5.1(3)

§ 460n–4. Hunting, fishing and trapping

The Secretary of the Interior shall permit hunting, fishing, and
trapping on the lands and waters under his jurisdiction within the
recreation area in accordance with the applicable laws and regulations of the United States and the respective States: *Provided*, That
the Secretary, after consultation with the respective State fish and
game commissions, may issue regulations designating zones where
and establishing periods when no hunting, fishing, or trapping shall
be permitted for reasons of public safety, administration, or public
use and enjoyment.

(Pub.L. 88–639, § 5, Oct. 8, 1964, 78 Stat. 1040.)

HISTORICAL AND STATUTORY NOTES

Revision Notes and Legislative Reports
  1964 Acts. House Report No. 1039, see
1964 U.S.Code Cong. and Adm.News, p.
3918.

LIBRARY REFERENCES

American Digest System
  Fish ☞8.
  Game ☞3.5.
  Key Number System Topic Nos. 176, 187.

§ 460n–5. Regulation of area; violations and penalties

Such national recreation area shall continue to be administered in
accordance with regulations heretofore issued by the Secretary of the
Interior relating to such areas, and the Secretary may revise such

regulations or issue new regulations to carry out the purposes of this subchapter. In his administration and regulation of the area, the Secretary shall exercise authority, subject to the provisions and limitations of this subchapter, comparable to his general administrative authority relating to areas of the national park system.

Any person who violates a rule or regulation issued pursuant to this subchapter shall be guilty of a misdemeanor, and may be punished by a fine of not more than $500, or by imprisonment not exceeding six months, or by both such fine and imprisonment.

(Pub.L. 88–639, § 6, Oct. 8, 1964, 78 Stat. 1040; Pub.L. 91–383, § 10(a) (4), as added Pub.L. 94–458, § 2, Oct. 7, 1976, 90 Stat. 1941.)

HISTORICAL AND STATUTORY NOTES

Revision Notes and Legislative Reports
   1964 Acts. House Report No. 1039, see 1964 U.S.Code Cong. and Adm.News, p. 3918.

   1976 Acts. House Report No. 94–1569, see 1976 U.S.Code Cong. and Adm.News, p. 4290.

Amendments
   1976 Amendments. Pub.L. 91–383, § 10(a)(4), as added by Pub.L. 94–458, struck out provisions relating to arrest powers of superintendent, caretakers, officers, or rangers of the Lake Mead National Recreation Area.

CODE OF FEDERAL REGULATIONS

Special regulations for particular areas of system, see 36 CFR § 7.1 et seq.

LIBRARY REFERENCES

American Digest System
   United States ⚲57.
   Woods and Forests ⚲5.
   Key Number System Topic Nos. 393, 411.

Notes of Decisions

Gambling regulation 1
Leasing of locatable materials 2

---

1. Gambling regulation
   National Park Service was within its authority in accepting state's cession of concurrent legislative authority over national recreational area, including private property located within its boundaries, and therefore, National Park Service Regulation, prohibiting gambling on federally-owned lands of a park area and on privately-owned lands within park areas, was applicable to the private property located within the national recreational area and condemnation award for such property, which was based on erroneous assumption that gambling was a permissible use of the property, was not legally competent and was excessive. U.S. v. 319.88 Acres of Land, More or Less, Situate in Clark County, Nev., D.C.Nev.1980, 498 F.Supp. 763. Eminent Domain ⚲ 150; United States ⚲ 57

2. Leasing of locatable materials
   Promulgation of regulations allowing leasing of "locatable" materials at Lake Mead National Recreation Area was not arbitrary and capricious. Sierra Club v. Watt, D.C.Utah 1983, 566 F.Supp. 380. Mines And Minerals ⚲ 5.1(3)

§ 460n–6. Political jurisdiction; taxing power; Hualapai Indians

Nothing in this subchapter shall deprive any State, or any political subdivision thereof, of its civil and criminal jurisdiction over the lands within the said national recreation area, or of its rights to tax persons, corporations, franchises, or property on the lands included in such area. Nothing in this subchapter shall modify or otherwise affect the existing jurisdiction of the Hualapai Tribe or alter the status of individual Hualapai Indians within that part of the Hualapai Indian Reservation included in said Lake Mead National Recreation Area.

(Pub.L. 88–639, § 7, Oct. 8, 1964, 78 Stat. 1041.)

HISTORICAL AND STATUTORY NOTES

Revision Notes and Legislative Reports
1964 Acts. House Report No. 1039, see 1964 U.S.Code Cong. and Adm.News, p. 3918.

LIBRARY REFERENCES

American Digest System
States ⊕4.19.
Key Number System Topic No. 360.

§ 460n–7. Revenues and fees; disposition

Revenues and fees obtained by the United States from operation of the national recreation area shall be subject to the same statutory provisions concerning the disposition thereof as are similar revenues collected in areas of the national park system with the exception, that those particular revenues and fees including those from mineral developments, which the Secretary of the Interior finds are reasonably attributable to Indian lands shall be paid to the Indian owner of the land, and with the further exception that other fees and revenues obtained from mineral development and from activities under other public land laws within the recreation area shall be disposed of in accordance with the provisions of the applicable laws.

(Pub.L. 88–639, § 8, Oct. 8, 1964, 78 Stat. 1041.)

HISTORICAL AND STATUTORY NOTES

Revision Notes and Legislative Reports
1964 Acts. House Report No. 1039, see 1964 U.S.Code Cong. and Adm.News, p. 3918.

LIBRARY REFERENCES

American Digest System
United States ⊕81.
Key Number System Topic No. 393.

§ 460n–8. United States magistrate judge: appointment; functions; probation; fees

A United States magistrate judge shall be appointed for that portion of the Lake Mead National Recreation Area that is situated in Mohave County, Arizona. Such magistrate judge shall be appointed by the United States district court having jurisdiction thereover, and the magistrate judge shall serve as directed by such court, as well as pursuant to, and within the limits of, the authority of said court.

The functions of the magistrate judge shall include the trial and sentencing of persons charged with the commission of misdemeanors and infractions as defined in section 3581 of Title 18. The exercise of additional functions by the magistrate judge shall be consistent with and be carried out in accordance with the authority, laws, and regulations, of general application to United States magistrate judges. The probation laws shall be applicable to persons tried by the magistrate judge and he shall have power to grant probation. The magistrate judge shall receive the fees, and none other, provided by law for like or similar services.

(Pub.L. 88–639, § 9, Oct. 8, 1964, 78 Stat. 1041; Pub.L. 98–473, Title II, § 222, Oct. 12, 1984, 98 Stat. 2028; Pub.L. 100–702, Title IV, § 404(c), Nov. 19, 1988, 102 Stat. 4651; Pub.L. 101–650, Title III, § 321, Dec. 1, 1990, 104 Stat. 5117.)

HISTORICAL AND STATUTORY NOTES

Revision Notes and Legislative Reports

1964 Acts. House Report No. 1039, see 1964 U.S.Code Cong. and Adm.News, p. 3918.

1984 Acts. House Report No. 98–1030 and House Conference Report No. 98–1159, see 1984 U.S.Code Cong. and Adm.News, p. 3182.

1988 Acts. House Report No. 100–889, see 1988 U.S.Code Cong. and Adm.News, p. 5982.

1990 Acts. Senate Report No. 101–416, see 1990 U.S.Code Cong. and Adm.News, p. 6802.

Amendments

1988 Amendments. Pub.L. 100–702 struck from the second par. the sentence "The provisions of Title 18, section 3402, and the rules of procedure and practice prescribed by the Supreme Court pursuant thereto, shall apply to all cases handled by such magistrate." which followed the sentence "The exercise of additional functions ....". See sections 2071 to 2074 of Title 28, Judiciary and Judicial Procedure.

1984 Amendments. Pub.L. 98–473, § 222(a) substituted "magistrate" for "commissioner" wherever appearing, which change in text had previously been made pursuant to Pub.L. 90–578 thereby requiring no further change in text.

Pub.L. 98–473, § 222(b), substituted provision relating to applicability to persons charged with misdemeanors and infractions under section 3581 of Title 18, for provisions relating to persons committing petty offenses under Title 18, section 1, and right of election of such persons to be tried in the district court of the United States.

Effective and Applicability Provisions
  1988 Acts. Amendment by Pub.L. 100–702 effective Dec. 1, 1988, see section 407 of Pub.L. 100–702, set out as a note under section 2071 of Title 28, Judiciary and Judicial Procedure.
  1984 Acts. Amendment by Pub.L. 98–473, effective Nov. 1, 1987, and applicable only to offenses committed after the taking effect of such amendment, see sec-

tion 235(a)(1) of Pub.L. 98–473, set out as a note under section 3551 of this title.

Change of Name
  "United States magistrate judge", "magistrate judge", and "United States magistrate judges" substituted for "United States magistrate", "magistrate", and "United States magistrates", respectively, wherever appearing in text pursuant to section 321 of Pub.L. 101–650, set out as a note under section 631 of Title 28, Judiciary and Judicial Procedure.

LIBRARY REFERENCES

American Digest System
  United States ☞35, 57.
  Key Number System Topic No. 393.

§ 460n–9. Authorization of appropriations

There are hereby authorized to be appropriated not more than $7,100,000 for the acquisition of land and interests in land pursuant to section 460n–1 of this title.

(Pub.L. 88–639, § 10, Oct. 8, 1964, 78 Stat. 1041; Pub.L. 93–477, Title I, § 101(12), Oct. 26, 1974, 88 Stat. 1445.)

HISTORICAL AND STATUTORY NOTES

Revision Notes and Legislative Reports
  1964 Acts. House Report No. 1039, see 1964 U.S.Code Cong. and Adm.News, p. 3918.

Amendments
  1974 Amendments. Pub.L. 93–477 substituted "$7,100,000" for "$1,200,000".

SUBCHAPTER LXXIII—DELAWARE WATER GAP NATIONAL RECREATION AREA

CROSS REFERENCES

Establishment of visitors facilities, see 16 USCA § 1274.

§ 460*o*. Establishment

In order to further the purposes of the joint resolution approved September 27, 1961 (re Delaware River Basin compact; 75 Stat. 688), and to provide, in a manner coordinated with the other purposes of the Tocks Island Reservoir project, for public outdoor recreation use and enjoyment of the proposed Tocks Island Reservoir and lands adjacent thereto by the people of the United States and for preservation of the scenic, scientific, and historic features contributing to public enjoyment of such lands and waters, the Secretary of the Interior is authorized, as herein provided, to establish and administer the Delaware Water Gap National Recreation Area, hereinafter referred to as the "area", as part of the Tocks Island Reservoir project, hereinafter referred to as "the project".

(Pub.L. 89–158, § 1, Sept. 1, 1965, 79 Stat. 612.)

HISTORICAL AND STATUTORY NOTES

References in Text

The joint resolution approved September 27, 1961, referred to in text, is Pub.L. 87–328, which was not classified to the Code.

Joseph M. McDade Recreational Trail at Delaware Water Gap National Recreation Area

Pub.L. 105–277, Div. A, § 101(e) [Title I, § 118], Oct. 21, 1998, 112 Stat. 2681–257, provided that: "The 37 mile River Valley Trail from the town of Delaware Gap to the edge of the town of Milford, Pennsylvania located within the Delaware Water Gap National Recreation Area shall hereafter be referred to in any law, regulation, document, or record of the United States as the Joseph M. McDade Recreational Trail."

Delaware Water Gap National Recreation Area Citizen Advisory Commission

Pub.L. 100–573, Oct. 31, 1988, 102 Stat. 2890, as amended Pub.L. 104–333, Div. I, Title VIII, § 814(d)(1)(K), Nov. 12, 1996, 110 Stat. 4196; Pub.L. 105–355, Title V, § 507, Nov. 6, 1998, 112 Stat. 3264; Pub.L. 106–176, Title III, § 301, Mar. 10, 2000, 114 Stat. 31, provided that:

"Sec. 1.   Establishment of Commission.

"There is established a commission to be known as the 'Delaware Water Gap National Recreation Area Citizen Advisory Commission' (hereafter in this Act [this note] referred to as the 'Commission'). The Commission shall advise the Secretary of the Interior on matters pertaining to the management and operation of the Delaware Water Gap National Recreation Area, as well as on other matters affecting the recreation area and its surrounding communities.

"Sec. 2.   Membership of Commission.

"(a) Appointment.—The Commission shall be composed of the following 11 members appointed not later than 60 days after the date of the enactment of this Act [Oct. 31, 1988] from among persons with knowledge of the recreation area:

"(1) 2 members appointed by the Secretary of the Interior (hereafter in this Act referred to as the 'Secretary').

"(2) 2 members appointed by the Secretary from among residents of New Jersey nominated by the Governor of New Jersey.

"(3) 2 members appointed by the Secretary from among residents of Pennsylvania nominated by the Governor of Pennsylvania.

"(4) 1 member appointed by the Secretary from among the residents of each of the following counties nominated by the county administrator of each such county: Sussex County, New Jersey, Warren County, New Jersey, Pike County, Pennsylvania, Monroe County, Pennsylvania, and Northampton County, Pennsylvania.

The Secretary shall ensure that the membership of the Commission is fairly balanced in terms of the points of view represented and the functions to be performed by the Commission.

"(b) Terms.—Members shall be appointed to the Commission for a term of 4 years. A member may serve after the expiration of his term until his successor has taken office.

"(c) Vacancies.—Any vacancy on the Commission shall be filled in the manner in which the original appointment was made.

"(d) Prohibition of additional pay.—Members of the Commission shall receive no additional pay, allowances, or benefits by reason of their service on the Commission, but the Secretary may pay expenses reasonably incurred in carrying out their responsibilities under this Act on vouchers signed by the Chairperson.

"(e) Chairperson.—The Commission shall elect a chairperson from among the members of the Commission.

"(f) Quorum.—A majority of the members of the Commission shall constitute a quorum but a lesser number may hold hearings.

"(g) Voting.—Each member of the Commission shall be entitled to 1 vote, which shall be equal to the vote of every other member of the Commission.

"(h) Charter.—The provisions of section 14(b) of the Federal Advisory Committee Act (Act of October 6, 1972; 86 Stat. 776) [set out in Appendix 2 to Title 5, Government organization and Employees], are hereby waived with respect to this Advisory Commission.

"Sec. 3. Powers of Commission.

"(a) Hearings.—The Commission may, for the purpose of carrying out its functions under section 1, hold such hearings, sit and act at such times and places, take such testimony, and receive such evidence, as the Commission considers appropriate.

"(b) Meetings with Secretary of the Interior.—Members of the Commission shall meet with the Secretary of the Interior or his designee at least once every 6 months. Such meetings shall be open to the public and shall be held at such times and in such places as to encourage public participation. The Commission shall provide the public with adequate notice of such meetings.

"(c) Rules and regulations.—The Commission may adopt such rules and regulations as may be necessary to establish its

procedures and to govern the manner of its operation.

"(d) Assistance from Federal agencies.—Upon request of the chairperson of the Commission, the head of any Federal agency or instrumentality shall, to the extent possible and subject to the discretion of such head make any of the facilities and services of such agency or instrumentality available to the Commission.

"(e) Mails.—The Commission may use the United States mails in the same manner and under the same conditions as other Federal agencies.

"Sec. 4. Repealed. Pub.L. 104–333, Div. I, Title VIII, § 814(d)(1)(K), Nov. 12, 1996, 110 Stat. 4196

"Sec. 5. Termination of Commission.

"The Commission shall terminate on the date that is 20 years after the date of the enactment of this Act [Oct. 31, 1988].

"Sec. 6. Authorization of appropriations.

"There are authorized to be appropriated such sums as may be necessary to carry out this Act."

[Pub.L. 105–355, § 507, which purported to amend section 5 of Pub.L. 101–573 by striking "10" and inserting "20" was executed to this note as the probable intent of Congress. Amendment by Pub.L. 106–176, § 301, correcting this error by changing the original reference to Pub.L. 101–573 to read Pub.L. 100–573, was effective as of Nov. 6, 1998.]

CODE OF FEDERAL REGULATIONS

National Park Service, general provisions, see 36 CFR § 1.1 et seq.

LIBRARY REFERENCES

American Digest System
    Water Law ⚮2519.
    Key Number System Topic No. 405.

§ 460*o*–1. Acquisition of lands

(a) Authority of Secretary of Army; transfer of jurisdiction over lands to Secretary of the Interior; authority of such Secretary; retention of use and occupancy rights; termination and transfer of authority and funds; acquisition priorities

The Secretary of the Army is authorized and directed to acquire, by such means as he may deem to be in the public interest, and as a part of his acquisition of properties for the project, lands and interests therein within the boundaries of the area, as generally depicted on the drawing entitled "Proposed Tocks Island National Recreation Area" dated and numbered September 1962, NRA–TI–7100, which drawing is on file in the Office of the National Park Service, Department of the Interior.   In acquiring these lands, the Secretary of the Army may utilize such statutory authorities as are available to him for the acquisition of project lands: *Provided*, That the Secretary of the Army shall acquire no lands or interests in land by exchange for lands or interests in land in Federal ownership unless the latter are in the States of Pennsylvania, New Jersey, or New York.   Periodically, and as soon as practicable after such lands and interests within the area are acquired, the Secretary of the Army shall transfer jurisdiction thereover to the Secretary of the Interior for the purposes of this subchapter.   Beginning on November 10, 1978, the Secretary of the Interior is authorized to acquire for purposes of the recreation area established under this subchapter all lands and interests therein within the exterior boundaries of the area depicted on the drawing referred to in this subsection (including any lands within such exterior boundaries designated for acquisition by the Secretary of the Army in connection with the project referred to in this subsection).   In exercising such authority, the Secretary of the Interior may permit the retention of rights of use and occupancy in the same manner as provided in the case of acquisitions by the Secretary of the Army under subsection (d) of this section.   On November 10, 1978, the acquisition authorities of any other Federal agency contained in this subsection shall terminate and the head of any other Federal agency shall transfer to the Secretary of the Interior jurisdiction over all lands and interests therein acquired by said agency under the authority of this subchapter, or any other authority of law which lands are within the exterior boundaries of the area depicted on the drawing referred to in this subsection.   On November 10, 1978, all unexpended balances available to any other Federal agency for acquisition of land within the exterior boundaries referred to in the preceding sentence shall be transferred to the Secretary of the Interior to be used for such purposes.   In carrying out his acquisition authority under this section the Secretary shall give priority to the following:

> **(1)** completion of acquisition of lands for which condemnation proceedings have been started pursuant to the authorization of the project referred to in this subsection;

> **(2)** acquisition of lands of beneficial owners, not being a corporation, who in the judgment of the Secretary would suffer hardship if acquisition of their lands were delayed;

(3) acquisition of lands on which, in the judgment of the Secretary, there is an imminent danger of development that would be incompatible with the purposes of the recreation area;

(4) acquisition of lands of beneficial owners, not being a corporation, who are willing to sell their lands provided they are able to continue to use it for noncommercial residential purposes for a limited period of time which will not, in the judgment of the Secretary, unduly interfere with the development of public use facilities for such national recreation area, pursuant to the authorization for such area;

(5) acquisition of scenic easements when, in the judgment of the Secretary, such easements are sufficient to carry out the purposes for which such national recreation area was authorized; and

(6) acquisition of lands necessary to preserve the integrity of the recreation area.

(b) Omission of designated lands from area

Notwithstanding the provisions of subsection (a) of this section, the Secretary of the Interior is authorized, after consultation with appropriate public officials of the affected political subdivisions of the States of Pennsylvania or New Jersey, as the case may be, to designate not more than three hundred acres adjacent and contiguous to the Borough of Milford, Pennsylvania, and not more than one thousand acres in Sussex County, New Jersey, for omission from the Delaware Valley National Recreation Area and the lands so designated shall not be acquired for said national recreation area under authority of this subchapter.

(c) Extension of boundaries; study and report to Congress

The Secretary of the Interior shall investigate, study, and report to the President and the Congress on the feasibility and usefulness of extending the boundaries of the Delaware Water Gap National Recreation Area to include, in whole or in part, that portion of Tocks Island Reservoir which lies upstream from the northern terminus of the national recreation area as shown on the map hereinbefore referred to and lands adjacent to said portion of said reservoir. No such extension of boundaries, however, shall be made until authorized by Act of Congress.

(d) Noncommercial residential occupancy for life or fixed term of years; price for property; "improved residential property" defined; waiver of relocation assistance benefits or rights

The beneficial owner, not being a corporation, of a freehold interest acquired before January 1, 1965, in improved residential property within the area to be acquired by the Secretary of the Army under authority of this subchapter, the continued use of which property for noncommercial residential purposes for a limited time will not, in the judgment of the Secretary of the Interior, unduly interfere with the development of public-use facilities for the national recreation area and will not, in the judgment of the Secretary of the Army, unduly interfere with the operation of the Tocks Island Reservoir project, may retain a right of use and occupancy of such property for noncommercial residential purposes for, as said owner may elect, either (i) a period terminating upon his death or the death of his spouse, whichever occurs later, or (ii) a term of not more than twenty-five years: *Provided*, That in no case shall the period or term for which such right of use and occupancy is retained extend beyond the term of the freehold interest acquired by the United States. The price payable to the owner of such property shall be reduced by an amount equal to the value of the right retained. As used in this subchapter "improved residential property" means a single-family year-round dwelling, the construction of which was begun before January 21, 1963, which dwelling serves as the owner's permanent place of abode at the time of its acquisition by the United States, together with not more than three acres of land on which the dwelling and appurtenant buildings are located which land the Secretary of the Interior or the Secretary of the Army, as the case may be, finds is reasonably necessary for the owner's continued use and occupancy of the dwelling: *Provided, further*, That whenever an owner of property elects to retain a right of use and occupancy pursuant to this subchapter, such owner shall be deemed to have waived any benefits or rights under the Uniform Relocation Assistance and Real Property Acquisition Policies Act of 1970 [42 U.S.C.A. § 4601 et seq.]

(Pub.L. 89–158, § 2, Sept. 1, 1965, 79 Stat. 612; Pub.L. 92–575, § 2, Oct. 27, 1972, 86 Stat. 1250; Pub.L. 95–625, Title III, § 316, Nov. 10, 1978, 92 Stat. 3483.)

HISTORICAL AND STATUTORY NOTES

References in Text

The Uniform Relocation Assistance and Real Property Acquisition Policies Act of 1970, referred to in subsec. (d), is Pub.L. 91–646, Jan. 2, 1991, 84 Stat. 1894, as amended, which is classified generally to chapter 61 (section 4601 et seq.) Title 42, The Public Health and Welfare. For complete classification of this Act to the Code see Short Title note set out under section 4601 of Title 42 and Tables.

Amendments

1978 Amendments. Subsec. (a). Pub.L. 95–625 authorized acquisition of lands within the exterior boundaries of the area by the Secretary of the Interior, retention of use and occupancy rights, termination of Federal agency authority over lands and transfer of authority and funds to the Secretary of the Interior, and prescribed acquisition priorities for the Secretary of the Interior.

1972   Amendments. Subsec.   (d). Pub.L. 92–575 provided for waiver of

benefits or rights under the Uniform Relocation Assistance and Real Property Acquisition Policies Act of 1970, upon election to retain right of use and occupancy
pursuant to sections 460o to 460o–7 of
this title.

LIBRARY REFERENCES

American Digest System
   United States ☞55.
   Key Number System Topic No. 393.

§ 460o–2. Designation of area; boundaries

(a) Publication in Federal Register; description of boundaries; administration of transferred lands and waters

As soon as practicable after September 1, 1965, and following the
transfer to the Secretary of the Interior by the Secretary of the Army
of jurisdiction over those lands and interests therein within the
boundary generally depicted on the drawing described in section
460o–1 of this title which, in the opinion of the Secretary of the
Interior, constitute an efficiently administrable unit, the Secretary of
the Interior shall declare establishment of the area by publication of
notice thereof in the Federal Register. Such notice shall contain a
detailed description of the boundaries of the area which shall encompass, to the extent practicable, the lands and waters shown on said
drawing. Prior to such establishment, the Secretary of the Interior
shall administer such transferred lands and waters, consistent with
the construction of the project, for purposes in contemplation of the
establishment of the area pursuant to this subchapter.

(b) Adjustments in boundaries; publication in Federal Register; acquisition of additional lands; acreage limitations

The Secretary of the Interior may subsequently make adjustments
in the boundary of the area by publication of the amended description thereof in the Federal Register and acquire, by such means as he
may deem to be in the public interest, including an exchange of
excluded for included lands or interests therein with or without the
payment or receipt of money to equalize values, additional lands and
interests therein included in the area by reason of the boundary
adjustment: *Provided*, That the area encompassed by such revised
boundary shall not exceed the acreage included within the detailed
boundary first described pursuant to this section.

(c) Continuance of existing uses

On lands acquired pursuant to this subchapter for recreation
purposes, the Secretary of the Army, with the concurrence of the

Secretary of the Interior, may permit the continuance of existing uses consistent with the purposes of this subchapter.

(Pub.L. 89–158, § 3, Sept. 1, 1965, 79 Stat. 613.)

LIBRARY REFERENCES

American Digest System
  Water Law ⊕2519.
  Key Number System Topic No. 405.

§ 460o–3. Administration authorities for conservation, management, or disposal of natural resources; coordination of administrative responsibilities of the Secretary of the Interior and Secretary of the Army

In the administration of the area for the purposes of this subchapter, the Secretary of the Interior may utilize such statutory authorities relating to areas of the national park system and such statutory authorities otherwise available to him for the conservation, management, or disposal of vegetative, mineral, or fish or wildlife resources as he deems appropriate to carry out the purposes of this subchapter. To assure consistent and effective planning, development, and operation for all purposes of the project, the Secretary of the Interior and the Secretary of the Army shall coordinate the administration of their respective responsibilities in the project; and such administration shall be consistent with the joint resolution approved September 27, 1961 (re Delaware River Basin compact; 75 Stat. 688).

(Pub.L. 89–158, § 4, Sept. 1, 1965, 79 Stat. 613.)

CODE OF FEDERAL REGULATIONS

Special regulations for particular areas of system, see 36 CFR § 7.1 et seq.

LIBRARY REFERENCES

American Digest System
  Woods and Forests ⊕5.
  Key Number System Topic No. 411.

§ 460o–4. Land and water use management plan; adoption, implementation, and revision; provisions

In the administration of the area for the purposes of this subchapter, the Secretary of the Interior, subject to provisions of section 460o–3 of this title, shall adopt and implement, and may from time to time revise, a land and water use management plan, which shall include specific provision for, in order of priority—

(1) public outdoor recreation benefits;

(2) preservation of scenic, scientific, and historic features contributing to public enjoyment;

(3) such utilization of natural resources as in the judgment of the Secretary of the Interior is consistent with, and does not significantly impair, public recreation and protection of scenic, scientific, and historic features contributing to public enjoyment.

(Pub.L. 89–158, § 5, Sept. 1, 1965, 79 Stat. 614.)

LIBRARY REFERENCES

American Digest System
    Water Law ☞2519.
    Key Number System Topic No. 405.

§ 460*o*–5. Hunting and fishing

The Secretary of the Interior shall permit hunting and fishing on lands and waters under his jurisdiction within the area in accordance with the applicable laws and regulations of the States concerned and of the United States. The Secretary of the Interior may designate zones where, and establish periods when, no hunting shall be permitted for reasons of public safety, wildlife management, administration, or public use and enjoyment not compatible with hunting, and may, in his plan for the area, provide areas for intensive fish and wildlife management, including public hunting and fishing, and shall issue appropriate regulations after consultation with appropriate officials of the States concerned. The Secretary of the Interior shall encourage such officials to adopt uniform regulations applicable to the whole of the Delaware Water Gap National Recreation Area.

(Pub.L. 89–158, § 6, Sept. 1, 1965, 79 Stat. 614.)

LIBRARY REFERENCES

American Digest System
    Fish ☞8.
    Game ☞3.5.
    Key Number System Topic Nos. 176, 187.

§ 460*o*–6. Civil and criminal jurisdiction and taxing power of State

Nothing in this subchapter shall be construed to deprive any State or political subdivision thereof, of its right to exercise civil and criminal jurisdiction over the lands and waters within the area or of its right to tax persons, corporations, franchises, or property on the lands and waters included in the area.

(Pub.L. 89–158, § 7, Sept. 1, 1965, 79 Stat. 614.)

§ 460o-7.   Authorization of appropriations

There are hereby authorized to be appropriated to the Secretary of the Interior for the acquisition of lands and interests in land pursuant to the provisions of section 460o-1 of this title and for expenses incident thereto not more than $65,000,000 which moneys shall be transferred to the Secretary of the Army.   There are also authorized to be appropriated not more than $18,200,000 for the cost of installing and constructing recreation facilities on the lands and interests in lands so acquired.   The amounts herein authorized to be appropriated are supplemental to those authorized to be appropriated for the Tocks Island project and related facilities by the Flood Control Act of 1962 (76 Stat. 1182).

(Pub.L. 89–158, § 8, Sept. 1, 1965, 79 Stat. 614; Pub.L. 92–575, § 1, Oct. 27, 1972, 86 Stat. 1250.)

HISTORICAL AND STATUTORY NOTES

References in Text
The amounts authorized to be appropriated for the Tocks Island project and related facilities by the Flood Control Act of 1962, referred to in text, appear at 76 Stat. 1182, and were not classified to the Code.   The Flood Control Act of 1962 is Title II of Pub.L. 87–874, Oct. 23, 1962, 76 Stat. 1173.   For complete classification of this Act to the Code, see Tables.

Amendments
1972 Amendments. Pub.L. 92–575 increased appropriations authorization to $65,000,000 from $37,412,000.

INDEX

TO

TITLE 16—CONSERVATION

See last volume of Title 16

END OF VOLUME

UNITED STATES CODE ANNOTATED

Title 16
Conservation
§§ 411 to 460o–7

2022
Cumulative Annual Pocket Part

Place in the back of 2010 bound volume

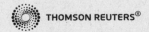

THOMSON REUTERS®

PREFACE

The 2022 Pocket Parts for U.S.C.A. contain the laws, classified to the United States Code, of a general and permanent nature enacted by Congress through the final law of the First Session of the 117th Congress and through Pub.L. 117–102 of the Second Session of the 117th Congress.

Notes of decisions of Federal courts include cases published on Thomson Reuters Westlaw as of March 2, 2022.

For scope of updates to Federal Court Rules, see individual rules sets.

Federal Sentencing Guidelines include amendments received to March 15, 2022.

The Pocket Parts also include updated Executive Orders, Proclamations, selected sections of the Code of Federal Regulations, and Reorganization Plans.

Contact Us

For additional information or research assistance, contact the Reference Attorneys at 1–800–REF–ATTY (1–800–733–2889) or by Live Chat: Access via Westlaw. Contact our U.S. legal editorial department directly with your questions and suggestions by e-mail at editors.us-legal@tr.com.

UNITED STATES CODE ANNOTATED

TITLE 16

CONSERVATION

CHAPTER 1—NATIONAL PARKS, MILITARY PARKS, MONUMENTS, AND SEASHORES

1

SUBCHAPTER LX—NATIONAL MILITARY PARKS

§ 411. Omitted

HISTORICAL NOTES

Codifications

Section, Act May 15, 1896, c. 182, § 1, 29 Stat. 120, which authorized the use of national military parks for military maneuvers, was editorially eliminated from the Code as a result of the enactment into positive law of Title 54, National Park Service and Related Programs, by Pub.L. 113–287, Dec. 19, 2014, 128 Stat. 3094.

§ 412. Omitted

HISTORICAL NOTES

Codifications

Section, Act May 15, 1896, c. 182, § 2, 29 Stat. 121, which authorized the Secretary of the Army to assemble cams for military instructions and to promulgate regulations regarding the assembling of the National Guard or militia, was editorially eliminated from the Code as a result of the enactment into positive law of Title 54, National Park Service and Related Programs, by Pub.L. 113–287, Dec. 19, 2014, 128 Stat. 3094.

§ 413. Omitted

HISTORICAL NOTES

Codifications

Section, Act March 3, 1897, c. 372, §§ 1, 5, 29 Stat. 621, 622, which authorized misdemeanor offenses relating to the destruction of structures and vegetation within any national military parks, was editorially eliminated from the Code as a result of the enactment into positive law of Title 54, National Park Service and Related Programs, by Pub.L. 113–287, Dec. 19, 2014, 128 Stat. 3094.

§ 414. Omitted

HISTORICAL NOTES

Codifications

Section, Act March 3, 1897, c. 1372 § 2, 5, 29 Stat. 621, 622, which authorized misdemeanor offenses relating to trespassing upon any national military parks for the purpose of hunting or shooting, was editorially eliminated from the Code as a result of the enactment into positive law of Title 54, National Park Service and Related Programs, by Pub.L. 113–287, Dec. 19, 2014, 128 Stat. 3094.

§ 416. Omitted

HISTORICAL NOTES

Codifications

Section, Act March 3, 1897, c. 372, §§ 4, 5, 29 Stat. 622, which related to refusal to surrender leased land within any national military parks after possession was demanded for by the United States by any park commissioner, and recovery action by the United States of such land, was editorially eliminated from the Code as a result of the enactment into positive law of Title

54, National Park Service and Related Programs, by Pub.L. 113–287, Dec. 19, 2014, 128 Stat. 3094.

§ 420. Omitted

HISTORICAL NOTES

Codifications

Section, Acts Mar. 4, 1911, c. 238, 36 Stat. 1253; May 27, 1952, c. 338, 66 Stat. 95; Pub.L. 94–579, Title VII, § 706(a), Oct. 21, 1976, 90 Stat. 2793; Pub.L. 113–287, § 7, Dec. 19, 2014, 128 Stat. 3272, which authorized heads of departments having jurisdiction over the lands to

grant easements for rights-of-way on the public lands, national forests, and reservations of the United States for electrical power and communications facilities, was editorially omitted because Act Mar. 4, 1911, is also classified to 43 U.S.C.A. § 961. It was also classified to sections 5 and 523 of this title, which were omitted from the Code.

§ 421. Omitted

HISTORICAL NOTES

Codifications

Section, Act Aug. 24, 1912, c. 355, § 1, 37 Stat. 442, which directed that vacancies occurring by death or resignation in the membership of the several commissions in charge of national mili-

tary parks shall not be filled, was editorially eliminated from the Code as a result of the enactment into positive law of Title 54, National Park Service and Related Programs, by Pub.L. 113–287, Dec. 19, 2014, 128 Stat. 3094. See 54 U.S.C.A. § 103303.

§ 422. Moores Creek National Battlefield; establishment

In order to preserve for historical and professional military study one of the most memorable battles of the Revolutionary War, the battlefield of Moores Creek, in the State of North Carolina, is declared to be a national battlefield whenever the title to the same shall have been acquired by the United States; that is to say, the area inclosed by the following lines:

Those tracts or parcels of land in the county of Pender, and State of North Carolina, more particularly described as follows:

First tract: Beginning at a stone at the run of Moores Creek, on the east bank of same, about twenty poles (in a straight line) above the new iron bridge, and running thence parallel to William Walker's line, south sixty-two and one-half degrees west eleven chains to a stake; thence south seven and one-half degrees east three and six-tenths chains to a stone at the south edge of the old stage road; thence along the south edge of said road south forty-six degrees east about five chains and eighty links to a stone; thence south thirty-seven and one-fourth degrees west fourteen chains and twelve links to a stone; thence north sixty-two and one-half degrees west ten chains and seventy-five links to a stone, a corner (4) of an eight-acre tract which the parties of the first part conveyed to Governor D. L. Russell, for the purposes aforesaid, by a deed dated January, 1898, and recorded in Pender County; thence with the lines of said tract north thirty-nine and one-half degrees east thirteen chains and twenty-seven links to a stake, the third corner of the said eight-acre tract; thence north fifty-one degrees west four chains to a stake about twenty feet from the old entrenchment (the second corner of the eight-acre tract); thence with the first line reversed north forty-four degrees west two chains to a sweet gum at the run of Moores Creek (the first corner of the eight-acre tract); thence up and with the run of said creek to the first station, containing twenty acres.

Second tract: Beginning at a sweet gum on the eastern edge of Moores Creek, running thence south forty-four degrees east two poles to a stake; thence south fifty-one degrees east four poles five links to a stake; thence south thirty-nine degrees west thirteen poles twenty-seven links to a stake; thence north fifty-one degrees west nine poles thirty-one links to a stake in the edge of Moores Creek; thence northerly with the creek to the beginning, containing eight acres more or less.

Third tract: Beginning at a cypress on the edge of the run of Moores Creek about twenty feet from the west end of the old entrenchments and running thence in a line parallel to and ten feet distance [1] from the outside or east edge of the old line of entrenchments in all the various courses of the same to a stake ten feet distant on the east side of the north end of said entrenchments; thence a direct line to the run of said Moores Creek; thence down said creek to the beginning, containing two acres, be the same more or less (the intention is to include all lands now known and designated as Moores Creek battlefield and now so recognized as such and owned by the State of North Carolina), together with all the privileges and appurtenances thereunto belonging.

The aforesaid tracts of land containing in the aggregate thirty acres, more or less, and being the property of the State of North Carolina, and the area thus inclosed shall be known as the Moores Creek National Battlefield.

[1] So in original. Probably should be "distant".

§ 423a–3. Petersburg National Battlefield boundary modification

(a) In general

The boundary of the Petersburg National Battlefield is modified to include the land and interests in land as generally depicted on the map titled "Petersburg National Battlefield Proposed Boundary Expansion", numbered 325/80,080, and dated June 2007/March 2016. The map shall be on file and available for public inspection in the appropriate offices of the National Park Service.

(b) Acquisition of properties

(1) Authority

The Secretary of the Interior (referred to in this section as the "Secretary") is authorized to acquire the land and interests in land described in subsection (a) from willing sellers only, by donation, purchase with donated or appropriated funds, exchange, or transfer.

(2) Omitted

(c) Administration

The Secretary shall administer any land or interests in land acquired under subsection (b) as part of the Petersburg National Battlefield in accordance with applicable laws and regulations.

(d) Administrative jurisdiction transfer

(1) In general

There is transferred—

    (A) from the Secretary to the Secretary of the Army administrative jurisdiction over the approximately 1.170-acre parcel of land depicted as "Area to be transferred to Fort Lee Military Reservation" on the map described in paragraph (2); and

    (B) from the Secretary of the Army to the Secretary administrative jurisdiction over the approximately 1.171-acre parcel of land depicted as "Area to be transferred to Petersburg National Battlefield" on the map described in paragraph (2).

(2) Map

The parcels of land described in paragraph (1) are depicted on the map titled "Petersburg National Battlefield Proposed Transfer of Administrative Jurisdiction", numbered 325/80,801A, dated May 2011/March 2016. The map shall be on file and available for public inspection in the appropriate offices of the National Park Service.

(3) Conditions of transfer

The transfer of administrative jurisdiction under paragraph (1) is subject to the following conditions:

(A) No reimbursement or consideration

The transfer shall be without reimbursement or consideration.

(B) Management

(i) Land transferred to the Secretary of the Army

The land transferred to the Secretary of the Army under paragraph (1)(A) shall be excluded from the boundary of the Petersburg National Battlefield.

(ii) Land transferred to the Secretary

The land transferred to the Secretary under paragraph (1)(B)—

(I) shall be included within the boundary of the Petersburg National Battlefield; and

(II) shall be administered as part of Petersburg National Battlefield in accordance with applicable laws and regulations.

(Pub.L. 114–328, Div. B, Title XXVIII, § 2834, Dec. 23, 2016, 130 Stat. 2740.)

HISTORICAL NOTES

Codifications

Section is comprised of section 2834 of Pub.L. 114–328. Subsec. (b)(2) of section 2834 of Pub.L. 114–328 amended section 313(a) of Pub.L. 95–625, 92 Stat. 3479, which is not classified to the Code.

§ 423h–2. Acquisition of lands; publication in Federal Register; administration

The Secretary of the Interior, in furtherance of the purposes of sections 423, 423a, and 423b to 423h of this title referred to in section 423h–1 of this title, may acquire by purchase with donated or appropriated funds, exchange, transfer, or by such other means as he deems to be in the public interest, not to exceed twelve hundred acres of land or interests in land at the site of the Battle of Five Forks for addition to the Petersburg National Battlefield. Lands and interests in lands acquired by the Secretary pursuant to this section shall, upon publication of a description thereof in the Federal Register, become a part of the Petersburg National Battlefield, and thereafter shall be administered by the Secretary of the Interior in accordance with the provisions of the Act entitled "An Act to establish a National Park Service, and for other purposes," approved August 25, 1916 (39 Stat. 535; 16 U.S.C. 1, 2, 3),[1] as amended and supplemented.

[1] See References in Text note set out under this section.

HISTORICAL NOTES

References in Text

The Act entitled "An Act to establish a National Park Service, and for other purposes," approved August 25, 1916 (39 Stat. 535; 16 U.S.C. 1, 2, 3), referred to in text, is Act Aug. 25, 1916, c. 408, 39 Stat. 535, known as the National Park Service Organic Act, which enacted 16 U.S.C.A. §§ 1, 2, 3, and 4 and provisions set out as a note under 54 U.S.C.A. § 100101.

Sections 1 to 4 of the Act were repealed and restated as 18 U.S.C.A. § 1865(a), and 54 U.S.C.A. § 100101(a), chapter 1003 of Title 54 (54 U.S.C.A. § 100301 et seq.), and 54 U.S.C.A. §§ 100751(a), 100752, 100753, and 102101 by Pub.L. 113–287, §§ 3, 4(a)(1), 7, Dec. 19, 2014, 128 Stat. 3094, 3260, 3272. For complete classification, see Tables. For disposition of former sections of this title, see Disposition Table preceding 54 U.S.C.A. § 100101.

§ 423l–3. Richmond National Battlefield Park; boundaries

[See main volume for text of (a)]

(b) Boundary adjustments

The Secretary may make minor adjustments in the boundaries of the battlefield park consistent with section 100506(c) of Title 54.

HISTORICAL NOTES

Codifications

In subsec. (b), "section 100506(c) of Title 54" substituted for "section 7(c) of the Land and Water Conservation Fund Act of 1965 (16 U.S.C. 460*l*–9(c))" on authority of Pub.L. 113–287, § 6(e), Dec. 19, 2014, 128 Stat. 3272, which Act enacted Title 54, 54 U.S.C.A. § 100101 et seq.

§ 423*l*–5. Park administration

(a) Applicable laws

The Secretary, acting through the Director of the National Park Service, shall administer the battlefield park in accordance with sections 423*l*-1 to 423*l*-6 of this title and laws generally applicable to units of the National Park System, including the Act of August 25, 1916 (16 U.S.C. 1 et seq.)[1] and the Act of August 21, 1935 (16 U.S.C. 461 et seq.).[1]

[See main volume for text of (b) to (d)]

[1] See References in Text note set out under this section.

HISTORICAL NOTES

References in Text

The Act of August 25, 1916 (16 U.S.C. 1 et seq.), referred to in subsec. (a), is Act Aug. 25, 1916, c. 408, 39 Stat. 535, known as the National Park Service Organic Act, which enacted 16 U.S.C.A. §§ 1, 2, 3, and 4 and provisions set out as a note under 54 U.S.C.A. § 100101. Sections 1 to 4 of the Act were repealed and restated as 18 U.S.C.A. § 1865(a), and 54 U.S.C.A. § 100101(a), chapter 1003 of Title 54 (54 U.S.C.A. § 100301 et seq.), and 54 U.S.C.A. §§ 100751(a), 100752, 100753, and 102101 by Pub.L. 113–287, §§ 3, 4(a)(1), 7, Dec. 19, 2014, 128 Stat. 3094, 3260, 3272. For complete classification, see Tables. For disposition of former sections of this title, see Disposition Table preceding 54 U.S.C.A. § 100101.

The Act of August 21, 1935 (16 U.S.C. 461 et seq.), referred to in subsec. (a), is Act Aug. 21, 1935, c. 593, 49 Stat. 666, known as the Historic Sites Act of 1935 and also as the Historic Sites, Buildings, and Antiquities Act, which enacted 16 U.S.C.A. §§ 461 to 467. The Act was repealed and restated as 18 U.S.C.A. § 1866(a), 54 U.S.C.A. §§ 102303 and 102304, and chapter 3201 of Title 54 (54 U.S.C.A. § 320101 et seq.) by Pub.L. 113–287, §§ 3, 4(a)(1), 7, Dec. 19, 2014, 128 Stat. 3094, 3260, 3272. For complete classification, see Tables. For disposition of former sections of this title, see Disposition Table preceding 54 U.S.C.A. § 100101.

§ 423n. Acceptance of lands and funds; acquisition of lands

HISTORICAL NOTES

Codifications

"Section 3113 of Title 40" substituted in text for "the Act of August 1, 1888" on authority of Pub.L. 107–217, § 5(c), Aug. 21, 2002, 116 Stat. 1303, the first section of which enacted Title 40, Public Buildings, Property, and Works.

§ 423*o*. Administration, protection, and development

The administration, protection, and development of the aforesaid battlefield site shall be exercised under the direction of the Secretary of the Interior by the National Park Service, subject to the provisions of the Act of August 25, 1916, entitled "An Act to establish a National Park Service, and for other purposes",[1] as amended.

[1] See References in Text note set out under this section.

HISTORICAL NOTES

References in Text

The Act of August 25, 1916, entitled "An Act to establish a National Park Service, and for other purposes", referred to in text, is Act Aug. 25, 1916, c. 408, 39 Stat. 535, known as the National Park Service Organic Act, which enacted 16 U.S.C.A. §§ 1, 2, 3, and 4 and provisions set out as a note under 54 U.S.C.A. § 100101. Sections 1 to 4 of the Act were repealed and restated as 18 U.S.C.A. § 1865(a), and 54 U.S.C.A. § 100101(a), chapter 1003 of Title 54 (54 U.S.C.A. § 100301 et seq.), and 54 U.S.C.A. §§ 100751(a), 100752, 100753, and 102101 by Pub.L. 113–287, §§ 3, 4(a)(1), 7, Dec. 19, 2014, 128 Stat. 3094, 3260, 3272. For complete classification, see Tables. For disposition of former sections of this title, see Disposition Table preceding 54 U.S.C.A. § 100101.

§ 425a. Acquisition of lands

HISTORICAL NOTES

Codifications

"Section 3113 of Title 40" substituted in text for "the Act of August 1, 1888, entitled 'An Act to authorize condemnation of lands for sites for public buildings, and for other purposes' (Twenty-fifth Statutes at Large, page 357)" on authority of Pub.L. 107–217, § 5(c), Aug. 21, 2002, 116 Stat. 1303, the first section of which enacted Title 40, Public Buildings, Property, and Works.

§ 426m. Administration, protection, and development

The administration, protection and development of the Stones River National Battlefield shall be exercised by the Secretary of the Interior in accordance with the provisions of the Act of August 25, 1916 (39 Stat. 535), entitled "An Act to establish a National Park Service, and for other purposes",[1] as amended.

[1] See References in Text note set out under this section.

HISTORICAL NOTES

References in Text

The Act of August 25, 1916 (39 Stat. 535), entitled "An Act to establish a National Park Service, and for other purposes", referred to in text, is Act Aug. 25, 1916, c. 408, 39 Stat. 535, known as the National Park Service Organic Act, which enacted 16 U.S.C.A. §§ 1, 2, 3, and 4 and provisions set out as a note under 54 U.S.C.A. § 100101. Sections 1 to 4 of the Act were repealed and restated as 18 U.S.C.A. § 1865(a), and 54 U.S.C.A. § 100101(a), chapter 1003 of Title 54 (54 U.S.C.A. § 100301 et seq.), and 54 U.S.C.A. §§ 100751(a), 100752, 100753, and 102101 by Pub.L. 113–287, §§ 3, 4(a)(1), 7, Dec. 19, 2014, 128 Stat. 3094, 3260, 3272. For complete classification, see Tables. For disposition of former sections of this title, see Disposition Table preceding 54 U.S.C.A. § 100101.

§ 426o–1. Planning

HISTORICAL NOTES

Prior Provisions

A prior section 3 of Pub.L. 100–205 was renumbered section 4 and is classified to section 426p of this title.

§ 428d–3. Administration, protection, and development

The administration, protection, and development of the lands authorized to be added to the Fort Donelson National Battlefield by sections 428d–1 and 428d–2 shall be exercised under the direction of the Secretary of the Interior by the National Park Service, subject to the provisions of the Act of August 25, 1916 (39 Stat. 535), entitled "An Act to establish a National Park Service, and for other purposes",[1] as amended.

[1] See References in Text note set out under this section.

HISTORICAL NOTES

References in Text

The Act of August 25, 1916 (39 Stat. 535), entitled "An Act to establish a National Park Service, and for other purposes", referred to in text, is Act Aug. 25, 1916, c. 408, 39 Stat. 535, known as the National Park Service Organic Act, which enacted 16 U.S.C.A. §§ 1, 2, 3, and 4 and provisions set out as a note under 54 U.S.C.A. § 100101. Sections 1 to 4 of the Act were repealed and restated as 18 U.S.C.A. § 1865(a), and 54 U.S.C.A. § 100101(a), chapter 1003 of Title 54 (54 U.S.C.A. § 100301 et seq.), and 54 U.S.C.A. §§ 100751(a), 100752, 100753, and 102101 by Pub.L. 113–287, §§ 3, 4(a)(1), 7, Dec. 19, 2014, 128 Stat. 3094, 3260, 3272. For complete classification, see Tables. For disposition of former sections of this title, see Disposition Table preceding 54 U.S.C.A. § 100101.

§ 428o. Administration, protection, and development

The administration, protection, and development of the Fort Donelson National Battlefield shall be exercised by the Secretary of the Interior in accordance with the provisions of the Act entitled "An Act to establish a National Park Service, and for other purposes", approved August 25, 1916 (39 Stat. 535),[1] as amended.

[1] See References in Text note set out under this section.

HISTORICAL NOTES

References in Text

The Act entitled "An Act to establish a National Park Service, and for other purposes", approved August 25, 1916 (39 Stat. 535), referred to in text, is Act Aug. 25, 1916, c. 408, 39 Stat. 535, known as the National Park Service Organic Act, which enacted 16 U.S.C.A. §§ 1, 2, 3, and 4 and provisions set out as a note under 54 U.S.C.A. § 100101. Sections 1 to 4 of the Act

were repealed and restated as 18 U.S.C.A. § 1865(a), and 54 U.S.C.A. § 100101(a), chapter 1003 of Title 54 (54 U.S.C.A. § 100301 et seq.), and 54 U.S.C.A. §§ 100751(a), 100752, 100753, and 102101 by Pub.L. 113–287, §§ 3, 4(a)(1), 7, Dec. 19, 2014, 128 Stat. 3094, 3260, 3272. For complete classification, see Tables. For disposition of former sections of this title, see Disposition Table preceding 54 U.S.C.A. § 100101.

§ 428p–2. Administration of Fort Donelson National Battlefield

The Secretary of the Interior shall administer the Fort Donelson National Battlefield in accordance with sections 428p to 428p–2 of this title and the laws generally applicable to units of the National Park System, including the Act of August 25, 1916 (commonly known as the National Park Service Organic Act; 16 U.S.C. 1 et seq.),[1] and the Act of August 21, 1935 (commonly known as the Historic Sites, Buildings, and Antiquities Act; 16 U.S.C. 461 et seq.).[1]

[1] See References in Text note set out under this section.

HISTORICAL NOTES

References in Text

The Act of August 25, 1916 (commonly known as the National Park Service Organic Act; 16 U.S.C. 1 et seq.), referred to in text, is Act Aug. 25, 1916, c. 408, 39 Stat. 535, known as the National Park Service Organic Act, which enacted 16 U.S.C.A. §§ 1, 2, 3, and 4 and provisions set out as a note under 54 U.S.C.A. § 100101. Sections 1 to 4 of the Act were repealed and restated as 18 U.S.C.A. § 1865(a), and 54 U.S.C.A. § 100101(a), chapter 1003 of Title 54 (54 U.S.C.A. § 100301 et seq.), and 54 U.S.C.A. §§ 100751(a), 100752, 100753, and 102101 by Pub.L. 113–287, §§ 3, 4(a)(1), 7, Dec. 19, 2014, 128 Stat. 3094, 3260, 3272. For complete classification, see Tables. For disposition of former

sections of this title, see Disposition Table preceding 54 U.S.C.A. § 100101.

The Act of August 21, 1935 (commonly known as the Historic Sites, Buildings, and Antiquities Act; 16 U.S.C. 461 et seq.), referred to in text, is Act Aug. 21, 1935, c. 593, 49 Stat. 666, also known as the Historic Sites Act of 1935, which enacted 16 U.S.C.A. §§ 461 to 467. The Act was repealed and restated as 18 U.S.C.A. §. 1866(a), 54 U.S.C.A. §§ 102303 and 102304, and chapter 3201 of Title 54 (54 U.S.C.A. § 320101 et seq.) by Pub.L. 113–287, §§ 3, 4(a)(1), 7, Dec. 19, 2014, 128 Stat. 3094, 3260, 3272. For complete classification, see Tables. For disposition of former sections of this title, see Disposition Table preceding 54 U.S.C.A. § 100101.

§ 429a. Jurisdiction and control; authorization of annual appropriation

HISTORICAL NOTES

Transfer of Functions

"Secretary of the Interior" substituted in text for "Secretary of War" pursuant to Reorg. Plan No. 3 of 1950, §§ 1, 2; Ex. Ord. No. 6166, § 2; and Ex. Ord. No. 6228, § 1. See below.

Reorg. Plan No. 3 of 1950, §§ 1, 2, eff. May 24, 1950, 15 F.R. 3174, 64 Stat. 1262, set out in the Appendix to Title 5, Government Organization and Employees, transferred the functions of

other officers, employees, and agencies of the Department of the Interior, with certain exceptions, to the Secretary of the Interior, with power to delegate.

Ex. Ord. No. 6166, § 2, and Ex. Ord. No. 6228, § 1, set out as a note under section 901 of Title 5, transferred the administrative functions of Brices Cross Roads and Tupelo battlefield sites to the Department of the Interior.

§ 429a–2. Change in name to Tupelo National Battlefield; administration

The Tupelo National Battlefield site is redesignated the Tupelo National Battlefield which shall continue to be administered pursuant to the Act of August 25, 1916 (39 Stat. 535), as amended and supplemented, entitled "An Act to establish a National Park Service, and for other purposes."[1]

[1] See References in Text note set out under this section.

HISTORICAL NOTES

References in Text

The Act of August 25, 1916 (39 Stat. 535), entitled "An Act to establish a National Park Service, and for other purposes.", referred to in

text, is Act Aug. 25, 1916, c. 408, 39 Stat. 535, known as the National Park Service Organic Act, which enacted 16 U.S.C.A. §§ 1, 2, 3, and 4 and provisions set out as a note under 54

U.S.C.A. § 100101. Sections 1 to 4 of the Act were repealed and restated as 18 U.S.C.A. § 1865(a), and 54 U.S.C.A. § 100101(a), chapter 1003 of Title 54 (54 U.S.C.A. § 100301 et seq.), and 54 U.S.C.A. §§ 100751(a), 100752, 100753, and 102101 by Pub.L. 113–287, §§ 3, 4(a)(1), 7, Dec. 19, 2014, 128 Stat. 3094, 3260, 3272. For complete classification, see Tables. For disposition of former sections of this title, see Disposition Table preceding 54 U.S.C.A. § 100101.

§ 429b. Manassas National Battlefield Park

(a) Establishment; boundaries

There is established as a unit of the national park system in the Commonwealth of Virginia the Manassas National Battlefield Park, which shall contain within its boundaries the important historical lands relating to the two battles of Manassas. The total area of the park shall not be greater than four thousand five hundred and twenty-five acres. The boundaries of the park shall be the boundaries depicted on the map entitled "Boundary Map, Manassas National Battlefield Park", dated October 1980, and numbered 379/80,009, which shall be on file and available for public inspection in the offices of the National Park Service, Department of the Interior. The Secretary shall publish in the Federal Register, as soon as practicable after the date of the enactment of this Act, but no later than one year from the effective date of this section, a detailed description and map of the boundaries. Notwithstanding section 100506(c) of Title 54, the Secretary may not make any changes in the boundaries of the park. The Secretary shall administer the park in accordance with laws, rules, and regulations applicable to the national park system.

[See main volume for text of (b) and (c)]

HISTORICAL NOTES

Codifications

In subsec. (a), "section 100506(c) of Title 54" substituted for "section 7(c) of the Land and Water Conservation Fund Act of 1965 (91 Stat. 211), as amended (16 U.S.C. 460*l*)" on authority of Pub.L. 113–287, § 6(e), Dec. 19, 2014, 128 Stat. 3272, which Act enacted Title 54, 54 U.S.C.A. § 100101 et seq.

§ 429b–4. Funds from Land and Water Conservation Fund

HISTORICAL NOTES

References in Text

The Land and Water Conservation Fund Act of 1965, referred to in subsec. (a), is Pub.L. 88–578, Sept. 3, 1964, 78 Stat. 897, which was classified principally to former part B of subchapter LXIX of chapter 1 of this title (16 U.S.C.A. § 460l–4 et seq.). Sections 2, 3, 4(i)(1)(C), (j) to (n), 5 to 13, and 201 of the Act were repealed and restated as 54 U.S.C.A. §§ 100506(c) and 100904 and chapter 2003 of Title 54 (54 U.S.C.A. § 200301 et seq.), by Pub.L. 113–287, §§ 3, 7, Dec. 19, 2014, 128 Stat. 3094, 3272. For complete classification, see Tables. For disposition of former sections of this title, see Disposition Table preceding 54 U.S.C.A. § 100101.

§ 430a. Acquisition of land

HISTORICAL NOTES

Codifications

"Sections 3111 and 3112 of Title 40" substituted in text for "section 355 of the Revised Statutes" and "section 3113 of Title 40" substituted in text for "the Act entitled 'An Act to authorize condemnation of lands for sites for public buildings, and for other purposes,' approved August 1, 1888" on authority of Pub.L. 107–217, § 5(c), Aug. 21, 2002, 116 Stat. 1303, the first section of which enacted Title 40, Public Buildings, Property, and Works.

§ 430a–2. Acquisition of lands within revised boundary

The Secretary of the Interior is authorized to acquire lands and interests in lands within the revised boundary by purchase, donation, with donated funds, or by exchange, utilizing for such exchanges federally owned lands of approximately equal value excluded from the park pursuant to sections 430a–1 to 430a–3 of this title. Federally owned lands so excluded which the Secretary of the Interior determines are not needed for such exchanges shall be disposed of in accordance with the provisions of chapters 1 to 11 of Title 40 and division C (except sections 3302, 3307(e), 3501(b), 3509, 3906, 4710, and 4711) of subtitle I of Title 41.

HISTORICAL NOTES

Codifications

In text, "chapters 1 to 11 of Title 40 and division C (except sections 3302, 3307(e), 3501(b), 3509, 3906, 4710, and 4711) of subtitle I of Title 41" was substituted for "the Federal Property and Administrative Services Act of 1949, as amended" on authority of Pub.L. 107–217, § 5(c), Aug. 21, 2002, 116 Stat. 1303, which Act enacted Title 40, Public Buildings, Property, and Works, and Pub.L. 111–350, § 6(c), Jan. 4, 2011, 124 Stat. 3854, which Act enacted Title 41, Public Contracts.

§ 430f–5. Siege and Battle of Corinth

[See main volume for text of (a) to (c)]

(d) Interpretive center and marking

[See main volume for text of (1) and (2)]

(3) Administration

The land and interests in land acquired, and the facilities constructed and maintained pursuant to this section, shall be administered by the Secretary as a part of Shiloh National Military Park, subject to the appropriate laws (including regulations) applicable to the Park, the Act entitled "An Act to establish a National Park Service, and for other purposes", approved August 25, 1916 (16 U.S.C. 1 et seq.),[1] and the Act entitled "An Act to provide for the preservation of historic American sites, buildings, objects, and antiquities of national significance, and for other purposes", approved August 21, 1935 (16 U.S.C. 461 et seq.).[1]

[See main volume for text of (e)]

[1] See References in Text note set out under this section.

HISTORICAL NOTES

References in Text

This title, referred to in subsec. (b), is Title VI of Div. I of Pub.L. 104–333, which enacted this section, former 16 U.S.C.A. § 469k, provisions formerly set out as a note under 16 U.S.C.A. § 1a–5, and provisions listed in a table of National Battlefield Sites set out under 54 U.S.C.A. § 320101.

The Act entitled "An Act to establish a National Park Service, and for other purposes", approved August 25, 1916 (16 U.S.C. 1 et seq.), referred to in subsec. (d)(3), is Act Aug. 25, 1916, c. 408, 39 Stat. 535, known as the National Park Service Organic Act, which enacted 16 U.S.C.A. §§ 1, 2, 3, and 4 provisions set out as a note under 54 U.S.C.A. § 100101. Sections 1 to 4 of the Act were repealed and restated as 18 U.S.C.A. § 1865(a), and 54 U.S.C.A. § 100101(a), chapter 1003 of Title 54 (54 U.S.C.A. § 100301 et seq.), and 54 U.S.C.A. §§ 100751(a), 100752, 100753, and 102101 by Pub.L. 113–287, §§ 3, 4(a)(1), 7, Dec. 19, 2014, 128 Stat. 3094, 3260, 3272. For complete classification, see Tables. For disposition of former sections of this title, see Disposition Table preceding 54 U.S.C.A. § 100101.

The Act entitled "An Act to provide for the preservation of historic American sites, buildings, objects, and antiquities of national significance, and for other purposes", approved August 21, 1935 (16 U.S.C. 461 et seq.), referred to in subsec. (d)(3), is Act Aug. 21, 1935, c. 593, 49 Stat. 666, known as the Historic Sites Act of 1935 and also as the Historic Sites, Buildings, and Antiquities Act, which enacted 16 U.S.C.A. §§ 461 to 467. The Act was repealed and restated as 18 U.S.C.A. § 1866(a), 54 U.S.C.A. §§ 102303 and 102304, and chapter 3201 of Title 54 (54 U.S.C.A. § 320101 et seq.) by Pub.L. 113–287, §§ 3, 4(a)(1), 7, Dec. 19, 2014, 128 Stat. 3094, 3260, 3272. For complete classification, see Tables. For disposition of former sections of this title, see Disposition Table preceding 54 U.S.C.A. § 100101.

§ 430f–10. Park management and administration

(a) In general

The Secretary shall administer the Unit in accordance with sections 430f–6 to 430f–12 of this title and the laws generally applicable to units of the National Park System, including—

(1) the Act entitled "An Act to establish a National Park Service, and for other purposes", approved August 25, 1916 (16 U.S.C. 1 et seq.);[1] and

(2) the Act entitled "An Act to provide for the preservation of historic American sites, buildings, objects, and antiquities of national significance, and for other purposes", approved August 21, 1935 (16 U.S.C. 461 et seq.).[1]

[See main volume for text of (b) to (d)]

1 See References in Text note set out under this section.

HISTORICAL NOTES

References in Text

The Act entitled "An Act to establish a National Park Service, and for other purposes", approved August 25, 1916 (16 U.S.C. 1 et seq.), referred to in subsec. (a)(1), is Act Aug. 25, 1916, c. 408, 39 Stat. 535, known as the National Park Service Organic Act, which enacted 16 U.S.C.A. §§ 1, 2, 3, and 4 and provisions set out as a note under 54 U.S.C.A. § 100101. Sections 1 to 4 of the Act were repealed and restated as 18 U.S.C.A. § 1865(a), and 54 U.S.C.A. § 100101(a), chapter 1003 of Title 54 (54 U.S.C.A. § 100301 et seq.), and 54 U.S.C.A. §§ 100751(a), 100752, 100753, and 102101 by Pub.L. 113–287, §§ 3, 4(a)(1), 7, Dec. 19, 2014, 128 Stat. 3094, 3260, 3272. For complete classification, see Tables. For disposition of former sections of this title, see Disposition Table preceding 54 U.S.C.A. § 100101.

The Act entitled "An Act to provide for the preservation of historic American sites, buildings, objects, and antiquities of national significance, and for other purposes", approved August 21, 1935 (16 U.S.C. 461 et seq.), referred to in subsec. (a)(2), is Act Aug. 21, 1935, c. 593, 49 Stat. 666, known as the Historic Sites Act of 1935 and also as the Historic Sites, Buildings, and Antiquities Act, which enacted 16 U.S.C.A. §§ 461 to 467. The Act was repealed and restated as 18 U.S.C.A. § 1866(a), 54 U.S.C.A. §§ 102303 and 102304, and chapter 3201 of Title 54 (54 U.S.C.A. § 320101 et seq.) by Pub.L. 113–287, §§ 3, 4(a)(1), 7, Dec. 19, 2014, 128 Stat. 3094, 3260, 3272. For complete classification, see Tables. For disposition of former sections of this title, see Disposition Table preceding 54 U.S.C.A. § 100101.

§ 430f–12. Authorization of appropriations

HISTORICAL NOTES

Prior Provisions

A prior section 7 of Pub.L. 106–271 was classified to section 430f–11 of this title, prior to repeal by Pub.L. 110–161.

§ 430f–13. Shiloh National Military Park boundary adjustment

(a) Definitions

In this section:

(1) Affiliated area

The term "affiliated area" means the Parker's Crossroads Battlefield established as an affiliated area of the National Park System by subsection (c)(1).

(2) Park

The term "Park" means Shiloh National Military Park, a unit of the National Park System.

(b) Areas to be added to Shiloh National Military Park

(1) Additional areas

The boundary of the Park is modified to include the areas that are generally depicted on the map entitled "Shiloh National Military Park, Proposed Boundary Adjustment", numbered 304/80,011, and dated July 2014, and which are comprised of the following:

(A) Fallen Timbers Battlefield.

(B) Russell House Battlefield.

(C) Davis Bridge Battlefield.

(2) Acquisition authority

The Secretary may acquire the land described in paragraph (1) by donation, purchase from willing sellers with donated or appropriated funds, or exchange.

(3) Administration

Any land acquired under this subsection shall be administered as part of the Park.

(c) Establishment of affiliated area

(1) In general

Parker's Crossroads Battlefield in the State of Tennessee is established as an affiliated area of the National Park System.

(2) Description of affiliated area

The affiliated area shall consist of the area generally depicted within the "Proposed Boundary" on the map entitled "Parker's Crossroads Battlefield, Proposed Boundary", numbered 903/80,073, and dated July 2014.

(3) Administration

The affiliated area shall be managed in accordance with—

(A) this section; and

(B) any law generally applicable to units of the National Park System.

(4) Management entity

The City of Parkers Crossroads and the Tennessee Historical Commission shall jointly be the management entity for the affiliated area.

(5) Cooperative agreements

The Secretary may provide technical assistance and enter into cooperative agreements with the management entity for the purpose of providing financial assistance for the marketing, marking, interpretation, and preservation of the affiliated area.

(6) Limited role of the Secretary

Nothing in this section authorizes the Secretary to acquire property at the affiliated area or to assume overall financial responsibility for the operation, maintenance, or management of the affiliated area.

(7) General management plan

(A) In general

The Secretary, in consultation with the management entity, shall develop a general management plan for the affiliated area in accordance with section 100502 of Title 54.

(B) Transmittal

Not later than 3 years after the date on which funds are made available to carry out this section, the Secretary shall submit to the Committee on Natural Resources of the House of Representatives and the Committee on Energy and Natural Resources of the Senate the general management plan developed under subparagraph (A).

(Pub.L. 116–9, Title II, § 2101, Mar. 12, 2019, 133 Stat. 723.)

STATUTORY NOTES

"Secretary" Defined for Pub.L. 116–9

"Secretary" as meaning the Secretary of the Interior, see section 2 of Pub.L. 116–9, set out as a note under 16 U.S.C.A. § 1.

§ 430g–4. Gettysburg National Military Park boundary revision

[See main volume for text of (a)]

(b) Additional land

In addition to the land identified in subsection (a), the park shall also include—

(1) the property commonly known as the Wills House located in the Borough of Gettysburg and identified as Tract P02–1 on the map entitled "Gettysburg National

Military Park" numbered MARO 305/80,011 Segment 2, and dated April 1981, revised May 14, 1999; and

(2) the properties depicted as "Proposed Addition" on the map entitled "Gettysburg National Military Park Proposed Boundary Addition", numbered 305/80,045, and dated January, 2010 (2 sheets), including—

(A) the property commonly known as the "Gettysburg Train Station"; and

(B) the property located adjacent to Plum Run in Cumberland Township.

[See main volume for text of (c)]

(Pub.L. 101–377, § 1, Aug. 17, 1990, 104 Stat. 464; Pub.L. 106–290, § 1, Oct. 10, 2000, 114 Stat. 921; Pub.L. 113–291, Div. B, Title XXX, § 3034(a), Dec. 19, 2014, 128 Stat. 3777.)

HISTORICAL NOTES

Amendments

2014 Amendments. Subsec. (b). Pub.L. 113–291, Div. B, § 3034(a), rewrote subsec. (b), which formerly read: "In addition to the land identified in subsection (a) of this section, the park shall also include the property commonly known as the Wills House located in the Borough of Gettysburg and identified as Tract P02–1 on the map entitled 'Gettysburg National Military Park' numbered MARO 305/80,011 Segment 2, and dated April 1981, revised May 14, 1999.".

§ 430g–5. Acquisition and disposal of lands

(a) General authority

(1) Authority to acquire land

The Secretary is authorized to acquire lands and interests in lands within the park by donation, purchase with donated or appropriated funds, exchange, or otherwise.

(2) Minimum Federal interests

In acquiring lands and interests in lands under sections 430g–4 to 430g–10 of this title, the Secretary shall acquire the minimum Federal interests necessary to achieve the objectives identified for specific areas and the park.

(3) Method of acquisition for certain land

Notwithstanding paragraph (1), the Secretary may acquire the properties added to the park by section 430g–4(b)(2) of this title only by donation.

(b) Authority to convey freehold and leasehold interests within park

The Secretary may convey lands and interests in lands within the park authorized in accordance with subsection (a) of section 102901 of Title 54, except that, notwithstanding subsection (d) of that section, the net proceeds from any such conveyance may be used, subject to appropriations, to acquire lands and interests within the park.

[See main volume for text of (c) and (d)]

(Pub.L. 101–377, § 2, Aug. 17, 1990, 104 Stat. 464; Pub.L. 106–290, § 2, Oct. 10, 2000, 114 Stat. 921; Pub.L. 113–291, Div. B, Title XXX, § 3034(b), Dec. 19, 2014, 128 Stat. 3777.)

HISTORICAL NOTES

Codifications

In subsec. (b), "subsection (a) of section 102901 of Title 54" substituted for "subsection (a) of the Act of July 15, 1968 (16 U.S.C. 460*l*–22)", meaning "subsection (a) of section 5 of the Act of July 15, 1968 (16 U.S.C. 460*l*–22)", on authority of Pub.L. 113–287, § 6(e), Dec. 19, 2014, 128 Stat. 3272, which Act enacted Title 54, 54 U.S.C.A. § 100101 et seq.

Amendments

2014 Amendments. Subsec. (a)(1). Pub.L. 113–291, Div. B, § 3034(b)(1), designated the first sentence as par. (1) and added "Authority to acquire land" as the heading.

Subsec. (a)(2). Pub.L. 113–291, Div. B, § 3034(b)(2), designated the second sentence as par. (2) and added "Minimum Federal interests" as the heading.

Subsec. (a)(3). Pub.L. 113–291, Div. B, § 3034(b)(3), added par. (3).

§ 430g–7. Conservation within Gettysburg Battlefield historic district

[See main volume for text of (a)]

(b) Prioritization of grants

Within the historic district, the Secretary shall give priority in making grants under sections 302902(a), 302903(a), and 302904 to 302908 of Title 54, and in providing technical assistance, information, and advice under section 303902 of Title 54, to those programs and activities in the historic district that will assure development and use of natural and cultural resources in a manner that is consistent with the conservation and maintenance of the district's historic character.

[See main volume for text of (c) to (e)]

(f) Federal consistency

(1) Any Federal or federally assisted activity or undertaking in the historic district, shall be consistent to the maximum extent possible with the purposes of the preservation of the historic district, including its rural, agricultural, and town elements, and shall also comply with the National Historic Preservation Act [1] and other applicable laws.

[See main volume for text of (2) and (3)]

[1] See References in Text note set out under this section.

HISTORICAL NOTES

References in Text

The National Historic Preservation Act, referred to in subsec. (f)(1), is Pub.L. 89–665, Oct. 15, 1966, 80 Stat. 915, which was classified generally to subchapter II of chapter 1A of this title, 16 U.S.C.A. § 470 et seq. The Act, except for section 1, was repealed and restated in division A of subtitle III of Title 54, 54 U.S.C.A. § 300101 et seq. by Pub.L. 113–287, §§ 3, 7, Dec. 19, 2014, 128 Stat. 3094, 3272. For complete classification, see Tables. For disposition of former sections of this title, see Disposition Table preceding 54 U.S.C.A. § 100101.

Codifications

In subsec. (b), "sections 302902(a), 302903(a), and 302904 to 302908 of Title 54" substituted for "section 101(d)" and "section 303902 of Title 54" substituted for "section 101(h), of the National Historic Preservation Act (16 U.S.C. 470a(d), (h))" on authority of Pub.L. 113–287, § 6(e), Dec. 19, 2014, 128 Stat. 3272, which Act enacted Title 54, 54 U.S.C.A. § 100101 et seq., and Pub.L. 102–575, Title XL, § 4006(a)(1), Oct. 30, 1992, 106 Stat. 4755, which redesignated subsecs. (d) and (h) of section 101 of the National Historic Preservation Act as subsecs. (e) and (i), respectively, of that section.

§ 430h. Vicksburg National Military Park

HISTORICAL NOTES

Change of Name

"United States magistrate judge" and "magistrate judge" substituted for "United States magistrate" and "magistrate", respectively, wherever appearing in text pursuant to section 321 of

Pub.L. 101–650, set out as a note under section 631 of Title 28, Judiciary and Judicial Procedure. Previously, "magistrate" substituted for "commissioner" pursuant to Pub.L. 90–578. See chapter 43 (§ 631 et seq.) of Title 28.

§ 430h–7. Exclusion of lands from park

[See main volume for text of (a) and (b)]

(c) Excess property

Any lands not conveyed pursuant to subsection (b) shall be reported to the Administrator of General Services as excess to the needs of the Department of the Interior and shall be subject to transfer or disposition in accordance with chapters 1 to 11 of Title 40 and division C (except sections 3302, 3307(e), 3501(b), 3509, 3906, 4710, and 4711) of subtitle I of Title 41.

HISTORICAL NOTES

Codifications

In (c), "chapters 1 to 11 of Title 40 and division C (except sections 3302, 3307(e), 3501(b), 3509, 3906, 4710, and 4711) of subtitle I of Title

41" was substituted for "the Federal Property and Administrative Services Act of 1949, as amended" on authority of Pub.L. 107–217, § 5(c), Aug. 21, 2002, 116 Stat. 1303, which Act enacted Title 40, Public Buildings, Property, and Works, and Pub.L. 111–350, § 6(c), Jan. 4, 2011,

124 Stat. 3854, which Act enacted Title 41, Public Contracts.

§ 430h–12. Administration

The Secretary shall administer any properties acquired under sections 430h–10 to 430h–13 of this title as part of the Vicksburg National Military Park in accordance with applicable laws and regulations.

§ 430h–14. Vicksburg National Military Park

(a) Acquisition of land

(1) In general

The Secretary of the Interior (referred to in this section as the "Secretary") may acquire the land or any interests in land within the area identified as "Modified Core Battlefield" for the Port Gibson Unit, the Champion Hill Unit, and the Raymond Unit as generally depicted on the map entitled "Vicksburg National Military Park—Proposed Battlefield Additions", numbered 306/100986A (4 sheets), and dated July 2012.

(2) Methods of acquisition

Land may be acquired under paragraph (1) by donation, purchase with donated or appropriated funds, or exchange, except that land owned by the State of Mississippi or any political subdivisions of the State may be acquired only by donation.

(b) Availability of map

The map described in subsection (a)(1) shall be on file and available for public inspection in the appropriate offices of the National Park Service.

(c) Boundary adjustment

On the acquisition of land by the Secretary under this section—

(1) the acquired land shall be added to Vicksburg National Military Park;

(2) the boundary of the Vicksburg National Military Park shall be adjusted to reflect the acquisition of the land; and

(3) the acquired land shall be administered as part of the Vicksburg National Military Park in accordance with applicable laws (including regulations).

(Pub.L. 113–291, Div. B, Title XXX, § 3044, Dec. 19, 2014, 128 Stat. 3798.)

§ 430k. Condemnation proceedings; purchase without condemnation; acceptance of donations of land

HISTORICAL NOTES

Codifications

"Section 3113 of Title 40" substituted in text for "the Act of August 1, 1888, entitled 'An Act to authorize condemnation of lands for sites for public buildings and for other purposes' (25 Stat.L. 357)" on authority of Pub.L. 107–217, § 5(c), Aug. 21, 2002, 116 Stat. 1303, the first section of which enacted Title 40, Public Buildings, Property, and Works.

§ 430m. Administration

The administration, development, preservation, and maintenance of the battlefield shall be exercised by the Secretary of the Interior in accordance with the Act of August 25, 1916 (39 Stat. 535; 16 U.S.C. 1 et seq.),[1] as amended and supplemented, and the Act of August 21, 1935 (49 Stat. 666).[1]

1 See References in Text note set out under this section.

HISTORICAL NOTES

References in Text

The Act of August 25, 1916 (39 Stat. 535; 16 U.S.C. 1 et seq.), referred to in text, is Act Aug. 25, 1916, c. 408, 39 Stat. 535, known as the National Park Service Organic Act, which enacted 16 U.S.C.A. §§ 1, 2, 3, and 4 and provisions set out as a note under 54 U.S.C.A. § 100101. Sections 1 to 4 of the Act were repealed and restated as 18 U.S.C.A. § 1865(a), and 54 U.S.C.A. § 100101(a), chapter 1003 of Title 54 (54 U.S.C.A. § 100301 et seq.), and 54 U.S.C.A. §§ 100751(a), 100752, 100753, and 102101 by Pub.L. 113–287, §§ 3, 4(a)(1), 7, Dec. 19, 2014, 128 Stat. 3094, 3260, 3272. For complete classification, see Tables. For disposition of former sections of this title, see Disposition Table preceding 54 U.S.C.A. § 100101.

The Act of August 21, 1935 (49 Stat. 666), referred to in text, is Act Aug. 21, 1935, c. 593, 49 Stat. 666, known as the Historic Sites Act of 1935 and also as the Historic Sites, Buildings, and Antiquities Act, which enacted 16 U.S.C.A. §§ 461 to 467. The Act was repealed and restated as 18 U.S.C.A. § 1866(a), 54 U.S.C.A. §§ 102303 and 102304, and chapter 3201 of Title 54 (54 U.S.C.A. § 320101 et seq.) by Pub.L. 113–287, §§ 3, 4(a)(1), 7, Dec. 19, 2014, 128 Stat. 3094, 3260, 3272. For complete classification, see Tables. For disposition of former sections of this title, see Disposition Table preceding 54 U.S.C.A. § 100101.

§ 430q. Offenses

HISTORICAL NOTES

Change of Name

"United States magistrate judge" substituted for "United States magistrate" wherever appearing in text pursuant to section 321 of Pub.L. 101–650, set out as a note under section 631 of Title 28, Judiciary and Judicial Procedure. Previously, "United States magistrate" substituted for "United States commissioner" pursuant to Pub.L. 90–578. See chapter 43 of Title 28 (28 U.S.C.A. § 631 et seq.).

§ 430s. Authorization of appropriations

HISTORICAL NOTES

Change of Name

Committee on Interior and Insular Affairs of the Senate abolished and replaced by Committee on Energy and Natural Resources of the Senate, effective Feb. 11, 1977. See Rule XXV of Standing Rules of the Senate, as amended by Senate Resolution No. 4 (popularly cited as the "Committee System Reorganization Amendments of 1977"), approved Feb. 4, 1977.

Committee on Interior and Insular Affairs of the House of Representatives changed to Committee on Natural Resources of the House of Representatives on Jan. 5, 1993, by House Resolution No. 5, One Hundred Third Congress. For references to Committees of the House of Representatives with new names, see Pub.L. 104–14, § 1(a), June 3, 1995, 109 Stat. 186, as amended, set out as a note preceding 2 U.S.C.A. § 21.

§ 430t-1. Kennesaw Mountain National Battlefield Park boundary

(a) Definitions

In this section:

(1) Map

The term "map" means the map entitled "Kennesaw Mountain National Battlefield Park, Proposed Boundary Adjustment", numbered 325/80,020, and dated February 2010.

(2) Park

The term "Park" means the Kennesaw Mountain National Battlefield Park.

(b) Kennesaw Mountain National Battlefield Park boundary adjustment

(1) Boundary adjustment

The boundary of the Park is modified to include the approximately 8 acres of land or interests in land identified as "Wallis House and Harriston Hill", as generally depicted on the map.

(2) Map

The map shall be on file and available for inspection in the appropriate offices of the National Park Service.

(3) Land acquisition

The Secretary may acquire land or interests in land described in paragraph (1) by donation, purchase from willing sellers, or exchange.

(4) Administration of acquired land

The Secretary shall administer land and interests in land acquired under this section as part of the Park in accordance with applicable laws (including regulations).

(Pub.L. 116–9, Title II, § 2103, Mar. 12, 2019, 133 Stat. 725.)

STATUTORY NOTES

"Secretary" Defined for Pub.L. 116–9

"Secretary" as meaning the Secretary of the Interior, see section 2 of Pub.L. 116–9, set out as a note under 16 U.S.C.A. § 1.

§ 430u. Donations of land; purchase and condemnation

HISTORICAL NOTES

Codifications

"Section 3113 of Title 40" substituted in text for "the Act of August 1, 1888" on authority of Pub.L. 107–217, § 5(c), Aug. 21, 2002, 116 Stat. 1303, the first section of which enacted Title 40, Public Buildings, Property, and Works.

§ 430w. Administration, protection, and development

The administration, protection, and development of the aforesaid national battlefield park shall be exercised under the direction of the Secretary of the Interior by the National Park Service subject to the provisions of the Act of August 25, 1916, entitled "An Act to establish a National Park Service, and for other purposes",[1] as amended.

[1] See References in Text note set out under this section.

HISTORICAL NOTES

References in Text

The Act of August 25, 1916, entitled "An Act to establish a National Park Service, and for other purposes", referred to in text, is Act Aug. 25, 1916, c. 408, 39 Stat. 535, known as the National Park Service Organic Act, which enacted 16 U.S.C.A. §§ 1, 2, 3, and 4 and provisions set out as a note under 54 U.S.C.A. § 100101. Sections 1 to 4 of the Act were repealed and restated as 18 U.S.C.A. § 1865(a), and 54 U.S.C.A. § 100101(a), chapter 1003 of Title 54 (54 U.S.C.A. § 100301 et seq.), and 54 U.S.C.A. §§ 100751(a), 100752, 100753, and 102101 by Pub.L. 113–287, §§ 3, 4(a)(1), 7, Dec. 19, 2014, 128 Stat. 3094, 3260, 3272. For complete classification, see Tables. For disposition of former sections of this title, see Disposition Table preceding 54 U.S.C.A. § 100101.

§ 430cc. Administration, protection, and development; improvements

(a) The National Park Service under the direction of the Secretary of the Interior, shall administer, protect, and develop the park, subject to the provisions of the Act entitled "An Act to establish a National Park Service, and for other purposes," approved August 25, 1916 (39 Stat. 535),[1] as amended.

[See main volume for text of (b)]

[1] See References in Text note set out under this section.

HISTORICAL NOTES

References in Text

The Act entitled "An Act to establish a National Park Service, and for other purposes," approved August 25, 1916 (39 Stat. 535), referred to in subsec. (a), is Act Aug. 25, 1916, c. 408, 39 Stat. 535, known as the National Park Service Organic Act, which enacted 16 U.S.C.A. §§ 1, 2, 3, and 4 and provisions set out as a note under 54 U.S.C.A. § 100101. Sections 1 to 4 of the Act were repealed and restated as 18 U.S.C.A. § 1865(a), and 54 U.S.C.A. § 100101(a), chapter 1003 of Title 54 (54 U.S.C.A. § 100301 et seq.), and 54 U.S.C.A. §§ 100751(a), 100752, 100753, and 102101 by Pub.L. 113–287, §§ 3, 4(a)(1), 7, Dec. 19, 2014, 128 Stat. 3094, 3260, 3272. For complete classification, see Tables. For disposition of former sections of this title, see Disposition Table preceding 54 U.S.C.A. § 100101.

§ 430hh. Administration, protection, and development; improvements

(a) The National Park Service, under the direction of the Secretary of the Interior, shall administer, protect, and develop the park, subject to the provisions of the Act entitled "An Act to establish a National Park Service, and for other purposes", approved August 25, 1916 (39 Stat. 535),[1] as amended.

[See main volume for text of (b)]

[1] See References in Text note set out under this section.

HISTORICAL NOTES

References in Text

The Act entitled "An Act to establish a National Park Service, and for other purposes", approved August 25, 1916 (39 Stat. 535), referred to in subsec. (a), is Act Aug. 25, 1916, c. 408, 39 Stat. 535, known as the National Park Service Organic Act, which enacted 16 U.S.C.A. §§ 1, 2, 3, and 4 and provisions set out as a note under 54 U.S.C.A. § 100101. Sections 1 to 4 of the Act were repealed and restated as 18 U.S.C.A. § 1865(a), and 54 U.S.C.A. § 100101(a), chapter 1003 of Title 54 (54 U.S.C.A. § 100301 et seq.), and 54 U.S.C.A. §§ 100751(a), 100752, 100753, and 102101 by Pub.L. 113–287, §§ 3, 4(a)(1), 7, Dec. 19, 2014, 128 Stat. 3094, 3260, 3272. For complete classification, see Tables. For disposition of former sections of this title, see Disposition Table preceding 54 U.S.C.A. § 100101.

§ 430*ll*. Designation

(a) Administration, protection, and development

The lands acquired under section 430kk of this title shall be set aside as a public park for the benefit and enjoyment of the people of the United States, and shall be designated as the Wilson's Creek National Battlefield. The National Park Service, under the direction of the Secretary of the Interior, shall administer, protect, and develop the park, subject to the provisions of the Act entitled "An Act to establish a National Park Service, and for other purposes", approved August 25, 1916 (39 Stat. 535).[1]

[See main volume for text of (b)]

[1] See References in Text note set out under this section.

HISTORICAL NOTES

References in Text

The Act entitled "An Act to establish a National Park Service, and for other purposes", approved August 25, 1916 (39 Stat. 535), referred to in subsec. (a), is Act Aug. 25, 1916, c. 408, 39 Stat. 535, known as the National Park Service Organic Act, which enacted 16 U.S.C.A. §§ 1, 2, 3, and 4 and provisions set out as a note under 54 U.S.C.A. § 100101. Sections 1 to 4 of the Act were repealed and restated as 18 U.S.C.A. § 1865(a), and 54 U.S.C.A. § 100101(a), chapter 1003 of Title 54 (54 U.S.C.A. § 100301 et seq.), and 54 U.S.C.A. §§ 100751(a), 100752, 100753, and 102101 by Pub.L. 113–287, §§ 3, 4(a)(1), 7, Dec. 19, 2014, 128 Stat. 3094, 3260, 3272. For complete classification, see Tables. For disposition of former sections of this title, see Disposition Table preceding 54 U.S.C.A. § 100101.

§ 430ss. Administration, protection, and development

The administration, protection, and development of the Fort Necessity National Battlefield shall be exercised by the Secretary of the Interior in accordance with provisions of the Act of August 25, 1916 (39 Stat. 535), entitled "An Act to establish a National Park Service, and for other purposes",[1] as amended and supplemented.

[1] See References in Text note set out under this section.

HISTORICAL NOTES

References in Text

The Act of August 25, 1916 (39 Stat. 535), entitled "An Act to establish a National Park Service, and for other purposes", referred to in text, is Act Aug. 25, 1916, c. 408, 39 Stat. 535, known as the National Park Service Organic Act, which enacted 16 U.S.C.A. §§ 1, 2, 3, and 4 and provisions set out as a note under 54 U.S.C.A. § 100101. Sections 1 to 4 of the Act were repealed and restated as 18 U.S.C.A. § 1865(a), and 54 U.S.C.A. § 100101(a), chapter 1003 of Title 54 (54 U.S.C.A. § 100301 et seq.), and 54 U.S.C.A. §§ 100751(a), 100752, 100753, and 102101 by Pub.L. 113–287, §§ 3, 4(a)(1), 7, Dec. 19, 2014, 128 Stat. 3094, 3260, 3272. For complete classification, see Tables. For disposition of former sections of this title, see Disposition Table preceding 54 U.S.C.A. § 100101.

§ 430uu–2. Acquisition of land; exclusion from Beaverhead National Forest; administration

[See main volume for text of (a) and (b)]

(c) Lands included in the Big Hole National Battlefield pursuant to sections 430uu to 430uu–4 of this title shall be administered in accordance with the provisions of the Act entitled "An Act to establish a National Park Service, and for other purposes", approved August 25, 1916 (39 Stat. 535; 16 U.S.C. 1–3),[1] as amended and supplemented.

1 See References in Text note set out under this section.

HISTORICAL NOTES

References in Text

The Act entitled "An Act to establish a National Park Service, and for other purposes", approved August 25, 1916 (39 Stat. 535; 16 U.S.C. 1–3), referred to in subsec. (c), is Act Aug. 25, 1916, c. 408, 39 Stat. 535, known as the National Park Service Organic Act, which enacted 16 U.S.C.A. §§ 1, 2, 3, and 4 and provisions set out as a note under 54 U.S.C.A. § 100101.

Sections 1 to 4 of the Act were repealed and restated as 18 U.S.C.A. § 1865(a), and 54 U.S.C.A. § 100101(a), chapter 1003 of Title 54 (54 U.S.C.A. § 100301 et seq.), and 54 U.S.C.A. §§ 100751(a), 100752, 100753, and 102101 by Pub.L. 113–287, §§ 3, 4(a)(1), 7, Dec. 19, 2014, 128 Stat. 3094, 3260, 3272. For complete classification, see Tables. For disposition of former sections of this title, see Disposition Table preceding 54 U.S.C.A. § 100101.

§ 430vv. River Raisin National Battlefield Park

[See main volume for text of (a)]

(b) Administration

(1) In general

The Secretary shall manage the Park for the purpose of preserving and interpreting the Battles of the River Raisin in accordance with the National Park Service Organic Act (16 U.S.C. 1 et seq.)[1] and the Act of August 21, 1935 (16 U.S.C. 461 et seq.).[1]

[See main volume for text of (2) and (3); (c) and (d)]

1 See References in Text note set out under this section.

HISTORICAL NOTES

References in Text

The National Park Service Organic Act (16 U.S.C. 1 et seq.), referred to in subsec. (b)(1), is Act Aug. 25, 1916, c. 408, 39 Stat. 535, which enacted 16 U.S.C.A. §§ 1, 2, 3, and 4 and provisions set out as a note under 54 U.S.C.A. § 100101. Sections 1 to 4 of the Act were repealed and restated as 18 U.S.C.A. § 1865(a), and 54 U.S.C.A. § 100101(a), chapter 1003 of Title 54 (54 U.S.C.A. § 100301 et seq.), and 54 U.S.C.A. §§ 100751(a), 100752, 100753, and 102101 by Pub.L. 113–287, §§ 3, 4(a)(1), 7, Dec. 19, 2014, 128 Stat. 3094, 3260, 3272. For complete classification, see Tables. For disposition of former sections of this title, see Disposition Table preceding 54 U.S.C.A. § 100101.

The Act of August 21, 1935 (16 U.S.C. 461 et seq.), referred to in subsec. (b)(1), is Act Aug. 21, 1935, c. 593, 49 Stat. 666, known as the Historic Sites Act of 1935 and also as the Historic Sites, Buildings, and Antiquities Act, which enacted 16 U.S.C.A. §§ 461 to 467. The Act was repealed and restated as 18 U.S.C.A. § 1866(a), 54 U.S.C.A. §§ 102303 and 102304, and chapter 3201 of Title 54 (54 U.S.C.A. § 320101 et seq.) by Pub.L. 113–287, §§ 3, 4(a)(1), 7, Dec. 19, 2014, 128 Stat. 3094, 3260, 3272. For complete classification, see Tables. For disposition of former sections of this title, see Disposition Table preceding 54 U.S.C.A. § 100101.

SUBCHAPTER LXI—NATIONAL AND INTERNATIONAL MONUMENTS AND MEMORIALS

§ 431. Repealed. Pub.L. 113–287, § 7, Dec. 19, 2014, 128 Stat. 3272

HISTORICAL NOTES

Section, Act June 8, 1906, c. 3060, § 2, 34 Stat. 225, related to national monuments, reservation of lands, and relinquishment of private claims.

See, generally, Title 54 Disposition Table preceding 54 U.S.C.A. § 100101.

STATUTORY NOTES

Albert Einstein Memorial

Pub.L. 95–625, Title VI, § 612, Nov. 10, 1978, 92 Stat. 3521, as amended Pub.L. 96–87, Title

IV, § 401(*o*), Oct. 12, 1979, 93 Stat. 666, was editorially transferred as a note set out under 54 U.S.C.A. § 320301, as a result of the enactment into positive law of Title 54, National Park Service and Related Programs, by Pub.L. 113–287, Dec. 19, 2014, 128 Stat. 3094.

National Law Enforcement Officers Memorial Maintenance Fund

Pub.L. 104–329, Title II, § 201, Oct. 20, 1996, 110 Stat. 4011, which provided for National Law Enforcement Officers Memorial Maintenance Fund, was editorially transferred to the National Memorials table by Pub.L. 109–314, §§ 1, 2, Oct. 6, 2006, 120 Stat. 1739.

National Monument Commission

Act Aug. 31, 1954, c. 1160, 68 Stat. 1029, was editorially eliminated from the Code as a result of the enactment into positive law of Title 54, National Park Service and Related Programs, by Pub.L. 113–287, Dec. 19, 2014, 128 Stat. 3094.

Study to Add Alaska and Hawaii to Lincoln National Memorial

Pub.L. 94–556, Oct. 19, 1976, 90 Stat. 2632, was editorially eliminated from the Code as a result of the enactment into positive law of Title 54, National Park Service and Related Programs, by Pub.L. 113–287, Dec. 19, 2014, 128 Stat. 3094.

National Monuments and National Memorials

Provisions relating to National Monuments Established Under Presidential Proclamations, establishing National Memorials, and establishing other National Monuments, were editorially transferred and are listed in tables set out under 54 U.S.C.A. § 320301, as a result of the enactment into positive law of Title 54, National Park Service and Related Programs, by Pub.L. 113–287, Dec. 19, 2014, 128 Stat. 3094.

§ 431a. Repealed. Pub.L. 113–287, § 7, Dec. 19, 2014, 128 Stat. 3272

HISTORICAL NOTES

Section, Sept. 14, 1950, c. 950, § 1 (part), 64 Stat. 849, related to limitation on further extension or establishment of national monuments in Wyoming. See 54 U.S.C.A. § 320301(d). Section comprised only part of the last sentence of section 1 of Act Sept. 14, 1950. The remainder of such section, except that part of the last sentence which repealed 16 U.S.C.A. §§ 406 to 406d, was classified to 16 U.S.C.A. § 406d–1 and former 16 U.S.C.A. § 451a. See, generally, Title 54 Disposition Table preceding 54 U.S.C.A. § 100101.

§ 432. Repealed. Pub.L. 113–287, § 7, Dec. 19, 2014, 128 Stat. 3272

HISTORICAL NOTES

Section, June 8, 1906, c. 3060, §§ 3, 4, 34 Stat. 225; July 26, 1947, c. 343, Title II, § 205(a), 61 Stat. 501, related to permits to examine ruins, excavations, and gathering of objects. See, generally, Title 54 Disposition Table preceding 54 U.S.C.A. § 100101.

§ 433. Repealed. Pub.L. 113–287, § 7, Dec. 19, 2014, 128 Stat. 3272

HISTORICAL NOTES

Section, June 8, 1906, c. 3060, § 1, 34 Stat. 225, related to American antiquities. See, generally, Title 54 Disposition Table preceding 54 U.S.C.A. § 100101.

§ 433b. Administration, protection, and development

The administration, protection and development of the aforesaid peace memorial shall be exercised under the direction of the Secretary of the Interior by the National Park Service, subject to the provisions of the Act of August 25, 1916, entitled "An Act to establish a National Park Service, and for other purposes",[1] as amended.

[1] See References in Text note set out under this section.

HISTORICAL NOTES

References in Text

The Act of August 25, 1916, entitled "An Act to establish a National Park Service, and for other purposes", referred to in text, is Act Aug. 25, 1916, c. 408, 39 Stat. 535, known as the National Park Service Organic Act, which enacted 16 U.S.C.A. §§ 1, 2, 3, and 4 and provisions set out as a note under 54 U.S.C.A. § 100101. Sections 1 to 4 of the Act were repealed and restated as 18 U.S.C.A. § 1865(a), and 54 U.S.C.A. § 100101(a), chapter 1003 of Title 54 (54 U.S.C.A. § 100301 et seq.), and 54 U.S.C.A. §§ 100751(a), 100752, 100753, and 102101 by Pub.L. 113–287, §§ 3, 4(a)(1), 7, Dec. 19, 2014, 128 Stat. 3094, 3260, 3272. For complete classification, see Tables. For disposition of former sections of this title, see Disposition Table preceding 54 U.S.C.A. § 100101.

§ 433c. Acceptance of donations of lands and funds; acquisition of land

HISTORICAL NOTES

Codifications

"Section 3113 of Title 40" substituted in text for "the Act of August 1, 1888" on authority of Pub.L. 107–217, § 5(c), Aug. 21, 2002, 116 Stat. 1303, the first section of which enacted Title 40, Public Buildings, Property, and Works.

§ 433g. Fort Frederica National Monument; establishment

When title to the site of Fort Frederica, on Saint Simon Island, Georgia, and such other related sites located thereon, as may be designated by the Secretary of the Interior, in the exercise of his discretion, as necessary or desirable for national-monument purposes, shall have been vested in the United States, said area not to exceed 305 acres shall be, and is, set apart as a national monument for the benefit and inspiration of the people, and shall be called the "Fort Frederica National Monument."

(May 26, 1936, c. 451, § 1, 49 Stat. 1373; Sept. 20, 1950, c. 957, § 1, 64 Stat. 869; Pub.L. 85–401, § 1, May 16, 1958, 72 Stat. 110; Pub.L. 116–9, Title II, § 2104(a), Mar. 12, 2019, 133 Stat. 726.)

HISTORICAL NOTES

Amendments

2019 Amendments. Pub.L. 116–9, § 2104(a), struck out "two hundred and fifty acres" and inserted "305 acres".

STATUTORY NOTES

Boundary Expansion

Pub.L. 116–9, Title II, § 2104(b), Mar. 12, 2019, 133 Stat. 726, provided that:

"(1) **In general.**—The boundary of the Fort Frederica National Monument in the State of Georgia is modified to include the land generally depicted as 'Proposed Acquisition Areas' on the map entitled 'Fort Frederica National Monument Proposed Boundary Expansion', numbered 369/132,469, and dated April 2016.

"(2) **Availability of map.**—The map described in paragraph (1) shall be on file and available for public inspection in the appropriate offices of the National Park Service.

"(3) **Acquisition of land.**—The Secretary [of the Interior] may acquire the land and interests in land described in paragraph (1) by donation or purchase with donated or appropriated funds from willing sellers only.

"(4) **No use of condemnation or eminent domain.**—The Secretary [of the Interior] may not acquire by condemnation or eminent domain any land or interests in land under this section or for the purposes of this section [Pub.L. 116–9, § 2104, amending this section and enacting this note]."

§ 433h. Donation of property; acquisition of lands

HISTORICAL NOTES

Codifications

"Section 3113 of Title 40" substituted in text for "the Act of August 1, 1888" on authority of Pub.L. 107–217, § 5(c), Aug. 21, 2002, 116 Stat. 1303, the first section of which enacted Title 40, Public Buildings, Property, and Works.

§ 433j. Administration, protection, and development

The administration, protection, and development of the aforesaid national monument shall be exercised under the direction of the Secretary of the Interior by the National Park Service, subject to the provisions of the Act of August 25, 1916, entitled "An Act to establish a National Park Service, and for other purposes",[1] as amended.

[1] See References in Text note set out under this section.

HISTORICAL NOTES

References in Text

The Act of August 25, 1916, entitled "An Act to establish a National Park Service, and for other purposes", referred to in text, is Act Aug. 25, 1916, c. 408, 39 Stat. 535, known as the National Park Service Organic Act, which enacted 16 U.S.C.A. §§ 1, 2, 3, and 4 and provisions set out as a note under 54 U.S.C.A. § 100101. Sections 1 to 4 of the Act were repealed and restated as 18 U.S.C.A. § 1865(a), and 54 U.S.C.A. § 100101(a), chapter 1003 of Title 54 (54 U.S.C.A. § 100101 et seq.), and 54 U.S.C.A. §§ 100751(a), 100752, 100753, and 102101 by Pub.L. 113–287, §§ 3, 4(a)(1), 7, Dec. 19, 2014, 128 Stat. 3094, 3260, 3272. For complete classification, see Tables. For disposition of former sections of this title, see Disposition Table preceding 54 U.S.C.A. § 100101.

§ 434. National monument in Riverside County, California

The Secretary of the Interior is authorized to set apart the following-described lands located in the county of Riverside, in the State of California, as a national monument, which shall be under the exclusive control of the Secretary of the Interior, who shall administer and protect the same under the provisions of the Act of Congress approved June 8, 1906, entitled "An Act for the preservation of American antiquities,"[1] and under such regulations as he may prescribe: The west half of the southwest quarter of section 2, the southeast quarter of section 3, all of section 10, the west half of the northwest quarter of section 11, all of section 14, all in township 5 south, range 4 east, San Bernardino base and meridian, containing one thousand six hundred acres: *Provided*, That before such reservation and dedication as herein authorized shall become effective the consent and relinquishment of the Agua Caliente Band of Indians shall first be obtained, covering its right, title, and interest in and to the lands herein described, and payment therefor to the members of said band on a per capita basis, at a price to be agreed upon, when there shall be donated for such purposes to the Secretary of the Interior a fund in an amount to be fixed and determined by him as sufficient to compensate the Indians therefor.

[1] See References in Text note set out under this section.

HISTORICAL NOTES

References in Text

The Act of Congress approved June 8, 1906, entitled "An Act for the preservation of American antiquities," referred to in text, is Act June 8, 1906, c. 3060, 34 Stat. 225, known as the Antiquities Act of 1906, which was classified generally to 16 U.S.C.A. §§ 431, 432, and 433.

The Act was repealed and restated as 18 U.S.C.A. § 1866(b), and 54 U.S.C.A. §§ 320301(a) to (c), 320302, and 320303 by Pub.L. 113–287, §§ 3, 4(a)(1), 7, Dec. 19, 2014, 128 Stat. 3094, 3260, 3272. For complete classification, see Tables. For disposition of former sections of this title, see Disposition Table preceding 54 U.S.C.A. § 100101.

§ 441a. Boundaries

STATUTORY NOTES

Extension of Boundaries

Act June 26, 1936, c. 842, Title II, 49 Stat. 1979, provided that the boundaries of the Badlands National Monument as established by this section shall be "extended to include such lands adjacent or contiguous thereto, in the State of South Dakota, including, but not being restricted to, lands designated as submarginal by the Resettlement Administration, as may be determined by the President, by proclamation, within five years following the approval of this Act, to be necessary for the proper rounding out of the boundaries of said Monument or the administration thereof, providing the entire area of such Monument shall not exceed 250,000 acres", and that the provisions of Act Aug. 25, 1916, c. 408, 39 Stat. 535, known as the National Park Service Organic Act (see Tables for classification), were applicable to the lands that were added to the Monument under such authority.

§ 441c. Administration, protection, and promotion; franchises for hotel and lodge accommodations

The administration, protection, and promotion of said Badlands National Park shall be exercised under the direction of the Secretary of the Interior by the National Park Service, subject to the provisions of the Act of August 25, 1916, entitled "An Act to establish a National Park Service, and for other purposes," as amended by the Act of June 2, 1920 (Forty-first United States Statutes at Large, page 732):[1] *Provided*, That in advance of the fulfillment of the conditions herein the Secretary of the Interior may grant franchises for hotel and for lodge accommodations under the provisions of this section.

[1] See References in Text note set out under this section.

HISTORICAL NOTES

References in Text

The Act of August 25, 1916, entitled "An Act to establish a National Park Service, and for other purposes," as amended by the Act of June 2, 1920 (Forty-first United States Statutes at Large, page 732), referred to in text, is Act Aug. 25, 1916, c. 408, 39 Stat. 535, known as the National Park Service Organic Act, which enacted 16 U.S.C.A. §§ 1, 2, 3, and 4 and provisions set out as a note under 54 U.S.C.A. § 100101. Sections 1 to 4 of the Act were repealed and restated as 18 U.S.C.A. § 1865(a), and 54 U.S.C.A. § 100101(a), chapter 1003 of Title 54 (54 U.S.C.A. § 100301 et seq.), and 54 U.S.C.A.

§§ 100751(a), 100752, 100753, and 102101 by Pub.L. 113–287, §§ 3, 4(a)(1), 7, Dec. 19, 2014, 128 Stat. 3094, 3260, 3272. For complete classi- fication, see Tables. For disposition of former sections of this title, see Disposition Table pre- ceding 54 U.S.C.A. § 100101.

§ 441i. Exchanges of land

In order that exchanges of land may be effectuated for the purposes of sections 441f to 441i of this title, the Secretary of the Interior is authorized, in his discretion and in accordance with the provisions of sections 3111 and 3112 of Title 40, to accept, on behalf of the United States, title to any land or interests in land within the exterior boundaries of the Badlands National Park as revised pursuant to sections 441f to 441i of this title, and, in exchange therefor, with the approval and concurrence of the Secretary of Agriculture, the Secretary of the Interior may patent lands of approximately equal value which were formerly set apart and reserved from the public domain within the Badlands Fall River soil conservation project, SD–LU–1. In effectuating such exchanges, in lieu of conveyances by the Secretary of the Interior, the Secretary of Agriculture may convey lands of approximately equal value within said project which have been acquired heretofore by the United States. All such exchanges shall, in all other respects, be considered as exchanges under the provisions of section 32c,[1] title III, of the Bankhead- Jones Farm Tenant Act and shall otherwise be in accordance with provisions of said Act, except that, upon acceptance of title to any lands so acquired by the United States under this section, such lands and any other lands acquired otherwise by the United States within the park boundaries shall be a part of that area. In consummating land exchanges hereunder upon an equitable basis, patents and instruments of conveyance may be issued, and property may be accepted, by the United States, subject to such reservations as may be necessary or in the public interest.

(May 7, 1952, c. 244, § 4, 66 Stat. 66; Pub.L. 95–625, Title VI, § 611, Nov. 10, 1978, 92 Stat. 3521.)

[1] So in original. Probably should be "32(c),".

HISTORICAL NOTES

Codifications

"Sections 3111 and 3112 of Title 40" substitut- ed in text for "section 355 of the Revised Stat- utes" on authority of Pub.L. 107–217, § 5(c), Aug. 21, 2002, 116 Stat. 1303, the first section of which enacted Title 40, Public Buildings, Prop- erty, and Works.

§ 441j. Revision of boundaries

CROSS REFERENCES

Pine Ridge Indian Reservation, conditions on conveyed lands, see 25 USCA § 5501.

§ 441k. Acquisition of property for park

CROSS REFERENCES

Pine Ridge Indian Reservation, conditions on conveyed lands, see 25 USCA § 5501.

§ 441l. Exchange of lands; transfer from Federal agency to administrative jurisdiction of Secretary; terms and conditions of purchase

Inasmuch as (A) most of the lands added to the Badlands National Park by section 441j of this title are inside the boundaries of the Pine Ridge Sioux Indian Reservation, (B) such lands are also within a tract of land forty-three miles long and twelve and one- half miles wide which is in the northwestern part of such Indian reservation and has been used by the United States Air Force as a gunnery range since the early part of World War II, (C) the tribal lands within such gunnery range were leased by the Federal Government and the other lands within such gunnery range were purchased by the Federal Government from the individual owners (mostly Indians), (D) the Depart- ment of the Air Force has declared most of such gunnery range lands excess to its needs and such excess lands have been requested by the National Park Service under chapters 1 to 11 of Title 40 and division C (except sections 3302, 3307(e), 3501(b), 3509, 3906, 4710, and 4711) of subtitle I of Title 41, (E) the leased tribal lands and the excess lands within the enlarged Badlands National Park are needed for the park, (F) the other excess lands in such gunnery range should be restored to the former Indian owners of such lands, and (G) the tribe is unwilling to sell its tribal lands for inclusion in the national park, but is willing to exchange them or interests therein for the excess gunnery range lands, which, insofar as the lands within the gunnery range formerly held by the tribe are concerned, should be returned to Indian ownership in any event, the Congress hereby finds that such exchange would be in the national interest and authorizes the following actions:

[See main volume for text of (a) and (b)]

HISTORICAL NOTES

Codifications

In subpar. (D) of introductory provisions, "chapters 1 to 11 of Title 40 and division C (except sections 3302, 3307(e), 3501(b), 3509, 3906, 4710, and 4711) of subtitle I of Title 41" was substituted for "the Federal Property and Administrative Services Act of 1949" on authority of Pub.L. 107–217, § 5(c), Aug. 21, 2002, 116 Stat. 1303, which Act enacted Title 40, Public Buildings, Property, and Works, and Pub.L. 111–350, § 6(c), Jan. 4, 2011, 124 Stat. 3854, which Act enacted Title 41, Public Contracts.

CROSS REFERENCES

Pine Ridge Indian Reservation, conditions on conveyed lands, see 25 USCA § 5501.

§ 441m. Disposition of excess gunnery range lands and reservation lands; purchase; terms and conditions; life estates and use restrictions

HISTORICAL NOTES

References in Text

The National Industrial Recovery Act of June 16, 1933, referred to in subsec. (a), is Act June 16, 1933, c. 90, 48 Stat. 195, as amended. Title II of the Act was classified principally to subchapter I (§ 401 et seq.) of chapter 8 of former Title 40, Public Buildings, Property, and Works, and was terminated June 30, 1943 by Act June 27, 1942, c. 450, § 1, 56 Stat. 410. Provisions of Title II of the Act which were classified to former Title 40 were repealed by Pub.L. 107–217, § 6(b), Aug. 21, 2002, 116 Stat. 1304. For complete classification of this Act to the Code, see Tables.

CROSS REFERENCES

Pine Ridge Indian Reservation, conditions on conveyed lands, see 25 USCA § 5501.

§ 441n. Lands outside gunnery range; exchange of lands; reservation of mineral rights; grazing and mineral development rights of Indians; execution of instruments; trust title

CROSS REFERENCES

Pine Ridge Indian Reservation, conditions on conveyed lands, see 25 USCA § 5501.

§ 441o. Facilities for interpretation of park and history of Sioux Nation; conveyance of reservation lands; submission of terms to Congressional committees

HISTORICAL NOTES

Change of Name

The word "park" was substituted in text for "monument" pursuant to Pub.L. 95–625, § 611, which is classified to section 441e–1 of this title and which redesignated Badlands National Monument as Badlands National Park.

The Committee on Interior and Insular Affairs of the Senate was abolished and replaced by the Committee on Energy and Natural Resources of the Senate, effective Feb. 11, 1977. See Rule XXV of the Standing Rules of the Senate, as amended by Senate Resolution 4 (popularly cited as the "Committee System Reorganization Amendments of 1977"), approved Feb. 4, 1977.

The Committee on Interior and Insular Affairs of the House of Representatives changed to Committee on Natural Resources of the House of Representatives on Jan. 5, 1993, by House Resolution No. 5, One Hundred Third Congress. For references to Committees of the House of Representatives with new names, see Pub.L. 104–14, § 1(a), June 3, 1995, 109 Stat. 186, as amended, set out as a note preceding 2 U.S.C.A. § 21.

§ 442. George Washington Birthplace National Monument

The land owned by the United States at Wakefield, Westmoreland County, Virginia, and all structures thereon shall constitute the George Washington Birthplace National Monument at Wakefield, Virginia, which is established and set apart for the preservation of the historical associations connected therewith, for the benefit and enjoyment of the people, and the said national monument shall be after January 23, 1930, administered by the National Park Service under the direction of the Secretary of the Interior subject to the provisions of the Act of August 25, 1916 (Thirty-ninth Statutes, page 535),[1] as amended.

[1] See References in Text note set out under this section.

HISTORICAL NOTES

References in Text

The Act of August 25, 1916 (Thirty-ninth Statutes, page 535), referred to in text, is Act Aug. 25, 1916, c. 408, 39 Stat. 535, known as the National Park Service Organic Act, which enacted 16 U.S.C.A. §§ 1, 2, 3, and 4 and provisions set out as a note under 54 U.S.C.A. § 100101. Sections 1 to 4 of the Act were repealed and restated as 18 U.S.C.A. § 1865(a), and 54 U.S.C.A. § 100101(a), chapter 1003 of Title 54 (54 U.S.C.A. § 100301 et seq.), and 54 U.S.C.A. §§ 100751(a), 100752, 100753, and 102101 by Pub.L. 113–287, §§ 3, 4(a)(1), 7, Dec. 19, 2014, 128 Stat. 3094, 3260, 3272. For complete classification, see Tables. For disposition of former sections of this title, see Disposition Table preceding 54 U.S.C.A. § 100101.

§ 445c. Pipestone National Monument

[See main volume for text of (a)]

(b) Administration, protection, and development

The administration, protection, and development of such monument shall be exercised under the direction of the Secretary of the Interior by the National Park Service, subject to the provisions of the Act entitled "An Act to establish a National Park Service, and for other purposes", approved August 25, 1916,[1] as amended.

[See main volume for text of (c)]

[1] See References in Text note set out under this section.

HISTORICAL NOTES

References in Text

The Act entitled "An Act to establish a National Park Service, and for other purposes", approved August 25, 1916, referred to in subsec. (b), is Act Aug. 25, 1916, c. 408, 39 Stat. 535, known as the National Park Service Organic Act, which enacted 16 U.S.C.A. §§ 1, 2, 3, and 4 and provisions set out as a note under 54 U.S.C.A. § 100101. Sections 1 to 4 of the Act were repealed and restated as 18 U.S.C.A. § 1865(a), and 54 U.S.C.A. § 100101(a), chapter 1003 of Title 54 (54 U.S.C.A. § 100301 et seq.), and 54 U.S.C.A. §§ 100751(a), 100752, 100753, and 102101 by Pub.L. 113–287, §§ 3, 4(a)(1), 7, Dec. 19, 2014, 128 Stat. 3094, 3260, 3272. For complete classification, see Tables. For disposition of former sections of this title, see Disposition Table preceding 54 U.S.C.A. § 100101.

§ 447a. Transferred to 16 U.S.C.A. § 410yyy

§ 447b. Transferred to 16 U.S.C.A. § 410yyy–1

§ 447c. Transferred to 16 U.S.C.A. § 410yyy–2

§ 449. Acceptance of donations of land and funds; acquisition of land

HISTORICAL NOTES

Codifications

"Section 3113 of Title 40" substituted in text for "the Act of August 1, 1888" on authority of Pub.L. 107–217, § 5(c), Aug. 21, 2002, 116 Stat. 1303, the first section of which enacted Title 40, Public Buildings, Property, and Works.

§ 450. Administration, protection, and development

The administration, protection, and development of the aforesaid national monument shall be exercised under the direction of the Secretary of the Interior by the National

Park Service, subject to the provisions of the Act of August 25, 1916, entitled "An Act to establish a National Park Service, and for other purposes",[1] as amended.

[1] See References in Text note set out under this section.

HISTORICAL NOTES

References in Text

The Act of August 25, 1916, entitled "An Act to establish a National Park Service, and for other purposes", referred to in text, is Act Aug. 25, 1916, c. 408, 39 Stat. 535, known as the National Park Service Organic Act, which enacted 16 U.S.C.A. §§ 1, 2, 3, and 4 and provisions set out as a note under 54 U.S.C.A. § 100101. Sections 1 to 4 of the Act were repealed and restated as 18 U.S.C.A. § 1865(a), and 54 U.S.C.A. § 100101(a), chapter 1003 of Title 54 (54 U.S.C.A. § 100301 et seq.), and 54 U.S.C.A. §§ 100751(a), 100752, 100753, and 102101 by Pub.L. 113–287, §§ 3, 4(a)(1), 7, Dec. 19, 2014, 128 Stat. 3094, 3260, 3272. For complete classification, see Tables. For disposition of former sections of this title, see Disposition Table preceding 54 U.S.C.A. § 100101.

§ 450e–1. Appomattox Court House National Historical Park

[See main volume for text of (a) to (c)]

(d) Administration

The Secretary shall administer the park in accordance with the Acts of August 25, 1916 (39 Stat. 535),[1] as amended and supplemented, and August 21, 1935 (49 Stat. 666)[1] as amended.

[See main volume for text of (e) and (f)]

[1] See References in Text note set out under this section.

HISTORICAL NOTES

References in Text

The Act of August 25, 1916 (39 Stat. 535), referred to in subsec. (d), is Act Aug. 25, 1916, c. 408, 39 Stat. 535, known as the National Park Service Organic Act, which enacted 16 U.S.C.A. §§ 1, 2, 3, and 4 and provisions set out as a note under 54 U.S.C.A. § 100101. Sections 1 to 4 of the Act were repealed and restated as 18 U.S.C.A. § 1865(a), and 54 U.S.C.A. § 100101(a), chapter 1003 of Title 54 (54 U.S.C.A. § 100301 et seq.), and 54 U.S.C.A. §§ 100751(a), 100752, 100753, and 102101 by Pub.L. 113–287, §§ 3, 4(a)(1), 7, Dec. 19, 2014, 128 Stat. 3094, 3260, 3272. For complete classification, see Tables. For disposition of former sections of this title, see Disposition Table preceding 54 U.S.C.A. § 100101.

The Act of August 21, 1935 (49 Stat. 666), referred to in subsec. (d), is Act Aug. 21, 1935, c. 593, 49 Stat. 666, known as the Historic Sites Act of 1935 and also as the Historic Sites, Buildings, and Antiquities Act, which enacted 16 U.S.C.A. §§ 461 to 467. The Act was repealed and restated as 18 U.S.C.A. § 1866(a), 54 U.S.C.A. §§ 102303 and 102304, and chapter 3201 of Title 54 (54 U.S.C.A. § 320101 et seq.) by Pub.L. 113–287, §§ 3, 4(a)(1), 7, Dec. 19, 2014, 128 Stat. 3094, 3260, 3272. For complete classification, see Tables. For disposition of former sections of this title, see Disposition Table preceding 54 U.S.C.A. § 100101.

§ 450m. Acceptance of donations of lands and funds; acquisition of land

HISTORICAL NOTES

Codifications

"Section 3113 of Title 40" substituted in text for "the Act of August 1, 1888" on authority of Pub.L. 107–217, § 5(c), Aug. 21, 2002, 116 Stat. 1303, the first section of which enacted Title 40, Public Buildings, Property, and Works.

§ 450n. Administration, protection, and development

The administration, protection, and development of the aforesaid national monument shall be exercised under the direction of the Secretary of the Interior by the National Park Service, subject to the provisions of the Act of August 25, 1916, entitled "An Act to establish a National Park Service, and for other purposes",[1] as amended.

[1] See References in Text note set out under this section.

HISTORICAL NOTES

References in Text

The Act of August 25, 1916, entitled "An Act to establish a National Park Service, and for other purposes", referred to in text, is Act Aug. 25, 1916, c. 408, 39 Stat. 535, known as the National Park Service Organic Act, which enacted 16 U.S.C.A. §§ 1, 2, 3, and 4 and provisions set out as a note under 54 U.S.C.A. § 100101. Sections 1 to 4 of the Act were repealed and restated as 18 U.S.C.A. § 1865(a), and 54 U.S.C.A. § 100101(a), chapter 1003 of Title 54 (54 U.S.C.A. § 100301 et seq.), and 54 U.S.C.A. §§ 100751(a), 100752, 100753, and 102101 by Pub.L. 113–287, §§ 3, 4(a)(1), 7, Dec. 19, 2014, 128 Stat. 3094, 3260, 3272. For complete classification, see Tables. For disposition of former sections of this title, see Disposition Table preceding 54 U.S.C.A. § 100101.

§ 450p. Acquisition of property; donations

HISTORICAL NOTES

Codifications

"Section 3113 of Title 40" substituted in text for "the Act of August 1, 1888" on authority of Pub.L. 107–217, § 5(c), Aug. 21, 2002, 116 Stat. 1303, the first section of which enacted Title 40, Public Buildings, Property, and Works.

§ 450q. Administration, protection, and development

The administration, protection, and development of the aforesaid national historic site shall be exercised under the direction of the Secretary of the Interior by the National Park Service, subject to the provisions of the Act of August 25, 1916 (39 Stat. 535), entitled "An Act to establish a National Park Service, and for other purposes",[1] as amended.

[1] See References in Text note set out under this section.

HISTORICAL NOTES

References in Text

The Act of August 25, 1916 (39 Stat. 535), entitled "An Act to establish a National Park Service, and for other purposes", referred to in text, is Act Aug. 25, 1916, c. 408, 39 Stat. 535, known as the National Park Service Organic Act, which enacted 16 U.S.C.A. §§ 1, 2, 3, and 4 and provisions set out as a note under 54 U.S.C.A. § 100101. Sections 1 to 4 of the Act were repealed and restated as 18 U.S.C.A. § 1865(a), and 54 U.S.C.A. § 100101(a), chapter 1003 of Title 54 (54 U.S.C.A. § 100301 et seq.), and 54 U.S.C.A. §§ 100751(a), 100752, 100753, and 102101 by Pub.L. 113–287, §§ 3, 4(a)(1), 7, Dec. 19, 2014, 128 Stat. 3094, 3260, 3272. For complete classification, see Tables. For disposition of former sections of this title, see Disposition Table preceding 54 U.S.C.A. § 100101.

§ 450t. Administration, protection, and development

The administration, protection, and development of the aforesaid national monument shall be exercised under the direction of the Secretary of the Interior by the National Park Service, subject to the provisions of the Act of August 25, 1916, entitled "An Act to establish a National Park Service, and for other purposes",[1] as amended.

[1] See References in Text note set out under this section.

HISTORICAL NOTES

References in Text

The Act of August 25, 1916, entitled "An Act to establish a National Park Service, and for other purposes", referred to in text, is Act Aug. 25, 1916, c. 408, 39 Stat. 535, known as the National Park Service Organic Act, which enacted 16 U.S.C.A. §§ 1, 2, 3, and 4 and provisions set out as a note under 54 U.S.C.A. § 100101. Sections 1 to 4 of the Act were repealed and restated as 18 U.S.C.A. § 1865(a), and 54 U.S.C.A. § 100101(a), chapter 1003 of Title 54 (54 U.S.C.A. § 100301 et seq.), and 54 U.S.C.A. §§ 100751(a), 100752, 100753, and 102101 by Pub.L. 113–287, §§ 3, 4(a)(1), 7, Dec. 19, 2014, 128 Stat. 3094, 3260, 3272. For complete classification, see Tables. For disposition of former sections of this title, see Disposition Table preceding 54 U.S.C.A. § 100101.

§ 450u. Transferred to 16 U.S.C.A. § 410gggg

§ 450w. Transferred to 16 U.S.C.A. § 410gggg–1

§ 450x. Transferred to 16 U.S.C.A. § 410gggg–2

§ 450y–1. Administration

The National Park Service, under the direction of the Secretary of the Interior, shall promote and regulate the use of the Coronado National Memorial for the benefit and enjoyment of the people of the United States. Insofar as applicable and not in conflict with sections 450y to 450y–4 of this title, the Act of August 25, 1916 (39 Stat. 535), providing for the establishment of a National Park Service,[1] as amended and supplemented, providing for the establishment of a National Park Service, shall govern the promotion and regulation of the designated memorial area: *Provided*, That nothing in sections 450y to 450y–4 of this title shall be construed to authorize any recreational or other development by the National Park Service within the sixty-foot strip north of the international boundary between the United States and Mexico withdrawn by proclamation of the President dated May 27, 1907 (35 Stat., part II, p. 2136), unless such development has received the prior approval of the Secretary of State.

[1] See References in Text note set out under this section.

HISTORICAL NOTES

References in Text

The Act of August 25, 1916 (39 Stat. 535), providing for the establishment of a National Park Service, referred to in text, is Act Aug. 25, 1916, c. 408, 39 Stat. 535, known as the National Park Service Organic Act, which enacted 16 U.S.C.A. §§ 1, 2, 3, and 4 and provisions set out as a note under 54 U.S.C.A. § 100101. Sections 1 to 4 of the Act were repealed and restated as 18 U.S.C.A. § 1865(a), and 54 U.S.C.A. § 100101(a), chapter 1003 of Title 54 (54 U.S.C.A. § 100301 et seq.), and 54 U.S.C.A. §§ 100751(a), 100752, 100753, and 102101 by Pub.L. 113–287, §§ 3, 4(a)(1), 7, Dec. 19, 2014, 128 Stat. 3094, 3260, 3272. For complete classification, see Tables. For disposition of former sections of this title, see Disposition Table preceding 54 U.S.C.A. § 100101.

§ 450y–6. Acquisition of lands; administration

The Secretary of the Interior is authorized to acquire lands and interests in lands within the revised boundaries of the Coronado National Memorial by purchase, donation, with donated funds, or by such other means as he may consider to be in the public interest. Lands and interests in lands acquired pursuant to this Act shall become a part of the Memorial and be administered by the Secretary of the Interior in accordance with the provisions of the Act of August 25, 1916 (39 Stat. 535),[1] as amended, and pursuant to sections 450y–1 to 450y–3 of this title.

[1] See References in Text note set out under this section.

HISTORICAL NOTES

References in Text

The Act of August 25, 1916 (39 Stat. 535), referred to in text, is Act Aug. 25, 1916, c. 408, 39 Stat. 535, known as the National Park Service Organic Act, which enacted 16 U.S.C.A. §§ 1, 2, 3, and 4 and provisions set out as a note under 54 U.S.C.A. § 100101. Sections 1 to 4 of the Act were repealed and restated as 18 U.S.C.A. § 1865(a), and 54 U.S.C.A. § 100101(a), chapter 1003 of Title 54 (54 U.S.C.A. § 100301 et seq.), and 54 U.S.C.A. §§ 100751(a), 100752, 100753, and 102101 by Pub.L. 113–287, §§ 3, 4(a)(1), 7, Dec. 19, 2014, 128 Stat. 3094, 3260, 3272. For complete classification, see Tables. For disposition of former sections of this title, see Disposition Table preceding 54 U.S.C.A. § 100101.

§ 450bb–1. Administration

The property acquired under the provisions of section 450bb of this title shall constitute the Harpers Ferry National Historical Park and shall be a public national memorial commemorating historical events at or near Harpers Ferry. The Director of the National Park Service under the direction of the Secretary, shall have the supervision, management, and control of such national historical park, and shall maintain and preserve it for the benefit and enjoyment of the people of the United States, subject to the provisions of the Act of August 25, 1916 (39 Stat. 535), entitled "An Act to establish a National Park Service, and for other purposes",[1] as amended.

[1] See References in Text note set out under this section.

HISTORICAL NOTES

References in Text

The Act of August 25, 1916 (39 Stat. 535), entitled "An Act to establish a National Park Service, and for other purposes", referred to in text, is Act Aug. 25, 1916, c. 408, 39 Stat. 535, known as the National Park Service Organic Act, which enacted 16 U.S.C.A. §§ 1, 2, 3, and 4 and provisions set out as a note under 54 U.S.C.A. § 100101. Sections 1 to 4 of the Act were repealed and restated as 18 U.S.C.A. § 1865(a), and 54 U.S.C.A. § 100101(a), chapter 1003 of Title 54 (54 U.S.C.A. § 100301 et seq.), and 54 U.S.C.A. §§ 100751(a), 100752, 100753, and 102101 by Pub.L. 113–287, §§ 3, 4(a)(1), 7, Dec. 19, 2014, 128 Stat. 3094, 3260, 3272. For complete classification, see Tables. For disposition of former sections of this title, see Disposition Table preceding 54 U.S.C.A. § 100101.

Amendments

2004 Amendments. Pub.L. 108–307, § 3, struck out "Secretary of the Interior" and inserted "Secretary".

§ 450cc–1. Administration, protection, and development

The administration, protection, and development of the Castle Clinton National Monument shall be under the supervision of the Secretary of the Interior, subject to the provisions of the Act entitled "An Act to establish a National Park Service, and for other purposes", approved August 25, 1916,[1] as amended.

[1] See References in Text note set out under this section.

HISTORICAL NOTES

References in Text

The Act entitled "An Act to establish a National Park Service, and for other purposes", approved August 25, 1916, referred to in text, is Act Aug. 25, 1916, c. 408, 39 Stat. 535, known as the National Park Service Organic Act, which enacted 16 U.S.C.A. §§ 1, 2, 3, and 4 and provisions set out as a note under 54 U.S.C.A. § 100101. Sections 1 to 4 of the Act were repealed and restated as 18 U.S.C.A. § 1865(a), and 54 U.S.C.A. § 100101(a), chapter 1003 of Title 54 (54 U.S.C.A. § 100301 et seq.), and 54 U.S.C.A. §§ 100751(a), 100752, 100753, and 102101 by Pub.L. 113–287, §§ 3, 4(a)(1), 7, Dec. 19, 2014, 128 Stat. 3094, 3260, 3272. For complete classification, see Tables. For disposition of former sections of this title, see Disposition Table preceding 54 U.S.C.A. § 100101.

§ 450dd–1. Administration

Upon a determination by the Secretary of the Interior that sufficient land has been acquired by the United States for the memorial, such property shall be established as the "De Soto National Memorial", and shall be administered by the Secretary of the Interior, through the National Park Service, for the benefit of the people of the United States. An order of the Secretary of the Interior, constituting notice of such establishment, shall be published in the Federal Register. Insofar as applicable and not in conflict with this section and section 450dd of this title, the Act of August 25, 1916 (39 Stat. 535), providing for the establishment of a National Park Service,[1] as amended and supplemented, shall govern the promotion and development of the national memorial.

[1] See References in Text note set out under this section.

HISTORICAL NOTES

References in Text

The Act of August 25, 1916 (39 Stat. 535), providing for the establishment of a National Park Service, referred to in text, is Act Aug. 25, 1916, c. 408, 39 Stat. 535, known as the National Park Service Organic Act, which enacted 16 U.S.C.A. §§ 1, 2, 3, and 4 and provisions set out as a note under 54 U.S.C.A. § 100101. Sections 1 to 4 of the Act were repealed and restated as 18 U.S.C.A. § 1865(a), and 54 U.S.C.A. § 100101(a), chapter 1003 of Title 54 (54 U.S.C.A. § 100301 et seq.), and 54 U.S.C.A. §§ 100751(a), 100752, 100753, and 102101 by Pub.L. 113–287, §§ 3, 4(a)(1), 7, Dec. 19, 2014, 128 Stat. 3094, 3260, 3272. For complete classification, see Tables. For disposition of former sections of this title, see Disposition Table preceding 54 U.S.C.A. § 100101.

§ 450ee–1. Repealed. Pub.L. 116–9, Title II, § 2203(g), Mar. 12, 2019, 133 Stat. 735

HISTORICAL NOTES

Section, Apr. 28, 1948, c. 239, § 2, 62 Stat. 204, related to the supervision, management, and control of the Fort Sumter National Monument.

§ 450ff–1. Size of site; effective date; additional lands

HISTORICAL NOTES

Change of Name

The words "national historic site" and "historic site" were substituted in text for "national monument" and "monument", respectively, in view of redesignation of Fort Vancouver National Monument as Fort Vancouver National Historic Site by Pub.L. 87–78, classified to section 450ff–6 of this title.

§ 450ff–2. Administration, protection, and development

The administration, protection, and development of the aforesaid national historic site shall be exercised under the direction of the Secretary of the Interior by the National Park Service, subject to the provisions of the Act of August 25, 1916 (39 Stat. 535), entitled "An Act to establish a National Park Service, and for other purposes",[1] as amended.

[1] See References in Text note set out under this section.

HISTORICAL NOTES

References in Text

The Act of August 25, 1916 (39 Stat. 535), entitled "An Act to establish a National Park Service, and for other purposes", referred to in text, is Act Aug. 25, 1916, c. 408, 39 Stat. 535, known as the National Park Service Organic Act, which enacted 16 U.S.C.A. §§ 1, 2, 3, and 4 and provisions set out as a note under 54 U.S.C.A. § 100101. Sections 1 to 4 of the Act were repealed and restated as 18 U.S.C.A. § 1865(a), and 54 U.S.C.A. § 100101(a), chapter 1003 of Title 54 (54 U.S.C.A. § 100301 et seq.), and 54 U.S.C.A. §§ 100751(a), 100752, 100753,

and 102101 by Pub.L. 113–287, §§ 3, 4(a)(1), 7, Dec. 19, 2014, 128 Stat. 3094, 3260, 3272. For complete classification, see Tables. For disposition of former sections of this title, see Disposition Table preceding 54 U.S.C.A. § 100101.

Change of Name

The words "national historic site" substituted in text for "national monument" in view of redesignation of Fort Vancouver National Monument as Fort Vancouver National Historic Site by Pub.L. 87–78, classified to section 450ff–6 of this title.

§ 450hh–2. Administration

The national monument shall be administered by the Secretary of the Interior, through the National Park Service, subject to the provisions of the Act of August 25, 1916 (39 Stat. 535; 16 U.S.C. 1–4),[1] as amended and supplemented, and the Act of August 21, 1935 (49 Stat. 666; 16 U.S.C. 461–467).[1]

[1] See References in Text note set out under this section.

HISTORICAL NOTES

References in Text

The Act of August 25, 1916 (39 Stat. 535; 16 U.S.C. 1–4), referred to in text, is Act Aug. 25, 1916, c. 408, 39 Stat. 535, known as the National Park Service Organic Act, which enacted 16 U.S.C.A. §§ 1, 2, 3, and 4 and provisions set out as a note under 54 U.S.C.A. § 100101. Sections 1 to 4 of the Act were repealed and restated as 18 U.S.C.A. § 1865(a), and 54 U.S.C.A. § 100101(a), chapter 1003 of Title 54 (54 U.S.C.A. § 100301 et seq.), and 54 U.S.C.A. §§ 100751(a), 100752, 100753, and 102101 by Pub.L. 113–287, §§ 3, 4(a)(1), 7, Dec. 19, 2014, 128 Stat. 3094, 3260, 3272. For complete classification, see Tables. For disposition of former

sections of this title, see Disposition Table preceding 54 U.S.C.A. § 100101.

The Act of August 21, 1935 (49 Stat. 666; 16 U.S.C. 461–467), referred to in text, is Act Aug. 21, 1935, c. 593, 49 Stat. 666, known as the Historic Sites Act of 1935 and also as the Historic Sites, Buildings, and Antiquities Act, which enacted 16 U.S.C.A. §§ 461 to 467. The Act was repealed and restated as 18 U.S.C.A. § 1866(a), 54 U.S.C.A. §§ 102303 and 102304, and chapter 3201 of Title 54 (54 U.S.C.A. § 320101 et seq.) by Pub.L. 113–287, §§ 3, 4(a)(1), 7, Dec. 19, 2014, 128 Stat. 3094, 3260, 3272. For complete classification, see Tables. For disposition of former sections of this title, see Disposition Table preceding 54 U.S.C.A. § 100101.

§ 450ii. Joshua Tree National Monument; revision of boundaries

STATUTORY NOTES

Abolition of Joshua Tree National Monument

Joshua Tree National Monument abolished and incorporated in Joshua Tree National Park, see section 410aaa–22 of this title.

§ 450ii–1. Excluded lands opened to entry under mining laws

STATUTORY NOTES

Abolition of Joshua Tree National Monument

Joshua Tree National Monument abolished and incorporated in Joshua Tree National Park, see section 410aaa–22 of this title.

§ 450ii–2. Continuation of leases, permits, and licenses

STATUTORY NOTES

Abolition of Joshua Tree National Monument

Joshua Tree National Monument abolished and incorporated in Joshua Tree National Park, see section 410aaa–22 of this title.

§ 450ii–3. Survey and report of mineral value

HISTORICAL NOTES

Change of Name

"United States Bureau of Mines" substituted in text for "Bureau of Mines" pursuant to Pub.L. 102–285, § 10(a), May 18, 1992, 106 Stat. 171, set out as a note under section 1 of Title 30, Mineral Lands and Mining. For provisions relating to closure and transfer of functions of the United States Bureau of Mines, see Transfer of Functions note set out under section 1 of Title 30.

"United States Geological Survey" substituted in text for "Geological Survey" pursuant to provision of Title I of Pub.L. 102–154, set out as a note under section 31 of Title 43, Public Lands.

STATUTORY NOTES

Abolition of Joshua Tree National Monument

Joshua Tree National Monument abolished and incorporated in Joshua Tree National Park, see section 410aaa–22 of this title.

§ 450jj. Jefferson National Expansion Memorial; authorization

There is authorized to be constructed by the Secretary of the Interior upon the Jefferson National Expansion Memorial National Historic Site,[1] Saint Louis, Missouri, an appropriate national memorial to those persons who made possible the territorial expansion of the United States, including President Thomas Jefferson and his aides, Livingston and Monroe, who negotiated the Louisiana Purchase, the great explorers, Lewis and Clark, and the hardy hunters, trappers, frontiersmen, pioneers, and others who contributed to such expansion.

[1] Redesignated "Gateway Arch National Park", see Change of Name note set out under this section and 16 U.S.C.A. § 450jj–10(b).

HISTORICAL NOTES

Change of Name

Any reference in a law, map, regulation, document, paper, or other record of the United States to the Jefferson National Expansion Memorial shall be considered to be a reference to the "Gateway Arch National Park", see Pub.L. 115–128, § 2(b), Feb. 22, 2018, 132 Stat. 328, which is classified to 16 U.S.C.A. § 450jj–10(b).

Short Title

2018 Amendments. Pub.L. 115–128, § 1, Feb. 22, 2018, 132 Stat. 328, provided that: "This Act [enacting 16 U.S.C.A. § 450jj–10] may be cited as the 'Gateway Arch National Park Designation Act'."

STATUTORY NOTES

Disposition of Funds Received by National Park Service as Reimbursement for Costs Incurred

Pub.L. 99–500, § 101(h) [Title I, § 100], Oct. 18, 1986, 100 Stat. 1783–251, provided: "That notwithstanding any other provision of law, hereafter funds received by the National Park Service as reimbursement for the cost of providing security, law enforcement, interpretive, and other services with respect to the operation of facilities at the Jefferson National Expansion Memorial National Historic Site [redesignated Gateway Arch National Park by Pub.L. 115–128, § 2, Feb. 22, 2018, 132 Stat. 328 (16 U.S.C.A. § 450jj–10)] shall be credited to the appropriation bearing the cost of providing such services."

[An identical provision is contained in Pub.L. 99–591, Title I, § 101(h) [Title I, § 100], Oct. 30, 1986, 100 Stat. 3341–251.]

§ 450jj–1. Construction of memorial

(a) Plan; contracts; employment and compensation of personnel

The memorial authorized herein shall be constructed in general, in accordance with the plan approved by the United States Territorial Expansion Memorial Commission on May 25, 1948. The Secretary of the Interior is authorized to enter into such contracts as may be necessary to carry out the purposes of sections 450jj to 450jj–9 of this title. The Secretary is also authorized to employ, in his discretion, by contract or otherwise, landscape architects, architects, engineers, sculptors, artists, other expert consultants, or firms, partnerships, or associations thereof, and to include in any such contract provision for the utilization of the services and facilities, and the payment of the travel and other expenses, of their respective organizations, in accordance with the usual customs of the several professions and at the prevailing rates for such services and facilities, without regard to the civil-service laws or regulations, chapter 51 and subchapter III of chapter

53 of Title 5, section 6101 of Title 41, or any other law or regulation relating to either employment or compensation.

[See main volume for text of (b) and (c)]

HISTORICAL NOTES

Codifications

In subsec. (a), "section 6101 of Title 41" substituted for "section 3709 of the Revised Statutes,

as amended" on authority of Pub.L. 111–350, § 6(c), Jan. 4, 2011, 124 Stat. 3854, which Act enacted Title 41, Public Contracts.

§ 450jj–2. Railroad agreement as condition precedent to undertaking memorial project

The memorial project authorized herein shall not be undertaken until there shall have been reached an agreement satisfactory to the Secretary of the Interior providing for the relocation of the railroad tracks and structures now situated on lands adjacent to the Jefferson National Expansion Memorial National Historic Site,[1] between the boundary of the site and the river. Such agreement shall contain such terms as may be deemed desirable by the Secretary but shall contain a provision limiting the Federal expenditure of funds in connection with such relocation of the tracks and structures to work undertaken within the historic site area.

[1] Redesignated "Gateway Arch National Park", see Change of Name note set out under this section and 16 U.S.C.A. § 450jj–10(b).

HISTORICAL NOTES

Change of Name

Any reference in a law, map, regulation, document, paper, or other record of the United States to the Jefferson National Expansion Memorial shall be considered to be a reference to the "Gateway Arch National Park", see Pub.L. 115–128, § 2(b), Feb. 22, 2018, 132 Stat. 328, which is classified to 16 U.S.C.A. § 450jj–10(b).

§ 450jj–3. Designation of additional land by Secretary; manner of acquiring additional land

(a) There is hereby designated for addition to the Jefferson National Expansion Memorial[1] (hereinafter in sections 450jj–3 to 450jj–9 of this title referred to as the "Memorial") approximately one hundred acres in the city of East Saint Louis, Illinois, contiguous with the Mississippi River and between the Eads Bridge and the Poplar Street Bridge, as generally depicted on the map entitled "Boundary Map, Jefferson National Expansion Memorial",[1] numbered 366–80013, dated January 1992, which shall be on file and available for public inspection in the offices of the National Park Service, Department of the Interior. The additional acreage authorized by this section is in recognition of the historical significance of the Memorial site to the westward expansion of the United States and the historical linkage of this site on the Mississippi in both Missouri and Illinois to such expansion, the international recognition of the Gateway Arch, designed by Eero Saarinen, as one of the world's great sculptural and architectural achievements, and the increasing use of the Memorial site by millions of people from all over the United States and the world.

[See main volume for text of (b)]

[1] Redesignated "Gateway Arch National Park", see Change of Name note set out under this section and 16 U.S.C.A. § 450jj–10(b).

HISTORICAL NOTES

Change of Name

Any reference in a law, map, regulation, document, paper, or other record of the United States to the Jefferson National Expansion Memorial shall be considered to be a reference to the "Gateway Arch National Park", see Pub.L. 115–128, § 2(b), Feb. 22, 2018, 132 Stat. 328, which is classified to 16 U.S.C.A. § 450jj–10(b).

§ 450jj–4. Transfer of land

Where appropriate in the discretion of the Secretary of the Interior, he may transfer by lease or otherwise, to any appropriate person or governmental entity, land owned by the United States (or any interest therein) which has been acquired by the Secretary under section 450jj–3 of this title. Any such transfer shall be consistent with the management plan for the area and with the requirements of sections 100903 and 102901 of Title 54 and shall be subject to such conditions and restrictions as the Secretary deems necessary to carry out the purposes of sections 450jj to 450jj–9 of this title, including terms and conditions which provide for—

[See main volume for text of (1) to (3)]

In transferring any lands or interest in lands under this section, the Secretary shall take into account the views of the Commission established under section 450jj–6 of this title.

HISTORICAL NOTES

Codifications

In introductory provisions, "sections 100903 and 102901 of Title 54" substituted for "section 5 of the Act of July 15, 1968 (82 Stat. 356; 16 U.S.C. 460l–22)" on authority of Pub.L. 113–287, § 6(e), Dec. 19, 2014, 128 Stat. 3272, which Act enacted Title 54, 54 U.S.C.A. § 100101 et seq.

§ 450jj–5. Administration of Memorial; cooperation with State and local governments and private sector

Lands and interests in lands acquired pursuant to section 450jj–3 of this title shall, upon acquisition, be a part of the Memorial. The Secretary of the Interior shall administer the Memorial in accordance with sections 450jj to 450jj–9 of this title and the provisions of law generally applicable to units of the national park system, including the Act entitled "An Act to establish a National Park Service, and for other purposes", approved August 25, 1916 (39 Stat. 535; 16 U.S.C. 1–4)[1] and the Act of August 21, 1935 (49 Stat. 666; 16 U.S.C. 461–467).[1] In the development, management, and operation of that portion of the Memorial which is added to the Memorial under section 450jj–3 of this title, the Secretary shall, to the maximum extent feasible, utilize the assistance of State and local government agencies and the private sector. For such purposes, the Secretary may, consistent with the management plan for the area, enter into cooperative agreements with the State, with any political subdivision of the State, or with any person. Any such cooperative agreement shall, at a minimum, establish procedures for providing notice to the Secretary of any action proposed by the State, such political subdivision, or such person, which may affect the area.

[1] See References in Text note set out under this section.

HISTORICAL NOTES

References in Text

The Act entitled "An Act to establish a National Park Service, and for other purposes", approved August 25, 1916 (39 Stat. 535; 16 U.S.C. 1–4), referred to in text, is Act Aug. 25, 1916, c. 408, 39 Stat. 535, known as the National Park Service Organic Act, which enacted 16 U.S.C.A. §§ 1, 2, 3, and 4 and provisions set out as a note under 54 U.S.C.A. § 100101. Sections 1 to 4 of the Act were repealed and restated as 18 U.S.C.A. § 1865(a), and 54 U.S.C.A. § 100101(a), chapter 1003 of Title 54 (54 U.S.C.A. § 100301 et seq.), and 54 U.S.C.A. §§ 100751(a), 100752, 100753, and 102101 by Pub.L. 113–287, §§ 3, 4(a)(1), 7, Dec. 19, 2014, 128 Stat. 3094, 3260, 3272. For complete classification, see Tables. For disposition of former

sections of this title, see Disposition Table preceding 54 U.S.C.A. § 100101.

The Act of August 21, 1935 (49 Stat. 666; 16 U.S.C. 461–467), referred to in text, is Act Aug. 21, 1935, c. 593, 49 Stat. 666, known as the Historic Sites Act of 1935 and also as the Historic Sites, Buildings, and Antiquities Act, which enacted 16 U.S.C.A. §§ 461 to 467. The Act was repealed and restated as 18 U.S.C.A. § 1866(a), 54 U.S.C.A. §§ 102303 and 102304, and chapter 3201 of Title 54 (54 U.S.C.A. § 320101 et seq.) by Pub.L. 113–287, §§ 3, 4(a)(1), 7, Dec. 19, 2014, 128 Stat. 3094, 3260, 3272. For complete classification, see Tables. For disposition of former sections of this title, see Disposition Table preceding 54 U.S.C.A. § 100101.

§ 450jj–10. Designation of Gateway Arch National Park

(a) Redesignation

The Jefferson National Expansion Memorial established under sections 450jj to 450jj–9 of this title shall be known and designated as the "Gateway Arch National Park".

(b) References

Any reference in a law, map, regulation, document, paper, or other record of the United States to the Jefferson National Expansion Memorial shall be considered to be a reference to the "Gateway Arch National Park".

(Pub.L. 115–128, § 2, Feb. 22, 2018, 132 Stat. 328.)

§ 450*oo*–9. Administration, protection, and development

When establishment of the monument has been effected, pursuant to sections 450*oo* to 450*oo*–10 of this title, the Secretary of the Interior shall administer, protect, and develop the monument in accordance with the provisions of the Act entitled "An Act to establish a National Park Service, and for other purposes" approved August 25, 1916 (39 Stat. 535),[1] as amended.

[1] See References in Text note set out under this section.

HISTORICAL NOTES

References in Text

The Act entitled "An Act to establish a National Park Service, and for other purposes" approved August 25, 1916 (39 Stat. 535), referred to in text, is Act Aug. 25, 1916, c. 408, 39 Stat. 535, known as the National Park Service Organic Act, which enacted 16 U.S.C.A. §§ 1, 2, 3, and 4 and provisions set out as a note under 54 U.S.C.A. § 100101. Sections 1 to 4 of the Act were repealed and restated as 18 U.S.C.A. § 1865(a), and 54 U.S.C.A. § 100101(a), chapter 1003 of Title 54 (54 U.S.C.A. § 100301 et seq.), and 54 U.S.C.A. §§ 100751(a), 100752, 100753, and 102101 by Pub.L. 113–287, §§ 3, 4(a)(1), 7, Dec. 19, 2014, 128 Stat. 3094, 3260, 3272. For complete classification, see Tables. For disposition of former sections of this title, see Disposition Table preceding 54 U.S.C.A. § 100101.

§ 450pp–1. Establishment; notice of establishment; administration

The property acquired pursuant to section 450pp of this title shall be established as the Roger Williams National Memorial and the Secretary of the Interior shall publish notice of such establishment in the Federal Register. Such national Memorial shall be administered by the Secretary subject to the provisions of the Act entitled "An Act to establish a National Park Service, and for other purposes," approved August 25, 1916 (39 Stat. 535),[1] as amended and supplemented, and the Act entitled "An Act to provide for the preservation of historic American sites, buildings, objects, and antiquities of national significance, and for other purposes," approved August 21, 1935 (49 Stat. 666).[1]

[1] See References in Text note set out under this section.

HISTORICAL NOTES

References in Text

The Act entitled "An Act to establish a National Park Service, and for other purposes," approved August 25, 1916 (39 Stat. 535), referred to in text, is Act Aug. 25, 1916, c. 408, 39 Stat. 535, known as the National Park Service Organic Act, which enacted 16 U.S.C.A. §§ 1, 2, 3, and 4 and provisions set out as a note under 54 U.S.C.A. § 100101. Sections 1 to 4 of the Act were repealed and restated as 18 U.S.C.A. § 1865(a), and 54 U.S.C.A. § 100101(a), chapter 1003 of Title 54 (54 U.S.C.A. § 100301 et seq.), and 54 U.S.C.A. §§ 100751(a), 100752, 100753, and 102101 by Pub.L. 113–287, §§ 3, 4(a)(1), 7, Dec. 19, 2014, 128 Stat. 3094, 3260, 3272. For complete classification, see Tables. For disposition of former sections of this title, see Disposition Table preceding 54 U.S.C.A. § 100101.

The Act entitled "An Act to provide for the preservation of historic American sites, buildings, objects, and antiquities of national significance, and for other purposes," approved August 21, 1935 (49 Stat. 666), referred to in text is Act Aug. 21, 1935, c. 593, 49 Stat. 666, known as the Historic Sites Act of 1935 and also as the Historic Sites, Buildings, and Antiquities Act, which enacted 16 U.S.C.A. §§ 461 to 467. The Act was repealed and restated as 18 U.S.C.A. § 1866(a), 54 U.S.C.A. §§ 102303 and 102304, and chapter 3201 of Title 54 (54 U.S.C.A. § 320101 et seq.) by Pub.L. 113–287, §§ 3, 4(a)(1), 7, Dec. 19, 2014, 128 Stat. 3094, 3260, 3272. For complete classification, see Tables. For disposition of former sections of this title, see Disposition Table preceding 54 U.S.C.A. § 100101.

§ 450ss–5. Limitations on funding

Authorization of Appropriations:[1]

(1) In general

In furtherance of the purposes of sections 450ss to 450ss–7 of this title, the Secretary may provide, from the National Park Service's National Recreation and Preservation account, the remainder of the sum of $5,000,000 for an endowment fund subject to paragraph (2), to remain available until expended.

[See main volume for text of (2)]

(Pub.L. 105–58, § 7, Oct. 9, 1997, 111 Stat. 1266; Pub.L. 108–199, Div. F, Title V, § 544(f), Jan. 23, 2004, 118 Stat. 348; Pub.L. 116–283, Div. H, Title XCV, § 9501, Jan. 1, 2021, 134 Stat. 4822.)

1 So in original. "Appropriations" probably should not be capitalized.

HISTORICAL NOTES

Amendments

2021 Amendments. Par. (1). Pub.L. 116-283, § 9501, struck out "there is hereby authorized" and inserted "the Secretary may provide, from the National Park Service's National Recreation and Preservation account, the remainder of".

SUBCHAPTER LXII—MISCELLANEOUS

§ 451a. Repealed. Pub.L. 113–287, § 7, Dec. 19, 2014, 128 Stat. 3272

HISTORICAL NOTES

Section, Act Sept. 14, 1950, c. 950, § 1 (part), 64 Stat. 849, limited further extension or establishment of national parks in Wyoming. See 54 U.S.C.A. § 104907. Section comprised only part of the last sentence of section 1 of Act Sept. 14, 1950. The remainder of such section, except that part of the last sentence which repealed 16 U.S.C.A. §§ 406 to 406d, was classified to 16 U.S.C.A. § 406d–1 and former 16 U.S.C.A. § 431a.

§ 452. Repealed. Pub.L. 113–287, § 7, Dec. 19, 2014, 128 Stat. 3272

HISTORICAL NOTES

Section, June 12, 1917, c. 27, § 1, 40 Stat. 153; May 24, 1922, c. 199, 42 Stat. 590; Sept. 12, 1950, c. 946, Title III, § 301(95), 64 Stat. 844, related to revenues of national parks covered into Treasury. See, generally, Title 54 Disposition Table preceding 54 U.S.C.A. § 100101.

§ 452a. Repealed. Pub.L. 113–287, § 7, Dec. 19, 2014, 128 Stat. 3272

HISTORICAL NOTES

Section, Aug. 31, 1954, c. 1163, 68 Stat. 1037, related to acquisition of non–Federal land within existing boundaries of any National Park, dona- tions, and authorization of appropriations. See, generally, Title 54 Disposition Table preceding 54 U.S.C.A. § 100101.

§ 455. Repealed. Pub.L. 113–287, § 7, Dec. 19, 2014, 128 Stat. 3272

HISTORICAL NOTES

Section, June 11, 1926, c. 555, § 1, 44 Stat. 726; July 26, 1947, c. 343, Title II, § 205(a), 61 Stat. 501, related to study of battlefields for commemorative purposes. See, generally, Title 54 Disposition Table preceding 54 U.S.C.A. § 100101.

§ 455a. Repealed. Pub.L. 113–287, § 7, Dec. 19, 2014, 128 Stat. 3272

HISTORICAL NOTES

Section, June 11, 1926, c. 555, § 2, 44 Stat. 727; July 26, 1947, c. 343, Title II, § 205(a), 61 Stat. 501, related to a report to Congress. See, generally, Title 54 Disposition Table preceding 54 U.S.C.A. § 100101.

§ 455b. Repealed. Pub.L. 113–287, § 7, Dec. 19, 2014, 128 Stat. 3272

HISTORICAL NOTES

Section, June 11, 1926, c. 555, § 3, 44 Stat. 727; July 26, 1947, c. 343, Title II, § 205(a), 61 Stat. 501, related to inclusion of estimate of cost of projected surveys in appropriation estimates. See, generally, Title 54 Disposition Table pre- ceding 54 U.S.C.A. § 100101.

§ 455c. Repealed. Pub.L. 113–287, § 7, Dec. 19, 2014, 128 Stat. 3272

HISTORICAL NOTES

Section, June 11, 1926, c. 555, § 4, 44 Stat. 727; July 26, 1947, c. 343, Title II, § 205(a), 61 Stat. 501, related to purchase of real estate for military park. See, generally, Title 54 Disposi- tion Table preceding 54 U.S.C.A. § 100101.

§ 456. Repealed. Pub.L. 113–287, § 7, Dec. 19, 2014, 128 Stat. 3272

HISTORICAL NOTES

Section, May 10, 1926, c. 277, § 1, 44 Stat. 491, related to availability of appropriations for expense of depositing public money. See, generally, Title 54 Disposition Table preceding 54 U.S.C.A. § 100101.

§ 456a. Repealed. Pub.L. 113–287, § 7, Dec. 19, 2014, 128 Stat. 3272

HISTORICAL NOTES

Section, May 9, 1935, c. 101, § 1, 49 Stat. 209, related to collections and payroll deductions for meals and quarters. See, generally, Title 54 Disposition Table preceding 54 U.S.C.A. § 100101.

§ 457. Repealed. Pub.L. 113–287, § 7, Dec. 19, 2014, 128 Stat. 3272

HISTORICAL NOTES

Section, Feb. 1, 1928, c. 15, 45 Stat. 54, related to actions for death or personal injury within national park or other place under jurisdiction of United States, and application of State laws. See, generally, Title 54 Disposition Table preceding 54 U.S.C.A. § 100101.

§ 458. Repealed. Pub.L. 113–287, § 7, Dec. 19, 2014, 128 Stat. 3272

HISTORICAL NOTES

Section, Mar. 8, 1928, c. 152, 45 Stat. 249, related to travel expenses incident to study of battlefields. See, generally, Title 54 Disposition Table preceding 54 U.S.C.A. § 100101.

§ 458a. Repealed. Pub.L. 113–287, § 7, Dec. 19, 2014, 128 Stat. 3272

HISTORICAL NOTES

Section, Aug. 27, 1940, c. 690, § 1, 54 Stat. 861, related to mats for reproduction in magazines and newspapers of photographs of scenery. See, generally, Title 54 Disposition Table preceding 54 U.S.C.A. § 100101.

SUBCHAPTER LXIII—NATIONAL SEASHORE RECREATIONAL AREAS

§ 459. Cape Hatteras National Seashore Recreational Area; conditional establishment; acquisition of lands

When title to all the lands, except those within the limits of established villages, within boundaries to be designated by the Secretary of the Interior within the area of approximately one hundred square miles on the islands of Chicamacomico, Ocracoke, Bodie, Roanoke, and Collington,[1] and the waters and the lands beneath the waters adjacent thereto shall have been vested in the United States, said area shall be, and is, established, dedicated, and set apart as a national seashore recreational area for the benefit and enjoyment of the people and shall be known as the Cape Hatteras National Seashore Recreational Area: *Provided,* That the United States shall not purchase by appropriation of public moneys any lands within the aforesaid area, but such lands shall be secured by the United States only by public or private donation.

[1] So in original. Probably should be "Colington,".

HISTORICAL NOTES

Change of Name

In text, substituted "national seashore recreational area" for "national seashore" pursuant to Act June 29, 1940.

§ 459a. Acceptance of donations; acquisition of property by purchase and condemnation

HISTORICAL NOTES

Codifications

"Section 3113 of Title 40" substituted in text for "the Act of August 1, 1888" on authority of Pub.L. 107–217, § 5(c), Aug. 21, 2002, 116 Stat. 1303, the first section of which enacted Title 40, Public Buildings, Property, and Works.

Change of Name

In text, substituted "national seashore recreational area" for "national seashore" pursuant to Act June 29, 1940.

§ 459a–1. Administration, protection, and development; commercial fishing by residents; hunting

The administration, protection, and development of the aforesaid national seashore recreational area shall be exercised under the direction of the Secretary of the Interior by the National Park Service, subject to the provisions of the Act of August 25, 1916 (39 Stat. 535), entitled "An Act to establish a National Park Service, and for other purposes",[1] as amended: *Provided*, That except as hereinafter provided nothing herein shall be construed to divest the jurisdiction of other agencies of the Government exercised on August 17, 1937, over Federal-owned lands within the area of the said Cape Hatteras National Seashore Recreational Area: *Provided further*, That the provisions of the Federal Power Act shall not apply to this national seashore recreational area: *And provided further*, That the legal residents of villages referred to in section 459 of this title shall have the right to earn a livelihood by fishing within the boundaries to be designated by the Secretary of the Interior, subject to such rules and regulations as the said Secretary may deem necessary in order to protect the area for recreational use as provided for in sections 459 to 459a–3 of this title: *And provided further*, That hunting shall be permitted, under such rules and regulations as may be prescribed by the Secretary of the Interior in conformity with the Migratory Bird Treaty Act of July 3, 1918 (40 Stat. 755) as follows: (a) Upon the waters of the sounds included within the national seashore recreational area, (b) in the area north of the Currituck County line, (c) on Ocracoke Island, and (d) within not more than two thousand acres of land in the remaining portion of said national seashore recreational area, as shall be designated by the Secretary of the Interior; except on lands and waters included in any existing or future wildlife or migratory bird refuge and adjacent closed waters.

1 See References in Text note set out under this section.

HISTORICAL NOTES

References in Text

The Act of August 25, 1916 (39 Stat. 535), entitled "An Act to establish a National Park Service, and for other purposes", referred to in text, is Act Aug. 25, 1916, c. 408, 39 Stat. 535, known as the National Park Service Organic Act, which enacted 16 U.S.C.A. §§ 1, 2, 3, and 4 and provisions set out as a note under 54 U.S.C.A. § 100101. Sections 1 to 4 of the Act were repealed and restated as 18 U.S.C.A. § 1865(a), and 54 U.S.C.A. § 100101(a), chapter 1003 of Title 54 (54 U.S.C.A. § 100301 et seq.), and 54 U.S.C.A. §§ 100751(a), 100752, 100753, and 102101 by Pub.L. 113–287, §§ 3, 4(a)(1), 7,

Dec. 19, 2014, 128 Stat. 3094, 3260, 3272. For complete classification, see Tables. For disposition of former sections of this title, see Disposition Table preceding 54 U.S.C.A. § 100101.

Amendments

1940 Amendments. Act June 29, 1940, § 2, added last proviso in respect to hunting.

Change of Name

In text, substituted "national seashore recreational area" for "national seashore" pursuant to Act June 29, 1940, § 1.

STATUTORY NOTES

Cape Hatteras National Seashore Recreational Area

Pub.L. 113–291, Div. B, Title XXX, § 3057, Dec. 19, 2014, 128 Stat. 3813, provided that:

"(a) **Definitions.**—In this section [this note]:

"(1) **Final Rule.**—The term 'Final Rule' means the final rule entitled 'Special Regulations, Areas of the National Park System, Cape Hatteras National Seashore—Off-Road

Vehicle Management' (77 Fed. Reg. 3123 (January 23, 2012)).

"(2) **National Seashore.**—The term 'National Seashore' means the Cape Hatteras National Seashore Recreational Area.

"(3) **Secretary.**—The term 'Secretary' means the Secretary of the Interior.

"(4) **State.**—The term 'State' means the State of North Carolina.

"(b) **Review and adjustment of wildlife protection buffers.**—

"(1) **In general.**—Not later than 180 days after the date of enactment of this Act [Dec. 19, 2014], the Secretary shall review and modify wildlife buffers in the National Seashore in accordance with this subsection and any other applicable law.

"(2) **Buffer modifications.**—In modifying wildlife buffers under paragraph (1), the Secretary shall, using adaptive management practices—

"(A) ensure that the buffers are of the shortest duration and cover the smallest area necessary to protect a species, as determined in accordance with peer-reviewed scientific data; and

"(B) designate pedestrian and vehicle corridors around areas of the National Seashore closed because of wildlife buffers, to allow access to areas that are open.

"(3) **Coordination with State.**—The Secretary, after coordinating with the State, shall determine appropriate buffer protections for species that are not listed under the Endangered Species Act of 1973 (16 U.S.C. 1531 et seq.) [Pub.L. 93–206, Dec. 28, 1973, 87 Stat. 884, enacting chapter 35 of this title, 16 U.S.C.A. § 1531 et seq.], but that are identified for protection under State law.

"(c) **Modifications to Final Rule.**—The Secretary shall undertake a public process to consider, consistent with management requirements at the National Seashore, the following changes to the Final Rule:

"(1) Opening beaches at the National Seashore that are closed to night driving restrictions, by opening beach segments each morning on a rolling basis as daily management reviews are completed.

"(2) Extending seasonal off-road vehicle routes for additional periods in the Fall and Spring if off-road vehicle use would not create resource management problems at the National Seashore.

"(3) Modifying the size and location of vehicle-free areas.

"(d) **Construction of new vehicle access points.**—The Secretary shall construct new vehicle access points and roads at the National Seashore—

"(1) as expeditiously as practicable; and

"(2) in accordance with applicable management plans for the National Seashore.

"(e) **Report.**—The Secretary shall report to Congress within 1 year after the date of enactment of this Act [Dec. 19, 2014] on measures taken to implement this section."

§ 459a–2. Preservation of natural features; acquisition of additional property; reversion of property on failure of conditions

HISTORICAL NOTES

Change of Name

In text, substituted "national seashore recreational area" for "national seashore" pursuant to Act June 29, 1940.

Notes of Decisions

Construction 1

---

1. Construction

Under Cape Hatteras National Seashore enabling legislation, natural resource protection took priority over recreational use on Seashore, and thus National Park Service's (NPS) final rule limiting off-road vehicle use within Seashore did not violate the enabling legislation; legislation provided that no plan for the convenience of visitors should be implemented if it was incompatible with preservation of the Seashore. Cape Hatteras Access Preservation Alliance v. Jewell, E.D.N.C.2014, 28 F.Supp.3d 537. Environmental Law ⟨⟩ 132; United States ⟨⟩ 298

§ 459a–3. Migratory bird refuges not to be affected

HISTORICAL NOTES

Change of Name

In text, substituted "national seashore recreational area" for "national seashore" pursuant to Act June 29, 1940.

§ 459a–6. Acquisition of non-Federal land within boundaries of recreational area

Section 101102 of Title 54 is amended to extend the authority of the Secretary of the Interior, contained therein, to the Cape Hatteras National Seashore Recreational Area.

HISTORICAL NOTES

Codifications

In text, "Section 101102 of Title 54" substituted for "the Act of August 31, 1954 (68 Stat.

1037)," on authority of Pub.L. 113–287, § 6(e), Dec. 19, 2014, 128 Stat. 3272, which Act enacted Title 54, 54 U.S.C.A. § 100101 et seq.

§ 459b–6. Administration of acquired property

(a) Utilization of authority for conservation and management of natural resources

Except as otherwise provided in sections 459b to 459b–8 of this title, the property acquired by the Secretary under such sections shall be administered by the Secretary subject to the provisions of the Act entitled "An Act to establish a National Park Service, and for other purposes", approved August 25, 1916 (39 Stat. 535),[1] as amended and supplemented, and in accordance with laws of general application relating to the national park system as defined by the Act of August 8, 1953 (67 Stat. 496);[1] except that authority otherwise available to the Secretary for the conservation and management of natural resources may be utilized to the extent he finds such authority will further the purposes of sections 459b to 459b–8 of this title.

[See main volume for text of (b) and (c)]

1 See References in Text note set out under this section.

HISTORICAL NOTES

References in Text

The Act entitled "An Act to establish a National Park Service, and for other purposes", approved August 25, 1916 (39 Stat. 535), referred to in subsec. (a), is Act Aug. 25, 1916, c. 408, 39 Stat. 535, known as the National Park Service Organic Act, which enacted 16 U.S.C.A. §§ 1, 2, 3, and 4 and provisions set out as a note under 54 U.S.C.A. § 100101. Sections 1 to 4 of the Act were repealed and restated as 18 U.S.C.A. § 1865(a), and 54 U.S.C.A. § 100101(a), chapter 1003 of Title 54 (54 U.S.C.A. § 100301 et seq.), and 54 U.S.C.A. §§ 100751(a), 100752, 100753, and 102101 by Pub.L. 113–287, §§ 3, 4(a)(1), 7, Dec. 19, 2014, 128 Stat. 3094, 3260, 3272. For complete classification, see Tables.

For disposition of former sections of this title, see Disposition Table preceding 54 U.S.C.A. § 100101.

The Act of August 8, 1953 (67 Stat. 496), referred to in subsec. (a), is Act Aug. 8, 1953, c. 384, 67 Stat. 496, which enacted 16 U.S.C.A. §§ 1b to 1d. The Act, except for section 1(3), was repealed and restated in 54 U.S.C.A. §§ 100501, 100755, 100901, 101901, 102711, and 103102 by Pub.L. 113–287, §§ 3, 7, Dec. 19, 2014, 128 Stat. 3094, 3272. Section 1(3) of the Act was transferred and is set out as a note under 16 U.S.C.A. § 407a. For complete classification, see Tables. For disposition of former sections of this title, see Disposition Table preceding 54 U.S.C.A. § 100101.

§ 459b–7. Cape Cod National Seashore Advisory Commission

HISTORICAL NOTES

References in Text

Sections 281, 283, 284, and 1914 of Title 18, referred to in subsec. (h)(1), were repealed by Pub.L. 87–849, § 2, Oct. 23, 1962, 76 Stat. 1126, "Except as they [sections 281 and 283] may

apply to retired officers of the armed forces of the United States)", and were supplanted by sections 203, 205, 207, and 209, respectively, of Title 18, Crimes and Criminal Procedure. For further details, see Exemptions note set out under section 203 of Title 18.

§ 459c–5. Owner's reservation of right of use and occupancy for fixed term of years or life

Notes of Decisions

Authority of Secretary of State 2
Injunctions 3
Jurisdiction 1

1. Jurisdiction

Court of Appeals had jurisdiction to review whether Secretary of Interior misunderstood his authority under Point Reyes National Seashore Act to issue special use permit for oyster farming on national shoreline and closely related question of whether he mistakenly interpreted

other statutory provisions as placing legal restriction on his authority. Drakes Bay Oyster Co. v. Jewell, C.A.9 (Cal.) 2013, 729 F.3d 967, amended and superseded on denial of rehearing en banc 747 F.3d 1073, certiorari denied 134 S.Ct. 2877, 573 U.S. 947, 189 L.Ed.2d 836. Environmental Law ⟐ 640; Fish ⟐ 7(2)

2. Authority of Secretary of State

Secretary of Interior did not misinterpret his authority under Point Reyes National Seashore Act to issue special use permit for oyster farming on national shoreline, where decision taken as a whole reflected that Secretary explicitly recognized that extending permit would be lawful and that he was not legally constrained by other laws. Drakes Bay Oyster Co. v. Jewell, C.A.9 (Cal.) 2013, 729 F.3d 967, amended and superseded on denial of rehearing en banc 747 F.3d 1073, certiorari denied 134 S.Ct. 2877, 573 U.S. 947, 189 L.Ed.2d 836. Environmental Law ⬅ 132; Fish ⬅ 7(2)

3. Injunctions

Oyster farmers seeking preliminary injunction requiring Secretary of Interior to issue a ten-year special use permit allowing farmers to continue their oyster farming operation on a nation-al shoreline were unlikely to prevail in showing decision was arbitrary and capricious, abuse of discretion, or in violation of any law; Secretary's decision had a rational basis in law, farmers were on notice seven years before their permit was denied that it would not be renewed, Secretary acted within his discretion to deny the permit, and policy considerations controlled Secretary's ultimate decision not to issue the permit. Drakes Bay Oyster Co. v. Jewell, C.A.9 (Cal.) 2013, 729 F.3d 967, amended and superseded on denial of rehearing en banc 747 F.3d 1073, certiorari denied 134 S.Ct. 2877, 573 U.S. 947, 189 L.Ed.2d 836. Environmental Law ⬅ 701

§ 459c–6. Administration of property

(a) Protection, restoration, and preservation of natural environment

Except as otherwise provided in sections 459c to 459c–7 of this title, the property acquired by the Secretary under such sections shall be administered by the Secretary without impairment of its natural values, in a manner which provides for such recreational, educational, historic preservation, interpretation, and scientific research opportunities as are consistent with, based upon, and supportive of the maximum protection, restoration, and preservation of the natural environment within the area, subject to the provisions of the Act entitled "An Act to establish a National Park Service, and for other purposes", approved August 25, 1916 (39 Stat. 535),[1] as amended and supplemented, and in accordance with other laws of general application relating to the national park system as defined by the Act of August 8, 1953 (67 Stat. 496),[1] except that authority otherwise available to the Secretary for the conservation and management of natural resources may be utilized to the extent he finds such authority will further the purposes of sections 459c to 459c–7 of this title.

[See main volume for text of (b)]

[1] See References in Text note set out under this section.

HISTORICAL NOTES

References in Text

The Act entitled "An Act to establish a National Park Service, and for other purposes", approved August 25, 1916 (39 Stat. 535), referred to in subsec. (a), is Act Aug. 25, 1916, c. 408, 39 Stat. 535, known as the National Park Service Organic Act, which enacted 16 U.S.C.A. §§ 1, 2, 3, and 4 and provisions set out as a note under 54 U.S.C.A. § 100101. Sections 1 to 4 of the Act were repealed and restated as 18 U.S.C.A. § 1865(a), and 54 U.S.C.A. § 100101(a), chapter 1003 of Title 54 (54 U.S.C.A. § 100301 et seq.), and 54 U.S.C.A. §§ 100751(a), 100752, 100753, and 102101 by Pub.L. 113–287, §§ 3, 4(a)(1), 7, Dec. 19, 2014, 128 Stat. 3094, 3260, 3272. For complete classification, see Tables.

For disposition of former sections of this title, see Disposition Table preceding 54 U.S.C.A. § 100101.

The Act of August 8, 1953 (67 Stat. 496), referred to in subsec. (a), is Act Aug. 8, 1953, c. 384, 67 Stat. 496 , which enacted 16 U.S.C.A. §§ 1b to 1d. The Act, except for section 1(3), was repealed and restated in 54 U.S.C.A. §§ 100501, 100755, 100901, 101901, 102711, and 103102 by Pub.L. 113–287, §§ 3, 7, Dec. 19, 2014, 128 Stat. 3094, 3272. Section 1(3) of the Act was transferred and is set out as a note under 16 U.S.C.A. § 407a. For complete classification, see Tables. For disposition of former sections of this title, see Disposition Table preceding 54 U.S.C.A. § 100101.

§ 459c–7. Authorization of appropriations; restriction on use of land

There are authorized to be appropriated such sums as may be necessary to carry out the provisions of sections 459c to 459c–7 of this title, except that no more than $57,500,000 shall be appropriated for the acquisition of land and waters and improvements thereon, and interests therein, and incidental costs relating thereto, in accordance with the provisions of such sections: *Provided,* That no freehold, leasehold, or lesser interest in any lands hereafter acquired within the boundaries of the Point Reyes National Seashore shall be conveyed for residential or commercial purposes except for public accommodations, facilities, and services provided pursuant to the Act of October 9, 1965 (Public Law 89–249; 79 Stat. 969).[1] In addition to the sums heretofore authorized by this section, there is further authorized to be appropriated $5,000,000 for the acquisition of lands or interests therein.

[1] See References in Text note set out under this section.

HISTORICAL NOTES

References in Text

The Act of October 9, 1965, referred to in text, is Pub.L. 89–249, Oct. 9, 1965, 79 Stat. 969, known as the National Park System Concessions Policy Act, which enacted subchapter IV of this chapter, 16 U.S.C.A. § 20 et seq., and amended 16 U.S.C.A. § 462, prior to being repealed by Pub.L. 105–391, Title IV, § 415(a), Nov. 13, 1998, 112 Stat. 3515.

§ 459d–4. Administration; utilization of authority for conservation and management of natural resources

Except as otherwise provided in sections 459d to 459d–7 of this title, the property acquired by the Secretary under such sections shall be administered by the Secretary, subject to the provisions of the Act entitled "An Act to establish a National Park Service and for other purposes", approved August 25, 1916 (39 Stat. 535),[1] as amended and supplemented, and in accordance with other laws of general application relating to the areas administered and supervised by the Secretary through the National Park Service; except that authority otherwise available to the Secretary for the conservation and management of natural resources may be utilized to the extent he finds such authority will further the purposes of sections 459d to 459d–7 of this title.

[1] See References in Text note set out under this section.

HISTORICAL NOTES

References in Text

The Act entitled "An Act to establish a National Park Service, and for other purposes", approved August 25, 1916 (39 Stat. 535), referred to in text, is Act Aug. 25, 1916, c. 408, 39 Stat. 535, known as the National Park Service Organic Act, which enacted 16 U.S.C.A. §§ 1, 2, 3, and 4 and provisions set out as a note under 54 U.S.C.A. § 100101. Sections 1 to 4 of the Act were repealed and restated as 18 U.S.C.A. § 1865(a), and 54 U.S.C.A. § 100101(a), chapter 1003 of Title 54 (54 U.S.C.A. § 100301 et seq.), and 54 U.S.C.A. §§ 100751(a), 100752, 100753, and 102101 by Pub.L. 113–287, §§ 3, 4(a)(1), 7, Dec. 19, 2014, 128 Stat. 3094, 3260, 3272. For complete classification, see Tables. For disposition of former sections of this title, see Disposition Table preceding 54 U.S.C.A. § 100101.

§ 459e–1. Acquisition of property

[See main volume for text of (a) to (g)]

(h) Sale of property acquired by condemnation; excepted properties; proceeds available for acquisition of property

(1)(A) The Secretary shall sell any property described in subparagraph (B) of this paragraph acquired by condemnation under sections 459e to 459e–9 of this title to the highest bidder; except that—

[See main volume for text of (i) and (ii)]

(B) The property referred to in subparagraph (A) of this paragraph is any property within the boundaries of the national seashore as delineated on the map mentioned in section 459e of this title except—

(i) property within the Dune district referred to in subsection (g) of this section;

(ii) beach or waters and adjoining land within the exempt communities referred to in the first sentence of subsection (e) of this section; and [1]

[See main volume for text of (iii) and (iv); (2); (i)]

[1] So in original. The word "and" probably should not appear.

§ 459f–5. Administration of Seashore

STATUTORY NOTES

Chincoteague National Wildlife Refuge; Establishment of Herbert H. Bateman Educational and Administrative Center

Pub.L. 106–291, Title I, § 141, Oct. 11, 2000, 114 Stat. 949, provided that the building housing the visitors center within the boundaries of the Chincoteague National Wildlife Refuge on Assateague Island, Virginia, was to be known and designated as the "Herbert H. Bateman Educational and Administrative Center".

§ 459f–11. Comprehensive plan for protection, management, and use of seashore

HISTORICAL NOTES

Change of Name

Committee on Interior and Insular Affairs of the Senate abolished and replaced by Committee on Energy and Natural Resources of the Senate, effective Feb. 11, 1977. See Rule XXV of Standing Rules of the Senate, as amended by Senate Resolution No. 4 (popularly cited as the "Committee System Reorganization Amendments of 1977"), approved Feb. 4, 1977.

Committee on Interior and Insular Affairs of the House of Representatives changed to Committee on Natural Resources of the House of Representatives on Jan. 5, 1993, by House Resolution No. 5, One Hundred Third Congress. For references to Committees of the House of Representatives with new names, see Pub.L. 104–14, § 1(a), June 3, 1995, 109 Stat. 186, as amended, set out as a note preceding 2 U.S.C.A. § 21.

§ 459g–7. Authorization of appropriations; master plan to Congressional committees; time; contents

HISTORICAL NOTES

Change of Name

Committee on Interior and Insular Affairs of the House of Representatives changed to Committee on Natural Resources of the House of Representatives on Jan. 5, 1993, by House Resolution No. 5, One Hundred Third Congress. For references to Committees of the House of Representatives with new names, see Pub.L. 104–14, § 1(a), June 3, 1995, 109 Stat. 186, as amended, set out as a note preceding 2 U.S.C.A. § 21.

§ 459h–1. Acquisition of property

[See main volume for text of (a)]

(b) Improved residential property owner's reservation of right of use and occupancy for residential purposes for life or fixed term of years; election by owner; transfer or assignment of right; adjustment of compensation

With respect to improved residential property acquired for the purposes of sections 459h to 459h–10 of this title, which is beneficially owned by a natural person and which the Secretary of the Interior determines can be continued in that use for a limited period of time without undue interference with the administration, development, or public use of the seashore, the owner thereof may on the date of its acquisition by the Secretary retain a right of use and occupancy of the property for noncommercial residential purposes for a term, as the owner may elect, ending either (1) at the death of the owner or his spouse, whichever occurs later, or (2) not more than twenty-five years from the date of acquisition. Any right so retained may during its existence be transferred or assigned. The Secretary shall pay to the owner the fair market value of the property on the date of such acquisition, less their [1] fair market value on such date of the right retained by the owner.

[See main volume for text of (c) to (e)]

[1] So in original. Probably should be "the".

STATUTORY NOTES

Gulf Islands National Seashore Land Exchange

Pub.L. 115–279, Nov. 20, 2018, 132 Stat. 4187, identified two parcels of land, one parcel owned by the Federal government, the other owned by Veterans of Foreign Wars Post 5699 [VFW Post] in the Gulf Islands National Seashore, Jackson County, Mississippi, and it authorized the Secretary of the Interior to make "equal value exchange[s]" of Federal land for land owned by the VFW Post.

§ 459h–2. Designation of hunting and fishing zones; regulation of maritime activities

HISTORICAL NOTES

References in Text

Sections 459h to 459h–10 of this title, referred to in subsec. (b), was in the original "this title", and was translated as reading "this Act", meaning Pub.L. 91–660, which enacted sections 459h to 459h–10 of this title, to reflect the probable intent of Congress, because Pub.L. 91–660 does not contain titles.

§ 459h–4. Administration of seashore; conservation and management of wildlife and natural resources; authority to designate areas as national historic sites; agreements

(a) In general

Except as otherwise provided in sections 459h to 459h–10 of this title, the Secretary shall administer the seashore in accordance with the Act of August 25, 1916 (30 Stat. 535), [1] as amended and supplemented (16 U.S.C. 1 et seq.).[2] In the administration of the seashore the Secretary may utilize such statutory authorities available to him for the conservation and management of wildlife and natural resources as he deems appropriate to carry out the purposes of sections 459h to 459h–10 of this title. With respect to Fort Redoubt, Fort San Carlos, Fort Barrancas at Pensacola Naval Air Station, Fort Pickens on Santa Rosa Island, and Fort McRee on Perdido Key, Florida, and Fort Massachusetts on Ship Island, Mississippi, together with such adjacent lands as the Secretary may designate, the Secretary shall administer such lands so as to recognize, preserve, and interpret their national historical significance in accordance with the Act of August 21, 1935 (49 Stat. 666; 16 U.S.C. 461–467), and he may designate them as national historic sites.

[See main volume for text of (b)]

[1] So in original. Probably should be "(39 Stat. 535),".

[2] See References in Text note set out under this section.

HISTORICAL NOTES

References in Text

The Act of August 25, 1916 (30 Stat. 535 [sic]), as amended and supplemented (16 U.S.C. 1 et seq.), referred to in subsec. (a), is Act Aug. 25, 1916, c. 408, 39 Stat. 535, known as the National Park Service Organic Act, which enacted 16 U.S.C.A. §§ 1, 2, 3, and 4 and provisions set out as a note under 54 U.S.C.A. § 100101. Sections 1 to 4 of the Act were repealed and restated as 18 U.S.C.A. § 1865(a), and 54 U.S.C.A. § 100101(a), chapter 1003 of Title 54 (54 U.S.C.A. § 100301 et seq.), and 54 U.S.C.A. §§ 100751(a), 100752, 100753, and 102101 by Pub.L. 113–287, §§ 3, 4(a)(1), 7, Dec. 19, 2014, 128 Stat. 3094, 3260, 3272. For complete classification, see Tables. For disposition of former sections of this title, see Disposition Table preceding 54 U.S.C.A. § 100101.

The Act of August 21, 1935 (49 Stat. 666; 16 U.S.C. 461–467), referred to in subsec. (a), is Act Aug. 21, 1935, c. 593, 49 Stat. 666, known as the Historic Sites Act of 1935 and also as the Historic Sites, Buildings, and Antiquities Act, which enacted 16 U.S.C.A. §§ 461 to 467. The Act was repealed and restated as 18 U.S.C.A. § 1866(a), 54 U.S.C.A. §§ 102303 and 102304, and chapter 3201 of Title 54 (54 U.S.C.A. § 320101 et seq.) by Pub.L. 113–287, §§ 3, 4(a)(1), 7, Dec. 19, 2014, 128 Stat. 3094, 3260, 3272. For complete classification, see Tables. For disposition of former sections of this title, see Disposition Table preceding 54 U.S.C.A. § 100101.

Codifications

Subsec. (a) is comprised of the first, second, and third sentences of subsec. (a) of section 5 of Pub.L. 91–660. The fourth sentence of subsec. (a) repealed 16 U.S.C.A. §§ 450gg to 450gg–3 and provisions formerly set out as a note under 16 U.S.C.A. § 450gg.

§ 459i–5. Administration, protection, and development

(a) Applicability of provisions; utilization of statutory authorities

The seashore shall be administered, protected, and developed in accordance with the provisions of the Act of August 25, 1916 (39 Stat. 535; 16 U.S.C. 1, 2–4),[1] as amended and supplemented, except that any other statutory authority available to the Secretary for the conservation and management of natural resources may be utilized to the extent he finds such authority will further the purposes of sections 459i to 459i–9 of this title.

(b) Preservation in primitive state; recreational activities exception

Except for certain portions of the seashore deemed to be especially adaptable for recreational uses, particularly swimming, boating, fishing, hiking, horseback riding, and other recreational activities of similar nature, which shall be developed for such uses as needed, the seashore shall be permanently preserved in its primitive state, and, except as provided in subsection (c), no development of the project or plan for the convenience of visitors shall be undertaken which would be incompatible with the preservation of the unique flora and fauna or the physiographic conditions now prevailing, nor shall any road or causeway connecting Cumberland Island to the mainland be constructed.

[See main volume for text of (c)]

(Pub.L. 92–536, § 6, Oct. 23, 1972, 86 Stat. 1068; Pub.L. 108–447, Div. E, Title I, § 145(b), Dec. 8, 2004, 118 Stat. 3073; Pub.L. 114–289, Title VI, § 601(c), Dec. 16, 2016, 130 Stat. 1491.)

1 See References in Text note set out under this section.

HISTORICAL NOTES

References in Text

The Act of August 25, 1916 (39 Stat. 535; 16 U.S.C. 1, 2–4), referred to in subsec. (a), is Act Aug. 25, 1916, c. 408, 39 Stat. 535, known as the National Park Service Organic Act, which enacted 16 U.S.C.A. §§ 1, 2, 3, and 4 and provisions set out as a note under 54 U.S.C.A. § 100101. Sections 1 to 4 of the Act were repealed and restated as 18 U.S.C.A. § 1865(a), and 54 U.S.C.A. § 100101(a), chapter 1003 of Title 54 (54 U.S.C.A. § 100301 et seq.), and 54 U.S.C.A. §§ 100751(a), 100752, 100753, and 102101 by

Pub.L. 113–287, §§ 3, 4(a)(1), 7, Dec. 19, 2014, 128 Stat. 3094, 3260, 3272. For complete classification, see Tables. For disposition of former sections of this title, see Disposition Table preceding 54 U.S.C.A. § 100101.

Amendments

2016 Amendments. Subsec. (b). Pub.L. 114–289, § 601(c), struck out "physiographic conditions not prevailing" and inserted "physiographic conditions now prevailing".

§ 459j–4. Administration, protection, and development

(a) Conservation and management of natural resources

The seashore shall be administered, protected, and developed in accordance with the provisions of the Act of August 25, 1916 (39 Stat. 535; 16 U.S.C. 1, 2–4),[1] as amended and supplemented, except that any other statutory authority available to the Secretary for the conservation management of natural resources may be utilized to the extent he finds such authority will further the purposes of sections 459j to 459j–8 of this title.

[See main volume for text of (b) and (c)]

1 See References in Text note set out under this section.

HISTORICAL NOTES

References in Text

The Act of August 25, 1916 (39 Stat. 535; 16 U.S.C. 1, 2–4), referred to in subsec. (a), is Act Aug. 25, 1916, c. 408, 39 Stat. 535, known as the National Park Service Organic Act, which enacted 16 U.S.C.A. §§ 1, 2, 3, and 4 and provisions set out as a note under 54 U.S.C.A. § 100101. Sections 1 to 4 of the Act were repealed and

restated as 18 U.S.C.A. § 1865(a), and 54 U.S.C.A. § 100101(a), chapter 1003 of Title 54 (54 U.S.C.A. § 100301 et seq.), and 54 U.S.C.A. §§ 100751(a), 100752, 100753, and 102101 by Pub.L. 113–287, §§ 3, 4(a)(1), 7, Dec. 19, 2014, 128 Stat. 3094, 3260, 3272. For complete classification, see Tables. For disposition of former sections of this title, see Disposition Table preceding 54 U.S.C.A. § 100101.

§ 459j–5. Canaveral National Seashore Advisory Commission

Notes of Decisions

Construction with other laws   1

---

1. Construction with other laws

Even if owner of life estate in property located on barrier island within national seashore managed by National Park Service (NPS) would extend portion of dock that was within area owned by state, rather than portion that was

within area owned by federal government, in order to maintain deep-water access to property, NPS' denial of permission for owner to make such change was not arbitrary and capricious under Administrative Procedure Act (APA), since NPS' establishing law in effect at time owner made request extended NPS' regulatory power to federal areas without mentioning federal ownership, and area owned by state fell within area designated as national seashore and as potential wilderness under Wilderness Act, as would authorize NPS to manage such designated state lands. High Point, LLLP v. National Park Service, C.A.11 (Ga.) 2017, 850 F.3d 1185. Environmental Law ⊕ 44

SUBCHAPTER LXIV—RECREATIONAL DEMONSTRATION PROJECTS

§ 459s. Lands for certain projects added to certain projects

HISTORICAL NOTES

Change of Name

Any reference relating to the White Sands National Monument shall be considered to be a reference to the White Sands National Park, see 16 U.S.C.A. § 410dddd(b)(3).

§ 459t. Secretary of the Interior authorized to execute deeds and leases for project lands; inclusion of conditional covenants

HISTORICAL NOTES

Codifications

"Section 1303 of Title 40" substituted in text for "the Act of August 27, 1935 (49 Stat. 885)" on authority of Pub.L. 107–217, § 5(c), Aug. 21, 2002, 116 Stat. 1303, the first section of which enacted Title 40, Public Buildings, Property, and Works.

SUBCHAPTER LXV—NATIONAL PARKWAYS

§ 460. Natchez Trace Parkway

All lands and easements heretofore and hereafter conveyed to the United States by the States of Mississippi, Alabama, and Tennessee for the right-of-way for the projected parkway between Natchez, Mississippi, and Nashville, Tennessee, together with sites acquired or to be acquired for recreational areas in connection therewith, and a right-of-way for said parkway of a width sufficient to include the highway and all bridges, ditches, cuts, and fills appurtenant thereto, but not exceeding a maximum of two hundred feet through Government-owned lands (except that where small parcels of Government-owned lands would otherwise be isolated, or where topographic conditions or scenic requirements are such that bridges, ditches, cuts, fills, parking overlooks, and landscape development could not reasonably be confined to a width of two hundred feet, the said maximum may be increased to such width as may be necessary, with the written approval of the department or agency having jurisdiction over such lands) as designated on maps heretofore or hereafter approved by the Secretary of the Interior, shall be known as the Natchez Trace Parkway and shall be administered and maintained by the Secretary of the Interior through the National Park Service, subject to the provisions of the Act of Congress approved August 25, 1916 (39 Stat. 535), entitled "An Act to establish a National Park Service, and for other purposes",[1] the provisions of which Act, as amended and supplemented, are extended over and made applicable to said parkway: *Provided,* That the Secretary of Agriculture is authorized, with the concurrence of the Secretary of the Interior, to connect with said parkway such roads and trails as may be necessary for the protection, administration, or utilization of adjacent and nearby national forests and the resources thereof: *And provided further,* That the Forest Service and the National Park Service shall, insofar as practicable, coordinate and correlate such recreational developments as each may plan, construct, or permit to be constructed, on lands within their respective jurisdictions, which, by mutual agreement, should be given special treatment for recreational purposes.

[1] See References in Text note set out under this section.

HISTORICAL NOTES

References in Text

The Act of Congress approved August 25, 1916 (39 Stat. 535), entitled "An Act to establish a National Park Service, and for other purposes", referred to in text, is Act Aug. 25, 1916, c. 408, 39 Stat. 535, known as the National Park Service Organic Act, which enacted 16 U.S.C.A. §§ 1, 2, 3, and 4 and provisions set out as a note under 54 U.S.C.A. § 100101. Sections 1 to 4 of the Act were repealed and restated as 18 U.S.C.A. § 1865(a), and 54 U.S.C.A. § 100101(a), chapter 1003 of Title 54 (54 U.S.C.A. § 100301 et seq.), and 54 U.S.C.A. §§ 100751(a), 100752, 100753, and 102101 by Pub.L. 113–287, §§ 3, 4(a)(1), 7, Dec. 19, 2014, 128 Stat. 3094, 3260,

3272. For complete classification, see Tables. For disposition of former sections of this title, see Disposition Table preceding 54 U.S.C.A. § 100101.

Transfer of Functions

Functions of Federal Works Agency and of all agencies thereof, together with functions of Federal Works Administrator transferred to Administrator of General Services by section 103(a) of act June 30, 1949, c. 288, Title I, 63 Stat. 380. Both Federal Works Agency and office of Federal Works Administrator abolished by section 103(b) of that Act. See Historical and Statutory Notes under section 303(b) of Title 40, Public Buildings, Property, and Works. Section 303(b) of Title 40 was amended generally by Pub.L. 109–313, § 2(a)(1), Oct. 6, 2006, 120 Stat. 1734, and, as so amended, no longer relates to the Federal Works Agency and Commissioner of

Public Buildings. See 2006 Amendments note under section 303 of Title 40.

Functions of Federal Works Agency and of all agencies thereof, together with functions of Federal Works Administrator transferred to Administrator of General Services by section 103(a) of act June 30, 1949, ch. 288, Title I, 63 Stat. 380. Both Federal Works Agency and office of Federal Works Administrator abolished by section 103(b) of that Act. See Historical and Revision Notes under section 303(b) of Title 40, Public Buildings, Property, and Works. Section 303(b) of Title 40 was amended generally by Pub.L. 109–313, § 2(a)(1), Oct. 6, 2006, 120 Stat. 1734, and, as so amended, no longer relates to the Federal Works Agency and Commissioner of Public Buildings. See 2006 Amendments note under section 303 of Title 40.

STATUTORY NOTES

Natchez Trace Parkway Land Conveyance Act of 2013

Pub.L. 113–35, Sept. 18, 2013, 127 Stat. 519, known as the Natchez Trace Parkway Land Conveyance Act of 2013, required the Secretary of the Interior to convey to the State of Mississippi, by quitclaim deed and without consideration, all right, title, and interest of the United States in and to the 2 parcels of land totaling approximately 67 acres generally depicted as "Proposed Conveyance" on the map entitled "Natchez Trace Parkway, Proposed Boundary Change" on file and available for public inspection in the appropriate offices of the National

Park Service. The deed of conveyance shall reserve an easement to the United States restricting the use of the parcel commonly known as the "bean field property" to only those uses which are compatible with the Natchez Trace Parkway. On completion of the conveyance the boundary of the Natchez Trace Parkway shall be adjusted to exclude the conveyed land and effective on Sept. 18, 2013, said boundary is adjusted to include the approximately 10 acres of land that is generally depicted as "Proposed Addition" on the above referenced map and such 10 acres shall be administered by the Secretary as part of the Natchez Trace Parkway.

Research References

ALR Library

32 American Law Reports, Federal 332, Validity, Construction, and Application of Endangered Species Act of 1973 (16 U.S.C.A. §§ 1531-1543).

33 American Law Reports, Federal 9, Uniform Relocation Assistance and Real Property Acquisition Policies Act of 1970 (42 U.S.C.A. §§ 4601-4655).

76 American Law Reports, Federal 279, Necessity and Sufficiency of Environmental Impact Statements Under § 102(2)(C) of National Environmental Policy Act of 1969 (42 U.S.C.A. § 4332(2)(C)) in Cases Involving Projects Relating to Acquisition, Construction, Alteration, or Disposition of Government Facilities.

47 American Law Reports 2nd 381, Right of Public to Fish in Stream Notwithstanding Objection by Riparian Owner.

§ 460a–2. Blue Ridge Parkway; establishment; administration and maintenance

All lands and easements heretofore or hereafter conveyed to the United States by the States of Virginia and North Carolina for the right-of-way for the projected parkway between the Shenandoah and Great Smoky Mountains National Parks, together with sites acquired or to be acquired for recreational areas in connection therewith, and a right-of-way for said parkway of a width sufficient to include the highway and all bridges, ditches, cuts, and fills appurtenant thereto, but not exceeding a maximum of two hundred feet through Government-owned lands (except that where small parcels of Government-owned lands would otherwise be isolated, or where topographic conditions or scenic requirements are such that bridges, ditches, cuts, fills, parking overlooks, landscape development, recreational and other facilities requisite to public use of said parkway could not reasonably be confined to a width of two hundred feet, the said maximum may be increased to such width as may be necessary, with the written approval of the department or agency having jurisdiction over such lands) as designated on maps heretofore or hereafter approved by the Secretary of the Interior, shall be known as the Blue Ridge Parkway and shall be administered and maintained by the Secretary of the Interior through the National Park Service, subject to the provisions of the Act of Congress approved August 25, 1916 (39 Stat. 535), entitled "An Act to establish a National Park Service, and for other purposes",[1] the provisions of which Act, as amended and supplemented, are extended over and made applicable to said parkway: *Provided,* That the Secretary of Agriculture is authorized, with the concurrence of the Secretary of the Interior, to connect with the parkway such roads and trails as may be necessary for the protection, administration, or utilization of adjacent and nearby national forests and the resources thereof: *And provided further,* That the Forest Service and the National Park Service shall, insofar as practicable, coordinate and correlate such recreational development as each may plan, construct, or permit to be constructed, on lands within their respective jurisdictions which, by mutual agreement, should be given special treatment for recreational purposes.

1 See References in Text note set out under this section.

HISTORICAL NOTES

References in Text

The Act of Congress approved August 25, 1916 (39 Stat. 535), entitled "An Act to establish a National Park Service, and for other purposes", referred to in text, is Act Aug. 25, 1916, c. 408, 39 Stat. 535, known as the National Park Service Organic Act, which enacted 16 U.S.C.A. §§ 1, 2, 3, and 4 and provisions set out as a note under 54 U.S.C.A. § 100101. Sections 1 to 4 of the Act were repealed and restated as 18 U.S.C.A. § 1865(a), and 54 U.S.C.A. § 100101(a), chapter 1003 of Title 54 (54 U.S.C.A. § 100301 et seq.), and 54 U.S.C.A. §§ 100751(a), 100752, 100753, and 102101 by Pub.L. 113–287, §§ 3, 4(a)(1), 7, Dec. 19, 2014, 128 Stat. 3094, 3260, 3272. For complete classification, see Tables. For disposition of former sections of this title, see Disposition Table preceding 54 U.S.C.A. § 100101.

Transfer of Functions

Functions of Federal Works Agency and of all agencies thereof, together with functions of Federal Works Administrator transferred to Administrator of General Services by section 103(a) of act June 30, 1949, c. 288, Title I, 63 Stat. 380. Both Federal Works Agency and office of Federal Works Administrator abolished by section 103(b) of that Act. See Historical and Statutory Notes under section 303(b) of Title 40, Public Buildings, Property, and Works. Section 303(b) of Title 40 was amended generally by Pub.L. 109–313, § 2(a)(1), Oct. 6, 2006, 120 Stat. 1734, and, as so amended, no longer relates to the Federal Works Agency and Commissioner of Public Buildings. See 2006 Amendments note under section 303 of Title 40.

§ 460a–3. Licenses or permits to owners of adjacent lands

Notes of Decisions

Arbitrary and capricious determinations 3
Deference 2
Jurisdiction of Court of Appeals 4
Standing 1

1. Standing

Environmental organizations had associational standing to file petition seeking judicial review of right of way issued by National Park Service (NPS) allowing natural gas pipeline to drill and pass underneath parkway surface, even though NPS did not manage forest visible from parkway, where organizations' members averred that they regularly used and enjoyed parkway and its scenic views and intended to visit it in future, and that one member owned home near where construction was expected to occur, pipeline's construction and maintenance corridor in forest would be visible from overlook and lessen parkway's aesthetic value, and pipeline would not exist in its proposed form if court invalidated right of way as requested. Sierra Club v. United States Department of the Interior, C.A.4 2018, 899 F.3d 260. Environmental Law ⬤⊐ 652

2. Deference

National Park Service's (NPS) interpretation of statute regarding licenses or permits for rights-of-way over parkway lands was not entitled to *Chevron* deference or *Skidmore* respect in action challenging NPS's issuance of right of way allowing natural gas pipeline to drill and

pass underneath parkway surface, where NPS gave one-sentence recitation of statutory text without any accompanying explanation, arguments that NPS's appellate counsel marshaled in agency's defense were merely litigation positions that did not reflect exercise of delegated legislative authority and agency expertise, and did not specifically address authorizations concerning natural gas pipelines, and right-of-way permit lacked virtually all procedural hallmarks of legislative-type determination. Sierra Club v. United States Department of the Interior, C.A.4 2018, 899 F.3d 260. Administrative Law And Procedure ⬤⊐ 2277; United States ⬤⊐ 307

3. Arbitrary and capricious determinations

National Park Service (NPS) acted arbitrarily and capriciously in granting right of way allowing natural gas pipeline to drill and pass underneath surface of Blue Ridge Parkway by failing to explain why pipeline was not inconsistent with Parkway's scenic value and public's enjoyment thereof, where NPS invoked inapplicable statutory provision and set of regulations as source of its authority, and visual impact study that NPS oversaw specifically concluded that effect of pipeline on views from Parkway "would likely be inconsistent with NPS management objectives." Sierra Club v. United States Department of the Interior, C.A.4 2018, 899 F.3d 260. United States ⬤⊐ 307

Natural Gas Act (NGA) did not preclude Court of Appeals from vacating incidental take statement (ITS) issued by United States Fish and Wildlife Service (FWS) authorizing natural gas pipeline to take listed species and right of way issued by National Park Service (NPS) allowing pipeline to drill and pass underneath parkway surface based on agencies' failures to comply with Endangered Species Act (ESA) and Blue Ridge Parkway Organic Act. Sierra Club v. United States Department of the Interior, C.A.4 2018, 899 F.3d 260. Environmental Law ⬢ 530; Gas ⬢ 9

4. Jurisdiction of Court of Appeals

Natural Gas Act (NGA) did not preclude Court of Appeals from vacating incidental take

statement (ITS) issued by United States Fish and Wildlife Service (FWS) authorizing natural gas pipeline to take listed species and right of way issued by National Park Service (NPS) allowing pipeline to drill and pass underneath parkway surface based on agencies' failures to comply with Endangered Species Act (ESA) and Blue Ridge Parkway Organic Act. Sierra Club v. United States Department of the Interior, C.A.4 2018, 899 F.3d 260. Environmental Law ⬢ 530; Gas ⬢ 9

SUBCHAPTER LXVI—PUBLIC PARK AND RECREATIONAL FACILITIES AT WATER RESOURCE DEVELOPMENT PROJECTS

§ 460d. Construction and operation of public parks and recreational facilities in water resource development projects; lease of lands; preference for use; penalty; application of section 3401 of Title 18; citations and arrests with and without process; limitations; disposition of receipts

HISTORICAL NOTES

Effective and Applicability Provisions

1964 Acts. Pub.L. 88–578, Title I, § (a), Sept. 3, 1964, 78 Stat. 897, provided in part that: "This

Act [amending this section, repealing 16 U.S.C.A. § 14, and amending provisions set out as a note under 23 U.S.C.A. § 120] shall become effective on January 1, 1965."

CODE OF FEDERAL REGULATIONS

Nondiscrimination in federally-assisted programs, see 36 CFR §§ 312.1 and 312.2.

Notes of Decisions

Judicial review   11

---

7. Leases and licenses

Preference clause in the Flood Control Act (FCA), requiring lease of lands at water resource development projects to be made for such purposes as Secretary of Army may deem reasonable in the public interest, does not create an entitlement to a lease of lands in favor of a local governmental entity, but the statute establishes general factors that United States Army Corps of Engineers must consider when it evaluates proposals for leases. Forsyth County v. U.S. Army Corps of Engineers, C.A.11 (Ga.) 2011, 633 F.3d 1032. Water Law ⬢ 2871

10. Injunction

District court did not abuse its discretion in denying county's motion for a preliminary injunction in action by county against United States Army Corps of Engineers in connection with Corps' decision to lease public park at water resource development project to nonprofit organization instead of to county; county failed to establish a substantial likelihood of success on merits of its complaint, as it offered no proof that Corps had wholly ignored preference clause of Flood Control Act (FCA), requiring lease of lands at water resource development projects to be made for such purposes as Secretary of Army may deem reasonable in the public inter-

est, and agency's weighing of factors in evaluating the competing proposals was not subject to judicial review under the Administrative Procedure Act (APA). Forsyth County v. U.S. Army Corps of Engineers, C.A.11 (Ga.) 2011, 633 F.3d 1032. Injunction ⬢ 1268

11. Judicial review

Under the Flood Control Act (FCA), requiring lease of lands at water resource development projects to be made for such purposes as Secretary of Army may deem reasonable in the public interest and requiring United States Army Corps of Engineers to give a preference to "local governmental agencies," among others, the weight accorded to a preference by the Corps is "committed to agency discretion by law" and is not subject to judicial review under the Administrative Procedure Act (APA); FCA requires the Secretary to consider the public interest, Corps' policy provides several additional factors that it has to consider in evaluating proposals for leases, no law provides how agency is to balance those factors in a particular case or what weight to assign to each factor, FCA instead grants Secretary broad discretion, and so the Court of Appeals is without "law to apply" to govern review of the weight accorded the preference for a particular lease. Forsyth County v. U.S. Army Corps of Engineers, C.A.11 (Ga.) 2011, 633 F.3d 1032. Water Law ⬢ 2871

§ 460d–3. Recreational user fees

Notes of Decisions

Personal injury claims 2

---

2. Personal injury claims

Fees charged by Army Corps of Engineers for use of federally-owned campground's overnight camping facilities were not admission fees charged for permission to enter campground for recreational use, and thus limited-liability provisions of Georgia's Recreational Property Act (RPA) barred personal injury claims brought against the federal government by campground visitor who fell down staircase in campground; Corps used the fees to defray some of the costs of services it provided at the campground, did not charge for any recreational activities at the campground, and charged the fee on a per-vehicle, not per-person, basis, and federal law expressly prohibited the Corps from charging an entrance fee for admission to its public recreation areas. Swafford v. United States, C.A.11 (Ga.) 2016, 839 F.3d 1365. Federal Courts ⟨key⟩ 3552

SUBCHAPTER LXVIII—NATIONAL CONSERVATION RECREATIONAL AREAS

§ 460k. Public recreation use of fish and wildlife conservation areas; compatibility with conservation purposes; appropriate incidental or secondary use; consistency with other Federal operations and primary objectives of particular areas; curtailment; forms of recreation not directly related to primary purposes of individual areas; repeal or amendment of provisions for particular areas

Notes of Decisions

Closed areas 4

---

4. Closed areas

Defendant's act of driving his off-road vehicle (ORV) on beach parallel to edge of an area in national wildlife refuge which had been posted as closed to public use, and then performing a three-point turn, during which his vehicle entered the closed area and crushed several plants inside it, violated statutes prohibiting entering a closed area on a national wildlife refuge and destroying a plant on a national wildlife refuge. U.S. v. Sams, E.D.N.C.2014, 45 F.Supp.3d 524. Environmental Law ⟨key⟩ 740; Environmental Law ⟨key⟩ 749

SUBCHAPTER LXIX—OUTDOOR RECREATION PROGRAMS

Part A—Coordination of Programs

§ 460l. Repealed. Pub.L. 113–287, § 7, Dec. 19, 2014, 128 Stat. 3272

HISTORICAL NOTES

Section, Pub.L. 88–29, § 1, May 28, 1963, 77 Stat. 49, related to congressional findings and declaration of policy. See 54 U.S.C.A. § 200101.

See, generally, Title 54 Disposition Table preceding 54 U.S.C.A. § 100101.

MEMORANDA OF PRESIDENT

PRESIDENTIAL MEMORANDUM

Memorandum of the President, A 21st Century Strategy for America's Great Outdoors, April 16, 2010, 75 F.R. 20767, was editorially transferred and set out under 54 U.S.C.A. § 200101, as a result of the enactment into positive law of Title 54, National Park Service and Related Programs, by Pub.L. 113–287, Dec. 19, 2014, 128 Stat. 3094.

§ 460l–1. Repealed. Pub.L. 113–287, § 7, Dec. 19, 2014, 128 Stat. 3272

HISTORICAL NOTES

Section, Pub.L. 88–29, § 2, May 28, 1963, 77 Stat. 49; Pub.L. 91–375, § 6(h), Aug. 12, 1970, 84 Stat. 776; Pub.L. 97–258, § 4(b), Sept. 13, 1982, 96 Stat. 1067, related to powers and duties of the Secretary of the Interior. See 54 U.S.C.A. § 200103. See, generally, Title 54 Disposition Table preceding 54 U.S.C.A. § 100101.

STATUTORY NOTES

Study Regarding Improved Outdoor Recreational Access for Persons With Disabilities

Pub.L. 105–359, § 1, Nov. 10, 1998, 112 Stat. 3275, was editorially eliminated from the Code as a result of the enactment into positive law of Title 54, National Park Service and Related Programs, by Pub.L. 113–287, Dec. 19, 2014, 128 Stat. 3094.

Connecticut River National Recreation Area Feasibility Study

Pub.L. 89–616, Oct. 3, 1966, 80 Stat. 867, was editorially eliminated from the Code as a result of the enactment into positive law of Title 54, National Park Service and Related Programs, by Pub.L. 113–287, Dec. 19, 2014, 128 Stat. 3094.

§ 460*l*–2. Repealed. Pub.L. 113–287, § 7, Dec. 19, 2014, 128 Stat. 3272

HISTORICAL NOTES

Section, Pub.L. 88–29, § 3, May 28, 1963, 77 Stat. 50, related to consultations of Secretary of the Interior with administrative officers, and execution of administrative responsibilities in conformity with nationwide plan. See 54 U.S.C.A. § 200104. See, generally, Title 54 Disposition Table preceding 54 U.S.C.A. § 100101.

§ 460*l*–3. Repealed. Pub.L. 113–287, § 7, Dec. 19, 2014, 128 Stat. 3272

HISTORICAL NOTES

Section, Pub.L. 88–29, § 4, May 28, 1963, 77 Stat. 50; Pub.L. 96–205, Title VI, § 608(c), Mar. 12, 1980, 94 Stat. 92, provided definitions. See 54 U.S.C.A. § 200102. See, generally, Title 54 Disposition Table preceding 54 U.S.C.A. § 100101.

PART B—LAND AND WATER CONSERVATION FUND

CROSS REFERENCES

State recreational boating safety programs, see 46 USCA § 13102.

§ 460*l*–4. Transferred to 54 U.S.C.A. § 100101 note

HISTORICAL NOTES

Codifications

Section, Pub.L. 88–578, Title I, § 1(b), Sept. 3, 1964, 78 Stat. 897, relating to land and water conservation provisions, and statement of purposes, was editorially transferred to be set out as a note under 54 U.S.C.A. § 100101, as a result of the enactment into positive law of Title 54, National Park Service and Related Programs, by Pub.L. 113–287, Dec. 19, 2014, 128 Stat. 3094.

STATUTORY NOTES

Survey of Entrance and User Fees

Pub.L. 91–308, § 4, July 7, 1970, 84 Stat. 410, was editorially eliminated from the Code as a result of the enactment into positive law of Title 54, National Park Service and Related Programs, by Pub.L. 113–287, Dec. 19, 2014, 128 Stat. 3094.

§ 460*l*–5. Repealed. Pub.L. 113–287, § 7, Dec. 19, 2014, 128 Stat. 3272

HISTORICAL NOTES

Section, Pub.L. 88–578, Title I, § 2, Sept. 3, 1964, 78 Stat. 897; Pub.L. 89–72, § 11, July 9, 1965, 79 Stat. 218; Pub.L. 90–401, §§ 1(a), 2, July 15, 1968, 82 Stat. 354, 355; Pub.L. 91–308, § 2, July 7, 1970, 84 Stat. 410; Pub.L. 91–485, § 1, Oct. 22, 1970, 84 Stat. 1084; Pub.L. 94–273, § 2(7), Apr. 21, 1976, 90 Stat. 375; Pub.L. 94–422, Title I, § 101(1), Sept. 28, 1976, 90 Stat. 1313; Pub.L. 95–42, § 1(1), June 10, 1977, 91 Stat. 210; Pub.L. 100–203, Title V, § 5201(f)(1), Dec. 22, 1987, 101 Stat. 1330–267, related to establishment of the land and water conservation fund. See 54 U.S.C.A. § 200302. See, generally, Title 54 Disposition Table preceding 54 U.S.C.A. § 100101.

EXECUTIVE ORDERS

EXECUTIVE ORDER NO. 11200

Executive Order No. 11200, Establishment of Recreation User Fees, Feb. 26, 1965, 30 F.R. 2645, was editorially transferred as a note set out under 54 U.S.C.A. § 200302, as a result of the enactment into positive law of Title 54, National Park Service and Related Programs, by Pub.L. 113–287, Dec. 19, 2014, 128 Stat. 3094.

§ 460*l*–6. Repealed. Pub.L. 113–287, § 7, Dec. 19, 2014, 128 Stat. 3272

HISTORICAL NOTES

Section, Pub.L. 88–578, Title I, § 3, Sept. 3, 1964, 78 Stat. 899; Pub.L. 100–203, Title V, § 5201(f)(2), Dec. 22, 1987, 101 Stat. 1330–267, related to appropriations for expenditure of land and water conservation fund moneys, and trans-

fers to miscellaneous receipts of Treasury. See 54 U.S.C.A. § 200303. See, generally, Title 54 Disposition Table preceding 54 U.S.C.A. § 100101.

§ 460*l*–6a. Repealed. Pub.L. 113–287, § 7, Dec. 19, 2014, 128 Stat. 3272

HISTORICAL NOTES

Section, Pub.L. 88–578, Title I, § 4, as added Pub.L. 92–347, § 2, July 11, 1972, 86 Stat. 459; amended Pub.L. 93–81, §§ 1, 2, Aug. 1, 1973, 87 Stat. 178, 179; Pub.L. 93–303, § 1, June 7, 1974, 88 Stat. 192; Pub.L. 96–344, § 9, Sept. 8, 1980, 94 Stat. 1135; Pub.L. 100–203, Title V, § 5201(a) to (c), Dec. 22, 1987, 101 Stat. 1330–263, 1330–264; Pub.L. 101–650, Title III, § 321, Dec. 1, 1990, 104 Stat. 5117; Pub.L. 103–66, Title V, § 5001(b), Title X, §§ 10001, 10002, Aug. 10, 1993, 107 Stat. 379, 402, 403; Pub.L. 103–437, § 6(p)(1), Nov. 2, 1994, 108 Stat. 4586; Pub.L. 104–66, Title I, § 1081(f), Dec. 21, 1995, 109

Stat. 721; Pub.L. 105–327, § 1, Oct. 30, 1998, 112 Stat. 3055; Pub.L. 108–447, Div. J, Title VIII, § 813(a), Dec. 8, 2004, 118 Stat. 3390; Pub.L. 109–54, Title I, § 132(a), (b), Aug. 2, 2005, 119 Stat. 526, related to admission and special recreation use fees. Subsecs. (a) to (h) and (i)(1)(A), (B), (2) to (4), which related to various fees and permits and reporting requirements, had been previously repealed. Subsecs. (i)(1)(C) and (j) to (n) were repealed and restated in 54 U.S.C.A. § 100904. See, generally, Title 54 Disposition Table preceding 54 U.S.C.A. § 100101.

STATUTORY NOTES

Construction

Pub.L. 109–54, Title I, § 132(d), Aug. 2, 2005, 119 Stat. 526, formerly set out as a note under this section, was editorially transferred as a note set out under 16 U.S.C.A. § 6812, as a result of the enactment into positive law of Title 54, National Park Service and Related Programs, by Pub.L. 113–287, Dec. 19, 2014, 128 Stat. 3094.

Limitations on Recreation Fee Demonstration Program

Pub.L. 108–447, Div. E, Title III, § 319, Dec. 8, 2004, 118 Stat. 3097, was editorially eliminated from the Code as a result of the enactment into positive law of Title 54, National Park Service and Related Programs, by Pub.L. 113–287, Dec. 19, 2014, 128 Stat. 3094.

National Park Service Entrance and Recreational Use Fees

Pub.L. 106–176, Title III, § 310, Mar. 10, 2000, 114 Stat. 34, was editorially eliminated from the Code as a result of the enactment into positive law of Title 54, National Park Service and Related Programs, by Pub.L. 113–287, Dec. 19, 2014, 128 Stat. 3094.

Recreation User Fees

Pub.L. 106–53, Title II, § 225, Aug. 17, 1999, 113 Stat. 297, was editorially eliminated from the Code as a result of the enactment into positive law of Title 54, National Park Service and Related Programs, by Pub.L. 113–287, Dec. 19, 2014, 128 Stat. 3094.

Recreational Fee Demonstration Program

Pub.L. 105–83, Title I, § 107, Nov. 14, 1997, 111 Stat. 1561, was editorially eliminated from the Code as a result of the enactment into positive law of Title 54, National Park Service

and Related Programs, by Pub.L. 113–287, Dec. 19, 2014, 128 Stat. 3094.

Study to Assess Traffic Congestion and Overcrowding at Certain Park System Units

Pub.L. 100–203, Title V, § 5201(e), Dec. 22, 1987, 110 Stat. 1330–267, was editorially eliminated from the Code as a result of the enactment into positive law of Title 54, National Park Service and Related Programs, by Pub.L. 113–287, Dec. 19, 2014, 128 Stat. 3094.

Prohibition on Entrance Fee at Statue of Liberty National Monument

Pub.L. 100–55, June 19, 1987, 101 Stat. 371, formerly set out as a note under this section, was editorially transferred as a note set out under 16 U.S.C.A. § 6802, as a result of the enactment into positive law of Title 54, National Park Service and Related Programs, by Pub.L. 113–287, Dec. 19, 2014, 128 Stat. 3094.

Establishment and Collection of Use or Royalty Fees for Manufacture, Reproduction, or Use of "Golden Eagle Insignia"

Pub.L. 92–347, § 3(a), July 11, 1972, 86 Stat. 459, formerly set out as a note under this section, was editorially transferred as a note set out under 54 U.S.C.A. § 200302, as a result of the enactment into positive law of Title 54, National Park Service and Related Programs, by Pub.L. 113–287, Dec. 19, 2014, 128 Stat. 3094.

Termination of Rights in "Golden Eagle Insignia"

Pub.L. 92–347, § 3(d), July 11, 1972, 86 Stat. 462, formerly set out as a note under this section, was editorially transferred as a note set out under 54 U.S.C.A. § 200302, as a result of the enactment into positive law of Title 54, National Park Service and Related Programs, by Pub.L. 113–287, Dec. 19, 2014, 128 Stat. 3094.

§ 460*l*–6c. Admission, entrance, and recreation fees

HISTORICAL NOTES

Codifications

Section was enacted as part of the Agricultural Reconciliation Act of 1993 and as part of the

Omnibus Budget Reconciliation Act of 1993, and not as part of the Land and Water Conservation Fund Act of 1965 which comprises this part.

§ 460*l*–6d. Commercial filming

(a) Commercial filming fee

(1) In general

The Secretary of the Interior or the Secretary of Agriculture (hereafter individually referred to as the "Secretary" with respect to land (except land in a System unit as defined in section 100102 of Title 54) under their respective jurisdictions) shall require a permit and shall establish a reasonable fee for commercial filming activities or similar projects on Federal land administered by the Secretary. The fee shall provide a fair return to the United States and shall be based on the following criteria:

(A) The number of days the filming activity or similar project takes place on Federal land under the Secretary's jurisdiction.

(B) The size of the film crew present on Federal land under the Secretary's jurisdiction.

(C) The amount and type of equipment present.

(2) Other factors

The Secretary may include other factors in determining an appropriate fee as the Secretary considers necessary.

(b) Recovery of costs

The Secretary shall collect any costs incurred as a result of filming activities or similar project, including administrative and personnel costs. All costs recovered shall be in addition to the fee assessed in subsection (a).

(c) Still photography

(1) In general

Except as provided in paragraph (2), the Secretary shall not require a permit nor assess a fee for still photography on land administered by the Secretary if such photography takes place where members of the public are generally allowed. The Secretary may require a permit, fee, or both, if such photography takes place at other locations where members of the public are generally not allowed, or where additional administrative costs are likely.

(2) Exception

The Secretary shall require and shall establish a reasonable fee for still photography that uses models or props which are not a part of the site's natural or cultural resources or administrative facilities.

(d) Protection of resources

The Secretary shall not permit any filming, still photography or other related activity if the Secretary determines that—

(1) there is a likelihood of resource damage;

(2) there would be an unreasonable disruption of the public's use and enjoyment of the site; or

(3) the activity poses health or safety risks to the public.

(e) Use of proceeds

(1) Fees

All fees collected under this section shall be available for expenditure by the Secretary, without further appropriation and shall remain available until expended.

(2) Costs

All costs recovered under this section shall be available for expenditure by the Secretary, without further appropriation, at the site where the costs are collected and shall remain available until expended.

(f) Processing of permit applications

The Secretary shall establish a process to ensure that the Secretary responds in a timely manner to permit applicants for commercial filming, still photography, or other activity.

(Pub.L. 106–206, § 1, May 26, 2000, 114 Stat. 314; Pub.L. 113–287, §§ 4(c), 7, Dec. 19, 2014, 128 Stat. 3261, 3272.)

Repeal

Section repealed by Pub.L. 113–287, § 7, Dec. 19, 2014, 128 Stat. 3272, insofar as applicable to the National Park System. See 54 U.S.C.A. § 100905.

HISTORICAL NOTES

Amendments

2014 Amendments. Pub.L. 113–287, § 4(c), rewrote the section, which formerly read:

"**(a) Commercial filming fee**

"The Secretary of the Interior and the Secretary of Agriculture (hereafter individually referred to as the 'Secretary' with respect to lands under their respective jurisdiction) shall require a permit and shall establish a reasonable fee for commercial filming activities or similar projects on Federal lands administered by the Secretary. Such fee shall provide a fair return to the United States and shall be based upon the following criteria:

"(1) The number of days the filming activity or similar project takes place on Federal land under the Secretary's jurisdiction.

"(2) The size of the film crew present on Federal land under the Secretary's jurisdiction.

"(3) The amount and type of equipment present.

"The Secretary may include other factors in determining an appropriate fee as the Secretary deems necessary.

"**(b) Recovery of costs**

"The Secretary shall also collect any costs incurred as a result of filming activities or similar project, including but not limited to administrative and personnel costs. All costs recovered shall be in addition to the fee assessed in subsection (a) of this section.

"**(c) Still photography**

"(1) Except as provided in paragraph (2), the Secretary shall not require a permit nor assess a fee for still photography on lands administered by the Secretary if such photography takes place where members of the public are generally allowed. The Secretary may require a permit,

fee, or both, if such photography takes place at other locations where members of the public are generally not allowed, or where additional administrative costs are likely.

"(2) The Secretary shall require and shall establish a reasonable fee for still photography that uses models or props which are not a part of the site's natural or cultural resources or administrative facilities.

"**(d) Protection of resources**

"The Secretary shall not permit any filming, still photography or other related activity if the Secretary determines—

"(1) there is a likelihood of resource damage;

"(2) there would be an unreasonable disruption of the public's use and enjoyment of the site; or

"(3) that the activity poses health or safety risks to the public.

"**(e) Use of proceeds**

"(1) All fees collected under this section shall be available for expenditure by the Secretary, without further appropriation, in accordance with the formula and purposes established for the Recreational Fee Demonstration Program (Public Law 104–134). All fees collected shall remain available until expended.

"(2) All costs recovered under this section shall be available for expenditure by the Secretary, without further appropriation, at the site where collected. All costs recovered shall remain available until expended.

"**(f) Processing of permit applications**

"The Secretary shall establish a process to ensure that permit applicants for commercial filming, still photography, or other activity are responded to in a timely manner."

§ 460*l*–7. Repealed. Pub.L. 113–287, § 7, Dec. 19, 2014, 128 Stat. 3272

HISTORICAL NOTES

Section, Pub.L. 88–578, Title I, § 5, formerly § 4, Sept. 3, 1964, 78 Stat. 900; Pub.L. 90–401, § 3, July 15, 1968, 82 Stat. 355, renumbered § 5, Pub.L. 92–347, § 2, July 11, 1972, 86 Stat. 459; amended Pub.L. 94–273, § 3(4), Apr. 21, 1976, 90 Stat. 376; Pub.L. 94–422, Title I, § 101(2), Sept. 28, 1976, 90 Stat. 1314; Pub.L. 95–42, § 1(2), June 10, 1977, 91 Stat. 210, related to allocation of land and water conservation fund for State and Federal purposes. See, generally, Title 54 Disposition Table preceding 54 U.S.C.A. § 100101.

§ 460*l*–8. Repealed. Pub.L. 113–287, § 7, Dec. 19, 2014, 128 Stat. 3272

HISTORICAL NOTES

Section, Pub.L. 88–578, Title I, § 6, formerly § 5, Sept. 3, 1964, 78 Stat. 900, renumbered § 6, Pub.L. 92–347, § 2, July 11, 1972, 86 Stat. 459; amended Pub.L. 93–303, § 2, June 7, 1974, 88 Stat. 194; Pub.L. 94–422, Title I, § 101(3), Sept. 28, 1976, 90 Stat. 1314; Pub.L. 95–625, Title VI, § 606, Nov. 10, 1978, 92 Stat. 3519; Pub.L. 99–645, Title III, § 303, Nov. 10, 1986, 100 Stat. 3587; Pub.L. 103–322, Title IV, § 40133, Sept. 13, 1994, 108 Stat. 1918; Pub.L. 103–437, § 6(p)(2), Nov. 2, 1994, 108 Stat. 4586; Pub.L. 104–333, Div. I, Title VIII, § 814(d)(1)(H), Nov. 12, 1996, 110 Stat. 4196, related to financial assistance to States. See, generally, Title 54 Disposition Table preceding 54 U.S.C.A. § 100101.

§ 460*l*–9. Repealed. Pub.L. 113–287, § 7, Dec. 19, 2014, 128 Stat. 3272

HISTORICAL NOTES

Section, Pub.L. 88–578, Title I, § 7, formerly § 6, Sept. 3, 1964, 78 Stat. 903; Pub.L. 90–401, § 1(c), July 15, 1968, 82 Stat. 355; renumbered § 7, Pub.L. 92–347, § 2, July 11, 1972, 86 Stat. 459; amended Pub.L. 93–205, § 13(c), Dec. 28, 1973, 87 Stat. 902; Pub.L. 94–422, Title I, § 101(4), Sept. 28, 1976, 90 Stat. 1317; Pub.L. 95–42, § 1(3)–(5), June 10, 1977, 91 Stat. 210, 211; Pub.L. 96–203, § 2, Mar. 10, 1980, 94 Stat. 81; Pub.L. 99–645, Title III, § 302, Nov. 10, 1986, 100 Stat. 3587; Pub.L. 103–437, § 6(p)(3), Nov. 2, 1994, 108 Stat. 4586; Pub.L. 104–333, Div. I, Title VIII, § 814(b), (d)(2)(C), Nov. 12, 1996, 110 Stat. 4194, 4196; Pub.L. 106–176, Title I, §§ 120(b), 129, Mar. 10, 2000, 114 Stat. 28, 30, related to allocation of land and water conservation fund moneys for Federal purposes. See, generally, Title 54 Disposition Table preceding 54 U.S.C.A. § 100101.

§ 460*l*–10. Repealed. Pub.L. 113–287, § 7, Dec. 19, 2014, 128 Stat. 3272

HISTORICAL NOTES

Section, Pub.L. 88–578, Title I, § 8, formerly § 7, Sept. 3, 1964, 78 Stat. 903, renumbered § 8, Pub.L. 92–347, § 2, July 11, 1972, 86 Stat. 459; amended Pub.L. 94–422, Title I, § 101(5), Sept. 28, 1976, 90 Stat. 1318, related to availability of land and water conservation fund for publicity purposes, standardized temporary signing, and standards and guidelines. See, generally, Title 54 Disposition Table preceding 54 U.S.C.A. § 100101.

§ 460*l*–10a. Repealed. Pub.L. 113–287, § 7, Dec. 19, 2014, 128 Stat. 3272

HISTORICAL NOTES

Section, Pub.L. 88–578, Title I, § 9, formerly § 8, as added Pub.L. 90–401, § 4, July 15, 1968, 82 Stat. 355; amended Pub.L. 91–308, § 3, July 7, 1970, 84 Stat. 410; renumbered § 9, Pub.L. 92–347, § 2, July 11, 1972, 86 Stat. 459; amended Pub.L. 93–303, § 3, June 7, 1974, 88 Stat. 194, related to contracts for acquisition of lands and waters. See, generally, Title 54 Disposition Table preceding 54 U.S.C.A. § 100101.

§ 460*l*–10b. Repealed. Pub.L. 113–287, § 7, Dec. 19, 2014, 128 Stat. 3272

HISTORICAL NOTES

Section, Pub.L. 88–578, Title I, § 10, formerly § 9, as added Pub.L. 90–401, § 4, July 15, 1968, 82 Stat. 355, and renumbered Pub.L. 92–347, § 2, July 11, 1972, 86 Stat. 459, related to contracts for options to acquire lands and waters in national park system. See, generally, Title 54 Disposition Table preceding 54 U.S.C.A. § 100101.

16 § 460*l*–10c
Repealed

CONSERVATION

§ 460*l*–10c.   Repealed.   Pub.L. 113–287, § 7, Dec. 19, 2014, 128 Stat. 3272

HISTORICAL NOTES

Section, Pub.L. 88–578, Title I, § 11, formerly § 2(a) (in part), Sept. 3, 1964, 78 Stat. 899; renumbered § 10, Pub.L. 90–401, § 1(a), July 15, 1968, 82 Stat. 354; renumbered § 11, Pub.L. 92–347, § 2, July 11, 1972, 86 Stat. 459, related to repeal of provisions prohibiting collection of recreation fees or user charges. See, generally, Title 54 Disposition Table preceding 54 U.S.C.A. § 100101.

§ 460*l*–10d.   Repealed.   Pub.L. 113–287, § 7, Dec. 19, 2014, 128 Stat. 3272

HISTORICAL NOTES

Section, Pub.L. 88–578, Title I, § 12, as added Pub.L. 94–422, Title I, § 101(6), Sept. 28, 1976, 90 Stat. 1318, related to a report on the needs, problems, and opportunities associated with urban recreation in highly populated regions. See, generally, Title 54 Disposition Table preceding 54 U.S.C.A. § 100101.

§ 460*l*–10e.   Repealed.   Pub.L. 113–287, § 7, Dec. 19, 2014, 128 Stat. 3272

HISTORICAL NOTES

Section, Pub.L. 88–578, Title I, § 13, as added Pub.L. 104–333, Div. I, Title X, § 1021(b), Nov. 12, 1996, 110 Stat. 4210; amended Pub.L. 105–83, Title V, § 505, Nov. 14, 1997, 111 Stat. 1617; Pub.L. 106–176, Title I, §§ 123(b), Mar. 10, 2000, 114 Stat. 29, related to an advisory commission on water–based recreation. See, generally, Title 54 Disposition Table preceding 54 U.S.C.A. § 100101.

STATUTORY NOTES

Recreational Opportunities at Federally Managed Man-made Lakes and Reservoirs

Pub.L. 104–333, Div. I, Title X, § 1021(a), Nov. 12, 1996, 110 Stat. 4210, as amended Pub.L. 106–176, Title I, § 123(a), Mar. 10, 2000, 114 Stat. 29, was editorially eliminated from the Code as a result of the enactment into positive law of Title 54, National Park Service and Related Programs, by Pub.L. 113–287, Dec. 19, 2014, 128 Stat. 3094.

§ 460*l*–11.   Repealed.   Pub.L. 113–287, § 7, Dec. 19, 2014, 128 Stat. 3272

HISTORICAL NOTES

Section, Pub.L. 88–578, Title II, § 201, Sept. 3, 1964, 78 Stat. 904; Pub.L. 91–605, Title III, § 302, Dec. 31, 1970, 84 Stat. 1743; Pub.L. 94–273, § 3(4), Apr. 21, 1976, 90 Stat. 376; Pub.L. 94–280, Title III, § 302, May 5, 1976, 90 Stat. 456; Pub.L. 95–599, Title V, § 503(b), Nov. 6, 1978, 92 Stat. 2757; Pub.L. 97–424, Title V, § 531(c), Jan. 6, 1983, 96 Stat. 2191; Pub.L. 99–514, § 2, Title XVIII, § 1875(e), Oct. 22, 1986, 100 Stat. 2095, 2897; Pub.L. 100–17, Title V, § 503(c), Apr. 2, 1987, 101 Stat. 258; Pub.L. 101–508, Title XI, § 11211(g)(2), Nov. 5, 1990, 104 Stat. 1388–427; Pub.L. 102–240, Title VIII, § 8002(d)(2)(B), Dec. 18, 1991, 105 Stat. 2204; Pub.L. 105–178, Title IX, § 9002(c)(2)(B), June 9, 1998, 112 Stat. 500; Pub.L. 109–59, Title XI, § 11101(c)(2)(B), Aug. 10, 2005, 119 Stat. 1944; Pub.L. 112–30, Title I, § 142(e)(2)(B), Sept. 16, 2011, 125 Stat. 356; Pub.L. 112–102, Title IV, § 402(e)(2)(B), Mar. 30, 2012, 126 Stat. 282; Pub.L. 112–140, Title IV, § 402(d)(2)(B), June 29, 2012, 126 Stat. 403; Pub.L. 112–141, Div. D, Title I, § 40102(e)(2)(B), July 6, 2012, 126 Stat. 845, related to transfers to and from the land and water conservation fund. See, generally, Title 54 Disposition Table preceding 54 U.S.C.A. § 100101.

PART C—WATER RESOURCES PROJECTS

§ 460*l*–17.   Miscellaneous provisions

(a) Project reports; outdoor recreation views; conformity to State comprehensive plan

The views of the Secretary of the Interior developed in accordance with section 200104 of Title 54, with respect to the outdoor recreation aspects shall be set forth in any report of any project or appropriate unit thereof within the purview of this part. Such views shall include a report on the extent to which the proposed recreation and fish and wildlife development conforms to and is in accord with the State comprehensive plan developed pursuant to section 200305(d) of Title 54.

[See main volume for text of (b) to (f)]

56

(g) Nonapplication of section 200306(a)(3) of Title 54 to nonreimbursable costs of the United States

section [1] 200306(a)(3) of Title 54 shall not apply to costs allocated to recreation and fish and wildlife enhancement which are borne by the United States as a nonreimbursable project cost pursuant to section 460*l*–13(a) or section 460*l*–14(b)(1) of this title.

[See main volume for text of (h)]

(Pub.L. 89–72, § 6, July 9, 1965, 79 Stat. 216; Pub.L. 94–576, Oct. 21, 1976, 90 Stat. 2728; Pub.L. 113–287, § 5(d)(1), Dec. 19, 2014, 128 Stat. 3264.)

[1] So in original. Probably should be capitalized.

HISTORICAL NOTES

Codifications

In subsec. (a), "section 200104 of Title 54" substituted for "section 3 of the Act of May 28, 1963 (77 Stat. 49)" on authority of Pub.L. 113–287, § 6(e), Dec. 19, 2014, 128 Stat. 3272, which Act enacted Title 54, 54 U.S.C.A. § 100101 et seq.

Amendments

2014 Amendments. Subsec. (a). Pub.L. 113–287, § 5(d)(1)(A), struck out "section

460*l*–8(d) of this title" and inserted "section 200305(d) of Title 54".

Subsec. (g). Pub.L. 113–287, § 5(d)(1)(B), struck out "Section 460*l*–9(a)(2) of this title" and inserted "Section 200306(a)(3) of Title 54".

PART D—LAND TRANSFERS

§ 460*l*–22. Repealed. Pub.L. 113–287, § 7, Dec. 19, 2014, 128 Stat. 3272

HISTORICAL NOTES

Section, Pub.L. 90–401, § 5, July 15, 1968, 82 Stat. 356; Pub.L. 98–506, § 2, Oct. 19, 1984, 98 Stat. 2338, related to conveyance of property and interests in property in national park sys-

tem and miscellaneous areas. See, generally, Title 54 Disposition Table preceding 54 U.S.C.A. § 100101.

PART E—RECLAMATION RECREATION MANAGEMENT

§ 460*l*–31. Findings

HISTORICAL NOTES

References in Text

This part, referred to in par. (6), was in the original "this title", meaning Title XXVIII of

Pub.L. 102–575, Oct. 30, 1992, 106 Stat. 4690, which enacted sections 460*l*–31 to 460*l*–34 of this title and amended sections 460*l*–13 to 460*l*–15 and 460*l*–18 of this title.

§ 460*l*–32. Definitions

HISTORICAL NOTES

References in Text

This part, referred to in text, was in the original "this title", meaning Title XXVIII of Pub.L. 102–575, Oct. 30, 1992, 106 Stat. 4690, which enacted sections 460*l*–31 to 460*l*–34 of this title and amended sections 460*l*–13 to 460*l*–15 and 460*l*–18 of this title.

Act of June 17, 1902, referred to in pars. (2) and (3), is Act June 17, 1902, c. 1093, 32 Stat.

388, popularly known as the Reclamation Act, which is classified generally to chapter 12 of Title 43, 43 U.S.C.A. § 371 et seq. However, section 371 of Title 43 is Act Dec. 5, 1924, c. 4, § 4, subsec. A, 43 Stat. 701. For complete classification, see Short Title note set out under 43 U.S.C.A. § 371 and Tables.

§ 460*l*–33. Management of reclamation lands

HISTORICAL NOTES

References in Text

This part, referred to in subsec. (d), was in the original "this title", meaning Title XXVIII of

Pub.L. 102–575, Oct. 30, 1992, 106 Stat. 4690, which enacted sections 460*l*–31 to 460*l*–34 of this title and amended sections 460*l*–13 to 460*l*–15 and 460*l*–18 of this title.

Act of June 17, 1902, referred to in subsec. (d), is Act June 17, 1902, ch. 1093, 32 Stat. 388, popularly known as the Reclamation Act, which

is classified generally to chapter 12 of Title 43, 43 U.S.C.A. § 371 et seq. However, section 371 of Title 43 is Act Dec. 5, 1924, c. 4, § 4, subsec. A, 43 Stat. 701. For complete classification, see Short Title note set out under 43 U.S.C.A. § 371 and Tables.

§ 460*l*–34. Protection of authorized purposes of reclamation projects

HISTORICAL NOTES

References in Text

This part, referred to in text, was in the original "this title", meaning Title XXVIII of Pub.L. 102–575, Oct. 30, 1992, 106 Stat. 4690, which enacted sections 460*l*–31 to 460*l*–34 of this title and amended sections 460*l*–13 to 460*l*–15 and 460*l*–18 of this title.

The Federal Water Project Recreation Act, referred to in subsec. (b), is Pub.L. 89–72, July 9, 1965, 79 Stat. 213 , as amended, which is classified principally to part C (§ 460*l*–12 et seq.) of this subchapter. For complete classification of this Act to the Code, see Short Title note set out under section 460*l*–12 of this title and Tables.

SUBCHAPTER LXX—OZARK NATIONAL SCENIC RIVERWAYS

§ 460m–5. Administration

The Ozark National Scenic Riverways shall be administered in accordance with the provisions of the Act of August 25, 1916 (39 Stat. 535),[1] as amended and supplemented, and in accordance with other laws of general application relating to the areas administered and supervised by the Secretary through the National Park Service; except that authority otherwise available to the Secretary for the conservation and management of natural resources may be utilized to the extent he finds such authority will further the purposes of this subchapter.

[1] See References in Text note set out under this section.

HISTORICAL NOTES

References in Text

The Act of August 25, 1916 (39 Stat. 535), referred to in text, is Act Aug. 25, 1916, c. 408, 39 Stat. 535, known as the National Park Service Organic Act, which enacted 16 U.S.C.A. §§ 1, 2, 3, and 4 and provisions set out as a note under 54 U.S.C.A. § 100101. Sections 1 to 4 of the Act were repealed and restated as 18 U.S.C.A.

§ 1865(a), and 54 U.S.C.A. § 100101(a), chapter 1003 of Title 54 (54 U.S.C.A. § 100301 et seq.), and 54 U.S.C.A. §§ 100751(a), 100752, 100753, and 102101 by Pub.L. 113–287, §§ 3, 4(a)(1), 7, Dec. 19, 2014, 128 Stat. 3094, 3260, 3272. For complete classification, see Tables. For disposition of former sections of this title, see Disposition Table preceding 54 U.S.C.A. § 100101.

SUBCHAPTER LXXI—BUFFALO NATIONAL RIVER

§ 460m–9. Acquisition of lands and waters

(a) Donation, purchase, and exchange; reimbursement of State of Arkansas

Within the boundaries of the Buffalo National River, the Secretary may acquire lands and waters or interests therein by donation, purchase or exchange, except that lands owned by the State of Arkansas or a political subdivision thereof may be acquired only by donation: *Provided,* That the Secretary may, with funds appropriated for development of the area, reimburse such State for its share of the cost of facilities developed on State park lands if such facilities were developed in a manner approved by the Secretary and if the development of such facilities commenced subsequent to March 1, 1972: *Provided further,* That such reimbursement shall not exceed a total of $375,000. When an individual tract of land is only partly within the boundaries of the national river, the Secretary may acquire all of the tract by any of the above methods in order to avoid the payment of severance costs. Land so acquired outside of the boundaries of the national river may be exchanged by the Secretary for non-Federal lands within the national river boundaries, and any portion of the land not utilized for such exchanges may be disposed of in accordance with the provisions of chapters 1 to 11 of Title 40 and division C (except sections 3302, 3307(e), 3501(b), 3509, 3906, 4710, and 4711) of subtitle I of Title 41. With the concurrence of the agency having custody thereof, any Federal property within the boundaries of the national river may be transferred without consideration to the administrative jurisdiction of the Secretary for administration as part of the national river.

[See main volume for text of (b) and (c)]

HISTORICAL NOTES

Codifications

In subsec. (a), "chapters 1 to 11 of Title 40 and division C (except sections 3302, 3307(e) 3501(b), 3509, 3906, 4710, and 4711) of subtitle I of Title 41" was substituted for "the Federal Property and Administrative Services Act of 1949, as amended" on authority of Pub.L. 107–217, § 5(c), Aug. 21, 2002, 116 Stat. 1303, which Act enacted Title 40, Public Buildings, Property, and Works, and Pub.L. 111–350, § 6(c), Jan. 4, 2011, 124 Stat. 3854, which Act enacted Title 41, Public Contracts.

§ 460m–12. Administration, protection, and development

The Secretary shall administer, protect, and develop the Buffalo National River in accordance with the provisions of the Act of August 25, 1916 (39 Stat. 535; 16 U.S.C. 1 et seq.),[1] as amended and supplemented; except that any other statutory authority available to the Secretary for the conservation and management of natural resources may be utilized to the extent he finds such authority will further the purposes of this subchapter.

[1] See References in Text note set out under this section.

HISTORICAL NOTES

References in Text

The Act of August 25, 1916 (39 Stat. 535; 16 U.S.C. 1 et seq.), referred to in text, is Act Aug. 25, 1916, c. 408, 39 Stat. 535, known as the National Park Service Organic Act, which enacted 16 U.S.C.A. §§ 1, 2, 3, and 4 and provisions set out as a note under 54 U.S.C.A. § 100101. Sections 1 to 4 of the Act were repealed and restated as 18 U.S.C.A. § 1865(a), and 54 U.S.C.A. § 100101(a), chapter 1003 of Title 54 (54 U.S.C.A. § 100301 et seq.), and 54 U.S.C.A. §§ 100751(a), 100752, 100753, and 102101 by Pub.L. 113–287, §§ 3, 4(a)(1), 7, Dec. 19, 2014, 128 Stat. 3094, 3260, 3272. For complete classification, see Tables. For disposition of former sections of this title, see Disposition Table preceding 54 U.S.C.A. § 100101.

SUBCHAPTER LXXI–A—NEW RIVER GORGE NATIONAL RIVER [TRANSFERRED]

§ 460m–15. Transferred to 16 U.S.C.A. § 410eeee–1

§ 460m–16. Transferred to 16 U.S.C.A. § 410eeee–2

§ 460m–17. Transferred to 16 U.S.C.A. § 410eeee–3

§ 460m–18. Transferred to 16 U.S.C.A. § 410eeee–4

§ 460m–19. Transferred to 16 U.S.C.A. § 410eeee–5

§ 460m–20. Transferred to 16 U.S.C.A. § 410eeee–6

§ 460m–21. Transferred to 16 U.S.C.A. § 410eeee–7

§ 460m–22. Transferred to 16 U.S.C.A. § 410eeee–8

§ 460m–23. Transferred to 16 U.S.C.A. § 410eeee–9

§ 460m–24. Transferred to 16 U.S.C.A. § 410eeee–10

§ 460m–25. Transferred to 16 U.S.C.A. § 410eeee–11

§ 460m–26. Transferred to 16 U.S.C.A. § 410eeee–12

§ 460m–27. Transferred to 16 U.S.C.A. § 410eeee–13

§ 460m–28. Transferred to 16 U.S.C.A. § 410eeee–14

§ 460m–29. Transferred to 16 U.S.C.A. § 410eeee–15

§ 460m–29a. Transferred to 16 U.S.C.A. § 410eeee–16

§ 460m–30. Transferred to 16 U.S.C.A. § 410eeee–17

SUBCHAPTER LXXII—LAKE MEAD NATIONAL RECREATION AREA

§ 460n–2. **Hualapai Indian lands; inclusion within area; mineral rights; leases and permits; hunting and fishing rights**

The authorities granted by this subchapter shall be subject to the following exceptions and qualifications when exercised with respect to any tribal or allotted lands of the Hualapai Indians that may be included within the exterior boundaries of the Lake Mead National Recreation Area:

[See main volume for text of (a) to (c)]

(d) Nothing in this subchapter shall deprive the members of the Hualapai Tribe of hunting and fishing privileges presently exercised by them, nor diminish those rights and privileges of that part of the reservation which is included in the Lake Mead Recreation Area.[1]

[1] So in original. Probably should be "Lake Mead National Recreation Area".

INDEX

CONSULT GENERAL INDEX